Fundamentals of
Organizational
Behaviour

THIRD CANADIAN EDITION

Fundamentals of
Organizational
Behaviour

NANCY LANGTON
University of British Columbia

STEPHEN P. ROBBINS
San Diego State University

PEARSON

Prentice
Hall

Toronto

Library and Archives Canada Cataloguing in Publication

Langton, Nancy
    Fundamentals of organizational behaviour / Nancy Langton, Stephen P.
Robbins. — 3rd Canadian ed.

Includes index.
Order of authors reversed on previous Canadian eds.

ISBN-10: 0-13-175737-7; ISBN-13: 978-0-13-175737-0

1. Organizational behaviour—Textbooks. I. Robbins, Stephen P., 1943– II. Title.

HD58.7.L35 2006   658.3   C2006-901435-3

ISBN-10: 0-13-175737-7
ISBN-13: 978-0-13-175737-0

Editor-in-Chief: Gary Bennett
Acquisitions Editor: Karen Elliott
Executive Marketing Manager: Cas Shields
Developmental Editor: Su Mei Ku
Production Editor: Jen Handel
Copy Editor: Claudia Forgas
Proofreader: Kathleen Richards
Production Coordinator: Andrea Falkenberg
Composition: Joan M. Wilson
Permissions and Photo Research: Lisa Brant
Cover and Interior Design: Alex Li
Cover Image: José Ortega / Images.com

2 3 4 5   11 10 09 08 07

Printed and bound in the United States of America.

BRIEF CONTENTS

CONTENTS

PREFACE

Welcome to the third Canadian edition of *Fundamentals of Organizational Behaviour* by Nancy Langton and Stephen P. Robbins. This edition takes a fresh approach to organizational behaviour coverage through more relevant examples, updated theory coverage, and a continued emphasis on pedagogically sound design. Based on earlier reviews we have found that potential users want chapters that have the right balance of theory and application material and are relevant to student learning.

GENERAL CONTENT AND APPROACH

- *Writing style.* Clarity and readability are hallmarks of this text. The style is described by reviewers as "conversational," "interesting," "student-friendly," and "very clear and understandable." We have given even greater attention to the needs of ESL students in this edition.

- *Examples, examples, examples.* From our teaching experience, we know that students may not remember a concept, but they will remember an example. Moreover, a good example goes a long way in helping students to better understand a concept. You will find this book to be packed full of recent real-world examples drawn from a variety of organizations: business and not-for-profit, large and small, and local and international. We have also used photos to provide additional examples and information by expanding the captions.

- *Comprehensive and leading-edge literature coverage.* This book follows in the path of Langton/Robbins, *Organizational Behaviour: Concepts, Controversies, and Applications,* Fourth Canadian Edition, in its comprehensive and up-to-date coverage of OB from both academic journals and business periodicals. It also includes the popular feature *OB on the Edge,* where we consider what's new and hot in organizational behaviour. *OB on the Edge* is unique to our Canadian editions. The feature provides an opportunity to explore challenging issues and encourages students to read more about these hot topics. We cover two such topics in this edition: *Stress at Work* and *The Toxic Workplace.*

- *Technology.* A Companion Website dedicated to the book is provided at **www.pearsoned.ca/langton**. The site includes an interactive study guide with practice tests consisting of true/false, multiple-choice, short essay, and Internet exercises; links to the websites of many of the organizations mentioned in the text; search tools; and a special section for instructors that includes a syllabus manager and other tools for effective teaching.

- *Skill-building emphasis.* Each chapter's *OB at Work* section is full of exercises to help students make the connections between theories and real-world applications. Exercises at the end of each chapter reinforce critical thinking, behavioural analysis, and team building.

- *Relevance.* The text reminds both instructors and students alike that we have entered the twenty-first century and must contend with a new paradigm of work that may be considerably different from the past. The new paradigm is more globally focused and competitive, relies more heavily on part-time and contract jobs, and places a higher premium on entrepreneurial acumen, either within the traditional workplace structure, as an individual seeking out an alternative job, or as the creator of your own new business.

When the first Canadian edition of our textbook *Organizational Behaviour: Concepts, Controversies, Applications* appeared, it emphasized that *OB is for everyone*, from the bottom-rung employee to the CEO, as well as anyone who has to interact with others to accomplish a task. We continue to emphasize this theme in *Fundamentals of Organizational Behaviour*. We remind readers of the material's relevance beyond a "9-to-5" job through each chapter's new feature, *OB for You*, which outlines how OB can be used by individuals in their daily lives. We continue the emphasis on *OB is for everyone* in the *From Concepts to Skills* ensemble at the end of each chapter.

HIGHLIGHTS OF THE THIRD CANADIAN EDITION
In this edition, we have

- Continued to focus on shorter chapters to capture student interest

- Added more exhibits to help clarify material and revised exhibits to make them clearer

- Introduced *OB in Action*, exhibits that provide tips or "take-aways" from each chapter—things that readers can put into action right now, based on what they've learned in the chapter

- Updated the research base significantly, and introduced more references to research in the text

CHAPTER-BY-CHAPTER HIGHLIGHTS: WHAT'S NEW
Here is a summary of the key changes that we made to this edition.

Chapter 1: What Is Organizational Behaviour?
- Reorganized the chapter and highlighted the challenges that organizations face that make the study of OB relevant

- Included a lengthier discussion of organizational citizenship behaviour

- Extended discussion of diversity in the workplace

- Added a section on "putting people first"

- Introduced *OB in Action—Practices of Successful Organizations*, to show what companies do to put people first

Chapter 2: Perception, Personality, and Emotions
- Added a number of new discussions, including

  - Prejudice

  - Self-fulfilling prophecy

  - The impact of locus of control in the workplace

  - How to increase self-esteem

  - Proactive personality

Chapter 3: Values, Attitudes, and Their Effects in the Workplace

- Included a section on Kent Hodgson's general moral principles
- Introduced *OB in Action—The Magnificent Seven Principles*, which illustrates universal values that managers should consider
- Expanded discussion of the Rokeach Value Survey
- Extensively revised the section on assessing cultural values. We emphasize the GLOBE research program and its relation to Hofstede's work.
- Extended discussion on the multicultural aspects of Canada
- Increased coverage of the differences (and similarities) of Francophone and Anglophone values
- Added more discussion on Aboriginal values
- Increased the coverage of job satisfaction and organizational citizenship
- Added a discussion on how job satisfaction affects customer satisfaction
- Expanded discussion of the exit-voice-loyalty-neglect model
- Provided additional discussion of organizational commitment

Chapter 4: Motivating Self and Others

- Expanded discussion on goal-setting theory, including
  - How goal setting motivates
  - SMART goals
  - The research findings related to goal setting
  - Contingency factors in goal setting, including the impact of self-efficacy
- Added the following new discussions:
  - What influences an employee's expectancy
  - The ranges for expectancy, instrumentality, and valence
  - Intrinsic and extrinsic rewards, including related research findings, and a discussion on how to increase intrinsic motivation
  - Job design, including a discussion of how jobs can be designed to increase motivation

Chapter 5: Working in Teams

- Added a number of new discussions, including
  - How groups become teams
  - Additional tips for managing virtual teams
  - How to use virtual workspaces to improve the productivity of virtual teams
  - The characteristics of ineffective and effective teams
- Restructured the discussion on conditions needed to create effective teams
- Introduced *OB in Action—Harming Your Team* to illustrate the problems of ineffective teams

- Increased discussion of the role of friendships in teams
- Expanded discussion of group cohesiveness, including tips for increasing cohesiveness
- Expanded coverage of dealing with team conflict
- Introduced *OB in Action—Creating a Team Charter* to help teams develop productivity norms when they first form

Chapter 6: Communication, Conflict, and Negotiation

- Introduced a new model of the communication process, indicating its iterative nature
- Included the following new discussions related to communication:
  - Information overload
  - How to communicate more effectively when under stress
  - The use of instant messaging in the workplace
  - Silence as a form of communication
- Expanded discussion of email in the workplace
- Significantly reorganized and revised the section on conflict, including the following:
  - Added a discussion on win-win vs. win-lose solutions
  - Added a new section on conflict resolution
  - Introduced *OB in Action—Choosing Strategies to Deal With Conflicts* to show the situations in which each conflict management strategy is best used
  - Introduced *OB in Action—Handling Personality Conflicts*, which suggests ways of dealing with personality conflicts in the workplace
  - Expanded the description of conflict management styles
- Significantly reorganized and revised the section on negotiation, including the following:
  - Added new material on the negotiation process, including an exhibit that shows the steps of the process
  - Introduced *OB in Action—Tips for Getting to Yes*, which gives you ideas on how to make negotiating work

Chapter 7: Power and Politics

- Shortened, focused section on bases of power including
  - The addition of information power
  - Research on the impact of bases of power on individual reactions
- Added a discussion on ways that individuals respond to influence tactics
- Updated discussion of influence tactics based on current research
- Added a new discussion of workplace bullying
- Added a new discussion on types of political activities
- Provided a section on research findings regarding organizational politics

Chapter 8: Leadership

- Added the following new discussions and sections
  - Trait theories of leadership, reflecting the latest research on this topic
  - Preferred leadership traits across cultures (includes an exhibit)
  - Research findings for behavioural theories of leadership
  - New discussion of downsides of charismatic leadership
  - Mentoring
  - How to create self-leaders
  - Cornerstones to a "moral foundation of leadership"
  - The effectiveness of women's style of leadership
  - Online leadership

Chapter 9: Decision Making, Creativity, and Ethics

- Shortened and focused the discussion on decision biases
- Introduced *OB in Action—Reducing Biases and Errors in Decision Making,* which provides ideas for improving decision making
- Added a discussion on what managers can do to reduce groupthink
- Included "focus on care" as a fourth ethical decision criterion
- Introduced *OB in Action—Developing a Meaningful Code of Ethics,* which shows how organizations implement codes of ethics
- Provided a definition of corporate social responsibility

Chapter 10: Organizational Culture and Change

- Reorganized the chapter to help focus on purposes of organizational culture at the beginning of the chapter
- Introduced *OB in Action—Finding Your Culture* to provide a checklist on types of organizational cultures one might prefer
- Focused more attention on strategies for merging organizational cultures
- Extended discussion on changing organizational culture, including more examples
- Created an exhibit that provides tips for changing organizational culture
- Completely rewrote and significantly reorganized the section on organizational change and added several new sections on
  - Kotter's eight-step plan for implementing change
  - Action research
  - Change agents
  - Appreciative inquiry, an approach to managing change
  - Focused discussion on tactics organizations can use to overcome resistance to change

PEDAGOGICAL FEATURES

The pedagogical features of *Fundamentals of Organizational Behaviour*, Third Canadian Edition, are designed to complement and reinforce the textual material. This book offers the most complete assortment of pedagogy available in any OB book on the market.

- The text is developed in a "story-line" format that emphasizes how the topics fit together. Each chapter opens with a concept map of key questions related to a main example that threads through the chapter. The opening vignette is shorter, and it is carried throughout the chapter to help students apply a story to the concepts they are learning. The questions from the concept map appear in the margin of the text to indicate where they are addressed. The chapter ends with each of the opening questions repeated and answered to summarize the contents of the chapter.

- Keyed examples, **OB in the Street**, **OB in the Workplace**, **Focus on Ethics**, and **Focus on Diversity** help students see the links between theoretical material and applications.

OB IN THE WORKPLACE

WestJet Airline's Employees Work Together

What do empowered employees do? Calgary-based WestJet Airlines employees are given lots of freedom to manage themselves.[23] Clive Beddoe, the company's president and CEO, was determined to create a company "where people wanted to manage themselves."

At WestJet, employees are asked to be responsible for their tasks, rather than rely on supervisors to tell them what to do. That includes Beddoe: "I don't direct things," he says. "We set some standards and expectations, but [I] don't interfere in how our people do their jobs." Instead, employees are given guidelines for behaviour. For instance, flight attendants are directed to serve customers in a caring, positive, and cheerful manner. How do they carry that out? It's up to them. Employees also share tasks. When a plane lands, all employees on the flight, even those who are flying off-duty, are expected to prepare the plane for its next takeoff.

Obviously, WestJet can lower its costs by keeping the number of supervisors down. The company operates with about 60 employees per aircraft, while a typical full-service airline such as Air Canada needs more than 140. But allowing employees to manage themselves has a bigger benefit. Beddoe believes it encourages employees to take pride in what they do. "They are the ones making the decisions about what they're doing and how they're doing it," says Beddoe. ⏴

- NEW! **OB in Action** features provide tips for using the concepts of OB in everyday life. For instance, OB in Action features includes *Practices of Successful Organizations*, *The Magnificent Seven Principles*, and *Managing Virtual Teams*.

- NEW! To help instructors and students readily spot significant discussions of research findings, we have included a research icon in the margin where these discussions appear. This helps emphasize the strong research foundation that underlies OB.

Theory Y The assumption that employees like work, are creative, seek responsibility, and will exercise self-direction and self-control if they are committed to the objectives.

- NEW! Margin definitions have been differentiated to help students separate concepts from theories. Definitions of terms and concepts appear in blue and definitions of theories appear in magenta, making them stand out for easier studying.

intrinsic motivators A person's internal desire to do something, due to such things as interest, challenge, and personal satisfaction.

- NEW! Integrated questions (in the form of yellow notes) throughout the chapters encourage students to think about how OB applies to their everyday lives and engage students in their reading of the material. These questions first appear in the chapter opener, under the heading OB Is For Everyone, and then appear throughout.

The examples in this textbook present va[...]
zations so that you gain a better understa[...]
many types that exist. Though you might n[...]
* Do you know what a "typical" organization looks like?
sidered this before, the college or university [...]
every bit as much a "real" organization as is [...]
Company or Air Canada or the Toronto Rap[...]
for-profit organization that hires people with [...]
to renovate and build in the inner city of W[...]
much a real organization as is London, Ontario-based EllisDon, one of No[...]
largest construction companies. Therefore, the theories we cover should b[...]
in light of the variety of organizations you may encounter. We try to point [...]
where the theory may be less applicable (or especially applicable) to a part[...]
organization. For the most part, however, you should expect that the discu[...]
textbook apply across the broad spectrum of organizations. Throughout, [...]
applications to a variety of organizations in our feature *OB in the Workpl[...]*

- Provided in the margins, Weblinks give students access to internet resources for companies and organizations discussed in the text, broadening their grasp of real-world issues. The Destinations button of the book's Companion Website provides hyperlinks and regular updating of the URLs for all weblinks.

- NEW! **Snapshot Summary** provides a study tool that helps students see the overall connection among concepts studied within each chapter.

- Each chapter concludes with **OB at Work,** a set of resources designed to help students apply the lessons of the chapter. Included in OB at Work are the following continuing and new features:

  - **For Review** and **For Critical Thinking** provide thought-provoking questions to review the chapter and consider ways to apply the material presented.

  - **OB for You** outlines how OB can be used by individuals in their daily lives.

  - **Point/CounterPoint** features promote debate on contentious OB issues. All have been shortened to present more focused arguments.

  - **Learning About Yourself Exercises, Breakout Group Exercise, Working with Others Exercises,** and **Ethical Dilemma Exercises** are all now featured in every chapter. We have found great value in using application exercises in the classroom. The many new exercises included here are ones that we have found particularly stimulating in our own classrooms. Our students say that they both like these exercises and learn from them.

  - **Case Incident** features deal with real-world scenarios and require students to exercise their decision-making skills. Each case will enable an instructor to quickly generate class discussion on a key theme within each chapter. The CD-ROM that accompanies this book includes additional Case Incidents.

  - **From Concepts to Skills** provides a wide range of applications for the *Fundamentals* user. The section begins with a practical set of tips on topics such as "Reading Emotions," "Setting Goals," and "Solving Problems Creatively," which demonstrate real-world applications of OB theories. This is followed by the features **Assessing Skills, Practising Skills,** and **Reinforcing Skills.** Assessing Skills encourages students to assess their personalities, leadership skills, conflict-handling intentions, and a variety of other traits and skills on the CD-ROM that accompanies this book. Students can therefore link their personal behaviours and traits to material covered in the chapter. Practising Skills presents an additional case or group activity to apply the chapter's learning objectives.

SNAPSHOT SUMMARY

1 Defining Organizational Behaviour
  OB Is for Everyone
  What Do We Mean by Organization?
2 OB: Making Sense of Behaviour in Organizations
  The Building Blocks of OB
  The Rigour of OB
3 How Will Knowing OB Make a Difference?
  In the Workplace
  For You as an Individual
4 Today's Challenges in the Canadian Workplace
  Challenges at the Individual Level
  Challenges at the Group Level
  Challenges at the Organizational Level

Reinforcing Skills asks students to talk about the material they have learned with others, or to apply it to their own personal experiences.

- **CBC Video Case Incidents** present CBC cases tied to the material in each chapter. The segments were carefully selected by Kyleen Myrah of Okanagan College, who also wrote the cases that appear in this text. The video cases provide instructors with audiovisual material to engage students' attention.

SUPPLEMENTS

We have created an outstanding supplements package for *Fundamentals of Organizational Behaviour*, Third Canadian Edition. The following materials are available.

Instructor's Resource CD-ROM (0-13-230489-9). This resource provides all of the following supplements in one convenient package:

Instructor's Resource Manual with CBC Video Guide (0-13-230493-7). The Instructor's Resource Manual includes learning objectives, chapter outlines and synopses, annotated lecture outlines, teaching guides for in-text exercises, a summary and analysis of the *Point/CounterPoint* features, and answers to questions found under *For Review, For Critical Thinking, Case Incidents*, and *CBC Video Case Incidents*. There are additional cases, exercises, and teaching materials as well. This supplement can be downloaded from Pearson Education Canada's online catalogue at vig.pearsoned.ca.

PowerPoint® Presentations (0-13-230492-9). This package includes over 400 slides of content and exhibits from the text, prepared for electronic presentation.

TestGen (0-13-230494-5). This test-generating and grading software allows instructors to assemble their own customized tests from the questions included in the TestGen. The TestGen contains over 1500 items, including multiple-choice, true/false, and discussion questions that relate not only to the body of the text but to *From Concepts to Skills, Point/Counterpoint*, and case materials. For each question, we have provided the correct answer, a page reference to the text, a difficulty rating (easy, moderate, or challenging), and a classification (recall or applied).

CBC/Pearson Education Canada Video Library (VHS 0-13-230495-3; DVD 0-13-229643-8). In an exclusive partnership, CBC and Pearson Education Canada have worked together to develop an exciting video package consisting of 10 segments in both VHS and DVD formats. These were specially chosen by Kyleen Myrah of Okanagan College. At an average of twelve minutes in length, these segments show students issues of organizational behaviour as they affect real Canadian individuals and companies. Teaching notes are provided in the *Instructor's Resource Manual with CBC Video Guide*.

Companion Website with Online Study Guide (0-13-179170-2). Our exciting new Companion Website includes a comprehensive online study guide that presents students with numerous study tools. Practice tests that consist of true/false, multiple-choice, short essay, and Internet exercises offer instant feedback to students. Destinations (hyperlinks to the text's weblinks) and search tools facilitate further research into key organizations and topics discussed in the text. A special section for instructors contains a syllabus manager and other materials. Go to **www.pearsoned.ca/langton** and explore.

Personal Response System (0-13-230490-2). Gauge your students' course progress with this Personal Response System that enables instructors to pose questions, record results, and display those results instantly in the classroom. Questions are provided in PowerPoint format.

Pearson Advantage. For qualified adopters, Pearson Education is proud to introduce the Pearson Advantage. The Pearson Advantage is the first integrated Canadian service program committed to meeting the customization, training, and support needs for your course. Our commitments are made in writing and in consultation with faculty. Your local Pearson Education sales representative can provide you with more details on this service program.

Content Media Specialists. Pearson's Content Media Specialists work with faculty and campus course designers to ensure that Pearson technology products, assessment tools, and online course materials are tailored to meet your specific needs. This highly qualified team is dedicated to helping schools take full advantage of a wide range of educational technology, by assisting in the integration of a variety of instructional materials and media formats.

ACKNOWLEDGMENTS

A number of people worked hard to give this third Canadian edition of *Fundamentals of Organizational Behaviour* a new look. Su Mei Ku, who has been the developmental editor on almost all of my projects, again outdid her always excellent performance. Her wit, good humour, helpfulness, support, and organizational skills made working on this textbook immensely easier. Su Mei served as a much-valued sounding board throughout the editorial process and also helped me significantly during manuscript preparation and the review of pages.

I received incredible support for this project from a variety of people at Pearson Education Canada. Karen Elliott, Acquisitions Editor, is a wonderful cheerleader for the project. Alex Li produced yet another beautiful interior and cover design. Jen Handel was terrific in her role as the Production Editor for this project. She was very responsive and patiently and calmly handled the production process with much grace and goodwill. Steve O'Hearn, President of Higher Education, Michael Young, former Vice President, Editorial Director of Higher Education, and Gary Bennett, Editor-in-Chief, are extremely supportive on the management side of Pearson Education Canada. This kind of support makes it much easier for an author to get work done and meet dreams and goals. Michael's support behind the scenes is particularly appreciated and valued and will be missed now that he's off to Australia. Lisa Brant was very helpful in doing the photo research, and made some incredible finds in her search for photos to highlight OB concepts. There are a variety of other people at Pearson who also had their hand in making sure that the manuscript would be transformed into this book and then delivered to your hands. To all of them I extend my thanks for jobs well done. The Pearson sales team is an exceptional group, and I know they will do everything possible to make this book successful. I continue to appreciate and value their support and interaction, particularly that of Cas Shields, Executive Marketing Manager.

Claudia Forgas was copyeditor for the project and did an amazing job of making sure everything was in place and written clearly. Kathleen Richards, as the proofreader, was extremely diligent about checking for consistency throughout the text. Both performed a number of helpful fact-checking activities. I enjoyed the opportunity to work with both of them. Their keen eyes helped to make these pages as clean as they are.

My family and friends are often ignored during the busier parts of writing a textbook. They accept this graciously and provide food, support, and encouragement, as necessary. I am grateful for their support. Particular thanks goes to the members of the Carnavaron Quilt Guild who provided Monday night breaks from gruelling writing sessions and always asked how things were going and encouraged me along the way.

Finally, I want to acknowledge the many reviewers of this textbook for their detailed helpful comments. I appreciate the time and care that they put into their reviewing:

Victoria Digby (Fanshawe College), Mark Giltrow, (British Columbia Institute of Technology), Scott Jeffrey (University of Waterloo), Beverley Linnell (Southern Alberta Institute of Technology), Kyleen Myrah (Okanagan College), Holly Seebach (Niagara College), Hoa Trinh (Conestoga College), Debra Warren (Centennial College), and Stephen Yurkiw (Red River College).

I dedicate this book to my father, Peter X. Langton. He was a man of many talents, and his understanding of organizational behaviour may have been greater than my own.

Nancy Langton

July 2006

ABOUT THE AUTHORS

Nancy Langton received her Ph.D. from Stanford University. Since completing her graduate studies, Dr. Langton has taught at the University of Oklahoma and the University of British Columbia. As a member of the Organizational Behaviour and Human Resources division at the Sauder School of Business, UBC, she teaches at the undergraduate, MBA and Ph.D. level and conducts executive programs on attracting and retaining employees, time management, family business issues, as well as women and management issues. Dr. Langton has received several major three-year research grants from the Social Sciences and Humanities Research Council of Canada, and her research interests have focused on human resource issues in the workplace, including pay equity, gender equity, and leadership and communication styles. She is currently conducting longitudinal research with entrepreneurs in the Greater Vancouver Region, trying to understand the relationship between their human resource practices and the success of their businesses. Her articles on these and other topics have appeared in such journals as *Administrative Science Quarterly, American Sociological Review, Sociological Quarterly, Journal of Management Education, Organization Studies,* and *Gender, Work and Organizations.* She has won Best Paper commendations from both the Academy of Management and the Administrative Sciences Association of Canada.

Dr. Langton routinely wins high marks from her students for teaching. She has been nominated many times for the Commerce Undergraduate Society Awards, and has won several honourable mention plaques. In 1998 she won the University of British Columbia Faculty of Commerce's most prestigious award for teaching innovation, The Talking Stick. The award was given for Dr. Langton's redesign of the undergraduate organizational behaviour course as well as the many activities that were a spin-off of these efforts. In 2001 she was part of the UBC MBA Core design team that won the Alan Blizzard award, a national award that recognizes innovation in teaching.

In Dr. Langton's "other life," she teaches the artistry of quiltmaking, and one day hopes to win first prize at *Visions,* the juried show for quilts as works of art. In the meantime she teaches art quilt courses on colour and design in her spare time. When she is not designing quilts, she is either reading novels (often suggested by a favourite correspondent), or studying cookbooks for new ideas. All of her friends would say that she makes from scratch the best pizza in all of Vancouver.

Stephen P. Robbins received his Ph.D. from the University of Arizona and has taught at the University of Nebraska at Omaha, Concordia University in Montreal, the University of Baltimore, Southern Illinois University at Edwardsville, and San Diego State University. Dr. Robbins' research interests have focused on conflict, power, and politics in organizations, as well as on the development of effective interpersonal skills. His articles on these and other topics have appeared in journals such as *Business Horizons, California Management Review, Business and Economic Perspectives, International Management, Management Review, Canadian Personnel and Industrial Relations,* and *The Journal of Management Education.*

In recent years, Dr. Robbins has been spending most of his professional time writing textbooks. These include *Essentials of Organizational Behavior,* 7th ed. (Prentice Hall,

2003); *Training in InterPersonal Skills*, 3rd ed., with Phillip Hunsaker (Prentice Hall, 2003); *Management*, 7th ed. with Mary Coulter (Prentice Hall, 2002); *Human Resource Management*, 7th ed., with David DeCenzo (Wiley, 2002); *The Self-Assessment Library* 2.0 (Prentice Hall, 2002); *Fundamentals of Management*, 3rd ed., with David DeCenzo (Prentice Hall, 2001); *Supervision Today!*, 3rd ed., with David DeCenzo (Prentice Hall, 2001); *Business Today* (Harcourt, 2001); *Managing Today!* 2nd ed. (Prentice Hall, 2000); and *Organization Theory*, 3rd ed. (Prentice Hall, 1990).

In Dr. Robbins' "other life," he participates in masters' track competition. Since turning 50 in 1993, he has set numerous indoor and outdoor age-group world sprint records; won more than a dozen indoor and outdoor U.S. championships at 60, 100, 200, and 400 meters; and captured seven gold medals at the World Masters Championships. Most recently, he won gold medals at 100 and 200 meters and as the anchor on the U.S. 4×100 relay in the Men's 55–59 age group at the 2001 World Championships in Brisbane, Australia.

A Great Way to Learn and Instruct Online

The Pearson Education Canada Companion Website is easy to navigate and is organized to correspond to the chapters in this textbook. Whether you are a student in the classroom or a distance learner you will discover helpful resources for in-depth study and research that empower you in your quest for greater knowledge and maximize your potential for success in the course.

Companion Website

[www.pearsoned.ca/langton]

Enter

PEARSON
Education Canada

Jump to...   http://www.pearsoned.ca/langton   ⬍   Home   Search   Help   Profile

Companion Website

Home >

Pearson Companion Website

Fundamentals of Organizational Behaviour, Third Canadian Edition, by Nancy Langton and Stephen P. Robbins

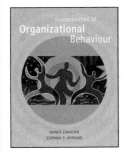

Student Resources

The modules for each chapter of the text provide students with tools for learning course material. These modules include:
- Chapter Overviews
- Study Guide with online quizzes
  — multiple choice
  — true/false
  — short essay
  — Internet exercises
- Web Destinations and Websearch
- PowerPoint Presentations
- Glossary Flashcards
- Electronic Glossary

Instructor Resources

A link to this book on the Pearson online catalogue (www.pearsoned.ca) provides instructors with additional teaching tools. Downloadable PowerPoint Presentations and an Instructor's Resource Manual are just some of the materials that may be available. The catalogue is password protected. To get a password, simply contact your Pearson Education Canada Representative or call Faculty Sales and Services at 1-800-850-5813.

CHAPTER **1**

What Is
Organizational
Behaviour?

An organization decides it will hire people with few skills and job experience. What challenges might its managers face?

1 What is organizational behaviour?

2 Isn't organizational behaviour common sense? Or just like psychology?

3 How does knowing about organizational behaviour make work and life more understandable?

4 What challenges do managers and employees face in the workplace of the twenty-first century?

Winnipeg-based Inner City Renovation (ICR) does renovation and construction work on rundown inner city residential and commercial buildings, with the aim of revitalizing the area.[1] As part of its mission, the company employs and trains low-income residents of the inner city. ICR is a for-profit company that was created by five not-for-profit joint venture partners: North End Housing Project (NEHP), Winnipeg Partners in Housing (WPH), Spence Neighbourhood Association (SNA), West Broadway Development Corporation (WBDC), and Community Ownership Solutions (COS). ICR has completed over 50 residential and commercial projects since opening its doors in August 2002.

Because ICR hires a number of employees who have few skills and little job experience, managers must teach the employees how to perform the role of employee. Managers must also teach employees about teamwork and leadership while working side by side with them on construction projects. Can a company like ICR survive as well as a company not as committed to social values?

The challenges that the managers at ICR face in running a successful organization and getting people to work well together illustrate several concepts you will find as you study the field of organizational behaviour. Let's take a look, then, at what organizational behaviour is.

DEFINING ORGANIZATIONAL BEHAVIOUR

Organizational behaviour (often abbreviated as OB) is a field of study that investigates how individuals, groups, and structure affect and are affected by behaviour within organizations. Behaviour refers to what people do in the organization, how they perform, and what their attitudes are. Because the organizations studied are often business organizations, OB is frequently applied to address workplace issues such as absenteeism, turnover, productivity, motivation, working in groups, and job satisfaction. Managers often apply the knowledge gained from OB research to help them manage their organizations more effectively.

1 What is organizational behaviour?

organizational behaviour A field of study that investigates the impact of individuals, groups, and structure on behaviour within organizations; the aim is to apply such knowledge toward improving organizational effectiveness.

OB IS FOR EVERYONE

* *Why do some people do well in organizational settings while others have difficulty?*

* *Do you know what a "typical" organization looks like?*

* *Does job satisfaction really make a difference?*

* *Are you ready to assume more responsibility at work?*

* *What people–related challenges have you noticed in the workplace?*

* *Why should you care about understanding other people?*

OB Is for Everyone

> ✳ *Why do some people do well in organizational settings while others have difficulty?*

Inner City Renovation
www.mts.net/~icri/

It may seem natural to think that the study of OB is for leaders and managers of organizations. After all, they often set the agenda for everyone else. However, OB is for everyone. For instance, many employees have informal leadership roles. They are often expected to move beyond simply providing labour to playing a more proactive role in achieving organizational success. As well, **managers** are increasingly asking employees to share in their decision-making processes rather than simply follow orders. For instance, employees in some retail stores can make decisions about when to accept returned items on their own, without involving the manager. Thus, in many organizations, the roles of managers and employees have become blurred.[2]

OB is not just for managers and employees. Entrepreneurs and self-employed individuals may not act as managers, but they certainly interact with other individuals and organizations as part of their work. In fact, much of OB is relevant beyond the workplace.

OB applies equally well to all situations in which you interact with others. In fact, OB is relevant anywhere that people come together and share experiences, work on goals, or meet to solve problems. The study of OB can shed light on the interactions among family members, the voluntary group that comes together to do something about reviving the downtown area, students working as a team on a class project, the parents

What is organizational behaviour? It's a field of study that focuses on three levels of behaviour in organizations. One level is the individual, such as the Wal-Mart greeter handing out smiley balloons. Another level is the group, such as the three employees of Praxair, a distributor of bottled industrial gases, who meet to discuss their work. The third level is structure, which is depicted here by employees working in cubicles at Bloomberg, a financial media company.

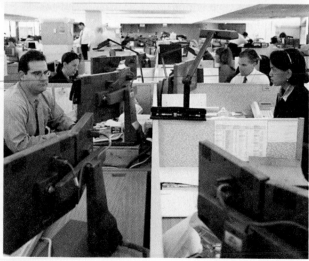

who sit on the board of their child's daycare centre, or even the members of a lunchtime pickup basketball team. Throughout the textbook, a feature called *OB in the Street* will help you understand these broader connections.

What Do We Mean by Organization?

An **organization** is a consciously coordinated social unit, made up of a group of people, who work together on common goals on a relatively continuous basis. Manufacturing and service firms are organizations, and so are schools, hospitals, churches, military units, retail stores, police departments, volunteer organizations, start-ups, and local, provincial, and federal government agencies. Inner City Renovation, which we discussed in the opening vignette, is a for-profit organization, but its partners are nonprofit organizations. Thus, when we say "organization" throughout this textbook, we are referring not only to large manufacturing firms but also to small mom-and-pop stores, as well as to the variety of other forms of organization that exist. Small businesses make up a significant part of the economy.[3] Businesses that employ no more than 20 people are responsible for about one-quarter of all Canadian jobs. Small businesses employing 50 or fewer people make up 24 percent of Canada's gross national product. Microbusinesses (companies with 5 or fewer employees managed by an owner/operator, often as sole proprietorships) account for about 8 percent of the employment in this country.

> **organization.** A consciously coordinated social unit, made up of a group of people, that functions on a relatively continuous basis to achieve common goals.

> ✱ *Do you know what a "typical" organization looks like?*

The examples in this textbook present various organizations so that you gain a better understanding of the many types that exist. Though you might not have considered this before, the college or university you attend is every bit as much a "real" organization as is Hudson's Bay Company or Air Canada or the Toronto Raptors. A small, for-profit organization that hires people with limited skills to renovate and build in the inner city of Winnipeg is as much a real organization as is London, Ontario-based EllisDon, one of North America's largest construction companies. Therefore, the theories we cover should be considered in light of the variety of organizations you may encounter. We try to point out instances where the theory may be less applicable (or especially applicable) to a particular type of organization. For the most part, however, you should expect that the discussions in this textbook apply across the broad spectrum of organizations. Throughout, we highlight applications to a variety of organizations in our feature *OB in the Workplace*.

OB: Making Sense of Behaviour in Organizations

> The managers at Inner City Renovation (ICR) quickly noticed that some of their employees had special challenges, such as their unemployment rates, their inconsistent job records, and their low education levels.[4] Managers interviewed employees about their career interests and their needs for skill development. In addition, employees have had one-on-one meetings with the ICR president and the employee support worker. Interviews and meetings are ways to collect data about employee behaviour. While ICR managers are not researchers, they understand the need for doing some research on their employees. How is OB research carried out, and in what situations does it apply?

We have thus far considered why OB can be applied in a variety of settings. In this next section, we consider the other fields of study that have contributed to OB and discuss the fact that OB is a scientific discipline, with careful research that is conducted to test and evaluate theories.

2 Isn't organizational behaviour common sense? Or just like psychology?

The Building Blocks of OB

OB is an applied behavioural science that is built upon contributions from a number of behavioural disciplines. The main areas are psychology, sociology, social psychology, anthropology, and political science.[5] As we will learn, psychology's contributions have been mainly at the individual or micro-level of analysis. The other four disciplines have contributed to our understanding of macro concepts, such as group processes and organization. Exhibit 1-1 presents an overview of the major contributions to the study of OB.

EXHIBIT 1-1   Toward an OB Discipline

The Rigour of OB

Whether you want to respond to the challenges of the Canadian workplace, which we discuss later in the chapter, manage well, guarantee satisfying and rewarding employment for yourself, or know how to work better in groups and teams, it pays to understand organizational behaviour. OB provides a systematic approach to the study of behaviour in organizations, as well as groups and teams. Underlying this systematic approach is the belief that behaviour is not random. Thus research studies are conducted and are the basis for all of the claims made in this textbook.

OB Looks at Consistencies

Certainly there are differences among individuals. Placed in similar situations, people don't all act exactly alike. However, there are certain fundamental consistencies underlying the behaviour of most individuals that can be identified and then modified to reflect individual differences.

These fundamental consistencies are very important because they allow predictability. For instance, when you get into your car, you make some definite and usually highly accurate predictions about how other people will behave.

What may be less obvious is that there are rules (written and unwritten) in almost every setting. Thus, it can be argued that it's possible to predict behaviour (undoubtedly, not always with 100-percent accuracy) in supermarkets, classrooms, doctors' offices, elevators, and in most structured situations. For instance, do you turn around and face the doors when you get into an elevator? Almost everyone does. Is there a sign inside the elevator that tells you to do this? Probably not! Just as we make predictions about drivers, where there are definite rules of the road, so we can make predictions about the behaviour of people in elevators, where there are few written rules. This example supports a major foundation of this textbook: Behaviour is generally predictable, and the *systematic study* of behaviour is a means to making reasonably accurate predictions.

OB Looks Beyond Common Sense

When we use the phrase **systematic study**, we mean looking at relationships, attempting to attribute causes and effects, and basing our conclusions on scientific evidence—that is, on data gathered under controlled conditions, and measured and interpreted in a reasonably rigorous manner—rather than relying on common sense. OB uses scientific research to uncover how behaviour works in organizations. Exhibit 1-2 on page 8 illustrates the common methods researchers use to study topics in OB.

A systematic approach does not mean that those things you have come to believe in an unsystematic way are necessarily incorrect. Some of the conclusions we make in this textbook, based on solid research findings, will support what you always knew was true. You will also be exposed to research evidence that runs counter to what you might have thought was common sense. In fact, one of the challenges to teaching a subject such as OB is to overcome the notion, held by many, that "it's all common sense."[6]

You will find that many of the so-called common-sense views you hold about human behaviour are wrong, on closer examination. Moreover, what one person considers common sense frequently runs counter to another's version. Are leaders born or made? What is it that motivates people at work nowadays? You probably have answers to such questions, and individuals who have not reviewed the research are likely to differ on their answers.

If understanding behaviour were simply common sense, we would not observe many of the problems that occur in the workplace, because managers and employees would know how to behave. For instance, we likely would not see people being bullied in the workplace, managers who don't know how to manage, and team members who don't inform teammates when their work is going to be late. Unfortunately, as you will see from

systematic study The examination of behaviour in order to draw conclusions, based on scientific evidence, about causes and effects in relationships.

EXHIBIT 1-2   Research Methods in OB

Source: J. R. Schermerhorn, J. G. Hunt, and R. N. Osborn, *Organizational Behavior,* 9th ed., 2005, p. 4. Copyright © 2005 John Wiley & Sons, Inc. Reprinted with permission of John Wiley & Sons, Inc.

examples throughout the textbook, many individuals exhibit less than desirable behaviour in the workplace. With a stronger grounding in the systematic analysis of OB, individuals would be able to avoid some of these mistakes. This chapter's *Point/Counterpoint* on page 22 looks at how systematic OB is.

One of the objectives of this textbook is to expose you to a systematic analysis of behaviour, in the belief that such analysis will improve your accuracy in explaining and predicting behaviour. Understanding OB may also help you behave better in organizations and groups as well. For example, after studying OB, you may realize that you should not discuss *The Apprentice* at 8:00 a.m. in the manager's office if your manager needs quiet time, is an introvert, and is production-oriented.[7]

OB Has Few Absolutes

There are few, if any, simple and universal principles that explain OB. In contrast, the physical sciences—chemistry, astronomy, and physics, for example—have laws that are consistent and apply in a wide range of situations. Such laws allow scientists to generalize about the pull of gravity or to confidently send astronauts into space to repair satellites. However, as one noted behavioural researcher concluded, "God gave all the easy problems to the physicists." Human beings are complex. Because we are not alike, our ability to make simple, accurate, and sweeping generalizations is limited. Two people often act differently in the same situation, and the same person's behaviour changes in different situations.

OB Takes a Contingency Approach

Just because people can behave differently at different times does not mean, of course, that we cannot offer reasonably accurate explanations of human behaviour or make valid predictions. It does mean, however, that OB must consider behaviour within the context in which it occurs—known as a **contingency approach**. So, for example, OB scholars would avoid stating that effective leaders should *always* seek the ideas of their employees before making a decision. Rather, we may find that in some situations a participative style is clearly superior, but in other situations an autocratic decision style is more effective. In other words, as you will see in Chapter 8, the effectiveness of a particular leadership style depends on the situation in which it is used. The OB scholar would therefore try to describe the situations to which each style is suited.

Consistent with the contingency approach, the *Point/Counterpoint* feature included in each chapter presents debates on some of the more controversial issues in OB. These debates highlight the fact that within OB there is disagreement on many issues. The *Point/Counterpoint* format gives you the opportunity to explore different points of view on an issue, discover how diverse perspectives complement and oppose each other, and gain insight into some of the current debates in the OB field.

contingency approach An approach taken by OB that considers behaviour within the context in which it occurs

HOW WILL KNOWING OB MAKE A DIFFERENCE?

When we talk about the impact of OB in each chapter, we consider the impact on both the workplace and the individual (see our features *OB in the Workplace* and *OB in the Street*). So let's begin our discussion of OB's impact by looking broadly at how knowing about OB makes a difference in the workplace, before we look at how OB affects us individually.

3 How does knowing about organizational behaviour make work and life more understandable?

In the Workplace

From a management point of view, understanding OB can help you manage well. Still, you might wonder whether managing well really makes a difference. Markham, Ontario-based Black Photo Corporation's president, Rod Smith, learned that not listening to employee demands can have undesirable consequences when he was confronted with a union drive at Black's. He notes the difficulties he has experienced in working with a union. "One of the things that you lose when you get unionized is that ability to be compassionate, because the rules are the rules, and they catch people in ways we prefer not to catch them."[8]

Black Photo Corporation
www.blackphoto.com

Consider another manager's perspective. Aris Kaplanis, president and CEO of Toronto-based Teranet, understands the importance of managing well. In the high-tech industry, where turnover is typically 10 to 20 percent, Teranet's annual turnover rate is less than 1 percent. Kaplanis believes that his turnover is low because Teranet developed a corporate culture that is both humane and family-friendly. "My perspective is that the company has two assets—one is the customers, the other is our employees. Both of these assets have to be serviced."[9]

Teranet
www.teranet.ca

The evidence indicates that managing people well makes for better corporations overall. Exhibit 1-3 on page 10 shows that many of the firms that made the KPMG/Ipsos Reid list of "Most Respected Corporations for Human Resource Management" also scored high on financial performance and best long-term investment value. Five of the companies placed in the top 10 on both financial measures.

Each year, *Report on Business* (*ROB*) magazine publishes a list of the "50 Best Employers in Canada." The magazine's 2005 survey identified three main traits of best-loved companies: (1) they show appreciation for their employees, (2) they coach employees to help them move up in the organization, and (3) they have good leaders who present the corporate strategy clearly and consistently.[10]

EXHIBIT 1-3	Most Respected Corporations for Human Resource Management (KPMG/Ipsos Reid's 2005 Survey)			
	Location	Industry	Rank on Financial Performance	Rank on Best Long-Term Investment Value
1. RBC Financial Group	Toronto	Financial Services	1	1
2. WestJet Airlines	Calgary	Air Transportation	n/a	n/a
3. Dofasco	Hamilton, ON	Steelmaker	n/a	n/a
4. TD Bank Financial Group	Toronto	Financial Services	6	5
5. EnCana Corporation	Calgary	Oil and Gas	3	2
6. Manulife Financial	Toronto	Financial Services	4	4
7. IBM Canada	Markham, ON	Computers	n/a	n/a
8. Toyota Canada	Scarborough, ON	Automotive	n/a	n/a
9. BMO Financial Group	Toronto	Financial Services	7	7

Source: KPMG/Ipsos Reid, *Eleventh Annual Survey of Canada's Most Respected Corporations,* www.mostrespected.ca/en/documents/CMRC2005En.pdf (accessed May 5, 2006).

organizational commitment The degree to which an employee identifies with the organization and wishes to remain with the organization.

affective commitment The strength of an individual's emotional attachment to, identification with, and involvement in the organization.

While the KPMG/Ipsos Reid survey shows that managing well adds to the bottom line, the *ROB* survey shows more directly that managing well provides managers with day-to-day returns. *ROB*'s 50 best employers have low turnover, and employees want to stay with their firms—even when they are offered higher-paying jobs by other companies. Employees with the 50 best employers who participated in the *ROB* survey did not mention money. Instead, they noted that the company recognizes their performance in little ways that make a difference.

The message from both surveys is this: Managing people well pays off. Doing so may also lead to greater **organizational commitment**. We use this term to describe the degree to which an employee identifies with the organization and wishes to maintain membership in the organization.[11] This type of commitment is often called **affective commitment**, which describes the strength of an individual's emotional attachment to, identification with, and involvement in the organization. Employees who are highly committed go beyond expected behaviours to provide extra service, extra insight, or whatever else is needed to get the job done. There is some concern that extreme organizational commitment can have negative effects, in that employees with strong organizational commitment may behave unethically to protect the organization. However, this concern should not be a reason to avoid encouraging commitment. One benefit of having committed employees is that they are less resistant to change when organizations need to carry out changes.

Finally, managing well may improve organizational citizenship behaviour, a topic we discuss later in the chapter.

For You as an Individual

You may be wondering exactly how OB applies to you if you are still in school and not yet working. Or you may want to know how OB applies to you if you are planning to run your own business or work for a small nonprofit organization, rather than a large organization. Or you may be asking yourself how OB applies to you if you are not planning on being a manager. We look at each of these scenarios below to help you see that OB is relevant in a variety of situations.

"What if I Am 'Just' a Student?"

You may think that OB is only useful once you reach the workplace. However, many of the concepts that apply to organizations also apply to teamwork, something many students have to do. As a team member, it's important to know how personality differences affect the ability of people to work together. You may need to motivate members of your team. Or you may want to know how to create a more effective team or solve conflict in a team. Individually or as part of a team, you also have decisions to make and need to know how to communicate with others. All of these topics are covered by OB.

"What if I Am Not Going to Work in a Large Organization?"

You may think that when we say "organization" we are referring to large financial firms in office towers, to the exclusion of the variety of other forms of organization that exist. You may be thinking that you want to work in a small business, or in your family's business, so OB has no relevance for you. But this would be short-sighted. Throughout your life you will work with a variety of organizations, and OB will help you better understand how those organizations work.

"What if I Do Not Want to Be a Manager?"

Many of us carry around a simplistic view of work organizations, with the participants divided into set categories: owners, leaders and/or managers, and employees. These distinct roles are found most often in large, publicly held organizations. Distinct organizational roles become more blurred when we discuss smaller, privately owned firms.

When we talk about leadership in organizations, we typically mean the person or persons responsible for setting the overall vision of the organization, although leadership can come from informal sources as well. While managers and leaders have seen their roles expand as a result of factors such as globalization and e-commerce, employees are also being asked to "move beyond their traditional role as inputs to the process of achieving organizational goals."[12] More and more employees are taking on this new role and responsibility. In particular, The Conference Board of Canada says that in high-performance organizations, "Employees are willing to be accountable for their own and the organization's success."[13] To be accountable means that employees "take charge of their own careers, decide what skills they need to acquire and determine where they wish to employ these skills."[14]

You may be thinking that you are not planning to work in an organization at all because you would prefer to be self-employed. While self-employed individuals often do not act as managers, they certainly interact with other individuals and organizations as part of their work. Thus, the study of OB is just as important for the sole proprietor or entrepreneur as for those who work in large organizations. It gives all of us more insight into how to work with others, and how to prepare to become employees in the twenty-first-century workplace.

TODAY'S CHALLENGES IN THE CANADIAN WORKPLACE

Inner City Renovation (ICR) employees are different from many typical for-profit organizations.[15] Forty-seven percent have not completed high school, 58 percent have criminal records, 79 percent were unemployed before being hired by ICR, and 37 percent had not held a job for more than 2 years. Employees often have had jobs that last only a few days to a month; 26 percent have held 30 jobs or more. The lives of these employees are marked by unstable employment, and thus, within the first year of employment at ICR, 42 percent missed or were not able to work because of domestic or family issues.

Because many of its employees lack job experience, ICR needed to establish a culture that would motivate employees to show up for work. Managers recognized the need to create a supportive work environment for its employees.

Many of ICR's employees are Aboriginal peoples who live in the inner city. To better understand the needs of these and its other employees, ICR managers conducted a formal survey of all employees and had a staff retreat near the end of the first year of operation. Because of the large number of Aboriginal peoples employed by ICR, the retreat incorporated certain Aboriginal traditions as part of the event. All discussions were held in a circle format, and the retreat included a sweat (a ceremony done for meditation and cleansing). In addition, employees had one-on-one meetings with the ICR president and the employee support worker.

ICR is a very committed employer. The company wants to change the life circumstances of its employees. What factors affect employee motivation? How can ICR socialize its employees to perform well in their jobs? How can ICR survive in the face of competition while maintaining its goal of employing people with limited skills and job experience?

4 What challenges do managers and employees face in the workplace of the twenty-first century?

OB considers that organizations are made up of levels, moving up from the individual, to the group, to the entire organizational structure. Each level contributes to the variety of activities that occur in today's workplace. Exhibit 1-4 presents the three levels of analysis we consider in this textbook, and shows that as we move from the individual level to the organization systems level, we deepen our understanding of behaviour in organizations. The three basic levels are like building blocks: Each level is constructed upon the previous level. Group concepts grow out of the foundation we lay out in the section on individual behaviour. We then overlay structural constraints on the individual and group in order to arrive at OB.

When we look at the different levels in the organization, we recognize that each has challenges that can affect how the levels above and/or below might operate. We consider the challenges at the individual, group, and organizational levels.

This chapter's *CBC Video Case Incident* further explores organizational challenges in the twenty-first century.

GM Woes

Challenges at the Individual Level

At the individual level, managers and employees need to learn how to work with people who may be different from themselves in a variety of dimensions, including personality, perception, values, and attitudes. This point is illustrated by the employee situation at ICR, where employees have a variety of experiences and come from several cultures.

Individuals also have different levels of job satisfaction and motivation, and these affect how managers manage employees. For instance, some of ICR's employees had drug and alcohol dependencies that affected their motivation and productivity.

More organizations expect employees to be empowered and to take on more responsibility than ever before. This expectation puts demands on both managers and employees. ICR initially created three committees where employees could give input on a variety of issues, but the managers were so busy trying to make sure the company met financial goals that they didn't have time to help the employees work on these committees.

Perhaps the greatest challenge facing individuals (and organizations) is how to behave ethically, as the findings from the Gomery Commission, looking into the $250-million sponsorship scandal of the Liberal party, show. At his sentencing hearing, Jean Brault, found guilty of defrauding the government of $1.23 million on contracts his company, Montreal-based Groupaction Marketing, obtained claimed the external pressures he faced led to his actions: "I'm not trying to excuse what I did, but essentially it's the political demands, the demands on me, that led me to take that first step."[16]

EXHIBIT 1-4   Basic OB Model

Individual Differences

People enter groups and organizations with certain characteristics that influence their behaviour, the more obvious of these being personality characteristics, perception, values, and attitudes. These characteristics are essentially intact when an individual joins an organization, and for the most part, there is little that those in the organization can do to alter them. Yet they have a very real impact on behaviour. In this light, we look at perception, personality, values, and attitudes, and their impact on individual behaviour in Chapters 2 and 3.

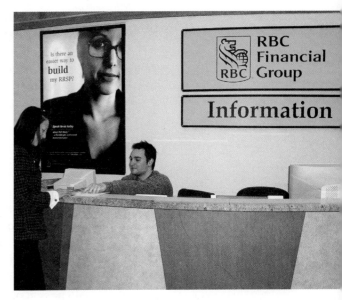

Job Satisfaction

✱ *Does job satisfaction really make a difference?*

Employees are increasingly demanding satisfying jobs. As we discuss in Chapter 3, less than half of Canadian employees are very satisfied with their jobs. The belief that satisfied employees are more productive than dissatisfied employees has been a basic assumption among managers for years. Although there is evidence that questions that causal relationship,[17] it can be argued that society should be concerned not only with the quantity of life—that is, with concerns such as higher productivity and material acquisitions—but also with its quality. Researchers with strong humanistic values argue that satisfaction is a legitimate objective of an organization. They believe that organizations should be responsible for providing employees with jobs that are challenging and intrinsically rewarding. This chapter's *Ethical Dilemma Exercise*, on page 24, questions the extent to which organizations should be responsible for helping individuals achieve balance in their lives.

Employers can pay the price when employees are not satisfied with working conditions. Bank tellers at Toronto-Dominion Bank and Canadian Imperial Bank of Commerce in Sudbury, Ontario, voted to join the United Steelworkers of America in 2005. Employees at a Sears Canada department store in Sudbury also pursued the possibility of joining the Steelworkers in 2005. Brian Whalen, a maintenance worker for the store, said that "job satisfaction levels . . . have declined dramatically over the past two years." He noted that employees were upset about low hourly wages, a benefits package that was not affordable, and job security.[18] While unionization does not necessarily increase job satisfaction, it does provide a mechanism for employees to have some bargaining power with their employers.

Toronto-based Royal Bank of Canada, Canada's largest financial institution in terms of assets, commands the respect of many business leaders. In a 2004 KPMG/Ipsos Reid poll of 250 Canadian CEOs, the company was ranked first in six out of nine categories, including "Top of Mind Most Respected Corporations," "Best Long-Term Investment Value," and "Human Resources Management."

Sears Canada
www.sears.ca

Motivation

An Angus Reid survey showed that 29 percent of employees do not feel they receive fair or reasonable rewards for the work that they do.[19] To address this concern, Chapter 4 discusses the importance of rewards in motivating employees. You may find the discussion of motivation and rewards particularly interesting in *Case Incident—How a UPS Manager Cut Turnover*, on page 25, where a manager faces the challenges of motivating different types of employees in order to reduce turnover.

Empowerment

At the same time that managers are being held responsible for employee satisfaction and happiness, they are also being asked to share more of their power. If you read any popular business magazine nowadays, you will find that managers are referred to as "coaches," "advisers," "sponsors," or "facilitators," rather than "bosses."[20]

Employees' responsibilities are increasing too. In many organizations, employees have become "associates" or "teammates."[21] Decision making is being pushed down to the operating level, where employees are being given the freedom to make choices about schedules, procedures, and solving work-related problems.

empowerment Giving employees responsibility for what they do.

> * *Are you ready to assume more responsibility at work?*

What is happening is that managers are empowering employees. **Empowerment** means managers are putting employees in charge of what they do. In the process, managers are learning how to give up control, and employees are learning how to take responsibility for their work and make appropriate decisions. The roles for both managers and employees are changing, often without much guidance on how to perform these new roles.

American Management Association
www.amanet.org

How widespread are these changes in the workplace? While we have no specific Canadian data, a survey by the American Management Association of 1040 executives found that 46 percent of their companies were still using a hierarchical structure, but 31 percent defined their companies as empowered.[22] *OB in the Workplace* looks at how WestJet Airlines empowers its employees.

OB IN THE WORKPLACE

WestJet Airline's Employees Work Together

What do empowered employees do? Calgary-based WestJet Airlines employees are given lots of freedom to manage themselves.[23] Clive Beddoe, the company's president and CEO, was determined to create a company "where people wanted to manage themselves."

At WestJet, employees are asked to be responsible for their tasks, rather than rely on supervisors to tell them what to do. That includes Beddoe: "I don't direct things," he says. "We set some standards and expectations, but [I] don't interfere in how our people do their jobs." Instead, employees are given guidelines for behaviour. For instance, flight attendants are directed to serve customers in a caring, positive, and cheerful manner. How do they carry that out? It's up to them. Employees also share tasks. When a plane lands, all employees on the flight, even those who are flying off-duty, are expected to prepare the plane for its next takeoff.

Obviously, WestJet can lower its costs by keeping the number of supervisors down. The company operates with about 60 employees per aircraft, while a typical full-service airline such as Air Canada needs more than 140. But allowing employees to manage themselves has a bigger benefit. Beddoe believes it encourages employees to take pride in what they do. "They are the ones making the decisions about what they're doing and how they're doing it," says Beddoe.

Throughout the textbook you will find references to empowerment. We discuss it in terms of power in Chapter 7, and we discuss how leaders contribute to empowerment in Chapter 8.

Behaving Ethically

In an organizational world characterized by cutbacks, expectations of increasing worker productivity, and tough competition in the marketplace, it's not altogether surprising that many employees feel pressured to cut corners, break rules, and engage in other forms of questionable practices.

The Enron scandal in the United States illustrated how casually some people treat the subject of ethics. Enron executives creatively changed how they reported their profits and losses. When challenged, the company's chair, Kenneth Lay, chose to look the other way. The reputation of accounting firm Arthur Andersen was destroyed because it failed to question Enron's accounting practices.

Ethics starts at the individual level. While the word refers to moral conduct, **ethics** is also the study of moral values or principles that guide our behaviour and inform us whether actions are right or wrong. Ethics helps us "do the right thing," such as not padding expense reports, or not phoning in sick to attend the opening of *Superman Returns*.

Individuals as well as organizations can face ethical dilemmas. As we show in Chapter 9, the study of ethics does not come with black and white answers. Rather, many factors need to be considered in determining the ethical thing to do. Those individuals who strive hard to create their own set of ethical values and those organizations that encourage an ethical climate in the face of financial and other pressures will be more likely to do the right thing.

Throughout this textbook you will find references to ethical and unethical behaviour. The *Focus on Ethics* vignettes provide thought-provoking illustrations of how various organizations deal with ethics.

Challenges at the Group Level

> ✳ *What people-related challenges have you noticed in the workplace?*

The behaviour of people in groups is more than the sum total of all the individuals acting in their own way. People's behaviour when they are in a group differs from their behaviour when they are alone. Therefore, the next step in developing an understanding of OB is the study of group behaviour.

Chapter 5 lays the foundation for an understanding of the dynamics of group and team behaviour. That chapter discusses how individuals are influenced by the patterns of behaviour they are expected to exhibit, what the team considers to be acceptable standards of behaviour, and how to make teams more effective.

Chapters 6 and 7 examine some of the more complex issues of interaction: communication, conflict, and negotiation; and power and politics. These two chapters give you an opportunity to think about how communication processes sometimes become complicated because of office politicking and interpersonal and group conflict.

Few people work entirely alone, and some organizations make widespread use of teams. Therefore, most individuals interact with others during the workday. This can lead to a need for greater interpersonal skills. The workplace is also made up of people from a variety of backgrounds. Thus, learning how to work with people from different cultures has become more important. We review some of the challenges that occur at the group level below.

Working With Others

Much of the success in any job involves developing good interpersonal, or "people," skills. In fact, The Conference Board of Canada identified the skills that form the foundation for a high-quality workforce in today's workplace as communication, thinking, learning, and working with others. Positive attitudes and behaviours and an ability to take responsibility for one's actions are also key skills, according to the Conference Board.[24] Because many people will work in small and medium-sized firms in the future, Human Resources and Skills Development Canada has noted that additional important skills are team building and priority management.[25]

In Canada's increasingly competitive and demanding workplace, neither managers nor employees can succeed on their technical skills alone. They must also have good people skills. Management professor Jin Nam Choi of McGill University reports that research shows that 40 percent of managers either leave or stop performing within 18 months of starting at an organization "because they have failed to develop relationships with bosses, colleagues or subordinates."[26] Choi's comment underscores the importance of developing interpersonal skills. This book has been written to help you develop those people skills, whether as an employee, manager, or potential manager.

To learn more about the interpersonal skills needed in today's workplace, read *From Concepts to Skills* on pages 27–29.

Workforce Diversity

> * *Why should you care about understanding other people?*

Organizations are becoming more diverse, employing a greater variety of people in terms of gender, race, ethnicity, sexual orientation, and age. A diverse workforce includes, for instance, women, Aboriginal peoples, Asian Canadians, African Canadians, Indo-Canadians, people with disabilities, gays and lesbians, and senior citizens. It also includes people with different demographic characteristics, such as education and socio-economic status. The ability to adapt to many different people is one of the most important and broad-based challenges facing organizations. We discuss **workforce diversity** issues in Chapter 3.

workforce diversity The mix of people in organizations in terms of gender, race, ethnicity, disability, sexual orientation, and age, and demographic characteristics such as education and socio-economic status.

One of the challenges in Canadian workplaces is the mix of generations working side by side: the Elders (those over 60), Baby Boomers (born between the mid-1940s and mid-1960s), Generation Xers (born between the mid-1960s and early 1980s), and the Net Generation (born between 1977 and 1997). Due to their very different life experiences, they bring different values and different expectations to the workplace.

We used to assume that people in organizations who differed from the stereotypical employee would somehow simply fit in. We now know that employees don't set aside their cultural values and lifestyle preferences when they come to work. Organizations therefore try to accommodate diverse groups of people by addressing their different lifestyles, family needs, and work styles.[27] We need to keep in mind that what motivates one person may not motivate another. One person may like a straightforward and open style of communication that another finds uncomfortable and threatening. To work effectively with different people, we need to understand how culture shapes them, and learn to adapt our interaction style.

The *Focus on Diversity* feature found throughout the textbook helps create awareness of the diversity issues that arise in organizations. Our first example looks at accommodations made to help Aboriginal cadets feel welcome at the RCMP training academy in Regina.

FOCUS ON **DIVERSITY**

Bringing Aboriginal Culture to the RCMP

How does a Heritage Room promote RCMP diversity? The sweet-smelling smoke of burning buffalo sage cleansed the air at opening ceremonies for the Aboriginal Heritage Room in the RCMP's Regina training academy. With cedar walls, Plains Indian artifacts, and reproductions of old photographs of Aboriginal Canadians, this is not a typical room in a police academy.[28]

The Heritage Room was set up to help Aboriginal cadets engage in spiritual practices while they train. They can now hold ceremonies, meet with elders, and discuss their culture in the Heritage Room. Dustin Ward, a cadet from the Mi'kmaq reserve in New Brunswick, praised the opening of the room as "one more sign that the RCMP welcomes First Nations Mounties. It shows the children hope that they can come here some day and be an RCMP cadet."

The Heritage Room is one of a series of RCMP programs to encourage diversity. In the late 1980s, the RCMP decided to allow Aboriginal Mounties to wear their hair in braids, if they wanted. Saskatchewan-born Aboriginal Pauline Busch, who helped get the Heritage Room opened, remembered that decision. "There's nothing that warms a child's heart and pride as seeing another Aboriginal person in the red serge, fully outlined with the braids."

Workforce diversity has important implications for management practice. Managers need to shift their philosophy from treating everyone alike to recognizing differences. They need to respond to those differences in ways that will ensure employee retention and greater productivity, while at the same time not discriminating against certain groups. This shift includes, for instance, providing diversity training and revising benefit programs to be more "family-friendly." At ICR, managers brought in a part-time social support worker to help new employees adjust to full-time employment. Many of ICR's employees faced family issues, domestic disputes, and substance abuse issues that made it difficult to meet work responsibilities. The support worker helped individual employees develop steps to deal with personal issues.

Diversity, if positively managed, can increase creativity and innovation in organizations, as well as improve decision making by providing different perspectives on problems.[29] When diversity is not managed properly, there is potential for higher turnover, miscommunication, and more interpersonal conflicts.

Challenges at the Organizational Level

OB becomes more complex when we move to the organizational level of analysis. Just as groups are not the sum total of individuals, so organizations are not the sum total of individuals and groups. There are many more interacting factors that place constraints on individual and group behaviour. In Chapter 8 we consider how leadership and management affect employee behaviour. In Chapter 9 we discuss decision making and creativity, and then look at the issues of ethics and corporate social responsibility. In Chapter 10 we look at organizational culture, which is generally considered the glue that holds organizations together. We also discuss organizational change in Chapter 10. As we have noted already, and as will become clear throughout the textbook, change has become a key issue for organizations.

Canadian businesses face many challenges in the twenty-first century. Their ability to be as productive as US businesses is constantly tested.[30] The need to develop effective employees, and to manage human resource issues such as absenteeism and turnover, is critical. Meanwhile, Canadian businesses face greater competition because of the global economy. Many companies have expanded their operations overseas, which means they have to learn how to manage people from different cultures.

Productivity

An organization or group is productive if it achieves its goals and does so by transferring inputs (labour and raw materials) to outputs (finished goods or services) at the lowest cost. **Productivity** implies a concern for both **effectiveness** (achieving goals) and **efficiency** (watching costs). The late management expert Peter Drucker stated that *effectiveness* is "doing the right thing," while *efficiency* is "doing things right."[31] For example, a hospital is *effective* when it successfully meets the needs of its patients. It is *efficient* when it can do so at a low cost. If a hospital manages to achieve higher output from its present staff—say, by reducing the average number of days a patient is confined to a bed, or

productivity A performance measure including effectiveness and efficiency.

effectiveness The achievement of goals.

efficiency The ratio of effective work output to the input required to produce the work.

by increasing the number of staff-patient contacts per day—we say that the hospital has gained productive *efficiency*. Similarly, a student team is effective when it puts together a group project that gets a high mark. It is efficient when all the members manage their time appropriately and are not at each other's throats. ICR faced effectiveness issues because it started out by having one team leader for three work teams. On paper, this appeared to be an efficient strategy. However, each team needed more supervision than the manager could provide while trying to manage three teams, which decreased each team's productivity. Therefore, ICR's strategy was not effective.

As you study OB, you will begin to understand those factors that influence the effectiveness and efficiency of individuals, groups, and the overall organization.

Developing Effective Employees

One of the major challenges facing organizations in the twenty-first century is how to engage employees effectively so that they are committed to the organization. We use the term **organizational citizenship behaviour (OCB)** to describe discretionary behaviour that is not part of an employee's formal job requirements, but that nevertheless promotes the effective functioning of the organization.[32] Recent research has also looked at expanding the work on OCB to team behaviour.[33]

Successful organizations need employees who will go beyond their usual job duties, providing performance that is beyond expectations. In today's dynamic workplace, where tasks are increasingly done in teams and where flexibility is critical, organizations need employees who will engage in "good citizenship" behaviours, such as making constructive statements about their work group and the organization, helping others on their team, volunteering for extra job activities, avoiding unnecessary conflicts, showing care for organizational property, respecting the spirit as well as the letter of rules and regulations, and gracefully tolerating the occasional work-related impositions and nuisances.

Toronto-based BBDO Canada encourages an entrepreneurial spirit as a way of inspiring OCB. The ad agency's president and CEO Gerry Frascione notes that a team leader on the Campbell Soup account overheard a Campbell's representative musing about a program that would launch Campbell's Soup ads when the temperature dipped. "Instead of waiting to get approvals, she acted very entrepreneurially and took it upon herself and made the whole thing happen in one week," says Frascione. "She went back to the client, analyzed the situation, fleshed out the opportunity, came up with an integrated communication plan, came up with a budget, and it was all done within five days."[34]

Organizations want and need employees who will do those things that are not in any job description. The evidence indicates that organizations that have such employees outperform those that don't.[35] As a result, OB is concerned with organizational citizenship behaviour.

Putting People First

Professor Jeffery Pfeffer of the Stanford Graduate School of Business advocates that managers should spend more time recognizing the value of the people who work for them. He emphasizes the need to "put people first" in considering organizational objectives and suggests the people-first strategy not only generates a committed workforce, but also significantly affects the bottom line.[36] Pfeffer notes that research shows that when organizations concern themselves with developing their employees, they are more successful. For instance, a study of 968 US firms found that those that used people-first strategies had significantly less turnover, and significantly greater sales, market value, and profits.[37] Similar results were found in a study of 100 German companies.[38]

organizational citizenship behaviour (OCB) Discretionary behaviour that is not part of an employee's formal job requirements, but that nevertheless promotes the effective functioning of the organization.

BBDO Canada
www.bbdo.ca

Pfeffer explains that people will work harder when they feel they have "more control and say in their work." They work smarter when they are "encouraged to build skills and competence." They work more responsibly when "responsibility is placed in the hands of employees farther down in the organization." *OB in Action—Practices of Successful Organizations* outlines the practices that successful people-first organizations use to encourage their employees to work harder, smarter, and more responsibly. *Case Incident—Great Plains Software: Pursuing a People-First Strategy* on the CD-ROM that accompanies this textbook asks you to examine the impact of "putting people first" in managing an organization.

Global Competition

In recent years, Canadian businesses have faced tough competition from the United States, Europe, Japan, and even China, as well as from other companies within our borders. To survive, they have had to reduce costs, increase productivity, and improve quality. A number of Canadian companies have found it necessary to merge in order to survive. For instance, Rona, the Boucherville, Quebec-based home improvement store, bought out Lansing, Revy, and Revelstoke in recent years in order to defend its turf against the Atlanta, Georgia-based Home Depot. That may not be enough to keep it from being swallowed up by the Mooresville, North Carolina-based Lowe's home improvement company, however.

Some employers are starting to outsource jobs to other countries, where labour costs are lower. For instance, Toronto-based Dell Canada's technical service lines are handled by technicians working in India. Toronto-based Wall & Associates, a full-service chartered accounting and management consulting firm, outsources document management to Uganda. Employees in Uganda are willing to work for $1 an hour to sort and record receipts. While these wages might seem low, on average, Ugandans make only $1 a day.

These changes in the workplace, and the loss of jobs to international outsourcing, mean that the actual jobs that employees perform, and even those of managers to whom they report, are in a permanent state of change. To stay employable under these conditions, employees need to continually update their knowledge and skills to meet new job requirements.[39] Today's managers and employees have to learn to live with flexibility, spontaneity, uncertainty, and unpredictability.

Managing and Working in a Multicultural World

Twenty or 30 years ago, national borders protected most firms from foreign competitive pressures. This is no longer the case. Trading blocks such as the North American Free Trade Agreement (NAFTA) and the European Union (EU) have greatly reduced tariffs and barriers to trade, and North America and Europe are no longer the only continents with highly skilled labour. The Internet also helps companies become more globally connected, by opening up international sales and by increasing opportunities to carry on business. Even small firms can bid on projects in different countries and compete with larger firms through the Internet. An implication of all these changes is that you could find yourself managing or working in a multicultural environment.

North American Free Trade Agreement (NAFTA)
www.nafta-sec-alena.org

European Union (EU)
http://europa.eu

OB IN ACTION

Practices of Successful Organizations

According to professor Jeffery Pfeffer of the Stanford Graduate School of Business, the following practices characterize organizations that benefit from how they manage their employees:

→ Providing **employment security** so that employees don't fear loss of jobs

→ **Hiring** people who have the **right skills and abilities**

→ Creating **self-managed teams** that have decision-making power

→ **Paying well**, and tying pay to organizational performance

→ Providing **extensive training** for skills, knowledge, and initiative

→ Reducing status differences so that **all employees feel valued**

→ **Sharing information** about organizational performance

Source: Adapted from J. Pfeffer and J. F. Veiga, "Putting People First for Organizational Success," *Academy of Management Executive* 13, no. 2 (May 1999), pp. 37–48.

SUMMARY AND IMPLICATIONS

1 **What is organizational behaviour?** Organizational behaviour (OB) is a field of study that investigates the impact that individuals, groups, and structure have on behaviour within an organization. It uses that knowledge to make organizations work more effectively. Specifically, OB focuses on how to improve productivity, reduce both absenteeism and turnover, and increase employee job satisfaction. OB also helps us understand how people can work together more effectively in the workplace.

OB recognizes differences, helps us see the value of workforce diversity, and calls attention to practices that may need to be changed when managing and working in different countries. It can help improve quality and employee productivity by showing managers how to empower their people, as well as how to design and implement change programs. It offers specific insights to improve people skills.

2 **Isn't organizational behaviour common sense? Or just like psychology?** OB is built on contributions from a number of behavioural disciplines, including psychology, sociology, social psychology, anthropology, and political science.

We all hold generalizations about the behaviour of people. Some of our generalizations may provide valid insights into human behaviour, but many are wrong. If understanding behaviour were simply common sense, we would see fewer problems in the workplace, because managers and employees would know how to behave. OB provides a systematic approach to improving predictions of behaviour that would be made from common sense alone.

3 **How does knowing about organizational behaviour make work and life more understandable?** From a management point of view, knowing OB can help you manage well. Managing people well pays off. It may also lead employees to have greater organizational commitment. From an individual point of view, knowing OB can help you understand why the workplace functions in the way it does. OB can also help you understand how to deal with others if you decide to start your own business.

4 **What challenges do managers and employees face in the workplace of the twenty-first century?** OB considers three levels of analysis—the individual, the group, and the organization—which, combined, help us understand behaviour in organizations. Each level has different challenges. At the individual level, we encounter employees who have different characteristics, and thus we consider how to better understand and make the most of these differences. Because employees have become more cynical about their employers, job satisfaction and motivation have become important issues in today's organizations. Employees are also confronted with the trend toward an empowered workplace. Perhaps the greatest challenge individuals (and organizations) face is how to behave ethically.

At the group level, individuals are increasingly expected to work in teams, which means that they need to do so effectively. Employees are expected to have good interpersonal skills. The workplace is now made up of people from many different backgrounds, requiring a greater ability to understand those different from ourselves.

At the organizational level, Canadian businesses face many challenges in the twenty-first century. They face ongoing competition at home and from US businesses, as well as growing competition from the global marketplace. Productivity is critical. It has become essential to develop effective employees who are committed to the organization. By putting people first, organizations can generate a committed workforce, but taking this approach becomes a challenge for businesses that focus solely on the bottom line. Organizations also have to learn how to be more sensitive to cultural differences, not only because Canada is a multicultural country, but also because competitive companies often develop global alliances or set up plants in foreign countries, where being aware of other cultures becomes a key to success.

For Review

1. Define *organizational behaviour.*

2. What is an organization? Is the family unit an organization? Explain.

3. "Behaviour is generally predictable, so there is no need to formally study OB." Do you agree or disagree with this statement? Why?

4. What does it mean to say OB takes a contingency approach in its analysis of behaviour?

5. What are the three levels of analysis in our OB model? Are they related? If so, how?

6. What are some of the challenges and opportunities that managers face as we move into the twenty-first century?

7. Why is job satisfaction an important consideration for OB?

8. What are effectiveness and efficiency, and how are they related to OB?

For Critical Thinking

1. "OB is for everyone." Build an argument to support this statement.

2. Why do you think the subject of OB might be criticized as being "only common sense," when we would rarely hear such a comment about a course in physics or statistics? Do you think this criticism of OB is fair?

3. On a scale of 1 to 10, measuring the sophistication of a scientific discipline in predicting phenomena, mathematical physics would probably be a 10. Where do you think OB would fall on the scale? Why?

4. Can empowerment lead to greater job satisfaction?

OB for You

- As you journey through this course in OB, bear in mind that the processes we describe are as relevant to you as an individual as they are to organizations, managers, and employees.

- When you work together with student teams, join a student organization, or volunteer time to a community group, know that your ability to get along with others has an effect on your interactions with the other people in the group and the achievement of the group's goals.

- If you are aware of how your perceptions and personality affect your interactions with others, you can be more careful in forming your initial impression of others.

- By knowing how to motivate others who are working with you, how to communicate effectively, and when to negotiate and compromise, you can get along in a variety of situations that are not necessarily work-related.

POINT

Looking for the Quick Fix to OB Issues

Walk into your nearest major bookstore. You will undoubtedly find a large section of books devoted to management and managing human behaviour. A close look at the titles will find there is certainly no shortage of popular books on topics related to OB. To illustrate the point, consider the following popular book titles that are currently available on the topic of leadership:

- *The Leadership Secrets of Attila the Hun* (Warner, 1990)

- *Make It So: Leadership Lessons from Star Trek, The Next Generation* (Pocket Books, 1996)

- *The Art of Leadership by Sun Tzu* (Premier, 2000)

- *Power Plays: Shakespeare's Lessons in Leadership and Management* (Simon & Schuster, 2000)

- *The Leadership Teachings of Geronimo* (Sterling House, 2002)

- *Leadership Wisdom from the Monk Who Sold His Ferrari* (Hay House, 2003)

- *Tony Soprano on Management: Leadership Lessons Inspired by America's Favorite Mobster* (Berkley, 2004)

Organizations are always looking for leaders; and managers and manager-wannabes are continually looking for ways to hone their leadership skills. Publishers respond to this demand by offering hundreds of titles that proclaim to provide insights into the complex subject of leadership. People hope that there are "shortcuts" to leadership success and that books like these can provide them with the secrets to leadership that others know about and which they can quickly learn through these books.

 COUNTERPOINT

Beware of the Quick Fix!

We all want to find quick and simple solutions to our complex problems. But here's the bad news: On problems related to OB, the quick and simple solutions are often wrong because they fail to consider the diversity among organizations, situations, and individuals. As Einstein said, "Everything should be made as simple as possible, but not simpler."

When it comes to trying to understand people at work, there is no shortage of simplistic ideas that books and consultants promote. And these books are not just on leadership. Consider three recent bestsellers. *Who Moved My Cheese?* is a metaphor about two mice that is meant to convey the benefits of accepting change. *Fish!* tells how a fish market in Seattle made its jobs motivating. And *Whale Done!* proposes that managers can learn a lot about motivating people from techniques used by whale trainers at Sea World in San Diego. Are the "insights" from these books generalizable to people working in hundreds of different countries, in a thousand different organizations, and doing a million different jobs? It's very unlikely.

Popular books on OB often have cute titles and are fun to read. But they can be dangerous. They make the job of managing people seem much simpler than it really is. They are also often based on the authors' opinions rather than substantive research.

OB is a complex subject. There are few, if any, simple statements about human behaviour that are generalizable to all people in all situations. Should you really try to apply leadership insights you got from a book on Shakespeare or Attila the Hun to managing software engineers in the twenty-first century?

The capitalist system ensures that when a need exists, opportunistic individuals will surface to fill that need. When it comes to managing people at work, there is clearly a need for valid and reliable insights to guide managers and those aspiring to managerial positions. However, most of the offerings available at your local bookstore tend to be simplistic solutions. To the degree that people buy these books and enthusiastically expect them to provide them with the secrets to effective management, they do a disservice to themselves and those they are trying to manage.

The Competing Values Framework: Identifying Your Interpersonal Skills

From the list below, identify what you believe to be your strongest skills, and then identify those in which you think your performance is weak. You should identify about 4 strong skills and 4 weak skills.

1. Taking initiative
2. Goal setting
3. Delegating effectively
4. Personal productivity and motivation
5. Motivating others
6. Time and stress management
7. Planning
8. Organizing
9. Controlling
10. Receiving and organizing information
11. Evaluating routine information
12. Responding to routine information
13. Understanding yourself and others
14. Interpersonal communication
15. Developing subordinates
16. Team building
17. Participative decision making
18. Conflict management
19. Living with change
20. Creative thinking
21. Managing change
22. Building and maintaining a power base
23. Negotiating agreement and commitment
24. Negotiating and selling ideas

Scoring Key:

These skills are based on the Competing Values Framework (pages 27–29), and they appear in detail in Exhibit 1-6 on page 28. Below, you will see how the individual skills relate to various managerial roles. Using the skills you identified as strongest, identify which roles you feel especially prepared for right now. Then, using the skills you identified as weakest, identify areas in which you might want to gain more skill. You should also use this information to determine whether you are currently more internally or externally focused, or oriented more toward flexibility or control.

Director: 1, 2, 3

Producer: 4, 5, 6

Coordinator: 7, 8, 9

Monitor: 10, 11, 12

Mentor: 13, 14, 15

Facilitator: 16, 17, 18

Innovator: 19, 20, 21

Broker: 22, 23, 24

After reviewing how your strengths and weaknesses relate to the skills that today's managers and leaders need, as illustrated in Exhibit 1-6, you should consider whether you need to develop a broader range of skills.

Source: Created based on material from R. E. Quinn, S. R. Faerman, M. P. Thompson, and M. R. McGrath, *Becoming a Master Manager: A Competency Framework* (New York: John Wiley and Sons, 1990), chapter 1.

BREAKOUT **GROUP** EXERCISES

Form small groups to discuss the following topics, as assigned by your instructor:

1. Consider a group situation in which you have worked. To what extent did the group rely on the technical skills of the group members vs. their interpersonal skills? Which skills seemed most important in helping the group function well?

2. Identify some examples of "worst jobs." What conditions of these jobs made them unpleasant? To what extent were these conditions related to behaviours of individuals?

3. Develop a list of "organizational puzzles," that is, behaviour you have observed in organizations that seemed to make little sense. As the term progresses, see if you can begin to explain these puzzles, using your knowledge of OB.

WORKING WITH **OTHERS** EXERCISE

Interpersonal Skills in the Workplace

This exercise asks you to consider the skills outlined in the Competing Values Framework on pages 27–29 to develop an understanding of managerial expertise. Steps 1–4 can be completed in 15–20 minutes.

1. Using the skills listed in the *Learning About Yourself Exercise,* identify the 4 skills that you think all managers should have.

2. Identify the 4 skills that you think are least important for managers to have.

3. In groups of 5–7, reach a consensus on the most-needed and least-needed skills identified in Steps 1 and 2.

4. Using Exhibit 1-6, determine whether your "ideal" managers would have trouble managing in some dimensions of organizational demands.

5. Your instructor will lead a general discussion of your results.

ETHICAL **DILEMMA** EXERCISE

What Is the Right Balance Between Work and Personal Life?

When you think of work/life conflicts, you may tend to think of people in lower levels of organizations who might not have as much flexibility in determining their workdays. However, a recent survey of 179 CEOs revealed that many of them struggle with this issue. For instance, 31 percent said they have a high level of stress in their lives; 47 percent admitted that they would sacrifice some compensation for more personal time; and 16 percent considered changing jobs in the past 6 months to reduce stress or sacrifices made in their personal lives.

Most of these surveyed executives conceded that they had given up, and continue to give up, a lot to get to the top in their organizations. They are often tired from the extensive and exhausting travel their jobs demand, not to mention an average 60-hour workweek. Yet most feel the climb to the CEO position was worth whatever sacrifices they have had to make.

Jean Stone, while not representative of the group, indicates the price that some of these executives have had to pay. As senior VP and chief operating officer of Dukane Corporation, an Illinois-based manufacturer of electronic communications equipment, Stone describes herself as highly achievement-oriented. She has an intense focus on her job and admits to having lost sight of her personal life. Recently divorced after a 10-year marriage, she acknowledges that "career and work pressures were a factor in that."

How much emphasis on work is *too much*? What is the right balance between work and personal life? How much would you be willing to give up to be CEO of a major company? And if you were a CEO, what ethical responsibilities,

if any, do you think you have to help your employees balance their work/family obligations?

Source: Based on M. J. Critelli, "Striking a Balance," *IndustryWeek,* November 20, 2000, pp. 26–36.

CASE INCIDENT

How a UPS Manager Cut Turnover

In 2002, Katriona Roeder was promoted to district manager for UPS's operation in Buffalo, New York. She was responsible for $225 million in revenue, 2300 employees, and the processing of some 45 000 packages an hour. When she took over in Buffalo, she faced a serious problem: turnover was out of control. Part-time employees—who load, unload, and sort packages, and who account for half of Buffalo's workforce—were leaving at the rate of 50 percent a year. Cutting this turnover rate became her highest priority.

The entire UPS organization relies heavily on part-time employees. In fact, it has historically been the primary inroad to becoming a full-time employee. Most of UPS's current executives, for instance, began as part-timers while attending college or university, then moved into full-time positions. In addition, UPS has always treated its part-timers well. They are given high pay, flexible work hours, full benefits, and substantial financial aid to go back to school. Yet these pluses did not seem to be enough to keep employees at UPS in Buffalo.

Roeder developed a comprehensive plan to reduce turnover. It focused on improving hiring, communication, the workplace, and supervisory training.

Roeder began by modifying the hiring process to screen out people who essentially wanted full-time jobs. She reasoned that unfulfilled expectations were frustrating the hires whose preferences were for full-time work. Given that it typically took new part-timers six years to work up to a full-time job, it made sense to try to identify people who actually preferred part-time work.

Next, Roeder analyzed the large database of information that UPS had on her district's employees. The data led her to the conclusion that she had five distinct groups working for her—differentiated by ages and stages in their careers. In addition, these groups had different needs and interests. In response, Roeder modified the communication style and motivation techniques she used with each employee to reflect the group to which he or she belonged. For instance, Roeder

found that college students are most interested in building skills that they can apply later in their careers. As long as these employees saw that they were learning new skills, they were content to keep working at UPS. So Roeder began offering them Saturday classes for computer-skill development and career-planning discussions.

Many new UPS employees in Buffalo were intimidated by the huge warehouse in which they had to work. To lessen that intimidation, Roeder improved lighting throughout the building and upgraded break rooms to make them more user-friendly. To further help new employees adjust, she turned some of her best shift supervisors into trainers who provided specific guidance during new hires' first week. She also installed more personal computers on the floor, which gave new employees easier access to training materials and human-resource information on UPS's internal network.

Finally, Roeder expanded training so supervisors had the skills to handle increased empowerment. Recognizing that her supervisors—most of whom were part-timers themselves—were the ones best equipped to understand the needs of part-time employees, supervisors learned how to assess difficult management situations, how to communicate in different ways, and how to identify the needs of different people. Supervisors learned to demonstrate interest in their employees as individuals. For instance, they were taught to inquire about employees' hobbies, where they went to school, and the like.

By 2006, Roeder's program was showing impressive results. Her district's attrition rate had dropped from 50 percent to 6 percent. During the first quarter of 2006, not one part-timer left a night shift. Annual savings attributed to reduced turnover, based largely on lower hiring costs, are estimated to be around $1 million. Additional benefits that the Buffalo district has gained from a more stable workforce include a 20 percent reduction in lost workdays due to work-related injuries and a drop from 4 percent to 1 percent in packages delivered on the wrong day or at the wrong time.

continued

OB *AT WORK*

Questions

1. In dollars-and-cents' terms, why did Katriona Roeder want to reduce turnover?

2. What are the implications from this case for motivating part-time employees?

3. What are the implications from this case for managing in future years when there may be a severe labour shortage?

4. Is it unethical to teach supervisors "to demonstrate interest in their employees as individuals"? Explain.

5. What facts in this case support the argument that OB should be approached from a contingency perspective?

Source: Based on K. H. Hammonds, "Handle With Care," *Fast Company,* August 2002, pp. 103–107.

 VIDEO CASE INCIDENT

GM Woes

In 32 countries around the world, General Motors (GM) produces approximately 20 000 cars and trucks each day. With over 300 000 employees, it may be the largest employer on the planet. However, once a highly profitable, successful company, GM is now struggling. Its inability to adapt to changing times and changing tastes has led to a steadily shrinking market share. Does GM have enough gas for the long haul?

Japanese and Korean automakers have muscled onto GM's turf, outspending GM two to one on research & development. For example, Toyota rolls out smaller, more fuel-efficient cars that consumers want and continues to build new assembly plants in North America. Toyota Canada enjoyed its biggest-ever Canadian sales month in April 2006, despite overall industry sales being down by 5 percent from last year. In contrast, GM took a major hit in April 2006 when it discontinued the deep discounts and incentives it was using to boost profits—sales for the month were 18.8 percent lower than sales in April 2005.

Joseph D'Cruz, business professor at the University of Toronto, equates GM's situation to that of a huge powerful ship, stuck in a sea full of dangerous icebergs. The treacherous thing about an iceberg, D'Cruz notes, is that you can see only 10 percent of it above the surface. D'Cruz sees five key problems lurking below the surface at GM, divided into two categories: people problems and production problems.

People problems include GM's crushing health care costs, a pension plan that is seriously underfunded, and a rigid top-down management structure known more for bureaucracy than decisiveness. Health care costs for GM's American workers have been in the spotlight, and for good reason. GM spent $5 billion (US) on health care costs in 2005, with more than $1 billion spent on drugs alone. Health care adds $1500 to the costs of every vehicle GM produces in the United States. It's a cost that GM's Japanese and Korean

rivals, who have a younger workforce, don't face. As a result, GM is threatening to cut health care for tens of thousands of its retired employees and is pressuring its unions to re-open contracts and give back some of the health benefits they won at the bargaining table.

On the production front, GM produces too many brands and a vehicle lineup that does not excite customers. Even GM bosses admit their vehicles don't have the same pizzazz they once did. The pressure to build more stylish vehicles is urgent because the competition is doing so.

The spike in oil prices has also hurt sales of GM's most important vehicle, the Sports Utility Vehicle (SUV). With gas prices heading higher and higher, consumers are now demanding fuel-efficient vehicles.

The problems are deep and vast at GM, says D'Cruz, and with all the menacing icebergs he believes it should seek help from the courts and apply for bankruptcy protection in the United States while it reorganizes itself. Swamped with so many problems, GM faces a turbulent future.

Questions

1. GM was compared with the *Titanic.* Do you agree with this comparison? Why or why not?

2. What challenges does GM face at the organizational level?

3. What challenges does GM face at the individual and group levels?

Sources: "GM Woes," *CBC—The National,* July 6, 2005; "Toyota Canada Has Huge Month," *Daily Courier* (Kelowna), May 3, 2006, p. B3; and J. Hyde, "Foreign? American? Auto Parts Go Global: U.S. Cars Add Content from Other Countries," *Knight Ridder Tribune Business News,* May 7, 2006, p. 1.

From **Concepts**
to **Skills**

Developing Interpersonal Skills

We note in the chapter that having a broad range of inter-personal skills to draw on makes us more effective organizational participants. So what kinds of interpersonal skills does an individual need in today's workplace? Robert Quinn, Kim Cameron, and their colleagues have developed a model known as the "Competing Values Framework" that can help us identify some of the most useful skills.[40] They note that the range of issues organizations face can be divided along two dimensions: an internal-external and a flexibility-control focus. This is illustrated in Exhibit 1-5. The internal-external dimension refers to the extent that organizations focus on one of two directions: either inwardly, toward employee needs and concerns and/or production processes and internal systems; or outwardly, toward such factors as the marketplace, government regulations, and the changing social, environmental, and technological conditions of the future. The flexibility-control dimension refers to the competing demands of organizations to stay focused on doing what has been done in the past vs. being more flexible in orientation and outlook.

Because organizations face the competing demands shown in Exhibit 1-5, it becomes obvious that managers and employees need a variety of skills to help them function within the various quadrants at different points. For instance, the skills needed to operate an efficient assembly-line process are not the same as those needed to scan the environment or to create opportunities in anticipation of changes in the environment. Quinn and his colleagues use the term *master manager* to indicate that successful managers learn and apply skills that will help them manage across the range of organizational demands; at some times moving toward flexibility, at others moving toward control, sometimes being more internally focused, sometimes being more externally driven.[41]

As organizations increasingly cut their layers, reducing the number of managers while also relying more on the use of teams in the workplace, the skills of the master manager apply as well to the employee. In other words, considering the Competing Values Framework, we can see that both managers and individual employees need to learn new skills and new ways of interpreting their organizational

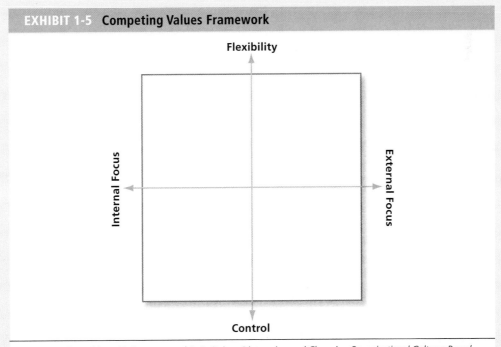

EXHIBIT 1-5 Competing Values Framework

Source: Adapted from K. Cameron and R. E. Quinn, *Diagnosing and Changing Organizational Culture: Based on the Competing Values Framework* (Reading, MA: Addison Wesley Longman, 1999).

continued

contexts. Continuing to use traditional skills and practices that worked in the past is not an option. The growth in self-employment also indicates a need to develop more interpersonal skills, particularly for anyone who goes on to build a business that involves hiring and managing employees.

Exhibit 1-6 outlines the many skills required of today's manager. It gives you an indication of the complex roles that managers and employees fill in the changing workplace. The skills are organized in terms of four major roles: maintaining flexibility, maintaining control, maintaining an external focus, and maintaining an internal focus. The *Learning About Yourself Exercise* on page 23 helps you identify your own strengths and weaknesses in these skill areas so that you can have a better sense of how close you are to becoming a successful manager. For instance, on the flexibility side, organizations want to inspire their employees toward high-performance behaviour. Such behaviour includes looking ahead to the future and imagining possible new directions for the organization. To do these things, employees need to think and act like mentors and facilitators. It is also important to have the skills of innovators and brokers. On the control side, organizations need to set clear goals about productivity expectations, and they have to

develop and implement systems to carry out the production process. To be effective on the production side, employees need to have the skills of monitors, coordinators, directors, and producers. The *Working With Others Exercise* on page 24 will help you better understand how closely your views on the ideal skills of managers and leaders match the skills needed to be successful in the broad range of activities that managers and leaders encounter.

At this point, you may wonder whether it is possible for people to learn all of the skills necessary to become a master manager. More important, you may wonder whether we can change our individual style, say from more controlling to more flexible. Here's what Peggy Witte, who used to be chair, president, and CEO of the now-defunct Royal Oak Mines, said about how her managerial style changed from controlling to more flexible over time: "I started out being very dictatorial. Everybody in head office reported to me. I had to learn to trust other executives so we could work out problems together."[42] So, while it is probably true that each of us has a preferred style of operating, it is also the case that we can enhance the skills we have or develop new ones if that is something we choose to do. Learning to

---

EXHIBIT 1-6   Skills for Mastery in the New Workplace

Source: R. E. Quinn, *Beyond Rational Management* (San Francisco: Jossey-Bass, 1988), p. 86.

work well with others, listening to others, and building trust are skills that are certainly worth trying to master.

Assessing Skills

After you've read this chapter, take the following Self-Assessments on your enclosed CD-ROM:

26. Am I Likely to Become an Entrepreneur?

47. How Motivated Am I to Manage?

48. Am I Well-Suited for a Career as a Global Manager?

Practising Skills

As the father of two young children, Marshall Rogers thought that serving on the board of Marysville Daycare would be a good way to stay in touch with those who cared for his children during the day.[43] But he never dreamed that he would become involved in union-management negotiations with daycare-centre workers.

Late one Sunday evening, in his ninth month as president of the daycare centre, Rogers received a phone call from Grace Ng, a union representative of the Provincial Government Employees' Union (PGEU). Ng informed Rogers that the daycare workers would be unionized the following week. Rogers was stunned to hear this news. Early the next morning, he had to present his new marketing plan to senior management at Techtronix Industries, where he was vice-president of marketing. Somehow he made it through the meeting, wondering why he had not been aware of the employees' unhappiness, and how this action would affect his children.

Following his presentation, Rogers received documentation from the Labour Relations Board indicating that the daycare employees had been working to unionize themselves for more than a year. Rogers immediately contacted Xavier Breslin, the board's vice-president, and together they determined that no one on the board had been aware that the daycare workers were unhappy, let alone prepared to join a union.

Hoping that there was some sort of misunderstanding, Rogers called Emma Reynaud, the Marysville supervisor. Reynaud attended most board meetings, but had never mentioned the union-organizing drive. Yet Reynaud now told Rogers that she had actively encouraged the other daycare workers to consider joining the PGEU because the board had not been interested in the employees' concerns, had not increased their wages sufficiently over the past two

years, and had not maintained communication channels between the board and the employees.

All of the board members had full-time jobs elsewhere, and many were upper- and middle-level managers in their own companies. They were used to dealing with unhappy employees in their own workplaces, although none had experienced a union-organizing drive. Like Rogers, they had chosen to serve on the board of Marysville to stay informed about the day-to-day events of the centre. They had not really thought of themselves as the centre's employer, although, as board members, they represented all the parents of children enrolled at Marysville. Their main tasks on the daycare-centre board had been setting fees for the children and wages for the daycare employees. The board members usually saw the staff members several times a week, when they picked up their children, yet the unhappiness represented by the union-organizing drive was surprising to all of them. When they met at an emergency board meeting that evening, they tried to evaluate what had gone wrong at Marysville.

Questions

1. If you were either a board member or a parent, how would you know that the employees taking care of your children were unhappy with their jobs?

2. What might you do if you learned about their unhappiness?

3. What might Rogers have done differently as president of the board?

4. In what ways does this case illustrate that knowledge of OB can be applied beyond your own workplace?

Reinforcing Skills

1. Talk to several managers you know and ask them what skills they think are most important in today's workplace. Ask them to specifically consider the use of teams in their workplaces, and what skills their team members most need to have but are least likely to have. How might you use this information to develop greater interpersonal skills?

2. Talk with several managers you know and ask them what skills they have found most important in doing their jobs. Why did they find these skills most important? What advice would they give a would-be manager about skills worth developing?

CHAPTER 2

Perception, Personality, and Emotions

At the Canadian Human Rights Commission, employees were unhappy with their jobs. Why would their dissatisfaction be regarded as perception rather than fact?

1 What is perception?

2 What causes people to have different perceptions of the same situation?

3 Can people be mistaken in their perceptions?

4 Does perception really affect outcomes?

5 What is personality and how does it affect behaviour?

6 Can emotions help or get in the way when we're dealing with others?

Many employees at the Canadian Human Rights Commission (CHRC) cheered in May 2001 when a commissioned report revealed widespread dissatisfaction in their workplace.[1] Ordinarily an exposé of on-the-job problems is not something to cheer about, but the CHRC workers were grateful their concerns were finally being made public.

Much to the employees' dismay, however, senior managers at CHRC suggested that the workplace problems were only a matter of employee "perception," not objective reality. Michelle Falardeau-Ramsay, who was chief commissioner at the time, even said, "It's a report that is based on perceptions and perceptions can become facts at one point."[2] The employees were left to wonder whether they and their managers were actually part of the same workplace.

All of our behaviour is somewhat shaped by our perceptions, personalities, emotions, and experiences. In this chapter, we consider the role that perception plays in affecting the way we see the world and the people around us. We also consider how personality characteristics affect our attitudes toward people and situations. We then consider how emotions shape many of our work-related behaviours.

PERCEPTION DEFINED

Perception is the process by which individuals select, organize, and interpret their sensory impressions in order to give meaning to their environment. However, what we perceive can be substantially different from objective reality. We often disagree about what is real. As we have seen, employees and senior management at the Canadian Human Rights Commission had very different views of their workplace conditions. Michelle Falardeau-Ramsay, the chief commissioner, even said it was all a matter of "perception."

Why is perception important in the study of organizational behaviour (OB)? Simply because people's behaviour is based on their perception of what reality is, not on reality itself. *The world as it is perceived is the world that is behaviourally important*. Paul Godfrey, CEO of Toronto-based Sun Media Corporation, notes that "a lot of things in life are

1 What is perception?

perception The process by which individuals select, organize, and interpret their sensory impressions in order to give meaning to their environment.

Canadian Human Rights Commission (CHRC)
www.chrc-ccdp.ca

OB IS FOR EVERYONE

✳ *Who do you tend to blame when someone makes a mistake? Ever wonder why?*

✳ *Have you ever misjudged a person? Do you know why?*

✳ *Are people born with their personalities?*

✳ *Do you think it is better to be a Type A or a Type B personality?*

✳ *Ever wonder why the grocery clerk is always smiling?*

31

perception." He claims that as chair of Metropolitan Toronto for 11 years, he had little real power, but people believed he could get things done, and so he did.[3]

FACTORS INFLUENCING PERCEPTION

> Comments by employees and managers illustrate different perceptions of the environment at the Canadian Human Rights Commission. For example, one unnamed employee said that Chief Commissioner Michelle Falardeau-Ramsay was an absentee manager who lacked important job skills. "When she does conduct a meeting she will occupy the time describing entertainment details of the latest trip she has taken at taxpayers' expense. She's out of touch."[4]
>
> Meanwhile, in responding to negative employee comments, Falardeau-Ramsay told reporters she felt complaints were directed against other senior managers, not her. "I was so overwhelmed, [the report] was so surprising that I didn't even think in those terms," she said.[5] Falardeau-Ramsay and her employees clearly had different perceptions of the same situation. What factors might have influenced these different perceptions?

2 What causes people to have different perceptions of the same situation?

How do we explain that individuals may look at the same thing, yet perceive it differently, and both be right? A number of factors affect perception. These factors can be found in the *perceiver,* in the object or *target* being perceived, or in the context of the *situation* in which the perception is made. Exhibit 2-1 summarizes the factors influencing perception. This chapter's *Working With Others Exercise* on page 67 will help you understand how your perceptions affect your evaluation of others.

The Perceiver

When an individual ("the perceiver") looks at something ("the target") and tries to interpret what he or she sees, that interpretation is heavily influenced by the perceiver's personal characteristics. Have you ever bought a new car and then suddenly noticed a large number of cars like yours on the road? It's unlikely that everyone else has suddenly bought the same model. Rather, your own purchase has influenced your perception so that you are now more likely to notice the other cars. This is an example of how factors related to the perceiver influence what he or she perceives.

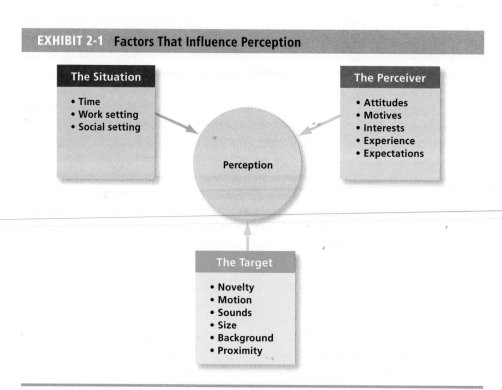

EXHIBIT 2-1   Factors That Influence Perception

The Situation
- Time
- Work setting
- Social setting

The Perceiver
- Attitudes
- Motives
- Interests
- Experience
- Expectations

Perception

The Target
- Novelty
- Motion
- Sounds
- Size
- Background
- Proximity

A variety of factors affects our perceptions. Our attitudes and motives, interests, and past experiences all shape the way we perceive an event.[6] When Chief Commissioner Michelle Falardeau-Ramsay suggested that employees' complaints about the CHRC were simply a matter of their perception, she was thinking about her own interests and motives in the situation. As head of the agency, she did not want to believe that she was responsible for any of the problems the employees reported.

We often interpret others' behaviours based on our own characteristics. People who take an optimistic approach to life act as if others will be just as upbeat, while those who are dishonest suspect others are equally dishonest.

Expectations can also distort our perceptions—we see what we expect to see. For example, if you expect police officers to be authoritarian, young people to have no ambitions, human resource directors to like people, or politicians to be unethical, you may perceive individuals from these categories in this way, regardless of their actual traits.

Finally, perceptions are likely to vary cross-culturally. Thus, something that you do in a friendly way may be viewed as too aggressive, or too informal, by someone from another country.

People's expectations about what employees working for a full-service web development agency should look like often leave them startled when they meet Jason Billingsley (left) and Justin Tilson (foreground), two of the founders of Vancouver-based Elastic Path Software (formerly Ekkon Technologies). Both men are in wheelchairs after a skiing accident for Billingsley and a mountain bike accident for Tilson. "It's an eye-opener sometimes," says Billingsley. "You've been talking on the phone for two or three weeks before you meet someone and they have no clue, and they kind of walk in and you see a little 'oh.'"

The Target

A target's characteristics can affect what is perceived. Loud people are more likely to be noticed in a group than are quiet ones. So, too, are extremely attractive or unattractive individuals. Novelty, motion, sound, size, and other attributes of a target shape the way we see it.

Because targets are not looked at in isolation, the relationship of a target to its background influences perception. Objects that are close to each other will tend to be perceived together rather than separately. Events that are close in time may also be seen as related, even if they are not. Employees in a particular department are seen as a group. If two people in a four-member department suddenly resign, we tend to assume that their departures were related when, in fact, they may be totally unrelated. Timing may also imply dependence when, for example, a new sales manager is assigned to a territory and, soon after, sales in that territory skyrocket. The assignment of the new sales manager and the increase in sales may not be related—the increase may be due to the introduction of a new product line or to one of many other reasons—but people would tend to see the two occurrences as related.

Persons, objects, or events that are similar to each other also tend to be grouped together. The greater the similarity, the greater the probability that we will tend to perceive them as a common group. People who are female, black, or members of any other clearly distinguishable group will tend to be perceived as similar not only in physical terms but in other unrelated characteristics as well.

The Situation

The context in which we see objects or events is important. Elements in the surrounding environment influence our perceptions. For instance, it might be entirely appropriate to wear shorts and T-shirts in a social setting, but not appropriate in a work setting.

Therefore, your interpretation of the same clothes will vary with the context. Similarly, you are more likely to notice your employees goofing off if your manager from head office happens to be in town. Your employees may be acting as they always do, but it is the situation that affects your perception. The time at which an object or event is seen can influence attention, as can location, light, heat, or any number of situational factors. Thus, it is possible to say that truth is often in the eye of the perceiver, rather than some objective fact. For instance, a recent study compared how women managers were perceived, depending upon whether they were wearing flat shoes, slacks, and a turtleneck or high heels, a tight skirt, and a low-cut blouse. Businesswomen wearing the sexy clothes were viewed as less competent. "A female manager whose appearance emphasized her sexiness elicited less positive emotions, more negative emotions, and perceptions of less competence on a subjective rating scale and less intelligence on an objective scale," the study's authors reported.[7]

PERCEPTUAL ERRORS

> In their workplace assessment report of the Canadian Human Rights Commission, consultants Watson Wyatt Worldwide identified numerous problems reported by employees. The employees suggested that three top managers should be replaced. They also claimed that female employees were discriminated against. The problems were considered so severe that some people outside the commission thought it should be closed. Chief Commissioner Michelle Falardeau-Ramsay disagreed. She said the findings were "unpleasant" and "painful," but suggested that those calling for the commission's closing had read the report in a "simplistic and irresponsible manner." These differences in response might suggest that the employees, Falardeau-Ramsay, or her critics were engaged in making perceptual errors. What might have caused this to happen?

3 Can people be mistaken in their perceptions?

It's difficult to perceive and interpret what others do. As a result, we develop shortcuts to make this task more manageable. These shortcuts are often very helpful—they allow us to make accurate perceptions quickly and provide valid information for making predictions. However, they are not foolproof. They can and do get us into trouble. For instance, when we make a bad first impression on someone, that perception may lead them to treat us poorly, or dismiss us as a prospective employee or teammate. Some of the errors that distort the perception process include attribution theory, selective perception, the halo effect, contrast effects, projection, and stereotyping.

Attribution Theory

attribution theory The theory that when we observe what seems to be atypical behaviour by an individual, we attempt to determine whether it is internally or externally caused.

✳ *Who do you tend to blame when someone makes a mistake? Ever wonder why?*

Attribution theory explains how we judge people differently, depending on the cause we attribute to a given behaviour.[8] Basically, the theory suggests that when we observe an individual's behaviour, we try to determine whether the individual is responsible for the behaviour (the cause is internal), or whether something outside the individual caused the behaviour (the cause is external). Whether we realize it or not, we use attribution theory whenever we try to come up with explanations for why people behaved the way they did.

In trying to understand another person's behaviour, then, we consider whether the behaviour was internally or externally caused. *Internally* caused behaviour is believed to be under the personal control of the individual; that is, the person *chooses* to engage in the behaviour. *Externally* caused behaviour is believed to result from outside causes; that is, the person does not have control over his or her actions and *is forced* into the behaviour by the situation. For example, while waiting for one of your team members who is late for a meeting, you could imagine either an internal or an external reason for the lateness. An internal reason might be that the team member must have partied into the wee hours of the morning and then overslept. An external attribution might be that there was a major automobile accident that tied up traffic.

Rules for Determining Attribution

In trying to determine whether behaviour is internally or externally caused, we rely on three rules about the behaviour: (1) distinctiveness, (2) consensus, and (3) consistency. Exhibit 2-2 summarizes the main elements in attribution theory.

Distinctiveness **Distinctiveness** refers to whether an individual acts similarly across a variety of situations. Is the student always underperforming (being late for class, goofing off in team meetings, not answering urgent emails) or is the student's behaviour in one situation unusual from what he shows in other situations? If the behaviour is unusual, the observer is likely to make an external attribution. If this action is not unusual, the observer will probably judge it as internally caused.

Consensus **Consensus** considers how an individual's behaviour compares with others in the same situation. If everyone who is faced with a similar situation responds in the same way, we can say the behaviour shows consensus. When consensus is high, an external attribution is given to an individual's behaviour. But if an individual's behaviour is different from everyone else's, you would conclude the cause for that individual's behaviour was internal.

Consistency Finally, an observer looks for **consistency** in an action that is repeated over time. If a student is usually on time for class (she has not been late all term), being 10 minutes late will be perceived differently from the way it is when the student is routinely late (almost every class). If a student is almost always late, the observer is likely to attribute lateness to internal causes. If the student is almost never late, then lateness will be attributed to external causes.

distinctiveness A behavioural rule that asks whether an individual acts similarly across a variety of situations.

consensus A behavioural rule that asks if everyone faced with a similar situation responds in the same way.

consistency A behavioural rule that asks whether the individual has been acting in the same way over time.

EXHIBIT 2-2 Attribution Theory

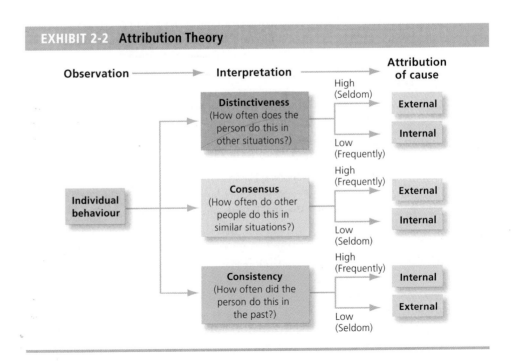

How Attributions Get Distorted

One of the more interesting findings from attribution theory is that there are errors or biases that distort attributions. For instance, there is substantial evidence that when we judge the behaviour of other people, we tend to put more emphasis on internal or personal factors and less emphasis on external factors.[9] This is called the **fundamental attribution error** and can explain why a sales manager is prone to attribute the poor performance of his or her sales agents to laziness rather than to the innovative product line introduced by a competitor. Recent research suggests that journalists often engage in the fundamental attribution error when they over-attribute firm performance to the CEO's characteristics. This attribution error results in the creation of "celebrity CEOs."[10]

Research suggests that individuals tend to overestimate their own good behaviour and underestimate the good behaviour of others.[11] We use **self-serving bias** when we judge ourselves. This means that when we are successful, we are more likely to believe it was because of internal factors, such as ability or effort. When we fail, however, we blame external factors, such as luck. In general, people tend to believe that their own behaviour is more positive than the behaviour of those around them. In a recent study, managers suggested that even though they were not responsible for the past poor performance of employees, they felt that they could help employees improve their behaviour in the future.[12]

Attribution theory was developed largely in the United States on the basis of experiments with Americans, but there is no particular reason to believe it would not apply in Canada. However, evidence from Japan[13] and Korea[14] suggests we should be careful in making attribution theory predictions in nonWestern countries or in those with strong collectivist traditions, such as Spain, Portugal, and some Eastern European countries.

fundamental attribution error The tendency to underestimate the influence of external factors and overestimate the influence of internal factors when making judgments about the behaviour of others.

self-serving bias The tendency for individuals to attribute their own successes to internal factors while putting the blame for failures on external factors.

Selective Perception

selective perception People's selective interpretation of what they see based on their interests, background, experience, and attitudes.

✳ *Have you ever misjudged a person? Do you know why?*

Because it is impossible for us to absorb everything we see, we engage in **selective perception**. Any characteristic that makes a person, object, or event stand out will increase the probability that we see that characteristic, rather than the whole package of characteristics. This tendency explains why, as we noted earlier, you are more likely to notice cars like your own.

How does selectivity work as a shortcut in judging other people? Since we cannot absorb all that we see, we take in bits and pieces. Those bits and pieces are not chosen randomly, but are selectively chosen according to our interests, background, experience, and attitudes. For instance, you are listening to your instructor while surfing the net. The next thing you know, the instructor is calling on you, asking a question, but you have no idea what to answer because you got involved in an online auction on eBay and lost track of the classroom discussion. While you were surfing, the eBay auction became more important than what your instructor was saying, and you tuned her out. However, had she said "tomorrow's test will cover the following topics," you might have snapped to attention again, knowing that you needed that information to study effectively.

Selective perception also allows us to "speed-read" others, but we may draw inaccurate pictures as a result. Because we see what we want to see, we can make unwarranted conclusions about an

Many day traders credited the gains they made in high-tech stocks between 1996 and early 2000 to their personal skills. But they blamed external sources for their losses when the prices of high-tech stocks took a nosedive.

ambiguous situation. Suppose there is a rumour going around the office that your company's sales are down and that large layoffs may be coming soon. If a senior executive from head office makes a routine visit around this time, it might be interpreted as management's first step in identifying which people to lay off. In reality, such an action might be the furthest thing from the senior executive's mind. Selective perception can also make us draw wrong conclusions about co-workers who have suffered serious illnesses, as *Focus on Diversity* shows.

FOCUS ON **DIVERSITY**

Underestimating Employees Who Have Been Seriously Ill

Does having had a serious illness mean that you cannot do your job? Lynda Davidson learned the hard way that suffering a mental illness and then getting treatment for it does not necessarily give one a clean bill of health at work.[15] When she returned to work after treatment, though she made her targets and earned her bonuses, her contract was not renewed. She later took a job as program manager at the Canadian Mental Health Association in Toronto.

Another Toronto woman suffered a similar fate when she was diagnosed with acute leukemia. After treatment, she returned to work at a large financial services organization only to find that she could not get any promotions. "I had the sense that people no longer took me seriously. I think people looked at me and thought, 'She's going to die,'" the woman said. It took moving to a different department where no one knew her before she could get ahead in her job.

It is not uncommon for employees with critical, chronic illnesses to feel that their jobs have been harmed by their illnesses. Employers and co-workers apparently perceive that those employees cannot function at the same level that they had prior to the illnesses. Describing a recent study done in the United States by the National Coalition for Cancer Survivorship, Dr. Ross Gray, a research psychologist at the Toronto-Sunnybrook Regional Cancer Centre, noted: "The study found that employers and co-workers overestimate the impact of cancer on people's lives. Decisions get made about advancement or capability that are out of line with the realities," Dr. Gray says.

Halo Effect

When we draw a general impression about an individual on the basis of a single characteristic, such as intelligence, likeability, or appearance, a **halo effect** is operating. This often happens when students evaluate their instructor. Students may give more weight to a single trait, such as enthusiasm, and allow their entire evaluation to be affected by how they judge the instructor on that one trait. Thus, an instructor may be quiet, assured, knowledgeable, and highly qualified, but if his or her presentation style lacks enthusiasm, those students would probably give the instructor a low rating.

halo effect Drawing a general impression of an individual on the basis of a single characteristic.

The reality of the halo effect was confirmed in a classic study. Subjects were given a list of traits and asked to evaluate the person to whom those traits applied.[16] When traits such as intelligent, skillful, practical, industrious, determined, and warm were used, the person was judged to be wise, humorous, popular, and imaginative. When cold was substituted for warm, a completely different set of perceptions was obtained, though otherwise the list was identical. Clearly, the subjects were allowing a single trait to influence their overall impression of the person being judged.

The halo effect does not operate at random. Research suggests that it is likely to be most extreme when the traits to be perceived are ambiguous in behavioural terms, when the traits have moral overtones, and when the perceiver is judging traits with which he or she has had limited experience.[17]

Contrast Effects

There is an old saying among entertainers who perform in variety shows: Never follow an act that has children or animals in it.

This example demonstrates how **contrast effects** can distort perceptions.[18] We don't evaluate a person in isolation. Our reaction to one person is often influenced by other people we have recently encountered.

Consider what happens when a manager interviews job candidates from a pool of applicants. The evaluation of a candidate can be affected by his or her place in the interview schedule. The candidate is likely to receive a better evaluation if interviewed after a mediocre applicant, and a worse evaluation if interviewed after a strong applicant.

contrast effects The concept that our reaction to one person is often influenced by other people we have recently encountered.

Projection

It is easy to judge others if we assume that they are similar to us. For instance, if you want challenge and responsibility in your job, you assume that others want the same. Or you are honest and trustworthy, so you take it for granted that other people are equally honest and trustworthy. This tendency for people to attribute their own characteristics to other people—which is called **projection**—can distort perceptions.

People who engage in projection tend to perceive others according to what they themselves are like rather than perceiving others as they really are. Because they always judge people as similar to themselves, when they observe someone who is actually like them their perceptions are naturally correct. But when they observe others who are not like them, their perceptions are not so accurate.

projection Attributing one's own characteristics to other people.

Stereotyping

When we judge someone on the basis of our perception of the group to which he or she belongs, we are using the shortcut called **stereotyping**. Stereotyping differs from the halo effect in that the latter is based on a single characteristic of the individual, rather than the individual's membership in a particular group. According to a popular literary anecdote, F. Scott Fitzgerald engaged in stereotyping when he told Ernest Hemingway, "the rich are very different from you and me," implying that the wealthy have values and behaviour unlike regular people. Hemingway's reply, "Yes, they have more money," indicated that he refused to generalize characteristics of people on the basis of their wealth.

stereotyping Judging someone on the basis of one's perception of the group to which that person belongs.

Generalization, of course, is not without advantages. It helps us simplify a complex world, and it permits us to maintain consistency. It is easier to deal with a large number of stimuli if we use stereotypes. As an example, assume you are a sales manager looking to fill a sales position in your territory and 100 people have applied. You want to hire someone who is ambitious and hard-working and who can deal well with adversity without spending too much time interviewing candidates. Your last five hires have been very successful and participated in athletics at university. So you eliminate from consideration candidates who have not participated in university sports, considerably reducing your search time. To the extent that athletes are ambitious, hard-working, and able to deal with adversity, the use of this stereotype can improve your decision making.

The problem, clearly, is when we inaccurately stereotype.[19] All university athletes are *not necessarily* ambitious, hard-working, or good at dealing with adversity, just as all accountants are *not necessarily* quiet and introspective. Moreover, when we stereotype like this, we run the risk of overlooking highly qualified people who do not meet our stereotypes. Recent research examining how Hollywood studio executives and producers judge the creative potential of relatively unknown screenwriters makes this clear.[20] When the screenwriters did not meet the stereotype of creative individuals in their presentation or appearance, they were judged as not creative (and often not taken seriously) without consideration of the content of their ideas. The researchers noted that this could result in hiring uncreative individuals simply because they fit the creative stereotype, and failing to hire truly creative individuals who did not fit the stereotype. A similar example is provided in the book *Blink,* in which trombone players auditioned for a seat in an orchestra from behind a curtain so that their gender would not be apparent.[21] While the interviewers all agreed on who was the best trombone player, they were shocked to discover that they had chosen a woman because in their view, "women don't play the trombone." In organizations, we frequently hear comments that represent stereotypes based on gender, age, race, ethnicity, and even weight:[22] "Women won't relocate for a promotion"; "men aren't interested in child care"; "older workers are more reliable"; "Asian immigrants are hard-working and conscientious"; "overweight people lack self-discipline." From a perceptual standpoint, if people expect to see these stereotypes, that is what they will see, whether or not the stereotypes are accurate.

Obviously, one of the problems of stereotypes is that they are widespread, despite the fact that they may not contain a shred of truth or that they may be irrelevant. Perhaps they are widespread only because many people are making the same inaccurate perception based on a false premise about a group. Stanford Graduate School of Business professor John Jost has uncovered another problem with stereotypes: They can be used to support the status quo.[23] He notes that when people buy into stereotypes about disadvantaged groups, they are less likely to challenge the consequences of the stereotype. For instance, subjects exposed to stereotypes such as "poor but happy," were less likely to respond negatively to ideas of social inequality. One implication of Jost's research is that we need to be aware of the effects of stereotypes on how we evaluate the world around us. Stereotypes can lead to strong negative reactions, such as prejudice, which we describe below.

Prejudice

Prejudice is an unfounded dislike of a person or group based on their belonging to a particular stereotyped group. For instance, an individual may dislike people of a particular religion, or state that she does not want to work with someone of a particular ethnicity. Prejudice can lead to negative consequences in the workplace and, in particular, to discrimination.[24] For instance, an individual of a particular ethnic group might be passed over for a management position because of the belief that employees might not see that person as a good manager. In another instance, an individual in his fifties who is looking for work but cannot find a job may be discriminated against because of the belief that younger workers are more appealing than older workers. Prejudice generally starts with stereotypes and then has negative emotional content added.

prejudice An unfounded dislike of a person or group based on their belonging to a particular stereotyped group.

WHY DO PERCEPTION AND JUDGMENT MATTER?

The employees at the Canadian Human Rights Commission (CHRC) felt that Chief Commissioner Michelle Falardeau-Ramsay was not living up to her role. They cited as evidence that she spent meeting time describing entertainment details of the latest trip she had taken at taxpayers' expense. This, and other perceptions of bad management, had led to high turnover at the commission and low morale. About 63 percent of the employees had left in the previous two years and 37 percent of those still working at the time of the survey were looking for other jobs. Falardeau-Ramsay was unaware of employee unhappiness. She said she had regularly met with employees and had never heard complaints of "managers openly showing favouritism, promoting men over women, and nurturing 'an anti-union culture.'"[25] Thus her perception led her to the judgment that there was nothing she needed to fix at the CHRC. It had not occurred to her that perhaps employees would be reluctant to share bad news with her. Did perceptions and judgments by both Falardeau-Ramsay and her employees lead to actions that were harmful to the organization?

4 Does perception really affect outcomes?

People in organizations are always judging each other. For instance, people typically go through an employment interview before being hired. Interviewers make perceptual judgments during the interview, which then affect whether the individual is hired. Studies show that if negative information is exposed early in the interview, it tends to be more heavily weighted than if that same information comes out later.[26] When multiple interviewers are present, agreement among interviewers is often poor; that is, different interviewers see different things in the same candidate and thus arrive at different conclusions about the applicant. If the employment interview is an important input into the hiring decision—and it usually is—you should recognize that perceptual factors influence who is hired and, eventually, the quality of an organization's labour force.

An employee's performance appraisal is another process that depends very much on the perceptual process.[27] An employee's future is closely tied to his or her appraisal—promotions, pay raises, and continuation of employment are among the most obvious outcomes. Although the appraisal can be objective (e.g., a salesperson is appraised on how many dollars of sales he or she generates in a given territory), many jobs are evaluated in subjective terms. Subjective measures are easier to implement, they provide managers with more freedom to do as they like, and many jobs do not readily lend themselves to objective measures. Subjective measures are, by definition, judgmental. The evaluator forms a general impression of an employee's work. To the degree that managers use subjective measures in appraising employees or choosing whom to promote, what the evaluator perceives to be good or bad employee characteristics or behaviours will significantly influence the outcome of the appraisal. One recent study found that managers in both Hong Kong and the United States were more likely to promote individuals who were more similar to themselves.[28] One's behaviour may also be affected by perceptions. Below we discuss how the self-fulfilling prophecy can lead to people's engaging in behaviour that is expected of them.

Managers are not the only people making judgments at work. When a new person joins a work team, he or she is immediately "sized up" by the other team members. McMaster University Professor Kathleen Martin found that even small things can make a difference in how a team member is viewed. In her study, students read descriptions of individuals and were then asked to evaluate 12 personality characteristics of "Tom" or "Mary."[29] Some of these descriptions included information about whether "Tom" or "Mary" exercised. Students evaluated nonexercisers more negatively on every personality and physical characteristic than those described as exercisers. In fact, those described as nonexercisers were rated more negatively than those for whom no information about exercise was provided. Martin noted, "When Mary and Tom were described as exercisers, they were considered to be harder workers, more confident, braver, smarter, neater, happier, and more sociable than the non-exerciser."

Self-Fulfilling Prophecy

There is an impressive amount of evidence that demonstrates that people will attempt to validate their perceptions of reality, even when those perceptions are faulty.[30] This characteristic is particularly relevant when we consider performance expectations on the job.

self-fulfilling prophecy A concept that proposes a person will behave in ways consistent with how he or she is perceived by others.

The terms **self-fulfilling prophecy** or *Pygmalion effect* have evolved to characterize the fact that people's expectations determine their behaviour. In other words, if a manager expects big things from his people, they are not likely to let him down. Similarly, if a manager expects people to perform minimally, they will tend to behave so as to meet those low expectations. The result then is that the expectations become reality.

An interesting illustration of the self-fulfilling prophecy is a study undertaken with 105 soldiers in the Israeli Defense Forces who were taking a 15-week combat command course.[31] The four course instructors were told that one-third of the specific incoming trainees had high potential, one-third had normal potential, and the potential of the rest was unknown. In reality, the trainees were randomly placed into those categories by the researchers. The results confirmed the existence of a self-fulfilling prophecy. The trainees whom instructors were told had high potential scored significantly higher on objective achievement tests, exhibited more positive attitudes, and held their leaders in higher regard than did the other two groups. The instructors of the supposedly high-potential trainees got better results from them because the instructors expected better performance. Expectations may not be the only factor leading to the self-fulfilling prophecy, however. In some cases, it is the treatment that individuals receive from instructors and others that accounts for higher performance. For instance, instructors might put more time and effort into those individuals who are expected to perform better.

As you can see, perception plays a large role in how people are evaluated. Personality, which we review below, is another major factor affecting how people relate in the workplace.

PERSONALITY

Why are some people quiet and passive, while others are loud and aggressive? Are certain personality types better adapted for certain job types? What do we know from theories of personality that can help us explain and predict the behaviour of leaders such as Stephen Harper, Paul Martin, or George W. Bush? How do we explain the risk-taking nature of Donald Trump, who still sees himself as the greatest businessman in America even though his hotel and casino businesses have gone through two bankruptcies? In this section, we will attempt to answer such questions.

What Is Personality?

When we talk of personality we don't mean that a person has charm, a positive attitude toward life, a smiling face, or is a finalist for "Miss Congeniality." When psychologists talk of personality, they mean a dynamic concept describing the growth and development of a person's whole psychological system. Rather than looking at parts of the person, personality looks at the whole person.

Gordon Allport produced the most frequently used definition of personality more than 60 years ago. He said personality is "the dynamic organization within the individual of those psychophysical systems that determine his unique adjustments to his environment."[32] For our purposes, you should think of **personality** as the stable patterns of behaviour and consistent internal states that determine how an individual reacts to and interacts with others. It is most often described in terms of measurable traits that a person exhibits. For an interesting look at how personality can affect business dealings, you might want to read this chapter's *Point/Counterpoint* discussion on page 58.[33] The discussion centres on how flexible and inflexible personality is. You may want to read the *Case Incident—The Rise and Fall of Dennis Kozlowski* to see how one man's early life might have affected how he later ran his business. In addition, this chapter's *CBC Video Case Incident* examines the personalities of two business partners.

Personality Determinants

An early argument in personality research centred on whether an individual's personality was predetermined at birth, or the result of the individual's interaction with his or her environment. Clearly, there is no simple answer. Personality appears to be a result of both influences. In addition, today we recognize a third factor—the situation. Thus, an adult's personality is now generally considered to be made up of both hereditary and environmental factors, moderated by situational conditions.

5 What is personality and how does it affect behaviour?

personality The stable patterns of behaviour and consistent internal states that determine how an individual reacts to and interacts with others.

NovaScotian Crystal

Early training and the culture in which we are raised are important environmental factors that shape our personalities. Other influences are family norms and memberships in social groups.

Heredity

Are people born with their personalities?

Heredity refers to those factors that were determined at conception. Physical stature, facial attractiveness, gender, temperament, muscle composition and reflexes, energy level, and biological rhythms are characteristics that are generally considered to be either completely or largely influenced by your parents' biological, physiological, and inherent psychological makeup. The heredity approach argues that the ultimate explanation of an individual's personality is genetic.

If personality characteristics were *completely* dictated by heredity, they would be fixed at birth and no amount of experience could alter them. If genetics resulted in your being tense and irritable as a child, for example, it would not be possible for you to change those characteristics as you grew into an adult. But personality characteristics are not completely dictated by heredity.

Environmental Factors

Among the factors that exert pressures on our personality formation are the culture in which we are raised; our early conditioning; the norms among our family, friends, and social groups; and other influences that we experience. The environment we are exposed to plays a substantial role in shaping our personalities.

For instance, North Americans have had the themes of industriousness, success, competition, independence, and the Protestant work ethic constantly drilled into them through books, the school system, family, and friends. North Americans, as a result, tend to be ambitious and aggressive compared with individuals raised in cultures that have emphasized getting along with others, cooperation, and the priority of family over work and career.

If we carefully consider the arguments favouring either heredity or environment as the main determinant of personality, we are forced to conclude that both are important. Heredity sets the parameters, or outer limits, but an individual's full potential will be determined by how well he or she adjusts to the demands and requirements of the environment.

3 Situational Conditions

A third factor, the situation, influences the effects of heredity and environment on personality. An individual's personality, although generally stable and consistent, does change in different situations. More specifically, the demands of different situations call forth different aspects of an individual's personality. We should not, therefore, look at personality patterns in isolation.[34]

Personality Traits

The early work in the structure of personality revolved around attempts to identify and label enduring characteristics that describe an individual's behaviour. Popular characteristics include shy, aggressive, submissive, lazy, ambitious, loyal, and timid. Those characteristics, when they are exhibited in a large number of situations, are called **personality traits**.[35] The more consistent the characteristic and the more often it occurs in different situations, the more important that trait is in describing the individual. The "Myers-Briggs Type Indicator" and "the Big Five Model," which we discuss below, are two methods that have been used to determine personality traits. A recent study suggests that personality traits are common across a variety of cultures.[36]

personality traits Enduring characteristics that describe an individual's behaviour.

Our personality traits, by the way, are evaluated differently by different people. This is partly a function of perception, which we discussed earlier in the chapter. In Exhibit 2-3, you will note that Lucy tells Linus a few things about his personality.

The Myers-Briggs Type Indicator

One of the most widely used personality frameworks is called the **Myers-Briggs Type Indicator (MBTI)**.[37] It is essentially a 100-question personality test that asks people how they usually feel or act in particular situations.

Myers-Briggs Type Indicator (MBTI) A personality test that taps four characteristics and classifies people into 1 of 16 personality types.

The MBTI classifies people based on how they prefer to focus their attention, collect information, process and evaluate information, and orient themselves to the outer world. These classifications are then combined into 16 personality types. Briefly, personality is classified along the following dimensions:

- *Extraversion/Introversion (E or I)*. This dimension refers to how people focus themselves: inside (introversion) or outside (extraversion).

- *Sensing/Intuiting (S or N)*. This dimension refers to how people gather information: very systematically (sensing) or relying on intuition (intuiting).

- *Thinking/Feeling (T or F)*. This dimension refers to how people prefer to make decisions: objectively and impersonally (thinking) or subjectively and interpersonally (feeling).

EXHIBIT 2-3

Source: Peanuts reprinted with permission of United Features Syndicate, Inc.

- *Judging/Perceiving (J or P).* This dimension refers to how people order their daily lives: being decisive and planned (judging) or spontaneous and flexible (perceiving).

Let's take a look at three examples of MBTI personality types:

- *INTJs are visionaries.* They usually have original minds and great drive for their own ideas and purposes. They are characterized as skeptical, critical, independent, determined, and often stubborn.

- *ESTJs are organizers.* They are realistic, logical, analytical, decisive, and have a natural head for business or mechanics. They like to organize and run activities.

- *ENTPs are conceptualizers.* They are innovative, individualistic, versatile, and attracted to entrepreneurial ideas. They tend to be resourceful in solving challenging problems but may neglect routine assignments.

Official Myers-Briggs tests can be administered only by trained professionals. However, if you are interested in learning about your personality type, you can get some understanding through the short test at the Personality Pathways website. One of the benefits of thinking about individuals by type is that it will give you some insight into how a particular person might react in a situation. If you browse in a library or bookstore, you will find a number of popular books designed to help you identify both your own and your colleagues' "personality types." However, as we noted above in our discussion of stereotyping, relying solely on personality measures to judge people can have its problems.

Ironically, there is no hard evidence that the MBTI is a valid measure of personality. But lack of evidence does not seem to deter its use in a wide range of organizations.

The Big Five Model

The most widely accepted model of personality is the five-factor model of personality—more typically called the "Big Five."[38] An impressive body of research supports the notion that five basic personality dimensions underlie all others and include most of the significant variations in human personality.[39] The Big Five personality factors are as follows:

- *Extraversion.* This dimension captures a person's comfort level with relationships. Extraverted individuals are sociable, talkative, and assertive.

- *Agreeableness.* This dimension refers to how readily a person will go along with others. Highly agreeable people are good-natured, cooperative, warm, and trusting.

- *Conscientiousness.* This dimension is a measure of a person's reliability. People who score high on conscientiousness are responsible, dependable, persistent, and achievement-oriented.

- *Emotional stability.* This dimension taps a person's ability to withstand stress. People high on emotional stability are calm, self-confident, and secure.

- *Openness to experience.* The final dimension addresses a person's range of interests and fascination with novelty. People high on openness to experience are imaginative, artistically sensitive, and intellectual.

Exhibit 2-4 on page 45 shows the characteristics for the high and low dimensions of each Big Five personality factor.

In addition to providing a unifying personality framework, research on the Big Five has found important relationships between these personality dimensions and job performance.[40] A broad spectrum of occupations was examined: professionals (including

Personality Pathways: Online Personality Test
www.personalitypathways.com/type
_inventory.html

extraversion A personality factor that describes the degree to which someone is sociable, talkative, and assertive.

agreeableness A personality factor that describes the degree to which someone is good-natured, cooperative, and trusting.

conscientiousness A personality factor that describes the degree to which someone is responsible, dependable, persistent, and achievement-oriented.

emotional stability A personality factor that describes the degree to which someone is calm, self-confident, and secure.

openness to experience A personality factor that describes the degree to which someone is imaginative, artistically sensitive, and intellectual.

EXHIBIT 2-4 Big Five Personality Factors

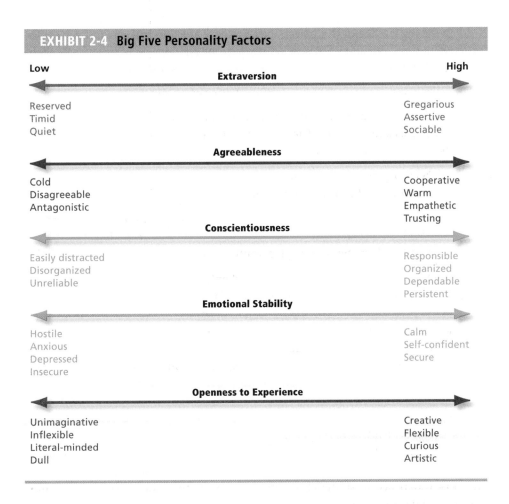

Low	**Extraversion**	High
Reserved		Gregarious
Timid		Assertive
Quiet		Sociable

	Agreeableness	
Cold		Cooperative
Disagreeable		Warm
Antagonistic		Empathetic
		Trusting

	Conscientiousness	
Easily distracted		Responsible
Disorganized		Organized
Unreliable		Dependable
		Persistent

	Emotional Stability	
Hostile		Calm
Anxious		Self-confident
Depressed		Secure
Insecure		

	Openness to Experience	
Unimaginative		Creative
Inflexible		Flexible
Literal-minded		Curious
Dull		Artistic

engineers, architects, accountants, and lawyers), as well as police officers, managers, salespeople, and semi-skilled and skilled employees. Job performance was defined in terms of performance ratings, training proficiency (performance during training programs), and information such as salary level.

It is not always easy for friends to share top management roles, but Anton Rabie (left), president and COO, and Ronnen Harary (right), CEO, of Toronto-based Spin Master like the arrangement. Rabie is an extravert, while Harary is an introvert. The childhood friends feel their personalities complement each other, making an ideal management team.

All of the Big Five factors have been found to have at least some relationship to performance in some situations.[41] Research finds a strong relationship between some of the Big Five factors and motivation. Lower emotional stability is associated with lower motivation, while conscientiousness appears to be positively related to motivation.[42] Finally, evidence finds a relatively strong and consistent relationship between conscientiousness and organizational citizenship behaviour (OCB).[43] This, however, seems to be the only personality dimension that predicts OCB.

Major Personality Attributes Influencing OB

In this section, we will evaluate specific personality attributes that have been found to be powerful predictors of behaviour in organizations. The first is related to locus of control—how much power over your destiny you think you have. The others are machiavellianism, self-esteem, self-monitoring, risk-taking, and Type A and proactive personalities. If you want to know more about your own personal characteristics, this chapter's *Learning About Yourself Exercises* on pages 59–66 present you with a variety of personality measures to explore.

Locus of Control

Some people believe that they are in control of their own destinies. Other people see themselves as pawns of fate, believing that what happens to them in their lives is due to luck or chance. The first type, those who believe that they control their destinies, have been labelled **internals**, whereas the latter, who see their lives as being controlled by outside forces, have been called **externals**.[44] A person's perception of the source of his or her fate is termed **locus of control**.

Individuals with an internal locus of control are more likely to problem solve when they encounter an obstacle while trying to achieve a goal. Individuals with an external locus of control are more likely to see the obstacle as caused by outside forces, and they will not necessarily know what to do in the face of that obstacle. Managers thus need to be more aware of obstacles facing employees who have an external locus of control, and do what they can to remove those obstacles.

A large amount of research has compared internals with externals. Internals report greater well-being, and this finding appears to be universal.[45] Internals show greater motivation, believe that their efforts will result in good performance, and get higher salaries and greater salary increases than externals.[46] Externals are less satisfied with their jobs, have higher absenteeism rates, are more alienated from the work setting, and are less involved in their jobs than are internals,[47] likely because they feel they have little control over organizational outcomes. Exhibit 2-5 on page 47 shows the relationship between locus of control and job performance.

If you are interested in determining your locus of control, you might want to complete *Learning About Yourself Exercise #1* on page 59.

Machiavellianism

The personality characteristic of **machiavellianism** (Mach) is named after Niccolò Machiavelli, who wrote in the sixteenth century on how to gain and use power. An individual high in machiavellianism is highly practical, maintains emotional distance, and believes that ends can justify means. "If it works, use it" is consistent with a high-Mach perspective.

A considerable amount of research has been directed toward relating high- and low-Mach personalities to certain behavioural outcomes.[48] High Machs manipulate more, win more, are persuaded less, and persuade others more than do low Machs.[49] Think of

---

internals Individuals who believe that they control their destinies.

externals Individuals who believe that their lives are controlled by outside forces, such as luck or chance.

locus of control The degree to which people believe they are in control of their own fates.

machiavellianism The degree to which an individual is pragmatic, maintains emotional distance, and believes that ends can justify means.

Niccolò Machiavelli
www.encyclopedia.com/html/M/Machiave.asp

EXHIBIT 2-5 The Effects of Locus of Control on Performance	
Conditions	**Performance**
Information Processing	
The work requires complex information processing and complex learning.	Internals perform better.
The work is quite simple and easy to learn.	Internals perform no better than externals.
Initiative	
The work requires initiative and independent action.	Internals perform better.
The work requires compliance and conformity.	Externals perform better.
Motivation	
The work requires high motivation and provides valued rewards in return for greater effort; it offers incentive pay for greater productivity.	Internals perform better.
The work does not require great effort and contingent rewards are lacking; hourly pay rates are determined by collective bargaining.	Externals perform at least as well as internals.

Source: J. B. Miner, *Industrial-Organizational Psychology* (New York: McGraw-Hill, 1992), p. 151. Reprinted with permission of The McGraw-Hill Companies.

Donald Trump interacting with the characters on *The Apprentice.* Yet these high-Mach outcomes are moderated by situational factors. It has been found that high Machs flourish (1) when they interact face to face with others rather than indirectly; (2) when the situation has a minimum number of rules and regulations, thus allowing latitude for improvisation; and (3) when low Machs get distracted by emotional involvement with details irrelevant to winning.[50]

Should we conclude that high Machs make good employees? That answer depends on the type of job and whether you consider ethical implications in evaluating performance. In jobs that require bargaining skills (such as labour negotiation) or that offer substantial rewards for winning (as in commissioned sales), high Machs will be productive. But if the ends cannot justify the means, if there are absolute standards of behaviour, or if the three situational factors noted in the preceding paragraph are not in evidence, our ability to predict a high Mach's performance will be severely curtailed. If you are interested in determining your level of machiavellianism, you might want to complete *Learning About Yourself Exercise #2* on page 60.

Self-Esteem

People differ in the degree to which they like or dislike themselves. This trait is called **self-esteem**.[51] The research on self-esteem (SE) offers interesting insights into OB. For example, self-esteem is directly related to expectations for success. High SEs believe that they have the ability to succeed at work. Individuals with high self-esteem will take more risks in job selection and are more likely to choose unconventional jobs than are people with low self-esteem. High SEs also tend to emphasize the positive when confronted with failure.[52]

The most generalizable finding on self-esteem is that low SEs are more easily influenced by external factors than are high SEs. Low SEs are dependent on the receipt of

self-esteem The degree to which individuals like or dislike themselves.

positive evaluations from others. As a result, they are more likely than high SEs to seek approval from others and more prone to conform to the beliefs and behaviours of those they respect. In managerial positions, low SEs tend to be concerned with pleasing others and, therefore, are less likely to take unpopular stands than are high SEs.

Not surprisingly, self-esteem has also been found to be related to job satisfaction. A number of studies confirm that high SEs are more satisfied with their jobs than are low SEs. If you are interested in determining your self-esteem score, you might want to complete *Learning About Yourself Exercise #3* on page 61. Recent research suggests that the factors that are used to measure self-esteem can be applied cross-culturally.[53]

Can you increase your self-esteem? Psychologist Nathaniel Branden suggests that people can increase their self-esteem by following his "Six Pillars of Self-Esteem," which is shown in Exhibit 2-6. By following the actions described, individuals can act with more confidence and integrity, which will lead to greater self-esteem. While Branden emphasizes that self-esteem comes from the choices we make, not from how others treat us, some recent research suggests that how leaders treat individuals in terms of fairness will have an impact on an individual's self-esteem.[54]

Articles by Nathaniel Branden
www.nathanielbranden.com/catalog
/articles.php#

Self-Monitoring

Some people are better able to pay attention to the external environment and respond accordingly, a characteristic known as **self-monitoring**.[55] Individuals high in self-monitoring show considerable ability to adjust and adapt their behaviour to the situations they are in. They are highly sensitive to external cues and can behave differently in different situations. High self-monitors are capable of presenting striking contradictions between their public personae and their private selves.

Low self-monitors cannot disguise themselves in the same way. They tend to display their true dispositions and attitudes in every situation; hence, there is high behavioural consistency between who they are and what they do.

Research suggests that high self-monitors tend to pay closer attention to the behaviour of others and are more capable of conforming than are low self-monitors.[56] In addition, high self-monitoring managers tend to be more mobile in their careers and receive more promotions (both internal and cross-organizational).[57] Recent research found that self-monitoring is also related to job performance and emerging leaders.[58] Specifically, high self-monitors are more likely to be high performers and more likely to become leaders. To determine whether you are a high or low self-monitor, you might want to complete *Learning About Yourself Exercise #4* on page 62.

self-monitoring A personality trait that measures an individual's ability to adjust behaviour to external, situational factors.

EXHIBIT 2-6   Branden's Six Pillars of Self-Esteem

1. *Living consciously:* Be aware of everything that affects your values and goals, and act with awareness.

2. *Self-acceptance:* Accept who you are without criticism and judgment.

3. *Personal responsibility:* Take responsibility for the decisions you make and the things you do.

4. *Self-assertiveness:* Honour your wants, needs, and values, and don't be afraid to speak up for things that are important to you.

5. *Living purposefully:* Develop short- and long-term goals, and make realistic plans to achieve your goals.

6. *Personal integrity:* Live up to your word and your values.

Source: Adapted from N. Branden, *Self-Esteem at Work: How Confident People Make Powerful Companies* (San Francisco: Jossey-Bass, 1998), pp. 33–36.

Risk-Taking

People differ in their willingness to take chances. Matthew Barrett, the former CEO and chair of Bank of Montreal, and Frank Stronach, chair of Magna International (and the subject of *Case Incident—Frank Stronach, Risk-Taker and Fair Enterprise Creator* on the CD-ROM that accompanies this textbook), are good examples of high risk-takers. The tendency to assume or avoid risk has been shown to have an impact on how long it takes managers to make a decision and how much information they require before making their choice. For instance, 79 managers worked on simulated exercises that required them to make hiring decisions.[59] High **risk-taking** managers made more rapid decisions and used less information in making their choices than did the low risk-taking managers. Interestingly, the decision accuracy was the same for both groups.

While it is generally correct to conclude that managers in organizations are risk-aversive,[60] there are still individual differences within this dimension.[61] As a result, it makes sense to recognize these differences and even to consider matching risk-taking tendencies with specific job demands. For instance, high risk-taking might lead to higher performance for a stock trader in a brokerage firm because that type of job demands rapid decision making. On the other hand, a willingness to take risks would not be suitable for an accountant who performs auditing activities. Organizations also send messages about how much risk is tolerated. Some managers convey to employees that they will be punished if they take risks that fail. This can dampen one's natural risk-taking tendencies. If you are interested in determining where you stand on risk-taking, you might want to complete *Learning About Yourself Exercise #5* on pages 63–64.

Richard Branson's tendency to take risks aligns with his job demands as an entrepreneur. Branson, founder and chairman of London-based Virgin Group, starts risky ventures that compete against industry giants. His Virgin Atlantic airline, for example, has taken market share from British Airways and has earned a reputation as one of the financially healthiest airlines in the world. Branson's risk-taking personality extends to his leisure activities of speedboat racing, skydiving, and ballooning.

risk-taking A person's willingness to take chances or risks.

Type A and Type B Personalities

> ✳ Do you think it is better to be a Type A or a Type B personality?

Do you know any people who are excessively competitive and always seem to be pushed for time? If you do, it's a good bet that those people have a **Type A personality**. An individual with a Type A personality is "aggressively involved in a chronic, incessant struggle to achieve more and more in less and less time, and, if required to do so, against the opposing efforts of other things or other persons."[62] In North American culture, such characteristics tend to be highly prized and positively associated with ambition and the successful acquisition of material goods.

Type A personality A personality with aggressive involvement in a chronic, incessant struggle to achieve more and more in less and less time and, if necessary, against the opposing efforts of other things or other people.

Type As

- Are always moving, walking, and eating rapidly
- Feel impatient with the rate at which most events take place
- Strive to think or do two or more things at once
- Cannot cope with leisure time
- Are obsessed with numbers, measuring their success in terms of how many or how much of everything they acquire

In contrast to the Type A personality is the Type B, who is exactly the opposite. Type Bs are "rarely harried by the desire to obtain a wildly increasing number of things or participate in an endless growing series of events in an ever-decreasing amount of time."[63]

Type Bs

- Never suffer from a sense of time urgency with its accompanying impatience

- Feel no need to display or discuss either their achievements or accomplishments unless such exposure is demanded by the situation

- Play for fun and relaxation, rather than to exhibit their superiority at any cost

- Can relax without guilt

Type As are often impatient, hurried, competitive, and hostile, but these traits tend to emerge most often when a Type A individual experiences stress or challenge.[64] Type As are fast workers because they emphasize quantity over quality. In managerial positions, Type As demonstrate their competitiveness by working long hours and, not infrequently, making poor decisions because they make them too fast. Stressed Type As are also rarely creative. Because of their concern with quantity and speed, they rely on past experiences when faced with problems. They will not allocate the time that is necessary to develop unique solutions to new problems. They seldom vary in their responses to specific challenges in their environment, and so their behaviour is easier to predict than that of Type Bs.

Are Type As or Type Bs more successful in organizations? Despite the hard work of Type As, Type Bs are the ones who appear to make it to the top. Great salespeople are usually Type As; senior executives are usually Type Bs. Why? The answer lies in the tendency of Type As to trade off quality of effort for quantity. Promotions in corporate and professional organizations "usually go to those who are wise rather than to those who are merely hasty, to those who are tactful rather than to those who are hostile, and to those who are creative rather than to those who are merely agile in competitive strife."[65]

Recent research has looked at the effect of job complexity on the cardiovascular health of both Type A and Type B individuals to see whether Type As always suffered negative health consequences.[66] Type B individuals did not suffer negative health consequences from jobs with psychological complexity. Type A workers who faced high job complexity had higher death rates from heart-related disorders than Type As who faced lower job complexity. These findings suggest that, health-wise, Type B workers suffer less when handling more complex jobs than do Type As. It also suggests that Type As who face lower job complexity do not encounter the same health risks as Type As who face higher job complexity.

If you are interested in determining whether you have a Type A or Type B personality, you might want to complete *Learning About Yourself Exercise #6* on page 65.

Proactive Personality

Did you ever notice that some people actively take the initiative to improve their current circumstances or create new ones while others sit by passively reacting to situations? The former individuals have been described as having proactive personalities.[67]

proactive personality A person who identifies opportunities, shows initiative, takes action, and perseveres until meaningful change occurs.

People with a **proactive personality** identify opportunities, show initiative, take action, and persevere until meaningful change occurs. They create positive change in their environment, regardless or even in spite of constraints or obstacles.[68]

Not surprisingly, proactives have many desirable behaviours that organizations look for. For instance, the evidence indicates that proactives are more likely to be seen as leaders and are more likely to act as change agents within the organization.[69] Other actions of proactives can be positive or negative, depending on the organization and the situation. For example, proactives are more likely to challenge the status quo or voice their displeasure when situations are not to their liking.[70] If an organization requires people with entrepreneurial initiative, proactives make good candidates; however, these are people who are also more likely to leave an organization to start their own business.[71] As individuals, proactives are more likely to achieve career success.[72] This is because they select, create, and influence work situations in their favour. Proactives are more likely to seek out job and organizational information, develop contacts in high places, engage in career planning, and demonstrate persistence in the face of career obstacles.

Personality and National Culture

There are certainly no common personality types for a given country. You can, for instance, find high and low risk-takers in almost any culture. Yet a country's culture should influence the dominant personality characteristics of its population. Let's build this case by looking at one personality attribute—locus of control.

There is evidence that cultures differ in terms of people's relationship to their environment.[73] In some cultures, such as those in North America, people believe that they can dominate their environment. People in other societies, such as Middle Eastern countries, believe that life is essentially preordained. Notice the close parallel to internal and external locus of control. We should expect a larger proportion of internals in the Canadian and American workforces than in the Saudi Arabian or Iranian workforces.

One caveat regarding personality tests is that they may be subject to cultural bias when used on samples of people other than those for whom the tests were designed. For instance, on common American personality tests, British people are characterized as "less dominant, achievement-orientated or flexible than Americans, but more self-controlled."[74] An example of a bias that can appear in such tests is that only 10 percent of British men answer "true" to the statement "I very much like hunting," while 70 percent of American men agree.[75] When these tests are used to select managers, they may result in the selection of individuals who are not as suitable in the British workplace as they would be in the American workplace.

EMOTIONS

Each of us has a range of personality characteristics, but we also bring with us a range of emotions. Given the obvious role that emotions play in our everyday lives, it might surprise you to learn that, until very recently, the topic of emotions was given little or no attention in the field of OB. When emotions were considered, the discussion focused on strong negative emotions—especially anger—that interfered with an employee's ability to do his or her job effectively. Emotions were rarely viewed as constructive or able to stimulate performance-enhancing behaviours.

6 Can emotions help or get in the way when we're dealing with others?

Certainly some emotions, particularly when exhibited at the wrong time, can reduce employee performance. But this does not change the reality that employees bring an emotional component with them to work every day, and that no study of OB could be comprehensive without considering the role of emotions in workplace behaviour.

What Are Emotions?

Emotions are intense feelings that are directed at someone or something.[76] Emotions are different from **moods**, which are feelings that tend to be less intense than emotions and that lack a contextual stimulus.[77]

Emotions are *reactions* to an object; they are not lasting personality traits. You show your emotions when you are "happy about something, angry at someone, afraid of something."[78] Moods, on the other hand, are not directed at an object. Emotions can turn into moods when you lose focus on the contextual object. So when a colleague criticizes

emotions Intense feelings that are directed at someone or something.

moods Feelings that tend to be less intense than emotions and that lack a contextual stimulus.

Source: Based on R. D. Woodworth, *Experimental Psychology* (New York: Holt, 1938).

you for the way you spoke to a client, you might become angry at him. That is, you show emotion (anger) toward a specific object (your colleague). But later in the day, you might find yourself just generally dispirited. You cannot attribute this feeling to any single event; you are just not your normal, upbeat self. This state describes a mood.

Research has identified six universal emotions: anger, fear, sadness, happiness, disgust, and surprise.[79] One factor that has strongly shaped what is and isn't listed in this basic set is the manner in which the emotions were identified. Researchers tended to look for universally identified facial expressions and then convert them into categories (see the facial expressions in *From Concepts to Skills* on page 71). Emotions that could not be identified readily by others through facial expressions, or that were considered a subset of one of the basic six, were not selected.

Exhibit 2-7 illustrates that the six emotions can be conceptualized as existing along a continuum.[80] The closer any two emotions are to each other on this continuum, the more people are likely to confuse them. For instance, happiness and surprise are frequently mistaken for each other, while happiness and disgust are rarely confused. Be aware that cultural factors can also influence interpretations of facial expressions.

Choosing Emotions: Emotional Labour

> * *Ever wonder why the grocery clerk is always smiling?*

Sometimes individuals are required to manage their emotions. For instance, you may be very angry with a co-worker or manager, but you may choose to suppress that anger in the interest of keeping the peace and/or your job. You may also decide not to kiss a co-worker in a moment of overwhelming exuberance, to make sure that your intentions are not misinterpreted. The display of emotions is governed somewhat by workplace norms and the demands of particular situations. For instance, crying is generally viewed as inappropriate in the workplace, particularly when it is a response to being criticized. Crying would be viewed more acceptably if someone were just notified of the death of a close relative, however. Peter Mackay was expected to show no emotion following his breakup with Belinda Stronach after she crossed the floor to the Liberal party. However, President George W. Bush was criticized for showing little emotion immediately following the devastating effects of Hurricane Katrina on New Orleans. Recent research suggests that negative emotions, even when controlled, generally lead to poorer performance.[81]

emotional labour   When an employee expresses organizationally desired emotions during interpersonal interactions.

University of California, Berkeley
www.berkeley.edu

Emotional labour refers to the requirement that employees express particular emotions at work (for instance, enthusiasm or cheerfulness) to maximize organizational productivity.[82] This term was first coined by Professor Arlie Hochschild of the University of California, Berkeley, and refers to the demand organizations make on their employees to display "appropriate" emotions during interpersonal transactions.[83]

The concept of emotional labour originally developed in relation to service jobs. Flight attendants, for instance, are expected to be cheerful, funeral counsellors sad, and doctors emotionally neutral. Studies of emotional labour have explored how smiling flight attendants, cheerful grocery clerks, gossipy hairdressers, and nasty bill collectors are expected to control their emotional expression to improve productivity, customer satisfaction, efficiency, and even profitability.[84] But today, the concept of emotional labour seems relevant to almost every job. You are expected, for example, to be courteous and not hostile in interactions with co-workers. And leaders are expected to draw on emotional labour to "charge the troops." Almost every great speech, for instance, contains a strong emotional component that stirs feelings in others.

As these studies show, however, managing emotions can take a toll when there is a discrepancy between the outward behaviour the person is required to display as part of his or her job and the inward feelings that the person has.[85] Therefore, while emotional labour can have positive implications within the workplace, it can also have negative personal consequences when a person consistently hides real emotions behind a work "face."[86] Flight attendants use the phrase "go robot" to describe how they separate their private feelings from their public behaviour.[87] Other researchers have discussed both the individual effects of emotional labour, such as distancing, burnout, and phoniness,[88] and the organizational effects, such as suppressed disagreements, reduced upward information flow, and loss of "voice."[89] A Vancouver Safeway employee described her company's requirement to smile at all shoppers: "My personal opinion is, they're expecting us not to be human. I just can't walk around with a smile on my face all day."[90] To further consider the issue of managing emotions at work, you may want to work on this chapter's *Ethical Dilemma Exercise* on page 68.

Emotional labour creates dilemmas for employees when their jobs require them to exhibit emotions that are inconsistent with their actual feelings. Not surprisingly, this is a frequent occurrence. There are people you have to work with to whom you find it very difficult to be friendly. Maybe you consider their personalities abrasive. Maybe you know they have said negative things about you behind your back. Regardless, your job requires you to interact with these people on a regular basis. So you are forced to pretend to be friendly.

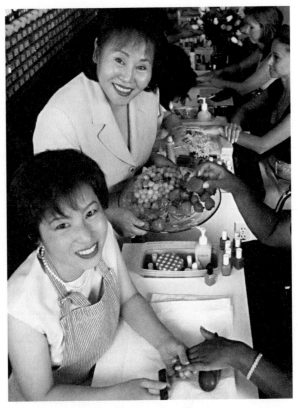

Emotional labour is an important component of effective job performance at the Happy Beauty Salon in Long Island, New York. Owner Happy Nomikos, shown here serving customers strawberries and grapes, requires that her nail technicians and hairstylists build customer loyalty by being courteous and cheerful. In interacting with her employees and customers, Nomikos says, "I have to keep everyone happy." She hugs loyal customers, jokes with her staff, and offers customers pizza and cake in celebration of employees' birthdays.

Canada Safeway
www.safeway.com

Why Should We Care About Emotions in the Workplace?

There are a number of reasons to be concerned about understanding emotions in the workplace.[91] People who know their own emotions and are good at reading others' emotions may be more effective in their jobs. That, in essence, is the theme underlying recent research on emotional intelligence.[92] The entire workplace can be affected by positive or negative workplace emotions, another issue we consider below. One recent study found that when leaders were in a positive mood, individual group members experienced better moods, and groups had a more positive tone. Groups whose leaders had a positive mood also found it easier to coordinate tasks, and expended less effort when doing their work.[93]

Emotional Intelligence

Emotional intelligence (EI) refers to an assortment of noncognitive skills, capabilities, and competencies that influence a person's ability to succeed in coping with environmental demands and pressures. It's composed of five dimensions:

- *Self-awareness.* Being aware of what you are feeling. It is exhibited by self-confidence, realistic self-assessment, and a self-deprecating sense of humour.

- *Self-management.* The ability to manage your own emotions and impulses. It is exhibited by trustworthiness and integrity, comfort with ambiguity, and openness to change.

- *Self-motivation.* The ability to persist in the face of setbacks and failures. It is exhibited by a strong drive to achieve, optimism, and high organizational commitment.

- *Empathy.* The ability to sense how others are feeling. It is exhibited by expertise in building and retaining talent, cross-cultural sensitivity, and service to clients and customers.

- *Social skills.* The ability to handle the emotions of others. It is exhibited by persuasiveness, and expertise in building and leading groups and teams.

EI differs from emotional labour because the latter is a job requirement (the demand to smile, express enthusiasm, etc.) while the former is regarded as a personality trait. A person with low EI may control his emotions because of a request from a manager (thus engaging in emotional labour), but might otherwise not do so.

Several studies suggest EI may play an important role in job performance.[94] For instance, one study looked at the characteristics of Bell Labs engineers who were rated as stars by their peers. The scientists concluded that stars were better at relating to others. That is, it was EI, not academic IQ, that characterized high performers.

Another study of US Air Force recruiters generated similar findings. Top-performing recruiters exhibited high levels of EI. Using these findings, the US Air Force revamped its selection criteria. A follow-up investigation found that hires who had high EI scores were 2.6 times more successful than those who did not.[95]

Corporations are acting on the results of these studies. A recent poll of human resource managers asked: How important is it for your workers to demonstrate EI to move up the corporate ladder? Forty percent replied "Very Important." Another 16 percent said "Moderately Important." Irene Taylor, a consultant with Toronto-based Praxis Canada, says her company "has conducted EQ assessments on about 300 Canadian lawyers over the past five years." She also says that demand to get into the company's EI coaching program is high. Professor John Oesch of the Joseph L. Rotman School of Management at the University of Toronto explains why coaching in EI has become popular: "It's a solid psychological construct that can be measured and, to a certain extent, taught."[96]

Tony Comper, president and CEO of the Bank of Montreal, certainly agrees with the importance of understanding EI. He cites Daniel Goleman's *Working With Emotional Intelligence*[97] as one of his favourite books on leadership.[98] This chapter's *From Concepts to Skills* gives you some insight into reading the emotions of others. To find out about your EI, complete *Learning About Yourself Exercise #7* on pages 65–66.

Negative Workplace Emotions

Negative emotions can lead to a number of deviant workplace behaviours. Anyone who has spent much time in an organization realizes that people often engage in voluntary actions that violate established norms and threaten the organization, its members, or both. These actions are called **employee deviance**.[99] They fall into categories such as production (leaving early, intentionally working slowly); property (stealing, sabotage); political (gossiping, blaming co-workers); and personal aggression (sexual harassment, verbal abuse).[100]

Many of these deviant behaviours can be traced to negative emotions. For instance, envy is an emotion that occurs when you resent someone for having something that you don't have but strongly desire.[101] It can lead to malicious deviant behaviours. Envy, for example, has been found to be associated with hostility, "backstabbing," and other forms of political behaviour, as well as with negatively distorting others' successes and positively distorting one's own accomplishments.[102]

> **employee deviance** Voluntary actions that violate established norms and threaten the organization, its members, or both.

SUMMARY AND IMPLICATIONS

1 **What is perception?** *Perception* is the process by which individuals organize and interpret their impressions in order to give meaning to their environment. Individuals behave in a given manner based not on the way their environment actually is but, rather, on what they see or believe it to be. An organization may spend millions of dollars to create a pleasant work environment for its employees. However, despite these expenditures, an employee who believes that his or her job is lousy will behave accordingly.

2 **What causes people to have different perceptions of the same situation?** A number of factors operate to shape and sometimes distort perception. These factors can be present in the *perceiver*, in the object or *target* being perceived, or in the context of the *situation* in which the perception is made. The perceiver's attitudes, motives, interests, and past experiences all shape the way he or she sees an event. The target's characteristics also affect what is perceived. Novelty, motion, sounds, size, and other characteristics of a target shape the way it is seen. Objects or events that are unrelated are often perceived together because they are close physically or in timing. Persons, objects, or events that are similar to each other also tend to be viewed as a group. The setting in which we see objects or events also affects how they are perceived.

3 **Can people be mistaken in their perceptions?** Perceiving and interpreting what others do is difficult and takes time. As a result, we develop shortcuts to make this task more manageable. These shortcuts, which include attribution theory, selective perception, the halo effect, contrast effects, projection, and stereotyping, are often valuable—they can sometimes allow us to make accurate perceptions quickly and provide valid data for making predictions. However, they are not foolproof. They can and do get us into trouble.

4 **Does perception really affect outcomes?** The evidence suggests that what individuals perceive about their work situations influences their productivity more than the situations do. Whether a job is actually interesting or challenging is irrelevant. Whether a manager actually helps employees to structure their work more efficiently and effectively is far less important than how employees perceive the manager's efforts. Similarly, issues such as fair pay, the validity of performance appraisals, and the adequacy of working conditions are not judged "objectively." Rather, individuals interpret conditions surrounding their jobs based on how they *perceive* their jobs.

SNAPSHOT SUMMARY

1 **Perception Defined**

2 **Factors Influencing Perception**
The Perceiver
The Target
The Situation

3 **Perceptual Errors**
Attribution Theory
Selective Perception
Halo Effect
Contrast Effects
Projection
Stereotyping

4 **Why Do Perception and Judgment Matter?**
Self-Fulfilling Prophecy

5 **Personality**
What Is Personality?
Personality Determinants
Personality Traits
Major Personality Attributes Influencing OB
Personality and National Culture

6 **Emotions**
What Are Emotions?
Choosing Emotions: Emotional Labour
Why Should We Care About Emotions in the Workplace?

5 What is personality and how does it affect behaviour? *Personality* is the stable patterns of behaviour and consistent internal states that determine how an individual reacts to and interacts with others. A review of the personality literature offers general guidelines that can lead to effective job performance. As such, it can improve hiring, transfer, and promotion decisions. Personality attributes give us a framework for predicting behaviour. Personality affects how people react to others and the types of jobs that they may desire. For example, individuals who are shy, introverted, and uncomfortable in social situations would probably make poor salespeople. Individuals who are submissive and conforming might not be effective as advertising "idea" people. Be aware, though, that measuring personality is not an exact science, and as you no doubt learned from the discussion of attribution theory it is easy to attribute personality characteristics in error.

6 Can emotions help or get in the way when were dealing with others? *Emotions* are intense feelings that are directed at someone or something. Positive emotions can be motivating for everyone in the workplace. Negative emotions may make it difficult to get along with others. Can managers control the emotions of their colleagues and employees? No. Emotions are a natural part of an individual's makeup. At the same time, managers err if they ignore the emotional elements in OB and assess individual behaviour as if it were completely rational. Managers who understand the role of emotions will significantly improve their ability to explain and predict individual behaviour.

Do emotions affect job performance? Yes. Emotions, especially negative ones, can hinder performance. That's probably why organizations, for the most part, try to remove emotions from the workplace. But emotions can also enhance performance. How? Two ways.[103] First, emotions can increase arousal levels, thus acting as motivators to higher performance. Second, emotional labour recognizes that feelings can be part of a job's required behaviour. So, for instance, the ability to effectively manage emotions in leadership and sales positions may be critical to success in those positions. Research also indicates the importance of emotional intelligence, the assortment of noncognitive skills, capabilities, and competencies that influence a person's ability to succeed in coping with environmental demands and pressures.

For Review

1. Define *perception*.

2. What is attribution theory? What are its implications for explaining behaviour in organizations?

3. What is stereotyping? Give an example of how stereotyping can create perceptual distortion.

4. Give some positive results of using shortcuts when judging others.

5. Describe the factors in the Big Five model. Evaluate which factor shows the greatest value in predicting behaviour.

6. What behavioural predictions might you make if you knew that an employee had (a) an external locus of control? (b) a low-Mach score? (c) low self-esteem? (d) a Type A personality?

7. To what extent do people's personalities affect how they are perceived?

8. What is emotional labour and why is it important to understanding OB?

9. What is emotional intelligence and why is it important?

For Critical Thinking

1. How might the differences in experience of students and instructors affect each of their perceptions of classroom behaviour (e.g., students' written work and class comments)?

2. An employee does an unsatisfactory job on an assigned project. Explain the attribution process that this person's manager will use to form judgments about this employee's job performance.

3. One day your boss comes in and he is nervous, edgy, and argumentative. The next day he is calm and relaxed. Does this behaviour suggest that personality traits are not consistent from day to day?

4. What, if anything, can managers do to manage emotions? Are there ethical implications in any of these actions? If so, what?

5. Give some examples of situations where expressing emotions openly might improve job performance.

OB for You

■ The discussion of perception might get you thinking about how you view the world. When we perceive someone as a troublemaker, for instance, this may be only a perception and not a real characteristic of the other person. It is always good to question your perceptions, just to be sure that you are not reading something into a situation that is not there.

■ One important thing to consider when looking for a job is whether your personality will fit the organization to which you are applying. For instance, it may be a highly structured organization. If you by nature are much less formal, this may not be a good fit for you.

■ Sometimes personalities get in the way when working in groups. You may want to see if you can figure out ways to get personality differences working in favour of group goals.

■ Emotions need not always be suppressed when working with others. While emotions can sometimes hinder performance, positive emotions can motivate you and those around you.

POINT

 COUNTERPOINT

Traits Are Powerful Predictors of Behaviour

The essence of trait approaches in OB is that employees possess stable personality characteristics that significantly influence their attitudes toward, and behavioural reactions to, organizational settings. People with particular traits tend to be relatively consistent in their attitudes and behaviour over time and across situations.[104]

Of course, trait theorists recognize that all traits are not equally powerful. They tend to put traits into one of three categories. *Cardinal traits* are those so strong and generalized that they influence every act a person performs. *Primary traits* are generally consistent influences on behaviour, but they may not show up in all situations. Finally, *secondary traits* are attributes that do not form a vital part of the personality, but come into play only in particular situations. For the most part, trait theories have focused on the power of primary traits to predict employee behaviour.

Trait theorists do a fairly good job of meeting the average person's common-sense beliefs. Think of friends, relatives, and acquaintances you have known for a number of years. Do they have traits that have remained essentially stable over time? Most of us would answer that question in the affirmative. If cousin Anne was shy and nervous when we last saw her 10 years ago, we would be surprised to find her outgoing and relaxed now.

Managers seem to have a strong belief in the power of traits to predict behaviour. If managers believed that situations determined behaviour, they would hire people almost at random and put great effort into structuring situations properly. But the employee selection process in most organizations places a great deal of emphasis on how applicants perform in interviews and on tests. Assume you are interviewing job candidates and ask yourself: What kind of person am I looking for? If you answer with terms such as *conscientious, hard-working, persistent, confident,* and *dependable,* you are a trait theorist!

Behaviour Is Determined by the Situation

Few people would dispute that there are some stable individual attributes that affect reactions to the workplace. But trait theorists go beyond that generality and argue that individual behaviour consistencies are widespread and account for much of the difference in behaviour among people.[105]

There are two important problems with using traits to explain a large proportion of behaviour in organizations. First, organizational settings are strong situations that have a large impact on employee behaviour. Second, individuals are highly adaptive and personality traits change in response to organizational situations.

It has been well known for some time that the effects of traits are likely to be strongest in relatively weak situations, and weakest in relatively strong situations. Organizational settings tend to be strong situations because they have rules and other formal regulations that define acceptable behaviour and punish deviant behaviour; and they have informal norms that dictate appropriate behaviours. These formal and informal constraints minimize the effects of personality traits.

By arguing that employees possess stable traits that lead to cross-situational consistencies in behaviours, trait theorists are implying that individuals don't really adapt to different situations. But there is a growing body of evidence that an individual's traits are changed by the organizations in which an individual participates. If the individual's personality changes as a result of exposure to organizational settings, in what sense can that individual be said to have traits that persistently and consistently affect his or her reactions to those very settings? Moreover, people typically belong to multiple organizations, which often include very different kinds of members. They adapt to those different situations. Instead of being the prisoners of a rigid and stable personality framework, as trait theorists propose, people regularly adjust their behaviour to reflect the requirements of various situations.

Assess Your Locus of Control

Read the following statements and indicate whether you agree more with choice A or choice B.

A

1. Making a lot of money is largely a matter of getting the right breaks.
2. I have noticed that there is a direct connection between how hard I study and the grades I get.
3. The number of divorces indicates that more and more people are not trying to make their marriages work.
4. It is silly to think that one can really change another person's basic attitudes.
5. Getting promoted is really a matter of being a little luckier than the next person.
6. If one knows how to deal with people, they are really quite easily led.
7. The grades I make are the result of my own efforts; luck has little or nothing to do with it.
8. People like me can change the course of world affairs if we make ourselves heard.
9. A great deal that happens to me is probably a matter of chance.
10. Getting along with people is a skill that must be practised.

B

1. Promotions are earned through hard work and persistence.
2. Many times, the reactions of teachers seem haphazard to me.
3. Marriage is largely a gamble.
4. When I am right, I can convince others.
5. In our society, a person's future earning power depends on his or her ability.
6. I have little influence over the way other people behave.
7. Sometimes I feel that I have little to do with the grades I get.
8. It is only wishful thinking to believe that one can readily influence what happens in our society.
9. I am in control of my destiny.
10. It is almost impossible to figure out how to please some people.

Scoring Key:

Give yourself 1 point for each of the following selections: 1B, 2A, 3A, 4B, 5B, 6A, 7A, 8A, 9B, and 10A.
   Scores can be interpreted as follows:

8–10 = **High internal locus of control**

6–7 = **Moderate internal locus of control**

5 = **Mixed**

3–4 = **Moderate external locus of control**

1–2 = **High external locus of control**

Source: Adapted from J. B. Rotter, "External Control and Internal Control," *Psychology Today,* June 1971, p. 42. Copyright 1971 by the American Psychological Association. Adapted with permission.

LEARNING ABOUT **YOURSELF** EXERCISE #2

How Machiavellian Are You?

For each statement, circle the number that most closely resembles your attitude.

Statement	Disagree			Agree	
	A Lot	A Little	Neutral	A Little	A Lot
1. The best way to handle people is to tell them what they want to hear.	1	2	3	4	5
2. When you ask someone to do something for you, it is best to give the real reason for wanting it rather than giving reasons that might carry more weight.	1	2	3	4	5
3. Anyone who completely trusts anyone else is asking for trouble.	1	2	3	4	5
4. It is hard to get ahead without cutting corners here and there.	1	2	3	4	5
5. It is safest to assume that all people have a vicious streak, and it will come out when given a chance.	1	2	3	4	5
6. One should take action only when it is morally right.	1	2	3	4	5
7. Most people are basically good and kind.	1	2	3	4	5
8. There is no excuse for lying to someone else.	1	2	3	4	5
9. Most people more easily forget the death of their fathers than the loss of their property.	1	2	3	4	5
10. Generally speaking, people will not work hard unless they are forced to do so.	1	2	3	4	5

Scoring Key:

To obtain your Mach score, add the number you have checked on questions 1, 3, 4, 5, 9, and 10. For the other 4 questions, reverse the numbers you have checked: 5 becomes 1, 4 is 2, 2 is 4, and 1 is 5. Total your 10 numbers to find your score. The higher your score, the more machiavellian you are. Among a random sample of American adults, the national average was 25.

Source: R. Christie and F. L. Geis, *Studies in Machiavellianism* (New York: Academic Press, 1970). Reprinted by permission.

How's Your Self-Esteem?

Answer each of the following questions honestly. Next to each question write a 1, 2, 3, 4, or 5, depending on which answer best describes you.

1 = Very often
2 = Fairly often
3 = Sometimes
4 = Once in a great while
5 = Practically never

_____ **1.** How often do you have the feeling that there is nothing that you can do well?

_____ **2.** When you talk in front of a class or group of people your own age, how often do you feel worried or afraid?

_____ **3.** How often do you feel that you have handled yourself well at social gatherings?

_____ **4.** How often do you have the feeling that you can do everything well?

_____ **5.** How often are you comfortable when starting a conversation with people you don't know?

_____ **6.** How often do you feel self-conscious?

_____ **7.** How often do you feel that you are a successful person?

_____ **8.** How often are you troubled with shyness?

_____ **9.** How often do you feel inferior to most people you know?

_____ **10.** How often do you feel that you are a worthless individual?

_____ **11.** How often do you feel confident that your success in your future job or career is assured?

_____ **12.** How often do you feel sure of yourself when among strangers?

_____ **13.** How often do you feel confident that some day people will look up to you and respect you?

_____ **14.** In general, how often do you feel confident about your abilities?

_____ **15.** How often do you worry about how well you get along with other people?

_____ **16.** How often do you feel that you dislike yourself?

_____ **17.** How often do you feel so discouraged with yourself that you wonder whether anything is worthwhile?

_____ **18.** How often do you worry about whether other people like to be with you?

_____ **19.** When you talk in front of a class or a group of people of your own age, how often are you pleased with your performance?

_____ **20.** How often do you feel sure of yourself when you speak in a class discussion?

Scoring Key:

Add up your score for the following 10 items: 1, 2, 6, 8, 9, 10, 15, 16, 17, and 18. For the other 10 items, reverse your scoring (that is, a 5 becomes 1, 4 is 2, 2 is 4, and 1 is 5). The higher your score, the higher your self-esteem.

Source: Developed by A. H. Eagly and adapted from J. R. Robinson and P. R. Shaver, *Measures of Social Psychological Attitudes* (Ann Arbor, MI: Institute of Social Research, 1973), pp. 79–80. With permission.

LEARNING ABOUT **YOURSELF** EXERCISE #4

Are You a High Self-Monitor?

Indicate the degree to which you think the following statements are true or false by circling the appropriate number. For example, if a statement is always true, circle the 5 next to that statement.

0 = Certainly, always false

1 = Generally false

2 = Somewhat false, but with exceptions

3 = Somewhat true, but with exceptions

4 = Generally true

5 = Certainly, always true

1.	In social situations, I have the ability to alter my behaviour if I feel that something else is called for.	0	1	2	3	4	5
2.	I am often able to read people's true emotions correctly through their eyes.	0	1	2	3	4	5
3.	I have the ability to control the way I come across to people, depending on the impression I wish to give them.	0	1	2	3	4	5
4.	In conversations, I am sensitive to even the slightest change in the facial expression of the person I'm conversing with.	0	1	2	3	4	5
5.	My powers of intuition are quite good when it comes to understanding others' emotions and motives.	0	1	2	3	4	5
6.	I can usually tell when others consider a joke in bad taste, even though they may laugh convincingly.	0	1	2	3	4	5
7.	When I feel that the image I am portraying isn't working, I can readily change it to something that does.	0	1	2	3	4	5
8.	I can usually tell when I've said something inappropriate by reading the listener's eyes.	0	1	2	3	4	5
9.	I have trouble changing my behaviour to suit different people and different situations.	0	1	2	3	4	5
10.	I have found that I can adjust my behaviour to meet the requirements of any situation I find myself in.	0	1	2	3	4	5
11.	If someone is lying to me, I usually know it at once from that person's manner of expression.	0	1	2	3	4	5
12.	Even when it might be to my advantage, I have difficulty putting up a good front.	0	1	2	3	4	5
13.	Once I know what the situation calls for, it's easy for me to regulate my actions accordingly.	0	1	2	3	4	5

Scoring Key:

To obtain your score, add up the numbers circled, except reverse scores for questions 9 and 12. On those, a circled 5 becomes a 0, 4 becomes 1, and so forth. High self-monitors are defined as those with scores of 53 or higher.

Source: R. D. Lennox and R. N. Wolfe, "Revision of the Self-Monitoring Scale," *Journal of Personality and Social Psychology,* June 1984, p. 1361. Copyright 1984 by the American Psychological Association. Reprinted by permission.

LEARNING ABOUT **YOURSELF** EXERCISE #5

Are You a Risk-Taker?

For each of the following situations, indicate the minimum odds of success you would demand before recommending that one alternative be chosen over another. Try to place yourself in the position of the adviser to the central person in each of the situations.

1. Mr. B, a 45-year-old accountant, has recently been informed by his physician that he has developed a severe heart ailment. The disease will be sufficiently serious to force Mr. B to change many of his strongest life habits—reducing his workload, drastically changing his diet, giving up favourite leisure-time pursuits. The physician suggests that a delicate medical operation could be attempted. If successful, the operation would completely relieve the heart condition. But its success cannot be assured, and in fact the operation might prove fatal.

   Imagine that you are advising Mr. B. Listed below are several probabilities or odds that the operation will prove successful. Check the *lowest probability* that you would consider acceptable for the operation to be performed.

   _____ Place a check mark here if you think that Mr. B should not have the operation, no matter what the probabilities.

   _____ The chances are 9 in 10 that the operation will be a success.

   _____ The chances are 7 in 10 that the operation will be a success.

   _____ The chances are 5 in 10 that the operation will be a success.

   _____ The chances are 3 in 10 that the operation will be a success.

   _____ The chances are 1 in 10 that the operation will be a success.

2. Mr. D is the captain of University X's varsity football team. University X is playing its traditional rival, University Y, in the final game of the season. The game is in its final seconds, and Mr. D's team, University X, is behind in the score. University X has time to make one more play. Mr. D, the captain, must decide on a strategy. Would it be best to try a play that would be almost certain to work and try to settle for a tie score? Or, on the other hand, should he try a more complicated and risky play that would bring victory if it succeeded or defeat if it failed?

   Imagine that you are advising Mr. D. Listed below are several probabilities or odds that the risky play will work. Check the *lowest probability* that you would consider acceptable for the risky play to be attempted.

   _____ Place a check mark here if you think that Mr. D should not attempt the risky play, no matter what the probabilities.

   _____ The chances are 9 in 10 that the risky play will work.

   _____ The chances are 7 in 10 that the risky play will work.

   _____ The chances are 5 in 10 that the risky play will work.

   _____ The chances are 3 in 10 that the risky play will work.

   _____ The chances are 1 in 10 that the risky play will work.

3. Ms. K is a successful businesswoman who has taken part in a number of civic activities of considerable value to the community. Ms. K has been approached by the leaders of her political party as a possible candidate in the next provincial election. Ms. K's party is a minority party in the constituency, though the party has won occasional elections in the past. Ms. K would like to hold political office, but to do so would involve a serious financial sacrifice, since the party does not have enough campaign funds. She would also have to endure the attacks of her political opponents in a heated campaign.

continued

LEARNING ABOUT **YOURSELF** EXERCISE #5 (Continued)

Imagine that you are advising Ms. K. Listed below are several probabilities or odds of Ms. K's winning the election in her constituency. Check the *lowest probability* that you would consider acceptable to make it worthwhile for Ms. K to run for political office.

_____   Place a check mark here if you think that Ms. K should not run for political office, no matter what the probabilities.

_____   The chances are 9 in 10 that Ms. K will win the election.

_____   The chances are 7 in 10 that Ms. K will win the election.

_____   The chances are 5 in 10 that Ms. K will win the election.

_____   The chances are 3 in 10 that Ms. K will win the election.

_____   The chances are 1 in 10 that Ms. K will win the election.

4. Ms. L, a 30-year-old research physicist, has been given a five-year appointment by a major university laboratory. As she considers the next five years, she realizes that she might work on a difficult long-term problem. If a solution to the problem could be found, it would resolve basic scientific issues in the field and bring high scientific honours. If no solution were found, however, Ms. L would have little to show for her five years in the laboratory, and it would be hard for her to get a good job afterward. On the other hand, she could, as most of her professional associates are doing, work on a series of short-term problems for which solutions would be easier to find. Those solutions would be of lesser scientific importance.

Imagine that you are advising Ms. L. Listed below are several probabilities or odds that a solution will be found to the difficult long-term problem that Ms. L has in mind. Check the *lowest probability* that you would consider acceptable to make it worthwhile for Ms. L to work on the more difficult long-term problem.

_____   Place a check mark here if you think Ms. L should not choose the long-term, difficult problem, no matter what the probabilities.

_____   The chances are 9 in 10 that Ms. L will solve the long-term problem.

_____   The chances are 7 in 10 that Ms. L will solve the long-term problem.

_____   The chances are 5 in 10 that Ms. L will solve the long-term problem.

_____   The chances are 3 in 10 that Ms. L will solve the long-term problem.

_____   The chances are 1 in 10 that Ms. L will solve the long-term problem.

Scoring Key:

These situations were based on a longer questionnaire. Your results are an indication of your general orientation toward risk rather than a precise measure. To calculate your risk-taking score, add up the chances you were willing to take and divide by 4. (For any of the situations in which you would not take the risk, regardless of the probabilities, give yourself a 10.) The lower your number, the more risk-taking you are.

Source: Adapted from N. Kogan and M. A. Wallach, *Risk Taking: A Study in Cognition and Personality* (New York: Holt, Rinehart and Winston, 1964), pp. 256–261.

Are You a Type A?

Circle the number on the scale below that best characterizes your behaviour for each trait.

1. Casual about appointments	1	2	3	4	5	6	7	8	Never late
2. Not competitive	1	2	3	4	5	6	7	8	Very competitive
3. Never feel rushed	1	2	3	4	5	6	7	8	Always feel rushed
4. Take things one at a time	1	2	3	4	5	6	7	8	Try to do many things at once
5. Slow doing things	1	2	3	4	5	6	7	8	Fast (eating, walking, etc.)
6. Express feelings	1	2	3	4	5	6	7	8	"Sit on" feelings
7. Many interests	1	2	3	4	5	6	7	8	Few interests outside work

Scoring Key:

Total your score on the 7 questions. Now multiply the total by 3. A total of 120 or more indicates that you are a hard-core Type A. Scores below 90 indicate that you are a hard-core Type B. The following gives you more specifics:

Points	Personality Type
120 or more	A1
106–119	A
100–105	A2
90–99	B1
Less than 90	B

Source: Adapted from R. W. Bortner, "Short Rating Scale as a Potential Measure of Pattern A Behavior," *Journal of Chronic Diseases,* June 1969, pp. 87–91. With permission.

What's Your EI at Work?

Evaluating the following 25 statements will allow you to rate your social skills and self-awareness, the components of emotional intelligence (EI). EI, the social equivalent of IQ, is complex, in no small part because it depends on some pretty slippery variables—including your innate compatibility, or lack thereof, with the people who happen to be your co-workers. But if you want to get a rough idea of how your EI stacks up, this quiz will help.

As honestly as you can, estimate how you rate in the eyes of peers, bosses, and subordinates on each of the following traits, on a scale of 1 to 4, with 4 representing strong agreement, and 1 representing strong disagreement.

_____ I usually stay composed, positive, and unflappable even in trying moments.

_____ I can think clearly and stay focused on the task at hand under pressure.

_____ I am able to admit my own mistakes.

continued

LEARNING ABOUT **YOURSELF** EXERCISE #7 (Continued)

_____   I usually or always meet commitments and keep promises.

_____   I hold myself accountable for meeting my goals.

_____   I am organized and careful in my work.

_____   I regularly seek out fresh ideas from a wide variety of sources.

_____   I am good at generating new ideas.

_____   I can smoothly handle multiple demands and changing priorities.

_____   I am results-oriented, with a strong drive to meet my objectives.

_____   I like to set challenging goals and take calculated risks to reach them.

_____   I am always trying to learn how to improve my performance, including asking advice from people younger than I am.

_____   I readily make sacrifices to meet an important organizational goal.

_____   The company's mission is something I understand and can identify with.

_____   The values of my team—or of our division or department, or the company—influence my decisions and clarify the choices I make.

_____   I actively seek out opportunities to further the overall goals of the organization and enlist others to help me.

_____   I pursue goals beyond what is required or expected of me in my current job.

_____   Obstacles and setbacks may delay me a little, but they don't stop me.

_____   Cutting through red tape and bending outdated rules are sometimes necessary.

_____   I seek fresh perspectives, even if that means trying something totally new.

_____   My impulses or distressing emotions don't often get the best of me at work.

_____   I can change tactics quickly when circumstances change.

_____   Pursuing new information is my best bet for cutting down on uncertainty and finding ways to do things better.

_____   I usually don't attribute setbacks to a personal flaw (mine or someone else's).

_____   I operate from an expectation of success rather than a fear of failure.

Scoring Key:

Total your score. A score below 70 indicates very low EI. EI can be improved. Says Daniel Goleman, author of _Working With Emotional Intelligence,_ "Emotional intelligence can be learned, and in fact we are each building it, in varying degrees, throughout life. It's sometimes called maturity. EQ is nothing more or less than a collection of tools that we can sharpen to help ensure our own survival."

Source: A. Fisher, "Success Secret: A High Emotional IQ," _Fortune,_ October 26, 1998, p. 298. Reprinted with permission of Time Warner Inc.

BREAKOUT **GROUP** EXERCISES

Form small groups to discuss the following topics, as assigned by your instructor:

1. Think back to your perception of this course and your instructor on the first day of class. What factors might have affected your perceptions of what the rest of the term would be like?

2. Describe a situation in which your perception turned out to be wrong. What perceptual errors did you make that might have caused this to happen?

3. Compare your scores on the *Learning About Yourself Exercises* at the end of the chapter. What conclusions could you draw about your group based on these scores?

WORKING WITH **OTHERS** EXERCISE

Evaluating Your Stereotypes

1. Your instructor will choose 4 volunteers willing to reveal an interesting true-life background fact about themselves. Examples of such background facts are as follows:

   • I can perform various dances, such as polka, rumba, bossa nova, and salsa.

   • I am the youngest of four children, and I attended a Catholic high school.

   • Neither of my parents attended school beyond grade 8.

   • My mother is a homemaker and my father is an author.

2. The instructor will put the 4 facts on the board without revealing to which person each belongs, and the 4 students will remain in the front of the room for the first part of the group discussion below.

3. Students in the class should silently decide which fact belongs to which person.

4. Students should break into groups of about 5 or 6 and try to reach consensus about which fact belongs to which person. Meanwhile, the 4 students can serve as observers to group discussions, listening in on rationales for how students decide to link the facts with the individuals.

5. After 15 minutes of group discussion, several groups will be asked to present their consensus to the class, with justifications.

6. The classroom discussion will focus on perceptions, assumptions, and stereotyping that led to the decisions made.

7. At the end of the discussion, the instructor will reveal which fact belongs to each student.

ETHICAL **DILEMMA** EXERCISE

Managing Emotions at Work

Our understanding of emotions at work has increased rapidly in the past decade. We are now at the point that we are capable (or close to it) of managing the emotions of employees. For instance, companies that want to create open and friendly workplaces are using the selection process to "select out" job applicants who are not outgoing and enthusiastic, and are providing training to teach employees how to smile and appear cheerful. Some organizations are going further in trying to create "emotionally humanistic" work environments not only by shaping the emotions that employees evoke in their daily contacts with customers but also by selecting employee applicants with high emotional intelligence; controlling the emotional atmosphere of teams and work groups; and using similar emotion-management practices.

Groucho Marx once joked that "the secret of success in show business is honesty and sincerity. Once you learn how to fake that, you've got it made." In many service organizations today, Groucho's remark is being applied. For instance, telephone-sales staff in a number of insurance companies are trained to evoke positive feelings from customers—to make it easy for them to say "yes." Employees are taught to avoid words with negative connotations and replace them with upbeat and confidence-building words such as "certainly," "rest assured," "immediate," and "great." Moreover, employees are taught to convey these "scripts" in a way that seems natural and spontaneous. To ensure that these "authentic" positive feelings are consistently evoked, the phone calls of these salespeople are often monitored.

Organizations such as McDonald's, Disney, and Starbucks select and program employees to be upbeat and friendly. They allow employees no choices. Moreover, these organizations export their emotional expectations to wherever they locate in the world. When the hamburgers or lattes come to town, the typical grimace of the Moscovite or shyness of the Finnish employee is subject to a similar genre of smile-training.

Is asking people to feign specific job-related emotions unethical if it conflicts with their basic personalities? Is exporting standardized emotional "rule books" to other cultures unethical? What do you think?

Source: This dilemma is based on S. Fineman, "Managing Emotions at Work: Some Political Reflections" (paper presented at a symposium at the Academy of Management Conference, Washington, DC, August 2001).

CASE INCIDENT

The Rise and Fall of Dennis Kozlowski

The Dennis Kozlowski story could be titled "The Good, the Bad, and the Ugly." The good: As CEO of Tyco International, Kozlowski oversaw the growth of a corporate giant. At its peak, Tyco was gobbling up 200 companies a year. Under his leadership, the value of Tyco increased 70-fold. In 2001, Kozlowski proclaimed his desire to be remembered as the world's greatest business executive.

The bad: Things turned sour when Kozlowski and his former chief financial officer were accused of running a criminal enterprise within Tyco. The two were charged with stealing $170 million (US) directly from the company and pocketing an additional $430 million through manipulated sales of stock, and found guilty in June 2005.

The ugly: Kozlowski's actions almost destroyed the company where he worked for 27 years. In 2002 alone, the value of the company's stock dropped $90 billion!

To understand Kozlowski's behaviour, we should look at the events that shaped his personality. He spent his early years in humble circumstances. He grew up in the 1950s and 1960s in Newark, New Jersey. He said he was the son of a Newark cop turned police detective. Only after he was indicted did it come out that his father was never a police officer in Newark or anywhere else. However, his mother did work for the Newark Police Department as a school crossing guard. His father, in actuality, was a wheeler-dealer who was a practised deceiver and an effective persuader. He had a strong personality but, for the most part, kept his misdeeds to little white lies.

Friends remember Dennis as an easygoing kid who did well in school without trying very hard. He was elected "class politician" by his high school graduating class in 1964. He went to Seton Hall, paying his way through college by playing guitar in a band. He served in Vietnam, held a few accounting jobs, and eventually joined Tyco in 1975.

Over the course of the 1980s, Kozlowski's happy-go-lucky demeanor disappeared. As he climbed the ladder at Tyco, he became a corporate tough guy, both respected and feared. He eventually become CEO in 1992 and oversaw the rapid expansion of the company.

Meanwhile, Kozlowski learned to live big. He had a $17 million apartment in New York, a $30 million mansion in Florida, and a $15 million yacht. He spent $20 million on art for his luxury homes. He took extravagance to the extreme—for instance, spending $6000 on a shower curtain! The more he made, the more he spent—and the more he allegedly stole. Although his total compensation was $170 million in 1999, it was not enough. He manipulated the company's employee relocation fund and Key Employee Loan Program (the latter created to help executives pay taxes due on stock options) to take hundreds of millions in interest-free funds. In 2001, for instance, he gave his wife $1.5 million to start a restaurant, spent $2.1 million on

a birthday party in the Greek Islands for his wife, and gave away $43 million in corporate funds to make philanthropic contributions in his own name.

A former Harvard professor suggests Kozlowski was undone by a rampant sense of entitlement: "By entitlement I mean an aspect of a narcissistic personality who comes to believe that he and the institution are one" and thus "that he can take what he wants when he wants it."

Questions

1. How did Kozlowski's past shape his personality?

2. Does this case contradict the view that personality is largely genetically derived? Explain.

3. What does this case say about corporate ethics?

4. In the movie *Wall Street,* Michael Douglas's character says, "Greed is good." Is this true? How does this apply to Kozlowski?

5. "Kozlowski just did what anybody would do if they had the chance. The people at fault in this story are Tyco's Board of Directors for not controlling their CEO." Do you agree or disagree? Discuss.

Source: Based on A. Bianco, W. Symonds, and N. Byrnes, "The Rise and Fall of Dennis Kozlowski," *BusinessWeek,* December 23, 2002, pp. 64–77.

 VIDEO CASE INCIDENT

NovaScotian Crystal

Do opposites attract? Meet Denis Ryan and Rod McCulloch—partners in NovaScotian Crystal, a small company situated on the quaint waterfront of Halifax.

NovaScotian Crystal makes fine crystal the traditional, old-fashioned, expensive way, with trained craftspeople. It is the only company in Canada that produces mouth-blown, hand-cut crystal.

Ryan started the company in the late 1990s on an impulse. He had already had successful careers in the entertainment and the financial services sectors. With a vision, intrigue, creativity, an impulsive nature, and a contagious enthusiasm for making crystal the traditional way, Ryan set up his glassworks. He even convinced craftspeople to come from Ireland to work for him.

After a few years of making crystal, but not many sales, Ryan found himself facing a serious financial crisis and pos-

sible bankruptcy. He needed someone who could focus on the financial side of the business. On another impulse, Ryan hired Rod McCulloch and a new partnership was born. Ryan took on the role of chair, figurehead, and liaison, while McCulloch became president.

McCulloch—a details, numbers, cost-conscious, organized kind of guy—looked for ways to turn the company around. Using his years of experience as an accountant, he thought about how to manage the company better, make it more efficient, and iron out production. He then began searching for more ways to cut costs and increase sales.

With each taking on different roles, Ryan and McCulloch worked well together. While McCulloch presented tough cost-cutting measures, Ryan brought impulsive ideas about new markets and, often, much-needed personal and emotional support. Even in the face of continuous failures and

continued

disappointments, the team never gave up. Out on the waterfront, over a mug of tea, Ryan could often be found giving McCulloch encouragement, a moment of peace, inspiration, and yet more creative, impulsive ideas for meeting their challenges. Take, for instance, how Ryan encouraged McCulloch to call investors for more money, or the suggestion to market their product to a high-end retail store in Toronto.

At long last, after a spring trade show, creative selling strategies, an expanded product line, and a Christmas craft show, NovaScotian Crystal finally turned a profit in the fall of 2001. Ryan and McCulloch celebrated their success over something stronger than tea. And wouldn't you know it: They didn't drink the same brand of beer.

Today, after years of operating near bankruptcy, NovaScotian Crystal has expanded its product lines, launched a series of online catalogues, and markets its products worldwide.

Questions

1. How would you describe the personalities of Denis Ryan and Rod McCulloch? Describe the extent to which personality plays a role in how Ryan and McCulloch run NovaScotian Crystal.

2. Evaluate the emotional side of running the business. How do Ryan and McCulloch each deal with the stress of running the business?

3. Explain the perceptions of each of these men. What role do these perceptions play in how each runs the company?

Sources: "NovaScotian Crystal," *CBC Venture*, April, 2002, 822; and NovaScotian Crystal, "About Us," http://www.novascotiancrystal.com (accessed October 25, 2005).

From **Concepts** to **Skills**

Reading Emotions

Understanding another person's felt emotions is very difficult. But we can learn to read others' displayed emotions.[106] We do this by focusing on verbal, nonverbal, and paralanguage cues.

The easiest way to find out what someone is feeling is to ask. Saying something as simple as "Are you OK? What's the problem?" can often provide you with the information to assess an individual's emotional state. But relying on a verbal response has two drawbacks. First, almost all of us conceal our emotions to some extent for privacy and to reflect social expectations. So we might be unwilling to share our true feelings. Second, even if we want to verbally convey our feelings, we may be unable to do so. As we noted earlier, some people have difficulty understanding their own emotions and, hence, are unable to express them verbally. So, at best, verbal responses provide only partial information.

You are talking with a co-worker. Does the fact that his back is rigid, his teeth are clenched, and his facial muscles tight tell you something about his emotional state? It probably should. Facial expressions, gestures, body movements, and physical distance are nonverbal cues that can provide additional insights into what a person is feeling. The facial expressions shown in Exhibit 2-8, for instance, are a window

into a person's feelings. Notice the difference in facial features: the height of the cheeks, the raising or lowering of the brow, the turn of the mouth, the positioning of the lips, and the configuration of muscles around the eyes. Even something as subtle as the distance someone chooses to put between him- or herself and you can convey how much intimacy, aggressiveness, repugnance, or withdrawal that person feels.

When you speak with someone, you may notice a sharp change in the tone of her voice and the speed at which she speaks. You are tapping into the third source of information on a person's emotions—paralanguage. This is communication that goes beyond the specific spoken words. It includes pitch, amplitude, rate, and voice quality of speech. Paralanguage reminds us that people convey their feelings not only in what they say, but also in how they say it.

Assessing Skills

After you've read this chapter, take the following Self-Assessments on your enclosed CD-ROM:

1. What's My Basic Personality?

23. What's My Emotional Intelligence Score?

EXHIBIT 2-8   Facial Expressions and Emotions

Each picture portrays a different emotion. Try to identify them before looking at the answers.

Top, left to right: neutral, surprise, happiness. Bottom: fear, sadness, anger.

Source: S. E. Taylor, L. A. Peplan, and D. O. Sears, *Social Psychology,* 9th ed. (Upper Saddle River, NJ: Prentice Hall, 1997), p. 98; photographs by Paul Eikman, Ph.D. Used with permission.

Practising Skills

Part A. Form groups of two. Each person is to spend a couple of minutes thinking of a time in the past when she or he was emotional about something. Examples might include being upset with a parent, sibling, or friend; being excited or disappointed about an academic or athletic achievement; being angry with someone over an insult or slight; being disgusted by something someone has said or done; or being happy because of something good that happened. Do not share this event with the other person in your group.

Part B. Now you will conduct two role plays. Each will be an interview. In the first, one person will play the interviewer and the other will play the job applicant. The job is for a summer management internship with a large retail chain. Each role play will last no longer than 10 minutes. The interviewer is to conduct a normal job interview, except you are to continually rethink the emotional episode you envisioned in Part A. Try hard to convey this emotion while, at the same time, being professional in interviewing the job applicant.

Part C. Now reverse positions for the second role play. The interviewer becomes the job applicant and vice versa. The new interviewer will conduct a normal job interview, except that he or she will continually rethink the emotional episode chosen in Part A.

Part D. Spend 10 minutes analyzing the interview, with specific attention focused on these questions: What emotion(s) do you think the other person was conveying? What cues did you pick up? How accurate were you in reading those cues?

Reinforcing Skills

1. Rent a DVD of an emotionally laden film such as *Death of a Salesman* or *12 Angry Men.* Carefully watch the actors for clues to the emotions they are exhibiting. Try to determine the various emotions projected and explain how you arrived at your conclusion.

2. Spend a day specifically looking for emotional cues in the people with whom you interact. Did this improve communication?

CHAPTER 3
Values, Attitudes, and Their Effects in the Workplace

At Procter & Gamble Canada, diversity is valued and respected. How does this affect the company's workplace?

1 What are values?

2 How can we understand values across cultures?

3 Are there unique Canadian values?

4 What are attitudes and why are they important?

Timothy Penner is president of Toronto-based Procter & Gamble (P&G) Canada. He leads a company that values diversity in its workplace. Consider P&G's statement on employee diversity:

Developing and managing a strong, diverse organization is essential to achieving our business purpose. We value the different perspectives that the diversity of Procter & Gamble people bring to the business. At Procter & Gamble, we operate on the fundamental belief that these diverse viewpoints are needed for organization creativity which produces genuine competitive advantage.[1]

Generally, we expect that an organization's values, like those of an individual, will be reflected in corresponding behaviour and attitudes. If a company stated that it valued workforce diversity and yet no behaviour followed from that statement, we would question whether that value was really so important to the company. However, in P&G's case, they back up their value statements with concrete policies and actions to show support for their values. Does having strong values make for a better workplace?

In this chapter, we look more carefully at how values influence behaviour, and consider the relationship between values and attitudes. We then consider two specific issues that arise from our discussion of values and attitudes: job satisfaction and organizational commitment.

VALUES

Is capital punishment right or wrong? How about employment equity guidelines in hiring? If a person likes power, is that good or bad? The answers to these questions are value-laden. Some might argue, for example, that capital punishment is right because it is a suitable punishment for crimes such as murder. However, others might argue just as strongly that no government has the right to take anyone's life.

Values are concepts or beliefs that guide how we make decisions about and evaluations of behaviours and events.[2] An individual's values can be ranked according to importance. Values tend to be relatively stable and enduring.[3] Most of our values are formed in our early years—with input from parents, teachers, friends, and others. As children, we are told that certain behaviours or outcomes are always desirable or always undesirable. There are few grey areas. It is this absolute or "black-or-white" learning of values that more or less ensures their stability and endurance.

We examine two frameworks for understanding values: Milton Rokeach's terminal and instrumental values and Kent Hodgson's general moral principles.

1 What are values?

Procter & Gamble Canada
www.pg.com/en_CA

values Concepts or beliefs that guide how we make decisions about and evaluations of behaviours and events.

OB IS FOR EVERYONE

* *How do countries differ in their values?*

* *What can you learn about OB from Aboriginal culture?*

* *What would you need to know to set up a business in Asia?*

* *Are Gen-Xers really different from their elders?*

EXHIBIT 3-1   Terminal and Instrumental Values in Rokeach Value Survey

Terminal Values	Instrumental Values
A comfortable life (a prosperous life)	Ambitious (hard-working, aspiring)
An exciting life (a stimulating, active life)	Broad-minded (open-minded)
A sense of accomplishment (lasting contribution)	Capable (competent, effective)
A world at peace (free of war and conflict)	Cheerful (lighthearted, joyful)
A world of beauty (beauty of nature and the arts)	Clean (neat, tidy)
Equality (brotherhood, equal opportunity for all)	Courageous (standing up for your beliefs)
Family security (taking care of loved ones)	Forgiving (willing to pardon others)
Freedom (independence, free choice)	Helpful (working for the welfare of others)
Happiness (contentedness)	Honest (sincere, truthful)
Inner harmony (freedom from inner conflict)	Imaginative (daring, creative)
Mature love (sexual and spiritual intimacy)	Independent (self-reliant, self-sufficient)
National security (protection from attack)	Intellectual (intelligent, reflective)
Pleasure (an enjoyable, leisurely life)	Logical (consistent, rational)
Salvation (saved, eternal life)	Loving (affectionate, tender)
Self-respect (self-esteem)	Obedient (dutiful, respectful)
Social recognition (respect, admiration)	Polite (courteous, well-mannered)
True friendship (close companionship)	Responsible (dependable, reliable)
Wisdom (a mature understanding of life)	Self-controlled (restrained, self-disciplined)

Source: M. Rokeach, *The Nature of Human Values* (New York: Free Press, 1973), p. 56.

Rokeach Value Survey

terminal values Goals that individuals would like to achieve during their lifetimes.

instrumental values Preferable ways of behaving.

Milton Rokeach classified the values that people hold into two sets, with each set containing 18 individual value items.[4] One set, called **terminal values**, refers to desirable end-states of existence. These are the goals that individuals would like to achieve during their lifetimes, such as a comfortable life, or happiness. The other set, called **instrumental values**, refers to preferable ways of behaving, such as being courageous or helpful. Exhibit 3-1 gives common examples for each of these sets.

Several studies confirm that these sets of values vary among groups.[5] People in the same occupations or categories (e.g., corporate managers, union members, parents, students) tend to hold similar values. For instance, one study compared corporate executives, members of the steelworkers' union, and members of a community activist group. Although a good deal of overlap was found among the three groups,[6] there were also some very significant differences (see Exhibit 3-2). The activists had value preferences

EXHIBIT 3-2   Mean Value Ranking of Executives, Union Members, and Activists (Top Five Only)

EXECUTIVES		UNION MEMBERS		ACTIVISTS	
Terminal	**Instrumental**	**Terminal**	**Instrumental**	**Terminal**	**Instrumental**
1. Self-respect	1. Honest	1. Family security	1. Responsible	1. Equality	1. Honest
2. Family security	2. Responsible	2. Freedom	2. Honest	2. A world of peace	2. Helpful
3. Freedom	3. Capable	3. Happiness	3. Courageous	3. Family security	3. Courageous
4. A sense of accomplishment	4. Ambitious	4. Self-respect	4. Independent	4. Self-respect	4. Responsible
5. Happiness	5. Independent	5. Mature love	5. Capable	5. Freedom	5. Capable

Source: Based on W. C. Frederick and J. Weber, "The Values of Corporate Managers and Their Critics: An Empirical Description and Normative Implications," in *Business Ethics: Research Issues and Imperative Studies,* ed. W. C. Frederick and L. E. Preston (Greenwich, CT: JAI Press, 1990), pp. 123–144.

that were quite different from those of the other two groups. They ranked "equality" as their most important terminal value; executives and union members ranked this value 12 and 13, respectively. Activists ranked "helpful" as their second-highest instrumental value. The other two groups both ranked it 14. These differences are important, because executives, union members, and activists all have a vested interest in what corporations do. These differences make it difficult when these groups have to negotiate with each other and can create serious conflicts when they contend with each other over the organization's economic and social policies.[7]

Ethical Values

Ethics is the study of moral values or principles that guide our behaviour and inform us whether actions are right or wrong. Thus ethical values are related to moral judgments about right and wrong.

In recent years, there has been concern that individuals are not grounded in moral values. It is believed that this lack of moral roots has resulted in a number of business scandals, such as those at WorldCom, Enron, Hollinger International, and in the sponsorship scandal of the Canadian government.

Management consultant Kent Hodgson has identified seven general moral principles that individuals should follow when making decisions about behaviour. He calls these "the Magnificent Seven" and suggests that they are universal values that managers should use to make *principled, appropriate,* and *defensible* decisions.[8] They are presented in *OB in Action—The Magnificent Seven Principles*. We discuss the issue of ethics further in Chapter 9.

ethics   The study of moral values or principles that guide our behaviour and inform us whether actions are right or wrong.

OB IN ACTION

The Magnificent Seven Principles

→ *Dignity of human life.* The lives of **people are to be respected.**

→ *Autonomy.* All **persons are intrinsically valuable** and **have the right to self-determination.**

→ *Honesty.* **The truth should be told** to those who have a right to know it.

→ *Loyalty.* **Promises, contracts,** and **commitments should be honoured.**

→ *Fairness.* **People should be treated justly.**

→ *Humaneness.* Our **actions ought to accomplish good,** and we should **avoid doing evil.**

→ *The common good.* Actions should accomplish **the greatest good for the greatest number** of people.

Source: K. Hodgson, "Adapting Ethical Decisions to a Global Marketplace," *Management Review* 81, no. 5 (May 1992), pp. 53–57. Reprinted by permission.

ASSESSING CULTURAL VALUES

Procter & Gamble (P&G) Canada's decision to value diversity in its workplace reflects a dominant value of Canada as a multicultural country. This value is very different from the United States, which considers itself a melting pot with respect to different cultures. P&G Canada has other values that guide employees. These include integrity, trust, ownership, leadership, and passion for winning. What do we know about the values of other countries? What values make Canada unique?

In Chapter 1, we noted that managers have to become capable of working with people from different cultures. Thus it is important to understand how values differ across cultures.

One of the most widely referenced approaches for analyzing variations among cultures has come from Geert Hofstede.[9] He surveyed more than 116 000 IBM employees in 40 countries about their work-related values. He found that managers and employees vary on five value dimensions of national culture.

Hofstede's original findings are based on research that is nearly three decades old. However, his work was updated and reaffirmed when a Canadian researcher at the Chinese University of Hong Kong, Michael Bond, conducted research on values in 22 countries on 5 continents.[10]

2 How can we understand values across cultures?

IBM Canada
www.ibm.com/ca/

| | | **EXHIBIT 3-3**   GLOBE Highlights | | |

Dimension	Countries Rating Low	Countries Rating Moderate	Countries Rating High
Assertiveness	Sweden New Zealand Switzerland	Egypt Ireland Philippines	Spain United States Greece
Future orientation	Russia Argentina Poland	Slovenia Egypt Ireland	Denmark Canada The Netherlands
Gender differentiation	Sweden Denmark Slovenia	Italy Brazil Argentina	South Korea Egypt Morocco
Uncertainty avoidance	Russia Hungary Bolivia	Israel United States Mexico	Austria Denmark Germany
Power distance	Denmark The Netherlands South Africa	England France Brazil	Russia Spain Thailand
Individualism/collectivism*	Denmark Singapore Japan	Hong Kong United States Egypt	Greece Hungary Germany
In-group collectivism	Denmark Sweden New Zealand	Japan Israel Qatar	Egypt China Morocco
Performance orientation	Russia Argentina Greece	Sweden Israel Spain	United States Taiwan New Zealand
Humane orientation	Germany Spain France	Hong Kong Sweden Taiwan	Indonesia Egypt Malaysia

* A low score on individualism is synonymous with collectivism.

Source: M. Javidan and R. J. House, "Cultural Acumen for the Global Manager: Lessons from Project GLOBE," *Organizational Dynamics,* Spring 2001, pp. 289–305. Reprinted with permission from Elsevier.

✳ *How do countries differ in their values?*

More recently, the Global Leadership and Organizational Behavior Effectiveness (GLOBE) research project identified nine dimensions on which national cultures differ.[11] This study is an ongoing cross-cultural investigation of leadership and national culture that has used data from 825 organizations in 62 countries. The GLOBE study confirms that Hofstede's five dimensions are still valid (his four original ones, plus the long-term orientation added through the merger of Bond's research with Hofstede's).[12] However, the GLOBE study has added four dimensions and provides us with an updated measure of where countries rate on each dimension. Exhibit 3-3 presents ratings by country on each of the dimensions.

The GLOBE dimensions are defined as follows:

- *Assertiveness.* The extent to which a society encourages people to be tough, confrontational, assertive, and competitive vs. modest and tender.

- *Future orientation.* The extent to which a society encourages and rewards future-oriented behaviours such as planning, investing in the future, and delaying gratification. This is essentially equivalent to Hofstede's long-term/short-term orientation.

- *Gender differentiation.* The extent to which a society maximizes gender role differences. This is essentially equivalent to Hofstede's masculinity/femininity dimension.

- *Uncertainty avoidance.* As identified by Hofstede, the GLOBE team defined this term as a society's reliance on social norms and procedures to alleviate the unpredictability of future events.

- *Power distance.* As did Hofstede, the GLOBE team defined this as the extent to which members of a society expect power to be shared unequally.

- *Individualism/collectivism.* Again, this term was defined, as was Hofstede's, as the extent to which individuals are encouraged by societal institutions to be integrated into groups within organizations and society.

- *In-group collectivism.* In contrast to focusing on societal institutions, this dimension encompasses the extent to which members of a society take pride in membership in small groups, such as their families and circles of close friends, and the organizations in which they are employed.

- *Performance orientation.* The extent to which a society encourages and rewards group members for performance improvement and excellence.

- *Humane orientation.* The extent to which a society encourages and rewards individuals for being fair, altruistic, generous, caring, and kind to others. This closely approximates Hofstede's quality-of-life dimension.

An awareness of the GLOBE study findings reminds us that (1) not all organizational behaviour theories and concepts are universally applicable to managing people around the world, especially in countries where work values are considerably different from those in Canada; and (2) you should consider cultural values when trying to understand the behaviour of people in different countries. To help you with this second point, we will stop regularly to consider the generalizability of theories and concepts presented in this book to different cultures.

In this chapter's *Working With Others Exercise* on page 94, you have the opportunity to compare the cultural values of two countries and determine how differences might affect group behaviour. The *Ethical Dilemma Exercise*, also on page 94, asks you to consider when something is a gift and when it is a bribe. Different cultures take different approaches to this question.

VALUES IN THE CANADIAN WORKPLACE

Studies have shown that when individual values align with organizational values, the results are positive. Individuals who have an accurate understanding of the job requirements and the organization's values adjust better to their jobs, and have greater levels of satisfaction and organizational commitment.[13] In addition, shared values between the employee and the organization lead to more positive work attitudes,[14] lower turnover,[15] and greater productivity.[16]

3 Are there unique Canadian values?

Individual and organizational values do not always align. Moreover, within organizations, individuals can have very different values. The *Case Incident—You Can't Do That*, on the CD-ROM that accompanies this textbook, asks you to consider whether particular values should be shut out from the workplace. Two major factors lead to a potential clash of values in the workplace: cultural differences and generational differences. Let's look at the implications of both factors in the Canadian workplace.

Cultural Differences

Canada is a multicultural country. "One in six Canadians in their 20s are immigrants, and one in five are the children of at least one immigrant parent."[17] In 2001, 44 percent of Metropolitan Toronto's population, 38 percent of Vancouver's, and 18.6 percent of Montreal's were made up of immigrants.[18] The 2001 census found that 17 percent of Canada's population over age five spoke neither of the country's two official languages as their first language. In Vancouver and Toronto, this rate was 38 percent and 41 percent, respectively, so considerably more than one-third of the population of those two cities does not speak either English or French as a first language.[19] Of those who speak other languages, 16 percent speak Chinese (mainly Mandarin or Cantonese). The other dominant languages in Canada are Italian in fourth place, followed by German, Punjabi, and Spanish.[20] These figures indicate the very different cultures that are part of the Canadian fabric of life.

Though we live in a multicultural society, there are some tensions among people from different races and ethnic groups. For instance, a 2002 Statistics Canada survey on ethnic diversity found that while most Canadians (93 percent) say they have never or rarely experienced unfair treatment because of their ethnicity or culture, 20 percent of visible minorities reported having been unfairly treated sometimes or often.[21]

Canadians often define themselves as "not Americans" and point out differences in the values of the two countries. A recent study, the Pew Global Attitudes Project, identified a number of differences between Canadian and American values.[22] Exhibit 3-4 on page 79 shows some of the highlights of that study.

In his recent book *Fire and Ice,* pollster Michael Adams finds that there is a growing dissimilarity between Canadian and American values. The two groups differ in 41 of the 56 values that Adams examined. For 24 values the gap has actually widened between 1992 and 2000, indicating that Canadians' social values are growing more distinct from those of Americans.[23] Adams suggests that the September 11, 2001, attacks have affected the personality of Americans. He finds Americans are more accepting of patriarchy and hierarchy these days, and he concludes that it is "the supposedly bold, individualistic Americans who are the nodding conformists, and the supposedly shy, deferential and law-abiding Canadians who are most likely to assert their personal autonomy and political agency."[24] This chapter's *CBC Video Case Incident* gives you additional insights into the differences between Canadians and Americans.

In what follows, we identify a number of cultural values that influence workplace behaviour in Canada. Be aware that these are generalizations, and it would be a mistake to assume that everyone coming from the same cultural background acts similarly. Rather, these overviews are meant to encourage you to think about cultural differences and similarities so that you can better understand people's behaviour.

Women wearing the *hajib*, the traditional head cover of Muslim women, face discrimination in getting jobs in Canada. A recent study found that visibly Muslim women were either told there were no jobs available or not given a chance to apply for a job almost 40 percent of the time that they asked an employer whether a job was available.

Diverging Ideologies

EXHIBIT 3-4   Canadian and American Value Differences

Statement	Percentage Who Completely Agree With Statement	
	Canadians	Americans
The impact of globalization on their country can be described as very good.	36	21
People are better off in a free market, despite inequality.	19	28
It is more important that government ensure that nobody is in need than that government stay out of the way.	52	34
It is the responsibility of government to tend to the very poor who cannot take care of themselves.	43	29
Immigrants have a very good influence on how well things are going.	19	8
Religion should be a matter of private faith, kept separate from government policy.	71	55
Homosexuality is a way of life that should be accepted by society.	69	51

Source: The Pew Research Center for the People and the Press, *Views of a Changing World 2003* (Washington, DC: The Pew Research Center for the People and the Press, June 2003).

Francophone and Anglophone Values

One of the larger cultural issues that confronts Canada is the question of Quebec separatism and anglophone-francophone differences. Thus, it may be of interest to managers and employees in Canadian firms to be aware of some of the potential cultural differences when managing in francophone environments compared with anglophone environments. A number of studies have shown that English-speaking Canadians and French-speaking Canadians have distinctive values. Francophones have been found to be more collectivist, or group-oriented, with a greater need for achievement, while anglophones have been found to be more individualist, or I-centred.[25] Francophones have also been shown to be more concerned about the interpersonal aspects of the workplace than task competence.[26] They have also been found to be more committed to their work organizations.[27] Anglophones have been shown to take more risks.[28] By contrast, a recent study examining work values in French- and English-speaking Canada found that French-speaking Canadians were not risk-takers and had the highest values for "reducing or avoiding ambiguity and uncertainty at work."[29]

Other studies have found that anglophone managers tended to value autonomy and intrinsic job values, such as achievement, and thus were more achievement-oriented, while francophone managers tended to value affiliation and extrinsic job values, such as technical supervision.[30]

A study conducted at the University of Ottawa and Laval University suggests that some of the differences reported in previous research may be decreasing.[31] Another study indicates that French Canadians have become more like English Canadians in valuing autonomy and self-fulfillment.[32] However, there is evidence of some continuing differences in lifestyle values. A recent Canadian Institute for Health Information report noted that Quebecers experience more stress than other Canadians.[33] The study also found that Quebecers smoke more, have the highest workplace absenteeism rate, and are less physically active than the rest of the country. Another study found that

Asked to define the fundamentals that give National Bank Financial its edge, senior vice-president and company director John Wells believes Montreal-based National Bank Financial's edge comes from company management that is largely francophone. He argues that French-speaking Canadians treat their employees well and will try to find *any* means of reducing expenses rather than lay off staff, in sharp contrast to the cost-cutting mechanisms of either English-speaking Canadian or American firms.

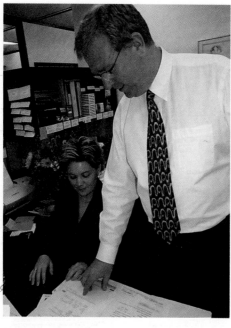

French-speaking Canadians and English-speaking Canadians have different values regarding cultural activities. For example, francophones are more likely to attend symphonic, classical, or choral music performances than anglophones. Anglophones are more likely to read newspapers, magazines, and books than francophones.[34]

Even though they have some cultural and lifestyle value differences, francophone and anglophone managers today have been exposed to similar types of organizational theories during their post-secondary school training, which might also influence their outlooks as managers. Thus we would not expect to find large differences in the way that firms in francophone Canada are managed, compared with those in the rest of Canada. Throughout the textbook, you will see a number of examples of Quebec-based businesses that support this conclusion.

Aboriginal Values

> ✱ What can you learn about OB from Aboriginal culture?

Entrepreneurial activity among Canada's Aboriginal peoples has been growing, as has the number of partnerships and alliances between Aboriginal and nonAboriginal businesses. There are now more than 27 000 Aboriginal-owned businesses in Canada. Fourteen percent of Aboriginal business owners live on reserves, while 86 percent live off reserves. Between 1996 and 2001, the growth rate of Aboriginal businesses was huge: They increased by nearly 31 percent, a rate nine times higher than Canadian businesses overall.[35]

With this strong increase in both the number of Aboriginal businesses and the number of partnerships and alliances between Aboriginal and nonAboriginal businesses, it is important to examine whether and how each culture manages differently.[36] "Aboriginal values are usually perceived (by non-Aboriginals) as an impediment to economic development and organizational effectiveness."[37] Such values include reluctance to compete, a time orientation different from the Western one, and an emphasis on consensus decision making.[38] Aboriginal peoples do not necessarily agree that these values are business impediments, however. Saskatoon-based First Nations Bank of Canada, for example, posted its fifth straight year of profitability in 2005.

Although Canadian businesses and government have historically assumed that "non-Native people must teach Native people how to run their own organizations," the First Nations of Canada are not convinced.[39] They believe that traditional culture, values, and languages can help build a self-sustaining economy. Moreover, they believe that their cultural values may actually be a positive force in conducting business.[40]

In recent years, Canadian businesses facing Native land claims have met some difficulties in trying to accommodate demands for appropriate land use. In some cases, *accommodation* can mean less logging or mining by businesses until land claims are worked out. In order to achieve better communication between businesses and native leaders, Cliff Hickey and David Natcher, two anthropologists from the University of Alberta, collaborated with the Little Red River Cree Nation in northern Alberta to develop

First Nations Bank of Canada
www.firstnationsbank.com/index.jsp

a new model for forestry operations on First Nations land.[41] The anthropologists sought to balance the Native community's traditional lifestyle with the economic concerns of forestry operations. *OB in Action—Ground Rules for Developing Business Partnerships With Aboriginal Peoples* outlines several of Hickey and Natcher's recommended ground rules, which they say could be used in oil and gas developments as well. Johnson Sewepegaham, chief of the Little Red River Cree, said his community will use these recommendations to resolve difficulties on treaty lands for which Vernon, BC-based Tolko Industries and High Level, Alberta-based Footner Forest Products jointly hold forest tenure.

Lindsay Redpath of Athabasca University has noted that Aboriginal cultures are more collectivist in orientation than are nonAboriginal cultures in Canada and the United States.[42] Aboriginal organizations are much more likely to reflect and advance the goals of the community. There is also a greater sense of family within the workplace, with greater affiliation and loyalty. Power distance in Aboriginal cultures is smaller than in nonAboriginal cultures of Canada and the United States, and there is an emphasis on consensual decision making. Aboriginal cultures are lower on uncertainty avoidance than nonAboriginal cultures in Canada and the United States. Aboriginal organizations and cultures tend to have fewer rules and regulations. Each of these differences suggests that businesses created by Aboriginal peoples will differ from nonAboriginal businesses, and both research and anecdotal evidence support this view.[43] For instance, Richard Prokopanko, director of corporate affairs for Montreal-based Alcan, says that a move from handling issues in a generally legalistic, contract-oriented manner to valuing more dialogue and collaboration has helped ease some of the tension that had built up over 48 years between Alcan and First Nations people.[44]

Asian Values

The largest visible minority group in Canada are the Chinese. Over 1 million people of this group live in Canada and represent 26 percent of the country's visible minority population.[45] The Chinese in this country are a diverse group; they come from different countries (e.g., China, Hong Kong, Malaysia), speak different languages, and practise different religions. The Chinese are only one part of the entire influence of East and Southeast Asian values that affect Canadian society. It is predicted that by 2017, almost one-half of all visible minorities in Canada will come from two groups, South Asian and Chinese, and that these groups will be represented in almost equal numbers.[46] As well, many Canadian organizations, particularly those in British Columbia, conduct significant business with Asian firms. Asian cultures differ from Canadian culture on many of the GLOBE dimensions discussed earlier. For instance, Asian cultures tend to exhibit greater power distance and greater collectivism. These differences in values can affect individual interactions.

Professor Rosalie Tung of Simon Fraser University and her student Irene Yeung examined the importance of *guanxi* (personal connections with the appropriate authorities or individuals) for a sample of North American, European, and Hong Kong firms doing business with companies in mainland China.[47] They suggest that their findings will also be relevant in understanding how to develop relationships with firms from Japan, South Korea, and Hong Kong.

Guanxi relationships
- based on reciprocation
- less self interest
- meant to be long term and enduring
- less on institutional law
- more on personal power + Authority
- governed b/more on emotion of Shame
- Seen to be extreamly important!

Guanxi

> ★ *What would you need to know to set up a business in Asia?*

"*Guanxi* refers to the establishment of a connection between two independent individuals to enable a bilateral flow of personal or social transactions. Both parties must derive benefits from the transaction to ensure the continuation of such a relationship."[48] *Guanxi* relations are based on reciprocation, unlike Western networked relationships, which may be characterized more by self-interest. *Guanxi* relationships are meant to be long-term and enduring, in contrast with the immediate gains sometimes expected in Western relationships. *Guanxi* also relies less on institutional law, and more on personal power and authority, than do Western relationships. Finally, *guanxi* relations are governed more by the notion of shame (i.e., external pressures on performance), while Western relations often rely on guilt (i.e., internal pressures on performance) to maintain agreements. *Guanxi* is seen as extremely important for business success in China—more than such factors as right location, price, or strategy, or product differentiation and quality. For Western firms wanting to do business with Asian firms, an understanding of *guanxi* and an effort to build relationships are important strategic advantages.

Our discussion about differences in cross-cultural values should suggest to you that understanding other cultures matters. When Canadian firms develop operations across Canada, south of the border, or overseas, employees need to understand other cultures in order to work more effectively and get along with others.

Generational Differences

Environics Research Group
http://erg.environics.net

In his book *Sex in the Snow*, pollster Michael Adams attempted to identify the social values of today's Canadians.[49] He found that within three broad age groups of adult Canadians—the Elders (those over 60), Baby Boomers (born between the mid-1940s and the mid-1960s), and Generation Xers (born between the mid-1960s and the early 1980s)—there are at least 12 quite distinct "value tribes." We present the age groups and discuss some of their values in what follows. For further information on these different value tribes and an opportunity to see where you might be classified in terms of your social values, visit the Environics Research Group website.

In the discussion of values that follows, bear in mind that we present broad generalizations, and you should certainly avoid stereotyping individuals on the basis of these generalizations. There are individual differences in values. For instance, not every Baby Boomer thinks alike, and neither does every member of Generation X. Thus, the important point about the values discussion is that you should try to understand how others might view things differently from you, even when they are exposed to the same situation.

The Elders

- Play by rules
- Core values + beliefs are in order

These individuals are characterized as "playing by the rules," and their core values are belief in order, authority, discipline, the Judeo-Christian moral code, and the Golden Rule (do unto others as you would have others do unto you). About 80 percent of the Elders resemble this description of traditional values, although there are variations within that 80 percent in the strength of fit.

Baby Boomers

Some what spoiled, hedonisitic, rebellious group belies the four categories of Boomers

- bit more fragmented in views.

The view of Baby Boomers as a somewhat spoiled, hedonistic, rebellious group belies the four categories of Boomers: autonomous rebels (25 percent), anxious communitarians (20 percent), connected enthusiasts (14 percent), and disengaged Darwinists (41 percent). So, unlike the Elders, the Boomers are a bit more fragmented in their views. Yet all but the disengaged Darwinists reflect, to some extent, the stereotypes of this generation: rejection of authority, skepticism regarding the motives of big business and government, a strong concern for the environment, and a strong desire for equality in the workplace and society. Of course, the disengaged Darwinists, the largest single group, do not fit this description well. The Darwinists are characterized as angry, intimidated by change, and anxious about their professional and financial futures.

Generation X

> ✳ Are Gen-Xers really different from their elders?

Although this group is quite fragmented in its values, research shows that the common values are experience-seeking, adaptability, and concern with personal image among peers. Despite these common values, Generation Xers can be divided into five tribes. Thrill-seeking materialists (25 percent) desire money and material possessions, as well as recognition, respect, and admiration. Aimless dependants (27 percent) seek financial independence, security, and stability. Social hedonists (15 percent) are experience-seeking, committed to their own pleasure, and seek immediate gratification. New Aquarians (13 percent) are experience-seeking, and also egalitarian and ecologically minded. Finally, autonomous post-materialists (20 percent) seek personal autonomy and self-fulfillment, and are concerned about human rights.

The Ne(x)t Generation

Since Adams' book appeared, another generation has been identified. Labelled the Net Generation,[50] millennials,[51] Generation Y, or the Echo Boomers, this generation, born between 1977 and 1997, consists of "creators, not recipients. And they are curious, contrarian, flexible, collaborative and high in self-esteem."[52] This generation is defined by its ease with technology, having grown up with cellphones, text messaging, and Internet access (hence the name "Net"). They are team players and optimists with a desire for order.[53]

In this chapter's *Learning About Yourself Exercise* on page 93, you have the opportunity to examine some of the things that you value.

The Generations Meet in the Workplace

Baby Boomers currently dominate the workplace, but their years of being in charge are limited. In 2013, half of them will be at least 55 and 18 percent will be over 60.[54] As

Vancouver-based Mainframe Entertainment, the company behind *Reboot* and *Zixx*, understands the values of its Generation X employees: experience, recognition, respect, and admiration. Mainframe's animators get leadership opportunities, including the opportunity to direct shows, which they would not get at higher-paying studios in Los Angeles. Mainframe has one of the lowest turnover rates in the animation business because of its emphasis on giving its young employees the opportunity to acquire new skills.

[Handwritten marginal notes:]
Baby Boomers, Workaholics,
- Generation Xers,
- Comfortable in adapting, but want more experience
- not in awe of authority
- not interested in copying the workaholic behaviour

Boomers move into head offices, the "play-by-the-rules," "boss-knows-best" Elders are being replaced by somewhat more egalitarian Boomers. They dislike the command-and-control rules that were part of their parents' lives, although the Boomers have also been described as workaholics. Meanwhile, the Generation Xers in the workplace are comfortable in adapting, but also want more experiences. They are not in awe of authority. Most important, they are not interested in copying the workaholic behaviour of their parents. Managing the expectations of each of these very different groups is not an easy task. It requires managers to be flexible, observant, and willing to adjust more to the individual needs of these different employees. Members of the Net Generation will certainly change the face of the workplace in significant ways. They have mastered a communication and information system that many of their parents have yet to understand.

[Handwritten: net Generation]

ATTITUDES

> The management at Procter & Gamble (P&G) Canada consider diversity a competitive advantage. They "believe that a diverse company will outperform a homogeneous company by inspiring more creative and innovative solutions."[55] To help employees foster a similar attitude toward diversity, P&G conducts mandatory diversity training for all employees. Thus, P&G recognizes the link between organizational values and employee attitudes. The training is meant to help employees have greater awareness of cultural and style differences. Managers are given additional training to help them improve their leadership in a diverse workplace. So how do attitudes get formed, and can they really be changed?

4 What are attitudes and why are they important?

attitudes Positive or negative feelings about objects, people, or events.

Attitudes are positive or negative feelings about objects, people, or events. When I say "I like my job," I am expressing my attitude to work. Attitudes are thus judgment responses to situations.

Attitudes are not the same as values because values are convictions about what is important, but the two are interrelated. In organizations, attitudes are important because they affect job behaviour. Employees may believe, for example, that supervisors, auditors, managers, and time-and-motion engineers are all conspiring to make employees work harder for the same or less money. This may then lead to a negative attitude toward management when an employee is asked to stay late and help on a special project. *Case Incident—Gourmet Foods Works on Employee Attitudes* on page 95 highlights how changes in attitudes can help a company's bottom line.

Employees may be negatively affected by the attitudes of their co-workers or clients. For instance, Debra Krakow, an architect with Kingston, Ontario-based Mill & Ross Architects, notes that client attitudes toward the competency of female architects discourage women from staying in that profession. "In my experience, if you're male, you're presumed competent or you wouldn't be there. If you're female, you're presumed incompetent until proven otherwise," she says.[56] In *From Concepts to Skills* on page 97, we discuss whether it is possible to change someone's attitude, and how that might happen in the workplace. *Focus on Diversity* looks at how attitudes toward who can make proper sushi affect who gets hired to be a sushi maker.

FOCUS ON **DIVERSITY**

Nontraditional Sushi Makers

What determines a good sushi maker?   For many sushi restaurants in Japan and in North America, a sushi chef "should" be male.[57] It's what's expected, and it's what's observed. Yoko Ogawa, 30, a female sushi chef at Yamaguchi in Midtown Manhattan, explains the problem women face: "They say that women cannot make sushi because their hands are too warm and that will ruin the fish."

Hiromi Suzuki, whose father is the chef and owner of Mie in the East Village of New York, shared some of her father's stories about women sushi makers: "Women can't make sushi because they wear perfume and makeup, and the smell of the perfume and makeup will ruin the food." Others believe that women can't become sushi chefs because the area behind the counter is sacred.

These attitudes have made it difficult not only for women but also for nonJapanese to become sushi makers in Japan and North America, although that is starting to change. When Toshi Sugiura started the California Sushi Academy in Venice, California, in 1998, he expected that his students would be Asian immigrants. Instead, most of the students were American. This required him to change his vision: "Sushi is becoming a worldwide food. Why can't black people and white people make sushi?"

All of these examples suggest that who gets hired into any position can be affected by attitudes about what the "right" person should look like. 🕴

A person can have thousands of attitudes, but organizational behaviour focuses our attention on a limited number of job-related attitudes. These job-related attitudes tap positive or negative evaluations that employees hold about aspects of their work environment. In the following, we consider two important attitudes that affect organizational performance: job satisfaction and organizational commitment.

Job Satisfaction

The term **job satisfaction** refers to an individual's general attitude toward his or her job. A person with a high level of job satisfaction holds positive attitudes toward the job, while a person who is dissatisfied with his or her job holds negative attitudes toward the job. When people speak of employee attitudes, more often than not they mean job satisfaction. In fact, the terms are frequently used interchangeably.

A recent Canadian Policy Research Networks survey on job satisfaction found that only 40 percent of Canadian employees are very satisfied with their jobs. By comparison, 47 percent of American employees are happy with their work and 54 percent of Danish employees are highly satisfied.[58] On the other hand, almost 40 percent of Canadian employees would not recommend their companies as good places to work. Forty percent also believe that they never see any of the benefits from their companies' making money. Almost 40 percent report that red tape and bureaucracy are among the biggest barriers to job satisfaction. A majority of the workforce (55 percent) says that they feel the "pressure of having too much to do."

So what are the consequences of lower job satisfaction? We examine this question below.

> **job satisfaction** An individual's general attitude toward his or her job.
>
> **Canadian Policy Research Networks**
> www.cprn.com/en/

Job Satisfaction and Individual Productivity

The evidence suggests that the link between an individual's job satisfaction and his or her productivity is very slightly positive.[59] It turns out the productivity can be affected as much by external conditions as it is by job satisfaction. For instance, a stockbroker's productivity is largely affected by the general movement of the stock market. When the market is moving up and volume is high, both satisfied and dissatisfied brokers will earn lots of commissions. Conversely, when the market is down, the level of broker satisfaction is not likely to mean much. One's position in the organization also seems to be an important moderating variable.

The relationship between job satisfaction and productivity is stronger when the employee's behaviour is not controlled by outside factors. An employee's productivity

Job Satisfaction Relationship

more among Professional, Supervisory, & manager positions.

on machine-paced jobs, for instance, will be much more influenced by the speed of the machine than by his or her level of satisfaction.

The evidence also shows that the satisfaction-productivity correlation is stronger for higher-level employees. Thus, we might expect the relationship to be more relevant for individuals in professional, supervisory, and managerial positions.

There is another complication in the satisfaction-productivity link. Some studies have found that productivity leads to satisfaction rather than the other way around.[60] In other words, an employee who does a good job feels good about it. Additionally, assuming that the organization rewards productivity, higher productivity should increase verbal recognition, pay level, and probabilities for promotion. These rewards, in turn, increase the employee's level of satisfaction with the job.

Some recent research has also looked at the idea of **perceived organizational support** and its effect on performance, absenteeism, job stress, and turnover.[61] Perceived organizational support reflects the degree to which employees believe that the organization values their contribution and cares about their well-being. An employee who believes the employer is supportive tends to perform better and feel a much stronger commitment to the organization.

Our *Point/Counterpoint* discussion on page 92 investigates the debate over whether job satisfaction is created by the situation or by an individual's characteristics.

Job Satisfaction and Organizational Productivity

The link between job satisfaction and productivity is much stronger when we look not at individuals, but at the organization as a whole.[62] When satisfaction and productivity data are gathered for the organization as a whole, rather than at the individual level, we find that organizations with more-satisfied employees tend to be more effective than organizations with less-satisfied employees.

Job Satisfaction and Organizational Citizenship Behaviour

In Chapter 1, we defined **organizational citizenship behaviour (OCB)** as discretionary behaviour that is not part of an employee's formal job requirements and is not usually rewarded, but that nevertheless promotes the effective functioning of the organization.[63] Individuals who are high in OCB will go beyond their usual job duties, providing performance that is beyond expectations. Examples of such behaviour include helping colleagues with their workloads, taking only limited breaks, and alerting others to work-related problems.[64] More recently OCB has been associated with the following workplace behaviours: "altruism, conscientiousness, loyalty, civic virtue, voice, functional participation, sportsmanship, courtesy, and advocacy participation."[65] Organizational citizenship is important, as it can help the organization function more efficiently and more effectively.[66] Recent work by York University professors Sabrina Salamon and Yuval Deutsch suggest that OCB may be a way for individuals to signal to managers and co-workers abilities that might not be immediately observable.[67]

It seems logical to assume that job satisfaction should be a major determinant of an employee's OCB.[68] Satisfied employees would seem more likely to talk positively about an organization, help others, and go beyond the normal expectations in their jobs.[69] Moreover, satisfied employees might be more prone to go beyond the call of duty because they want to reciprocate their positive experiences. Consistent with this thinking, early discussions of OCB assumed that it was closely linked with satisfaction.[70] Some evidence, however, suggests that satisfaction does influence OCB, but through perceptions of fairness.[71]

There is, then, a modest overall relationship between job satisfaction and OCB.[72] But job satisfaction is unrelated to OCB when fairness is considered.[73] What does this mean? Basically, job satisfaction comes down to a belief that there are fair outcomes, treatment, and procedures in the workplace.[74] If you do not feel that your manager, the

perceived organizational support The degree to which employees believe that the employer values their contribution to the organization and cares about employee well-being.

organizational citizenship behaviour (OCB) Discretionary behaviour that is not part of an employee's formal job requirements, but that nevertheless promotes the effective functioning of the organization.

organization's procedures, or its pay policies are fair, your job satisfaction is likely to suffer significantly. However, when you perceive organizational processes and outcomes to be fair, trust is developed. When you trust your employer, your job satisfaction increases, and you are more willing to voluntarily go beyond your formal job requirements. Recent research suggests that OCB can be applied cross-culturally, although the exact form of OCB might be different in non–North American countries.[75]

Job Satisfaction and Customer Satisfaction

Employees in service jobs often interact with customers. Since the management of service organizations should be concerned with pleasing those customers, it is reasonable to ask: Is employee satisfaction related to positive customer outcomes? For front-line employees who have regular contact with customers, the answer is yes.

The evidence indicates that satisfied employees increase customer satisfaction and loyalty.[76] Why? In service organizations, customer retention and defection are highly dependent on how front-line employees deal with customers. Satisfied employees are more likely to be friendly, upbeat, and responsive—which customers appreciate. Because satisfied employees are less prone to turnover, customers are more likely to encounter familiar faces and receive experienced service. These qualities build customer satisfaction and loyalty. In addition, the relationship seems to apply in reverse: Dissatisfied customers can increase an employee's job dissatisfaction. Employees who have regular contact with customers report that rude, thoughtless, or unreasonably demanding customers adversely affect the employees' job satisfaction.[77]

How Employees Can Express Dissatisfaction

Dissatisfied employees are more likely to miss work, but the correlation is moderate—usually less than −0.40.[78] Dissatisfied employees are also more likely to quit their jobs, and the correlation is stronger than what we found for absenteeism.[79] However, a person's general disposition toward life moderates the job satisfaction-turnover relationship.[80] Some individuals gripe more than others and such individuals, when dissatisfied with their jobs, are less likely to quit than those who are more positively disposed toward life. So if two employees are equally dissatisfied, the one most likely to quit is the one with the highest predisposition to be happy or satisfied with life in general. Likely these individuals do not feel trapped and are willing to exert more control over the situation and look for another job.

The evidence suggests that employees express dissatisfaction in a number of ways.[81] For example, rather than quit, employees can complain, be insubordinate, steal organizational property, or avoid some of their work responsibilities. Exhibit 3-5 on page 88 illustrates a model that can be used to examine individual responses to dissatisfaction along two dimensions: whether they are constructive or destructive and whether they are active or passive. Four types of behaviour result:[82]

- **Exit**. Actively attempting to leave the organization, including looking for a new position as well as resigning. This is a destructive action from the point of view of the organization.

- **Voice**. Actively and constructively trying to improve conditions, including suggesting improvements, discussing problems with superiors, and some forms of union activity.

- **Loyalty**. Passively but optimistically waiting for conditions to improve, including speaking up for the organization in the face of external criticism and trusting the organization and its management to do the right thing.

- **Neglect**. Passively allowing conditions to worsen, including chronic absenteeism or lateness, reduced effort, and increased error rate.

exit Dissatisfaction expressed by actively attempting to leave the organization.

voice Dissatisfaction expressed by actively and constructively attempting to improve conditions.

loyalty Dissatisfaction expressed by passively waiting for conditions to improve.

neglect Dissatisfaction expressed by passively allowing conditions to worsen.

EXHIBIT 3-5 Responses to Job Dissatisfaction

Exit and neglect behaviours encompass our performance variables—productivity, absenteeism, and turnover. But this list expands employee response to include voice and loyalty—constructive behaviours that allow individuals to tolerate unpleasant situations or to revive satisfactory working conditions. It helps us to understand situations, such as those sometimes found among unionized employees, where low job satisfaction is coupled with low turnover.[83] Union members often express dissatisfaction through the grievance procedure or through formal contract negotiations. These voice mechanisms allow the union members to continue in their jobs while convincing themselves that they are acting to improve the situation.

Organizational Commitment

organizational commitment
A state in which an employee identifies with a particular organization and its goals, and wishes to maintain membership in the organization.

Organizational commitment is defined as a state in which an employee identifies with a particular organization and its goals, and wishes to maintain membership in the organization.[84]

Professor John Meyer at the University of Western Ontario and his colleagues have identified and developed measures for three types of commitment:[85]

- *Affective commitment.* An individual's relationship to the organization: his or her emotional attachment to, identification with, and involvement in the organization.

- *Normative commitment.* The obligation an individual feels to staying with the organization.

- *Continuance commitment.* An individual's calculation that it is in his or her best interest to stay with the organization based on the perceived costs of leaving the organization.

Affective commitment is strongly associated with positive work behaviours such as performance, attendance, and citizenship. Normative commitment is less strongly associated with positive work behaviours. However, when affective and normative commitment decline, individuals are much more likely to quit their jobs.[86]

Because continuance commitment reflects an individual's calculation that it is in his or her best interest to stay with the organization (perhaps because it would be difficult to find a job elsewhere), it is often associated with negative work behaviours.

Arnold Carbone (centre) receives a high level of job satisfaction and has a positive attitude about his job. Carbone, as "Conductor of Bizarre and D" at Ben & Jerry's, travels the world and eats as many desserts as he can in his job as developer of new ice-cream flavours for Ben & Jerry's. Carbone created flavours such as Phish Food and Wavy Gravy.

People in highly paid jobs and union members with good benefits may exhibit continuance commitment because of the rewards received from the job, rather than their preference for the job itself.[87]

The notion of organizational commitment has changed in recent years. Twenty years ago, employees and employers had an unwritten loyalty contract, with employees typically remaining with a single organization for most of their careers. This notion has become increasingly obsolete. As such, "measures of employee-firm attachment, such as commitment, are problematic for new employment relations."[88] Canadian business consultant Barbara Moses notes that "40-somethings still value loyalty: they think people should be prepared to make sacrifices, to earn their way. The 20-somethings are saying, 'No, I want to be paid for my work; I have no belief in the goodness of organizations, so I'm going to be here as long as my work is meaningful.'"[89]

How can companies increase organizational commitment? Research on a number of companies known for employees with high organizational commitment identified five reasons why employees commit themselves:[90]

- They are proud of [the company's] aspirations, accomplishments, and legacy; they share its values.

- They know what each person is expected to do, how performance is measured, and why it matters.

- They are in control of their own destinies; they savour the high-risk, high-reward work environment.

- They are recognized mostly for the quality of their individual performance.

- They have fun and enjoy the supportive and highly interactive environment.

These findings suggest a variety of ways for organizations to increase the commitment of employees. Additionally, a recent study conducted in five countries suggests that an individual's organizational commitment is strongly associated with whether the employee finds the work interesting.[91] Earlier in the chapter we discussed the role of satisfaction on organizational citizenship behaviour (OCB). We should also note that when individuals have high organizational commitment, they are likely to engage in more OCB.

SUMMARY AND IMPLICATIONS

1 **What are values?**   Values guide how we make decisions about and evaluations of behaviours and events. They represent basic convictions about what is important, right, and good to the individual. Although they do not have a direct impact on behaviour, values strongly influence a person's attitudes. So knowledge of an individual's values can provide insight into his or her attitudes.

2 **How can we understand values across cultures?**   Geert Hofstede found that managers and employees vary on five value dimensions of national culture. His insights were expanded by the GLOBE project, an ongoing cross-cultural investigation of leadership and national culture. That study has identified nine dimensions in which cultures can vary: assertiveness, future orientation, gender differentiation, uncertainty avoidance, power distance, individualism/collectivism, in-group collectivism, performance orientation, and humane orientation.

3 **Are there unique Canadian values?**   In his recent books, pollster Michael Adams identifies the social values of today's Canadians. He finds that within three broad age groups of adult Canadians—the Elders (those over 60), Baby Boomers (born between the mid-1940s and mid-1960s), and Generation Xers (born between the mid-1960s and the early 1980s)—there are at least 12 quite distinct "value tribes." More recently, discussion has turned to the Net Generation, now in their early 20s, who are the newest entrants to the workplace. Canada is a multicultural country, and there are a number of groups that contribute to its diverse values, such as Aboriginal peoples, French Canadians, and various immigrant groups. Canadian values differ from American values and those of its other trading partners in a variety of ways.

4 **What are attitudes and why are they important?**   Attitudes are positive or negative feelings about objects, people, or events. Attitudes affect the way people respond to situations. When I say "I like my job," I am expressing my attitude to work and I am likely to be more committed in my behaviour than if my attitude was one of not liking my job. A person can have thousands of attitudes, but OB focuses our attention on a limited number of job-related attitudes. These job-related attitudes tap positive or negative evaluations that employees hold about aspects of their work environment. Most of the research in OB has been concerned with two attitudes: job satisfaction and organizational commitment.

For Review

1. Describe the GLOBE project's dimensions of national culture.

2. Compare Aboriginal and nonAboriginal values.

3. How might differences in generational values affect the workplace?

4. What might explain low levels of employee job satisfaction in recent years?

5. Are satisfied employees productive employees? Explain your answer.

6. What is the relationship between job satisfaction and absenteeism? Job satisfaction and turnover? Which is the stronger relationship?

7. Contrast exit, voice, loyalty, and neglect as employee responses to job satisfaction.

For Critical Thinking

1. "Thirty-five years ago, young employees we hired were ambitious, conscientious, hard-working, and honest. Today's young employees don't have the same values." Do you agree or disagree with this manager's comments? Support your position.

2. Do you think there might be any positive and significant relationship between the possession of certain personal values and successful career progression in organizations such as Merrill Lynch, the Canadian Union of Postal Workers (CUPW), and the City of Regina's police department? Discuss.

3. "Managers should do everything they can to enhance the job satisfaction of their employees." Do you agree or disagree? Support your position.

4. When employees are asked whether they would again choose the same work or whether they would want their children to follow in their footsteps, fewer than half typically answer "yes." What, if anything, do you think this implies about employee job satisfaction?

OB for You

- You will encounter many people who have values different from yours in the classroom, in various kinds of activities in which you participate, as well as in the workplace. You should try to understand value differences, and to figure out ways to work positively with people who are different from you.

- Though we often try to generalize about people's values based on either their generation or their culture, not all people in a group hold the same values. Be prepared to look beyond the group characteristics to understand the person.

- The variety of possible responses to dissatisfaction (exit, voice, loyalty, neglect) gives you alternatives to consider when you are feeling dissatisfied with a situation. Neglect may be an easy way to respond, but consider whether voice might be more effective.

POINT

Managers Create Job Satisfaction

A review of the evidence has identified four factors conducive to high levels of employee job satisfaction: mentally challenging work, equitable rewards, supportive working conditions, and supportive colleagues.[92] Importantly, each of these factors is controllable by management.

Mentally challenging work. People prefer jobs that give them opportunities to use their skills and abilities and offer a variety of tasks, freedom, and feedback on how well they are doing. These characteristics make work mentally challenging.

Equitable rewards. Employees want pay systems and promotion policies that they perceive as just, unambiguous, and in line with their expectations. When pay is seen as fair based on job demands, individual skill level, and community pay standards, satisfaction is likely to result. Similarly, employees seek fair promotion policies and practices. Promotions provide opportunities for personal growth, more responsibilities, and increased social status. Individuals who perceive that promotion decisions are made in a fair and just manner, therefore, are likely to experience satisfaction from their jobs.

Supportive working conditions. Employees want work environments that support personal comfort and good job performance. Studies demonstrate that employees prefer physical surroundings that are not dangerous or uncomfortable. Most employees also prefer working relatively close to home, in clean and relatively modern facilities, and with adequate tools and equipment.

Supportive colleagues. People get more out of work than merely money or tangible achievements. For most employees, work also fills the need for social interaction. Not surprisingly, therefore, having friendly and supportive co-workers leads to increased job satisfaction. The behaviour of an employee's manager is also a major determinant of satisfaction. Studies generally find that employee satisfaction increases when the immediate supervisor is understanding and friendly, offers praise for good performance, listens to employees' opinions, and shows a personal interest in them.

COUNTERPOINT

Satisfaction Is Individually Determined

The notion that managers and organizations can control the level of employee job satisfaction is inherently attractive. It fits nicely with the view that managers directly influence organizational processes and outcomes. Unfortunately there is a growing body of evidence challenging the notion that managers control the factors that influence employee job satisfaction. Contemporary research indicates that employee job satisfaction is largely genetically determined.[93]

Whether people are happy or not is essentially determined by their gene structure. You either have happy genes or you don't. Approximately 80 percent of people's differences in happiness, or subjective well-being, has been found to be attributable to their different genes.

Analysis of satisfaction data for a selected sample of individuals over a 50-year period found that individual results were consistently stable over time, even when these people changed employers and occupations. This and other research suggests that an individual's disposition toward life—positive or negative—is established by his or her genetic makeup, holds over time, and carries over into his or her disposition toward work.

Given these findings, there is probably little that most managers can do to influence employee satisfaction. In spite of the fact that managers and organizations go to extensive lengths to try to improve employee job satisfaction through manipulating job characteristics, working conditions, and rewards, these actions are likely to have little effect. The only place where managers will have significant influence is through their control of the selection process. If managers want satisfied employees, they need to make sure their selection process screens out the negative, maladjusted, troublemaking fault-finders who derive little satisfaction in anything job-related. This is probably best achieved through personality testing, in-depth interviewing, and careful checking of applicants' previous work records.

LEARNING ABOUT **YOURSELF** EXERCISE

What Do You Value?

There are 16 items in the list below. Rate how important each one is to you on a scale of 0 (not important) to 100 (very important). Write a number between 0 and 100 on the line to the left of each item.

Not Important				**Somewhat Important**							**Very Important**	
0	10	20	30	40	50	60	70	80	90	100		

_____ **1.** An enjoyable, satisfying job.

_____ **2.** A high-paying job.

_____ **3.** A good marriage.

_____ **4.** Meeting new people; social events.

_____ **5.** Involvement in community activities.

_____ **6.** My religion.

_____ **7.** Exercising, playing sports.

_____ **8.** Intellectual development.

_____ **9.** A career with challenging opportunities.

_____ **10.** Nice cars, clothes, home, and so on.

_____ **11.** Spending time with family.

_____ **12.** Having several close friends.

_____ **13.** Volunteer work for nonprofit organizations, such as the Canadian Cancer Society.

_____ **14.** Meditation, quiet time to think, pray, and so on.

_____ **15.** A healthy, balanced diet.

_____ **16.** Educational reading, television, self-improvement programs, and so on.

Scoring Key:

Transfer the numbers for each of the 16 items to the appropriate column; then add up the 2 numbers in each column.

	Professional	**Financial**	**Family**	**Social**
	1. _____	2. _____	3. _____	4. _____
	9. _____	10. _____	11. _____	12. _____
Totals	_____	_____	_____	_____

	Community	**Spiritual**	**Physical**	**Intellectual**
	5. _____	6. _____	7. _____	8. _____
	13. _____	14. _____	15. _____	16. _____
Totals	_____	_____	_____	_____

The higher the total in any value dimension, the higher the importance you place on that value set. The closer the numbers are in all 8 dimensions, the more well rounded you are.

Source: R. N. Lussier, *Human Relations in Organizations: A Skill Building Approach,* 2nd ed. (Homewood, IL: Richard D. Irwin, 1993). Reprinted by permission of the McGraw-Hill Companies, Inc.

Form small groups to discuss the following topics, as assigned by your instructor. Each person in the group should first identify 3 to 5 key personal values.

1. Identify the extent to which values overlap in your group.

2. Try to uncover with your group members the source of some of your key values (e.g., parents, peer group, teachers, church).

3. What kind of workplace would be most suitable for the values that you hold most closely?

WORKING WITH **OTHERS** EXERCISE

Understanding Cultural Values

Objective   To compare the cultural values of two countries, and determine how differences might affect group behaviour.

Time   Approximately 30 minutes.

Procedure

1. Break into groups of 5 or 6.

2. Pretend that you are a group of students working on a project. Half of you are from Canada and hold typically "Canadian" cultural values; the other half are from the country assigned and hold that country's cultural values.

3. Consider the values of power distance, individualism/collectivism, and uncertainty avoidance, and discuss the differences between Canadian cultural values and the values of the country assigned to you. (Refer to Exhibit 3-3 on page 76 to identify the values of your assigned country.)

4. Answer the following questions: What challenges might you expect in working together? What steps could be taken to work together more effectively?

ETHICAL **DILEMMA** EXERCISE

Is It a Bribe or a Gift?

The Corruption of Foreign Public Officials Act prohibits Canadian firms from making payments to foreign government officials with the aim of gaining or maintaining business. But payments are acceptable if they don't violate local laws. For instance, payments to officers working for foreign corporations are legal. Many countries don't have such legal guidelines.

Bribery is a common way of doing business in many underdeveloped countries. Government jobs there often don't pay very well, so it's tempting for officials to supplement their income with bribes. In addition, in many countries, the penalties for demanding and receiving bribes are few or nonexistent.

You are a Canadian who works for a large European multinational computer manufacturer. You are currently working to sell a $5 million system to a government agency in Nigeria. The Nigerian official who heads up the team that will decide who gets this contract has asked you for a payment of $20 000. He says this payment will not guarantee you get the order, but without it he cannot be very encouraging. Your company's policy is very flexible on the issue of "gifts" to facilitate sales. Your boss says that it's OK to pay the $20 000, but only if you can be relatively assured of the order.

You are not sure what you should do. The Nigerian official has told you specifically that any payment to him is not to be mentioned to anyone else on the Nigerian team. You know for certain that three other companies are also negotiating, but it's unconfirmed whether two of those companies have turned down the payment request.

What would you do?

Source: This exercise is based on M. Allen, "Here Comes the Bribe," *Entrepreneur,* October 2000, p. 48.

CASE INCIDENT

Gourmet Foods Works on Employee Attitudes

Gourmet Foods is a huge grocery and drug company. It has more than 2400 supermarkets, and its Premier and Polar brands make it the fifth-largest drugstore company in North America. In a typical year, shoppers will make 1.4 billion trips through its stores.

Gourmet Foods competes against tough businesses. Wal-Mart, in particular, has been eating away at its market share. In 2001, with revenues flat and profits falling, the company hired Larry Johnston to turn the business around.

Johnston came to Gourmet Foods from General Living Medical Systems. It was while he was at General Living that Johnston met a training specialist named Roger Nelson. Nelson endeared himself to Johnston when the latter hired Nelson to help him with a serious problem. At the time, Johnston had been sent to Paris to fix General Living's European division. The division made CT scanners. Over the previous decade, four executives had been brought in to turn the division around and try to make it profitable. All had failed. Johnston responded to the challenge by initiating some important changes—he made a number of acquisitions, he closed down inefficient plants, and he moved factories to Eastern European countries to take advantage of lower labour costs. Then he brought in Nelson to charge up the troops. "After we got Roger in," says Johnston, "people began to live their lives differently. They came to work with a spring in their step." In three years, the division was bringing in annual profits of $100 million. Johnston gives a large part of the credit for this turnaround to Nelson.

What is Nelson's secret? He provides motivation and attitude training. Here is an example of Nelson's primary program—called the Successful Life Course. It lasts three days and begins each morning at 6 a.m. The first day begins with a chapter from an inspirational handout, followed by 12 minutes of yoga-like stretching. Then participants march up a hill, chanting, "I know I can, I know I can." This is followed by breakfast and then a variety of lectures on attitude, diet, and exercise. But the primary focus of the program is on attitude. Says Nelson, "It's your attitude, not your aptitude, that determines your altitude." Other parts of the program include group hugs, team activities, and mind-control relaxation exercises.

Johnston believes strongly in Nelson's program. "Positive attitude is the single biggest thing that can change a business," says Johnston. He sees Nelson's program as a critical bridge linking employees with customers: "We're in the business of maintenance and acquisition of customers." With so many shoppers going through his stores, Johnston says there are "a lot of opportunities for customer service. We've got to energize the associates." To prove he is willing to put his money where his mouth is, Johnston has committed $10 million to this training. By the end of 2006, 10 000 managers will have taken the course. They, in turn, will train all 190 000 Gourmet Foods "associates," with the help of tapes and books.

Nelson claims his program works. He cites success at companies such as Allstate, Milliken & Co., and Abbott Labs. "The goal is to improve mental, physical, and emotional well-being," he says. "We as individuals determine the success of our lives. Positive thoughts create positive actions."

Questions

1. Explain the logic as to how Nelson's three-day course could positively influence Gourmet Foods' profitability.

2. Johnston says, "Positive attitude is the single biggest thing that can change a business." How valid and generalizable do you think this statement is?

3. If you were Johnston, what could you do to evaluate the effectiveness of your $10 million investment in Nelson's training program?

4. If you were a Gourmet Foods employee, how would you feel about going through Nelson's course? Explain your position.

Source: Based on M. Burke, "The Guru in the Vegetable Bin," *Forbes,* March 3, 2003, pp. 56–58.

CBC ⊕ VIDEO CASE INCIDENT

Diverging Ideologies

When it comes to what Canadians and Americans say is important, there is a continental divide, one that is growing ever wider, every day. Although Canada has become more integrated economically with its largest trading partner, it appears that Canadians and Americans have diverging ideologies. Canadians and Americans have distinct points of views on a variety of issues, such as the Kyoto Accord, the decriminalization of marijuana, and same sex marriage.

L'École nationale de cirque, a circus school founded in Montreal over 20 years ago, is symbolic of the ideological differences between Canada and the United States. The school encourages risk-taking and boundary-breaking and is completely different from anything found south of the border. The unique circus arts taught at the school speak to the new Canadian image: bilingual, multinational, government-funded, postmodern, multicultural, and avant-garde.

Pollster Michael Adams states that although most polls show that Canadians believe they are gradually becoming more and more like Americans, his research shows the opposite: Canadians are questioning and turning away from traditional hierarchies and old authorities and are actually becoming more like Europeans. So where are the gaps on values, perspectives, and world view between the two countries?

In Canada, the belief in the father's supremacy is in decline, whereas in the United States it is growing. What is the significance of this finding? It has implications for how Canadians and Americans perceive the role of women in society, who should be boss in the workplace, and who should be the leader of the country.

Religion is another area in which Canadians and Americans show differences. Americans are becoming more religious than Canadians, with weekly church attendance in the United States at 50 percent. In contrast, weekly church attendance in Canada is at 20 percent.

Adams points out other distinctions, including the view of urban life. Canadians are comfortable with ethnicity and diversity, settling in cities where they can find a sense of community in both the downtown and the suburbs.

Americans, driven by racial issues in downtown cores, are moving to the suburbs and beyond.

Another difference, according to Adams, is that Canadians believe government can provide solutions—national daycare, Old Age Security, revitalized cities—whereas Americans want less government intervention in their lives.

Michael Byers, political scientist at the University of British Columbia, says Canadians are becoming more socially tolerant. The Canadian political spectrum, Byers states, is also further to the left as a whole than the American system. According to Michael Adams, the American ideal of rugged individualism and emphasis on moral values, terrorism, and economy excludes the social agenda. In contrast, Canadian values are more tailored to compromise, accommodation, and shared responsibility. In terms of values and beliefs, it appears that Canadians and Americans are, more often than not, on different paths.

Questions

1. Are Canadian values becoming more similar or dissimilar to American values? Explain.

2. Suppose a large Canadian telecommunications firm merges with a large American telecommunications firm. To what extent might the differences in values between these Canadian and American employees affect how they interact and work together?

3. Imagine that a Canadian company is producing computer products and shipping them across the border to the United States and overseas to Europe. Should management be concerned about the impact of Canadian values on customer relations? What should customer service representatives keep in mind when dealing with American and European customers?

Sources: Based on "Diverging Ideologies," *CBC—The National,* November 30, 2004; and S. Maich, "The Worst President in 100 Years?" *Maclean's,* April 17, 2006, pp. 28–33.

From **Concepts**
to **Skills**

Changing Attitudes

Can you change unfavourable employee attitudes? Sometimes! It depends on who you are, the strength of the employee's attitude, the magnitude of the change, and the technique you choose to try to change the attitude.

People are most likely to respond to changes suggested by someone who is liked, credible, and convincing. If people like you, they are more apt to identify and adopt your message. Credibility implies trust, expertise, and objectivity. So you are more likely to change someone's attitude if that person views you as believable, knowledgeable about what you're saying, and unbiased in your presentation. Finally, successful attitude change is enhanced when you present your arguments clearly and persuasively.

It's easier to change a person's attitude if he or she is not strongly committed to it. Conversely, the stronger the belief in the attitude, the harder it is to change it. Also, attitudes that have been expressed publicly are more difficult to change because doing so requires admitting having made a mistake.

It's also easier to change attitudes when the change required is not very significant. To get a person to accept a new attitude that varies greatly from his or her current position requires more effort. It may also threaten other deeply held attitudes.

All attitude-change techniques are not equally effective across situations. Oral persuasion techniques are most effective when you use a positive, tactful tone; present strong evidence to support your position; tailor your argument to the listener; use logic; and support your evidence by appealing to the person's fears, frustrations, and other emotions. But people are more likely to embrace change when they can experience it. The use of training sessions where employees share and personalize experiences, and practise new behaviours, can be powerful stimulants for change. Consistent with self-perception theory, changes in behaviour can lead to changes in attitudes.

Assessing Skills

After you've read this chapter, take the following Self-Assessments on your enclosed CD-ROM.

  6. What Do I Value?

  7. How Involved Am I in My Job?

  8. How Satisfied Am I With My Job?

  9. What Are My Attitudes Toward Workplace Diversity?

  16. What's My Attitude Toward Achievement?

  45. How Committed Am I to My Organization?

Practising Skills

Form groups of 2. Person A is to choose any topic that he or she feels strongly about and state his or her position on the topic in 30 words or less. Person B's task will be to try to change Person A's attitude on this topic. Person B will have 10 minutes to make his or her case. When the time is up, the roles are reversed. Person B picks the topic and Person A has 10 minutes to try to change Person B's attitude.

Potential topics (you can choose *either* side of a topic) include the following: politics; the economy; world events; social practices; or specific management issues, such as that organizations should require all employees to undergo regular drug testing, there is no such thing as organizational loyalty any more, the customer is always right, and layoffs are an indication of management failures.

Questions

  1. Were you successful in changing the other person's attitude? Why or why not?

  2. Was the other person successful in changing your attitude? Why or why not?

  3. What conclusions can you draw about changing the attitudes of yourself and others?

Reinforcing Skills

  1. Try to convince a friend or relative to go with you to see a movie or play that you know he or she does not want to see.

  2. Try to convince a friend or relative to try a different brand of toothpaste.

Stress at Work

Celebrated clothing designer and entrepreneur Linda Lundström (shown relaxing above), founder of Toronto-based Linda Lundström, knew she was under too much stress the day she started crying uncontrollably after she couldn't find a parking spot near her doctor's office.[1] "It was the proverbial last straw," she says about the parking incident. At the time, she was dealing with success, recognition, a growing business, and two small children. She had started to develop physical symptoms: skin rashes, intestinal disorders, neuralgia, and insomnia. That day, she walked into her doctor's office chanting over and over again, "I can't do it any more." Lundström has since learned to manage her stress and help her employees do the same.

Calgary school bus driver Marvin Franks had a much more negative response to stress.[2] Franks was arrested in March 2002 when a scared student on his bus phoned 911 from her cellphone after smelling alcohol on his breath and finding his driving erratic. When police stopped Franks, his blood alcohol level was three times the legal limit. Franks' excuse? "If you had these kids on your bus, you'd drink too." He admitted that he was unable to control the children, but said that he smelled of alcohol only because he had a hangover, and had drunk only two beers before starting his route.

Are We Overstressed?

Stress appears to be a major factor in the lives of many Canadians. A recent survey conducted by Statistics Canada found that Canadians experience a great deal of stress, with those from Quebec topping the list.[3] The survey also found that women were more stressed than men. The inset *Stress Across the Country, 2001–2002* reports the findings.

For employees, stress is also a fact of life—and it continues to increase over time. Recent research conducted at the University of Montreal found that of the 12 job categories examined, including unskilled white- and blue-collar employees and semi-skilled blue-collar employees, only upper-level managers reported no increase in stress levels from 1987 to 1998.[4] A 2001 survey done by Ipsos-Reid of 1500 Canadians with employer-sponsored health care plans found that 62 percent reported experiencing "a great deal of stress on the job." Workplace stress was bad enough to cause 34 percent of those surveyed to say that it had made them physically ill.[5] In a 2000 Statistics Canada survey, one-third of employees blamed long hours or overwork for their stress, while 15 percent blamed "poor interpersonal relations," and 13 percent blamed risk of accident or injury.[6] Front-line employees are not the only members of the organization who experience stress, however. In a study conducted by researchers Darren Larose and Bernadette Schell at Ontario's Laurentian University, 88 percent of the executives surveyed indicated elevated levels of stress and/or unhealthy personality traits.[7] They also had higher levels of predisposition to serious illnesses such as cancer and heart disease.

Perhaps one of the biggest problems for employees is that they are increasingly asked to donate labour to their employers, according to Professor Linda Duxbury of Carleton University's Sprott School of Business and Professor Chris Higgins of the Richard Ivey School of Business at the University of Western Ontario. Their survey of 31 571 Canadians found that in the previous month half of them had worked an extra 2.5 days of unpaid overtime, and more than half had donated 3.5 days of working at home to catch up.[8] Canadians are frequently reporting that they want more balance in their work and family lives.[9]

The Most Stressful Jobs

How do jobs rate in terms of stress? The inset *The Most Stressful Jobs* shows how selected occupations ranked in an evaluation of 250 jobs. Among the criteria used in the rankings were overtime, quotas, deadlines, competitiveness, physical demands, environmental conditions, hazards encountered, initiative required, stamina required, win-lose situations, and working in the public eye.

Stress is not something that can be ignored in the workplace. A 2005 poll by Ipsos-Reid found that 66 percent of the CEOs surveyed said that "stress, burnout or other physical and mental health issues" have a negative effect on productivity.[10] A 2001 study conducted in 15 developed countries found that individuals who report that they are stressed in their jobs are 25 percent more likely to quit and 25 percent more likely to miss days of work.[11] Canadian, French, and Swedish employees reported the highest stress levels. In Canada, 41 percent of employees noted that they "often" or "always" experience stress at work, while only 31 percent of employees in Denmark and Switzerland reported stress levels this high. "In the wake of years of fiscal downsizing, workers across all sectors are working harder and longer than ever while trying to balance family responsibilities," said Scott Morris, former head of the Vancouver-based consulting firm Priority Management Systems.[12] Daniel Ondrack, a professor at the University of Toronto's Joseph L. Rotman School of Management, notes that "one of the major reasons for absenteeism is the logistical problems workers face in just getting to work, including transporting children to school and finding daycare. Single parents, especially female, have to juggle all the daycare and family responsibilities, and that makes it extremely difficult for people to keep up with work demands."[13]

Stress Across the Country, 2001–2002

Region	% with no life stresses	% with quite a lot of stress
Alberta	9.8	26.0
Atlantic Canada	14.6	18.7
British Columbia	12.0	23.6
Ontario	10.7	25.7
The Prairies	8.7	24.5
Quebec	18.0	30.0

Source: Compiled using data from Statistics Canada, "Life Stress, by Sex, Household Population Aged 18 and Over, Canada, Provinces, Territories, Health Regions and Peer Groups, 2000/01," www.statcan.ca/english/freepub/82-221-XIE/00503/tables/html/2336.htm (accessed August 4, 2005).

The Most Stressful Jobs

How do jobs rate in terms of stress? The following shows how selected occupations ranked in an evaluation of 250 jobs. Criteria used in the rankings included overtime, quotas, deadlines, competitiveness, physical demands, environmental conditions, hazards encountered, initiative required, stamina required, win-lose situations, and working in the public eye.

Rank Score		Stress Score	Rank Score		Stress Score
1.	US president	176.6	47.	Auto salesperson	56.3
2.	Firefighter	110.9	50.	College professor	54.2
3.	Senior executive	108.6	60.	School principal	51.7
6.	Surgeon	99.5	103.	Market research analyst	42.1
10.	Air traffic controller	83.1	104.	Personnel recruiter	41.8
12.	Public relations executive	78.5	113.	Hospital administrator	39.6
16.	Advertising account executive	74.6	119.	Economist	38.7
17.	Real estate agent	73.1	122.	Mechanical engineer	38.3
20.	Stockbroker	71.7	124.	Chiropractor	37.9
22.	Pilot	68.7	132.	Technical writer	36.5
25.	Architect	66.9	149.	Retail salesperson	34.9
31.	Lawyer	64.3	173.	Accountant	31.1
33.	General physician	64.0	193.	Purchasing agent	28.9
35.	Insurance agent	63.3	229.	Broadcast technician	24.2
42.	Advertising salesperson	59.9	245.	Actuary	20.2

Source: Reprinted by permission of the *Wall Street Journal*, © 1996 Dow Jones & Company. All rights reserved worldwide.

What Is Stress?

Stress is usually defined in terms of a situation that creates excessive psychological or physiological demands on a person. Thus the situation, often referred to as the stressor, and the response *together* create the stress that an individual experiences. This distinction is important because what is stressful to one person may be enjoyable or at least viewed as neutral by another. Although almost anyone might feel stress if followed by a stranger in a dark alley, not everyone feels stressed when given the opportunity for public speaking.

Dr. Hans Selye, a Montreal-based researcher, pioneered the study of stress and its effects. His model, the general adaptation syndrome (GAS), suggests that stress occurs in three stages: alarm, resistance, and exhaustion.[14] The alarm stage occurs when the body tries to meet the initial challenge of the stressor. The brain reacts by sending a message to the rest of the body's systems, causing such symptoms as increased respiration, raised blood pressure, dilated pupils, and tensed muscles.

The resistance stage occurs if the stressor continues. At this stage, a person feels such symptoms as fatigue, anxiety, and tension due to the body's attempt to fight the stressor. The exhaustion stage occurs from prolonged and continual exposure to the same stressor. The important thing to remember about how GAS works is that it puts heavy demands on the body. The more that GAS is activated and the longer that it goes on, the more wear and tear your body experiences. Individuals who frequently go through alarm, resistance, and exhaustion cycles are more likely to be susceptible to fatigue, disease, aging, and other negative physical and psychological consequences.

Stress is not necessarily bad in and of itself. It is typically discussed in a negative context, but it also has a positive value. Consider, for example, athletes or stage performers who use stress positively to rise to the occasion and perform at or near their maximum potential. On the other hand, students who put off studying for exams until the last moment and then develop the flu are not able to use their stress to perform at a maximum level.

Causes of Stress

A variety of sources of stress have been identified, including "work overload; role conflict; ineffective, hostile and incompetent bosses; lack of personal fit with a job; lack of recognition; lack of a clear job description or chain of command; fear, uncertainty, and doubt about career progress; and prejudice based on age, gender, ethnicity or religion."[15] In their research on stress, Professors Duxbury and Higgins found that more than 50 percent of employees feel they will not advance unless they put in long hours, and that turning down extra work is unacceptable.[16] They also found that although only 10 percent of employees worked 50 or more hours a week in 1991, 25 percent were working those hours in 2001.[17]

A variety of changes in the workplace have resulted in additional causes of stress. We identify some of these key changes below:[18]

- *Competition and change.* With globalization has come increasing pressure to compete and innovate, which has led to an increase in re-engineering and restructuring. Alicja Muszynski, a sociology professor at the University of Waterloo, notes that "as corporations, including universities, have been asked to tighten their belts, there are fewer jobs and people that are left have to take on more responsibility."[19] Meanwhile, she adds, "people are afraid to take on less in the workplace, or to complain, because they're afraid they're going to get downsized."

- *Technological change.* Employees are often expected to learn new technologies without being given adequate training. Or they are not consulted when new technology is introduced. In addition, employees at all levels are flooded with information because of technological changes. As well, employees are frequently asked to be "on" for their jobs more hours each day: Pagers, voice mail, faxes, email, the Internet, and intranets make it possible to stay in touch with the workplace 24 hours a day. Research by Professor Christina Cavanagh of the Richard Ivey School of Business at the University of Western Ontario shows that email is an increasing cause of stress. Individuals receive an average of 80 or 90 emails daily, and devote an hour more each day to handling it than they did two years ago. The frustration is not just with quantity or time. When Cavanagh asked 10 middle managers to keep track of their emails, she discovered that nearly half of the messages were "junk or notes with little relevance."[20]

- *Increasingly diverse workforce.* "If diversity is not managed effectively it may lead to interper-

sonal stress, competition among different groups for attention and resources, and decreased interaction because of the perceived need for political correctness in speech, interaction, and recognition." In diverse groups, individuals experience differences in beliefs and values, differences in role expectations, and differences in perceptions about fairness in procedures.

- *Downsizing.* With downsizing seemingly a routine procedure in many companies, even the threat of layoffs can be stressful. Moreover, after downsizing, firms often increase the workload of remaining employees, which leads to more stress.

- *Employee empowerment and teamwork.* Both empowerment and teamwork require greater decision-making responsibility and interaction skills from employees. Although this alone is stressful, it is particularly stressful for individuals who "have little or no interest in empowerment or teamwork structures and processes. Many people do not function well in a group setting, and they and their work may suffer if forced into a team environment."

- *Work/home conflict.* Trying to balance work life and family life is difficult at the best of times, but more employees are finding that their jobs are demanding longer hours, either formally or informally. This makes it difficult to manage the nonwork parts of life. Families with children where both parents work, or where parents are raising children alone, often have the added stress of managing childcare arrangements.

About one in eight workers was responsible for providing some form of care for aging parents in 1997, and one survey found that one in three was doing so in 2002.[21] Being a caregiver is an additional stress both at home and at work. Studies indicate that those who have difficulties finding effective child care or eldercare have lower work performance and increased absenteeism, decreased satisfaction, and lower physical and psychological well-being.[22] A fact that tends to be overlooked when stressors are reviewed individually is that stress is an additive phenomenon.[23] Stress builds up. Each new and persistent stressor adds to an individual's stress level. A single stressor may seem relatively unimportant in and of itself, but if it is added to an already high level of stress, it can be "the straw that breaks the camel's back." You may recall that the final straw for Linda Lundström was not being able to find a parking space.

Consequences of Stress
Stress manifests itself in a number of ways. For instance, an individual who is experiencing a high level of stress may develop high blood pressure, ulcers, irritability, difficulty in making routine decisions, loss of appetite, accident proneness, and the like. These symptoms can be placed under three general categories: physiological, psychological, and behavioural symptoms.[24]

- *Physiological symptoms.* Most of the research on stress suggests that it can create changes in metabolism, increase heart and breathing rates, increase blood pressure, cause headaches, and induce heart attacks. An interesting aspect of illness in today's workplace is the considerable change in how stress shows up. In the past, older workers were the ones claiming sick leave, workers' compensation, and short- and long-term disability—most often in cases of catastrophic illness such as heart attacks, cancer, and major back surgeries. These days, however, it is not unusual for long-term disability programs to be filled with employees in their 20s, 30s, and 40s. Employees are claiming illnesses that are either psychiatric (such as depression) or more difficult to diagnose (such as chronic fatigue syndrome or fibromyalgia, a musculoskeletal discomfort). The increase in disability claims may be the result of downsizing taking its toll on the psyches of those in the workforce.[25]

- *Psychological symptoms.* Job dissatisfaction is "the simplest and most obvious psychological effect" of stress.[26] However, stress also manifests itself in other psychological states—for instance, tension, anxiety, irritability, boredom, and procrastination.

The evidence indicates that when people are placed in jobs that make multiple and conflicting demands or in which there is a lack of clarity as to the person's duties, authority, and responsibilities, both stress and dissatisfaction increase.[27] Similarly, the less control that people have over the pace of their work, the greater the stress and dissatisfaction. More research is needed to clarify the relationship, but the evidence suggests that jobs providing a low level of variety, significance, autonomy, feedback, and identity create stress and reduce satisfaction and involvement in the job.[28]

- *Behavioural symptoms.* Behaviourally related stress symptoms include changes in productivity, absence, and turnover, as well as changes in eating habits, increased smoking or consumption of alcohol, rapid speech, fidgeting, and sleep disorders. More recently stress has been linked to aggression and violence in the workplace.

Why Do Individuals Differ in Their Experience of Stress?

Some people thrive on stressful situations, while others are overwhelmed by them. What is it that differentiates people in terms of their ability to handle stress? What individual difference variables moderate the relationship between *potential* stressors and *experienced* stress? At least five variables—perception, job experience, social support, belief in locus of control, and hostility—have been found to be relevant moderators.

- *Perception.* Individuals react in response to their *perception* of reality rather than to reality itself. Perception, therefore, moderates the relationship between a potential stress condition and an employee's reaction to it. For example, one person might fear losing his job because the company is laying off staff, while another might perceive the situation as an opportunity to receive a large severance allowance and start a small business. Similarly, what one employee perceives as a challenging job may be viewed as threatening and demanding by others.[29] So the stress potential in environmental, organizational, and individual factors does not lie in objective conditions. Rather, it lies in an employee's interpretation of those factors.

- *Job experience.* Experience on the job tends to be negatively related to work stress. Two explanations have been offered.[30] First, people who experience more stress on the job when they are first hired may be more likely to quit. Therefore, people who remain with the organization longer are those with more stress-resistant traits or those who are more resistant to the stress characteristics of their organization. Second, people eventually develop coping mechanisms to deal with stress. Because this takes time, senior members of the organization are more likely to be fully adapted and should experience less stress.

- *Social support.* There is increasing evidence that social support— that is, collegial relationships with co-workers or supervisors—can buffer the impact of stress.[31] The logic underlying this moderating variable is that social support helps ease the negative effects of even high-strain jobs.

For individuals whose work associates are unhelpful or even actively hostile, social support may be found outside the job. Involvement with family, friends, and community can provide the support—especially for those with a high social need—that is missing at work, and this can make job stressors more tolerable.

- *Belief in locus of control.* The personality trait locus of control determines the extent to which individuals believe they have control over the things that happen in their lives. Those with an internal locus of control believe they control their own destiny. Those with an external locus of control believe their lives are controlled by outside forces. Evidence indicates that internals perceive their jobs to be less stressful than do externals.[32]

When internals and externals confront a similar stressful situation, the internals are likely to believe that they can have a significant effect on the results. They therefore act to take control of events. Externals are more likely to experience stress because they frequently act helpless, often by being passive and defensive, while feeling helpless.

- *Hostility.* Some people's personality includes a high degree of hostility and anger. These people are chronically suspicious and mistrustful of others. Recent evidence indicates that such *hostility* significantly increases a person's stress and risk for heart disease.[33] More specifically, people who are quick to anger, maintain a persistently hostile outlook, and project a cynical mistrust of others are more likely to experience stress in situations.

How Do We Manage Stress?

Both the individual and the organization can take steps to help the individual manage stress. Below we discuss ways that individuals can manage stress, and then we examine programs that organizations use to help employees manage stress.

Individual Approaches

An employee can take personal responsibility for reducing his or her stress level. Individual strategies that have proven effective include time management techniques, physical exercise, relaxation training, and a close social support network.

- *Time management.* Many people manage their time poorly. The things we have to accomplish in any given day or week are not necessarily beyond completion if we manage our time properly.

The well-organized employee, like the well-organized student, can often accomplish twice as much as the person who is poorly organized. So understanding and using basic *time management* principles can help individuals cope better with tensions created by job demands.[34] A few of the more well-known time management principles are: (1) making daily lists of activities to be accomplished; (2) prioritizing activities by importance and urgency; (3) scheduling activities according to the priorities set; and (4) knowing your daily cycle and handling the most demanding parts of your job during the high part of your cycle, when you are most alert and productive.[35]

- *Physical activity.* Noncompetitive physical exercise, such as aerobics, walking, jogging, swimming, and riding a bicycle, has long been recommended by physicians as a way to deal with excessive stress levels. These forms of *physical exercise* increase heart capacity, lower at-rest heart rate, provide a mental diversion from work pressures, and offer a means to "let off steam."[36]

- *Relaxation techniques.* Individuals can teach themselves to reduce tension through *relaxation techniques* such as meditation, hypnosis, and biofeedback. The objective is to reach a state of deep relaxation, where you feel physically relaxed, somewhat detached from the immediate environment, and detached from body sensations.[37] Fifteen or 20 minutes a day of deep relaxation releases tension and provides a person with a pronounced sense of peacefulness. Importantly, significant changes

FactBox[38]

- One in three Canadians between the ages of 25 and 44 claims to be a workaholic.

- 38% of people in management report being workaholics.

- 85% of married women who are employed full-time and have at least one child at home, and 75% of similarly situated men, say that weekdays are too short to accomplish what needs to get done.

- The financial cost to companies because employees are trying to balance work and family obligations is estimated to be at least $2.7 billion a year.

- 1/3 of Canadians don't take all of their vacation days, saving their employers $8 billion a year.

- When Canadians do go on holiday, 36% of them take work, and check their office voice mail and email.

in heart rate, blood pressure, and other physiological factors result from achieving the deep relaxation condition.

- *Building social supports.* Having friends, family, or colleagues to talk to provides an outlet when stress levels become excessive. Expanding your *social support network*, therefore, can be a means for tension reduction. It provides you with someone to listen to your problems and to offer a more objective perspective on the situation. Research also demonstrates that social support moderates the stress-burnout relationship.[39] That is, high support reduces the likelihood that heavy work stress will result in job burnout.

The inset *Tips for Reducing Stress* offers additional ideas for reducing stress.

Organizational Approaches

Employees who work at Toronto-based BCS Communications, a publishing, advertising, and public relations agency, receive biweekly shiatsu massages, paid for by the company. The company spends about $700 a month for the massages, equivalent to the amount it used to spend providing coffee to the employees. "It's in my company's best interest to have my employees be healthy," says Caroline Tapp-McDougall, the BCS group publisher.[40]

Vancouver-based QLT, which develops pharmaceuticals that are activated when exposed to light, has an in-house gym and offers aerobics

Tips for Reducing Stress

- At least two or three times a week, spend time with supportive friends or family.

- Ask for support when you are under pressure. This is a sign of health, not weakness.

- If you have spiritual or religious beliefs, increase or maintain your involvement.

- Use a variety of methods to reduce stress. Consider exercise, nutrition, hobbies, positive thinking, and relaxation techniques such as meditation or yoga.

Source: J. Lee, "How to Fight That Debilitating Stress in Your Workplace," *The Vancouver Sun,* April 5, 1999, p. C3. Reprinted with permission.

and stretch classes and Friday-morning shiatsu massage treatments to its employees. QLT's cafeteria has healthy food choices, and Weight Watchers products. Robyn Crisanti, a QLT spokesperson, explains the company's investment in wellness: "Corporate wellness is good for employees and there is a lot of research that shows healthy employees take fewer sick days and are more productive."[41] The programs also make it easier for QLT to attract talented employees.

Most firms that have introduced wellness programs have found significant benefits. Health Canada reports that businesses get back $3.39 for each corporate dollar they invest in wellness initiatives. For individuals with three to five risk factors (such as high cholesterol, being overweight, or smoking) the return was $2.04 for each dollar spent.[42] The savings come about because there is less turnover, greater productivity, and reduced medical claims.[43] About 64 percent of Canadian companies surveyed by Health Canada offered some sort of wellness initiative, including stop-smoking programs, stress courses, and back-pain management programs; 17.5 percent of companies offered on-site wellness programs.[44]

So what can organizations do to reduce employee stress? In general, strategies to reduce stress include improved processes for choosing employees, placement of employees in appropriate jobs, realistic goal setting, designing jobs with employee needs and skills in mind, increased employee involvement, improved organizational communication, and, as mentioned, establishment of corporate wellness programs.

Certain jobs are more stressful than others, but individuals also differ in their response to stress situations. We know, for example, that

individuals with little experience or an external locus of control tend to be more prone to stress. Selection and placement decisions should take these facts into consideration. Although management should not restrict hiring to only experienced individuals with an internal locus of control, such individuals may adapt better to high-stress jobs and perform those jobs more effectively.

Research shows that individuals perform better when they have specific and challenging goals and receive feedback on how well they are progressing toward them.[45] The use of goals can reduce stress as well as provide motivation. Specific goals that are perceived as attainable clarify performance expectations. Additionally, goal feedback reduces uncertainties as to actual job performance. The result is less employee frustration, role ambiguity, and stress.

Creating jobs that give employees more responsibility, more meaningful work, more autonomy, and increased feedback can reduce stress because these factors give the employee greater control over work activities and lessen dependence on others. Of course, not all employees want jobs with increased responsibility. The right job for employees with a low need for growth might be less responsibility and increased specialization. If individuals prefer structure and routine, more structured jobs should also reduce uncertainties and stress levels.

One idea that has received considerable recent attention is allowing employees to take short naps during the workday.[46] Nap time, apparently, isn't just for preschool kids any more! An increasing number of companies are finding that allowing employees to catch 10 to 30 minutes of sleep in the afternoon

Reducing Stress in the Workplace

- Avoid electronic monitoring of staff. Personal supervision generates considerably less stress.

- Allow workers time to recharge after periods of intense or demanding work.

- Deliver important information that significantly affects employees face to face.

- Encourage positive social interactions between staff to promote problem solving around work issues and increase emotional support.

- Keep in mind that staff need to balance privacy and social interaction at work. Extremes can generate stress.

Source: J. Lee, "How to Fight That Debilitating Stress in Your Workplace," *Vancouver Sun*, April 5, 1999, p. C3. Reprinted with permission of the *Vancouver Sun*.

increases productivity and makes them less prone to errors.

Increasing formal organizational communication with employees reduces uncertainty by lessening role ambiguity and role conflict. Given the importance that perceptions play in moderating the stress-response relationship, management can also use effective communications as a means to shape employee perceptions. Remember that what employees categorize as demands, threats, or opportunities are merely interpretations, and those interpretations can be affected by the symbols and actions communicated by management.

Our final suggestion is to offer organizationally supported wellness programs, such as those provided by QLT and BCS Communications. These programs focus on the employee's total physical and mental condition.[47] For example, they typically include workshops to help people quit smoking, control alcohol use, lose weight, eat better, and develop a regular exercise program. The assumption underlying most wellness programs is that employees need to take personal responsibility for their physical and mental health. The organi-zation is merely a vehicle to make this happen. The inset *Reducing Stress in the Workplace* offers additional ideas.

Research Exercises

1. Look for data on stress levels in other countries. How do these data compare with the Canadian data presented above? Are the sources of stress the same in different countries? What might you conclude about how stress affects people in different cultures?

2. Find out what three Canadian organizations in three different industries have done to help employees manage stress. Are there common themes in these programs? Did you find any unusual programs? To what extent are these programs tailored to the needs of the employees in those industries?

Your Perspective

1. Think of all of the technological changes that have happened in the workplace in recent years, including email, BlackBerrys, and intranets. What are the positive benefits of this change? What are the downsides? As an employee facing the demand to "stay connected" to your workplace, how would you try to maintain a balance in your life?

2. How much responsibility should individuals take for managing their own stress? To what extent should organizations become involved in the personal lives of their employees when trying to help them manage stress? What are the pros and cons for whether employees or organizations take responsibility for managing stress?

Want to Know More?

If you are wondering how stressed you are, go to **www.heartandstroke.ca** and click on "Your Heart & Stroke Risk Assessment." The site also offers tips on how to relax and manage stress.

FACE**OFF**

When organizations provide on-site daycare facilities, they are filling a needed role in parents' lives, and making it easier for parents to attend to their job demands rather than worry about child-care arrangements.

When employees expect organizations to provide child care, they are shifting their responsibilities to their employers, rather than keeping their family needs and concerns private. Moreover, it is unfair to give child-care benefits when not all employees have children.

CHAPTER **4**

Motivating Self
and **Others**

The BC Lions football team holds one of the longest winning streaks in CFL history. How does motivation affect how the team performs?

1 What is motivation?

2 How do needs motivate people?

3 Are there other ways to motivate people?

4 Do equity and fairness matter?

5 How can rewards and job design motivate employees?

6 What kinds of mistakes are made in reward systems?

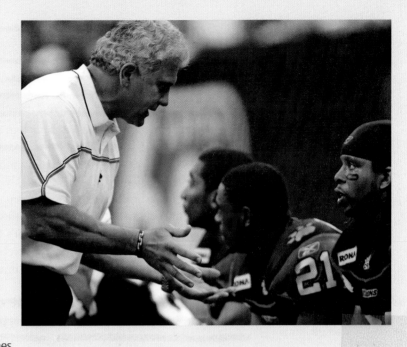

By most accounts, Vancouver-based BC Lions head coach Wally Buono is not a particularly warm person.[1] Buono is a hard taskmaster with his BC Lions players and coaches, and is not afraid to make tough decisions. "In this business, if you stay with the status quo you haven't improved yourself," he said after his team lost in the 2005 Western final.

Buono wants to coach winners, not losers. As a coach, Buono has one of the winningest records in the Canadian Football League (CFL). His teams have been to seven Grey Cups, and the BC Lions had the third-longest winning streak in CFL history by the middle of the season in 2005. But then they started losing games.

Buono seems to motivate by being tough. He's not afraid to criticize his players publicly, and will give them a long list of their faults during contract negotiations. He claims that he gives only two performance reviews to players: "Once when I warn you and once when I cut you."

Buono's players may not like him personally, but at the beginning of the 2005 season they performed well. Players spent hours in training each day because "guys wanna get better," explained slotback Geroy Simon. Then the team fell apart.

This chapter examines the subject of motivation and rewards in some detail. It looks at what motivation is, key motivation theories, and how motivation theories and reward systems can be used effectively in the workplace.

DEFINING MOTIVATION

Following the lead of professors Gary Latham of the Joseph L. Rotman School of Management at the University of Toronto and Craig Pinder of the Faculty of Business at the University of Victoria, we define **motivation** as the internal and external factors that lead an individual to engage in goal-related behaviour. Motivation can affect the intensity, direction, and persistence a person shows in working toward a goal.[2] *Intensity* is concerned with how hard a person tries. This is what most of us focus on when we talk about motivation. However, high intensity is unlikely to positively affect job performance unless the effort is channelled in a *direction* that is useful. Finally, the effort requires *persistence*. This is a measure of how long a person can maintain his or her effort. Motivated individuals stay with a task long enough to achieve their goal.

1 What is motivation?

motivation The internal and external forces that lead an individual to work toward a goal.

OB IS FOR EVERYONE

* Are managers manipulating employees when they link rewards to productivity? Is this ethical?

* Why do some managers do a better job of motivating people than others?

* How important is fairness to you?

* What can you do if you think your salary is "unfair"?

* When might job redesign be an appropriate motivational tool?

* Ever wonder why employees do some strange things?

Theory X The assumption that employees dislike work, will attempt to avoid it, and must be coerced, controlled, or threatened with punishment to achieve goals.

Theory Y The assumption that employees like work, are creative, seek responsibility, and will exercise self-direction and self-control if they are committed to the objectives.

intrinsic motivators A person's internal desire to do something, due to such things as interest, challenge, and personal satisfaction.

extrinsic motivators Motivation that comes from outside the person and includes such things as pay, bonuses, and other tangible rewards.

Many people incorrectly view motivation as a personal trait—that is, some have it and others don't. Along these lines, Douglas McGregor has proposed two distinct views of human beings. **Theory X**, which is basically negative, suggests that employees dislike work, will try to avoid it, and must be coerced, controlled, or threatened with punishment to achieve goals. **Theory Y**, which is basically positive, suggests that employees will use self-direction and self-control if they are committed to the goals.[3]

Our knowledge of motivation tells us that neither of these theories fully accounts for employee behaviour. What we know is that motivation is the result of the interaction of the individual and the situation. Certainly, individuals differ in their basic motivational drives. But the same employee who is quickly bored when pulling the lever on a drill press may enthusiastically pull a slot machine lever in Casino Windsor for hours. You may read a thriller at one sitting, yet find it difficult to concentrate on a textbook for more than 20 minutes. It's not necessarily you—it's the situation. So as we analyze the concept of motivation, keep in mind that the level of motivation varies both between individuals and within individuals at different times. What motivates people will also vary for both the individual and the situation.

Motivation theorists talk about **intrinsic motivators** and **extrinsic motivators**. Extrinsic motivators come from outside the person and include such things as pay, bonuses, and other tangible rewards. Intrinsic motivators come from a person's internal desire to do something, motivated by such things as interest, challenge, and personal satisfaction. Individuals are intrinsically motivated when they genuinely care about their work, look for better ways to do it, and are energized and fulfilled by doing it well.[4] The rewards the individual gets from intrinsic motivation come from the work itself, rather than from external factors such as increases in pay or compliments from the boss.

Are individuals mainly intrinsically or extrinsically motivated? Theory X suggests that people are almost exclusively driven by extrinsic motivators. However, Theory Y suggests that people are more intrinsically motivated. Intrinsic and extrinsic motivation may reflect the situation, however, rather than individual personalities.

For example, suppose your mother has asked you to take her to a meeting an hour away and then drop off your twin brother somewhere else. You may be willing to drive her, without any thought of compensation, because it will make you feel nice to do something for her. That is intrinsic motivation. But if you have a love-hate relationship with your brother, you may insist that he buy you lunch for helping out. Lunch would then be an extrinsic motivator—something that came from outside yourself and motivated you to do the task.

Recent research suggests that perceptions of managers regarding whether employees are intrinsically or extrinsically motivated vary by culture.[5] North American managers perceive employees as more extrinsically than intrinsically motivated, and tend to give better performance appraisals to employees whom they perceive to be intrinsically motivated. Asian managers perceive employees as equally motivated by intrinsic and extrinsic factors. Latin American managers perceive employees as more intrinsically than extrinsically motivated, and give higher performance evaluations to those they believe are more intrinsically motivated. Though managers from the three cultures have different perceptions of their employees, employees in all three cultures said that they were motivated more by intrinsic than extrinsic rewards. If you think money is a powerful motivator, you may be surprised to read an opposing viewpoint in this chapter's *Point/Counterpoint* on page 142.

NEEDS THEORIES OF MOTIVATION

2 How do needs motivate people?

The main theories of motivation fall into one of two categories: needs theories and process theories. *Needs theories* describe the types of needs that must be met in order to motivate individuals. *Process theories* help us understand the actual ways in which we and others can be motivated. There are a variety of needs theories, including Maslow's hierarchy of needs, Alderfer's ERG theory,[6] McClelland's theory of needs,[7] and Herzberg's motivation-hygiene theory (sometimes called the *two-factor theory*). We briefly review these to illustrate the basic properties of needs theories.

Maslow's Hierarchy of Needs Theory

It is probably safe to say that the best-known theory of motivation is Abraham Maslow's hierarchy of needs.[8] He hypothesized that every human being has a hierarchy of five needs:

Abraham Maslow
www.ship.edu/~cgboeree/
maslow.html

- *Physiological.* Includes hunger, thirst, shelter, sex, and other bodily needs.

- *Safety.* Includes security and protection from physical and emotional harm.

- *Social.* Includes affection, belongingness, acceptance, and friendship.

- *Esteem.* Includes internal esteem factors such as self-respect, autonomy, and achievement; and external esteem factors such as status, recognition, and attention.

- *Self-actualization.* Includes growth, achieving one's potential, and self-fulfillment. This is the drive to become what one is capable of becoming.

As each of these needs becomes substantially satisfied, the next need becomes more important to fulfill. In terms of Exhibit 4-1, the individual moves up the steps of the needs hierarchy. From the perspective of motivation, the theory would say that while no need is ever fully satisfied, a substantially satisfied need no longer motivates. So if you want to motivate someone, according to Maslow, you need to understand what level of the hierarchy that person is currently on and focus on satisfying the needs at or above that level.

Maslow's needs theory continues to be widely recognized some 60 years after he proposed it, particularly among practising managers. The practical significance of Maslow's theory is widely accepted.[9] The theory is intuitive and easy to understand. Unfortunately, research does not generally validate the theory, although research does suggest that people have basic needs that are important to them and motivate them to get along with others.[10] Maslow himself provided no empirical evidence for his theory. Several studies that examined the theory found little support for the prediction that needs form the hierarchy proposed by Maslow, that unsatisfied needs motivate, or that a satisfied need moves a person to seek satisfaction at a new need level.[11]

EXHIBIT 4-1   Maslow's Hierarchy of Needs

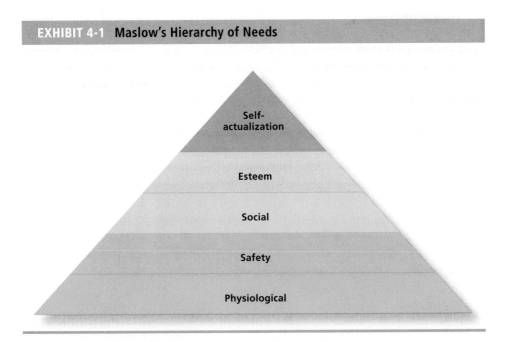

ERG Theory

Clayton Alderfer has reworked Maslow's hierarchy of needs to align it more closely with the empirical research. His revised need hierarchy is called **ERG theory**.[12]

Alderfer argues that there are three groups of core needs—existence, relatedness, and growth—hence, the name: ERG theory. The *existence* group is concerned with our basic material existence requirements. They include the items that Maslow considered to be physiological and safety needs. The *relatedness* group is concerned with our desire for maintaining important interpersonal relationships. These social and status desires require interaction with others if they are to be satisfied, and they align with Maslow's social need and the external component of Maslow's esteem need. Finally, the *growth* group is concerned with our intrinsic desire for personal development. This group includes the intrinsic component of Maslow's esteem need and the characteristics included under self-actualization.

Aside from substituting three needs for five, how does Alderfer's ERG theory differ from Maslow's? In contrast to the hierarchy of needs theory, the ERG theory demonstrates that (1) more than one need may be working at the same time, and (2) if the gratification of a higher-level need is stifled, the desire to satisfy a lower-level need increases. ERG theory is more consistent with our knowledge of individual differences among people. Variables such as education, family background, and cultural environment can alter the importance or driving force that a group of needs holds for a particular person.

Several studies have supported ERG theory,[13] but there is also evidence that it does not work in some organizations.[14] Overall, however, ERG theory represents a more valid version of the need hierarchy.

McClelland's Theory of Needs

McClelland's theory of needs was developed by David McClelland and his associates to help explain motivation.[15] The theory focuses on three needs: achievement, power, and affiliation. They are defined as follows:

- *Need for achievement*. The drive to excel, to achieve in relation to a set of standards, to strive to succeed.

- *Need for power*. The need to make others behave in a way that they would not have behaved otherwise.

- *Need for affiliation*. The desire for friendly and close interpersonal relationships.

Some people have a compelling drive to succeed. They are striving for personal achievement rather than the rewards of success per se. They have a desire to do something better or more efficiently than it has been done before. This drive is the achievement need (*nAch*). From research into the achievement need, McClelland found that high achievers differentiate themselves from others by their desire to do things better.[16]

The need for power (*nPow*) is the desire to have impact, to be influential, and to control others. Individuals high in nPow enjoy being "in charge," strive for influence over others, prefer to be placed in competitive and status-oriented situations, and tend to be more concerned with prestige and gaining influence over others than with effective performance.

The third need isolated by McClelland is affiliation (*nAff*). This need has received the least attention from researchers. Individuals with a high affiliation motive strive for friendship, prefer cooperative situations rather than competitive ones, and desire relationships that involve a high degree of mutual understanding.

Relying on an extensive amount of research, some reasonably well-supported predictions can be made based on the relationship of these needs to job performance. First, individuals with a high need to achieve prefer and will be motivated by job situations with personal responsibility, feedback, and an intermediate degree of risk. Second, people with a high achievement need are interested in how well they do personally and not in influencing others to do well. Thus, they may not make good managers.[17] Third, the best managers are high in their need for power and low in their need for affiliation.[18]

Motivation-Hygiene Theory

The motivation-hygiene theory was proposed by psychologist Frederick Herzberg.[19] Herzberg investigated the question "What do people want from their jobs?" in an effort to determine what might lead to a person's success or failure at work.

Frederick Herzberg
www.lib.uwo.ca/business/
herzberg.html

He found that intrinsic factors—such as achievement, recognition, the work itself, responsibility, advancement, and growth—seem to be related to job satisfaction. Herzberg also found that there were characteristics that led to job dissatisfaction. The factors that caused dissatisfaction were extrinsic—such as company policy and administration, supervision, interpersonal relations, and working conditions.

Herzberg's research led him to conclude that the opposite of satisfaction is not dissatisfaction, as was traditionally believed. Removing dissatisfying characteristics from a job does not necessarily make the job satisfying. As illustrated in Exhibit 4-2, Herzberg proposes a dual continuum: the opposite of "Satisfaction" is "No Satisfaction," and the opposite of "Dissatisfaction" is "No Dissatisfaction."

Herzberg explained that the factors leading to job satisfaction were *motivators* that are separate and distinct from the *hygiene factors* that lead to job dissatisfaction. Thus managers who try to get rid of factors that create job dissatisfaction can create more pleasant workplaces, but not necessarily more motivated ones. Hygiene factors include company policy and administration, supervision, interpersonal relations, working conditions, and salary. When these factors are adequate, people will not be dissatisfied; however, neither will they be satisfied. Motivating factors include achievement, recognition, the work itself, responsibility, and growth. These are the characteristics that people find intrinsically rewarding or motivating.

EXHIBIT 4-2   Contrasting Views of Satisfaction and Dissatisfaction

Traditional view

Dissatisfaction   Satisfaction

Herzberg's view

Hygiene Factors

Dissatisfaction   No Dissatisfaction

Motivators

No Satisfaction   Satisfaction

Herzberg's theory has received some criticism.[20] However, it has been widely read and few managers are unfamiliar with his recommendations. Over the past 40 years the popularity of jobs that allow employees greater responsibility in planning and controlling their work can probably be attributed largely to Herzberg's findings and recommendations.

Summarizing Needs Theories

All needs theories of motivation, including Maslow's hierarchy of needs, Alderfer's ERG theory, McClelland's theory of needs, and Herzberg's motivation-hygiene theory (or the two-factor theory), propose a similar idea: Individuals have needs that, when unsatisfied, will result in motivation. For instance, if you have a need to be praised, you may work harder at your task in order to receive recognition from your manager or other co-workers. Similarly, if you need money and you are asked to do something, within reason, that offers money as a reward, you will be motivated to complete the task in order to earn the money. Where needs theories differ is in the types of needs they consider, and whether they propose a hierarchy of needs (where some needs have to be satisfied before others) or simply a list of needs. Exhibit 4-3 illustrates the relationship of the four needs theories to each other. While the theories use different names for the needs, and also have different numbers of needs, we can see that they are somewhat consistent in the types of needs addressed. Exhibit 4-4 on page 113 indicates the contribution of and empirical support for each theory.

Needs Theories in the Workplace

What can we conclude from the needs theories? We can safely say that individuals have needs and that they can be highly motivated to achieve those needs. The types of needs, and their importance, vary by individual, and probably vary over time for the same individual as well. When rewarding individuals, one should consider their specific needs. Some employees may be struggling to make ends meet, while others are looking for more opportunities to reach self-actualization. Individual needs also change over time, depending on one's stage in life. Obviously, in a workplace it would be difficult to design a reward structure that could completely take into account the specific needs of each employee. At Burnaby, BC-based TELUS, employees earn points through a variety of job-related activities. They then choose gifts from a catalogue

EXHIBIT 4-3 **Relationship of Various Needs Theories**

EXHIBIT 4-4 Summarizing the Various Needs Theories				
Theory	**Maslow**	**Herzberg**	**Alderfer**	**McClelland**
Is there a hierarchy of needs?	The theory argues that lower-order needs must be satisfied before one progresses to higher-order needs.	Hygiene factors must be met if a person is not to be dissatisfied. They will not lead to satisfaction, however. Motivators lead to satisfaction.	More than one need can be important at the same time. If a higher-order need is not being met, the desire to satisfy a lower-level need increases.	People vary in the types of needs they have. Their motivation and how well they perform in a work situation are related to whether they have a need for achievement, power, or affiliation.
What is the theory's impact/ contribution?	The theory enjoys wide recognition among practising managers. Most managers are familiar with it.	The popularity of giving employees greater responsibility for planning and controlling their work can be attributed to his findings (see, for instance, the job characteristics model on page 134). It shows that more than one need may operate at the same time.	The theory is seen as a more valid version of the need hierarchy. It tells us that achievers will be motivated by jobs that offer personal responsibility, feedback, and moderate risks.	The theory tells us that high need achievers do not necessarily make good managers, since high achievers are more interested in how they do personally.
What empirical support/ criticisms exist?	Research does not generally validate the theory. In particular, there is little support for the hierarchical nature of needs. The theory is criticized for how data were collected and interpreted.	It is not really a *theory* of motivation: It assumes a link between satisfaction and productivity that was not measured or demonstrated.	It ignores situational variables.	It has mixed empirical support, but the theory is consistent with our knowledge of individual differences among people. Good empirical support exists on needs achievement in particular.

that lists rewards and their point values. To get an idea of the factors that might motivate you in the workplace, turn to this chapter's *Learning About Yourself Exercise* on page 143.

PROCESS THEORIES OF MOTIVATION

What does the life of a Canadian Football League assistant coach look like? It's definitely not glamorous.[21] The coaches work long hours, they can be fired without notice if the team's owner or head coach think they are responsible for the poor play of the team, and they work long hours without pensions or benefits.

Dan Dorazio, an offensive line coach with the BC Lions, faced a choice after his team beat the Calgary Stampeders in August 2005: stay in Calgary overnight, or drive home to Abbotsford, BC, and arrive just before midnight. Tired after a long day of coaching, he still was not able to

> rest. He was expected to have the Calgary game tape analyzed before sunrise, so that the coaches could plan the post-game practice with the players later in the afternoon. Dorazio chose to drive home, and, after a brief nap, go into his office at 4 a.m.
>
> What would make an assistant coach show up for work, day after day, under these conditions?

③ Are there other ways to motivate people?

Process theories include: expectance + goal setting [handwritten]

While needs theories identify the different needs that could be used to motivate individuals, process theories focus on the broader picture of *how* someone can set about motivating another individual. Process theories include *expectancy theory* and *goal-setting theory*. Focusing greater attention on these process theories might help you understand how to motivate yourself or someone else.

Expectancy Theory

expectancy theory The theory that individuals are motivated based upon their evaluation of whether their effort will lead to good performance, whether good performance will be followed by a given outcome, and whether that outcome is attractive to them.

Currently, one of the most widely accepted explanations of motivation is Victor Vroom's **expectancy theory**.[22]

From a practical perspective, expectancy theory says that an employee will be motivated to exert a high level of effort when he or she believes the following:

- That the effort will lead to good performance
- That good performance will lead to organizational rewards, such as a bonus, a salary increase, or a promotion
- That the rewards will satisfy his or her personal goals

The theory, therefore, focuses on the three relationships (expectancy, instrumentality, and valence) illustrated in Exhibit 4-5 on page 115 and described below. This exhibit also provides an example of how you might apply the theory.

Effort-Performance Relationship

expectancy The belief that effort is related to performance.

The effort-performance relationship is commonly called **expectancy**. It refers to the individual's perception of how probable it is that exerting a given amount of effort will lead to good performance. For example, employees are sometimes asked to perform tasks for *question* [handwritten] which they do not have suitable skills or training. When that is the case, they will be less motivated to try hard, because they already believe that they will not be able to accomplish what they are being asked to do. Expectancy can be expressed as a probability, and ranges from 0 to 1.

In the opening vignette, we saw that the BC Lions players were willing to work hard for a demanding coach. These players likely felt that their efforts, such as spending extra time training, would lead to good performance.

In general, an employee's expectancy is influenced by the following:

- Self-esteem
- Previous success
- Help from supervisors and subordinates
- Information
- Proper materials and equipment[23]

Coach Wally Buono's observation on motivation highlights the importance of the expectancy link in motivating individuals. According to Buono, motivation "is really the function of the person that you hire ... You need to be able to give [staff and

Golfers such as Prince Edward Island's Lorie Kane illustrate the effectiveness of the expectancy theory of motivation, where rewards are tied to effort and outcome. Players on the LPGA tour are paid strictly according to their performance, unlike members of professional team sports. Kane's first LPGA tour victory came in 2000, at the Michelob Light Classic. It ended a string of nine runner-up finishes. She had two more victories in 2000 and won the 2001 LPGA Takefuji Classic. As Kane has put more effort into her play, she has been increasing her earnings each year.

EXHIBIT 4-5 How Does Expectancy Theory Work?

players] the proper setting . . . atmosphere . . . tools so they're not hindered from doing what they have to do."[24]

Performance-Rewards Relationship

✳ *Are managers manipulating employees when they link rewards to productivity? Is this ethical?*

The performance-rewards relationship is commonly called **instrumentality**. It refers to the individual's perception of whether performing at a particular level will lead to the attainment of a desired outcome. In particular, will the performance be acknowledged by those who have the power to allocate rewards? Instrumentality ranges from −1 to +1. A negative instrumentality indicates that high performance reduces the chances of getting the desired outcome. An instrumentality of 0 indicates that there is no relationship between performance and receiving the desired outcome.

instrumentality The belief that performance is related to rewards.

In a study by the Angus Reid Group, only 44 percent of employees said the workplace recognizes employees who excel at their job.[25] Thus, one possible source of low motivation is the employee's belief that no matter how hard he or she works, the performance will not be recognized. BC Lions offensive line coach Dan Dorazio works long hours at his job because he does feel that his efforts are recognized by the head coach and by the players on the team.

Rewards–Personal Goals Relationship

✳ *Why do some managers do a better job of motivating people than others?*

The rewards–personal goals relationship is commonly called **valence**. It refers to the degree to which organizational rewards satisfy an individual's personal goals or needs and the attractiveness of those potential rewards for the individual. Unfortunately, many managers are limited in the rewards they can distribute, which makes it difficult to personalize rewards. Moreover, some managers incorrectly assume that all employees want the same thing. They overlook the motivational effects of differentiating rewards. In either case, employee motivation may be lower because the specific need the employee has is not being met through the reward structure. Valence ranges from −1 (very undersirable reward) to +1 (very desirable reward).

valence The value or importance an individual places on a reward.

Vancouver-based Radical Entertainment, creator of such digital entertainment as *The Incredible Hulk* and *The Simpsons Road Rage,* makes sure it meets the needs of its employees, because it does not want to lose them to the United States.[26] The company employs

Radical Entertainment
www.radical.ca

EXHIBIT 4-6   Steps to Increasing Motivation, Using Expectancy Theory

Improving Expectancy	Improving Instrumentality	Improving Valence
Improve the ability of the individual to perform.	Increase the individual's belief that performance will lead to reward.	Make sure that the reward is meaningful to the individual.
• Make sure employees have skills for the task. • Provide training. • Assign reasonable tasks and goals.	• Observe and recognize performance. • Deliver rewards as promised. • Indicate to employees how previous good performance led to greater rewards.	• Ask employees what rewards they value. • Give rewards that are valued.

a "Radical fun guru" whose job is to make the workplace so much fun that no one wants to leave. The company provides free food all day, including catered lunches a few times a week, and there is a log cabin on-site, fitted out with big screens, DVDs, and gaming equipment, where employees can take time out to recharge during their long workdays. Radical Entertainment offers these benefits to meet the needs of its young employees, who find greater motivation from being part of a cool workplace than having a bigger pension plan.

Expectancy Theory in the Workplace

Does expectancy theory work? Although it has its critics,[27] most of the research evidence supports the theory.[28] Research in cross-cultural settings has also indicated support for expectancy theory.[29]

Exhibit 4-6 shows how managers can increase the motivation of employees, using insights from expectancy theory. Managers can take steps to improve expectancy, instrumentality, and valence. To further appreciate how expectancy theory might apply in the workplace, see this chapter's *Case Incident—Wage Reduction Proposal* on the CD-ROM that accompanies this textbook for an example of what happens when expected rewards are withdrawn.

Goal-Setting Theory

You have heard the phrase a number of times: "Just do your best. That's all anyone can ask." But what does "do your best" mean? Do we ever know if we have achieved that vague goal? Might you have done better in your high school English class if your parents had said, "You should strive for 75 percent or higher on all your work in English" instead of "do your best"?

The research on goal setting by Edwin Locke and his colleague Professor Gary Latham at the University of Toronto shows that intentions to work toward a goal are a major source of work motivation.[30] A **goal** is "what an individual is trying to accomplish; it is the object or aim of an action."[31] Goals tell an employee what needs to be done and how much effort will need to be expended.[32]

goal   What an individual is trying to accomplish.

How Does Goal Setting Motivate?

According to Locke, goal setting motivates in four ways (see Exhibit 4-7 on page 117):[33]

- *Goals direct attention.* Goals indicate where individuals should direct their efforts when they are choosing among things to do. For instance, recognizing that an important assignment is due in a few days, goal setting may encourage you to say no when friends invite you to a movie this evening.

- *Goals regulate effort.* Goals suggest how much effort an individual should put into a given task. For instance, if earning a high mark in accounting is more important to you than earning a high mark in organizational behaviour (OB), you will likely put more effort into studying accounting.

EXHIBIT 4-7 Locke's Model of Goal Setting

Source: Adapted from E. A. Locke and G. P. Latham, *A Theory of Goal Setting and Task Performance* (Englewood Cliffs, NJ: Prentice Hall, 1980). Reprinted with permission of Edwin A. Locke.

- *Goals increase persistence.* Persistence represents the effort spent on a task over time. When people keep goals in mind, they will work hard on them, even in the face of obstacles.

- *Goals encourage the development of strategies and action plans.* Once goals are set, individuals can develop plans for achieving those goals. For instance, a goal to become more fit may include plans to join a gym, workout with friends, and change eating habits.

In order for goals to be effective, they should be "SMART." SMART stands for

- **Specific:** Individuals know exactly what is to be achieved.
- **Measurable:** The goals proposed can be tracked and reviewed.
- **Attainable:** The goals, even if difficult, are reasonable and achievable.
- **Results-oriented:** The goals should support the vision of the organization.
- **Time-bound:** The goals are to be achieved within a stated time.

Employees can respond quite positively to frequent goal-setting, as *OB in the Workplace* shows.

OB IN THE WORKPLACE

Employees Hold Meetings to Achieve Goals

Will employees police themselves to meet goals? Raj Narayanaswamy, CEO of Calgary-based Replicon, which develops time-management software, thinks so.[34] He offered his employees a deal in the last quarter of 1998. His employees wanted him to close the office over Christmas holidays. He wanted to make sure all of his shipments got out on time. "Meet these goals before then, and we will think about it," he told them.

Replicon
www.replicon.com

To achieve this goal, the employees developed a plan, and scheduled daily 10-minute meetings to make sure everything stayed on track. They ended up surpassing their goal, and getting the vacation days they wanted.

Narayanaswamy has encouraged his employees to set departmental and personal goals to increase revenue and solve problems each quarter ever since. He rewards them with trips and events when goals are met. The employees continue to hold daily meetings to assess how well the goals are being met, and Narayanaswamy thinks the "cringe factor" motivates individuals. "It's difficult for someone to attend a daily meeting and say every day, 'I didn't get it done,'" he points out. Because the employees set the goals, they are also more likely to work hard to achieve them.

From Concepts to Skills on pages 148–149 gives further ideas of how to effectively engage in goal setting.

Goal-setting theory is consistent with expectancy theory. The goals can be considered the effort-performance link—in other words, the goals determine what must be done. Feedback can be considered the performance-rewards relationship, where the individual's efforts are recognized. Finally, the implication of goal setting is that the achievement of the goals will result in intrinsic satisfaction (and may of course be linked to external rewards).

Contingency Factors in Goal Setting

Are there any contingencies in goal-setting theory, or can we take it as a universal truth that difficult and specific goals will always lead to higher performance? Feedback is one of the most important factors that influences the relationship between goals and performance. Recent research suggests that when individuals receive negative feedback, they lower their goals, and when they receive positive feedback, they raise their goals.[35]

Self-efficacy may explain how feedback affects goal behaviour. **Self-efficacy** refers to an individual's belief that he or she is capable of performing a task.[36] The higher your self-efficacy, the more confidence you have in your ability to succeed in a task. So, in difficult situations, we find that people with low self-efficacy are more likely to lessen their effort or give up altogether, while those with high self-efficacy will try harder to master the challenge.[37] In addition, individuals high in self-efficacy seem to respond to negative feedback with increased effort and motivation, whereas those low in self-efficacy are likely to lessen their effort when given negative feedback.[38]

self-efficacy An individual's belief that he or she is capable of performing a task.

In addition to feedback, four other factors have been found to influence the goals-performance relationship. These are goal commitment, adequate self-efficacy, task characteristics, and national culture. Goal-setting theory presupposes that an individual is committed to the goal; that is, he or she is determined not to lower or abandon the goal. This is most likely to occur when goals are made public, when the individual has an internal locus of control, and when the goals are self-set rather than assigned.[39]

Research indicates that individual goal setting does not work equally well on all tasks. The evidence suggests that goals seem to have a greater effect on performance when tasks are simple rather than complex, well-learned rather than new, and independent rather than interdependent.[40] On interdependent tasks, group goals are preferable. Finally, goal-setting theory is culture bound. It's well adapted to countries like Canada and the United States because its key components align reasonably well with North American cultures. Following the GLOBE measures from Chapter 3, it assumes that employees will be reasonably independent (not too high a score on power distance), that managers and employees will seek challenging goals (low in uncertainty avoidance), and that performance is considered important by both (high in performance orientation). So don't expect goal setting to necessarily lead to higher employee performance in countries such as Portugal or Chile, where the opposite conditions exist.

Our overall conclusion is that intentions—as articulated in terms of hard and specific goals—are a potent motivating force. Under the proper conditions, they can lead to higher performance.

RESPONSES TO THE REWARD SYSTEM

As one of four quarterbacks for the BC Lions football team, Casey Printers was not a happy player when the football season started in summer 2005.[41] He was the CFL's most outstanding player in the 2004 season, after stepping in when starting quarterback Dave Dickenson was injured. Subsequently, Printers led the BC Lions to an eight-game winning streak, and he thought that should have entitled him to a better contract for 2005.

> Printers signed his first contract with the BC Lions in 2004, for $65 000 a year. He asked for a new four-year contract that would pay him more than $400 000 a year. The team turned him down, countering with an offer of $1 million over three years. Printers turned that down.
>
> Printers' rationale for the seemingly high salary demand was that his teammate and fellow quarterback Dave Dickenson makes $400 000 a year, as does Edmonton Eskimos quarterback Ricky Ray and Montreal Alouettes quarterback Anthony Calvillo. "My value is just as equal as these guys, so why not try to get equal or more? It just makes perfect business sense," he explains. Will Printers continue to be motivated to play for the BC Lions? And is he making the right salary comparisons?

To a large extent, motivation theories are about rewards. The theories suggest that individuals have needs, and will exert effort to have those needs met. The needs theories specifically identify those needs. Goal-setting and expectancy theories portray processes by which individuals act and then receive desirable rewards (intrinsic or extrinsic) for their behaviour.

Three additional process theories ask us to consider how individuals respond to rewards. *Equity theory* suggests that individuals evaluate and interpret rewards. *Fair process* goes one step further, suggesting that employees are sensitive to a variety of fairness issues in the workplace that extend beyond the reward system but also affect employee motivation. *Cognitive evaluation theory* examines how individuals respond to the introduction of extrinsic rewards for intrinsically satisfying activities.

4 Do equity and fairness matter?

Equity Theory

✳ *How important is fairness to you?*

Equity theory suggests that employees compare their job inputs (i.e., effort, experience, education, competence, creativity) and outcomes (i.e., salary levels, raises, recognition, challenging assignments, working conditions) with those of others. We perceive what we get from a job situation (the outcomes mentioned above) in relation to what we put into it (the inputs mentioned above), and then we compare our outcome-input ratio with the outcome-input ratio of relevant others. (This idea is illustrated in Exhibit 4-8.) If we

equity theory Individuals compare their job inputs and outcomes with those of others and then respond so as to eliminate any inequities.

EXHIBIT 4-8   Equity Theory

Ratio of Output to Input	Person 1's Perception
Person 1 / Person 2	Inequity, underrewarded
Person 1 / Person 2	Equity
Person 1 / Person 2	Inequity, overrewarded

Because of the financial crisis in Russia, many firms do not have money to pay their employees. Instead of receiving a salary, employees get paid in goods the factories produce. Velta Company, a bicycle maker in Russia, gives workers one bicycle a month instead of a paycheque. Workers then have to sell their bikes for cash or barter it for food. Some workers deal with the inequity of not getting a salary by using a different referent. "We are luckier than people over at the chemical plant," says one Velta employee. "At least our factory gives us something we can sell."

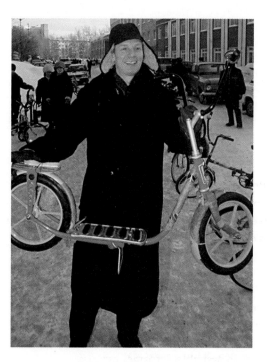

perceive our ratio to be equal to that of the relevant others with whom we compare ourselves, a state of equity is said to exist. We perceive our situation as fair—that justice prevails. When we see the ratio as unequal, we experience this as inequity.

Imagine that you wrote a case analysis for your marketing professor and spent 18 hours researching and writing it up. Your classmate spent 6 hours doing her analysis. Each of you received a mark of 75 percent. It is likely that you would perceive this as unfair, as you worked considerably harder (i.e., exerted more effort) than your classmate. J. Stacy Adams has proposed that those experiencing inequity are motivated to do something to correct it.[42] Thus, you might be inclined to spend considerably less time on your next assignment for your marketing professor.

What Happens When We Feel Treated Inequitably?

✳ *What can you do if you think your salary is "unfair"?*

When individuals feel that they have been treated inequitably, they generally act to reduce that inequity. Based on equity theory, they can be predicted to make one of six choices, with some of them being more negative to the organization than others.[43] We can illustrate these choices by noting possible responses that quarterback Casey Printers could have had when he compared his salary with the higher salaries of other quarterbacks in his reference group.

- *Change their inputs* (for example, Casey Printers could have decided to exert less effort playing quarterback).

- *Change their outcomes* (for example, Printers could have tried to renegotiate his contract to get himself a higher salary).

- *Adjust perceptions of self* (for example, Printers could have thought, "I've only been in the Canadian Football League for two years. Maybe I don't really have the same experience as the other guys").

- *Adjust perceptions of others* (for example, Printers could have thought, "Anthony Cavillo of the Alouettes has been a quarterback for a lot longer, and maybe he deserves greater pay").

- *Choose a different referent* (for example, Printers could have considered what other quarterbacks who have been in the league for only two years receive).

- *Leave the field* (for example, Printers could hope that he would be picked up by another team at the end of the season, which in fact is what happened when he decided to leave the BC Lions for the Kansas City Chiefs in 2006).

Case Incident—Frustrated at Age 32 on page 147 describes what happens when a Generation Xer feels he does not have the same opportunities in the workplace as a Baby Boomer.

Bear in mind that being treated equitably is not the same as being treated equally. Equity theory tells us that people who perform better should observe that they are rewarded better than those who do not perform as well. Thus poor performers should also observe that they receive lesser rewards than those who perform at a higher level. Paying equally would mean that everyone is paid the same, regardless of performance.

RESEARCH FINDINGS   Equity Theory

Equity theory has generally been supported, with a few minor qualifications.[44] First, inequities created by overpayment do not seem to have a significant impact on behaviour in most work situations. Apparently, people have a great deal more tolerance of overpayment inequities than of underpayment inequities, or are better able to rationalize them. Second, not all people are equity sensitive.[45] For example, some employees simply do not worry about how their rewards compare with those of others. Predictions from equity theory are unlikely to be very accurate with these individuals.

Equity Theory in the Workplace

It is important to note that while most research on equity theory has focused on pay, employees seem to look for equity in the distribution of other organizational rewards. For instance, it has been shown that the use of high-status job titles, as well as large and lavishly furnished offices, may function as desirable outcomes for some employees in their equity equations.[46]

Equity theory demonstrates that, for most employees, motivation is influenced significantly by relative rewards, as well as by absolute rewards. However, some key issues are still unclear.[47] For instance, how do employees handle conflicting equity signals, such as when unions point to other employee groups who are substantially *better off*, while management argues how much things have *improved*? How do employees define inputs and outcomes? How do they combine and weigh their inputs and outcomes to arrive at totals? Despite these problems, equity theory continues to offer some important insights into employee motivation.

Fair Process and Treatment

Recent research has been directed at redefining what is meant by equity, or fairness.[48] Historically, equity theory focused on **distributive justice**, or the perceived fairness of the *amount* and *allocation* of rewards among individuals. But people also care about **procedural justice**—the perceived fairness of the *process* used to determine the distribution of rewards. (This includes having a voice in a decision and finding accuracy in decision making.) And they care, too, about **interactional justice**—the quality of the *interpersonal treatment* received from a manager.[49] (Being treated sensitively and being provided an explanation for decisions are examples.)

distributive justice The perceived fairness of the amount and allocation of rewards among individuals.

procedural justice The perceived fairness of the process used to determine the distribution of rewards.

interactional justice The quality of the interpersonal treatment received from a manager.

The evidence indicates that distributive justice has a greater influence on employee satisfaction than procedural justice, while procedural and interactional justice tend to affect an employee's organizational commitment, trust in his or her manager, and intention to quit.[50] Researchers have found that when managers and employees believed that the company's processes were fair, they were more likely to show a high level of trust and commitment to the organization. Employees engaged in negative behaviour when they felt the process was unfair.[51]

For example, employees at Volkswagen's plant in Puebla, Mexico, staged a lengthy walkout *after* being offered a 20-percent raise. The reason? Their union leaders had agreed to work-rule concessions without consulting them. The employees, even though happy about the raise, did not believe that the process leading to the change in the work rules was fair. This behaviour is consistent with economist Alan Blinder's findings that "Changing the way workers are *treated* may boost productivity more than changing the way they are *paid*."[52]

Volkswagen Canada
www.vw.ca

W. L. Gore, maker of Gore-Tex fabric and Elixir guitar strings, has a compensation and reward system based on procedural justice. At Gore, motivation comes from approval of co-workers. Compensation is determined by employees, who rank their team members each year. Gore openly shares information about how pay decisions are made based on consistent procedures. Procedural fairness helps create a strong organizational commitment among employees.

Sauder School of Business
www.sauder.ubc.ca

Air Canada Employee Morale Flies Low

To increase employees' perception of procedural justice, managers should consider openly sharing information on how allocation decisions are made and follow consistent and unbiased procedures. With increased procedural and interactional fairness, employees are likely to view their managers and the organization as positive, even if they are dissatisfied with pay, promotions, and other personal outcomes. Professor Daniel Skarlicki at the Sauder School of Business at the University of British Columbia has found that it is when unfavourable outcomes are combined with unfair procedures or poor interpersonal treatment that resentment and retaliation (e.g., theft, bad-mouthing, sabotage) are most likely.[53] This explains why Casey Printers left the BC Lions and signed a three-year contract with the Kansas City Chiefs: He did not think he was being treated fairly and suggested that the coaching staff did not have confidence in him.[54]

This chapter's *CBC Video Case Incident* shows what can happen when employees feel they have been treated unfairly.

Cognitive Evaluation Theory

cognitive evaluation theory
Offering extrinsic rewards (e.g., pay) for work effort that was previously rewarding intrinsically will tend to decrease the overall level of a person's motivation.

Several researchers suggest that the introduction of extrinsic rewards, such as pay, for work effort that was *previously rewarding intrinsically* (i.e., that was personally satisfying) will tend to decrease the overall level of a person's motivation.[55] This proposal—which has come to be called **cognitive evaluation theory**—has been extensively researched, and a large number of studies have been supportive.[56] Additionally, Alfie Kohn, often cited for his work on rewards, argues that people are actually punished by rewards, and do inferior work when they are enticed by money, grades, or other incentives. His extensive review of incentive studies concluded that "rewards usually improve performance only at extremely simple—indeed, mindless—tasks, and even then they improve only quantitative performance."[57]

Extrinsic vs. Intrinsic Rewards

Historically, motivation theorists have generally assumed that intrinsic motivators are independent of extrinsic motivators. That is, the stimulation of one would not affect the other. But cognitive evaluation theory suggests otherwise. It argues that when extrinsic rewards are used by organizations as payoffs for superior performance, the intrinsic rewards, which are derived from individuals doing what they like, are reduced.

In other words, when extrinsic rewards are given to someone for performing an interesting task, it causes intrinsic interest in the task itself to decline. For instance, although a taxi driver expects to be paid for taking your best friend to the airport, you do not expect your friend to pay you if you volunteer to drive her to the airport. In fact, the offer of pay might diminish your pleasure in doing a favour for your friend.

Why would such an outcome occur? The popular explanation is that the individual experiences a loss of control over his or her own behaviour when it is being rewarded by external sources. This causes the previous intrinsic motivation to diminish. Extrinsic rewards can produce a shift—from an internal to an external explanation—in an individual's perception of why he or she works on a task. If you are reading a novel a week because your contemporary literature instructor requires you to, you can attribute your reading behaviour to an external source. If you stop reading novels the moment the course ends, this is more evidence that your behaviour was due to an external source. However, if you find yourself continuing to read a novel a week when the course ends, your natural inclination is to say, "I must enjoy reading novels because I'm still reading one a week!"

RESEARCH FINDINGS   Extrinsic and Intrinsic Rewards

Although further research is needed to clarify some of the current ambiguity, the evidence does lead us to conclude that the interdependence of extrinsic and intrinsic rewards is a real phenomenon.[58] A large body of research shows that large external rewards can undermine the positive performance of employees.[59] When employees work for a large reward, they will explain their behaviour through that reward—"I did it for the money." However, in the absence of large rewards, employees are more likely to reflect on the interesting nature of the work or the benefits of being an organizational member to explain their behaviour. When an organization provides employees with intrinsically interesting work, they will often work longer and harder than one might predict from the actual external rewards.

In studies dating back to the 1940s, employees have always ranked other items, such as being shown appreciation for work done, feeling "in" on things, and having interesting work, as being more important to them than their salaries.[60] Employees at both Southwest Airlines and AES, an independent producer of electrical power with offices in the United States, Argentina, China, Hungary, and other countries, indicated that they appreciated the positive working climates of these organizations more than the financial rewards they received.[61]

Increasing Intrinsic Motivation

Our discussion of motivation theories and our discussion of how to apply motivation theories in the workplace focuses mainly on improving extrinsic motivation. Recently Professor Kenneth Thomas of the Naval Postgraduate School in Monterey, California, has developed a model of intrinsic motivation that draws from the job characteristics model and cognitive evaluation theory.[62] He identifies four key rewards that increase an individual's intrinsic motivation:

- *Sense of choice.* The opportunity to select what one will do, and perform the way one thinks best. Individuals can use their own judgment to carry out the task.

- *Sense of competence.* The feeling of accomplishment for doing a good job. People are more likely to feel a sense of accomplishment when they carry out challenging tasks.

- *Sense of meaningfulness.* The opportunity to pursue worthwhile tasks. Individuals feel good about what they are doing, and believe that what they are doing matters.

- *Sense of progress.* The feeling of accomplishment that one is making progress on a task, and that it is moving forward. Individuals feel that they are spending their time wisely in doing their jobs.

EXHIBIT 4-9 Building Blocks for Intrinsic Rewards

Leading for Choice	Leading for Competence
• Delegated authority • Trust in workers • Security (no punishment) for honest mistakes • A clear purpose • Information	• Knowledge • Positive feedback • Skill recognition • Challenge • High, noncomparative standards
Leading for Meaningfulness	**Leading for Progress**
• A noncynical climate • Clearly identified passions • An exciting vision • Relevant task purposes • Whole tasks	• A collaborative climate • Milestones • Celebrations • Access to customers • Measurement of improvement

Source: Reprinted with permission from the publisher. From *Intrinsic Motivation at Work: Building Energy and Commitment.* Copyright © K. Thomas. Berrett-Koehler Publishers Inc., San Francisco, CA. All rights reserved. www.bkconnection.com.

Thomas also identified four sets of behaviours managers can use to create intrinsic rewards for their employees:

- *Leading for choice.* Empowering employees and delegating tasks

- *Leading for competence.* Supporting and coaching employees

- *Leading for meaningfulness.* Inspiring employees and modelling desired behaviours

- *Leading for progress.* Monitoring and rewarding employees

Exhibit 4-9 presents the building blocks that increase the likelihood that intrinsic rewards are motivational.

CREATING A MOTIVATING WORKPLACE: REWARDS AND JOB REDESIGN

5 How can rewards and job design motivate employees?

Organizations use specific incentives to motivate individuals, teams, and the entire organization to achieve organizational goals such as productivity, reduced turnover, and leadership effectiveness. They can also redesign jobs to create more motivating workplaces.

Employee Recognition: Showing People That They Matter

Expectancy theory tells us that a key component of motivation is the link between performance and reward (that is, having your behaviour recognized). Employee recognition programs cover a wide spectrum of activities. They range from a spontaneous and private "thank you" on up to widely publicized formal programs in which specific types of behaviour are encouraged and the procedures for attaining recognition are clearly identified.[63]

Recognition may not be enough for some jobs, however, as Exhibit 4-10 on page 125 suggests.

Sometimes, however, the link between reward and performance is unclear, as *Ethical Dilemma Exercise* on page 146 shows.

A survey of Canadian firms in 2004 by Hewitt Associates found that 34 percent of companies recognized individual or group achievements with cash or merchandise.[64] At the same time, recognizing employees can cost little or no money. Toronto-based KPMG is one company that has created a "thank-you culture" to recognize good work and deeds. Recognition is a way of "reinforcing our corporate values," says Val Duffey, KPMG's Toronto-based human resource director. "We acknowledge that recognition is critical to motivating, satisfying and retaining the best employees."[65] Not all employees feel they get recognition, however. In a recent *Globe and Mail* Web poll, 27 percent of respondents said that they had never received a compliment from their bosses, and 10 percent said that they had received the last compliment from their bosses over a year ago.[66]

Organizations can recognize employees in numerous ways. The *Globe and Mail* awards the Stephen Godfrey Prize for Newsroom Citizenship. Vancouver-based Purdy's Chocolates recognizes employees on their birthdays and when they move, get married, or have children. As well, Purdy's recognizes employees who reach their five-year anniversary with the company at an annual luncheon, with out-of-town employees flown in for the event.[67] Other ways of recognizing performance include sending personal notes or emails for good performance, putting employees on prestigious committees, sending them for training, and giving someone an assistant for a day to help clear backlogs.

Employee recognition may reduce turnover in organizations, particularly that of good employees. When executives were asked the reasons why employees left for jobs with other companies, 34 percent said it was due to lack of recognition and praise,

EXHIBIT 4-10

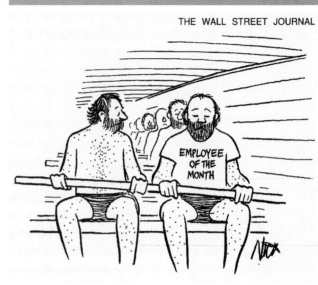

THE WALL STREET JOURNAL

EMPLOYEE OF THE MONTH

Source: From the *Wall Street Journal,* October 21, 1997. Reprinted by permission of Cartoon Features Syndicate.

Hewitt Associates
www.hewitt.com/canada

At Toronto-based Snap Promotions, rewards are given spontaneously, for extraordinary effort. CEO Warren Kotler (kneeling at right, with employees Leilani Nolan and Mez Lalji) shows his deep appreciation for his entire team by giving them tickets to shows and concerts, buying them lunch, and even sending a masseuse to someone's home. Kotler recently organized a "Steak & Beans" contest, dividing the company into two teams that received points for meetings set, quotes generated, and sales achieved. At the end of the period, the losing team ate beans at Morton's Steakhouse in Toronto (a well-known upscale restaurant) while watching the winners feast on steak.

compared with 29 percent who mentioned low compensation, 13 percent who mentioned limited authority, and 8 percent who cited personality problems.[68]

Variable-Pay Programs: Improving Productivity

A large body of research suggests that pay is far more motivational than some motivation theorists such as Maslow and Herzberg suggest.[69] Consistent with this research, managers generally look at ways to manipulate pay to improve performance by considering a variety of incentive schemes. Some of these are individually based, some are team based, and some reward all members of the organization for working together toward productivity goals. The rewards used are all forms of **variable-pay programs**. What differentiates these forms of compensation from more traditional programs is that they do not pay a person only for time on the job or seniority. Instead, a portion of an employee's pay is based on some individual and/or organizational measure of performance. Unlike more traditional base-pay programs, with variable pay there is no guarantee that just because you made $60 000 last year, you will make the same amount this year. Instead, earnings fluctuate annually, based on performance.[70]

The number of employees who have variable-pay programs has been rising in Canada. A 2005 survey of 360 firms by Hewitt Associates found that 81 percent of them have variable-pay programs in place, compared with 43 percent in 1994.[71] That same year, 80 percent of large US companies had some form of variable-pay program.[72] About 22 percent of Japanese companies have company-wide pay-for-performance (or variable-pay) programs.[73]

These programs are more common among non-unionized companies, although more than 30 percent of unionized companies had such plans in 2002.[74] Prem Benimadhu, an analyst with The Conference Board of Canada, notes, "Canadian unions have been very allergic to variable compensation."[75] Under variable-pay programs, individuals are not guaranteed specific annual wages, making their work experience riskier. People paid under a variable-pay structure may worry about not being able to predict wages ahead of time. However, the Conference Board study suggests that in a unionized setting, variable pay is used as an add-on to base pay, which means there is somewhat less uncertainty about wages. Those working under a variable-pay structure may also be concerned that factors out of their control might affect whether bonuses are awarded, and whether rewards are set by political processes rather than objective factors.

Variable-based pay can be applied at individual, team, and company-wide levels, making it possible to link rewards to the appropriate level of performance. Below, we briefly describe some examples of incentives at these different levels of the organization.

Individual-Based Incentives

Piece-Rate Wages   Piece-rate wages are one of the earliest forms of individual performance pay. They have long been popular as a means for compensating production employees. In a **piece-rate pay plan**, employees are paid a fixed sum for each unit of production completed. When an employee gets no base salary and is paid only for what he or she produces, this is a pure piece-rate plan. People who work at baseball parks selling peanuts and soft drinks frequently are paid this way. They might get to keep 25 cents for every bag of peanuts they sell. If they sell 200 bags during a game, they make $50. If they sell only 40 bags, their take is a mere $10. Sales associates who are paid commissions based on sales also have a form of piece-rate pay plan.

Many organizations use a modified piece-rate pay plan, where employees earn a base hourly wage plus a piece-rate differential. For example, a legal typist might be paid an hourly wage plus a certain rate per typed page. Or a sales associate might be paid a base salary plus commissions on sales. Such modified plans provide a basic security net, while still offering a productivity incentive.

variable-pay programs   Reward programs in which a portion of an employee's pay is based on some individual and/or organizational measure of performance.

piece-rate pay plan   An individual-based incentive plan in which employees are paid a fixed sum for each unit of production completed.

Even though the cost of the gun registry grew from $2 million to over $1 billion and an internal Justice Department investigation reported problems with the usability of the data, 96 percent of civil servants at the Department of Justice received bonuses for their performance in 2002. This calls into question whether the federal government actually uses a pay-for-performance system when giving out rewards to employees.

Bonuses   Bonuses are becoming an increasingly popular form of individual incentive in Canada.[76] They are used by such companies as Molson Coors Brewing Company, Ontario Hydro Energy, and the Bank of Montreal. Bonuses are more common in the United States than in Canada, with more employees receiving them and larger rewards given.[77] This is because Canada has a more unionized economy, a relative lack of competition, and a large public sector. Until recently, the only bonus for federal public servants was $800, awarded to those in bilingual jobs. More recently, both federal and provincial governments introduced bonuses for public sector employees to acknowledge superior performance.

Bonuses can be used for reasons other than improving performance. A recent study showed that 39 percent of small and medium-sized companies used bonuses as a retention strategy, so that employees would not look for jobs elsewhere.[78] In spring 2006, in the hopes of having no labour unrest during the 2010 Olympics, the BC provincial government offered bonuses of about $3000 to every public sector employee whose union signed a four-year (or longer) collective agreement. As a result of the bonus offer, all affected unions settled their contracts before the March 31 deadline set by the provincial government.

Bonuses are not free from organizational politics (which we discuss in Chapter 7), and they can sometimes result in negative behaviour. When using bonuses, managers should be mindful of potential unexpected behaviours that may arise when employees try to ensure that they will receive bonuses.

Group-Based Incentives

Gainsharing   The variable-pay program that has received the most attention in recent years is undoubtedly **gainsharing**.[79] This is a formula-based group incentive plan. Improvements in group productivity—from one period to another—determine the total amount of money that is to be allocated. The productivity savings can be divided between the company and employees in any number of ways, but 50-50 is fairly typical.

Gainsharing differs from profit-sharing, discussed on the next page. Gainsharing focuses on productivity gains rather than profits, and so it rewards specific behaviours

gainsharing A group-based incentive plan in which improvements in group productivity determine the total amount of money to be shared.

that are less influenced by external factors. Employees in a gainsharing plan can receive incentive awards even when the organization is not profitable.

Gainsharing was initially popular only in large unionized manufacturing companies,[80] such as Montreal-based Molson Coors Brewing Company and Montreal-based Hydro-Québec. This has changed in recent years, with smaller companies, such as Delta, BC-based Avcorp Industries, and governments, such as Ontario's Kingston Township and Town of Ajax, also introducing gainsharing. Gainsharing has been found to improve productivity in a majority of cases and often has a positive impact on employee attitudes.[81]

Organizational-Based Incentives

There are two major forms of organizational-based pay-for-performance programs: profit-sharing and stock option plans, including employee stock ownership plans.

profit-sharing plan An organization-wide plan in which the employer shares profits with employees based on a predetermined formula.

IKEA Canada
www.ikea.ca

Profit-Sharing Plans   A **profit-sharing plan** is an organization-wide plan in which the employer shares profits with employees based on a predetermined formula. The plan can distribute direct cash outlays or stock options. Though senior executives are most likely to be rewarded through profit-sharing plans, employees at any level can be recipients. For instance, IKEA divided every penny rung up in its 152 stores on October 8, 1999, among its 44 000 staffers in 28 countries. This amounted to $2500 for each employee.[82]

Be aware that profit-sharing plans focus on past financial results. They don't necessarily focus employees on the future, because employees and managers look for ways to cut costs today, without considering longer-term organizational needs. They also tend to ignore factors such as customer service and employee development, which may not be seen as directly linked to profits. In addition, employees who work in companies in cyclical industries would see inconsistent rewards in such a plan. For example, a financial services company would offer few or no rewards during slumping economic periods, and substantial rewards during times of economic growth. Fluctuating rewards may not work for all employees. Employees at St. John's, Newfoundland-based Fishery Products International were quite upset when the $750 profit-sharing cheques they received in 2000 were reduced to just 10 percent of that for 2001 because of lower profits. Allan Moulton, a union representative of the employees, said, "It's extremely hard for [employees] . . . to see that [the company] realized profits, and they expected to see some benefits from the profits they generated."[83]

employee stock ownership plan (ESOP) A company-established benefit plan in which employees acquire stock as part of their benefits.

Stock Options and Employee Stock Ownership Plans   Some companies try to encourage employees to adopt the values of top management by making them owners of their firms. The idea is that employees will be more likely to think about the consequences of their behaviour on the bottom line if they own part of the company. Employees can become owners of the company either through being granted stock options or through an **employee stock ownership plan (ESOP)**.[84] Stock options give employees the right to buy stocks in the company at a later date for a guaranteed price. ESOPs are company-established benefit plans in which employees acquire stock as part of their benefits.

Canadian companies lag far behind the United States in the use of ESOPs because Canada's tax environment is less conducive to such plans. More recently, both the dot-com meltdown and the high-tech meltdown have made employees more reluctant to accept stock options instead of cash. Lisa Slipp, head of executive compensation at Toronto-based consulting firm Mercer Human Resource Consulting, notes that "people are recognizing the reality of stock options, that they are attractive in an up market and less so in a down market."[85]

Mercer Human Resource Consulting
www.mercerhr.com

RESEARCH FINDINGS ESOPs

The research on ESOPs indicates that they increase employee satisfaction.[86] But their impact on performance is less clear. For instance, one study compared 45 companies with ESOPs against 238 companies without ESOPs.[87] Companies with ESOPs outperformed those without, both in terms of employment and sales growth. Other studies on companies with ESOPs have shown disappointing results.[88] More important, ESOPs can sometimes focus employees on trying to increase short-term stock prices while not worrying about the impact of their behaviour on the long-term effectiveness of the organization.

ESOPs have the potential to increase employee job satisfaction and work motivation. For this potential to be realized, employees need to experience ownership psychologically.[89] Some employees may not be fully aware of how their performance affects company performance, or they may not feel that they have any control over company performance. So, in addition to having a financial stake in the company, employees need to be kept regularly informed on the status of the business and also have the opportunity to exercise influence over the business.

Linking Productivity-Related Incentives to Motivation Theories

Variable pay is probably most compatible with expectancy theory predictions. Specifically, under these plans, individuals should perceive a strong relationship between their performance and the rewards they receive, and thus be more motivated. They should also be more productive.

However, the evidence is mixed, at best.[90] One recent study that followed the careers of 1000 top economists found that they put in more effort early in their careers, at a time when productivity-related incentives had a larger impact.[91] A recent study of Finnish white collar employees found that higher levels of pay and more frequent payments positively affected productivity, while lower levels of pay did not improve productivity.[92] Other studies generally support that organizations with profit-sharing plans or gainsharing plans have higher levels of profitability and productivity than those without.[93] But there are studies that question the effectiveness of pay-for-performance approaches, suggesting they can lead to less group cohesiveness.[94] Although some researchers note that much of the evidence supporting pay for performance "is based on anecdotal testimonials and one-time company cases, rather than on methodologically more rigorous empirical studies,"[95] a number of researchers have shown that the connection between pay and performance is linked to productivity improvement.[96] This is supported by a recent study in Canada that looked at both unionized and non-unionized workplaces, and found that variable-pay plans result in "increased productivity, a safer work environment, a better understanding of the business by employees, and little risk of employees losing base pay," according to Prem Benimadhu, an analyst with The Conference Board of Canada.[97]

Using pay for performance can be difficult for some managers. They worry about what should constitute performance and how it should be measured. There is also some belief by managers and employees alike that wages should keep pace with inflation, independent of performance issues. Other barriers include salary scales keyed to what the competition is paying; traditional compensation systems that rely heavily on specific pay grades and relatively narrow pay ranges; and performance appraisal practices that produce inflated evaluations and expectations of full rewards.

Of course, from the employees' perspective, the major concern about pay-for-performance programs is a potential drop in earnings. *Pay for performance* means employees must share in the risks as well as the rewards of their employers' businesses. They are not guaranteed the same salary each year under this system. A recent Conference Board of Canada study may ease some fears about this particular concern. There was no evidence that pay for performance led to a reduction in salary in unionized settings. Instead, it "is used as an 'add-on' to the employees' base salary."[98] Pay for performance may also be more successful when organizations are more transparent about financial conditions. Ottawa-based Lee Valley Tools, which has a pay-for-performance program, uses quarterly newsletters to let employees know how much profit is forecast. Being informed helps employees understand how their efforts will pay off for them. Robin Lee, the company's president, says "sharing information and profits promotes an atmosphere in which hard work, innovation and efficiency pay off for everybody."[99]

What About Teamwork?

Incentive pay, especially when it is awarded to individuals, can have a negative effect on group cohesiveness and productivity, and in some cases may not offer significant benefits to a company.[100] For example, Montreal-based National Bank of Canada offered a $5 employee bonus for every time employees referred clients for loans, mutual funds, or other bank products. But the bonus so upset employees that the plan was abandoned after just three months.[101] Tellers complained that the bonus caused colleagues to compete against one another. Meanwhile, the bank could not determine whether the referrals actually generated new business.

Organized labour is, in general, cool to the idea of pay for performance. Andrew Jackson, director of the Social and Economic Policy Department at the Canadian Labour Congress, explains that "it hurts co-operation in the workplace. It can lead to competition between workers, speeding up the pace of work. It's a bad thing if it creates a stressful work environment where older workers can't keep up."[102] Pay for performance can also be problematic if work is speeded up to such unfair levels that employees can injure themselves. Still, not all unions oppose pay for performance, and the benefits and drawbacks of such incentive plans must be carefully considered before they are introduced.

If an organization wants a group of individuals to function as a "team" (which we define in Chapter 5), emphasis needs to be placed on team-based rewards rather than individual rewards. We will discuss the nature of team-based rewards in Chapter 5.

Motivating Beyond Productivity

In recent years, organizations have been paying for performance on bases other than strict productivity. Compensation experts Patricia Zingheim and Jay Schuster note the following activities that merit additional compensation:[103]

- *Commissions beyond sales.* Commissions might be determined by customer satisfaction and/or sales team outcomes, such as meeting revenue or profit targets.
- *Leadership effectiveness.* Rewards can be determined by employee satisfaction or measures of how the manager handles his or her employees.
- *New goals.* Rewards go to all employees who contribute to specific organizational goals, such as customer satisfaction, cycle time, or quality measures.
- *Knowledge workers in teams.* Rewards are linked to the performance of knowledge workers and/or professional employees who work on teams.
- *Competency and/or skills.* Rewards are based on employees' abstract knowledge or competencies—for example, knowledge of technology, the international business context, customer service, or social skills.

Exhibit 4-11 on page 131 compares the strengths and weaknesses of variable-pay programs, team-based rewards, and skill-based pay programs. **Skill-based pay** is based on how many skills an employee has or how many jobs he or she can do.

skill-based pay Pay based on how many skills an employee has or how many jobs he or she can do.

While rewarding individuals for something other than performance may make sense in some instances, not everyone agrees that these rewards are fair. *OB in the Street* questions whether athletic scholarships should be given for athletic skills only, with little concern for academic merit or financial need.

OB IN THE STREET

Scholarships for Jocks: Skills or Smarts?

Should university athletes be awarded money just for their athletic abilities? Jack Drover, athletic director at Mount Allison University in Sackville, New Brunswick, thinks not.[104] He objects to student-athlete awards that are often offered because of what coaches and teams need rather than what the individual student needs.

Many university presidents react negatively to schools using financial rewards to recruit athletes. Some high school athletes can get full-tuition scholarships to university, even though they have not achieved high marks in school. While not every university finds this problematic, others feel awarding scholarships that don't recognize academic achievement or financial need is "an affront to the values of higher education."

Schools across the country interpret the rules for scholarships differently, which may affect the quality of school sports teams. Universities in Ontario (which rarely give scholarships to first-year students) have had particular difficulty competing with schools across the country. For example, since 1995 only two football teams in Ontario have won the Vanier Cup: the Ottawa Gee Gees (2000) and the Wilfrid Laurier Golden Hawks (2005); the University of Ottawa is one of the few schools in the province that gives many athletic scholarships. In contrast, the Saint Mary's Huskies of Halifax, Nova Scotia, has been in the Vanier Cup final four times since 1999, winning twice. Rivals claim that a reason for the team's successes is its "plentiful" athletic scholarships.[105] Some members of Canadian Interuniversity Sport (CIS) suggest that a level playing field, with no scholarships granted to first-year athletes except in cases of financial need and academic merit, would be fairer to all teams. CIS president Marg MacGregor, however, argues that "We're asking a lot of our students when we say compete every weekend and practise all the time without any support."

EXHIBIT 4-11 **Comparing Various Pay Programs**

Approach	Strengths	Weaknesses
Variable pay	• Motivates for performance. • Cost-effective. • Clearly links organizational goals and individual rewards.	• Individuals do not always have control over factors that affect productivity. • Earnings vary from year to year. • Can cause unhealthy competition among employees.
Team-based rewards	• Encourages individuals to work together effectively. • Promotes goal of team-based work.	• Difficult to evaluate team performance sometimes. • Equity problems could arise if all members paid equally.
Skill-based pay	• Increases the skill levels of employees. • Increases the flexibility of the workforce. • Can reduce the number of employees needed.	• Employers may end up paying for unneeded skills. • Employees may not be able to learn some skills, and thus feel demotivated.

Designing Motivating Jobs

✳ *When might job redesign be an appropriate motivational tool?*

Either as an alternative or a supplement to various reward programs, managers can consider redesigning jobs to make them more motivating. OB researchers Richard Hackman from Harvard University and Greg Oldham from the University of Illinois explored the nature of good jobs through their **job characteristics model (JCM)**.[106] The JCM identifies five core job dimensions and their relationship to personal and work outcomes. Building on Herzberg's motivation-hygiene theory, the JCM focuses on the content of jobs rather than the context of jobs and can be considered as a way of motivating employees and increasing job satisfaction.

job characteristics model (JCM) A model that identifies five core job dimensions and their relationship to personal and work outcomes.

Job enrichment, an application of the JCM, refers to the vertical expansion of jobs. It increases the degree to which employees control the planning, execution, and evaluation of their work. An enriched job organizes tasks so that an employee does a complete activity. It expands employees' freedom and independence, increases responsibility, and provides feedback, so individuals will be able to assess and correct their own performance.[107]

job enrichment The vertical expansion of jobs.

Core Job Dimensions

According to the JCM, any job can be described in terms of five core job dimensions:

skill variety The degree to which the job requires a variety of different activities.

- *Skill variety*. The degree to which the job requires a variety of different activities so the employee can use a number of different skills and talents.

task identity The degree to which the job requires completion of a whole and identifiable piece of work.

- *Task identity*. The degree to which the job requires completion of a whole and identifiable piece of work.

task significance The degree to which the job has a substantial impact on the lives or work of other people.

- *Task significance*. The degree to which the job has a substantial impact on the lives or work of other people.

autonomy The degree to which the job provides substantial freedom, independence, and discretion to the individual in scheduling the work and determining the procedures to be used in carrying it out.

- *Autonomy*. The degree to which the job provides substantial freedom, independence, and discretion to the individual in scheduling the work and determining the procedures to be used in carrying it out.

McDonald's sends its employees to Hamburger University to train them to give good service. Employees working in fast-food stores are often part-time, and they view their jobs as temporary. McDonald's uses the experience at Hamburger U and other training opportunities to help employees feel part of the organization and more committed to their work.

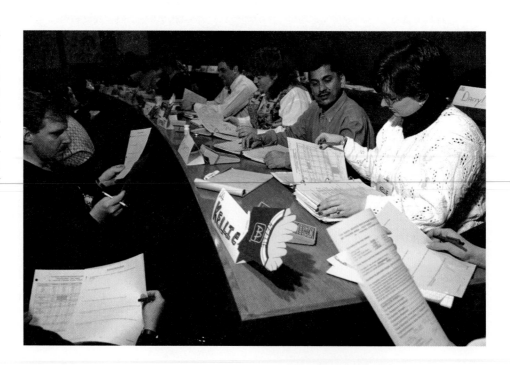

EXHIBIT 4-12	Examples of High and Low Job Characteristics

Skill Variety

| High variety | The owner-operator of a garage who does electrical repair, rebuilds engines, does body work, and interacts with customers |
| Low variety | A body shop employee who sprays paint eight hours a day |

Task Identity

| High identity | A cabinet maker who designs a piece of furniture, selects the wood, builds the object, and finishes it to perfection |
| Low identity | An employee in a furniture factory who operates a lathe solely to make table legs |

Task Significance

| High significance | Nursing the sick in a hospital intensive care unit |
| Low significance | Sweeping hospital floors |

Autonomy

| High autonomy | A telephone installer who schedules his or her own work for the day, makes visits without supervision, and decides on the most effective techniques for a particular installation |
| Low autonomy | A telephone operator who must handle calls as they come according to a routine, highly specified procedure |

Feedback

| High feedback | An electronics factory employee who assembles a radio and then tests it to determine if it operates properly |
| Low feedback | An electronics factory employee who assembles a radio and then routes it to a quality control inspector who tests it for proper operation and makes needed adjustments |

Source: G. Johns, *Organizational Behavior: Understanding and Managing Life at Work,* 4th ed. Copyright © 1997. Adapted by permission of Pearson Education, Inc., Upper Saddle River, NJ.

- *Feedback*. The degree to which carrying out the work activities required by the job results in the individual's obtaining direct and clear information about the effectiveness of his or her performance.

feedback The degree to which individuals obtain direct and clear information about the effectiveness of their performance.

Jobs can be rated as high or low on these dimensions. Examples of jobs with high and low ratings appear in Exhibit 4-12.

Critical Psychological States

The JCM, presented in Exhibit 4-13 on page 134, links the five core job dimensions to three critical psychological states:[108]

- *Experienced meaningfulness.* The model predicts that if an employee's task is meaningful, the employee will view the job as important, valuable, and worthwhile. (Notice how in Exhibit 4-13 skill variety, task identity, and task significance combine to create meaningful work.)

- *Experienced responsibility for outcomes.* Employees feel a sense of personal responsibility for results when their jobs give them greater autonomy.

- *Knowledge of the actual results.* Feedback helps employees know whether they are performing effectively. The feedback can come from managers, clients, co-workers, or the nature of the task itself.

EXHIBIT 4-13   The Job Characteristics Model

Source: J. R. Hackman and G. R. Oldham, *Work Design* (excerpted from pages 78–80). Copyright © 1980 by Addison-Wesley Publishing Co. Reprinted by permission of Addison-Wesley Longman.

The model suggests that the more employees experience meaningfulness, responsibility, and knowledge of the actual results, the greater their motivation, performance, and satisfaction, and the lower their absenteeism and likelihood of leaving the organization.[109] As Exhibit 4-13 shows, the links between the job dimensions and the outcomes are moderated or adjusted by the strength of the individual's growth need—in other words, the employee's desire for self-esteem and self-actualization. This means, for example, that not every employee will respond favourably to a job with skill variety, task identity, task significance, autonomy, or feedback. Those with high self-esteem and self-actualization needs will respond more favourably than others with different needs.

EVALUATING THE USE OF REWARDS IN THE WORKPLACE

6 What kinds of mistakes are made in reward systems?

When applying motivation theories in the workplace, managers should be aware of the kinds of signals rewards send, how rewards are viewed in different cultures, and whether rewards are essential.

Beware the Signals That Rewards Send

✳ *Ever wonder why employees do some strange things?*

In 1998, Vancouver's bus drivers claimed, on average, 18.6 sick days. Victoria's bus drivers averaged only 16.6 sick days.[110] Are Vancouver's drivers more likely to catch cold than Victoria's? Not likely! Rather, differences in the way that sick days are paid may account for the differences. Victoria's drivers get paid in full for six sick days, no matter how the days are taken. But once Vancouver drivers take their second "sick time," they are paid only if they are off more than three days for their illness, so it makes sense for them to stay home sick longer. At Carignan, Quebec-based hardware store Centre de rénovation Pointe et Meunier, owner Daniel Blais had to revise his plan to give commissions to employees based on profit per sales. An "employee [who] happened to be near someone who was looking at a big-ticket item tended to shadow that person rather than going to help the next customer who was looking at something less costly," says Blais. He found that employees gave better overall service when he switched the performance plan to a group commission divided evenly among staff and based on overall profits for the department.[111]

Perhaps more often than we would like, organizations engage in what has been called "the folly of rewarding A, while hoping for B."[112] Organizations do this when they hope that employees will engage in one type of behaviour, yet they reward another type. Managers of Vancouver's bus drivers had hoped that by increasing the number of days a driver had to be out sick to get paid, bus drivers would take fewer days off. Instead, managers might have considered giving bonuses for perfect attendance. Hoping for a behaviour you are not rewarding is unlikely to make it happen to any great extent. In fact, as expectancy theory suggests, individuals will generally perform in ways to raise the probability of receiving the rewards offered.

Exhibit 4-14 provides further examples of common management reward follies. Research suggests that there are three major obstacles to ending these follies:[113]

- *Individuals are unable to break out of old ways of thinking about reward and recognition practices.* This approach is demonstrated when management emphasizes quantifiable behaviours, to the exclusion of nonquantifiable behaviours; when management is reluctant to change the existing performance system; and when employees have an entitlement mentality (i.e., they don't support changing the reward system because they are comfortable with the current behaviours that are rewarded).

EXHIBIT 4-14 Management Reward Follies	
We hope for . . .	**But we reward . . .**
Teamwork and collaboration	The best team members
Innovative thinking and risk-taking	Proven methods and not making mistakes
Development of people skills	Technical achievements and accomplishments
Employee involvement and empowerment	Tight control over operations and resources
High achievement	Another year's effort
Long-term growth; environmental responsibility	Quarterly earnings
Commitment to total quality	Shipping on schedule, even with defects
Candour; surfacing bad news early	Reporting good news, whether it's true or not; agreeing with the manager, whether or not (s)he's right

Sources: Constructed from S. Kerr, "On the Folly of Rewarding A, While Hoping for B," *Academy of Management Executive* 9, no. 1 (1995), pp. 7–14; and "More on the Folly," *Academy of Management Executive* 9, no. 1 (1995), pp. 15–16. Reprinted by permission.

- *Organizations often do not look at the big picture of their performance system.* Thus, rewards are allocated at subunit levels, with the result that units often compete against each other.

- *Both management and shareholders often focus on short-term results.* They don't reward employees for longer-range planning.

Organizations would do well to ensure that they do not send the wrong message when offering rewards. When organizations outline an organizational objective of "team performance," for example, but reward each employee according to individual productivity, does this send a message that teams are valued? Or when a retailer tells commissioned employees that they are responsible for monitoring and replacing stock as necessary, are employees more likely to concentrate on making sales or stocking the floor? Employees motivated by the promise of rewards will do those things that earn them the rewards they value.

Caveat Emptor: Motivation Theories Are Culture-Bound

Reward strategies that have been used successfully in Canada and the United States do not always work successfully in other cultures. Take, for instance, a study comparing sales representatives at a large electronics company in the United States with one in Japan. The study found that while Rolex watches, expensive dinners, and fancy vacations were valued rewards for star performers in the United States, taking the whole sales team bowling was more appreciated in Japan. The study's authors found that "being a member of a successful team with shared goals and values, rather than financial rewards, is what drives Japanese sales representatives to succeed."[114]

Why do our motivation theories perform less well when we look at their use in countries beyond Canada and the United States? Most current motivation theories were developed in the United States and so take US cultural norms for granted.[115] That may account for why Canada and the United States, which have more individualistic cultures, rely more heavily on extrinsic motivating factors than some other countries.[116] Japanese and German firms rarely make use of individual work incentives because their cultures are more collectivist.[117]

Many of the social-psychological theories of motivation rely heavily on the idea of motivating the individual through individual rewards. Thus they emphasize, particularly in an organizational context, the meaning of "pay," and give little attention to the informal rewards that come from group norms and prestige from peers.[118] Exhibit 4-15 on page 137 presents a quick summary of the cultural differences in motivation observed by a number of studies.

Motivation theories also assume that needs are similar across societies. For instance, Maslow's needs hierarchy argues that people start at the physiological level and then move progressively up the hierarchy in this order: physiological, safety, social, esteem, and self-actualization. This hierarchy, if it applies at all, aligns well with American culture and reasonably well with Canadian culture. However, in countries such as Austria, Denmark, and Germany, where uncertainty avoidance characteristics are strong, security needs would be at the top of the needs hierarchy. Countries that score high on humane orientation characteristics—Indonesia, Egypt, and Malaysia—would have social needs on top.[119] We would predict, for instance, that group work will motivate employees more when the country's culture scores high on the humane orientation criterion.

Equity theory has gained a relatively strong following in Canada and United States. That is no surprise, since North American reward systems assume that employees are highly sensitive to equity in the granting of rewards, and expect pay to be tied closely to performance. However, recent evidence suggests that in collectivist cultures, especially in the former socialist countries of Central and Eastern Europe, employees expect rewards to

---

EXHIBIT 4-15 **Snapshots of Cultural Differences in Motivation**

Japan: Sales representatives prefer being members of a successful team with shared goals and values, rather than receiving financial rewards.

Russia: Cotton mill employees given either valued extrinsic rewards (North American T-shirts with logos, children's sweatpants, tapes of North American music, etc.) or praise and recognition are more productive. However, rewards do not help for those who work on Saturdays.

China: Bonuses are often given to everyone, regardless of individual productivity. Many employees expect jobs for life, rather than jobs based on performance.

Mexico: Employees prefer immediate feedback on their work. Therefore daily rewards for exceeding quotas are preferred.

Canada and the United States: Managers rely more heavily on extrinsic motivators.

Japan and Germany: Firms rarely give rewards based on individual performance.

---

reflect their individual needs as well as their performance.[120] Moreover, consistent with a legacy of Communism and centrally planned economies, employees show an entitlement attitude—they expect outcomes to be *greater* than their inputs.[121] These findings suggest that Canadian- and US-style pay practices may need modification, especially in Russia and former Communist countries, in order to be perceived as fair by employees.

These international findings indicate that it is important to consider the internal norms of a country when developing an incentive plan rather than simply import a plan that works well in Canada and the United States.

Can We Just Eliminate Rewards?

Alfie Kohn, in his book *Punished by Rewards*, argues that "the desire to do something, much less to do it well, simply cannot be imposed; in this sense, it is a mistake to talk about motivating other people. All we can do is set up certain conditions that will maximize the probability of their developing an interest in what they are doing and remove the conditions that function as constraints."[122]

Alfie Kohn
www.alfiekohn.org

Creating a Motivating Work Environment

Based on his research and consulting experience, Kohn proposes actions that organizations can take to create a motivating work environment.[123]

Abolish Incentive Pay   Paying people generously and fairly makes sure they don't feel exploited, and takes pay off their minds. As a result, employees will be more able to focus on the goals of the organization rather than have their paycheques as their main goal.

Re-evaluate Evaluation   Instead of making performance appraisals look and feel like a punitive effort—who gets raises, who gets promoted, who is told he or she is performing poorly—the performance evaluation system might be structured more like a two-way conversation to trade ideas and questions, done continuously, not as a competition. The discussion of performance should not be tied to compensation. "Providing feedback that employees can use to do a better job ought never to be confused or combined with controlling them by offering (or withholding) rewards."[124]

Create the Conditions for Authentic Motivation   A noted economist recently summarized the evidence about pay for productivity as follows: "Changing the way workers are *treated* may boost productivity more than changing the way they are *paid.*"[125] There is some consensus about what the conditions for creating authentic motivation might be: helping employees rather than putting them under surveillance; listening to employee concerns and thinking about problems from their viewpoint; and providing plenty of feedback so they know what they have done right and what they need to improve.[126]

Support Collaboration   People are more likely to perform better in well-functioning groups where they can get feedback and learn from each other.[127] Therefore, it is important to provide the necessary supports to create well-functioning teams.

Pay Attention to Content   People are generally the most motivated when their jobs give them an opportunity to learn new skills, provide variety in the tasks that are performed, and enable them to demonstrate competence. Some of this can be fostered by carefully matching people to their jobs and by giving them the opportunity to try new jobs. It is also possible to increase the meaningfulness of many jobs.

But what about jobs that don't seem inherently interesting? One psychologist suggests that in cases where the jobs are fundamentally unappealing, the manager might acknowledge frankly that the task is not fun, give a meaningful rationale for why it must be done, and then give people as much choice as possible in how the task is completed.[128] One sociologist studying a group of garbage collectors in San Francisco discovered that they were quite satisfied with their work.[129] Their satisfaction came from the way the work and the company were organized: Relationships among the crew were important, the tasks and routes were varied to provide interest, and the company was set up as a cooperative, so that each employee owned a share of the company, and thus felt "pride of ownership."

Provide Choice   "We are most likely to become enthusiastic about what we are doing—and all else being equal, to do it well—when we are free to make decisions about the way we carry out a task."[130] Extrinsic rewards (and punishments too) actually remove choice, because they focus us on rewards, rather than on tasks or goals. Research suggests that burnout, dissatisfaction, absenteeism, stress, and coronary heart disease are related to situations where individuals did not have enough control over their work.[131] By *choice* we do not mean lack of management, but rather involving people in the decisions that are to be made. A number of case studies indicate that participative management, when it includes full participation by everyone, is successful.[132]

These actions represent an alternative to simply providing more and different kinds of incentives to try to induce people to work more effectively. They suggest that providing the proper environment may be more important than the reward structure.

Putting It All Together

While it is always dangerous to synthesize a large number of complex ideas into a few simple guidelines, the following suggestions summarize the essence of what we know about motivating employees in organizations:

- *Recognize individual differences.* Employees have different needs and should not be treated alike. Managers should spend the time necessary to understand what is important to each employee and then align goals, level of involvement, and rewards with individual needs. This chapter's *Working With Others Exercise* on pages 144–145 gives you an opportunity to understand the different needs of a diverse workforce.

- *Use goals and feedback.* Employees should have hard, specific goals, as well as feedback on how well they are faring in pursuit of those goals.

- *Allow employees to participate in decisions that affect them.* Employees can contribute to a number of decisions that affect them: setting work goals, choosing their own benefits packages, solving productivity and quality problems, and the like. This can increase employee productivity, commitment to work goals, motivation, and job satisfaction.

- *When giving rewards, be sure that they are clearly related to the performance desired.* It is important that employees perceive a clear link between rewards and the type of performance expected. How closely rewards are *actually* correlated to performance criteria is less important than the *perception* of this relationship. If individuals perceive that there is little relation between the performance desired and the rewards they receive, the results will be low performance, a decrease in job satisfaction, and an increase in turnover and absenteeism.

- *Check the system for equity.* Employees should be able to perceive rewards as matching the inputs they bring to the job. At a simplistic level, this means that experience, skills, abilities, effort, and other obvious inputs should explain differences in performance and, hence, pay, job assignments, and other obvious rewards.

SUMMARY AND IMPLICATIONS

1 What is motivation? Motivation is the process that accounts for an individual's intensity, direction, and persistence of effort toward reaching a goal. *Intensity* is concerned with how hard a person tries. This is the element most of us focus on when we talk about motivation. However, high intensity is unlikely to lead to good job performance unless the effort is channelled in a useful *direction*. Finally, the effort requires *persistence*.

2 How do needs motivate people? All needs theories of motivation, including Maslow's hierarchy of needs, Alderfer's ERG theory, McClelland's theory of needs, and Herzberg's motivation-hygiene theory (sometimes called the *two-factor theory*) propose a similar idea: Individuals have needs that will result in motivation. Needs theories suggest that motivation will be high to the degree that the rewards individuals receive for high performance satisfy their dominant needs.

3 Are there other ways to motivate people? Process theories focus on the broader picture of how someone can set about motivating another individual. Process theories include expectancy theory and goal-setting theory. Expectancy theory says that an employee will be motivated to exert a high level of effort when he or she believes (1) that the effort will lead to good performance; (2) that good performance will lead to organizational rewards, such as a bonus, a salary increase, or a promotion; and (3) that the rewards will satisfy his or her personal goals.

Goal-setting theory suggests that intentions to work toward a goal are a major source of work motivation. That is, goals tell an employee what needs to be done and how much effort will need to be expended. Specific goals increase performance; difficult goals, when accepted, result in higher performance than do easy goals; and feedback leads to higher performance than does nonfeedback.

4 **Do equity and fairness matter?**   Individuals look for fairness in the reward system. Rewards should be perceived by employees as related to the inputs they bring to the job. At a simplistic level, this means that experience, skills, abilities, effort, and other obvious inputs should explain differences in performance and, hence, pay, job assignments, and other obvious rewards.

5 **How can rewards and job design motivate employees?**   When organizations want to reward individuals for specific high performance, they often turn to employee recognition programs. Recognizing an employee's superior performance often costs little or no money.

When organizations want to improve productivity, they often use variable-pay programs. With these programs, a portion of an employee's pay is based on some individual and/or organizational measure of performance.

Managers can enrich jobs following the job characteristics model. The model tells us that jobs that offer skill variety, task identity, task significance, autonomy, and feedback tend to be more motivating for employees.

6 **What kinds of mistakes are made in reward systems?**   Individuals are responsive to the signals sent out by organizations, and if they determine that some activities are not valued, they may not engage in them, even when the firm expects employees to do so. Rewards should be linked to the type of performance expected. Rewards are also culture-bound. Individuals respond to rewards in general, and specific rewards, differently, depending upon what culture they come from. Finally, rewards are not always necessary. In the right context, individuals often motivate themselves intrinsically and can achieve quite high levels of performance doing so. We also know that giving rewards for things that were previously done for intrinsic motivation will decrease motivation.

For Review

1. What are the implications of Theories X and Y for motivation practices?

2. Identify the variables in expectancy theory.

3. Describe the four ways in which goal setting motivates.

4. Explain cognitive evaluation theory. How applicable is it to management practice?

5. What are the pluses and minuses of variable-pay programs from an employee's viewpoint? From management's viewpoint?

6. What is an ESOP? How might it positively influence employee motivation?

7. Define the five core dimensions in the JCM.

8. Describe three jobs that score high on the JCM. Describe three jobs that score low.

9. What can firms do to create more motivating environments for their employees?

For Critical Thinking

1. Identify three activities you really enjoy (for example, playing tennis, reading a novel, going shopping). Next, identify three activities you really dislike (for example, visiting the dentist, cleaning the house, following a low-fat diet). Using expectancy theory, analyze each of your answers to assess why some activities stimulate your effort while others don't.

2. Identify five different bases by which organizations can compensate employees. Based on your knowledge and experience, is performance the basis most used in practice? Discuss.

3. "Employee recognition may be motivational for the moment, but it doesn't have any staying power. Why? Because employees can't take recognition to Roots or The Bay!" Do you agree or disagree? Discuss.

4. "Performance can't be measured, so any effort to link pay with performance is a fantasy. Differences in performance are often caused by the system, which means the organization ends up rewarding the circumstances. It's the same thing as rewarding the weather forecaster for a pleasant day." Do you agree or disagree with this statement? Support your position.

5. Your textbook argues for recognizing individual differences. It also suggests paying attention to members of diverse groups. Does this view contradict the principles of equity theory? Discuss.

OB for You

- To motivate yourself to finish a particularly long and dry chapter in a textbook, plan a snack break. Or buy yourself a new CD once that major accounting assignment is finished.

- The people you interact with appreciate recognition. Consider including a brief note on a nice card to show thanks for a job well done. Or you might send a basket of flowers. Sometimes just sending a pleasant, thankful email is enough to make a person feel valued. All of these things are easy enough to do, and appreciated greatly by the recipient.

- Be aware of the kinds of things that motivate you, so you can choose jobs and activities that suit you better.

OB *AT WORK*

POINT

Money Motivates!

The importance of money as a motivator has been consistently downgraded by most behavioural scientists. They prefer to point out the value of challenging jobs, goals, participation in decision making, feedback, cohesive work teams, and other nonmonetary factors as stimulants to employee motivation. We argue otherwise here—that money is the crucial incentive to work motivation. As a medium of exchange, it is the vehicle by which employees can purchase the numerous need-satisfying things they desire. Money also performs the function of a scorecard, by which employees assess the value that the organization places on their services and by which employees can compare their value to others.[133]

Money's value as a medium of exchange is obvious. People may not work only for money, but remove the money and how many people would come to work? A study of nearly 2500 employees found that while these people disagreed over what their primary motivator was, they unanimously ranked money as their number two.[134] This study reaffirms that for the vast majority of the workforce, a regular paycheque is absolutely necessary in order to meet basic physiological and safety needs.

The best case for money as a motivator is presented by Professor Ed Locke at the Robert H. Smith School of Business at the University of Maryland, who reviewed a number of studies.[135] Locke looked at four methods of motivating employee performance: money, goal setting, participation in decision making, and redesigning jobs to give employees more challenge and responsibility. He found that the average improvement from money was 30 percent; goal setting increased performance 16 percent; participation improved performance by less than 1 percent; and job redesign positively affected performance by an average of 17 percent. Moreover, every study Locke reviewed that used money as a method of motivation resulted in some improvement in employee performance. Such evidence demonstrates that money may not be the only motivator, but it's difficult to argue that it does not motivate!

COUNTERPOINT

Money Doesn't Motivate Most Employees Today!

Money can motivate some people under some conditions, so the issue isn't really whether money can motivate. The answer to that is "It can!" The more relevant question is this: Does money motivate most employees in the workforce today to higher performance? The answer to this question, we will argue, is "no."[136]

For money to motivate an individual's performance, certain conditions must be met. First, money must be important to the individual. Second, money must be perceived by the individual as being a direct reward for performance. Third, the marginal amount of money offered for the performance must be perceived by the individual as significant. Finally, management must have the discretion to reward high performers with more money. Let's take a look at each of these conditions.

Money is not important to all employees. High achievers, for instance, are intrinsically motivated. Money should have little impact on these people. Similarly, money is relevant to those individuals with strong lower-order needs; but for most of the workforce, lower-order needs are substantially satisfied.

Money would motivate if employees perceived a strong link between performance and rewards in organizations. Unfortunately, pay increases are far more often determined by levels of skills and experience, community pay standards, the consumer price index, and the organization's current and future financial prospects than by each employee's level of performance.

For money to motivate, the marginal difference in pay increases between a high performer and an average performer must be significant. In practice, it rarely is. How much motivation is there in knowing that if you work really hard you will end up with $20 a week more than someone who is doing just enough to get by? For a large number of people, not much! Research indicates that merit raises must be at least 7 percent of base pay for employees to perceive them as motivating. Unfortunately, recent surveys find nonmanagerial employees averaging merit increases of only 4.9 percent.[137]

In most organizations, managers have a very small area of discretion within which they can reward their higher-performing employees. So money might be theoretically capable of motivating employees to higher levels of performance, but most managers are not given enough flexibility to do much about it.

LEARNING ABOUT **YOURSELF** EXERCISE

What Motivates You?

Circle the number that most closely agrees with how you feel. Consider your answers in the context of your current job or a past work experience.

	Strongly Disagree				Strongly Agree
1. I try very hard to improve on my past performance at work.	1	2	3	4	5
2. I enjoy competition and winning.	1	2	3	4	5
3. I often find myself talking to those around me about nonwork matters.	1	2	3	4	5
4. I enjoy a difficult challenge.	1	2	3	4	5
5. I enjoy being in charge.	1	2	3	4	5
6. I want to be liked by others.	1	2	3	4	5
7. I want to know how I am progressing as I complete tasks.	1	2	3	4	5
8. I confront people who do things I disagree with.	1	2	3	4	5
9. I tend to build close relationships with co-workers.	1	2	3	4	5
10. I enjoy setting and achieving realistic goals.	1	2	3	4	5
11. I enjoy influencing other people to get my way.	1	2	3	4	5
12. I enjoy belonging to groups and organizations.	1	2	3	4	5
13. I enjoy the satisfaction of completing a difficult task.	1	2	3	4	5
14. I often work to gain more control over the events around me.	1	2	3	4	5
15. I enjoy working with others more than working alone.	1	2	3	4	5

Scoring Key:

To determine your dominant needs—and what motivates you—place the number 1 through 5 that represents your score for each statement next to the number for that statement.

Achievement	Power	Affiliation
1. _____	2. _____	3. _____
4. _____	5. _____	6. _____
7. _____	8. _____	9. _____
10. _____	11. _____	12. _____
13. _____	14. _____	15. _____
Totals: _____	_____	_____

Add up the total of each column. The sum of the numbers in each column will be between 5 and 25 points. The column with the highest score tells you your dominant need.

Source: Based on R. Steers and D. Braunstein, "A Behaviorally Based Measure of Manifest Needs in Work Settings," *Journal of Vocational Behavior,* October 1976, p. 254; and R. N. Lussier, *Human Relations in Organizations: A Skill Building Approach* (Homewood, IL: Richard D. Irwin, 1990), p. 120.

BREAKOUT **GROUP** EXERCISES

Form small groups to discuss the following topics, as assigned by your instructor:

1. One of the members of your team continually arrives late for meetings and does not turn drafts of assignments in on time. Choose one of the available theories and indicate how the theory explains the member's current behaviour and how the theory could be used to motivate the group member to perform more responsibly.

2. You are unhappy with the performance of one of your instructors and would like to encourage the instructor to present livelier classes. Choose one of the available theories and indicate how the theory explains the instructor's current behaviour. How could you as a student use the theory to motivate the instructor to present livelier classes?

3. Harvard University recently changed its grading policy to recommend to instructors that the average course mark should be a B. This was the result of a study showing that more than 50 percent of students were receiving an A or A– for coursework. Harvard students are often referred to as "the best and the brightest," and they pay $27 000 (US) for their education, so they expect high grades. Discuss the impact of this change in policy on the motivation of Harvard students to study harder.

WORKING WITH **OTHERS** EXERCISE

Rewards for a Diverse Workforce

Purpose   To learn about the different needs of a diverse workforce.

Time   Approximately 40 minutes.

Directions   Divide the class into groups of approximately 6 students. Each group is assigned 1 of the following people and is to determine the best benefits package for that person.

- Lise is 28 years old. She is a divorced mother of 3 children, aged 3, 5, and 7. She is the department head. She earns $37 000 a year in her job and receives another $3600 a year in child support from her ex-husband.

- Ethel is a 72-year-old widow. She works 25 hours a week to supplement her $8000 annual pension. Including her hourly wage of $7.75, she earns $18 075 a year.

- John is a 34-year-old black male born in Trinidad who is now a Canadian resident. He is married and the father of two small children. John attends college at night and is within a year of earning his bachelor's degree. His salary is $24 000 a year. His wife is an attorney and earns approximately $54 000 a year.

- Sanjay is a 26-year-old physically impaired Indo-Canadian male. He is single and has a master's degree in education. Sanjay is paralyzed and confined to a wheelchair as a result of a car accident. He earns $29 000 a year.

- Wei Mei is a single 22-year-old immigrant. Born and raised in China, she came to Canada only three months ago. Wei Mei's English needs considerable improvement. She earns $18 000 a year.

- Mike is a 16-year-old white male in his 2nd year of high school. He works 15 hours a week after school and during vacations. He earns $7.75 an hour, or approximately $6045 a year.

Background

Our 6 participants work for a company that has recently installed a flexible benefits program. Instead of the traditional "one benefits package fits all," the company is allocating an additional 25 percent of each employee's annual pay to be used for discretionary benefits. Those benefits and their annual costs are listed on the next page.

Benefit Yearly Cost

Extended medical care (for services such as private hospital room, eyeglasses, and dental care that are not provided by the province's health insurance plan) for employee:

Plan A (No deductible and pays 90%)	$3000
Plan B ($200 deductible and pays 80%)	$2000
Plan C ($1000 deductible and pays 70%)	$ 500

Extended medical care for dependants (same deductibles and percentages as above):

Plan A	$2000
Plan B	$1500
Plan C	$ 500
Supplementary dental plan	$ 500

Life insurance:

Plan A ($25 000 coverage)	$ 500
Plan B ($50 000 coverage)	$1000
Plan C ($100 000 coverage)	$2000
Plan D ($250 000 coverage)	$3000
Mental health plan	$ 500
Prepaid legal assistance	$ 300
Vacation	2% of annual pay for each week, up to 6 weeks a year
Pension at retirement equal to approximately 50% of final annual earnings	$1500
Four-day workweek during the three summer months	4% of annual pay (available only to full-time employees)
Daycare services (after company contribution) for all of an employee's children, regardless of number	$2000
Company-provided transportation to and from work	$ 750
University tuition reimbursement	$1000
Language class tuition reimbursement	$ 500

The Task

1. Each group has 15 minutes to develop a flexible benefits package that consumes 25 percent (and no more!) of its character's pay.

2. After completing Step 1, each group appoints a spokesperson who describes to the entire class the benefits package the group has arrived at for its character.

3. The entire class then discusses the results. How did the needs, concerns, and problems of each participant influence the group's decision? What do the results suggest for trying to motivate a diverse workforce?

Source: Exercise developed by Steve Robbins, with special thanks to Professor Penny Wright (San Diego State University) for her suggestions during the development of this exercise. Exercise modified by Nancy Langton.

OB *AT WORK*

ETHICAL **DILEMMA** EXERCISE

Are CEOs Paid Too Much?

Critics have described the astronomical pay packages given to Canadian and American CEOs as "rampant greed." In 2004, the average compensation of CEOs of Canadian companies that make up the S&P/TSX index was $5.5-million, nearly doubling the $3.5 million in compensation awarded in 2003. By comparison, the S&P/TSX index rose 14.5 in 2004 and profits at TSX companies were up 30 percent.

How do you explain such large pay packages to CEOs? Some say this represents a classic economic response to a situation in which the demand is great for high quality top-executive talent and the supply is low. Other arguments in favour of paying executives $1 million a year or more are the need to compensate people for the tremendous responsibilities and stress that go with such jobs; the motivating potential that 7- and 8-figure annual incomes provide to senior executives and those who might aspire to be; and the influence of senior executives on the company's bottom line. (For example, research findings cited on page 271 of Chapter 8 attribute a 15- to 25-percent variation in profitability to the leadership quality of CEOs.)

Critics of executive pay practices in Canada and the United States argue that CEOs choose board members whom they can count on to support ever-increasing pay for top management. If board members fail to "play along,"

they risk losing their positions, their fees, and the prestige and power inherent in board membership.

In addition, it is not clear that executive compensation is tied to firm performance. For instance, KPMG found in one survey that for 40 percent of the respondents, there was no correlation between the size of the bonus and how poorly or well the company fared. Consider the data in Exhibit 4-16, which illustrates the disconnect that can sometimes happen between CEO compensation and firm performance. *National Post Business* writers calculated that the CEOs noted in the exhibit were overpaid, based on their companies' performances for the year.

Is high compensation of CEOs a problem? If so, does the blame for the problem lie with CEOs or with the shareholders and boards that knowingly allow the practice? Are Canadian and American CEOs greedy? Are these CEOs acting unethically? Should their pay reflect more closely some multiple of their employees' wages? What do you think?

Sources: E. Church, "Market Recovery Delivers Executive Payout Bonanza," *Globe and Mail,* May 4, 2005, pp. B1, B9; "Gimme Gimme: Greed, the Most Insidious of Sins, Has Once Again Embraced a Decade," *Financial Post,* September 28/30, 1996, pp. 24–25; and I. McGugan, "A Crapshoot Called Compensation," *Canadian Business,* July 1995, pp. 67–70.

EXHIBIT 4-16	2005 Compensation of Canada's "Most Overpaid" CEOs		
CEO(s)	**Was Paid (3-Yr Avg.)**	**Should Have Been Paid***	**Amount Overpaid**
1. Ian Telfer/Robert McEwen Goldcorp Vancouver, British Columbia	$32 823 000	$1 313 000	$31 510 000
2. E. Melnyk Biovail Mississauga, Ontario	$23 392 000	$1 404 000	$21 988 000
3. Richard Smith/David Stein CoolBrands Markham, Ontario	$9 647 000	$675 000	$8 972 000
4. Jeffrey Orr/Robert Gratton Power Financial Corporation Montreal, Quebec	$76 139 000	$9 898 000	$66 241 000
5. Gerald Schwartz Onex Toronto, Ontario	$26 163 000	$4 709 000	$21 454 000

**National Post Business*'s calculations take into account CEO performance variables.

Source: Based on D. Dias, "Bang for the Buck: CEO Scorecard," *National Post Business,* November 2005, p. 79. Material reprinted with the express permission of National Post Company, a CanWest Partnership.

Frustrated at Age 32

Bob Wood is 32. But if you listened to him, you would think he was 65 and washed up. "I graduated from university at a great time. It was 1996. I started as an analyst for Accenture, worked as a health care IT consultant for two other firms, and then became chief technology officer at Claimshop.com, a medical claims processor." By 2001, Bob was making $80 000 a year plus bonus, driving an expensive European sports car, and optimistic about his future. But Bob Wood has become a statistic. He's one of the Canadians born between 1966 and 1975 whose peak earnings may be behind them. Bob now makes $44 000 as a technology analyst at a hospital and is trying to adjust to the fact that the go-go years of the late 1990s are history.

Like many of his generation, Bob is mired in debt. He owes $23 000 on his university loans and has run up more than $4500 on his credit cards. He faces a world very different from the one his father found when he graduated from college in the early 1960s.

"The rules have changed. And we Generations Xers are getting hit hard. We had to go to university to get a decent job. But the majority of us graduated with tuition debt. The good news was that when we graduated, the job market was great. I got a $5000 hiring bonus on my first job! The competition by employers for good people drove salaries up. When I was 28, I was making more money than my dad, who had been with the same company for over 20 years. But my dad has job security. And he has a nice retirement plan that will pay him a guaranteed pension when he turns 58. Now look at me. I don't know if I'll ever make $80 000 again. If I do, it'll be in 20 or more years. I have no job security. I'm paying $350 a month on my university

loans. I'm paying another $250 more in payments on my BMW. And my girlfriend says it's time for us to settle down and get married. It would be nice to own a house, but how can I commit myself to a 30-year mortgage when I don't know if I'll have a job in six months?"

"I'm very frustrated. I feel like my generation got a bad deal. We initially got great jobs with unrealistically high pay. I admit it; we were spoiled. We got used to working one job for six months, quitting, then taking another and getting ourselves a 25 or 30 percent raise. We thought we'd be rich and retired by 40. The truth is that we're now lucky to have a job and, if we do, it probably pays half what we were making a few years ago. We have no job security. The competition for jobs, combined with pressures by business to keep costs down, means a future with minimal salary increases. It is pretty weird to be only 32 years old and to have your best years behind you!"

Questions

1. Analyze Bob using Maslow's hierarchy of needs.

2. Analyze Bob's lack of motivation using equity theory and expectancy theory.

3. If you were Bob's boss, what could you do to positively influence his motivation?

4. What are the implications of this case for employers hiring Generation Xers?

Source: Ideas for this case are based on N. Watson, "Generation Wrecked," *Fortune*, October 14, 2002, pp. 183–190.

Air Canada Employee Morale Flies Low

Air Canada, Canada's national airline, has cut costs extensively in recent years while fighting possible bankruptcy. However, the difficulties faced by Air Canada have taken a toll on employee morale to the extent that staff could derail the company's current course of action.

Much of employee anger is directed toward CEO Robert Milton. Employees were particularly upset when Milton negotiated a $20 million bonus for himself from proposed new investor Victor Li of Li Investments, on the condition that Milton remain in the top leadership position for four

continued

years. Meanwhile, Milton asked his employees to take over $1 billion in cuts to their pay and benefits.

Despite severe financial trouble in the airline industry in recent years, some airlines have been a success. For example, Southwest Airlines of Texas has been listed among the 100 best companies to work for in America. The company uses a no-layoff policy as a positive motivator. Southwest is a profitable airline known for recruiting the best and brightest people it can find, and has a reputation for providing its staff with excellent compensation packages, opportunities for rapid advancement and professional growth, and challenging and interesting assignments. Management uses special interviewing and screening methods to hire people who can have fun on the job and demonstrate outgoing personality traits that create a high-spirited, fun-loving in-flight atmosphere for passengers. The hiring process is so selective that only 3 percent of people who apply at Southwest are offered jobs.

While Air Canada employees may question Milton's style, the CEO does have supporters. Karl Moore, a leadership and aviation expert, claims that Milton is one of the top airline CEOs in the world. Sunny Gordon of Li Investments believes that leaders should have a stake in their companies to produce expected results. He also believes Milton deserves a bonus if results are appropriate and Milton is able to repair relationships with employees.

Canadian-born Don Carty provides an example of what happens when airline employees feel they have not been treated fairly. Carty joined American Airlines (AA) as CEO in 1998. His employees agreed to almost $2 billion in concessions in 2003 to try to save the company from bank-

ruptcy before discovering that the year before, Carty and other senior executives were quietly offered big bonuses ($1.6 million just for Carty) to encourage them to keep their jobs. Outraged employees threatened to back out of their agreements and Carty resigned. For Carty, the mistake was not just in accepting the bonus but in hiding it as well. Carty's message to Milton: "If you take a bonus while your employees take cuts, your credibility is shot."

Questions

1. Using needs theories of motivation, explain how Southwest Airlines motivates its employees.

2. How can expectancy theory, equity theory, and fair process explain the outrage employees at American Airlines felt when they found out about Don Carty's hidden executive bonus? What could senior management do at American Airlines to improve motivation?

3. One Air Canada employee stated, "Milton treats us all the same—complete disregard and hatred." Using the lessons and examples from Southwest Airlines and American Airlines, how can CEO Robert Milton rebuild morale and improve motivation?

Sources: "The Hostile Skies," *CBC Venture,* February 15, 2004, VA2070D, 914; A. A. Thompson Jr., A. J. Strickland III, and J. E. Gamble, *Crafting and Executing Strategy: The Quest for Competitive Advantage, Concepts and Cases* (Boston: McGraw-Hill Irwin, 2005); and "Major Investor Walks Away from Air Canada Deal," *CTV.ca,* April 4, 2004, http://www.ctv.ca/servlet/ArticleNews/story/CTVNews/1080943752094_76352952///?hub=Canada (accessed June 7, 2006).

From **Concepts**
to **Skills**

Setting Goals

You can be more effective at setting goals if you use the following eight suggestions.

1. *Identify the key tasks you want to accomplish.* Goal setting begins by defining what it is that you want to accomplish.

2. *Establish specific and challenging goals for each key task.* Identify the level of performance you want to accomplish for each task. Specify the targets toward which you are working.

3. *Specify the deadlines for each goal.* Putting deadlines on each goal reduces ambiguity. Deadlines, however, should not be set arbitrarily. Rather, they need to be realistic given the tasks to be completed.

4. *Allow the employee to participate actively.* When employees participate in goal setting, they are more likely to accept the goals. However, it must be sincere participation. That is, employees must perceive that you are truly seeking their input, not just going through the motions.

5. *Prioritize goals.* When you have more than one goal, it's important to rank the goals in order of importance. The purpose of prioritizing is to encourage you to take action and expend effort on each goal in proportion to its importance.

6. *Rate goals for difficulty and importance.* Goal setting should not encourage people to choose easy goals. Instead, goals should be rated for their difficulty and importance. When goals are rated, individuals can be given credit for trying to reach difficult goals, even if they don't fully achieve them.

7. *Build in feedback mechanisms to assess goal progress.* Feedback lets you know whether your level of effort is sufficient to attain the goal. Set deadlines for when you will evaluate how you are performing. You should review your progress frequently.

8. *Link rewards to goal attainment.* It's natural for you to get discouraged when working toward your goals. Link rewards to the achievement of goals to help encourage you more.

Source: Based on S. P. Robbins and D. A. DeCenzo, *Fundamentals of Management,* 4th ed. (Upper Saddle River, NJ: Prentice Hall, 2004), p. 85.

Assessing Skills

After you've read this chapter, take the following Self-Assessments on your enclosed CD-ROM.

10. What Motivates Me?

11. What Are My Dominant Needs?

12. What Rewards Do I Value Most?

13. What's My View on the Nature of People?

14. What Are My Course Performance Goals?

17. How Sensitive Am I to Equity Differences?

Practising Skills

Tammie Arnold worked her way through college while holding down a part-time job bagging groceries at the Food Town supermarket chain. She liked working in the food industry, and when she graduated she accepted a position with Food Town as a management trainee. Over the next three years, Arnold gained experience in the grocery store industry and in operating a large supermarket. About a year ago, Arnold received a promotion to store manager at one of the chain's locations. One of the things she has liked about Food Town is that it gives store managers a great deal of autonomy in running their stores. The company provides very general guidelines to its managers. Top management is concerned with the bottom line; for the most part, how the store manager gets there is up to him or her. Now that Arnold is finally a store manager, she wants to use goal setting to motivate her employees. She likes the idea that everyone should have clear goals to work toward and then be evaluated against those goals.

The store employs 70 people, although except for the managers most work only 20 to 30 hours per week. There are 6 people reporting to Arnold: an assistant manager; a weekend manager; and grocery, produce, meat, and bakery managers. The only highly skilled jobs belong to the butchers, who have strict training and regulatory guidelines. Other less skilled jobs include cashier, shelf stocker, maintenance employee, and grocery bagger.

Arnold has come to you for advice on how to design a goal-setting program for her store. Specifically describe how she should go about setting goals in her new position. Include examples of goals for the jobs of butcher, cashier, and bakery manager.

Reinforcing Skills

1. Set personal and academic goals you want to achieve by the end of this term. Prioritize and rate them for difficulty.

2. Where do you want to be in five years? Do you have specific five-year goals? Establish three goals you want to achieve in five years. Make sure these goals are specific, challenging, and measurable.

CHAPTER 5
Working in Teams

How do you get teenagers to devote their spare time to learning more about science and technology? Make it a competition and put them on a team.

1 What are teams and groups?

2 Does everyone use teams?

3 Do groups and teams go through stages while they work?

4 How do we create effective teams?

5 How do virtual teams work?

6 Are teams always the answer?

The students at Glenforest Secondary School in Mississauga, Ontario, took part in the ninth annual Canada FIRST Robotics Games in spring 2002.[1] They had eight weeks to design and build a remotely operated robot that would compete with other robots built by secondary school teams across the country. The students wanted to do a better job than they had in 2001. The team's previous robot moved well, but it could not meet the challenge of firing balls at pie plates. The students suspected that to improve their entry, they needed a better team and more coaching from adults. Although they knew little about teamwork, they had support and encouragement from teachers, engineering mentors, and corporate sponsors. What factors could help the students have a better team and build a better robot than their previous attempt?

For teams to excel, a number of conditions need to be met. Effective teams need wise leadership, a variety of

resources, and a way to solve problems. Team members need to be dedicated, and they need to build trust. In this chapter, we examine why teams have become so popular in the workplace, how groups and teams develop, how to create effective teams, how virtual teams work, and when a team is your best option to get work done.

TEAMS VS. GROUPS: WHAT'S THE DIFFERENCE?

There is some debate whether groups and teams are really separate concepts, or whether the terms can be used interchangeably. We think that there is a subtle difference between the terms. A **group** is two or more people with a common relationship. Thus a group could be co-workers or people meeting for lunch or standing at the bus stop. Unlike teams, groups do not necessarily engage in collective work that requires interdependent effort.

A **team** is "a small number of people with complementary skills who are committed to a common purpose, performance goals, and approach for which they hold them-

1 What are teams and groups?

Glenforest Secondary School
www.glenforestlibrary.com

group Two or more people with a common relationship.

team A small number of people who work closely together toward a common objective and are accountable to one another.

selves mutually accountable."[2] Groups become teams when they meet the following conditions:[3]

- Team members share *leadership.*

- Both individuals and the team as a whole share *accountability* for the work of the team.

- The team develops its own *purpose* or *mission.*

- The team works on *problem solving* continuously, rather than just at scheduled meeting times.

- The team's measure of *effectiveness* is the team's outcomes and goals, not individual outcomes and goals.

Thus while not all groups are teams, all teams can be considered groups. Much of what we discuss in this chapter applies equally well to both. We will offer some suggestions on creating effective teams later in the chapter. This chapter's *Point/Counterpoint* on page 177 discusses whether sports teams are good models for helping us understand how teams function in the workplace.

WHY HAVE TEAMS BECOME SO POPULAR?

When Glenforest Secondary School teachers decided that students should enter the Canada FIRST Robotics Games, they could have asked each of the smartest kids in the science class to build their own robots. This is not what the teachers and students chose to do, however. Instead, they created a team. Was this a reasonable way for Glenforest Secondary to proceed?

2 Does everyone use teams?

Pick up almost any business newspaper or magazine today and you will read how teams have become an essential part of the way business is done in companies such as Zellers, Xerox, Sears Canada, General Electric, AT&T, Hewlett-Packard, Motorola, Apple Computer, DaimlerChrysler AG, 3M, Australian Airlines, Johnson & Johnson, and London Life

Many employees are asked to work in teams in order to accomplish their tasks. In a self-managed work team, such as the one from Xerox shown here, members make decisions about how to manage and schedule production, and also monitor the quality of their output.

Insurance Company. A Conference Board of Canada report found that more than 80 percent of its 109 respondents used teams in the workplace.[4] This finding is similar in the United States, where 80 percent of *Fortune* 500 companies have half or more of their employees on teams. As well, 68 percent of small US manufacturers use teams in their production areas.[5] Thus, it is not surprising that Glenforest Secondary also selected a team to build a robot. The extensive use of teams creates the *potential* for an organization to generate greater outputs with no increase in inputs. Notice, however, we said "potential." Creating a team does not lead magically to positive results. As well, merely calling a group a *team* will not automatically increase its performance.

Do teams work? The evidence suggests that teams typically outperform individuals when the tasks being done require multiple skills, judgment, and experience.[6] As organizations have restructured to compete more effectively and efficiently, they have turned to teams as a way to better use employee talents. Management has found that teams are more flexible and responsive to changing events than traditional departments or other forms of permanent groupings. Teams can quickly assemble, deploy, refocus, and disband. Teams also can be more motivational. Recall from the job characteristics model in Chapter 4 that having greater task identity is one way of increasing motivation. Teams allow for greater task identity, with team members working on tasks together.

As we show later in this chapter, successful, or high-performing, teams have certain common characteristics. If management hopes to gain increases in organizational performance through the use of teams, it must ensure that its teams possess these characteristics.

STAGES OF GROUP AND TEAM DEVELOPMENT

Consider when the Glenforest Secondary School students first started working together to build the robot. If they were anything like most ordinary teams, they all might not have known each other, or trusted each other. They might not have known who should be the leader or how to form the plans for what they had to do. Besides building a successful robot, they had to raise $16 000 to take part in the Canada FIRST Robotics Games. They also had several deadlines to meet. To build a successful team that would achieve their goals, the students would have had to go through several stages. So what stages do teams go through as they develop?

While we make a distinction between groups and teams, some of the stages of development they go through are similar. In this section, we discuss two models of group development. The five-stage model describes the standardized sequence of stages groups pass through. The recently discovered punctuated-equilibrium model describes the pattern of development specific to temporary groups with deadlines. These models apply as readily to teams.

3 Do groups and teams go through stages while they work?

The Five-Stage Model

From the mid-1960s, it was believed that groups passed through a standard sequence of five stages.[7] As shown in Exhibit 5-1 on page 154, these five stages have been labelled *forming, storming, norming, performing,* and *adjourning.* Although we now know that not all groups pass through these stages in a linear fashion, the five-stage model of group development can still help in addressing your anxieties about working in groups and teams. The model shows how individuals move from being independent to working interdependently with group members.

- *Stage I: Forming.* Think about the first time you met with a new group that had been put together to accomplish a task. Do you remember how some people seemed silent and others felt confused about the task you were to accomplish? Those feelings arise during the first stage of group development, know as

EXHIBIT 5-1 Stages of Group Development and Accompanying Issues

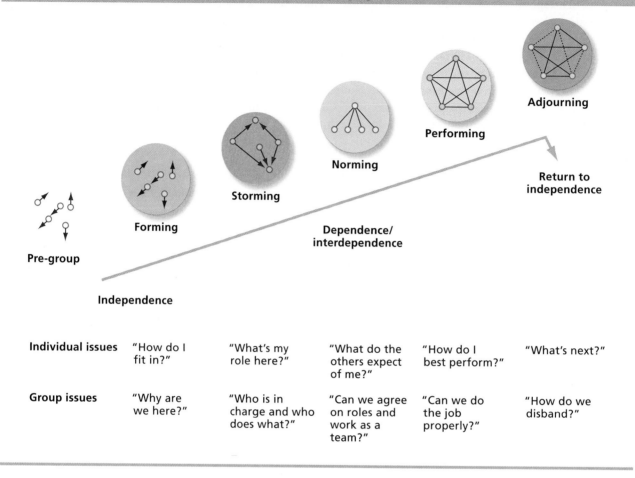

Individual issues	"How do I fit in?"	"What's my role here?"	"What do the others expect of me?"	"How do I best perform?"	"What's next?"
Group issues	"Why are we here?"	"Who is in charge and who does what?"	"Can we agree on roles and work as a team?"	"Can we do the job properly?"	"How do we disband?"

---

forming The first stage in group development, characterized by much uncertainty.

storming The second stage in group development, characterized by intragroup conflict.

norms Acceptable standards of behaviour within a group that are shared by the group's members.

forming. **Forming** is characterized by a great deal of uncertainty about the group's purpose, structure, and leadership. Members are "testing the waters" to determine what types of behaviour are acceptable. This stage is complete when members have begun to think of themselves as part of a group.

- *Stage II: Storming.* Do you remember how some people in your group just didn't seem to get along, and sometimes power struggles even emerged? These reactions are typical of the **storming** stage, which is one of intragroup conflict. Members accept the existence of the group, but resist the constraints that the group imposes on individuality. Furthermore, there is conflict over who will control the group. When this stage is complete, a relatively clear hierarchy of leadership will emerge within the group.

  Some groups never really emerge from the storming stage, or they move back and forth through storming and the other stages. A group that remains forever planted in the storming stage may have less ability to complete the task because of all the interpersonal problems.

- *Stage III: Norming.* Many groups resolve the interpersonal conflict and reach the third stage, in which close relationships develop and the group demonstrates cohesiveness. There is now a strong sense of group identity and camaraderie. The group develops **norms**, acceptable standards of behaviour that are shared by the group's members. All groups have established norms that tell members what they ought and ought not to do under certain circumstances. When agreed to and accepted by the group, norms act as a means of influencing the behaviour of group members with a minimum of external controls. This **norming** stage is complete when the group structure solidifies, and the group has assimilated a common set of expectations about what defines correct member behaviour.

- *Stage IV: Performing.* Next, and you may have noticed this in some of your own group interactions, some groups just seem to come together well and start to do their work. This fourth stage, when significant task progress is being made, is called **performing**. The structure at this point is fully functional and accepted. Group energy has moved from getting to know and understand each other to performing the task at hand. In this chapter's opening vignette, when Glenforest Secondary School raced its robot in the Canada FIRST Robotics Games, it was performing.

- *Stage V: Adjourning.* For permanent work groups, performing is the last stage in their development. However, for temporary committees, teams, task forces, and similar groups that have a limited task to perform, there is an **adjourning** stage. In this stage, the group prepares to split up. High task performance is no longer the group's top priority. Instead, attention is directed toward wrapping up activities. Group members' responses vary at this stage. Some members are upbeat, basking in the group's accomplishments. Others may be depressed over the loss of camaraderie and friendships gained during the work group's life.

norming The third stage in group development, characterized by close relationships and cohesiveness.

performing The fourth stage in group development, when the group is fully functional.

adjourning The final stage in group development for temporary groups, where attention is directed toward wrapping up activities rather than task performance.

Putting the Five-Stage Model into Perspective

Many interpreters of the five-stage model have assumed that a group becomes more effective as it progresses through the first four stages. While that is usually true, what makes a group effective is more complex than this model acknowledges. Under some conditions, high levels of conflict lead to high group performance, as long as the conflict is directed toward the task and not toward group members. So we might expect to find situations in which groups in Stage II outperform those in Stages III or IV. Similarly, groups do not always proceed clearly from one stage to the next. Sometimes, in fact, several stages go on simultaneously, as when groups are storming and performing at the same time. Groups even occasionally move backwards to previous stages. Therefore, you should not assume that all groups follow the five-stage process precisely or that Stage IV is always the most preferable.

The five-stage model ignores organizational context.[8] For instance, a study of a cockpit crew in an airliner found that, within 10 minutes, three strangers assigned to fly together for the first time had become a high-performing group. How could a group come together so quickly? The answer lies in the strong organizational context surrounding the tasks of the cockpit crew. This context provided the rules, task definitions, information, and resources needed for the group to perform. They didn't need to develop plans, assign roles, determine and allocate resources, resolve conflicts, and set norms the way the five-stage model predicts.

Within the workplace, some group behaviour takes place within a strong organizational context, and the five-stage development model might have limited applicability for those groups. However, there are a variety of situations in the workplace in which groups are assigned to tasks, and the individuals do not know each other. They must therefore work out interpersonal differences at the same time that they work through the assigned tasks.

EXHIBIT 5-2   **The Punctuated-Equilibrium Model**

The Punctuated-Equilibrium Model

Temporary groups with deadlines don't seem to follow the previous model. Studies indicate that temporary groups with deadlines have their own unique sequence of action (or inaction):[9]

- The first meeting sets the group's direction.

- The first phase of group activity is one of inertia.

- A transition takes place at the end of the first phase, which occurs exactly when the group has used up half its allotted time.

- The transition initiates major changes.

- A second phase of inertia follows the transition.

- The group's last meeting is characterized by high levels of productive activity.

✳ *Ever wonder what causes flurries of activity in groups?*

This pattern is called the *punctuated-equilibrium model*, developed by Professor Connie Gersick, a Visiting Scholar at the Yale University School of Management, and is shown in Exhibit 5-2.[10] It is important for you to understand these shifts in group behaviour. If you are ever in a group that is not working well, knowing about the shifts could help you think of ways to make the group move to a more productive phase.

Phase 1

As a group member and possibly a group leader, you need to recognize that the first meeting sets the group's direction. A framework of behavioural patterns and assumptions through which the group will approach its project emerges in this first meeting. These lasting patterns can appear as early as the first few seconds of the group's life.

Once set, the group's direction becomes accepted and is unlikely to be re-examined throughout the first half of the group's life. This is a period of inertia—that is, the group tends to stand still or become locked into a fixed course of action. Even if it gains new insights that challenge initial patterns and assumptions, the group does not act on these new insights in Phase 1. You may recognize that in some groups, during the early period of trying to get things accomplished, no one really did his or her assigned tasks. You may also recognize this phase as one where everyone carries out the tasks, but not in a very coordinated fashion. Thus, the group is performing at a relatively low level. This does not necessarily mean that it is doing nothing at all, however.

Phase 2

At some point, the group moves out of the inertia stage and recognizes that work needs to get completed. One of the more interesting discoveries made in these studies was that each group experienced its transition at the same point in its calendar—precisely halfway between its first meeting and its official deadline. The similarity occurred despite the fact that some groups spent as little as an hour on their projects while others spent six months. It was as if the groups universally experienced a mid-life crisis at this point. The midpoint appears to work like an alarm clock, heightening members' awareness that their time is limited and that they need to "get moving." When you work on your next group project, you might want to examine when your group starts to "get moving."

This transition ends Phase 1 and is characterized by a concentrated burst of changes, dropping of old patterns, and adoption of new perspectives. The transition sets a revised direction for Phase 2, which is a new equilibrium or period of inertia. In this phase, the group executes plans created during the transition period. The group's last meeting is characterized by a final burst of activity to finish its work. There have been a number of studies that support the basic premise of punctuated equilibrium, though not all of them found that the transition in the group occurred exactly at the midpoint.[11]

Applying the Punctuated-Equilibrium Model

Let's use this model to describe some of your experiences with student teams created for doing group term projects. At the first meeting, a basic timetable is established. Members size up one another. They agree they have nine weeks to complete their projects. The instructor's requirements are discussed and debated. From that point, the group meets regularly to carry out its activities. About four or five weeks into the project, however, problems are confronted. Criticism begins to be taken seriously. Discussion becomes more open. The group reassesses where it has been and aggressively moves to make necessary changes. If the right changes are made, the next four or five weeks find the group developing a first-rate project. The group's last meeting, which will probably occur just before the project is due, lasts longer than the others. In it, all final issues are discussed and details resolved.

In summary, the punctuated-equilibrium model characterizes deadline-oriented groups and teams as exhibiting long periods of inertia interspersed with brief revolutionary changes triggered primarily by members' awareness of time and deadlines. To use the terminology of the five-stage model, the group begins by combining the *forming* and *norming* stages, then goes through a period of *low performing*, followed by *storming*, then a period of *high performing*, and, finally, *adjourning*.

Several researchers have suggested that the five-stage and punctuated-equilibrium models are at odds with each other.[12] However, it makes more sense to view the models as complementary: The five-stage model considers the interpersonal process of the group, while the punctuated-equilibrium model considers the time challenges that the group faces.[13] Group members and managers may want to use the implications of the punctuated-equilibrium model to either shorten the deadlines for tasks (so that less time is wasted getting to the midpoint of the time period) or to build in more goals and rewards for the first half of the time period (to help overcome the inertia that occurs during that phase).

CREATING EFFECTIVE TEAMS

Beatrice Sze, Glenforest Secondary School's robotics team co-captain, gave her teammates a sense of responsibility and ownership over their work. For example, when a team member came to her with questions about what to do next, she would say encouragingly, "Use your brain. You can figure this out. You know how to do this."

The students at Glenforest Secondary also had to be resourceful. One team member's parents provided the family basement for a team gathering place. That enabled the students to get extra parts from the family's snowblower and dehumidifier. Sometimes they worked so late into the evening that they had sleepovers on the basement floor, huddled in sleeping bags. They also got a mentor—a computer and electrical engineer with Bell Mobility—who tried to guide the students in the right direction without telling them what to do. What other factors might have contributed to the effectiveness of Glenforest Secondary's robotics team?

4 How do we create effective teams?

When we consider team effectiveness, we refer to such objective measures as the team's productivity, managers' ratings of the team's performance, and aggregate measures of member satisfaction. Some of the considerations necessary to create effective teams are outlined next. However, we are also interested in team process. Exhibit 5-3 provides a checklist of the characteristics of an effective team.

There is no shortage of efforts that try to identify the factors that lead to team effectiveness.[14] However, studies have taken what was once a "veritable laundry list of characteristics"[15] and organized them into a relatively focused model with four general categories (summarized in Exhibit 5-4 on page 159):[16]

- Resources and other contextual influences that make teams effective

- The team's composition

EXHIBIT 5-3	**Characteristics of an Effective Team**
1. **Clear purpose**	The vision, mission, goal, or task of the team has been defined and is now accepted by everyone. There is an action plan.
2. **Informality**	The climate tends to be informal, comfortable, and relaxed. There are no obvious tensions or signs of boredom.
3. **Participation**	There is much discussion, and everyone is encouraged to participate.
4. **Listening**	The members use effective listening techniques such as questioning, paraphrasing, and summarizing to get out ideas.
5. **Civilized disagreement**	There is disagreement, but the team is comfortable with this and shows no signs of avoiding, smoothing over, or suppressing conflict.
6. **Consensus decisions**	For important decisions, the goal is substantial but not necessarily unanimous agreement through open discussion of everyone's ideas, avoidance of formal voting, or easy compromises.
7. **Open communication**	Team members feel free to express their feelings on the tasks as well as on the group's operation. There are few hidden agendas. Communication takes place outside meetings.
8. **Clear rules and work assignments**	There are clear expectations about the roles played by each team member. When action is taken, clear assignments are made, accepted, and carried out. Work is distributed among team members.
9. **Shared leadership**	While the team has a formal leader, leadership functions shift from time to time depending on the circumstances, the needs of the group, and the skills of the members. The formal leader models the appropriate behaviour and helps establish positive norms.
10. **External relations**	The team spends time developing key outside relationships, mobilizing resources, and building credibility with important players in other parts of the organization.
11. **Style diversity**	The team has a broad spectrum of team-player types including members who emphasize attention to task, goal setting, focus on process, and questions about how the team is functioning.
12. **Self-assessment**	Periodically, the team stops to examine how well it is functioning and what may be interfering with its effectiveness.

Source: G. M. Parker, *Team Players and Teamwork: The New Competitive Business Strategy* (San Francisco: Jossey-Bass, 1990), table 2, p. 33.
Copyright © 1990 by Jossey-Bass, Inc., Publishers. Reprinted by permission of John Wiley & Sons, Inc.

EXHIBIT 5-4   A Model of Team Effectiveness

Context
- Adequate resources
- Leadership and structure
- Climate of trust
- Performance evaluation and rewards

Composition
- Skills
- Personality
- Roles
- Diversity
- Size
- Members' flexibility
- Members' preference for teamwork

Team effectiveness

Work design
- Autonomy
- Skill variety
- Task identity
- Task significance

Process
- Common purpose
- Specific goals
- Team efficacy
- Managed level of conflict
- Accountability

- Work design

- Process variables (those things that go on in the team that influence how effective the team is)

Becoming a team player is not easy, as *OB in the Street* demonstrates.

OB IN THE STREET

Top Skeleton Racer Finds Teamwork a Real Challenge

Is being a team player all that tough?   Jeff Pain spent much of the 2000s so far try-ing his best not to be a team player.[17] Before the 2006 Olympic Winter Games, Pain was ranked the top skeleton racer in Canada.

Much of Pain's negativity toward teamwork was directed at team member Duff Gibson. The two have been intense rivals for over five years.

"When Duff started skeleton [in 1999], I had a difficult time with my team dynam-ics because I felt that I knew a lot more than the people I was sliding with," says Pain. "I didn't want to share information with them and I carried that mistaken belief right up to last year [2004]. That was probably my and Duff's worst year."[18]

In summer 2004, Pain, Gibson, and fellow team member Paul Boehm decided to work together to share information about the tracks they were competing on, and then tried to help each other out.

Pain and Gibson improved their times and reached the highest level in interna-tional standings. Pain admits that learning how to be more of a team player has helped him improve in a sport that he was thinking of quitting because of his unhap-piness with other team members. "I really insulated myself, and that didn't create a good environment for me or the team," Pain says.[19] At the 2006 Olympics, the two teammates wound up taking the top spots in skeleton racing: Gibson won gold, and Pain won silver.

At Montreal-based PEAK Financial Group, CEO Robert Frances (left) lets his teams do their own hiring. Everyone who might work with the potential hire, including subordinates, is invited to sit in on the interview. "If a team is to work properly as a team, then they should have a say in who the other team members are," says Frances. His philosophy is that if those involved don't think they will get along at the start, it's better to know this before they are hired. At right, we see a couple of PEAK's client services employees getting ready for the RRSP season.

PEAK Financial Group
www.peakgroup.com

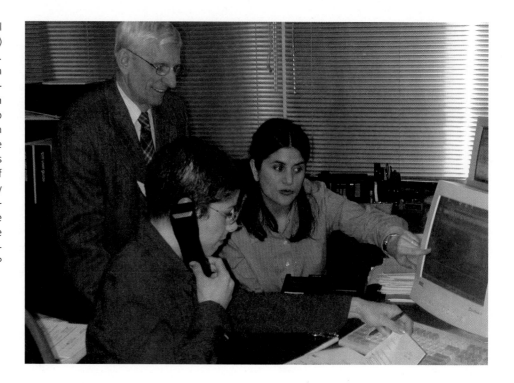

Keep in mind two caveats as you review the issues that lead to effective teams:

- First, teams differ in form and structure. Since the model we present attempts to generalize across all varieties of teams, you need to be careful not to rigidly apply the model's predictions to all teams.[20] The model should be used as a guide, not as an inflexible prescription.

- Second, the model assumes that it's already been determined that teamwork is preferable over individual work. Creating "effective" teams in situations in which individuals can do the job better is equivalent to solving the wrong problem perfectly.

OB in Action—Harming Your Team on page 161 presents actions that can make a team ineffective. You might want to evaluate your own team experiences against this checklist to give you some idea of how well your team is functioning or to understand what might be causing problems for your team. Then consider the factors that lead to more effective teams below. For an applied look at the process of building an effective team, see the *Working With Others Exercise* on pages 179–180, which asks you to build a paper tower with teammates and then analyze how the team performed.

Context

Teams can require a great deal of maintenance to function properly. They need management support as well as an organizational structure that supports teamwork. The four contextual factors that appear to be most significantly related to team performance are adequate resources, effective leadership, a climate of trust, and a performance evaluation and reward system that reflects team contributions. Hamilton, Ontario-based Dofasco is a clear example of getting the context right for team performance. Dofasco started using teams in the early 1990s, putting almost 7000 employees through team-building exercises. Today, multidisciplinary teams are given improvement goals; the teams assume responsibility for developing plans to reach the goals. To a large extent, the teams are self-managed. "The supervisor became less of an ass-kicker and more of a resource person," explained former CEO John Mayberry.[21] Pay is tied partly to how well Dofasco

Dofasco
www.dofasco.ca

does each year, which helps motivate employees to work with their teams, rather than as individuals.

Adequate Resources

All work teams rely on resources outside the team to sustain them. A scarcity of resources directly reduces the ability of a team to perform its job effectively. As one set of researchers concluded, after looking at 13 factors potentially related to team performance, "perhaps one of the most important characteristics of an effective work group is the support the group receives from the organization."[22] This includes technology, adequate staffing, administrative assistance, encouragement, and timely information.

Teams must receive the necessary support from management and the larger organization if they are going to succeed in achieving their goals. You may recall from the opening vignette that one of the reasons for the Glenforest Secondary School team's failure in 2001 was that it didn't have the kind of coaching it needed to build a great robot. For the 2002 competition, the team found a mentor and also created a workshop at one of the team member's homes.

Leadership and Structure

Leadership plays a crucial role in the development and success of teams. Professor Richard Hackman of Harvard University, who is the leading expert on teams, suggests that the role of team leader involves the following:[23]

- Creating a real team rather than a team in name only

- Setting a clear and meaningful direction for the team's work

- Making sure that the team structure will support its working effectively

- Ensuring that the team operates within a supportive organizational context

- Providing expert coaching

There are some practical problems that must be resolved when a team first starts working together. Team members must agree on who is to do what and ensure that all members contribute equally in sharing the workload. The team also needs to determine how schedules will be set, what skills need to be developed, how the team will resolve conflicts, and how the team will make and modify decisions. Agreeing on the specifics of work and how they fit together to integrate individual skills requires team leadership and structure. This, incidentally, can be provided directly by management or by the team members themselves. In the case of the Glenforest Secondary School students in this chapter's vignette, the team was led by two student co-captains. The adult advisers did not try to tell the students what to do.

On traditionally managed teams, we find that two factors seem to be important in influencing team performance—the leader's expectations and his or her mood. Leaders who expect good things from their team are more likely to get them! For instance, military platoons under leaders who held high expectations performed significantly better in training than platoons whose leaders did not set expectations.[24] Additionally, studies have found that leaders who exhibit positive moods get better team performance and lower turnover.[25] The *Learning About Yourself Exercise* on pages 178–179 will help you evaluate how suited you are to building and leading a team.

OB IN ACTION

Harming Your Team

→ **Refuse to share** issues and concerns. Team members refuse to share information and engage in silence, avoidance, and meetings behind closed doors where not all members are included.

→ **Depend** too much **on the leader**. Members rely too much on the leader and do not carry out their responsibilities.

→ **Fail to follow through** on decisions. Teams do not take action after decision making, showing that the needs of the team have low priority, or members are not committed to the decisions that were made.

→ **Hide conflict.** Team members do not reveal that they have a difference of opinion and this causes tension.

→ **Fail at conflict resolution.** Infighting, put-downs, and attempts to hurt other members damage the team.

→ **Form subgroups.** The team breaks up into smaller groups that put their needs ahead of the team as a whole.

Source: Based on W. G. Dyer, R. H. Daines, and W. C. Giauque, *The Challenge of Management* (New York: Harcourt Brace Jovanovich, 1990), p. 343.

OB IN ACTION

Building Trust

The following actions, in order of importance, help build one's trustworthiness.

→ **Integrity**—built through **honesty** and **truthfulness**.

→ **Competence**—demonstrated by technical and interpersonal **knowledge** and **skills**.

→ **Consistency**—shown by **reliability, predictability**, and **good judgment** in handling situations.

→ **Loyalty**—one's willingness to **protect** and **stand up** for another person.

→ **Openness**—one's willingness to **share ideas** and **information** freely.

Source: P. L. Schindler and C. C. Thomas, "The Structure of Interpersonal Trust in the Workplace," *Psychological Reports*, October 1993, pp. 563–573.

Recent research suggests that women may make better team leaders than men. "The more women participating equally in a project, the better the outcome," suggests Professor Jennifer Berdahl, of the Joseph L. Rotman School of Management at the University of Toronto.[26] Berdahl's research, which looked at 169 students enrolled in her organizational behaviour courses, found that in predominantly female teams, women shared leadership roles and were more egalitarian in how they worked. Male-led teams, whether they were predominantly male groups or mixed-gender groups, received poorer grades on their projects than teams where women shared leadership roles.[27]

Sometimes teams need coaches more than they need leaders. Though workplace teams often report that they receive little coaching compared with leadership,[28] productivity-related coaching may help teams perform more effectively. In particular, coaching may be best at three particular stages in the team's history: "at the beginning for effort-related (motivational) interventions, near the midpoint for strategy-related (consultative) interventions, and at the end of a task cycle for (educational) interventions that address knowledge and skill."[29]

Teams do not always need a leader. For instance, the evidence indicates that self-managed work teams often perform better than teams with formally appointed leaders.[30] Leaders can also obstruct high performance when they interfere with self-managed teams.[31] On self-managed teams, team members absorb many of the duties typically assumed by managers.

Climate of Trust

Members of effective teams trust each other. For team members to do this, they must feel that the team is capable of getting the task done and they must believe that "the team will not harm the individual or his or her interests."[32] Interpersonal trust among team members facilitates cooperation, reduces the need to monitor one another's behaviour, and bonds members around the belief that others on the team won't take advantage of them. Team members are more likely to take risks and expose vulnerabilities when they believe they can trust others on their team. *OB in Action—Building Trust* shows the dimensions that underlie the concept of trust.

Team members must also trust their leaders.[33] Trust in leadership is important in that it allows the team to be willing to accept and commit to their leader's goals and decisions.

Performance Evaluation and Rewards

> * *Should individuals be paid for their "teamwork" or their individual performance?*

How do you get team members to be both individually and jointly accountable? The traditional individually oriented evaluation must be modified to reflect team performance.[34] Individual performance evaluations, fixed hourly wages, individual incentives, and the like are not consistent with the development of high-performance teams. So in addition to evaluating and rewarding employees for their individual contributions, management should consider group-based appraisals, profit sharing, gainsharing, small-group incentives, and other system modifications that will reinforce team effort and commitment. Ignoring these factors may affect the level of trust that develops in the team.[35]

One additional consideration when deciding whether and how to reward team members is the effect of pay dispersion on team performance. Research by Nancy Langton, your Vancouver-based author, shows that when there is a large discrepancy in wages among group members, collaboration is lowered.[36] A study of baseball players' salaries also found that teams where players were paid more similarly often outperformed teams with highly paid "stars" and lowly paid "scrubs."[37]

Composition

> ✳ Why do some teams seem to get along better than others?

This category includes variables that relate to how teams should be staffed. In this section, we address the skills, personality, and roles of team members, the diversity and size of the team, member flexibility, and members' preference for teamwork. This chapter's *CBC Video Case Incident* demonstrates how putting together a good team can lead to a very successful company.

CBC ◉

Earth Buddies

Skills

To perform effectively, a team requires three different types of skills:

1. It needs people with *technical expertise*.

2. It needs people with the *problem-solving* and *decision-making skills* to be able to identify problems, generate alternatives, evaluate those alternatives, and make competent choices.

3. It needs people with good listening, feedback, conflict resolution, and other *interpersonal skills*.[38]

No team can achieve its performance potential without developing all three types of skills. The right mix is crucial. Too much of one at the expense of others will result in lower team performance. But teams don't need to have all the complementary skills in place at the beginning. It's not uncommon for one or more members to take responsibility to learn the skills in which the group is deficient, thereby allowing the team to reach its full potential.

Personality

Teams have different needs, and people should be selected for the team on the basis of their personalities and preferences, as well as the team's needs for diversity and specific roles. We demonstrated in Chapter 2 that personality has a significant influence on individual employee behaviour. Personality also influences team behaviour. Many of the dimensions identified in the Big Five model of personality have been shown to be relevant to team effectiveness. Specifically, teams that rate higher in mean levels of extraversion, agreeableness, conscientiousness, and emotional stability tend to receive higher managerial ratings for team performance.[39]

Very interestingly, the evidence indicates that the variance in personality characteristics may be more important than the mean.[40] So, for example, although higher mean levels of conscientiousness on a team are desirable, mixing both conscientious and not-so-conscientious members tends to lower performance. Including just one person who is low on agreeableness, conscientiousness, or extraversion can result in strained internal processes and decreased overall performance.[41]

Being a gracious team member can make a difference. When Atlanta-based CNN decided to revise its morning program *American Morning* in summer 2005, CNN/US President Jonathan Klein decided to replace co-anchor Bill Hemmer, who had held the anchor position for several years. In explaining the decision, Klein noted that he wanted a male anchor who would work with female co-anchor Soledad O'Brien and help her look good too, rather than trying to take all the attention himself.

Roles

role   A set of expected behaviours of a person in a given position in a social unit.

task-oriented roles   Roles performed by group members to ensure that the tasks of the group are carried out.

maintenance roles   Roles performed by group members to maintain good relations within the group.

In groups, each individual fills a particular **role**. By this term, we mean a set of expected behaviour patterns of a person in a given position in a social unit. Within almost any group, two sets of role relationships need to be considered: task-oriented roles and maintenance roles. **Task-oriented roles** are performed by group members to ensure that the tasks of the group are accomplished. These roles include initiators, information seekers, information providers, elaborators, summarizers, and consensus makers. **Maintenance roles** are carried out to ensure that group members maintain good relations. These roles include harmonizers, compromisers, gatekeepers, and encouragers. You may recall from this chapter's vignette that Beatrice Sze was an encourager—helping team members achieve their best.

Effective teams maintain some balance between task orientation and maintenance of relations. Exhibit 5-5 on page 165 identifies a number of task-oriented and maintenance behaviours in the key roles that you might find in a team.

On many teams, there are individuals who will be flexible enough to play multiple roles and/or complete each other's tasks. This is an obvious plus to a team because it greatly improves its adaptability and makes it less reliant on any single member.[42] Selecting members who themselves value flexibility, and then cross-training them to be able to do one another's jobs, should lead to higher team performance over time.

individual roles   Roles performed by group members that are not productive for keeping the team on task.

role expectations   How others believe a person should act in a given situation.

role conflict   A situation in which an individual finds that complying with one role requirement may make it more difficult to comply with another.

Occasionally within teams, you will see people take on **individual roles** that are not productive for keeping the team on task. When this happens, the individual is demonstrating more concern for himself or herself than the team as a whole.

Most roles, whether in the workplace or in our personal lives, are governed by **role expectations**, that is, how others believe a person should act in a given situation. **Role conflict** exists when an individual finds that complying with one role requirement may make it more difficult to comply with another.[43] At the extreme, it can include situations in which two or more role expectations are mutually contradictory! *Case Incident—Role Conflict Among Telephone Service Employees* on the CD-ROM that accompanies this textbook looks at how role conflict affects one's work life.

Diversity

group diversity   The heterogeneous mix of individuals within a group.

Group diversity refers to the presence of a heterogeneous mix of individuals within a group.[44] Individuals can be different not only in functional characteristics (jobs, positions, expertise, or work experiences) but also in demographic or cultural characteristics (age, race, sex, and citizenship).

RESEARCH FINDINGS   Team Diversity

Managing diversity on teams is a balancing act (see Exhibit 5-6 on page 166).[45] On the one hand, a number of researchers have suggested that diversity brings a greater number of ideas, perspectives, knowledge, and skills to the group, which can be used to perform at a higher level.[46] On the other hand, researchers have suggested that diversity can lead people to recall stereotypes and therefore bring bias into their evaluations of people who are different from them.[47] Diversity can thus make it more difficult to unify the team and reach agreements.[48] We consider some of the evidence to help us resolve these opposing views.

* *Is building a team just from people who are friends a good idea?*

In a study examining the effectiveness of teams of strangers and teams of friends on bargaining, researchers found that teams of strangers gained greater profit than teams of friends, when teams reported to a supervisor.[49] However, teams of friends were more cohesive than teams of strangers. Another study of 60 teams found that in effective teams, about 50 percent of the individuals considered themselves friends, which underscores the importance of teams'

EXHIBIT 5-5 Roles Required for Effective Team Functioning

	Function	Description	Example
Roles that build task accomplishment	Initiating	Stating the goal or problem, making proposals about how to work on it, setting time limits.	"Let's set up an agenda for discussing each of the problems we have to consider."
	Seeking information and opinions	Asking group members for specific factual information related to the task or problem, or for their opinions about it.	"What do you think would be the best approach to this, Jack?"
	Providing information and opinions	Sharing information or opinions related to the task or problems.	"I worked on a similar problem last year and found . . ."
	Clarifying	Helping one another understand ideas and suggestions that come up in the group.	"What you mean, Sue, is that we could . . . ?"
	Elaborating	Building on one another's ideas and suggestions.	"Building on Don's idea, I think we could . . ."
	Summarizing	Reviewing the points covered by the group and the different ideas stated so that decisions can be based on full information.	Appointing a recorder to take notes on a blackboard.
	Consensus testing	Providing periodic testing on whether the group is nearing a decision or needs to continue discussion.	"Is the group ready to decide about this?"
Roles that build and maintain a team	Harmonizing	Mediating conflict among other members, reconciling disagreements, relieving tensions.	"Don, I don't think you and Sue really see the question that differently."
	Compromising	Admitting error at times of group conflict.	"Well, I'd be willing to change if you provided some help on . . ."
	Gatekeeping	Making sure all members have a chance to express their ideas and feelings and preventing members from being interrupted.	"Sue, we haven't heard from you on this issue."
	Encouraging	Helping a group member make his or her point. Establishing a climate of acceptance in the group.	"I think what you started to say is important, Jack. Please continue."

Source: "Team Processes," in *Managing for the Future,* ed. D. Ancona, T. Kochan, M. Scully, J. Van Maanen, and D. E. Westney (Cincinnati, OH: South-Western College Publishing, 1996), p. 9.

developing friendships.[50] However, the researchers also found that in teams that reported almost 100 percent friendship, performance was much lower. These groups tended to isolate themselves from others and not seek outside influences. The research on friendships in teams suggests that teams of friends may be less concerned with productivity and more concerned with maintaining their relationship than are teams of strangers.

EXHIBIT 5-6	Advantages and Disadvantages of Diversity
Advantages	**Disadvantages**
Multiple perspectives	Ambiguity
Greater openness to new ideas	Complexity
Multiple interpretations	Confusion
Increased creativity	Miscommunication
Increased flexibility	Difficulty in reaching a single agreement
Increased problem-solving skills	Difficulty in agreeing on specific actions

Source: Adapted from N. J. Adler, *International Dimensions of Organizational Behavior,* 4th ed., p. 109. Copyright © 2002. By permission of South-Western College Publishing, a division of International Thomson Publishing, Cincinnati, OH 45227.

Recent studies have examined the effect of heterogeneous values on performance and suggest that value differences may have a greater influence than functional, demographic, or cultural differences.[51] Professor Margaret Neale of Stanford University's Graduate School of Business examined the impact of three types of diversity on group performance: informational, demographic, and value-goal diversity.[52] She found that these different forms of diversity generate different types of conflict. Informational diversity is associated with constructive conflict, with team members debating about the best course of action. Neale considers this positive conflict. Demographic diversity can result in interpersonal conflict, which, if left unresolved, can destroy the group. Groups that have value-goal diversity may face the most damage from the diversity. When team members do not agree on values and goals, it is hard for them to function. However, if a team works through differences to reach consensus on values and goals, team members then know one another's intentions.

Overall, studies suggest that the strongest case for diversity on work teams can be made when these teams are engaged in problem-solving and decision-making tasks.[53] Heterogeneous teams may have qualities that lead to creative or unique solutions.[54] The lack of a common perspective also means diverse teams usually spend more time discussing issues, which decreases the possibility that a weak alternative will be chosen. Although diverse groups have more difficulty working together and solving problems, this goes away with time as the members come to know one another. A recent study supports this idea; teams with high expertise diversity were found to perform better when team members were committed to the team than when team members showed low commitment.[55]

Recent research suggests that when team members share a common belief that diversity will affect their performance positively, they set the foundation for the team to manage the diversity in a positive way. Specifically, if team members set out early to try to learn about one another in order to understand and make the most of their differences, this will have a positive effect on the team.[56] Laurie Milton, at the Haskayne School of Business at the University of Calgary, and several co-authors found that even 10 minutes spent sharing personal information when group members first started working together lowered group conflict and improved creative performance.[57] When group members didn't share personal information at the beginning of their work, they were less likely to do so later.

The research findings, taken as a whole, suggest that diversity can bring added benefits to the team, but to do so, team members must have some common values, and they need to be willing to share information about themselves early on. Thus we can expect that diversity begins to provide extra value to the team once team members get to know one another and the team becomes more cohesive. *Focus on Diversity* on page 167 examines the impact of diversity on learning to work together in teams.

FOCUS ON **DIVERSITY**

Questioning the Impact of Diversity

Do diverse teams really have more difficulty learning how to work together? The late Professor Barbara Kelsey of Ryerson University studied groups of Caucasian and Chinese men living in Canada to see how being a token ethnic member in a group (the only Chinese or the only Caucasian) would affect participation and influence levels in groups.[58] Some groups worked face to face, others by computer only.

What Kelsey found in the face-to-face groups was that Caucasian males, whether tokens or dominants in their groups, had higher participation levels on average than Chinese males. However, in face-to-face groups dominated by Chinese males, the Chinese males also had relatively high participation rates. Only the token Chinese males scored low in participation or influence on their groups.

In the computer-only groups, the ethnicity of group members could be determined in some groups, while for others it could not. In those groups where the ethnicity of team members was unknown, there were no differences in the participation rates of Chinese and Caucasian men.

Kelsey's research suggests that participation and influence may be less a cultural issue, and more related to how individuals respond to visible differences when interacting with diverse team members.

Size

Generally speaking, the most effective teams have fewer than 10 members. And experts suggest using the smallest number of people who can do the task. Unfortunately, there is a tendency for managers to make teams too large. While a minimum of four or five members may be necessary to develop a diversity of views and skills, managers seem to seriously underestimate how coordination problems can dramatically increase as team members are added. When teams have excess members, cohesiveness and mutual accountability decline, social loafing increases, and more and more people do less talking compared to others. So in designing effective teams, managers should try to keep the number of members at less than 10. If a work unit is larger and you want a team effort, consider breaking the unit into subteams. Uneven numbers in teams may help build in a mechanism to break ties and resolve conflicts, while an even number of team members may foster the need to create more consensus.

Separated workstations, such as these at a Hong Kong toy factory, reduce work group interactions.

Size and Social Loafing   One of the most important findings related to the size of a team has been labelled **social loafing**. Social loafing is the tendency of individuals to expend less effort when working collectively than when working individually.[59] It directly challenges the logic that the productivity of the team as a whole should at least equal the sum of the productivity of each individual in that team.

✳ *Why don't some team members pull their weight?*

What causes this social loafing effect? It may be due to a belief that others in the team are not carrying their fair share. If you view others as lazy or inept, you can re-establish equity by reducing your effort. Another explanation is the dispersion of responsibility. Because the results of the team cannot be attributed to any single person, the relationship between an individual's input and the team's output is clouded. In such situations, individuals may be tempted to become "free riders" and coast on the team's efforts. In other words, there will be a reduction in efficiency when individuals believe that their contribution cannot be measured. To reduce social loafing, teams should not be larger than necessary, and individuals should be held accountable for their actions.

Member Flexibility

Teams made up of flexible individuals have members who can complete each other's tasks. This is an obvious plus to a team because it greatly improves its adaptability and makes it less reliant on any single member.[60] So selecting members who themselves value flexibility, then cross-training them to be able to do each other's jobs, should lead to higher team performance over time.

Members' Preference for Teamwork

Not every employee is a team player. Given the option, many employees will "select themselves out" of team participation. When people who would prefer to work alone are required to team up, there is a direct threat to the team's morale.[61] This suggests that, when selecting team members, individual preferences should be considered, as well as abilities, personalities, and skills. High-performing teams are likely to be composed of people who prefer working as part of a team.

Work Design

Effective teams need to work together and take collective responsibility to complete significant tasks. They must be more than a "team-in-name-only."[62] The work design category includes variables such as freedom and autonomy, the opportunity to use a variety of skills and talents, the ability to complete a whole and identifiable task or product, and the participation in a task or project that has a substantial impact on others. The evidence indicates that these characteristics enhance member motivation and increase team effectiveness.[63] These work design characteristics motivate teams because they increase members' sense of responsibility for and ownership of the work, and because they make the work more interesting to perform.[64] These recommendations are consistent with the job characteristics model we presented in Chapter 4.

Process

Process variables make up the final component of team effectiveness. The process category includes member commitment to a common purpose; establishment of specific goals; team efficacy; a managed level of conflict; and a system of accountability.

Common Purpose

Effective teams have a common and meaningful purpose that provides direction, momentum, and commitment for members.[65] This purpose is a vision. It's broader than specific goals.

Members of successful teams put a tremendous amount of time and effort into discussing, shaping, and agreeing on a purpose that belongs to them both collectively and individually. This common purpose, when accepted by the team, becomes the equivalent of what celestial navigation is to a ship's captain—it provides direction and guidance under any and all conditions.

Specific Goals

Successful teams translate their common purpose into specific, measurable, and realistic performance goals. Just as we demonstrated in Chapter 4 how goals lead individuals to higher performance, so goals also energize teams. These specific goals facilitate clear communication. They also help teams maintain their focus on achieving results.

Consistent with the research on individual goals, team goals should be challenging. Difficult goals have been found to raise team performance on those criteria for which they are set. So, for instance, goals for quantity tend to raise quantity, goals for speed tend to raise speed, goals for accuracy tend to raise accuracy, and so on.[66]

Teams should also be encouraged to develop milestones—tangible steps toward completion of the project. This allows teams to focus on their goals and evaluate progress toward the goals. The milestones should be sufficiently important and readily accomplished so that teams can celebrate some of their accomplishments along the way.

Team Efficacy

Effective teams have confidence in themselves. They believe they can succeed. We call this *team efficacy*.[67]

Success breeds success. Teams that have been successful raise their beliefs about future success which, in turn, motivates them to work harder. One of the factors that helps teams build their efficacy is **cohesiveness**—the degree to which members are attracted to one another and are motivated to stay on the team.[68] Though teams differ in their cohesiveness, it is important because it has been found to be related to the team's productivity.[69]

Studies consistently show that the relation between cohesiveness and productivity depends on the performance-related norms established by the group.[70] If performance-related norms are high (for example, high output, quality work, cooperation with individuals outside the group), a cohesive group will be more productive than a less cohesive group. If cohesiveness is high and performance norms are low, productivity will be low. If cohesiveness is low and performance norms are high, productivity increases—but less than in the high cohesiveness–high norms situation. Where cohesiveness and performance-related norms are both low, productivity will tend to fall into the low-to-moderate range. These conclusions are summarized in Exhibit 5-7 on page 170. *OB in Action—Creating a Team Charter* provides a way for teams to develop productivity norms when the team first forms.

Most studies of cohesiveness focus on *socio-emotional cohesiveness,* the "sense of togetherness that develops when individuals derive emotional satisfaction from group participation."[71]

A recent study of 23 National Basketball Association (NBA) teams found that "shared experience"—tenure on the team and time on court—tended to reduce turnover and boost win-loss performance significantly. Why do you think teams that stay together longer tend to play better?

cohesiveness   The degree to which team members are attracted to one another and are motivated to stay on the team.

OB IN ACTION

Creating a Team Charter

When you form a new team, you may want to develop a team charter, so that everyone agrees on the basic norms for group performance. Consider including answers to the following in your charter:

→ What are team members' **names and contact information** (phone, email)?

→ How will **communication** among team members take place (phone, email)?

→ What will the **team ground rules** be (where and when to meet, attendance expectations, workload expectations)?

→ How will **decisions** be made (consensus, majority vote, leader rules)?

→ What **potential conflicts** may arise within the team? Among team members?

→ How will **conflicts be resolved** by the group?

Source: Submitted by Don Miskiman, Chair, Department of Management, and U-C Professor of Management, Malaspina University-College, Nanaimo, BC. With permission.

EXHIBIT 5-7	Relationship Among Team Cohesiveness, Performance Norms, and Productivity

Cohesiveness

		High	Low
Performance Norms	**High**	High productivity	Moderate productivity
	Low	Low productivity	Moderate to low productivity

There is also *instrumental cohesiveness*: the "sense of togetherness that develops when group members are mutually dependent on one another because they believe they could not achieve the group's goal by acting separately." Teams need to achieve a balance of these two types of cohesiveness to function well. *OB in Action—Increasing Group Cohesiveness* indicates how to increase both socio-emotional and instrumental cohesiveness.

OB IN ACTION

Increasing Group Cohesiveness

Increasing socio-emotional cohesiveness

→ Keep the group relatively **small**.

→ Strive for a **favourable public image** to increase the status and prestige of belonging.

→ Encourage **interaction** and **cooperation**.

→ Emphasize members' **common characteristics** and interests.

→ **Point out environmental threats** (e.g., competitors' achievements) to rally the group.

Increasing instrumental cohesiveness

→ Regularly update and **clarify the group's goal(s)**.

→ Give every group member a **vital "piece of the action."**

→ Channel each group member's special talents toward the **common goal(s)**.

→ **Recognize** and equitably reinforce **every member's contributions**.

→ Frequently remind group members they **need one another** to get the job done.

Source: R. Kreitner and A. Kinicki, *Organizational Behavior,* 6th ed. (New York: Irwin, 2004), p. 460. Reprinted by permission of McGraw Hill Education.

What, if anything, can management do to increase team efficacy? Two possible options are helping the team to achieve small successes and skill training. Small successes build team confidence. As a team develops an increasingly stronger performance record, it also increases the collective belief that future efforts will lead to success. In addition, managers should consider providing training to improve members' technical and interpersonal skills. The greater the abilities of team members, the greater the likelihood that the team will develop confidence and the capability to deliver on that confidence.

Managed Level of Conflict

Conflict on a team is not necessarily bad. Though relationship conflicts—those based on interpersonal incompatibilities, tension, and animosity toward others—are almost always dysfunctional, teams that are completely void of conflict are likely to be less effective, with the members becoming withdrawn and only superficially harmonious. Often, if there were no conflict, the alternative was not agreement, but apathy and disengagement. Teams that avoid conflict also tend to have lower performance levels, forget to consider key issues, or remain unaware of important aspects of their situation.[72] So effective teams are characterized by an appropriate level of conflict.[73]

Kathleen Eisenhardt of the Stanford Graduate School of Business and her colleagues studied top management teams in technology-based companies to understand how they manage conflict.[74] Their research identified six tactics that helped the teams successfully manage the interpersonal conflict that can accompany group interactions. These are presented in *OB in Action—Reducing Team Conflict* on page 171. By handling the interpersonal conflict well, the teams were able to achieve their goals without letting conflict get in the way.

Groups need mechanisms by which they can manage the conflict, however. From the research reported above, we could conclude that sharing information and goals and striving to be open and get along are helpful strategies for negotiating our way through the maze of conflict. A sense of humour and a willingness to understand the points of others without insisting that everyone agree on all points are also important. Group members should try to focus on the issues rather than on personalities, and strive to achieve fairness and equity in the group process.

Accountability

Successful teams make members individually and jointly accountable for the team's purpose, goals, and approach.[75] They clearly define what they are individually responsible for and what they are jointly responsible for. *From Concepts to Skills* on pages 182–183 discusses how to conduct effective team meetings.

TWENTY-FIRST CENTURY TEAMWORK: VIRTUAL TEAMS

When we think of teams, we often picture face-to-face interactions. **Virtual teams**, however, seldom interact face-to-face and they use computer technology to tie together physically separated members in order to achieve a common goal.[76] They enable people to collaborate online—using communication links such as wide-area networks, videoconferencing, and email—whether team members are only a room away or continents apart. With the greater availability of technology and increasing globalization, virtual teams have become not only possible, but necessary. To the extent that work is knowledge-based rather than production-oriented, virtual teams are also becoming more common.

Providing that team members are comfortable with using technology, virtual teams can do all the things that other teams do—share information, make decisions, complete tasks. They can include members from the same organization or link an organization's members with employees from other organizations (suppliers and joint partners). They can convene for a few days to solve a problem, a few months to complete a project, or exist permanently.[77] Often they can be more efficient at tasks as well, because of the ease of sharing information through email and voice mail. Virtual teams also make it possible for people who are in different geographical and time zones to work together.

Virtual teams can suffer from the limited social contact of team members. This can lead to bonding problems, which the research on teams suggests is important for team performance. One recent meta-analysis of 27 studies of virtual teams questioned whether members of virtual teams ever bonded in the traditional sense.[78] Lack of bonding can lead to slower and less accurate performance than is the case for face-to-face teams.

Virtual teams can also suffer from the absence of *paraverbal* and *nonverbal* cues in their communications. In face-to-face conversation, people use paraverbal (tone of voice, inflection, voice volume) and nonverbal (eye movement, facial expression, hand gestures, and other body language) cues to provide increased meaning. In virtual communications, team members are not able to duplicate the normal give-and-take of face-to-face discussion. As a result, virtual team members often have less social rapport and are more at risk of misunderstanding one another.

O B IN ACTION

Reducing Team Conflict

→ Work with **more, rather than less, information**, and debate on the basis of **facts**.

→ Develop **multiple alternatives** to enrich the level of debate.

→ Develop commonly agreed-upon **goals**.

→ Use **humour** when making tough decisions.

→ Maintain a **balanced power** structure.

→ Resolve issues **without forcing consensus**.

Source: Based on K. M. Eisenhardt, J. L. Kahwajy, and L. J. Bourgeois III, "How Management Teams Can Have a Good Fight," *Harvard Business Review,* July–August 1997, p. 78.

---

5 How do virtual teams work?

virtual teams Teams that seldom interact face-to-face and use computer technology to tie together physically dispersed members in order to achieve a common goal.

Virtual Teams and Trust

There has been some concern that, because virtual teams lack face-to-face interaction, it may be more difficult to build trust among individuals. However, two recent studies examining how virtual teams work on projects indicate that virtual teams can develop close interaction and trust; these qualities simply evolve differently than in face-to-face groups.[79] In face-to-face groups, trust comes from direct interaction, over time. In virtual teams, trust is either established at the outset or it generally does not develop. The researchers found that initial electronic messages set the tone for how interactions occurred throughout the entire project. In one team, for instance, when the appointed leader sent an introductory message that had a distrustful tone, the team suffered low morale and poor performance throughout the duration of the project. The researchers suggest that virtual teams should start with an electronic "courtship," where members provide some personal information. Then the teams should assign clear roles to members, helping members to identify with each other. Finally, the researchers noted that teams whose members had a positive attitude (eagerness, enthusiasm, and intense action orientation in messages) did considerably better than teams that had one or more pessimists. The article by S. L. Jarvenpaa, K. Knoll, and D. E. Leidner cited in endnote 79 of this chapter provides more detail on this subject; you might find the team experience reported there interesting.

Creating Virtual Workspaces

It is obvious that virtual teams must rely on technology to communicate. But what is the best way to do this? Team members can be overwhelmed with email, drowning in messages to the point of failing to read them. To better understand the problem, a recent study looked at 54 teams from 26 companies operating in a wide variety of industries.[80] The researchers found that 83 percent of the teams they studied used virtual workspaces (also known as virtual meeting rooms) to communicate. The virtual workspace is a team website on a company's intranet, designed to help remind team members of their "decisions, rationales, and commitments." The virtual workspace can have "walls" or links to information about each person, and discussion forums with topic threads that cover important issues and problems. The discussion forums can also serve as places to post work-in-progress to get feedback. Exhibit 5-8 on page 173 shows an example of a virtual workspace for a project at Shell.

Tips for managers who want to improve the way virtual teams function include the following: ensure that the team addresses feelings of isolation that members might have; ensure that team members have a mix of interpersonal and technical skills; and pay careful attention to evaluating performance and providing recognition and feedback.[81] By engaging in spontaneous communication with virtual team members, managers can also reduce the likelihood and impact of conflict.[82] For more tips on improving the way virtual teams function, see *OB in Action—Managing Virtual Teams*.

O B IN ACTION

Managing Virtual Teams

Establishing trust and commitment, encouraging communication, and assessing team members pose tremendous challenges for virtual team managers. Here are a few tips to make the process easier:

→ Establish **regular times** for group interaction.

→ Set up **firm rules** for communication.

→ Use **visual forms of communication** where possible.

→ **Copy** the good points of **on-site teams**. For example, allow time for informal chitchat and socializing, and celebrate achievements.

→ **Give and receive feedback** and offer assistance on a regular basis. Be persistent with people who are not communicating with you or each other.

→ Agree on **standard technology** so all team members can work together easily.

→ Consider using **360-degree feedback** to better understand and evaluate team members. This type of feedback comes from the full circle of daily contacts that an employee might have, including supervisors, peers, subordinates, and clients.

→ Provide a **virtual workspace** via an intranet, website, or bulletin board.

→ Note which employees **effectively use email** to build team rapport.

→ **Smooth the way for the next assignment** if membership on the team, or the team itself, is not permanent.

→ **Be available** to employees, but don't wait for them to seek you out.

→ Encourage **informal, off-line conversation** between team members.

Source: C. Joinson, "Managing Virtual Teams," *HR Magazine*, June 2002, p. 71. Reprinted with the permission of *HR Magazine*, published by the Society for Human Resource Management, Alexandria, VA.

EXHIBIT 5-8 An Illustration of a Virtual Workspace

Chemicals Value Network

Leader
Houston

Treasury
London

Consultant
London

Customer Service
Houston

IT
London

Product Manager
Singapore

Product Manager
Houston

Manufacturing
The Netherlands

Strategy Analyst
Houston

Consultant
Boston

New Business Dev.
London

Technology
Houston

Source: Reprinted by permission of Shell Chemical LP.

Case Incident—A Virtual Team at T. A. Sterns on pages 180–181 further explores how virtual teams work.

BEWARE! TEAMS ARE NOT ALWAYS THE ANSWER

When the Glenforest Secondary School students got together to build a robot, it made sense for them to form a team. No student had all the knowledge and skills required to complete the task, as we saw in the opening vignette. But does every task need a team?

Despite considerable success in the use of teams, they are not necessarily appropriate in all situations, as Exhibit 5-9 on page 174 suggests. Teamwork takes more time and often more resources than individual work. Teams, for instance, have greater communication demands, conflicts to be managed, and meetings to be run. In their enthusiasm to enjoy the benefits of teams, some managers have introduced them into situations where the work is better done by individuals. A 2003 study done by Statistics Canada found that the introduction of teamwork lowered turnover in the service industries, for both high- and low-skilled employees. However, manufacturing companies experienced higher turnover if they introduced teamwork and formal teamwork training, compared with not doing so (15.8 percent vs. 10.7 percent).[83]

Another consideration is ethics. This chapter's *Ethical Dilemma Exercise* on page 180 asks you to think about whether it is ethical to force employees to be team players.

How do you know if the work of your group would be better done in teams? It has been suggested that three tests be applied to see if a team fits the situation:[84]

6 Are teams always the answer?

- *Can the work be done better by more than one person?* Simple tasks that don't require diverse input are probably better left to individuals.

EXHIBIT 5-9

Source: S. Adams, *Build a Better Life by Stealing Office Supplies* (Kansas City: MO: Andrews and McMeal, 1991), p. 31. Dilbert reprinted with permission of United Features Syndicate.

- *Does the work create a common purpose or set of goals for the people in the group that is more than the sum of individual goals?* For instance, the service departments of many new-car dealers have introduced teams that link customer service personnel, mechanics, parts specialists, and sales representatives. Such teams can better manage collective responsibility for ensuring that customers' needs are properly met.

- *Are the members of the group interdependent?* Teams make sense where there is interdependence between tasks—where the success of the whole depends on the success of each one, *and* the success of each one depends on the success of the others. Soccer, for instance, is an obvious *team* sport because of the interdependence of the players. Swim teams, by contrast, are not really teams, but groups of individuals whose total performance is merely the sum of the individual performances. Others have outlined the conditions under which organizations would find teams more useful: "when work processes cut across functional lines; when speed is important (and complex relationships are involved); when the organization mirrors a complex, differentiated, and rapidly changing market environment; when innovation and learning have priority; and when the tasks that have to be done require online integration of highly interdependent performers."[85]

SUMMARY AND IMPLICATIONS

1 **What are teams and groups?** Groups and teams differ. The output of a group is simply the sum of individual efforts. A team, because of the close collaboration among members, produces output that is greater than the sum of individual efforts.

2 **Does everyone use teams?** Teams have become an essential part of the way business is being done these days. A Conference Board of Canada report found that more than 80 percent of its 109 respondents used teams in the workplace. This finding is similar in the United States, where 80 percent of *Fortune* 500 companies have half or more of their employees on teams. As well, 68 percent of small US manufacturers use teams in their production areas.

3 **Do groups and teams go through stages while they work?** Two different models illustrate how teams and groups develop. The first, the five-stage model, describes the standard sequence of stages groups pass through: forming, storming, norming, performing, and adjourning. Through these stages, group members learn how to settle conflicts and develop norms, which enable them to perform. The second, the punctuated-equilibrium model, describes the pattern of development specific to temporary groups with deadlines. In this model, the group shows two great periods of activity. The first peak in activity takes place after the midpoint of the project, a time in which the team performs at a higher level than it did previously. The second peak takes place right before the project comes due.

4 **How do we create effective teams?** For teams to be effective, careful consideration must be given to resources, the team's composition, work design, and process variables. The four contextual factors that appear to be most significantly related to team performance are the presence of adequate resources, effective leadership, a climate of trust, and a performance evaluation and reward system that reflects team contributions. Effective teams are neither too large nor too small—typically they range in size from 5 to 12 people. They have members who fill role demands, are flexible, and who prefer to be part of a group. Teams will be more effective if members have freedom and autonomy to do their tasks and believe that the task will have a substantial impact on others. Finally, effective teams have members committed to a common purpose and specific team goals.

5 **How do virtual teams work?** Virtual teams can do many of the same things face-to-face teams can, but they have more challenges, especially when it comes to team-member bonding and building trust. To help build understanding among teammates, members should provide some personal information early on, and they should also be clear on one another's roles from the outset. Researchers have found that virtual teams with members who have positive attitudes do better than teams with pessimistic members. Often, virtual teams communicate, discuss ideas, post work-in-progress, and exchange feedback through a virtual workspace via an intranet, website, or bulletin board.

6 **Are teams always the answer?** Teams are not necessarily appropriate in every situation. How do you know if the work of your group would be better done in teams? It's been suggested that three tests be applied to see if a team fits the situation: (1) Can the work be done better by more than one person? (2) Does the work create a common purpose or set of goals for the people in the group that is more than the sum of individual goals? and (3) Are the members of the group interdependent? This third test asks whether the success of the whole depends on the success of each one *and* the success of each one depends on the success of the others.

For Review

1. How can teams increase employee motivation?

2. Describe the five-stage model of group development.

3. Describe the punctuated-equilibrium model of group development.

4. What are the characteristics of an effective team?

5. How can team members harm their team?

6. What is the difference between task-oriented roles and maintenance roles?

7. What are the effects of team size on performance?

8. How can a team minimize social loafing?

9. Contrast virtual and face-to-face teams.

10. What conditions favour creating a team, rather than letting an individual perform a given task?

For Critical Thinking

1. How could you use the punctuated-equilibrium model to understand group behaviour better?

2. Have you experienced social loafing as a team member? What did you do to prevent this problem?

3. Would you prefer to work alone or as part of a team? Why? How do you think your answer compares with that of others in your class?

4. What effect, if any, do you expect that workforce diversity has on a team's performance and satisfaction?

OB for You

- Know that you will be asked to work on teams and groups both during your post-secondary years and later in life, so understanding how teams work is an important skill to have.

- Think about the roles that you play on teams. Teams need task-oriented people to get the job done, but they also need maintenance-oriented people who help keep people working together and feeling committed to the team.

- Help your team set specific, measurable, realistic goals, as this leads to more successful outcomes.

POINT

 COUNTERPOINT

Sports Teams Are Good Models for Workplace Teams

Studies from hockey, football, soccer, basketball, and baseball have found a number of elements in successful sports teams that can be applied to successful work teams.[86]

Successful teams integrate cooperation and competition. Effective team coaches get athletes to help one another but also push one another to perform at their best. Sports teams with the best win-loss records had coaches who promoted a strong spirit of cooperation and a high level of healthy competition among their players.

Successful teams score early wins. Early successes build teammates' faith in themselves and their capacity as a team. For instance, research on hockey teams of relatively equal ability found that 72 percent of the time the team that was ahead at the end of the first period went on to win the game. So managers should provide teams with early tasks that are simple and provide "easy wins."

Successful teams avoid losing streaks. Losing can become a self-fulfilling prophecy. A couple of failures can lead to a downward spiral if a team becomes demoralized and believes it is helpless to end its losing streak. Managers need to instill the confidence in team members that they can turn things around when they encounter setbacks.

Practice makes perfect. Successful sports teams execute on game day but learn from their mistakes in practice. A wise manager carves out time and space in which work teams can experiment and learn.

Successful teams use halftime breaks. The best coaches in basketball and football use halftime during a game to reassess what is working and what is not. Managers of work teams should build in similar assessments at about the halfway point in a team project to evaluate how the team can improve.

Winning teams have a stable membership. Studies of professional basketball teams have found that the more stable a team's membership, the more likely the team is to win. The more time teammates have together, the more able they are to anticipate one another's moves and the clearer they are about one another's roles.

Successful teams debrief after failures and successes. The best sports teams study the game video. Similarly, work teams need to take time to routinely reflect on both their successes and failures and to learn from them.

Sports Teams Are Not the Model for All Teams

There are flaws in using sports as a model for developing effective work teams. Here are just four caveats.[87]

All sport teams are not alike. In baseball, for instance, there is little interaction among teammates. Rarely are more than two or three players directly involved in a play. The performance of the team is largely the sum of the performance of its individual players. In contrast, basketball has much more interdependence among players. Usually all players are involved in every play, team members have to be able to switch from offence to defence at a moment's notice, and there is continuous movement by all, not just the player with the ball. The performance of the team is more than the sum of its individual players. So when using sports teams as a model for work teams, you have to make sure you are making the correct comparison.

Work teams are more varied and complex. In an athletic league, teams vary little in their context, the design of the team, and the design of the task. But from one work team to the next, these factors can vary tremendously. As a result, coaching plays a much more significant part in a sports team's performance than in the workplace. Performance of work teams is more a function of getting the team's structural and design variables right. So, in contrast to sports, managers of work teams should focus less on coaching and more on getting the team set up for success.

A lot of employees cannot relate to sports metaphors. Not everyone on work teams is conversant in sports. Team members from different cultures also may not know the sports metaphors you are using. Most Canadians, for instance, are unfamiliar with the rules and terminology of Australian football.

Work team outcomes are not easily defined in terms of wins and losses. Sports teams usually measure success in terms of wins and losses. Such measures of success are rarely as clear for work teams. Managers who try to define success in wins and losses imply that the workplace is ethically no more complex than the playing field, which is rarely true.

LEARNING ABOUT YOURSELF EXERCISE

How Good Am I at Building and Leading a Team?

Use the following rating scale to respond to the 18 questions on building and leading an effective team:

Strongly Disagree 1	Disagree 2	Slightly Disagree 3	Slightly Agree 4	Agree 5	Strongly Agree 6

1. I am knowledgeable about the different stages of development that teams can go through in their life cycles.   1   2   3   4   5   6

2. When a team forms, I make certain that all team members are introduced to one another at the outset.   1   2   3   4   5   6

3. When the team first comes together, I provide directions, answer team members' questions, and clarify goals, expectations, and procedures.   1   2   3   4   5   6

4. I help team members establish a foundation of trust among themselves and between themselves and me.   1   2   3   4   5   6

5. I ensure that standards of excellence, not mediocrity or mere acceptability, characterize the team's work.   1   2   3   4   5   6

6. I provide a great deal of feedback to team members regarding their performance.   1   2   3   4   5   6

7. I encourage team members to balance individual autonomy with interdependence among other team members.   1   2   3   4   5   6

8. I help team members become at least as committed to the success of the team as to their own personal success.   1   2   3   4   5   6

9. I help team members learn to play roles that assist the team in accomplishing its tasks, as well as building strong interpersonal relationships.   1   2   3   4   5   6

10. I articulate a clear, exciting, passionate vision of what the team can achieve.   1   2   3   4   5   6

11. I help team members become committed to the team vision.   1   2   3   4   5   6

12. I encourage a win-win philosophy in the team; that is, when one member wins, every member wins.   1   2   3   4   5   6

13. I help the team avoid making the group's survival more important than accomplishing its goal.   1   2   3   4   5   6

14. I use formal process-management procedures to help the group become faster, more efficient, and more productive, and to prevent errors.   1   2   3   4   5   6

15. I encourage team members to represent the team's vision, goals, and accomplishments to outsiders.   1   2   3   4   5   6

16. I diagnose and capitalize on the team's core competence.   1   2   3   4   5   6

17. I encourage the team to achieve dramatic breakthrough innovations, as well as small continuous improvements.   1   2   3   4   5   6

18. I help the team work toward preventing mistakes, not just correcting them after the fact.   1   2   3   4   5   6

Scoring Key:

The authors of this instrument propose that it assesses team development behaviours in five areas: diagnosing team development (items 1, 16); managing the forming stage (items 2–4); managing the storming stage (items 10–12, 14, 15); managing the norming stage (items 6–9, 13); and managing the performing stage (items 5, 17, 18). Add up your score. Your total score will range between 18 and 108.

Based on a norm group of 500 business students, the following can help estimate where you are relative to others:

95 or above = **You are in the top quartile of being able to build and lead a team**

72–94 = **You are in the second quartile**

60–71 = **You are in the third quartile**

Below 60 = **You are in the bottom quartile**

Source: Adapted from D. A. Whetten and K. S. Cameron, *Developing Management Skills,* 3rd ed. © 1995, pp. 534–535. Adapted by permission of Pearson Education, Inc., Upper Saddle River, NJ.

BREAKOUT **GROUP** EXERCISES

Form small groups to discuss the following topics, as assigned by your instructor:

1. One of the members of your team continually arrives late for meetings and does not turn drafts of assignments in on time. In general this group member is engaging in social loafing. What can the members of your group do to reduce social loafing?

2. Consider a team with which you've worked. Using the information in Exhibit 5-5 on page 165, consider whether there were more task-oriented or maintenance-oriented roles in the group. What impact did this have on the group's performance?

3. Identify 4 or 5 norms that a team could put into place near the beginning of its life to help it function better over time.

WORKING WITH **OTHERS** EXERCISE

The Paper Tower Exercise

Step 1   Each group will receive 20 index cards, 12 paper clips, and 2 marking pens. Groups have 10 minutes to plan a paper tower that will be judged on the basis of 3 criteria: height, stability, and beauty. No physical work (building) is allowed during this planning period.

Step 2   Each group has 15 minutes for the actual construction of the paper tower.

Step 3   Each tower will be identified by a number assigned by your instructor. Each student is to individually examine all the paper towers. Your group is then to come to a consensus as to which tower is the winner (5 minutes). A spokesperson from your group should report its decision and the criteria the group used in reaching it.

Step 4   In your small groups, discuss the following questions (your instructor may choose to have you discuss only a subset of these questions):

    a. What percentage of the plan did each member of your group contribute, on average?

    b. Did your group have a leader? Why or why not?

    c. How did the group generally respond to the ideas that were expressed during the planning period?

    d. To what extent did your group follow the five-stage model of group development?

continued

e. List specific behaviours exhibited during the planning and building sessions that you felt were helpful to the group. Explain why you found them helpful.

f. List specific behaviours exhibited during the planning and building sessions that you felt were dysfunctional to the group. Explain why you found them dysfunctional.

Source: This exercise is based on "The Paper Tower Exercise: Experiencing Leadership and Group Dynamics" by Phillip L. Hunsaker and Johanna S. Hunsaker, unpublished manuscript. A brief description is included in "Exchange," *Organizational Behavior Teaching Journal* 4, no. 2 (1979), p. 49. Reprinted by permission of the authors. The materials list was suggested by Sally Maitlis, Sauder School of Business, UBC.

ETHICAL **DILEMMA** EXERCISE

Pressure to Be a Team Player

"OK I admit it. I'm not a team player. I work best when I work alone and am left alone," says Zach Sanders.

Zach's employer, an office furniture manufacturer, recently reorganized around teams. All production in the company's Winnipeg factory is now done in teams. Zach's design department has been broken up into three design teams.

"I've worked here for four years. I'm very good at what I do. And my performance reviews confirm that. I've scored 96 percent or higher on my evaluations every year I've been here. But now everything is changing. I'm expected to be part of our modular-office design team. My evaluations and

pay raises are going to depend on how well the team does. And, get this, 50 percent of my evaluation will be on how well I facilitate the performance of the team. I'm really frustrated and demoralized. They hired me for my design skills. They knew I wasn't a social type. Now they're forcing me to be a team player. This doesn't play to my strengths at all."

Is it unethical for Zach's employer to force him to be a team player? Is Zach's employer breaking an implied contract that it made with him at the time he was hired? Does the employer have any responsibility to provide Zach with an alternative that would allow him to continue to work independently?

CASE INCIDENT

A Virtual Team at T. A. Stearns

T. A. Stearns is a national tax accounting firm whose main business is tax preparation services for individuals. Stearns' superior reputation is based on the high quality of its advice and the excellence of its service. Key to the achievement of its reputation are the state-of-the-art computer databases and analysis tools that its people use when counselling clients. These programs were developed by highly trained individuals.

The programs are highly technical, in terms of both the code in which they are written and the tax laws they cover. Perfecting them requires high levels of programming skill as well as the ability to understand the law. New laws and interpretations of existing laws have to be integrated quickly and flawlessly into the existing regulations and analysis tools.

The creation of these programs is carried out in a virtual environment by four programmers in the greater Vancouver area. The four work at home and are connected to each other and to the company by email, telephone, and conference software. Formal on-site meetings among all of the pro-

grammers take place only a few times a year, although the workers sometimes meet informally at other times. The four members of the team are Tom Andrews, Cy Crane, Marge Dector, and Megan Harris.

These four people exchange email messages many times every day. In fact, it's not unusual for them to step away from guests or family to log on and check in with the others. Often their emails are amusing as well as work-related. Sometimes, for instance, when they were facing a deadline and one of Marge's kids was home sick, they helped each other with the work. Tom has occasionally invited the others to visit his farm; and Marge and Cy have gotten their families together several times for dinner. About once a month the whole team gets together for lunch.

All four of these Stearns employees are on salary, which, consistent with company custom, is negotiated separately and secretly with management. Although each is required to check in regularly during every workday, they were told when they were hired that they could work wherever they wanted. Clearly, flexibility is one of the pluses of these jobs. When the four get together, they often joke about the managers and workers who are tied to the office, referring to them as "face timers" and to themselves as "free agents."

When the programmers are asked to make a major program change, they often develop programming tools called macros to help them do their work more efficiently. These macros greatly enhance the speed at which a change can be written into the programs. Cy in particular really enjoys hacking around with macros. On one recent project, for instance, he became obsessed with the prospect of creating a shortcut that could save him a huge amount of time. One week after turning in his code and his release notes to the company, Cy bragged to Tom that he had created a new macro that had saved him eight hours of work that week. Tom was skeptical of the shortcut, but after trying it out he found that it actually saved him many hours too.

Stearns has a suggestion program that rewards employees for innovations that save the company money. The program gives an employee 5 percent of the savings generated by his or her innovation over three months. The company also has a profit-sharing plan. Tom and Cy felt that the small amount of money that would be generated by a company reward would not offset the free time that they gained using their new macro. They wanted the time for leisure or consulting work. They also feared their group might suffer if management learned about the innovation. It would enable three people to do the work of four, which could lead to one of them being let go. So they didn't share their innovative macro with management.

Although Tom and Cy wouldn't share the innovation with management, they were concerned that they were entering their busy season and they knew everyone on the team would be stressed by the heavy workload. They decided to distribute the macro to the other members of their team and swore them to secrecy.

Over lunch one day, the team set itself a level of production that it felt would not arouse management's suspicion. Several months passed and the four used some of their extra time to push the quality of their work even higher. But they also now had more time to pursue their own personal interests.

Dave Regan, the in-house manager of the work group, picked up on the innovation several weeks after it was first implemented. He had wondered why production time had gone down a bit while quality had shot up, and he got his first inkling of an answer when he saw an email from Marge to Cy thanking him for saving her so much time with his "brilliant mind." Not wanting to embarrass his employees, the manager hinted to Tom that he wanted to know what was happening, but he got nowhere. He did not tell his own manager about his suspicions, reasoning that since both quality and productivity were up he did not really need to pursue the matter further.

Dave very recently learned that Cy had boasted about his trick to a member of another virtual work group in the company. Suddenly, the situation seemed to have gotten out of control. Dave decided to take Cy to lunch. During the meal, Dave asked Cy to explain what was happening. Cy told him about the innovation, but he insisted the group's actions had been justified to protect itself.

Dave knew that his own boss would soon hear of the situation and that he would be looking for answers—from him.

Questions

1. Is this group a team?
2. What role have norms played in how this team acted?
3. Has anyone in this case acted unethically?
4. What should Dave do now?

Source: Adapted from "The Virtual Environment Work Team," a case prepared by R. Andre, professor, Northeastern University. With permission.

CBC ◉ VIDEO CASE INCIDENT

Earth Buddies

On December 11, 1998, Anton Rabie, Ronnen Harary, and Ben Varadi found themselves on the cover of *Canadian Business* magazine. In the article, they were referred to as "Marketing Maniacs," examples of the young and enthusiastic entrepreneurs in today's marketplace.

Fresh out of business school in 1993 and based in Toronto, the partnership between Rabie, Harary, and Varadi quickly

flourished with the initial success of their product release: Earth Buddy, a small novelty head that sprouted grass hair when set in water. Thanks to successful negotiations with retail giants such as K-Mart, Canadian Tire, and Zellers, sales grew steadily for the first few years. In 1995, the partnership changed the company name to Spin Master Toys. After only four years of operating, Spin Master reported $10 million in sales in 1998.

continued

Over the years, the friends have had their share of disagreements, triumphs, and failures. Together, they have recruited talented outsiders to join their executive committee, researched and successfully launched innovative toy products from Asia, and nurtured the company to where it is today. Although a private company, Spin Master reported $103 million in sales in 2000.

Today, the executive team at Spin Master has grown to 12 members. Rabie is the president, Harary is the CEO, and Varadi is the executive vice-president. In 2002, the firm introduced a variety of new products, including the Air Hogs Helicopter, Air Hogs Radio Control, and Air Hogs Quick Charge. In addition, the company re-branded itself by changing the corporate logo and name. In 2004, Rabie, Harary, and Varadi celebrated Spin Master's 10-year anniversary, the achievements of their fledgling business, and what it truly means to work together as a team.

Questions

1. Describe the partnership norms at Spin Master Toys.

2. Describe the roles displayed by the firm's executive team members: Anton Rabie, Ronnen Harary, and Ben Varadi.

3. Using the five-stage model of group development, analyze the changes on the executive team. Be sure to address how the team's decision-making process was affected by the introduction of Michelle (Harary's sister) and Austin (Michelle's husband) to the team.

Sources: Based on "Earthbuddies," *CBC Venture*, July 21, 2002, VA2035H & I; Spin Master Toys, "Company History," http://www.spinmaster.com; and S. Steinberg and J. Chidley, "Fun for the Money," *Canadian Business*, December 11, 1998, pp. 44–52.

From **Concepts** to **Skills**

Conducting a Team Meeting

Team meetings have a reputation for inefficiency. For instance, noted Canadian-born economist John Kenneth Galbraith has said, "Meetings are indispensable when you don't want to do anything."

When you are responsible for conducting a meeting, what can you do to make it more efficient and effective? Follow these 12 steps:[88]

1. *Prepare a meeting agenda.* An agenda defines what you hope to accomplish at the meeting. It should state the meeting's purpose; who will be in attendance; what, if any, preparation is required of each participant; a detailed list of items to be covered; the specific time and location of the meeting; and a specific finishing time.

2. *Distribute the agenda in advance.* Participants should have the agenda far enough in advance that they can adequately prepare for the meeting.

3. *Consult with participants before the meeting.* An unprepared participant cannot contribute to his or her full potential. It is your responsibility to ensure that members are prepared, so check with them ahead of time.

4. *Get participants to go over the agenda.* The first thing to do at the meeting is to have participants review the agenda, make any changes, and then approve the final agenda.

5. *Establish specific time limits.* Meetings should begin on time and have a specific time for completion. It is your responsibility to specify these times and to hold to them.

6. *Maintain focused discussion.* It is your responsibility to give direction to the discussion; to keep it focused on the issues; and to minimize interruptions, disruptions, and irrelevant comments.

7. *Encourage and support participation of all members.* To maximize the effectiveness of problem-oriented meetings, each participant must be encouraged to contribute. Quiet or reserved personalities need to be drawn out so their ideas can be heard.

8. *Maintain a balanced style.* The effective group leader pushes when necessary and is passive when need be.

9. *Encourage the clash of ideas.* You need to encourage different points of view, critical thinking, and constructive disagreement.

10. *Discourage the clash of personalities.* An effective meeting is characterized by the critical assessment of ideas, not attacks on people. When running a meeting, you must quickly intercede to stop personal attacks or other forms of verbal insult.

11. *Be an effective listener.* You need to listen with intensity, empathy, and objectivity, and do whatever is necessary to get the full intended meaning from each participant's comments.

12. *Bring proper closure.* You should close a meeting by summarizing the group's accomplishments; clarifying what actions, if any, need to follow the meeting; and allocating follow-up assignments. If any decisions are made, you also need to determine who will be responsible for communicating and implementing them.

Assessing Skills

After you've read this chapter, take the following Self-Assessment on your enclosed CD-ROM:

31. Do I Trust Others?

32. Do Others See Me as Trustworthy?

Practising Skills

Jameel Saumur is the leader of a five-member project team that has been assigned the task of moving his engineering firm into the booming area of high-speed intercity rail construction. Saumur and his team members have been researching the field, identifying specific business opportunities, negotiating alliances with equipment vendors, and evaluating high-speed rail experts and consultants from around the world. Throughout the process, Tonya Eckler, a highly qualified and respected engineer, has challenged a number of things Saumur has said during team meetings and in the workplace. For example, at a meeting two weeks ago, Saumur presented the team with a list of 10 possible high-speed rail projects and started evaluating the company's ability to compete for them. Eckler contradicted virtually all of Saumur's comments, questioned his statistics, and was quite pessimistic about the possibility of getting contracts on these projects. After this latest display of displeasure, two other group members, Bryan Worth and Maggie Ames, are complaining that Eckler's actions are damaging the team's effectiveness. Eckler was originally assigned to the team for her unique expertise and insight. If you had to advise this team, what suggestions would you make to get the team on the right track to achieve its fullest potential?

Reinforcing Skills

1. Interview three mana'gers at different organizations. Ask them about their experiences in managing teams. Have each describe teams that they thought were effective and why they succeeded. Have each also describe teams that they thought were ineffective and the reasons that might have caused this.

2. Contrast a team you have been in where members trusted one another with another team you have been in where members lacked trust in one another. How did the conditions in each team develop? What were the consequences in terms of interaction patterns and performance?

CHAPTER **6**

Communication, Conflict, and Negotiation

What do you do when a group of former employees think they have been treated unfairly and current employees are thinking about joining a union? Will communication help reduce tensions?

1 How does communication work?

2 What are the barriers to communication?

3 What are other issues in communication?

4 What is conflict?

5 How can conflict be resolved?

6 How does one negotiate effectively?

In late 1997, mill employees of Hamilton, Ontario-based Dofasco were unhappy with the company.[1] The number of jobs had fallen from 10 300 to 7000 in the previous five years. Former employees had started a group called SHAFT (So How Many Are Fired Tomorrow) to press grievances against the company for what they claimed was unfair dismissal. The Canadian Auto Workers and the United Steelworkers unions were approached by employees with requests to form a union at Dofasco.

John Mayberry, then CEO, showed little respect for his employees. From his early days as a manager, he was not popular: He was disliked "for his habit of springing surprise inspections, and there were rumours that he had threatened to fire employees he thought were malingering."

The culture at Dofasco in the early 1990s did not support open communication, and there was a great deal of conflict between Mayberry and his employees. Mayberry tended to use one-way communication: He would talk and employees were to listen. His concern that employees had been treated too kindly by the previous management meant that he was not open to negotiating resolutions to the challenges the company faced. Would Mayberry learn to work with his employees more effectively?

In this chapter we explore the foundations of communication and then consider the effects of communication on conflict and negotiation.

THE COMMUNICATION PROCESS

Research indicates that poor communication is probably the most frequently cited source of interpersonal conflict.[2] Individuals spend nearly 70 percent of their waking hours communicating—writing, reading, speaking, listening—which means that they have many opportunities in which to engage in poor communication. A WorkCanada survey of 2039 Canadians in six industrial and service categories explored the state of

1 How does communication work?

Dofasco
www.dofasco.ca

OB IS FOR EVERYONE

* *What information should be sent by which communication channel?*

* *What factors hinder cross-cultural communication?*

* *How can you communicate better when you're stressed out?*

* *Is conflict always bad?*

* *Ever notice that communicating via email can lead to misunderstandings?*

* *Should you try to win at any cost when you bargain?*

* *Does body language really make a difference?*

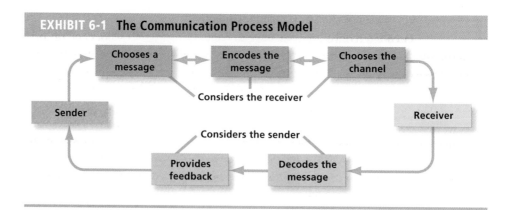

EXHIBIT 6-1   The Communication Process Model

Sender → Chooses a message ↔ Encodes the message ↔ Chooses the channel

Considers the receiver

Chooses the channel → Receiver

Considers the sender

Sender ← Provides feedback ← Decodes the message ← Receiver

communication in Canadian businesses.[3] The survey found that 61 percent of senior executives believed they did a good job of communicating with employees. However, those who worked below the senior executives did not share this feeling—only 33 percent of the managers and department heads believed that senior executives were effective communicators. Lower-level employees reported that communication was even worse:

communication The transfer and understanding of a message between two or more people.

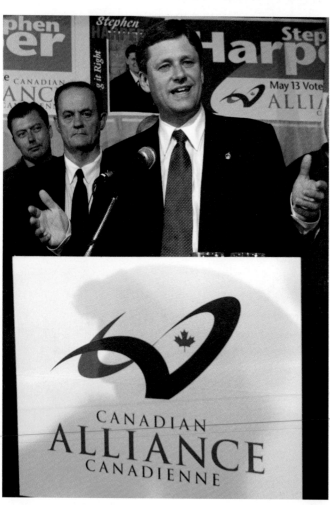

The former Canadian Alliance learned in its early days that it's easy to communicate unintended messages. The party's first choice of name, Canadian Conservative Reform Alliance Party, caused quite a stir for its acronym (CCRAP). People across the country wondered what the new party was trying to communicate about its objectives.

Only 22 percent of hourly workers, 27 percent of clerical employees, and 22 percent of professional staff reported that senior executives did a good job of communicating with them. Moreover, a recent study found that Canadians reported less favourable perceptions about their companies' communications than did Americans.[4]

Despite these communication problems, no group can exist without **communication**, which is the transfer and understanding of a message between two or more people. Communication can be thought of as a process, or flow, as shown in Exhibit 6-1. The model indicates that communication is both an interactive and iterative process. The sender has to keep in mind the receiver (or audience) and in finalizing the communication, may decide to revisit decisions about the message, the encoding, and/or the feedback. For instance, a manager may want to convey a message face to face, and then may not be able to do so for some reason. The message sent by email or voice mail may need to be framed differently than the message that would have been delivered face to face. Similarly, you may decide on a message, and then realize the medium that you have chosen will make the message too complicated. Writing 10 emails to set up a simple lunch appointment may convince you midway through the process to pick up the telephone to finalize the details.

We discussed perception in Chapter 2. The communication process is significantly affected by the sender's perception of the receiver and the receiver's perception of the sender. For instance, if the receiver does not trust the sender, he or she may interpret intended positive statements in a negative manner.

Encoding and Decoding

Messages are **encoded** (converting a message to symbolic form) by a sender and **decoded** (interpreting a sender's message) by a receiver. Four factors have been described that affect message encoding and decoding: skill, attitudes, knowledge, and the socio-cultural system. For example, our success in communicating to you depends on our writing skills and your reading skills. Communication success also includes speaking, listening, and reasoning skills. As we discussed in Chapter 3, our interactions with others are affected by our attitudes, values, and beliefs. Thus, the attitudes of the sender and receiver toward each other will affect how the message is transmitted. Clearly, the amount of knowledge the source and receiver hold about a subject will affect the clarity of the message that is transferred. Finally, our position in the social-cultural system affects our ability to successfully engage in communication. Messages sent and received by people of equal rank are sometimes interpreted differently than messages sent and received by people in very different positions.

encoding   Converting a message to symbolic form.

decoding   Interpreting a sender's message.

The Message

The **message** is the actual physical product from the source encoding. "When we speak, the speech is the message. When we write, the writing is the message. When we paint, the picture is the message. When we gesture, the movements of our arms, the expressions on our face are the message."[5] Our message is affected by the code, or group of symbols, that we use to transfer meaning; the content of the message itself; and the decisions that we make in selecting and arranging both codes and content. A poor choice of symbols, and confusion in the content of the message, can cause problems. McDonald's recently settled a lawsuit over its choice of words, as *Focus on Ethics* reveals.

message   What is communicated.

FOCUS ON **ETHICS**

Vegetarian or Not Vegetarian?

Does "no beef" really mean what it implies?   In March 2002, Oak Brook, Illinois-based McDonald's Corporation agreed to pay $19 million (CDN) to settle lawsuits from vegetarians who suggested the company had deceived them about how it produced french fries.[6] Under the agreement, McDonald's had to pay $10 million to charities that support vegetarianism. The company was also ordered to publicly apologize and learn about vegetarian dietary issues.

McDonald's communication practices were questioned in the lawsuit. In 1990, the company had announced that its restaurants would no longer use beef fat to cook french fries. Instead, only pure vegetable oil would be used. What the company did not say was that it would continue to add beef tallow to the fries as a flavouring agent.

When vegetarians discovered that they had been unwittingly eating beef-flavoured fries, they were upset. McDonald's claimed that it never said the french fries were vegetarian. The company did apologize for any confusion its announcement caused, however.

Messages can also get "lost in translation" when two parties formalize their understanding through contracts. Contracts are meant to be written in legal terms, for lawyers, but these may not always capture the underlying meaning of the parties' understandings. Collective agreements written between management and unions sometimes suffer from this problem as well. When either management or union leaders point to the collective agreement for every interaction in the workplace, they are relying on the encoding of their negotiations, but this may not permit some of the flexibility that was intended in some cases.

The Channel

channel The medium through which a message travels.

The **channel** is the medium through which a message travels. It is selected by the source, who must determine which channel is formal and which one is informal. Formal channels are established by organizations to transmit messages about the job-related activities of members. Traditionally, they follow the authority network within the organization. Other forms of messages, such as personal or social messages, follow the informal channels in the organization. Examples of channels include formal memos, voice mail, email, and meetings. Choosing a poor channel, or one with a high noise level, can distort communication.

Why do people choose one channel of communication over another—for instance, a phone call instead of a face-to-face talk? One answer might be anxiety! An estimated 5 to 20 percent of the population suffers from debilitating **communication apprehension**, or anxiety, which is undue tension and anxiety about oral communication, written communication, or both.[7] We all know people who dread speaking in front of a group, but some people may find it extremely difficult to talk with others face to face or become extremely anxious when they have to use the telephone. As a result, they may rely on memos, letters, or email to convey messages when a phone call would not only be faster but also more appropriate.

communication apprehension Undue tension and anxiety about oral communication, written communication, or both.

But what about the 80 to 95 percent of the population who do not suffer from this problem? Is there any general insight we might be able to provide regarding choice of communication channel? The answer is a qualified "yes." A model of media richness has been developed to explain channel selection among managers.[8]

Research has found that channels differ in their capacity to convey information. Some are rich in that they have the ability to (1) handle multiple cues at the same time, (2) allow rapid feedback, and (3) be very personal. Others are lean in that they score low on these three factors. As Exhibit 6-2 illustrates, face-to-face conversation scores highest in terms of **channel richness** because it provides for the maximum amount of information to be transmitted during a communication episode. That is, it offers multiple information cues (words, postures, facial expressions, gestures, intonations), immediate feedback (both verbal and nonverbal), and the personal touch of "being there." Impersonal written media such as formal reports and bulletins rate lowest in richness.

channel richness The amount of information that can be transmitted during a communication episode.

EXHIBIT 6-2   Information Richness of Communication Channels

Sources: Based on R. H. Lengel and R. L. Daft, "The Selection of Communication Media as an Executive Skill," *Academy of Management Executive,* August 1988, pp. 225–232; and R. L. Daft and R. H. Lengel, "Organizational Information Requirements, Media Richness, and Structural Design," *Managerial Science,* May 1996, pp. 554–572. Reproduced from R. L. Daft and R. A. Noe, *Organizational Behavior* (Fort Worth, TX: Harcourt, 2001), p. 311.

> *❋ What information should be sent by which communication channel?*

The choice of one channel over another depends on whether the message is routine or nonroutine. Routine messages tend to be straightforward and have a minimum of ambiguity. Nonroutine messages are likely to be complicated and have the potential for misunderstanding. Individuals can communicate routine messages efficiently through channels that are lower in richness. However, they can communicate nonroutine messages more effectively by selecting rich channels. Evidence indicates that high-performing managers tend to be more media-sensitive than low-performing managers.[9] In other words, they are better able to match appropriate media richness with the ambiguity involved in the communication.

A 1999 study at Boston University revealed that managers found it easier to deliver bad news (layoffs, promotion denials, and negative feedback) via email, and that the messages were delivered more accurately this way. This does not mean that sending negative information through email is always recommended. One of the co-authors of the study noted that "offering negative comments face-to-face is often taken as a sign that the news is important and the deliverer cares about the recipient."[10]

The Feedback Loop

The final link in the communication process is the **feedback loop**. Feedback lets us know whether understanding has been achieved. If the feedback loop is to succeed in preventing miscommunication, the receiver needs to give feedback and the sender needs to check for it. Many receivers forget that there is a responsibility involved in communication: to give feedback. For instance, if you sit in a boring lecture, but never discuss with the instructor ways that the delivery could be improved, you have not engaged in communication with your instructor.

When either the sender or the receiver fails to engage in the feedback process, the communication is effectively one-way communication. Two-way communication involves both talking and listening. Many managers communicate badly because they fail to use two-way communication.[11]

One of the greatest difficulties managers have is providing performance feedback. In *From Concepts to Skills*, on pages 217–218, we discuss strategies for providing performance feedback. We also provide some practice exercises for doing so.

The Context

All communication takes place within a context, and violations of that context may create additional problems in sending and receiving messages. For instance, the context of a workplace presents different expectations about how to interact with people than does the context of a bus stop. The workplace may demand more formal interaction, while communication at a bus stop is generally expected to be informal. In some situations, informal communication can look unprofessional, and thus be viewed negatively. In other situations, formal communication can make others feel awkward, if the formality is out of place. Thus, it is important to consider context in both encoding the message and choosing the channel.

feedback loop The final link in the communication process; it puts the message back into the system as a check against misunderstandings.

Companies use the technique of 360-degree feedback to ensure that individuals get feedback from co-workers and subordinates. As a senior vice-president with Scotiabank, Claude Norfolk found that sometimes feedback hurts. "I was really surprised, for example, to find out that I needed to work on my listening skills, because I thought I was a pretty good listener." Turns out his wife agreed with Norfolk's colleagues. Still, he found value in the exercise. Feedback almost always brings with it valuable insights, which we can use for greater understanding.

BARRIERS TO EFFECTIVE COMMUNICATION

> Dofasco's former CEO, John Mayberry, initially had difficulty communicating with his employees. He didn't really respect them, because he felt they represented an entitlement culture ("good day's work, a day's pay, nice retirement package").[12] Thus, he used selective perception when evaluating their concerns. Because he carried out surprise inspections, employees worried they would be fired for any little problem. This made them defensive. What are other ways that communication can be negatively affected?

2 What are the barriers to communication?

A number of factors have been identified as barriers to communication. The more prominent ones are filtering, selective perception, defensiveness, information overload, and language.

Filtering

filtering A sender's manipulation of information so that it will be seen more favourably by the receiver.

Filtering occurs when a sender manipulates information so that the receiver will view it more favourably. For example, when a manager tells a senior executive what the manager thinks the executive wants to hear, the manager is filtering information. Does this happen much in organizations? Sure! As information is passed up to senior executives, employees must condense and summarize it so that those on top don't become overloaded with information. The personal interests and perceptions of what is important by those doing the summarizing will result in filtering.

The major determinant of filtering is the number of levels in an organization's structure. The more levels in an organization's hierarchy, the more opportunities there are for filtering information.

Selective Perception

Receivers in the communication process selectively see and hear based on their needs, motivations, experience, background, and other personal characteristics. Receivers also project their interests and expectations into communications as they decode them. For example, the employment interviewer who believes that young people are more interested in spending time on leisure and social activities than working extra hours to further their careers is likely to be influenced by that stereotype when interviewing young job applicants. As we discussed in Chapter 2, we do not see reality; rather, we interpret what we see and call it "reality."

Enron's former CEO, Jeff Skilling, is a good example of a person with selective perception. When he was interviewed in November 2001 as information about Enron's accounting problems was just starting to emerge, he refused to acknowledge that anything wrong had gone on at the company. To him, Enron represented "a totally different way of thinking about business—we got it," he said.[13] His implication was that it was everyone else who was using selective perception in failing to recognize Enron's greatness. As the scandal continued to unfold, it became obvious that it was Skilling who was using selective perception.

Defensiveness

When people feel that they are being threatened, they tend to react in ways that reduce their ability to achieve mutual understanding. That is, they become defensive—engaging in behaviours such as verbally attacking others, making sarcastic remarks, being overly judgmental, and questioning others' motives. So when individuals interpret another's message as threatening, they often respond in ways that hinder effective communication. *OB in the Workplace* on page 191 shows how defensiveness between the new head of FPI and the company's employees led to the breakdown of an acquisitions deal.

Seafood Companies Fail to Reach Acquisition Agreement

Why does defensiveness harm communication? John Risley, chair and co-founder of Halifax-based Clearwater Seafood, aimed to create a seafood giant by acquiring St. John's, Newfoundland-based Fishery Products International (FPI).[14]

At first Risley was successful in his goal, when in May 2001 he engineered a takeover of the FPI board. Immediately, he promised Newfoundlanders that they would lose no jobs. This was a relief to the fishery workers, who had seen jobs tumble by two-thirds in the past decades.

However, in January 2002 union representatives were told that to cut costs, up to 580 jobs would be lost from three rural Newfoundland plants. This announcement angered workers and politicians alike. Risley defensively argued that the culture of Newfoundland was the real problem: "This is a culture in which people think there's value in the number of jobs that become eligible for unemployment insurance," he said.

Allan Moulton, a union leader and employee at FPI's Marystown plant for 30 years, spoke up at a public hearing on the FPI-Clearwater acquisition: "We're not the only seasonal workers in Canada and it's unfortunate Newfoundland really got pegged with this," he added. "We worked long hours in this industry and every single worker worked hard to save Fishery Products International, and we were successful and we want to get back to doing that."

During 2002, the acquisition was called off because the two companies could not reach agreement, and plans to modernize FPI's plants were scrapped. In mid-2006, FPI was still having difficulties and hoping to sell off some of its holdings. More considerate communication by Risley might have led to fewer problems and less defensiveness, and might have allowed his planned acquisition to go through.

Clearwater Seafood
www.clearwater.ca

Information Overload

Individuals have a finite capacity for processing data. When the information we have to work with exceeds our ability to process it, the result is **information overload**. With emails, phone calls, faxes, meetings, and the need to keep current in one's field, more and more managers and professionals are complaining that they are suffering from too much information. A related issue is the question of how much information managers should share with employees.

What happens when individuals have more information than they can sort out and use? They tend to select out, ignore, pass over, or forget information. Or they may put off further processing until the overload situation is over. Regardless, the result is lost information and less effective communication.

information overload The state of having more information than one can process.

Language

Words mean different things to different people. "The meanings of words are not in the words; they are in us."[15] Age, education, and cultural background are three of the more obvious variables that influence the language a person uses and the definitions he or she gives to words. For instance, when Alanis Morissette sang "Isn't It Ironic?" middle-aged English professors complained that she completely misunderstood the meaning of "irony"—but the millions who bought her CD understood what she meant.

THE FAR SIDE   BY GARY LARSON

"Well, actually, Doreen, I rather resent being
called a 'swamp thing.' ... I prefer the
term 'wetlands-challenged-mutant.'"

Source: The Far Side by Gary Larson, Copyright © 1994 for
Works, Inc. All rights reserved. Used with permission.

Even with a common language, such as English, our usage of that language is far from uniform. For example, in many organizations, employees come from diverse backgrounds and, therefore, have different patterns of speech. Additionally, the grouping of employees into departments creates specialists who develop their own jargon or technical language. In large organizations, members are also often widely dispersed geographically—even operating in different countries—and individuals in each location will use terms and phrases that are unique to their area. In hierarchical organizations, sometimes the language of senior executives can be confusing to operative employees who are unfamiliar with management jargon.

Senders tend to assume that the words and terms they use mean the same to the receiver that they do to them. This, of course, is often incorrect and can create communication difficulties. The multicultural environment of many of today's workplaces makes communication issues even more complex. In many workplaces, there are people whose first language is something other than English. This means that even more opportunities arise for confusion about meaning. It is therefore important to be aware that your understanding of the particular meaning of a word or phrase may not be shared by all. Exhibit 6-3 shows individuals who have very different views on what words to use.

Communicating Under Stress

* *How can you communicate better when you're stressed out?*

One of the most difficult times to communicate properly is when one is under stress. While stress can arise from any number of situations, it can be particularly stressful to have to communicate in something other than one's first language. One consultant has identified several tips for communicating under stress. These tips are also appropriate for less stressful communication.[16]

- *Speak clearly.* Be direct about what you want to say, and avoid hiding behind words. For instance, as difficult as it might be to say "You did not receive the position," the listener is better able to process the information when it is spoken that directly.

- *Be aware of the nonverbal part of communicating.* Tone, facial expression, and body language send signals that may or may not be consistent with your message. In a stressful situation, it is best to speak in a neutral manner.

- *Think carefully about how you state things.* In many situations, it is better to be restrained so that you do not offend your listener. For instance, when you threaten someone if they do not do exactly what you want ("I insist on speaking to your manager this minute"), you simply escalate the situation. It is better to state what you want calmly, so that you can be heard accurately.

CURRENT ISSUES IN COMMUNICATION

How are electronics changing the way people communicate with each other in organizations? How important is nonverbal communication? What does silence have to do with communicating? Why do men and women often have difficulty communicating with each other? How can individuals improve their cross-cultural communication? We address each of these issues below.

❸ What are other issues in communication?

Electronic Communications

Since the early 1980s, we have been subjected to an onslaught of new electronic ways to communicate. Electronic communications (including pagers, fax machines, videoconferencing, electronic meetings, email, cellphones, voice mail, and BlackBerrys) make it possible for you to work even if you are away from your workstation. These technologies are largely reshaping the way we communicate in organizations.[17] You can be reached when you are in a meeting; having a lunch break; visiting a customer's office across town; watching a movie in a crowded theatre; or playing golf on a Saturday morning. The line between an employee's work and nonwork life is no longer distinct, meaning all employees theoretically can be "on call" 24 hours a day.

Organizational boundaries become less relevant as a result of electronic communications. Why? Because networked computers allow employees to jump vertical levels within the organization, work full-time at home or someplace other than "the office," and have ongoing communications with people in other organizations.

Email

Email has added considerably to the number of hours worked per week, according to a recent study by Christina Cavanagh, professor of management communications at the Richard Ivey School of Business, University of Western Ontario. Between 2000 and 2002, business professionals and executives said they were working six more hours a week, responding to email.[18] Researchers calculate that 141 billion email messages circulate the globe each day. Five years ago, that number was 5.1 billion email messages.[19] One researcher suggests that knowledge workers devote about 28 percent of their days to email.[20]

Despite the large investment of time, email is not always the best way to communicate. It does not provide either the verbal or nonverbal nuances that a face-to-face meeting does. There has been some attempt to remedy this through the development of "emoticons" (for example, the smiley face :-)) to indicate a friendly tone, and abbreviations (for example, *IMHO*, "in my humble opinion") to indicate that individuals are respectfully trying to convey their own viewpoints. There is also the standard warning not to write emails in ALL CAPS, as doing so is an indication that one is shouting. Exhibit 6-4 on page 194 illustrates some of the conventional symbols used in email.

✳ *Ever notice that communicating via email can lead to misunderstandings?*

The information overload caused by the use of email in the workplace deserves greater consideration by managers and employees alike. Individuals may use email to hide from direct interaction, to protect their

Christina Cavanagh: Thinking Outside the Inbox
www.christinacavanagh.com

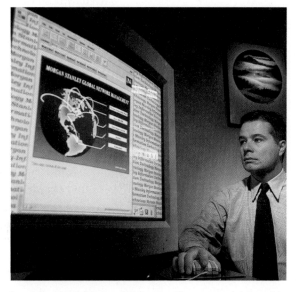

Investment bank Morgan Stanley uses the company's intranet to distribute data and information to employees at its 600 offices around the world. For example, the global network allows traders in Japan to receive up-to-the-minute information on securities transactions from colleagues in New York. Morgan Stanley has also connected its "hoot-and-holler" worldwide voice-messaging system to its intranet, allowing salespeople to receive messages from their workstation speakers on the trading floor.

Electronic mail need not be emotion-free. Over the years, email users have developed a set of symbols (*emoticons*) for expressing emotions. For instance, the use of all caps (as in THIS PROJECT NEEDS YOUR IMMEDIATE ATTEN-TION!) is the email equivalent of shouting. The following highlights some emoticons:

:)	Smile	:-|	Disappointed
<g>	Grin	:-@	Scream
:(	Frown	:-0	Yell
;)	Wink	:-D	Shock or surprise
:-[	Really sad face	:'(	Crying

Pfizer Canada
www.pfizer.ca

power, or to create a one-way communication tool. Email has also become a tool to create paper trails for interaction, allowing people to avoid face-to-face communication on difficult topics. Moreover, for people with a high need for social contact, a heavy reliance on electronic communications is likely to lead to lower job satisfaction.

Some managers are starting to respond to the negative effects of email in the workplace. At the beginning of 2005, Jon Coleman, vice-president and general manager of Markham, Ontario-based Pfizer Consumer Healthcare, asked his staff to cut the number of emails they sent by 25 percent over the next year. In July 2005, Coleman's group introduced Freedom Six to Six to help meet their goal. This program bans employees from sending email messages between 6 p.m. and 6 a.m., and on weekends. Coleman notes that employees should not measure their productivity based on the number of emails they handle. Rather, they should spend more time doing their actual work.[21]

Considerations for Writing and Sending Email   Despite many advantages to email, it is important to realize that it is virtually indestructible once it gets backed up on your company's server. Also, its very speed and accessibility can cause miscommunication and misdirected messages. Individuals often make stronger negative statements when using email than they would in holding a face-to-face conversation.[22] Individuals often give little thought to how their emails might be interpreted, and assume that their intent will be readily apparent to the recipient, even though this is not always the case.[23]

With these issues in mind, consider the following tips for writing and sending email offered by business professor Christina Cavanagh of the University of Western Ontario:[24]

- Don't send emails without a subject line.
- Be careful in your use of emoticons and acronyms for business communication.
- Write your message clearly, and briefly.
- Copy emails to others only if they really need the information.
- Sleep on angry emails before sending to be sure you are sending the right message.

Case Incident—Emailing "Lazy" Employees on page 216 asks you to evaluate one manager's use of email to tell his employees to work harder.

Employees should also be aware that email is not necessarily private, and companies often take the position that they have the right to read your email. Some wonder, however, whether reading employee email is ethical. *Focus on Ethics* illustrates that employees cannot assume that their email is private.

FOCUS ON **ETHICS**

Your Email Can Get You Fired

Canadian Auto Workers (CAW)
www.caw.ca

Canadian National Railway (CN)
www.cn.ca

Should your email be safe from your manager's eyes? The Canadian Auto Workers (CAW) union expressed outrage in early 1998 when it discovered that Montreal-based Canadian National Railway (CN) was reading employees' email messages.[25]

"Our people feel violated. You're given an email address and you have a password, and it's yours. It's personal" is the view of Abe Rosner, a national CAW representative. CN, however, disagrees: "Email is to be used for CN business-approved activities only. Flowing from this is that any communication exchanged on the system is viewed as company property," explains Mark Hallman, a CN spokesperson.

While most employees do not think managers should listen to their subordinates' voice mail messages or read their emails, some managers disagree. More than 20 percent of managers surveyed recently said that they monitored their employees' voice mail, email, and/or computer files. The managers argue that the company owns the systems used to produce this material, and therefore they should have access to the information.

Fred Jones (not his real name) was fired from a Canadian company for forwarding dirty jokes to his clients.[26] Until this incident, Jones had been a high-performing employee who sold network computers for his company. Jones thought that he was only sending the jokes to clients who liked them, and assumed the clients would tell him if they didn't want to receive the jokes. Instead, a client complained to the company about receiving the dirty jokes. After an investigation, the company fired Jones. Jones is still puzzled about being fired. He views his email as private; to him, sending jokes is the same as telling them at the water cooler.

Jones was not aware that under current law, employee information, including email, is not necessarily private. Most federal employees, provincial public sector employees, and employees working for federally regulated industries are covered by the federal Privacy Act and Access to Information Act, in place since 1985. Many private sector employees are not covered by privacy legislation, however.

Ann Cavoukian, Information and Privacy Commissioner of Ontario, notes that "employees deserve to be treated like adults and companies should limit surveillance to rare instances, such as when there is suspicion of criminal activity or harassment."[27] She suggests that employers use respect and courtesy when dealing with employees' email, and she likens email to office phone calls, which generally are not monitored by the employer. It is clearly important, in any event, that employees be aware of their companies' policies on email.

Instant Messaging

Instant messaging (IM), which has been popular among teens for more than a decade, is now rapidly moving into business.[28]

Instant messaging is essentially real-time email. Its growth has been spectacular. In 2002 Canadians sent 174 million text messages, in 2003 they sent 352 million text messages, and in 2004 they sent more than 710 million text messages.[29] Experts estimate that by 2005, more people will be using IM than email as their primary communication tool at work.[30]

IM is a fast and inexpensive means for managers to stay in touch with employees and for employees to stay in touch with each other. It also provides several advantages over email. There's no delay, no inbox clutter of messages, and no uncertainty as to whether the message was received. Managers also find that IM is an excellent means for monitoring employees' physical presence at their workstations. "With a glance at their contact lists, users can tell who's logged on and available right now."[31] Service technicians at Ajax, Ontario-based Pitney Bowes Canada started using IM rather than pagers, because "it's cheaper and it's two-way."[32] The company knows if messages are received.

IM isn't going to replace email. Email is still probably a better device for conveying long messages that need to be saved. IM is preferred for sending one or two-line messages that would just clutter up an email inbox. On the downside, some IM users find the technology intrusive and distracting. IM's continual online presence can make it hard for employees to concentrate and stay focused. Managers also express concern that IM will be used by employees to chat with friends and colleagues about nonwork issues. Finally, because instant messages are easily broken into, many organizations are concerned about IM security.[33]

Nonverbal Communication

Anyone who has ever paid a visit to a singles bar or a nightclub is aware that communication need not be verbal in order to convey a message. A glance, a stare, a smile, a frown, a provocative body movement—they all convey meaning. This example illustrates that no discussion of communication would be complete without a discussion of **nonverbal communication**. This includes body movements, facial expressions, and the physical distance between the sender and the receiver.

The academic study of body motions has been labelled **kinesics**. It refers to gestures, facial configurations, and other movements of the body. Because it is a relatively new field, there is not complete agreement on findings. Still, body movement is an important segment of the study of communication.

nonverbal communication Messages conveyed through body movements, facial expressions, and the physical distance between the sender and the receiver.

kinesics The study of body motions, such as gestures, facial configurations, and other movements of the body.

✳ *Does body language really make a difference?*

It has been argued that every body movement has a meaning and that no movement is accidental.[34] Through body language, we can say "Help me, I'm confused," or "Leave me alone, I'm really angry." Rarely do we send our messages consciously. We act out our state of being with nonverbal body language, even if we are not aware of doing so. In North America, we lift one eyebrow for disbelief. We rub our noses for puzzlement. We clasp our arms to isolate ourselves or to protect ourselves. We shrug our shoulders for indifference, wink one eye for intimacy, tap our fingers for impatience, slap our foreheads for forgetfulness.[35] Babies and young children provide another good illustration of effective use of nonverbal communication. Although they lack developed language skills, they often use fairly sophisticated body language to communicate their physical and emotional needs. Such use of body language underscores its importance in communicating needs throughout life.

While we may disagree on the specific meaning of these movements (and different cultures may interpret specific body movements differently), body language adds to and often complicates verbal communication. For instance, if you read the transcript of a meeting, you do not grasp the impact of what was said in the same way you would if you had been there or had seen the meeting on video. Why? There is no record of nonverbal communication. The *intonations*, or emphasis, given to words or phrases is missing.

The *facial expression* of a person also conveys meaning. A snarling face says something different from a smile. Facial expressions, along with intonations, can show arrogance, aggressiveness, fear, shyness, and other characteristics that would never be communicated if you read a transcript of the meeting.

Studies indicate that those who maintain *eye contact* while speaking are viewed with more credibility than those whose eye contact wanders. People who make eye contact are also deemed more competent than those who do not.

The way individuals space themselves in terms of *physical distance*, commonly called **proxemics**, also has meaning. What is considered proper spacing largely depends on cultural norms. For instance, studies have shown that those from "contact" cultures (e.g., Arabs, Latin Americans, southern Europeans) are more comfortable with body closeness and touch than those from "noncontact" cultures (Asians, North Americans, northern Europeans).[36] These differences can lead to confusion. If someone stands closer to you than expected according to your cultural norms, you may interpret the action as an expression of aggressiveness or sexual interest. However, if the person stands farther away than you expect, you might think he or she is displeased with you

proxemics The study of physical space in interpersonal relationships.

or uninterested. Someone whose cultural norms differ from yours might be very surprised by your interpretation.

Environmental factors such as seating arrangements or the conditions of the room can also send intended or unintended messages. A person whose desk faces the doorway demonstrates command of his or her physical space, while perhaps also conveying that one should not come too close.

It is important for the receiver to be alert to these nonverbal aspects of communication. You should look for nonverbal cues as well as listen to the literal meaning of a sender's words. In particular, you should be aware of contradictions between the messages. The manager may say that she is free to talk to you about that raise you have been seeking, but you may see nonverbal signals from her (such as looking at her watch) that suggest that this is not the time to discuss the subject. It is not uncommon for people to express one emotion verbally and another nonverbally. These contradictions often suggest that actions speak louder (and more accurately) than words.

We should monitor body language with some care. For instance, while it is often thought that individuals who cross their arms in front of their chests are showing resistance to a message, they might also do this if they are feeling cold, regardless of their reactions to a message.

Silence as Communication

Sherlock Holmes once solved a murder mystery based not on what happened but on what *didn't* happen. Holmes remarked to his assistant, Dr. Watson, about "the curious incident of the dog in the nighttime." Watson, surprised, responds, "But the dog did nothing in the nighttime." To which Holmes replied, "That was the curious incident." Holmes concluded the crime had to be committed by someone with whom the dog was familiar because the watchdog did not bark.

The dog that did not bark in the night is often used as a metaphor for an event that is significant by reason of its absence. That story is also an excellent illustration of the importance of silence in communication.

Professors Craig Pinder of the University of Victoria and Karen Harlos of McGill University have noted that silence—defined here as an absence of speech or noise— generally has been ignored as a form of communication in organizational behaviour because it represents *in*action or *non*behaviour. But silence is not necessarily inaction. Nor is it, as many believe, a failure to communicate. Silence can, in fact, be a powerful form of communication.[37] It can mean someone is thinking or contemplating a response to a question. It can mean a person is anxious and fearful of speaking. It can signal agreement, dissent, frustration, or anger.

In terms of organizational behaviour, we can see several links between silence and work-related behaviour. For instance, silence is a critical element of groupthink because it implies agreement with the majority. It can be a way for employees to express dissatisfaction, as when they "suffer in silence." It can be a sign that someone is upset, as when a typically talkative person suddenly says nothing—"What's the matter with him? Is he all right?" It's a powerful tool used by individuals to signal disfavour by shunning or ignoring someone with "silent insults." As well, it's a crucial element of group decision making, allowing individuals to think over and contemplate what others have said.

Failing to pay close attention to the silent portion of a conversation can result in missing a vital part of the message. Astute communicators watch for gaps, pauses, and hesitations. They hear and interpret silence. They treat pauses, for instance, as analogous to a flashing yellow light at an intersection—they pay attention to what comes next. Is the person thinking, deciding how to frame an answer? Is the person suffering from communication apprehension? Sometimes the real message in a communication is buried in the silence.

Communication Barriers Between Women and Men

Research indicates that women use language to create connection while men use language to emphasize status and power. The businesswomen conversing here illustrate that women speak and hear a language of connection and intimacy.

Research by Deborah Tannen provides us with important insights into differences in the conversation styles of men and women.[38] In particular, Tannen has been able to explain why gender often creates oral communication barriers. Her research does not suggest that *all* men or *all* women behave the same way in their communication, but she illustrates some important generalizations.

The essence of Tannen's research is that men use talk to emphasize status, while women use it to create connection. According to Tannen, women speak and hear a language of connection and intimacy, while men speak and hear a language of status and independence. So, for many men, conversations are primarily a way to preserve independence and maintain status in a hierarchical social order. For many women, however, conversations are negotiations for closeness in which people try to seek and give confirmation and support. The following examples will illustrate Tannen's thesis.

Men often complain that women talk on and on about their problems. Women criticize men for not listening. What is happening is that when men hear a problem, they often assert their desire for independence and control by offering solutions. Many women, on the other hand, view telling a problem as a means to promote closeness. The women present the problem to gain support and connection, not to get the male's advice. Mutual understanding, as sought by women, is symmetrical. But giving advice is asymmetrical—it sets up the (male) advice giver as more knowledgeable, more reasonable, and more in control; this contributes to distancing men and women in their efforts to communicate.

Men often criticize women for seeming to apologize all the time. Men tend to see the phrase "I'm sorry" as a weakness because they interpret the phrase to mean the woman is accepting blame. However, women typically use "I'm sorry" to express empathy: "I know you must feel bad about this. I probably would too in the same position."

While Tannen has received wide acknowledgment of her work, some suggest that it is anecdotal and/or based on faulty research. Goldsmith and Fulfs argue that men and women have more similarities than differences as communicators, although they acknowledge that when communication difficulties do appear, it is appealing to attribute them to gender.[39] Despite this, Nancy Langton, your Vancouver-based author, has noted, based on evidence from role plays, that men and women make requests for raises differently, and men are more likely to state that men were more effective at making requests, while women are more likely to indicate that it was women who handled the interaction more favourably.[40]

Cross-Cultural Communication

Effective communication is difficult under the best of conditions. Cross-cultural factors clearly create the potential for increased communication problems.

Cultural Barriers

✳ *What factors hinder cross-cultural communication?*

One author has identified four specific problems related to language difficulties in cross-cultural communications.[41] First, there are *barriers caused by semantics.* As we have noted previously, words mean different things to different people. This is particularly true for people from different national cultures. Some words, for instance, do not translate

Ottawa-based Donna Cona made history when it designed and installed the computer network for the Government of Nunavut. Two-thirds of the firm's software engineers are Aboriginal. Peter Baril, Nunavut's director of informatics services, notes: "Donna Cona's quiet and knowledgeable approach was perhaps the most important skill brought to our project. No other style could have worked in this predominantly Aboriginal environment."

between cultures. For instance, the new capitalists in Russia may have difficulty communicating with their English-speaking counterparts because English terms such as *efficiency, free market,* and *regulation* cannot be translated directly into Russian.

Second, there are *barriers caused by word connotations.* Words imply different things in different languages. The Japanese word *hai* translates as "yes," but its connotation may be "yes, I am listening," rather than "yes, I agree." Western executives may be hampered in their negotiations if they do not understand this connotation.

Third are *barriers caused by tone differences.* In some cultures language is formal, and in others it's informal. In some cultures, the tone changes depending on the context: People speak differently at home, in social situations, and at work. Using a personal, informal style in a situation where a more formal style is expected can be embarrassing and offensive.

Fourth, there are *barriers caused by differences in perceptions.* People who speak different languages actually view the world in different ways. The Inuit perceive snow differently because they have many words for it. They also perceive "no" differently from English speakers because the Inuit have no such word in their vocabulary.

Overcoming Cross-Cultural Difficulties

When communicating with people from a different culture, what can you do to reduce misperceptions, misinterpretations, and misevaluations? Following these four rules can be helpful:[42]

- *Assume differences until similarity is proven.* Most of us assume that others are more similar to us than they actually are. But people from different countries often are very different from us. So you are far less likely to make an error if you assume others are different from you rather than assuming similarity until difference is proven.

- *Emphasize description rather than interpretation or evaluation.* Interpreting or evaluating what someone has said or done, in contrast with describing, is based more on the observer's culture and background than on the observed situation. As a result, delay judgment until you have had sufficient time to observe and interpret the situation from the differing viewpoints of all the cultures involved.

- *Be empathetic.* Before sending a message, put yourself in the recipient's shoes. What are his or her values, experiences, and frames of reference? What do you know about his or her education, upbringing, and background that can give you added insight? Try to see the other person as he or she really is.

- *Treat your interpretations as a working hypothesis.* Once you have developed an explanation for a new situation or think you empathize with someone from a foreign culture, treat your interpretation as a hypothesis that needs further testing rather than as a certainty. Carefully assess the feedback provided by recipients to see if it confirms your hypothesis. For important decisions or communiqués, you can also check with other foreign and home-country colleagues to ensure that your interpretations are on target.

HOW COMMUNICATION BREAKDOWN LEADS TO CONFLICT

In response to massive layoffs in the 1990s, Dofasco's mill employees became unhappy and sought ways to press grievances against the company and protect their jobs. Employees were kept out of the loop, felt they were not respected, and looked to alternative arrangements to get their voices heard by management. The communication breakdown led to a major conflict between the employees and the company's CEO. What can be done about conflict to make sure it does not get out of control?

4 What is conflict?

Conflict can be a serious problem in *any* organization. It might not lead to co-CEOs going after each other in court, as happened when brothers Wallace and Harrison McCain battled over command of McCain Foods, the New Brunswick-based french-fry empire they had built together. Still, it can certainly hurt an organization's performance and lead to the loss of good employees.

Conflict Defined

conflict A process that begins when one party perceives that another party has negatively affected, or is about to negatively affect, something that the first party cares about.

Several common themes underlie most definitions of conflict.[43] Conflict must be *perceived* by the parties to it; if no one is aware of a conflict, it is generally agreed that no conflict exists. Conflict also involves opposition or incompatibility, and some form of interaction between the parties.[44] These factors set the conditions that determine the beginning point of the conflict process. We can define **conflict**, then, as a process that begins when one party perceives that another party has negatively affected, or is about to negatively affect, something that the first party cares about.[45]

This definition is deliberately broad. It describes that point in any ongoing activity when an interaction "crosses over" to become conflict. It includes the wide range of conflicts that people experience in groups and organizations—incompatibility of goals, differences over interpretations of facts, disagreements based on behavioural expectations, and the like. Finally, our definition is flexible enough to cover the full range of conflict levels—from subtle forms of disagreement to overt and violent acts.

Conflict has positive sides and negative sides, which we will discuss further when we cover functional and dysfunctional conflict. For more on this debate, refer to the *Point/Counterpoint* discussion on page 212.

Functional vs. Dysfunctional Conflict

functional conflict Conflict that supports the goals of the group and improves its performance.

dysfunctional conflict Conflict that hinders group performance.

Not all conflict is bad. Some conflicts support the goals of the group and improve its performance; these are **functional**, or constructive, forms of conflict. But there are conflicts that hinder group performance; these are **dysfunctional**, or destructive, forms of conflict. The criterion that differentiates functional from dysfunctional conflict is group performance. If a group is unable to achieve its goals because of conflict, then the conflict is dysfunctional.

> ✳ *Is conflict always bad?*

Exhibit 6-5 provides a way of visualizing conflict behaviour. All conflicts exist somewhere along this continuum. At the lower part of the continuum, we have conflicts characterized by subtle, indirect, and highly controlled forms of tension. An illustration might be a student politely objecting to a point the instructor has just made in class. Conflict intensities escalate as they move upward along the continuum, until they become highly destructive. Strikes and lockouts, riots, and wars clearly fall into this upper range. For the most part, you should assume that conflicts that reach the upper ranges of the continuum are almost always dysfunctional. Functional conflicts are typically confined to the lower range of the continuum. *Case Incident—Managing Conflict at Schneider National* on the CD-ROM that accompanies this textbook describes how functional conflict improves an organization.

EXHIBIT 6-5	Conflict Intensity Continuum

Annihilatory conflict	Overt efforts to destroy the other party
	Aggressive physical attacks
	Threats and ultimatums
	Assertive verbal attacks
	Overt questioning or challenging of others
No conflict	Minor disagreements or misunderstandings

Sources: Based on S. P. Robbins, *Managing Organizational Conflict: A Nontraditional Approach* (Upper Saddle River, NJ: Prentice Hall, 1974), pp. 93–97; and F. Glasl, "The Process of Conflict Escalation and the Roles of Third Parties," in *Conflict Management and Industrial Relations,* ed. G. B. J. Bomers and R. Peterson (Boston: Kluwer-Nijhoff, 1982), pp. 119–140.

RESEARCH FINDINGS   Conflict

Research on conflict has yet to clearly identify those situations in which conflict is more likely to be constructive than destructive. However, there is growing evidence that the source of the conflict is a significant factor determining functionality.[46] **Cognitive conflict**, which is task-oriented and occurs because of differences in perspectives and judgments, can often result in identifying potential solutions to problems. Thus it would be regarded as functional conflict. **Affective conflict**, which is emotional and aimed at a person rather than an issue, tends to be dysfunctional conflict.

cognitive conflict Conflict that is task-oriented and related to differences in perspectives and judgments.

affective conflict Conflict that is emotional and aimed at a person rather than an issue.

One study of 53 teams found that cognitive conflict, because it generates more alternatives, led to better decisions, more acceptance of the decisions, and ownership of the decisions. Teams experiencing affective conflict, where members had personality incompatibilities and disputes, showed poorer decisions and lower levels of acceptance of the decisions.[47]

Because conflict can involve our emotions in a variety of ways, it can also lead to stress. You may want to refer to the *OB on the Edge—Stress at Work* on pages 98–105 to get some ideas on how to manage the stress that might arise from conflicts you experience.

CONFLICT RESOLUTION

Conflict in the workplace can affect the effectiveness of individuals, teams, and the entire organization.[48] One study found 20 percent of managers' time is spent managing conflict.[49]

5 How can conflict be resolved?

Once conflict arises, what can be done to resolve it? The way a conflict is defined goes a long way toward establishing the sort of outcomes that might settle it. For instance, if I define our salary disagreement as a zero-sum or *win-lose situation*—that is, if you get the increase in pay you want, there will be just that amount less for me—I am going to be far less willing to look for mutual solutions than if I frame the conflict as a potential *win-win situation*. So individual attitudes toward a conflict are important, because attitudes typically define the set of possible settlements.

Conflict Management Strategies

Conflict researchers often use dual concern theory to describe people's conflict management strategies. Dual concern theory considers how one's degree of *cooperativeness* (the degree to which one tries to satisfy the other person's concerns) and *assertiveness* (the degree to which one tries to satisfy one's own concerns) determine how a conflict is handled.[50] The five conflict-handling strategies identified by the theory are as follows:[51]

- *Forcing.* Imposing one's will on the other party.
- *Problem solving.* Trying to reach an agreement that satisfies both one's own and the other party's aspirations as much as possible.
- *Avoiding.* Ignoring or minimizing the importance of the issues creating the conflict.
- *Yielding.* Accepting and incorporating the will of the other party.
- *Compromising.* Balancing concern for oneself with concern for the other party in order to reach a solution.

Forcing is a win-lose solution, as is yielding, while problem solving seeks a win-win solution. Avoiding conflict and pretending it does not exist, and compromising, so that neither person gets what they want, can yield lose-lose solutions. Exhibit 6-6 illustrates these five strategies, along with specific actions that one might take when using them.

Choosing a particular strategy for resolving conflict depends on a variety of factors. Research shows that while people may choose among the strategies, they have an underlying disposition to handle conflicts in certain ways.[52] In addition, some situations call for particular strategies. For instance, when a small child insists on trying to run into the street, a parent may need a forcing strategy to restrain the child. Co-workers who are

EXHIBIT 6-6   Conflict-Handling Strategies and Accompanying Behaviours

ASSERTIVENESS
Trying to satisfy one's own concerns

Assertive — Unassertive

Forcing
Satisfying one's own interests without concern for the other's interests
- Make threats and bluffs
- Make persuasive arguments
- Make positional commitments

Problem solving
Clarifying differences to find mutually beneficial outcomes
- Exchange information about priorities and preferences
- Show insights
- Make trade-offs between important and unimportant issues

Compromising
Giving up something to reach an outcome (done by both parties)
- Match other's concessions
- Make conditional promises and threats
- Search for a middle ground

Avoiding
Withdrawing from or ignoring conflict
- Don't think about the issues

Yielding
Placing the other's interests above one's own
- Make unilateral concessions
- Make unconditional promises
- Offer help

Uncooperative — Cooperative

COOPERATIVENESS

Trying to satisfy the other person's concerns

Sources: Based on K. W. Thomas, "Conflict and Negotiation Processes in Organizations," in *Handbook of Industrial and Organizational Psychology,* vol. 3, 2nd ed., ed. M. D. Dunnette and L. M. Hough (Palo Alto, CA: Consulting Psychologists Press, 1992), p. 668; C. K. W. De Dreu, A. Evers, B. Beersma, E. S. Kluwer, and A. Nauta, "A Theory-Based Measure of Conflict Management Strategies in the Workplace," *Journal of Organizational Behavior* 22, no. 6 (September 2001), pp. 645–668; and D. G. Pruitt and J. Rubin, *Social Conflict: Escalation, Stalemate and Settlement* (New York: Random House, 1986).

having a conflict over setting deadlines to complete a project on time may decide that problem solving is the best strategy to use.

This chapter's *Learning About Yourself Exercise* on page 213–214 gives you the opportunity to discover your preferred conflict-handling strategy. As well, this chapter's *CBC Video Case Incident* shows two men's preference in handling their conflict. *OB in Action—Choosing Strategies to Deal With Conflicts* indicates the situations in which each strategy is best used.

The disagreement between the City of Vancouver and developer Peter Wall produced a compromise that could be called a lose-lose solution, as the following *OB in the Street* shows.

CBC
Buggy Wars

OB IN THE STREET

One Wall Centre Goes Two-Toned

Is compromise necessarily the best way to go? When developer Peter Wall hired architect Peter Busby to design One Wall Centre in downtown Vancouver, the two planned a massive glass skyscraper.[53] City council reviewed the plans and okayed the design, even granting a building height considerably higher than those in the surrounding neighbourhood.

The plans made the building look translucent, but as the tower went up, the glass looked black and impenetrable. Complaints started coming in to City Hall, because the assumption had been that the building would use clear glass. The architect said that Wall had changed his mind about the colour of the glass once construction started. Wall claimed, however, that the city had approved the darker glass sample in use. Unfortunately, no one could find the glass samples.

A planned lawsuit by the city was stopped for lack of evidence. So the two sides reached a compromise: The 48-storey building would have its lower levels in blackened glass, and the top 17 floors in lighter glass, rather than tearing down the building and starting over. Neither the city nor the developer obtained their preferred solution, and meanwhile residents of Vancouver will have the two-tone building, a visible reminder of the outcome of compromise, towering over them for many years to come. 🕱

What Can Individuals Do to Manage Conflict?

There are a number of conflict resolution techniques that individuals can use to try to defuse conflict inside and outside the workplace. These include the following:[54]

- *Problem solving.* Requesting a face-to-face meeting to identify the problem and resolve it through open discussion.

- *Developing superordinate goals.* Creating a shared goal that requires both parties to work together, and motivates them to do so.

- *Smoothing.* Playing down differences while emphasizing common interests with the other party.

OB IN ACTION

Choosing Strategies to Deal With Conflicts[55]

Forcing

→ In emergencies

→ On important but unpopular issues

→ On vital issues when you know you are right

→ Against people who take advantage of noncompetitive behaviour

Problem solving

→ If both sets of concerns are too important to be compromised

→ To merge different perspectives

→ To gain commitment through a consensus

→ To mend a relationship

Avoiding

→ When an issue is trivial

→ When your concerns won't be met

→ When potential disruption outweighs the benefits of resolution

→ To let people cool down and regain perspective

continued

Choosing Strategies to Deal With Conflicts (continued)

Yielding

→ When you find you are wrong

→ To show your reasonableness

→ When issues are more important to others than yourself

→ To build social credits for later issues

→ When harmony and stability are especially important

Compromising

→ When goals are important but not worth more assertive approaches

→ When opponents are committed to mutually exclusive goals

→ To achieve temporary settlements to complex issues

→ To arrive at expedient solutions under time pressure

- *Compromising.* Agreeing with the other party that each will give up something of value to reach an accord.

- *Avoidance.* Withdrawing from, or suppressing, the conflict. The choice of technique may depend on how serious the issue is to you, whether you take a win-win or a win-lose approach, and your preferred conflict management style.

When the conflict is specifically work-related, there are additional techniques that might be used:

- *Expansion of resources.* The scarcity of a resource—say, money, promotion opportunities, office space—can create conflict. Expansion of the resource can create a win-win solution.

- *Authoritative command.* Management can use its formal authority to resolve the conflict and then communicate its desires to the parties involved.

- *Altering the human variable.* Behavioural change techniques such as human relations training can alter attitudes and behaviours that cause conflict.

- *Altering the structural variables.* The formal organization structure and the interaction patterns of conflicting parties can be changed through job redesign, transfers, creation of coordinating positions, and the like.

Resolving Personality Conflicts

Personality conflicts are an everyday occurrence in the workplace. While there is no available data for Canada, supervisors in the United States spend about 18 percent of their time handling personality conflicts among employees.[56] A variety of factors leads to personality conflicts, including the following:[57]

- Misunderstandings based on age, race, or cultural differences

- Intolerance, prejudice, discrimination, or bigotry

- Perceived inequities

- Misunderstandings, rumours, or falsehoods about an individual or group

- Blaming for mistakes or mishaps (finger-pointing)

Personality conflicts can result in lowered productivity when people find it difficult to work together. The individuals experiencing the conflict may seek sympathy from other members of the work group, causing co-workers to take sides. The ideal solution would be for the two people in conflict to work it out between themselves, without involving others, but this does not always happen. However, it is not always possible for people to talk things out, and it may be a Western cultural bias to expect that individuals should generally be able to do so.[58] *OB in Action—Handling Personality Conflicts* on page 205 suggests ways of dealing with personality conflicts in the workplace.

NEGOTIATION

When management-employee relations break down, it is not unusual that employees start to consider joining a labour union. If the employees are successful in their bid for unionization, then it is the labour union that negotiates with management over wage and working conditions. While Dofasco's mill employees did consider joining either the Canadian Auto Workers or the United Steelworkers union, they have not done so yet. One reason might be that CEO John Mayberry worked hard to negotiate effectively with his employees and to foster a supportive environment for all. He did this by creating a performance culture, where employee bonuses and pay are tied to how well the company does. He also encouraged employees to learn from other companies, and even sent a few employees around the world to see what other companies do and how they do it. Mayberry organized employees into teams, getting them to be accountable and to work together to solve problems, make plans and schedules, and provide team members with feedback. In other words, Mayberry created a win-win situation. What steps can help ensure negotiations are effective?

When parties are potentially in conflict, they may choose to negotiate a resolution. Negotiation occurs in the interactions of almost everyone in groups and organizations: Labour bargains with management; managers negotiate with employees, peers, and senior management; salespeople negotiate with customers; purchasing agents negotiate with suppliers; employees agree to answer a colleague's phone for a few minutes in exchange for some past or future benefit. In today's team-based organizations, negotiation skills become critical so that teams can work together effectively.

We define **negotiation** as a process in which two or more parties try to agree on the exchange rate for goods or services they are trading.[59] Note that we use the terms *negotiation* and *bargaining* interchangeably.

Within a negotiation, one should be aware that individuals have *issues, positions,* and *interests. Issues* are items that are specifically placed on the bargaining table for discussion. *Positions* are the individual's stand on the issues. For instance, salary may be an issue for discussion. The salary you hope to receive is your position. Finally, *interests* are the underlying concerns that are affected by the negotiation resolution. For instance, the reason that you might want a six-figure salary is that you are trying to buy a house in Vancouver, and that is your only hope of being able to make mortgage payments.

Negotiators who recognize the underlying interests of themselves and the other party may have more flexibility in achieving a resolution. For instance, in the example just given, an employer who offers you a mortgage at a lower rate than the bank does, or who provides you with an interest-free loan that can be used against the mortgage, may be able to address your underlying interests without actually meeting your salary position. You may be satisfied with this alternative, if you understand what your interest is.

Interest-based bargaining enabled Vancouver-based NorskeCanada (now Catalyst Paper Corporation) to sign a mutually beneficial five-year contract with the Communications, Energy and Paperworkers Union of Canada in fall 2002, after just nine days of negotiations.[60] While the union and NorkseCanada had experienced bitter conflict in previous negotiations, in this particular situation both sides agreed to focus more on the interests of the parties, rather than on demands and concessions. Both sides were pleased with the outcome.

Bargaining Strategies

There are two general approaches to negotiation—*distributive bargaining* and *integrative bargaining.*[61] These are compared in Exhibit 6-7 on page 206.

6 How does one negotiate effectively?

negotiation A process in which two or more parties exchange goods or services and try to agree upon the exchange rate for them.

OB IN ACTION

Handling Personality Conflicts

Tips for employees having a personality conflict

→ **Communicate directly** with the other person to resolve the perceived conflict (emphasize problem solving and common objectives, not personalities).

→ **Avoid dragging** co-workers into the conflict.

→ If dysfunctional conflict persists, **seek help** from direct supervisors or human resource specialists.

Tips for third-party observers of a personality conflict

→ **Do not take sides** in someone else's personality conflict.

→ **Suggest the parties work things out** themselves in a constructive and positive way.

→ If dysfunctional conflict persists, **refer the problem to the parties' direct supervisors**.

Tips for managers whose employees are having a personality conflict

→ **Investigate and document** conflict.

→ If appropriate, **take corrective action** (e.g., feedback or behaviour shaping).

→ If necessary, **attempt informal dispute resolution**.

→ **Refer difficult conflicts** to human resource specialists or hired counsellors for formal resolution attempts and other interventions.

Source: R. Kreitner and A. Kinicki, *Organizational Behavior,* 6th ed. (New York: McGraw Hill, 2004), p. 492, table 14-1. Reprinted by permission of McGraw Hill Education.

EXHIBIT 6-7 Distributive vs. Integrative Bargaining		
Bargaining Characteristic	Distributive Bargaining	Integrative Bargaining
Available resources	Fixed amount of resources to be divided	Variable amount of resources to be divided
Primary motivations	I win, you lose	I win, you win
Primary interests	Opposed to each other	Convergent or congruent with each other
Focus of relationships	Short-term	Long-term

Source: Based on R. J. Lewicki and J. A. Litterer, *Negotiation* (Homewood, IL: Irwin, 1985), p. 280.

Distributive Bargaining

distributive bargaining
Negotiation that seeks to divide up a fixed amount of resources; a win-lose solution.

✳ *Should you try to win at any cost when you bargain?*

Distributive bargaining is a negotiating strategy that operates under zero-sum (win-lose) conditions. That is, any gain I make is at your expense, and vice versa. Probably the most widely cited example of distributive bargaining is in labour-management negotiations over wages. Typically, management comes to the bargaining table determined to keep its labour costs as low as possible. Since every cent more that labour negotiates increases management's costs, each party bargains aggressively and treats the other as an opponent who must be defeated.

When engaged in distributive bargaining, a party focuses on trying to get the opponent to agree to a specific target point, or to get as close to it as possible. Examples of such tactics are persuading your opponent of the impossibility of reaching his or her target point and the advisability of accepting a settlement near yours; arguing that your target is fair, while your opponent's is not; and trying to get your opponent to feel emotionally generous toward you and thus accept an outcome close to your target point.

Integrative Bargaining

integrative bargaining
Negotiation that seeks one or more settlements that can create a win-win solution.

In contrast to distributive bargaining, **integrative bargaining** operates under the assumption that there exists one or more settlements that can create a win-win solution. In terms of intraorganizational behaviour, all things being equal, integrative bargaining is preferable to distributive bargaining. Why? Because the former builds long-term relationships and makes working together in the future easier. It bonds negotiators and allows both sides to leave the bargaining table feeling that they have achieved a victory. For instance, in union-management negotiations, both sides might sit down to figure out other ways to reduce costs within an organization, so that it is possible to have greater wage increases. Distributive bargaining, on the other hand, leaves one party a loser. It tends to build animosities and deepen divisions when people must work together on an ongoing basis.

How to Negotiate

Exhibit 6-8 on page 207 provides a simplified model of the negotiation process. It views negotiation as made up of five steps: (1) developing a strategy; (2) defining ground rules; (3) clarification and justification; (4) bargaining and problem solving; and (5) closure and implementation.

> **EXHIBIT 6-8** **The Negotiation Process**
>
> Developing a strategy → Defining ground rules → Clarification and justification → Bargaining and problem solving → Closure and implementation
>
> *Source:* This model is based on R. J. Lewicki, "Bargaining and Negotiation," *Exchange: The Organizational Behavior Teaching Journal* 6, no. 2 (1981), pp. 39–40.

Developing a Strategy

Before you start negotiating, you need to do your homework. What is the nature of the conflict? What is the history leading up to this negotiation? Who is involved and what are their perceptions of the conflict? What do you want from the negotiation? What are *your* goals? It often helps to put your goals in writing and develop a range of outcomes—from "most hopeful" to "minimally acceptable"—to keep your attention focused.

You also want to prepare an assessment of what you think the other party to your negotiation's goals are. What are they likely to ask for? How entrenched are they likely to be in their position? What intangible or hidden interests may be important to them? What might they be willing to settle for? When you can anticipate your opponent's position, you are better equipped to counter his or her arguments with the facts and figures that support your position.

In determining goals, parties are well advised to consider their "target and resistance" points, as well as their *best alternative to a negotiated agreement* (**BATNA**).[62] The buyer and the seller represent two negotiators. Each has a *target point* that defines what he or she would like to achieve. Each also has a *resistance point,* which marks the lowest outcome that is acceptable—the point below which each would break off negotiations rather than accept a less favourable settlement. The area between these two points makes up each negotiator's aspiration range. As long as there is some overlap between the buyer's and seller's aspiration ranges, there exists a **bargaining zone** where each side's aspirations can be met. Referring to Exhibit 6-9, if the buyer's resistance point is $450, and the seller's resistance point is $500, then the two may not be able to reach agreement because there is no overlap in their aspiration ranges. Recent research suggests that having an attractive BATNA is particularly powerful to a negotiator when the bargaining zone is small.[63] The lengthy and bitter negotiations between the National Hockey League Players' Association and the National Hockey League owners underscored that there was no overlap in the bargaining zone on where the salary cap should be set, as the following *OB in the Workplace* on page 208 shows.

BATNA The *best alternative to a negotiated agreement;* the outcome an individual faces if negotiations fail.

bargaining zone The zone between each party's resistance point, assuming there is overlap in this range.

Eric C. Gould's Negotiation Site www.batna.com

> **EXHIBIT 6-9** **Staking Out the Bargaining Zone**
>
> $400 $475 $525 $600
>
> ← Buyers aspiration range →   Seller's aspiration range →
> Bargaining zone
>
> Buyer's target point   Seller's resistance point   Buyer's resistance point   Seller's target point

OB IN THE WORKPLACE

Hockey Union and Management Fail to Score a Goal

How could an entire hockey season be cancelled? In early February 2005, Gary Bettman, National Hockey League (NHL) commissioner, was signalling to hockey fans throughout North America that the 2004–2005 hockey season was about to be called off.[64] Hockey players had been trying to negotiate a new contract with NHL management since 2003, meeting 14 times in 2003, 14 in 2004, and 9 times by early February to try to resolve their differences. Little success had been made, despite all of those meetings.

Gary Bettman (left), the NHL commissioner, shakes hands with former head of the NHLPA, Bob Goodenow, after they finally reached an end to the stalemate that led to the cancellation of the 2004–2005 hockey season. Neither man seemed able to celebrate victory at the end of their lengthy negotiations.

Each side blamed the other for the stalemate and indicated that their BATNA—not playing any hockey at all for an entire season—was more desirable than ending the dispute.

"Their [the hockey players'] outright rejection of our proposal yesterday [February 9, 2005] I think speaks more to the fact that the union is never, ever, ever, ever—under any circumstances—prepared to play under any kind of cost-certain, economic partnership, salary cap—you pick the term—type of system," said Bill Daly, executive vice-president and chief legal officer of the NHL.

Hockey players saw the issue somewhat differently. "They [management] have made it clear they have only one way of doing things, and that's through their hard-cap system," claimed National Hockey League Players' Association (NHLPA) senior director Ted Saskin.

The NHL and the NHLPA settled their differences in July 2005, and the players agreed to a salary cap, something they had said they absolutely would not do throughout most of the negotiations. The 2004–2005 season's 1230 regular-season games were cancelled and there was no Stanley Cup champion for the first time since 1919, when the final between Montreal and Seattle was cancelled because of a flu epidemic.

One's BATNA represents the alternative that an individual will face if negotiations fail. For instance, during the winter 2005 hockey negotiations, for both hockey players and owners, the BATNA was the loss of the 2004–2005 season.

As part of your strategy, you should determine not only your BATNA but some estimate of the other side's as well.[65] If you go into your negotiation having a good idea of what the other party's BATNA is, you will have a better understanding of how far you can press to achieve the results you desire.

You can practise your negotiating skills in the *Working With Others Exercise* on pages 214–215.

Defining Ground Rules

Once you have done your planning and developed a strategy, you are ready to begin defining the ground rules and procedures with the other party over the negotiation itself. Who will do the negotiating? Where will it take place? What time constraints, if any, will apply? To what issues will negotiation be limited? Will there be a specific

Negotiation skills are critical in the buyer-seller relationship. At this open-air cheese market in Alkmaar, the Netherlands, two purchasing agents for food buyers taste a sample of Edam cheese before they negotiate prices with the seller of the cheese.

procedure to follow if an impasse is reached? During this phase, the parties will also exchange their initial proposals or demands. The *Ethical Dilemma Exercise* on pages 215–216 considers whether it is ever appropriate to lie during negotiations.

Clarification and Justification

When initial positions have been exchanged, both you and the other party will explain, amplify, clarify, bolster, and justify your original demands. This part of the process need not be confrontational. Rather, it is an opportunity for educating and informing each other on the issues, why they are important, and how each arrived at their initial demands. This is the point at which you might want to provide the other party with any documentation that helps support your position.

Bargaining and Problem Solving

The essence of the negotiation process is the actual give and take in trying to hash out an agreement. It is here that concessions will undoubtedly need to be made by both parties. *OB in Action—Tips for Getting to Yes* gives you further ideas on how to make negotiating work for you, based on the popular book *Getting to Yes*.[66]

Closure and Implementation

The final step in the negotiation process is formalizing the agreement that has been worked out and developing procedures that are necessary for implementation and monitoring. For major negotiations—which would include everything from labour-management negotiations such as in the National Hockey League situation, to bargaining over lease terms, to buying real estate, to negotiating a job offer for a senior management position—this will require hammering out the specifics in a formal contract. In most cases, however, closing of the negotiation process is nothing more formal than a handshake.

OB IN ACTION

Tips for Getting to Yes

R. Fisher and W. Ury present four principles for win-win negotiations in their book *Getting to Yes:*

- **Separate** the **people from** the **problem.** Work on the issues at hand, rather than getting involved in personality issues between the parties.

- Focus on **interests, not positions.** Try to identify what each person needs or wants, rather than coming up with an unmovable position.

- Look for ways to achieve **mutual gains.** Rather than focusing on one "right" solution for your position, brainstorm for solutions that will satisfy the needs of both parties.

- Use **objective criteria** to achieve a fair solution. Try to focus on fair standards, such as market value, expert opinion, norms, or laws to help guide decision making.

Source: R. Fisher and W. Ury, *Getting to Yes* (New York: Penguin Books, 1991).

SUMMARY AND IMPLICATIONS

1 **How does communication work?** Findings in this chapter suggest that the goal of perfect communication is unattainable. Yet there is evidence that demonstrates a positive relationship between effective communication (which includes factors such as perceived trust, perceived accuracy, desire for interaction, top-management receptiveness, and upward information requirements) and employee productivity.[67] Therefore, choosing the correct channel, being a good listener, and using feedback well may make for more effective communication.

2 **What are the barriers to communication?** Human beings will always be subject to errors in communication because of filtering, selective perception, defensiveness, information overload, and language. What is said may not be what is heard. Whatever the sender's expectations, the decoded message in the mind of the receiver represents his or her reality. This "reality" will determine the individual's reactions, including performance, motivation, and degree of satisfaction in the workplace.

3 **What are other issues in communication?** The big topics in communication are electronic communications, the importance of nonverbal communication and silence, gender differences in communication, and cross-cultural differences in communication. As we saw in this chapter, email, among other electronic communications, has become far more prevalent, is causing more stress, and can be misused so that it is not always the most effective means of communication. Nonverbal cues help provide a clearer picture of what someone is trying to say. Silence can be an important communication clue, and failing to pay attention to silence can result in missing some or all of a message. Good communicators hear and interpret silence. We can make some generalizations about differences in the conversational style of men and women; men are more likely to use talk to emphasize status, while women use talk to create connection. We noted that there are a variety of barriers when communicating with someone from a different culture, and that it is best to assume differences until similarity is proven, emphasize description rather than *interpretation or evaluation*, practise empathy, and treat your interpretations as a working hypothesis.

4 **What is conflict?** Conflict occurs when one person perceives that another person's actions will have a negative effect on something the first party cares about. Many people automatically assume that all conflict is bad. However, conflict can be either functional (constructive) or dysfunctional (destructive) to the performance of a group or unit. An optimal level of conflict encourages communication, prevents stagnation, stimulates creativity, allows tensions to be released, and plants the seeds of change, yet not so much as to be disruptive or to deter activities.

5 **How can conflict be resolved?** The way a conflict is defined goes a long way toward establishing the sort of outcomes that might settle it. One can work toward a *win-lose solution* or a *win-win solution*. Conflict management strategies are determined by the extent to which one wants to cooperate with another party, and the extent to which one asserts his or her own concerns.

6 **How does one negotiate effectively?** Negotiation is a process in which two or more parties try to agree on the exchange rate for goods or services they are trading. Negotiation is an ongoing activity in groups and organizations. Distributive bargaining can resolve disputes, but it often negatively affects one or more negotiators' satisfaction because it is focused on the short term and because it is confrontational. Integrative bargaining, by contrast, tends to provide outcomes that satisfy all parties and build lasting relationships.

For Review

1. Describe the communication process and identify its key components. Give an example of how this process operates with both oral and written messages.

2. Contrast encoding and decoding.

3. What are the advantages and disadvantages of email? Of instant messaging?

4. What is nonverbal communication? Does it aid or hinder verbal communication?

5. What does the phrase "sometimes the real message in a communication is buried in the silence" mean?

6. What are the managerial implications from the research contrasting male and female communication styles?

7. List four specific problems related to language difficulties in cross-cultural communication.

8. What is the difference between functional and dysfunctional conflict? What determines functionality?

9. What defines the bargaining zone in distributive bargaining?

10. How can you improve your negotiating effectiveness?

For Critical Thinking

1. "Ineffective communication is the fault of the sender." Do you agree or disagree? Discuss.

2. Using the concept of channel richness, give examples of messages best conveyed by email, in face-to-face communication, and on the company bulletin board.

3. Why do you think so many people are poor listeners?

4. Assume one of your co-workers had to negotiate a contract with someone from China. What problems might he or she face? If the co-worker asked for advice, what suggestions would you make to help facilitate a settlement?

5. From your own experience, describe a situation you were involved in where the conflict was dysfunctional. Describe another example, from your experience, where the conflict was functional. Would the other parties in the conflicts agree with your assessment of what is functional or dysfunctional?

OB for You

- If you are having difficulty communicating with someone, you might consider that both you and the other person are contributing something to that breakdown. This tends to be true even if you are inclined to believe that the other person is the party more responsible for the breakdown.

- Often either selective perception or defensiveness gets in the way of communication. As you work in your groups on student projects, you may want to observe communication flows more critically to help you understand ways that communication can be improved and dysfunctional conflict avoided.

- It may seem easier, but avoiding conflict does not necessarily have a more positive outcome than working with someone to resolve the conflict.

- Trying to achieve a win-win solution in a conflict situation tends to lead to better relationships and greater trust.

OB *AT WORK*

POINT

COUNTERPOINT

Conflict Is Good for an Organization

We have made considerable progress in the last 25 years toward overcoming the negative stereotype given to conflict. Most behavioural scientists and an increasing number of practising managers now accept that the goal of effective management is not to eliminate conflict. Rather, it is to create the right intensity of conflict so as to reap its functional benefits.

Let's briefly review how stimulating conflict can provide benefits to the organization.[68]

- *Conflict is a means by which to bring about radical change.* It is an effective device by which management can drastically change the existing power structure, current interaction patterns, and entrenched attitudes.

- *Conflict facilitates group cohesiveness.* While conflict increases hostility between groups, external threats tend to cause a group to pull together as a unit. Intergroup conflicts raise the extent to which members identify with their own group and increase feelings of solidarity, while, at the same time, internal differences and irritations dissolve.

- *Conflict improves group and organizational effectiveness.* The stimulation of conflict sparks the search for new means and goals and clears the way for innovation. The successful resolution of a conflict leads to greater effectiveness, to more trust and openness, to greater attraction of members for one another, and to the depersonalization of future conflicts. In fact, it has been found that as the number of minor disagreements increases, the number of major clashes decreases.

- *Conflict brings about a slightly higher, more constructive level of tension.* Constructive levels of tension improve the chances of solving the conflicts in a way satisfactory to all parties concerned. When the level of tension is very low, the parties are not sufficiently motivated to do something about a conflict.

These points are clearly not comprehensive. As noted in this chapter, conflict provides a number of benefits to an organization. However, groups or organizations that lack conflict are likely to suffer from apathy, stagnation, groupthink, and other debilitating problems. In fact, more organizations probably fail because they have too little conflict rather than too much.

All Conflicts Are Dysfunctional!

It may be true that conflict is an inherent part of any group or organization. It may not be possible to eliminate it completely. However, just because conflicts exist is no reason to worship them. All conflicts are dysfunctional, and it is one of management's major responsibilities to keep conflict intensity as low as humanly possible. A few points support this case:

- *The negative consequences from conflict can be devastating.* The list of negatives associated with conflict is impressive. Obvious negatives include increased turnover, decreased employee satisfaction, labour grievances and strikes, sabotage, physical aggression, and inefficiencies between work units.

- *Effective managers build teamwork.* A good manager builds a coordinated team. Conflict works against such an objective. A successful work group is like a successful sports team: Each member knows his or her role and supports his or her teammates. When a team works well, the whole becomes greater than the sum of the parts. Management creates teamwork by minimizing internal conflicts and facilitating internal coordination.

- *Competition is good for an organization, but not conflict.* Competition and conflict should not be confused with each other. Conflict is behaviour directed against another party, whereas competition is behaviour aimed at obtaining a goal without interference from another party. Competition is healthy; it is the source of organizational vitality. Conflict, on the other hand, is destructive.

- *Managers who accept and stimulate conflict don't survive in organizations.* The whole argument over the value of conflict may be open to question as long as most senior executives in organizations view conflict traditionally. In the traditional view, any conflict is seen as bad. Since the evaluation of a manager's performance is made by higher-level executives, those managers who do not succeed in eliminating conflicts are likely to be appraised negatively. This in turn will reduce opportunities for advancement. Any manager who aspires to move up in such an environment would be wise to follow the traditional view and eliminate any outward signs of conflict. Failure to follow this advice might result in the premature departure of the manager.

What Is Your Primary Conflict-Handling Style?

Indicate how often you rely on each of the following tactics by circling the number you feel is most appropriate. When I have a conflict at work, I do the following:

		Not at All				Very Much
1.	I give in to the wishes of the other party.	1	2	3	4	5
2.	I try to realize a middle-of-the-road solution.	1	2	3	4	5
3.	I push my own point of view.	1	2	3	4	5
4.	I examine issues until I find a solution that really satisfies me and the other party.	1	2	3	4	5
5.	I avoid a confrontation about our differences.	1	2	3	4	5
6.	I concur with the other party.	1	2	3	4	5
7.	I emphasize that we have to find a compromise solution.	1	2	3	4	5
8.	I search for gains.	1	2	3	4	5
9.	I stand for my own and the other party's goals and interests.	1	2	3	4	5
10.	I avoid differences of opinion as much as possible.	1	2	3	4	5
11.	I try to accommodate the other party.	1	2	3	4	5
12.	I insist we both give in a little.	1	2	3	4	5
13.	I fight for a good outcome for myself.	1	2	3	4	5
14.	I examine ideas from both sides to find a mutually optimal solution.	1	2	3	4	5
15.	I try to make differences loom less large.	1	2	3	4	5
16.	I adapt to the other party's goals and interests.	1	2	3	4	5
17.	I strive whenever possible toward a 50-50 compromise.	1	2	3	4	5
18.	I do everything to win.	1	2	3	4	5
19.	I work out a solution that serves my own as well as the other party's interests as well as possible.	1	2	3	4	5
20.	I try to avoid a confrontation with the other party.	1	2	3	4	5

Scoring Key:

To determine your primary conflict-handling strategy, place the number 1 through 5 that represents your score for each statement next to the number for that statement. Then add up the columns.

continued

Yielding	Compromising	Forcing	Problem solving	Avoiding
1. _____	2. _____	3. _____	4. _____	5. _____
6. _____	7. _____	8. _____	9. _____	10. _____
11. _____	12. _____	13. _____	14. _____	15. _____
16. _____	17. _____	18. _____	19. _____	20. _____
Totals _____	_____	_____	_____	_____

Your primary conflict-handling style is the category with the highest total. Your fallback intention is the category with the second-highest total.

Source: C. K. W. De Dreu, A. Evers, B. Beersma, E. S. Kluwer, and A. Nauta, "A Theory-Based Measure of Conflict Management Strategies in the Workplace," *Journal of Organizational Behavior* 22, no. 6 (September 2001), pp. 645–668. Copyright © John Wiley & Sons Limited. Reproduced with permission.

BREAKOUT **GROUP** EXERCISES

Form small groups to discuss the following topics, as assigned by your instructor:

1. Describe a situation in which you ignored someone. What impact did it have on that person's subsequent communication behaviours?

2. What differences have you observed in the ways that men and women communicate?

3. You and 2 other students carpool to school every day. The driver has recently taken to playing a new radio station quite loudly. You do not like the music, or the loudness. Using one of the conflict-handling strategies outlined in Exhibit 6-6 on page 202, indicate how you might go about resolving this conflict. Identify a number of BATNAs (*best* alternative *to a negotiated agreement*) available to you, and then decide whether you should continue carpooling.

WORKING WITH **OTHERS** EXERCISE

A Negotiation Role Play

This role play is designed to help you develop your negotiating skills. The class is to break into pairs. One person will play the role of Terry, the department supervisor. The other person will play Dale, Terry's boss.

The Situation: Terry and Dale work for hockey-equipment manufacturer Bauer. Terry supervises a research laboratory. Dale is the manager of research and development (R & D). Terry and Dale are former skaters who have worked for Bauer for more than 6 years. Dale has been Terry's boss for 2 years.

One of Terry's employees has greatly impressed Terry. This employee is Lisa Roland. Lisa was hired 11 months ago. She is 24 years old and holds a master's degree in mechanical engineering. Her entry-level salary was $52 500 a year. She was told by Terry that, in accordance with corporation policy, she would receive an initial performance evaluation at 6 months and a comprehensive review after 1 year. Based on her performance record, Lisa was told she could expect a salary adjustment at the time of the 1-year evaluation.

Terry's evaluation of Lisa after 6 months was very positive. Terry commented on the long hours Lisa was working, her cooperative spirit, the fact that others in the lab enjoyed working with her, and her immediate positive impact on the project to which she had been assigned. Now that Lisa's first anniversary is coming up, Terry has again reviewed Lisa's performance. Terry thinks Lisa may be the best new person the R & D group has ever hired. After only a year, Terry has ranked Lisa third highest in a department of 11.

Salaries in the department vary greatly. Terry, for instance, has a basic salary of $93 800, plus eligibility for a bonus that might add another $7000 to $11 000 a year. The salary range of the 11 department members is $42 500 to $79 000. The lowest salary is a recent hire with a bachelor's degree in physics. The two people that Terry has rated above Lisa earn base salaries of $73 800 and $78 900. They are both 27 years old and have been at Bauer for 3 and 4 years, respectively. The median salary in Terry's department is $65 300.

Terry's Role: You want to give Lisa a big raise. While she is young, she has proven to be an excellent addition to the department. You don't want to lose her. More important, she knows in general what other people in the department are earning, and she thinks she is underpaid. The company typically gives 1-year raises of 5 percent, although 10 percent is not unusual and 20 to 30 percent increases have been approved on occasion. You would like to get Lisa as large an increase as Dale will approve.

Dale's Role: All your supervisors typically try to squeeze you for as much money as they can for their people. You understand this because you did the same thing when you were a supervisor, but your boss wants to keep a lid on costs. He wants you to keep raises for recent hires generally in the range of 5 to 8 percent. In fact, he has sent a memo to all managers and supervisors stating this objective. However, your boss is also very concerned with equity and paying people what they are worth. You feel assured that he will support any salary recommendation you make, as long as it can be justified. Your goal, consistent with cost reduction, is to keep salary increases as low as possible.

The Negotiation: Terry has a meeting scheduled with Dale to discuss Lisa's performance review and salary adjustment. In your role of either Dale or Terry, take a couple of minutes to think through the facts in this exercise and to prepare a strategy. Determine what your target and resistance points are and what your BATNA is. Then you have up to 15 minutes to conduct your negotiation. When your negotiation is complete, the class will compare the various strategies used and the outcomes that resulted.

ETHICAL **DILEMMA** EXERCISE

Is It Unethical to Lie and Deceive During Negotiations?

It has been said that the whole notion of negotiation is built on ethical quicksand: To succeed, you must deceive. Is this true? Apparently a lot of people think so. For instance, one study found that 28 percent of negotiators lied about a common interest issue during negotiations, while another study found that 100 percent of negotiators either failed to reveal a problem or actively lied about it during negotiations if they were not directly asked about the issue.

Is it possible for someone to maintain high ethical standards and, at the same time, deal with the daily need to negotiate with bosses, peers, staff, people from other organizations, friends, and even relatives?

continued

We can probably agree that bald-faced lies during negotiation are wrong. At least most ethicists would probably agree. The universal dilemma surrounds the little lies—the omissions, evasions, and concealments that are often necessary to best an opponent.

During negotiations, when is a lie a lie? Is exaggerating benefits, downplaying negatives, ignoring flaws, or saying "I don't know" when in reality you do considered lying? Is declaring that "this is my final offer and nonnegotiable" (even when you are posturing) a lie? Is pretending to bend over backward to make meaningful concessions lying? Rather than being unethical practices, the use of these "lies" is considered by many as indicators that a negotiator is strong, smart, and savvy.

When are evasiveness and deception out of bounds? Is it naive to be completely honest and bare your soul during negotiations? Or are the rules of negotiations unique: Is any tactic that will improve your chance of winning acceptable?

Sources: Based on M. E. Schweitzer, "Deception in Negotiations," in *Wharton on Making Decisions*, ed. S. J. Hoch and H. C. Kunreuther (New York: Wiley, 2001), pp. 187–200; and M. Diener, "Fair Enough," *Entrepreneur*, January 2002, pp. 100–102.

CASE INCIDENT

Emailing "Lazy" Employees

Imagine receiving the following email from your CEO:

We are getting less than 40 hours of work from a large number of our EMPLOYEES. The parking lot is sparsely used at 8 a.m.; likewise at 5 p.m. As managers, you either do not know what your EMPLOYEES are doing or you do not CARE. In either case, you have a problem and you will fix it or I will replace you. :-{{

NEVER in my career have I allowed a team which worked for me to think they had a 40-hour job. I have allowed YOU to create a culture which is permitting this. NO LONGER. :-|

The note (paraphrased) continues: "Hell will freeze over before any more employee benefits are given out. I will be watching the parking lot and expect it to be substantially full at 7:30 a.m. and 6:30 p.m. on weekdays and half full on Saturdays. You have two weeks. Tick, tock. **: ("**

:-{{ = very angry	:-| = dissappointed	: (= frowing

Questions

1. What impact would this message have on you if you received it?

2. Is email the best way to convey such a message?

3. What problems might arise if people outside the organization saw this email?

4. What suggestions, if any, would you make to the CEO to help improve communication effectiveness?

5. What conflict-handling style is this CEO using? What might be a more effective style? Why?

Sources: Based on E. Wong, "Stinging Office E-Mail Lights 'Firestorm,'" *Globe and Mail,* April 9, 2001, p. M1; P. D. Broughton, "Boss's Angry Email Sends Shares Plunging," *Daily Telegraph of London*, April 6, 2001; D. Stafford, "Shattering the Illusion of Respect," *Kansas City Star,* March 29, 2001, p. C1.

CBC (●) VIDEO CASE INCIDENT

Buggy Wars

Two friends and neighbours arrange to go into business together and then become bitter rivals: This is the story of Bob Bell and Michael Sharpe, who once lived just four houses apart on Oxford Street in Guelph, Ontario.

Bell and Sharpe thought they had a good idea for a new business venture—a bicycle trailer—but the good idea turned into a long, sizzling struggle.

Bell invented the bicycle trailer. Shortly after coming up with the idea, he began to design and build the bicycle trailer in his garage. Once he shared his idea with Sharpe, both thought they could form a successful partnership by drawing upon each other's expertise. Bell, an engineer by trade, would take on research and development; Sharpe, a former computer software sales manager and career manager, would focus on marketing. Sharpe put together the business plan—but before it was finalized, the deal fell apart.

The major point of conflict between Bell and Sharpe was royalties. Bell wanted to license the bicycle trailer design to Sharpe and collect a fee for each bicycle trailer produced. Sharpe wanted Bell to invest more in the venture and share the financial risk. However, Bell did not see any grounds for negotiation. Bell considered the bicycle trailer his idea. He had designed it, he had bought the materials to build it, and he had put in the time to develop the final product. When both parties hired lawyers and Bell demanded intellectual property rights, the great Canadian buggy war began.

Bell planned a slow, steady campaign, working from the basement of his home with one employee. He started selling his cargo trailer, the WIKE, at the local farmers' market. His goal was to sell 20 trailers the first year and 500 in the coming year. Bell continued his "go slow, get it right" campaign, selling locally and fine-tuning his trailer to carry children. However, he eventually decided that making every bicycle trailer himself was not a good strategy. By 2002, Bob Bell just wanted his life back.

Meanwhile, Sharpe had his own grand plan. He established his new company, Greenways, mortgaged his home,

took a bank loan, rented a factory, and hired five employees. Sharpe began mass production of his version of the trailer, the Wonder Wagon, which accommodated small children. He projected sales of 2500 nationwide for the coming year. By the spring of 1994, Sharpe was selling to big specialty retailers and Toronto's largest sporting goods store. Later, bike shops across the country and two national retailers were selling his wagon. He was even a corporate sponsor in Vancouver's Ride for Life.

So how did this end? Bell won the patent infringement case against Sharpe. Bell's company has expanded to six different versions of the bicycle trailer. It also has a licensed manufacturer in China, from whom Bell collects royalties. Sharpe eventually abandoned the whole buggy idea, and switched careers to . . . the fitness industry.

Questions

1. What were the sources of conflict between Bell and Sharpe?

2. Which of the five conflict resolution techniques does each man prefer in handling his conflict? Is there another conflict resolution approach you would recommend? Why?

3. How would you have handled the conflict? How would your personality have affected your approach to resolving the conflict?

Source: Based on "Buggy Wars," *CBC Venture,* August 18, 2002, 841.

From **Concepts**
to **Skills**

Providing Performance Feedback

One of the most difficult communication challenges for individuals is providing feedback to others. For instance, in a study conducted by Watson Wyatt Worldwide, only 60 percent of Canadian employees said they understood the measures used to evaluate their performance; only 47 percent said that their managers clearly expressed goals and

assignments.[69] We review some of these communication difficulties below.

For many managers, few activities are more unpleasant than providing performance feedback to employees.[70] In fact, unless pressured by organizational policies and controls, managers are likely to ignore this responsibility.[71]

continued

Why the reluctance to give performance feedback? There seem to be at least three reasons. First, managers are often uncomfortable discussing performance weaknesses directly with employees. Given that almost every employee could undoubtedly improve in some areas, managers fear a confrontation when presenting negative feedback. This discomfort apparently applies even when people give negative feedback to a computer! Bill Gates reports that Microsoft conducted a project requiring users to rate their experience with a computer. "When we had the computer the users had worked with ask for an evaluation of its performance, the responses tended to be positive. But when we had a second computer ask the same people to evaluate their encounters with the first machine, the people were significantly more critical. Their reluctance to criticize the first computer 'to its face' suggested that they didn't want to hurt its feelings, even though they knew it was only a machine."[72]

Second, many employees tend to become defensive when their weaknesses are pointed out. Instead of accepting the feedback as constructive and a basis for improving performance, some employees challenge the evaluation by criticizing the manager or redirecting blame to someone else.

Finally, employees tend to have an inflated assessment of their own performance. Statistically speaking, half of all employees must be below-average performers. But the evidence indicates that the average employee's estimate of his or her own performance level generally falls around the 75th percentile.[73] So even when managers are providing good news, employees are likely to perceive it as not good enough!

The solution to the performance feedback problem is not to ignore it, but to train managers in how to conduct constructive feedback sessions. An effective review in which the employee perceives the appraisal as fair, the manager as sincere, and the climate as constructive can result in the employee leaving the interview in an upbeat mood. The employee will be informed about the performance areas in which he or she needs to improve and feel determined to correct the deficiencies.[74] In addition, the performance review should be designed more as a counselling activity than a judgmental process. This can best be accomplished by allowing the review to evolve out of the employee's own self-evaluation, but be aware that some individuals can over- or underestimate their performance and have a self-serving bias.

Managers can use the following tips to give more effective feedback:

- Relate feedback to existing performance **goals** and clear **expectations**.
- Give **specific** feedback tied to observable behaviour or measurable results.
- Channel feedback toward **key result areas**.
- Give feedback as soon as possible.
- Give positive feedback for **improvement**, not just final results.
- Focus feedback on **performance**, not personalities.
- Base feedback on **accurate** and **credible** information.[75]

Assessing Skills

After you've read this chapter, take the following Self-Assessments on your enclosed CD-ROM:

27. What's My Face-to-Face Communication Style?

28. How Good Are My Listening Skills?

39. What's My Preferred Conflict-Handling Style?

40. What's My Negotiating Style?

43. How Good Am I at Giving Performance Feedback?

Practising Skills

Choose a person with whom you've worked as a member of a team, and practise giving feedback to each other. Person A should begin by identifying behaviours that directly helped meet the goals of the project, and then give feedback about what needs to be improved. Person B should summarize the feedback to demonstrate that the key points have been heard. Persons A and B should then switch roles. How comfortable did you feel in giving feedback? In receiving feedback?

Reinforcing Skills

1. In one of your classes practise giving feedback to your instructor. Talk with your instructor outside class, indicating what you like about the class, and what you think might make the class better. What was the instructor's response?

2. The next time you are working with someone, and their performance is really helpful, give them positive feedback.

3. If you are in a situation where someone's performance is bothering you, instead of getting upset, figure out a way of giving constructive feedback to that person.

CHAPTER 7
Power and Politics

How could Jamie Salé and David Pelletier first lose and later win the 2002 Winter Olympics gold medal for figure skating? Power and politics tell much of the story.

1 What is power?

2 How does one get power?

3 How does dependency affect power?

4 What tactics can be used to increase power?

5 What does it mean to be empowered?

6 How are power and harassment related?

7 Why do people engage in politics?

Any Canadian, and many Americans, watching the pairs figure skating competition in the 2002 Winter Olympics seemed sure they had watched a gold-medal performance when Jamie Salé and David Pelletier gave their final bow.[1] Moments later, however, fans looked on in horror as the gold medal was awarded to Russian skaters Yelena Berezhnaya and Anton Sikharulidze. North Americans were shocked: What they remembered was a flawed performance by the Russians, with Sikharulidze shaky on a double axel and Berezhnaya stiff in some of her landings, and a perfect performance by the Canadian duo.

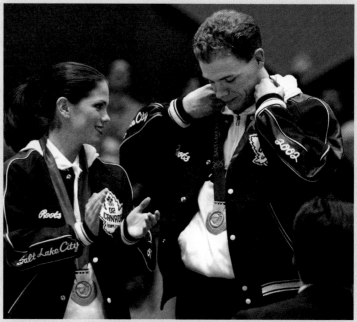

Figure skating has long been considered a political rather than an artistic event, in which the Soviet Union influenced its allies to support Russian skaters while Western judges tended to side with US skaters. Thus it was not surprising that charges of politics and abuse of power surfaced quickly.

A major theme throughout this chapter is that power and politics are a natural process in any group or organization. Although you might have heard the saying "Power corrupts, and absolute power corrupts absolutely," power is not always bad. Understanding how to use power and politics effectively makes organizational life more manageable, because it can help you gain the support you need to do your job effectively.

A DEFINITION OF POWER

Power refers to a capacity that A has to influence the behaviour of B, so that B acts in accordance with A's wishes.[2] This definition implies that there is a *potential* for power if someone is dependent on another. But one can have power and not impose it.

Probably the most important aspect of power is that it is a function of **dependency**. The more that B depends on A, the more power A has in the relationship. Dependence, in turn, is based on the alternatives that B perceives and the importance that B places on the alternative(s) that A controls. A person can have power over you only if he or she controls something you desire. If you are attending college or university on funds totally provided by your parents, you probably recognize the power that your parents hold over you. You are dependent on them for financial support. But once you are out of school, have a job, and are making a good income, your parents' power is reduced significantly. Who among us, though, has not known or heard of the rich relative who is able to control a large number of family members merely through the implicit or explicit threat of "writing them out of the will"?

1 What is power?

power A capacity that A has to influence the behaviour of B, so that B acts in accordance with A's wishes.

dependency B's relationship to A when A possesses something that B needs.

Jamie Salé and David Pelletier Official Website
www.sale-pelletier.com/english/

OB IS FOR EVERYONE

* Have you ever wondered how you might increase your power?

* Do workplaces empower people?

* Why do some people seem to engage in politics more than others?

* In what situations does impression management work best?

Within larger organizations, the information technology (IT) group often has considerable power, because everyone, right up to the CEO, is dependent on this group to keep computers and networks running. Since few people have the technical expertise to do so, IT personnel end up being viewed as irreplaceable. This gives them a lot of power within the organization.

Power should not be considered a bad thing, however. "Power, if used appropriately, should actually be a positive influence in your organization," says Professor Patricia Bradshaw of the Schulich School of Business at York University. "Having more power doesn't necessarily turn you into a Machiavellian monster. It can help your team and your organization achieve its goals and increase its potential."[3] The positive benefits of power (and politics) have also been explored by Professor Tom Lawrence of SFU Business and his colleagues.[4]

BASES OF POWER

> As the Olympics figure skating controversy swirled, International Skating Union (ISU) president Ottavio Cinquanta tried to contain the uproar by announcing three days after the event that "We cannot change the result of the competition." He was sending out a signal to the Americans, who had taken to the airwaves to protest the results of the competition, that lobbying could not turn judges' scores around or change ISU procedures. Forty-eight hours later, however, he changed his mind and announced that the results would be changed, and Salé and Pelletier would receive gold medals as well. What could have made Cinquanta change his decision so quickly?

2 How does one get power?

Where does power come from? What is it that gives an individual or a group influence over others? The answer to these questions was developed by social scientists John French and Bertrand Raven, who first presented a five-category classification scheme of sources or bases of power: coercive, reward, legitimate, expert, and referent.[5] They subsequently added information power to that schema (see Exhibit 7-1).[6]

Coercive Power

coercive power Power that is based on fear.

Coercive power is defined by French and Raven as dependent on fear. One reacts to this power base out of fear of the negative results that might occur if one fails to comply. It

---

EXHIBIT 7-1   Measuring Bases of Power

Does a person have one or more of the six bases of power? These descriptions help identify the person's power base.

Power Base	Statement
Coercive	The person can make things difficult for people, and you want to avoid getting him or her angry.
Reward	The person is able to give special benefits or rewards to people, and you find it advantageous to trade favours with him or her.
Legitimate	The person has the right, considering his or her position and your job responsibilities, to expect you to comply with legitimate requests.
Expert	The person has the experience and knowledge to earn your respect, and you defer to his or her judgment in some matters.
Referent	You like the person and enjoy doing things for him or her.
Information	The person has data or knowledge that you need.

Source: Adapted from G. Yukl and C. M. Falbe, "Importance of Different Power Sources in Downward and Lateral Relations," *Journal of Applied Psychology,* June 1991, p. 417. With permission.

rests on the application, or the threat of the application, of physical sanctions such as the infliction of pain, the generation of frustration through restriction of movement, or the controlling by force of basic physiological or safety needs. When Jacques Rogge, president of the International Olympic Committee (IOC), threatened to ban judged sports from the Olympics because of the skating scandal, he was using a form of coercion. He was trying to intimidate the International Skating Union (ISU), making them fear that if the controversy was not ended quickly, figure skaters would no longer compete in the Olympics.

International Olympic Committee (IOC) www.olympic.org

International Skating Union (ISU) www.isu.org

Of all the bases of power available, the power to hurt others is possibly the most often used, most often condemned, and most difficult to control. The state relies on its military and legal resources to intimidate nations, or even its own citizens; businesses rely upon the control of economic resources to request tax reductions; and religious institutions threaten individuals with dire consequences in the afterlife if they do not conduct themselves properly in this life. At the personal level, individuals use coercive power through a reliance on physical strength, words, or the ability to grant or withhold emotional support from others. These bases provide the individual with the means to physically harm, bully, humiliate, or deny love to others.[7]

At the organizational level, A has coercive power over B if A can dismiss, suspend, or demote B, assuming that B values his or her job. Similarly, if A can assign B work activities that B finds unpleasant or treat B in a manner that B finds embarrassing, A possesses coercive power over B.

Reward Power

The opposite of coercive power is **reward power**. People will go along with the wishes or directives of another if doing so produces positive benefits; therefore, one who can distribute rewards that others view as valuable will have power over those others. These rewards can be anything that another person values. In an organizational context, we think of money, favourable performance appraisals, promotions, interesting work assignments, friendly colleagues, important information, and preferred work shifts or sales territories.[8]

As with coercive power, you do not have to be a manager to be able to exert influence through rewards. Rewards such as friendliness, acceptance, and praise are available to everyone in an organization. To the degree that an individual seeks such rewards, your ability to give or withhold them gives you power over that individual.

reward power   Power that achieves compliance based on the ability to distribute rewards that others view as valuable.

legitimate power   Power that a person receives as a result of his or her position in the formal hierarchy of an organization.

Legitimate Power

In formal groups and organizations, probably the most frequent access to one or more of the bases of power is through a person's structural position. This is called **legitimate power**. It represents the power a person receives as a result of his or her position in the formal hierarchy of an organization.

Positions of authority include coercive and reward powers. Legitimate power, however, is broader than the power to coerce and reward. Specifically, it includes acceptance by members of an organization of the authority of a position. When school principals, bank presidents, or generals speak (assuming that their directives are viewed as within the authority of their positions), teachers, tellers, and privates listen and usually comply. You will note in Exhibit 7-2 on page 224 that one of the men in the meeting identifies himself as the rule maker, which means that he has legitimate power. IOC president Jacques Rogge was one of the few individuals who had legitimate power to try to resolve the skating controversy.

In India, Naina Lal Kidwai is a powerful woman in the banking industry. She is the chief executive of the Hongkong and Shanghai Banking Corporation (HSBC), India. Kidwai's formal power is based on her position at the bank.

EXHIBIT 7-2

"*I was just going to say 'Well, I don't make the rules.' But, of course, I do make the rules.*"

Source: Drawing by Leo Cullum in *The New Yorker.* Copyright © 1986 *The New Yorker Magazine.* Reprinted by permission.

Expert Power

expert power   Influence based on special skills or knowledge.

Expert power is influence based on expertise, special skills, or knowledge. Expertise has become one of the most powerful sources of influence as the world has become more technologically oriented. While it is generally acknowledged that physicians have expertise and hence expert power—most of us follow the advice that our doctors give us— you should also recognize that computer specialists, tax accountants, economists, and other specialists can have power as a result of their expertise. Young people may find they have increased power in the workplace these days because of the technical knowledge and expertise that their Baby-Boomer managers may not have.

Expert power relies on trust that all relevant information is given out honestly and completely. Of course, since knowledge is power, the more that information is shared, the less expert power a person has. Thus, some individuals try to protect their power by withholding information.[9] This tactic can result in poor-quality performance by those who need the information.[10] The *Working With Others Exercise* on pages 245–246 gives you the opportunity to explore the effectiveness of different bases of power in changing someone's behaviour.

Referent Power

referent power   Influence based on possession by an individual of desirable resources or personal traits.

Roots Canada
www.roots.com/new_canada/html/index_canada.shtml

Referent power develops out of admiration of another and a desire to be like that person. In a sense, then, it is a lot like charisma. If you admire someone to the point of modelling your behaviour and attitudes after him or her, that person possesses referent power over you. Sometimes teachers and coaches have referent power because of our admiration of them. Referent power explains why celebrities are paid millions of dollars to endorse products in commercials. Companies such as Toronto-based Roots Canada have

EXHIBIT 7-3   Continuum of Responses to Power

Resistance   Compliance   Commitment

Bases of
Leader
Power

Most likely employee response

Coercive

Reward

Legitimate

Expert

Referent

Source: R. M. Steers and J. S. Black, *Organizational Behavior,* 5th ed. (New York: HarperCollins, 1994), p. 487. Reprinted by permission of Pearson Education Inc., Upper Saddle River, New Jersey.

developed advertising themes around popular Canadians, such as "bad boy" Olympic gold-medallist and snowboarder Ross Rebagliati, to convince people to buy specific products.[11] Similarly, Nike has used sports celebrities such as former Toronto Raptors star centre Vince Carter to promote its products. In some ads, stars have provided their own music, as was the case in Canadian jazz diva Diana Krall's TV commercials for Chrysler.

Information Power

Information power comes from access to and control over information. People in an organization who have data or knowledge that others need can make those others dependent on them. Managers, for instance, because of their access to privileged sales, cost, salary, profit, and similar data, can use this information to control and shape subordinates' behaviour. Similarly, departments that possess information that is critical to a company's performance in times of high uncertainty—for example, the legal department when a firm faces a major lawsuit or the human resource department during critical labour negotiations—will gain increased power in their organizations until those uncertainties are resolved. This chapter's *Case Incident—The Power of Bill Fowler at Blackmer/Dover Resources* on pages 246–247 shows the power that one man can have in a manufacturing organization.

information power   Power that comes from access to and control over information.

Evaluating the Bases of Power

Generally, people will respond in one of three ways when faced with the people who use the bases of power described above:

- *Commitment.* The person is enthusiastic about the request and shows initiative and persistence in carrying it out.

- *Compliance.* The person goes along with the request grudgingly, puts in minimal effort, and takes little initiative in carrying out the request.

- *Resistance.* The person is opposed to the request and tries to avoid it with such tactics as refusing, stalling, or arguing about it.[12]

A review of the research on the effectiveness of these forms of power finds that they differ in their impact on a person's performance.[13] Exhibit 7-3 summarizes some of this research. Coercive power leads to resistance from individuals, decreased satisfaction, and increased mistrust. Reward power results in compliance if the rewards are consistent with what individuals want as rewards, something the *Ethical Dilemma Exercise* on page 246 shows clearly. Legitimate power also results in compliance, but it does not generally result in increased commitment. In other words, legitimate power does not inspire individuals to act beyond the basic level. Expert and referent powers are the most likely to lead to commitment from individuals. Research shows that deadline pressures increase group members' reliance on individuals with expert and information power.[14] Ironically, the least effective bases of power for improving commitment—coercive, reward, and legitimate—are the ones most often used by managers, perhaps because they are the easiest to introduce.[15]

DEPENDENCY: THE KEY TO POWER

As the Olympics figure skating furor unfolded, some claimed that French judge Marie-Reine Le Gougne was pressured by the French figure skating federation to vote for the Russians, in exchange for which the Russian judge would vote for the French skaters in the Olympic ice dancing competition. In August 2002, a Russian mobster was arrested for possible bribery charges in the case, suggesting that external pressures were applied to higher-ups in the skating organizations, who then pressured judges to fix votes. "Though it doesn't excuse them for not judging honestly, it suggests that individuals highly ranked within their federations are indeed setting the tone for their [the judges'] behaviour," noted US dance judge Sharon Rogers.[16] The French judge was dependent on her superiors to keep her judging job, something she valued very much. Meanwhile, a dependence on bribes from the Russian mobster made higher-ups pressure their judges. What factors might lead to one person's having greater power over another?

3 How does dependency affect power?

In this section, we show how an understanding of dependency is central to furthering your understanding of power itself.

The General Dependency Postulate

Let's begin with a general postulate: *The greater B's dependency on A, the greater the power A has over B.* When you possess anything that others require but that you alone control, you make them dependent upon you and therefore you gain power over them.[17] Another way to frame dependency is to think about a relationship in terms of "who needs whom?" The person who has the most need is the one most dependent on the relationship.[18]

Dependency is inversely proportional to the alternative sources of supply. If something is plentiful, possession of it will not increase your power. If everyone is intelligent, intelligence gives no special advantage. Similarly, in the circles of the super rich, money does not result in power. But if you can create a monopoly by controlling information, prestige, or anything that others crave, they become dependent on you. Alternatively, the more options you have, the less power you place in the hands of others. This explains, for example, why most organizations develop multiple suppliers rather than give their business to only one.

What Creates Dependency?

Dependency is increased when the resource you control is important, scarce, and cannot be substituted.[19]

Importance

If nobody wants what you have, there is no dependency. To create dependency, the thing(s) you control must be perceived as important. In some organizations, people

The location of power varies among organizations. At Walt Disney, enormous power is held by high-tech scientists in the research and development group of Walt Disney Imagineering, a division formed by Walt Disney in 1952 to create Disneyland. The company relies on these highly skilled and creative staffers to develop cyberland fantasies such as virtual-reality theme parks, websites for kids, and smart TV sets that learn viewers' programming preferences and automatically record programs they forget to watch.

who control the budget have a great deal of importance. In other organizations, those who possess the knowledge to keep technology working smoothly are viewed as important. What is important is situational. It varies among organizations and undoubtedly also varies over time within any given organization. Individuals or organizations that are regarded as important may pressure others to engage in unethical behaviour, however, as *Focus on Ethics* suggests.

FOCUS ON **ETHICS**

Enron Requests Action from UBS PaineWebber

Did Enron use its power to cause a UBS PaineWebber employee to be fired?   In August 2001, months before the Enron scandal broke, executives of Enron pressured UBS PaineWebber (now UBS Financial Services) to discipline one of its brokers.[20] The broker, Chung Wu, had advised Enron employees to sell their stock options. Within hours of the complaint, the broker was fired.

When the Enron executive in charge of the stock option program learned that Wu had warned employees that the company's "financial situation is deteriorating," he notified PaineWebber immediately via email. His message stated: "Please handle this situation. This is extremely disturbing to me."

PaineWebber went even further than firing Wu, however. It also sent his clients a report that Enron was "likely heading higher than lower from here on out."

PaineWebber has since suggested that Wu acted unethically because his email messages to Enron clients were unauthorized and because he did not tell them that PaineWebber's research analyst rated Enron a "strong buy."

One might question PaineWebber's behaviour, however. When Wu sent the email messages, the stock was worth $36. Only a few months later, it was worthless. PaineWebber managed Enron's stock option program and handled large personal accounts for many of Enron's executives. It also did investment banking for Enron. Thus, it did not want to risk losing Enron's business by suggesting the stock was in trouble.

Scarcity

As noted previously, if something is plentiful, possession of it will not increase your power. A resource must be perceived as scarce to create dependency.

Scarcity can help explain how low-ranking employees gain power if they have important knowledge not available to high-ranking employees. Possession of a scarce resource—in this case, important knowledge—makes those who don't have it dependent on those who do. Thus, an individual might refuse to show others how to do a job, or might refuse to share information, thereby increasing his or her importance.

Nonsubstitutability

The fewer substitutes for a resource, the more power comes from control over that resource. At Apple Computer, for example, most observers, as well as the board, believed that no one other than Steve Jobs could turn the company around when they returned him to the role of CEO in 1997. In another example, when a union goes on strike and management is not permitted to replace the striking employees, the union has considerable control over the organization's ability to carry out its tasks.

People are often able to ask for special rewards (higher pay or better assignments) because they have skills that others do not. This chapter's *Point/Counterpoint* feature on page 243 considers the fairness of rewarding some people better than others.

Steve Jobs
www.apple.com/pr/bios/jobs.html

INFLUENCE TACTICS

> Looking at the 2002 Winter Olympics figure skating controversy, we can find a number of instances where the various people involved in the controversy used influence tactics to get their way. There is some evidence that the French and Russian judges formed a coalition to ensure that the French ice dancers would get a gold medal in a later event. The Russian mobster used bargaining, trading bribes for votes. International Olympic Committee president Jacques Rogge used assertiveness to convince International Skating Union (ISU) president Ottavio Cinquanta that in fact there would be two gold medals. He also threatened the ISU with sanctions, including banning judged sports from the Olympics, if they did not award the second medal. So how and why do influence tactics work?

4 What tactics can be used to increase power?

influence tactics Ways that individuals translate power bases into specific actions.

> * Have you ever wondered how you might increase your power?

How do individuals translate their bases of power into specific, desired actions? Research indicates that people use common tactics to influence outcomes.[21] One study identifies the nine **influence tactics** managers and employees use to increase their power:[22]

1. *Rational persuasion.* Using facts and data to make a logical or rational presentation of ideas.

2. *Inspirational appeals.* Appealing to values, ideals, and goals when making a request.

3. *Consultation.* Getting others involved to support one's objectives.

4. *Ingratiation.* Using flattery, creating goodwill, and being friendly prior to making a request.

5. *Personal appeals.* Appealing to loyalty and friendship when asking for something.

6. *Exchange.* Offering favours or benefits in exchange for support.

7. *Coalition tactics.* Getting the support of other people to provide backing when making a request.

8. *Pressure.* Using demands, threats, and reminders to get someone to do something.

9. *Legitimating tactics.* Claiming the authority or right to make a request, or showing that it supports organizational goals or policies.

Which influence tactics were used by participants in the figure skating controversy?

Researchers found that there are significant differences in the tactics used to influence actions, depending upon whether people are interacting with someone above or below them in rank. While all individuals favour rational persuasion, those managing upward are even more likely to use it (77 percent vs. 52 percent of those managing downward). Those managing downward are next most likely to use pressure (22 percent) or ingratiation (15 percent). The other favoured choices of those managing upward were coalition tactics (15 percent) and pressure (15 percent).[23]

This chapter's *CBC Video Case Incident* illustrates how the key players of the Liberal Party's sponsorship scandal used influence tactics to win government contracts.

Management at Flextronics plants in China used legitimating tactics and rational persuasion in establishing a series of rigid rules and procedures to guard against the threat of severe acute respiratory syndrome (SARS). Employees complied with the rules—such as twice-daily hand washing after eating meals in the company canteen—because they understood the mandates were made for their own safety.

CBC 🔴

Jean Brault and the Sponsorship Scandal

EMPOWERMENT: GIVING POWER TO EMPLOYEES

Thus far our discussion has implied that—to some extent, at least—power is most likely to rest in the hands of managers, to be used as part of their interaction with employees. However, in today's workplace, there is a movement toward sharing more power with employees by putting them in teams and also by making them responsible for some of the decisions regarding their jobs. With the flattening of organizations, so that there are fewer middle managers, employees also end up with more responsibilities. Organizational specialists refer to this increasing responsibility as *empowerment*. We briefly mention in Chapter 8 that one of the current trends in leadership is empowering employees. Between 1995 and 2005, nearly 50 000 articles about empowerment have appeared in the print media in the United States and Canada, with almost 6000 articles appearing in Canadian newspapers during that time.[24]

5 What does it mean to be empowered?

Definition of Empowerment

The definition of **empowerment** that we use here refers to the freedom and the ability of employees to make decisions and commitments.[25] Unfortunately, neither managers nor researchers can agree on the definition of empowerment. Robert E. Quinn and Gretchen M. Spreitzer, in their consulting work with a *Fortune* 500 manufacturing company, found that executives were split about 50-50 in their definition.[26] One group of executives "believed that empowerment was about delegating decision making within a set of clear boundaries." Empowerment would start at the top, specific goals and tasks would be assigned, responsibility would be delegated, and people would be held accountable for their results. The other group believed that empowerment was "a process of risk taking and personal growth." This type of empowerment starts at the bottom, with considering the employees' needs, showing them what empowered behaviour looks like, building teams, encouraging risk-taking, and demonstrating trust in employees' ability to perform.

Much of the press on empowerment has been positive, with both executives and employees applauding the ability of front-line workers to make and execute important decisions.[27] However, not all reports are favourable. One management expert noted that much of the talk about empowerment is simply lip service,[28] with organizations telling employees that they have decision-making responsibility but not giving them

empowerment The freedom and the ability of employees to make decisions and commitments.

Empowered employees, whether they work individually or in teams, like this one at Carbon Five, need the tools and training to take responsibility for their work. Teams at Carbon Five have a great deal of freedom to make decisions, while their managers act as advisers and coaches.

the authority to carry out their decisions. In order for an employee to be fully empowered, he or she needs access to the information required to make decisions; rewards for acting in appropriate, responsible ways; and the authority to make the necessary decisions. Empowerment means that employees understand how their jobs fit into the organization and that they are able to make decisions regarding job action in light of the organization's purpose and mission. Managers at Montague, PEI-based Durabelt recognize that to be empowered, employees need to have the appropriate skills to handle their jobs. The company sells customized conveyor belts used to harvest some vegetable and fruit crops. Employees need to be responsive to customer concerns when manufacturing the belts. In order to empower employees to manage customer relations successfully, Durabelt created Duraschool, an ongoing training program that provides employees with the skills they need to be more effective.[29]

Empowerment in the Workplace

✳ *Do workplaces empower people?*

The concept of empowerment has caused much cynicism in many workplaces. Employees are told that they are empowered and yet they do not feel that they have the authority to act, or they feel that their managers still micromanage their performance. Some managers are reluctant to empower their employees because this means sharing or even relinquishing their own power. Other managers worry that empowered employees may decide to work on goals and jobs that are not as closely aligned to organizational goals. Some managers, of course, do not fully understand how to go about empowering their employees.

In some cases, employees do not want to be empowered, and having more power can even make them ill. A study carried out by Professor Jia Lin Xie, of the University of Toronto's Joseph L. Rotman School of Management, and colleagues found that when people are put in charge at work but don't have the confidence to handle their responsibilities, they can become ill.[30] Specifically, people who blame themselves when things go wrong are more likely to suffer colds and infections if they have high levels of control at work. This finding by Professor Xie and her colleagues was somewhat unexpected, as some have hypothesized that greater control at work would lead to less stress. The study showed, instead, that the impact of empowerment depended on personality and job factors. Those who had control, but did not blame themselves when things went wrong, suffered less stress, even if the job was demanding. The study's findings suggest the importance of choosing carefully which employees to empower when doing so. These findings are also consistent with the Hackman-Oldham job characteristics model presented in Chapter 4.[31] Empowerment will be positive if a person has high growth-needs strengths (see Exhibit 4-13 on page 134) but those with low growth-needs strengths may be more likely to experience stress when empowered.

When employees are empowered, it means that they are expected to act, at least in a small way, as owners of the company, rather than just as employees. Ownership is not

Joseph L. Rotman School of Management, University of Toronto
www.rotman.utoronto.ca

necessary in the financial sense, but in terms of identifying with the goals and mission of the organization. For employees to be empowered, however, and have an ownership mentality, four conditions need to be met, according to Professor Dan Ondrack at the Rotman School of Management:

- There must be a clear definition of the values and mission of the company.

- The company must help employees gain the relevant skills.

- Employees need to be supported in their decision making and not criticized when they try to do something extraordinary.

- Employees need to be recognized for their efforts.[32]

At Vancouver-based Great Little Box Company (GLBC), which designs and manufactures corrugated containers, employees are given the freedom to do whatever they feel is necessary and appropriate to make customers happy. If a customer is dissatisfied with the product, the employee can say, "OK, I'll bring this product back and return it for you" without having to get prior authorization.

Great Little Box Company (GLBC)
www.greatlittlebox.com

Exhibit 7-4 outlines what two researchers discovered in studying the characteristics of empowered employees.

Effects of Empowerment

Does empowerment work? Researchers have shown that at both the individual level[33] and the team level,[34] empowerment leads to greater productivity. At Winnipeg-based Melet Plastics, a manufacturer of plastic components, employees can come in for two extra hours each week (for which they are paid overtime) to work on projects of their choice that help improve the performance of the company. As a result, employees are less

---

EXHIBIT 7-4   Characteristics of Empowered People

Robert E. Quinn and Gretchen M. Spreitzer, in their research on the characteristics of empowered people (through both in-depth interviews and survey analysis), found four characteristics that most empowered people have in common:

- Empowered people have a sense of *self-determination* (this means that they are free to choose how to do their work; they are not micromanaged).

- Empowered people have a sense of *meaning* (they feel that their work is important to them; they care about what they are doing).

- Empowered people have a sense of *competence* (this means that they are confident about their ability to do their work well; they know they can perform).

- Empowered people have a sense of *impact* (this means that people believe they can have influence on their work unit; others listen to their ideas).

Source: R. E. Quinn and G. M. Spreitzer, "The Road to Empowerment: Seven Questions Every Leader Should Consider," *Organizational Dynamics,* Autumn 1997, p. 41.

likely to see Melet "as a place where they simply arrive, park their brains at the door and do what they're told."[35]

Four US researchers investigated whether empowerment works similarly in different countries.[36] Their findings showed that employees in India gave their supervisors low ratings when empowerment was high, while employees in the United States, Mexico, and Poland rated their supervisors favourably when empowerment was high. In both the United States and Mexico, empowerment had no effect on satisfaction with co-workers. However, satisfaction with co-workers was higher when employees were empowered in Poland. In India, empowerment led to lower satisfaction with co-workers.

Similar findings in a study comparing empowerment in the United States, Brazil, and Argentina indicate that in hierarchical societies, empowerment may need to be introduced with care.[37] Employees in such societies may be more used to working in teams, but they also expect their managers to be the people with all the answers.

Our discussion of empowerment suggests that a number of problems can arise when organizations decide they want to empower employees. First, some managers do not want empowered employees, because this can take away some of their own base of power. Second, some employees have little or no interest in being empowered, and therefore resist any attempts to be empowered. And finally, empowerment is not something that works well in every workplace throughout the world.

THE ABUSE OF POWER: HARASSMENT IN THE WORKPLACE

6 How are power and harassment related?

People who engage in harassment in the workplace are typically abusing their power positions. The manager-employee relationship best characterizes an unequal power relationship, where position power gives the managers the capacity to reward and coerce. Managers give employees their assignments, evaluate their performance, make recommendations for salary adjustments and promotions, and even decide whether employees retain their jobs. These decisions give managers power. Since employees want favourable performance reviews, salary increases, and the like, it is clear that managers control the resources that most employees consider important and scarce. It is also worth noting that individuals who occupy high-status roles (such as management positions) sometimes believe that harassing employees is merely an extension of their right to make demands on lower-status individuals.

Although co-workers do not have position power, they can have influence and use it to harass peers. In fact, although co-workers appear to engage in somewhat less severe forms of harassment than do managers, co-workers are the most frequent perpetrators of harassment, particularly sexual harassment, in organizations. How do co-workers exercise power? Most often they provide or withhold information, cooperation, and support. For example, the effective performance of most jobs requires interaction and support from co-workers. This is especially true these days as work is assigned to teams. By threatening to withhold or delay providing information that is necessary for the successful achievement of your work goals, co-workers can exert power over you.

Some categories of harassment have long been illegal in Canada, including those based on race, religion, and national origin, as well as sexual harassment. Unfortunately, some types of harassment that occur in the workplace are not deemed illegal, even if they create problems for employees and managers. We focus here on two types of harassment that have received considerable attention in the press: workplace bullying and sexual harassment.

Workplace Bullying

Many of us are aware, anecdotally if not personally, of managers who harass employees, demanding overtime without pay or excessive work performance. Further, some of the recent stories of workplace violence have reportedly been the result of an employee's feeling intimidated at work. In research conducted in the private and public sector in southern Saskatchewan, Céleste Brotheridge, a professor at the Université du Québec à Montréal, found that bullying was rather prevalent in the workplace. Forty percent of the respondents noted that they had experienced one or more forms of bullying weekly in the past six months. Ten percent experienced bullying at a much greater level: five or more incidents a week. Brotheridge notes that bullying has a negative effect on the workplace: "Given bullying's [negative] effects on employee health, it is reason for concern."[38]

There is no clear definition of workplace bullying, and Marilyn Noble, a Fredericton-based adult educator, remarks that in some instances there can be a fine line between managing and bullying. However, Noble, who co-chaired a research team on workplace violence and abuse at the University of New Brunswick, notes that "when it becomes a question of shaming people, embarrassing people, holding them up to ridicule, just constantly being on their case for no apparent reason, then [management] is becoming unreasonable." Moreover, "a bully often acts by isolating an individual. And they may be a serial bully, who always has a victim on the go. They may, in fact, have multiple victims on the go, but their strategy is to isolate them from one another."[39]

Sexual Harassment

The issue of sexual harassment has received increasing attention by corporations and the media because of the growing ranks of female employees, especially in nontraditional work environments, and because of a number of high-profile cases. For example, in March 2006, it was reported that all four female firefighters in the Richmond, BC, fire department had taken a leave of absence, alleging that they had faced repeated sexual harassment and discrimination from male firefighters in the department. The city has since introduced a code of conduct for its firefighters.[40] A survey by York University found that 48 percent of working women in Canada reported they had experienced some form of "gender harassment" in the year before they were surveyed.[41] Sexual harassment is also occurring among young people. A survey of 3000 high school students from eight schools in Toronto, Montreal, and Kingston, Ontario, found that three-quarters of them said they had been sexually harassed at least once by peers.[42]

Barbara Orser, a research affiliate with The Conference Board of Canada, notes that "sexual harassment is more likely to occur in environments that tolerate bullying, intimidation, yelling, innuendo and other forms of discourteous behaviour."[43] Recent research supports this view, finding that within work environments, general incivility, gender harassment, and sexual harassment tended to occur together.[44] These behaviours indicate that one person is trying to use power over another.

The Supreme Court of Canada defines **sexual harassment** as unwelcome behaviour of a sexual nature in the workplace that negatively affects the work environment or leads to adverse job-related consequences for the employee.[45] Despite the legal framework for defining sexual harassment, there continues to be disagreement as to what *specifically* constitutes sexual harassment. Sexual harassment includes unwanted physical touching, recurring requests for dates when it is made clear the person is not interested, and coercive threats that a person will lose her or his job if she or he refuses a sexual proposition. The problems of interpreting sexual harassment often surface around some of its more subtle forms—unwanted looks or comments, off-colour jokes, sexual artifacts such as nude calendars in the workplace, sexual innuendo, or misinterpretations of where the line between "being friendly" ends and "harassment" begins. *Case Incident—Damned if You Do; Damned if You Don't* on the CD-ROM that accompanies this textbook illustrates how these problems can make people feel uncomfortable in the workplace. Most studies confirm that the concept of power is central to understanding sexual harassment.[46] This seems to be true whether the harassment comes from a manager, a co-worker, or even an employee.

sexual harassment Unwelcome behaviour of a sexual nature in the workplace that negatively affects the work environment or leads to adverse job-related consequences for the employee.

Supreme Court of Canada
www.scc-csc.gc.ca

Because of power inequities, sexual harassment by one's manager typically creates the greatest difficulty for the person being harassed. If there are no witnesses, it is the manager's word against the employee's word. Are there others whom this manager has harassed, and if so, will they come forward? Because of the manager's control over resources, many of those who are harassed are afraid of speaking out for fear of retaliation by the manager.

One of the places where there has been a dramatic increase in the number of sexual harassment complaints is at university campuses across Canada, according to Paddy Stamp, sexual harassment officer at the University of Toronto.[47] However, agreement on what constitutes sexual harassment, and how it should be investigated, is no clearer for universities than for industry.

While nonconsensual sex between professors and students is rape and subject to criminal charges, it is harder to evaluate apparently consensual relationships that occur outside the classroom. There is some argument over whether truly consensual sex is ever possible between students and professors. In an effort to underscore the power discrepancy and potential for abuse of it by professors, in the late 1990s Yale University decided that there could be no sexual relations between students and professors. In 2003, the University of California, which includes Berkeley, implemented a policy that went further, forbidding romantic relationships between professors and their students as well.[48] Most universities have been unwilling to take such a strong stance. However, this issue is certainly one of concern, because the power distance between professors and students is considerable.

In concluding this discussion, we would like to point out that sexual harassment is about power. It is about an individual controlling or threatening another individual. It is wrong. Moreover, it is illegal. You can understand how sexual harassment surfaces in organizations if you analyze it in power terms. We should also point out that sexual harassment is not something done only by men to women. There have been several cases of males reporting sexual harassment by male managers.[49] While there have been no media reports of women sexually harassing either men or women in Canada, under the framework of the law, it is certainly feasible.

POLITICS: POWER IN ACTION

Both International Olympic Committee president Jacques Rogge and International Skating Union president Ottavio Cinquanta paid a lot of attention to what the media had to say about the figure skating controversy. The event had taken place in the United States, and Americans made it clear that they were dismayed when the Canadians lost. As a result, the controversy was discussed on a variety of talk shows and news programs, and in newspapers. This was a way of keeping the controversy alive and trying to persuade the Olympics head that the decision needed to be changed. Rogge arguably was affected by the pressure, fearing that the negative publicity surrounding the skating controversy was harming the rest of the Olympics. Thus, when he decided to award the unprecedented second gold medal, it might have been less about making the "right" decision and more about making a political decision to silence dissent. So why is politics so prevalent? Is it merely a fact of life?

7 Why do people engage in politics?

Organizational behaviour researchers have learned a lot in recent years about how people gain and use power in organizations. Part of using power in organizations is engaging in organizational politics to influence others to help you achieve your personal objectives. Lobbying others to get them to vote with you on a particular decision is engaging in organizational politics.

When people get together in groups, power will be exerted. People want to carve out niches from which to exert influence, to earn rewards, and to advance their careers.[50] When employees in organizations convert their power into action, we describe them as engaged in politics. Those with good political skills have the ability to use their bases of power effectively.[51] Below we cover the types of political activity people use to try to influence others as well as impression management. Political skills are not confined to adults, of course. When your Vancouver author's six-year-old nephew wanted the latest Game Boy knowing full well his parents did not approve, he waged a careful, deliberate campaign to wear them down, explaining how he would use the toy only at assigned times, etc. His politicking paid off: Within six weeks he succeeded in getting the toy.

Definition of Political Behaviour

There has been no shortage of definitions for organizational politics. One clever definition of *politics* comes from Tom Jakobek, Toronto's former budget chief, who said, "In politics, you may have to go from A to C to D to E to F to G and then to B."[52]

For our purposes, we will define **political behaviour** in organizations as those activities that are outside one's formal role (i.e., not part of one's specific job duties), and that influence, or try to influence, the distribution of advantages and disadvantages within the organization.[53]

This definition encompasses key elements from what most people mean when they talk about organizational politics. Political behaviour is *outside* one's specified job requirements. The behaviour attempts to use one's *bases of power.* Our definition also encompasses efforts to influence the goals, criteria, or processes used for decision making when we state that politics is concerned with "the distribution of advantages and disadvantages within the organization." Our definition is broad enough to include such varied political behaviours as whistle-blowing, spreading rumours, withholding key information from decision makers, leaking confidential information about organizational activities to the media, exchanging favours with others in the organization for mutual benefit, and lobbying on behalf of or against a particular individual or decision alternative. Exhibit 7-5 on page 236 provides a quick measure to help you assess how political your workplace is.

Now that you have learned a bit about political behaviour, you may want to assess your own political behaviour in our *Learning About Yourself Exercise* on page 244.

Political behaviour is not confined to just individual hopes and goals. Politics might also be used to achieve organizational goals.[54] For instance, if a CEO wants to change the way employees are paid, say from salaries to commissions, this might not be a popular choice to the employees. While it might make good organizational sense to make this change (perhaps the CEO believes this will increase productivity), simply imposing the change through the use of power (go along with this or you're fired) might not be very popular. Instead, the CEO may try to pitch the reasons for the change to sympathetic managers and employees, trying to get them to understand the necessity for the change. Burnaby, BC-based TELUS used a direct approach with its employees after four and a half years of unsuccessful bargaining with union leaders. Management became frustrated with the impasse and explained their wage and benefit offer directly to employees in the hopes of getting the employees to side with management rather than their union leaders. The union was outraged by this behaviour, and it took several more months for union members and management to finally complete a new collective agreement in fall 2005.

The Reality of Politics

Why, you may wonder, must politics exist? Isn't it possible for an organization to be politics-free? It's *possible,* but most unlikely. Organizations are made up of individuals and groups with different values, goals, and interests.[55] This sets up the potential for conflict over resources. The allocation of departmental budgets, space, project responsibilities, and bonuses are the kind of resource issues about which organizational members will disagree.

political behaviour Those activities that influence, or attempt to influence, the distribution of advantages and disadvantages within the organization.

EXHIBIT 7-5   A Quick Measure of How Political Your Workplace Is

How political is your workplace? Answer the 12 questions using the following scale:

SD = **Strongly disagree**   1   5

D = **Disagree**   2   4

U = **Uncertain**   3   3

A = **Agree**   4   2

SA = **Strongly agree**   5   1

1. Managers often use the selection system to hire only people who can help them in their future.   *SA 5*

2. The rules and policies concerning promotion and pay are fair; it's how managers carry out the policies that is unfair and self-serving.   *D 2*

3. The performance ratings people receive from their managers reflect more of the managers' "own agenda" than the actual performance of the employee.   *D 2*

4. Although a lot of what my manager does around here appears to be directed at helping employees, it's actually intended to protect my manager.   *A 4*

5. There are cliques or "in-groups" that hinder effectiveness around here.   *A 4*

6. My co-workers help themselves, not others.   *A 4*

7. I have seen people deliberately distort information requested by others for purposes of personal gain, either by withholding it or by selectively reporting it.   *A 4*

8. If co-workers offer to lend some assistance, it is because they expect to get something out of it.   *A 4*

9. Favouritism rather than merit determines who gets ahead around here.   *A 4*

10. You can usually get what you want around here if you know the right person to ask.   *SA 5*

11. Overall, the rules and policies concerning promotion and pay are specific and well-defined.   *A 2*

12. Pay and promotion policies are generally communicated clearly in this organization.   *A 2*

42

This questionnaire taps the three salient dimensions that have been found to be related to perceptions of politics: manager behaviour, co-worker behaviour, and organizational policies and practices. To calculate your score for items 1 to 10, give yourself 1 point for Strongly disagree; 2 points for Disagree; and so forth (through 5 points for Strongly agree). For items 11 and 12, reverse the score (that is, 1 point for Strongly agree, etc.). Add up the total: The higher the total score, the greater the degree of perceived organizational politics.

Source: G. R. Ferris, D. D. Frink, D. P. S. Bhawuk, J. Zhou, and D. C. Gilmore, "Reactions of Diverse Groups to Politics in the Workplace," *Journal of Management* 22, no. 1 (1996), pp. 32–33.

Resources in organizations are also limited, which often turns potential conflict into real conflict. If resources were abundant, then all the various constituencies within the organization could satisfy their goals. Because they are limited, not everyone's interests can be provided for. Moreover, whether true or not, gains by one individual or group are often *perceived* as being at the expense of others within the organization. These forces create a competition among members for the organization's limited resources. Peter Godsoe, former CEO of Toronto-based Scotiabank, demonstrated an awareness of how to get the most resources for whatever unit he headed, while enhancing his own career, as the *OB in the Workplace* on page 237 shows.

OB IN THE WORKPLACE

Godsoe Makes the Most of Resources to Become CEO of Scotiabank

How do you ensure your way to the top?   Peter Godsoe was determined to become CEO of Scotiabank. In his quest for this job, he learned how to "outlast and outwit other hopefuls."[56] When he was put in charge of the bank's lending in the United States and Latin America, he made the operation his own by giving it a new name, the Western Hemisphere International Regional Office (WHIRO). While heading WHIRO, he reported to Scott McDonald, who was regarded as a potential successor to then CEO Ced Ritchie. In order to raise his profile, Godsoe built "a loyal following by making WHIRO the hot shop," thus making himself look better than McDonald. Godsoe developed cartoons, WHIRO hero awards, a crest, jackets, and a Latin motto that translated: "If you don't have a hernia, you're not pulling your weight," all with the aim of strengthening his unit's culture and making it more prominent within the bank. After his time at WHIRO, Godsoe demonstrated a remarkable knack for getting himself appointed the head of every organizational division created. Eventually, McDonald ended up leaving the bank, while Godsoe replaced Ritchie (but not before he threatened to leave to accept another job offer).

Scotiabank
www.scotiabank.com

Maybe the most important factor behind politics within organizations is the realization that most of the "facts" that are used to allocate the limited resources are open to interpretation. What, for instance, is *good* performance? What is an *adequate* improvement? What constitutes an *unsatisfactory* job? It is in this large and ambiguous middle ground of organizational life—where the facts *don't* speak for themselves—that politics flourish.

Finally, because most decisions must be made in a climate of ambiguity—where facts are rarely fully objective and thus are open to interpretation—people within organizations will use whatever influence they can to taint the facts to support their goals and interests. That, of course, creates the activities we call *politicking*. For more about how one engages in politicking, see *From Concepts to Skills* on pages 248–249.

President and CEO Aris Kaplanis of Toronto-based high-tech firm Teranet (shown here at far right with his senior management group) discourages negative office politics by his employees. The company employs the Golden Rule, "Do unto others as you would have others do unto you." He tells his employees, "If you're here to play a game, you're in the wrong business."

Therefore, to answer the earlier question of whether it is possible for an organization to be politics-free, we can say "yes"—but only if all the members of that organization hold the same goals and interests, organizational resources are not scarce, and performance outcomes are completely clear and objective. However, that does not describe the organizational world that most of us live in!

 RESEARCH FINDINGS   Politicking

Our earlier discussion focused on the favourable outcomes for individuals who successfully engage in politicking. But for most people—who have modest political skills or are unwilling to play the politics game—outcomes tend to be mainly negative.[57] There is, for instance, very strong evidence indicating that perceptions of organizational politics are negatively related to job satisfaction.[58] The perception of politics also tends to increase job anxiety and stress. This seems to be because of the belief that, by not engaging in politics, a person may be losing ground to others who are active politickers, or, conversely, because of the additional pressures individuals feel of having entered into and competing in the political arena.[59] Not surprisingly, when politicking becomes too much to handle, it can lead employees to quit.[60] Finally, there is preliminary evidence suggesting that politics leads to self-reported declines in employee performance.[61] Perceived organizational politics appears to have a demotivating effect on individuals, and thus leads to decreased performance levels.

Types of Political Activity

> * *Why do some people seem to engage in politics more than others?*

Within organizations, we can find a variety of political activities in which people engage. These include the following:[62]

- *Attacking or blaming others.* Used when trying to avoid responsibility for failure.

- *Using information.* Withholding or distorting information, particularly to hide negative information.

- *Managing impressions.* Bringing positive attention to one's self or taking credit for the positive accomplishments of others.

- *Building support for ideas.* Making sure that others will support one's ideas before they are presented.

- *Praising others.* Making important people feel good.

- *Building coalitions.* Joining with other people to create a powerful group.

- *Associating with influential people.* Building support networks.

- *Creating obligations.* Doing favours for others so they will owe you favours later.

Individuals will use these political activities for different purposes. Some of these activities are more likely to be used to defend one's position (such as attacking or blaming others), while other activities are meant to enhance one's image (such as building support for ideas and managing impressions).

Impression Management

impression management The process by which individuals attempt to control the impression others form of them.

The process by which individuals attempt to control the impression others form of them is called **impression management**.[63] Being perceived positively by others should have benefits for people in organizations. It might, for instance, help them initially to get the jobs they want in an organization and, once hired, to get favourable evaluations, superior salary increases, and more rapid promotions. In a political context, it might help bring more advantages their way. For instance, during the Olympics figure skating controversy, Jamie Salé and David Pelletier were seen in many television shows and news conferences, always giving the impression that they were not lobbying for a gold medal after the fact, and presenting an image of clean-cut, soft-spoken individuals. This led to even more sympathy for their plight.

Impression management does not imply that the impressions people convey are necessarily false (although, of course, they sometimes are).[64] Some activities may be done with great sincerity. For instance, you may *actually* believe that ads contribute little to sales in your region or that you are the key to the tripling of your division's sales. However, if the image claimed is false, you may be discredited.[65] The impression manager must be cautious not to be perceived as insincere or manipulative.[66]

RESEARCH FINDINGS   Impression Management

Below we explore research findings in two areas: the *use* of impression management and the *effectiveness* of impression management.

Use of Impression Management Impression management is more likely to be used by high self-monitors than low self-monitors.[67] Low self-monitors tend to present images of themselves that are consistent with their personalities, regardless of the beneficial or detrimental effects for them. In contrast, high self-monitors are skilled at reading situations and moulding their appearances and behaviour to fit each situation.

> ✳ *In what situations does impression management work best?*

Research by Marc-David Seidel at the Sauder School of Business, University of British Columbia, and his colleagues suggests that impression management is engaged in more frequently by those who spend at least some time telecommuting. These employees feel the need to keep their supervisors more informed about their activities, because they are physically absent.[68]

Sauder School of Business, University of British Columbia
www.sauder.ubc.ca

Effectiveness of Impression Management A number of studies have examined the effectiveness of impression management techniques in a variety of work situations. Studies show that impression management behaviour is positively associated with job-interview success.[69] For instance, one study found that recent university graduates who used more self-promotion tactics got higher evaluations by interviewers and more follow-up job-site visits, even after adjusting for grade point average, gender, and job type.[70] Other studies have found that those using impression management techniques received better performance evaluations from their managers,[71] were liked more by their managers,[72] and were criticized less.[73] Impression management effects seem to work more strongly when the measures of performance are subjective, however, than when they can be measured more objectively.[74] For instance, those using impression management techniques were rated more highly for interpersonal effectiveness, but they could be more negatively evaluated on their business competence.[75] Overall, the findings of these studies suggest that there is some advantage to engaging in impression management as long as the person delivers on the objective measures of performance as well. For those who intend to become leaders, engaging in impression management techniques makes it more likely that they will be chosen.[76]

Making Office Politics Work

One thing to be aware of is that extreme office politics can have a negative effect on employees. Researchers have found that organizational politics is associated with less organizational commitment,[77] lower job satisfaction,[78] and decreased job performance.[79]

Individuals who experience greater organizational politics are more likely to report higher levels of job anxiety,[80] and they are more likely to consider leaving the organization.[81]

Is there an effective way to engage in office politics that is less likely to be disruptive or negative? We discussed different negotiation strategies in Chapter 6, including a *win-lose* strategy, which means that if I win, you lose, and a *win-win* strategy, which means creating situations where both of us can win. *Fast Company*, a business magazine, identifies several rules that may help you make your way through the office politics maze:[82]

Fast Company Magazine
www.fastcompany.com

- *Nobody wins unless everybody wins.* The most successful proposals look for ways to acknowledge, if not include, the interests of others. This requires building support for your ideas across the organization. "Real political skill isn't about campaign tactics," says Lou DiNatale, a veteran political consultant at the University of Massachusetts. "It's about pulling people toward your ideas and then pushing those ideas through to other people." When ideas are packaged to look as if they are best for the organization as a whole and will help others, it is harder for others to counteract your proposal.

- *Don't just ask for opinions—change them.* It is helpful to find out what people think and then, if necessary, set out to change their opinions so that they can see what you want to do. It is also important to seek out the opinions of those you don't know well, or who are less likely to agree with you. Gathering together people who always support you is often not enough to build an effective coalition.

- *Everyone expects to be paid back.* In organizations, as in life, we develop personal relationships with those around us. It is those personal relationships that affect much of the behaviour in organizations. By building good relationships with colleagues, supporting them in their endeavours, and showing appreciation for what they accomplish, you are building a foundation of support for your own ideas.

- *Success can create opposition.* As part of the office politics, success can be viewed as a *win-lose* strategy, which we identified above. Some people may feel that your success comes at their expense. So, for instance, your higher profile may mean that a project of theirs will be received less favourably. You have to be prepared to deal with this opposition.

SUMMARY AND IMPLICATIONS

1 What is power? Power refers to a capacity that A has to influence the behaviour of B, so that B acts in accordance with A's wishes.

2 How does one get power? There are six bases or sources of power: coercive, reward, legitimate, expert, referent, and information. These forms of power differ in their ability to improve a person's performance. *Coercive power* tends to result in negative performance responses from individuals; it decreases satisfaction, increases mistrust, and creates fear. *Reward power* may improve performance, but it can also lead to unethical behaviour. *Legitimate power* does not have a negative effect, but does not generally stimulate employees to improve their attitudes or performance, and it does not generally result in increased commitment. Ironically, the least effective bases of power—coercive, legitimate, and reward—are the ones most likely to be used by managers, perhaps because they are the easiest to implement. By contrast, effective leaders use *expert* and/or *referent power*; these forms of power are not derived from the person's position. *Information power* comes from access to and control over information and can be used in both positive (sharing) and negative (withholding) ways in the organization.

3 **How does dependency affect power?** To maximize your power, you will want to increase others' dependence on you. You can, for instance, increase your power in relation to your employer by developing knowledge or a skill that he or she needs and for which there is no ready substitute. However, you will not be alone in trying to build your bases of power. Others, particularly employees and peers, will seek to make you dependent on them. While you try to maximize others' dependence on you, you will be trying to minimize your dependence on others. Of course, others you work with will be trying to do the same. The result is a continual struggle for power.

4 **What tactics can be used to increase power?** One particular study identified nine tactics, or strategies, that managers and employees use to increase their power: rational persuasion, inspirational appeals, consultation, ingratiation, personal appeals, exchange, coalition tactics, pressure, and legitimating tactics.[83]

5 **What does it mean to be empowered?** Empowerment refers to the freedom and the ability of employees to make decisions and commitments. There is a lot of positive press on empowerment. However, much of the talk of empowerment in organizations does not result in employees' being empowered. Some managers do not fully understand how to go about empowering their employees, and others find it difficult to share their power with employees. As well, some employees have little or no interest in being empowered, and empowerment is not something that works well in every culture.

6 **How are power and harassment related?** People who engage in harassment in the workplace are typically abusing their power position. Harassment can come in many forms, from gross abuse of power toward anyone of lower rank, to abuse of individuals because of their personal characteristics, such as race, religion, national origin, and gender.

7 **Why do people engage in politics?** People use politics to influence others to help them achieve their personal objectives. Whenever people get together in groups, power will be exerted. People also use impression management to influence people. Impression management is the process by which individuals attempt to control the impression others form of them. Though politics is a natural occurrence in organizations, when it is carried to an extreme it can damage relationships among individuals.

For Review

1. What is power? How do you get it?

2. Contrast the bases of power and influence tactics.

3. What are some of the key contingency variables that determine which tactic a power holder is likely to use?

4. Which of the six bases of power lie with the individual? Which are derived from the organization?

5. State the general dependency postulate. What does it mean?

6. What creates dependency? Give an applied example.

7. Identify the range of empowerment that might be available to employees.

8. Define *sexual harassment.* Who is most likely to harass an employee: a boss, a co-worker, or a subordinate? Explain.

9. How are power and politics related?

10. Define *political behaviour.* Why is politics a fact of life in organizations?

For Critical Thinking

1. Based on the information presented in this chapter, if you were a recent graduate entering a new job, what would you do to maximize your power and accelerate your career progress?

2. "Politics isn't inherently bad. It is merely a way to get things accomplished within organizations." Do you agree or disagree? Defend your position.

3. You are a sales representative for an international software company. After four excellent years, sales in your territory are off 30 percent this year. Describe three impression management techniques you might use to convince your manager that your sales record is better than one could have expected under the circumstances.

4. "Sexual harassment should not be tolerated in the workplace." "Workplace romances are a natural occurrence in organizations." Are both of these statements true? Can they be reconciled?

5. Which impression management techniques have you used? What ethical implications, if any, are there in using impression management?

OB for You

- There are a variety of ways to increase your power in an organization. As an example, you could acquire more knowledge about a situation and then use that information to negotiate a bonus with your employer. Even if you don't get the bonus, the knowledge may help you in other ways.

- To increase your power, consider how dependent others are on you. Dependency is affected by your importance, substitutability, and scarcity options. If you have needed skills that no one else has, you will have more power.

- You can develop political skills. Remembering to take time to join in an office birthday celebration for someone is part of developing the skill of working with others effectively.

POINT

"Special Deals" for "Special Employees" Make Sense

In countries such as France, Belgium, and the Netherlands, terms of employment are largely mandated by law and hence highly standardized.[84] In contrast, in countries such as Canada, the United States, the United Kingdom, and New Zealand, managers have considerable leeway to negotiate idiosyncratic deals with employees. In these latter countries, managers are increasingly using this latitude to customize their treatment of "special" individuals.

Two trends help explain the growth in special deals for certain employees. First, the demand for knowledge workers with distinctive competencies in a competitive market means workers have greater power to negotiate employment conditions suited to their tastes and preferences. Second, the decline in unionization and the weakening of the job security–based model of organizational careers have led to less-standardized conditions of employment.

In order to hire, motivate, and keep highly skilled workers, managers are negotiating special treatment for certain employees. Examples of this special treatment include higher pay than others for doing similar work, allowing an employee to work from home several days a week, permitting an employee to leave early to fulfill family obligations, upgrading travel arrangements, and allowing certain employees to spend time on personal projects during work time.

What do these employees have that allow them to make idiosyncratic arrangements? It can be unique credentials, special skills, high status, important contacts, or high marketability. But it must also include the willingness of an employee or prospective employee to speak up and ask for special treatment. These deals are typically offered as bargaining chips when negotiating initial employment terms or after the employee has been on the job a while, built a trusting relationship with his or her manager, and become a valued performer.

These special deals have advantages for both employees and managers. They provide greater rewards for employees and allow them to tailor their jobs to better meet their personal needs. They also give individual managers greater latitude in motivating their employees and the flexibility to adapt to changing circumstances.

COUNTERPOINT

"Special Deals" Hurt the Work Environment

Making special deals with certain employees is bound to undermine whatever trust there is in an organization. Although management may desire flexibility in its relationships with employees, maintaining standardized practices is more likely to provide the appearance of fairness that is needed to create a climate of trust. Customization of employment relationships, under the guise of flexibility, only increases politics in the workplace.

There is no shortage of arguments against special deals for special employees. Here are just a few:

- *Special deals give too much power to managers.* They allow managers to negotiate favourable treatment with employees they like, politicizing the work environment.

- *Special deals are unlikely to be perceived as fair by those who do not receive them.* One person's merit is another's favouritism.

- *Special deals reward the wrong behaviours.* They encourage employees to "kiss up" to their bosses and to treat every attempt to get a raise or time off as a bargaining opportunity.

- *Special deals tend to go to aggressive employees, whether or not they are contributing the most.* Shy, quiet, and less demanding employees who are good performers are likely to be excluded.

- *Special deals are not cost-free.* One employee's gain is often at another's expense. So allowing one employee in a department to take off two hours early every Thursday afternoon to coach his son's baseball team often means others in that department will have to take up some of his work. This has the potential to create conflicts. For instance, evidence indicates that many single and childless employees resent the "family-friendly" benefits—such as helping to find an employee's spouse employment or paid daycare—that many companies offer to married workers and those with children.

Our position is that special deals undermine trust and cooperation at work. We have spent three-quarters of a century building formal human resource systems that ensure consistent treatment of the workforce. These systems are critical to promoting fairness, cooperation, and efficiency. Using idiosyncratic deals to supposedly enhance flexibility is a major step toward trashing these systems.

LEARNING ABOUT **YOURSELF** EXERCISE

How Political Are You?

To determine your political tendencies, please review the following statements. Check the answer that best represents your behaviour or belief, even if that particular behaviour or belief is not present all the time.

		True	False
1.	You should make others feel important through an open appreciation of their ideas and work.	____	____
2.	Because people tend to judge you when they first meet you, always try to make a good first impression.	____	____
3.	Try to let others do most of the talking, be sympathetic to their problems, and resist telling people that they are totally wrong.	____	____
4.	Praise the good traits of the people you meet, and always give people an opportunity to save face if they are wrong or make a mistake.	____	____
5.	Spreading false rumours, planting misleading information, and backstabbing are necessary, if somewhat unpleasant, methods of dealing with your enemies.	____	____
6.	Sometimes it is necessary to make promises that you know you will not or cannot keep.	____	____
7.	It is important to get along with everybody, even with those who are generally recognized as windbags, abrasive, or constant complainers.	____	____
8.	It is vital to do favours for others so that you can call in these IOUs at times when they will do you the most good.	____	____
9.	Be willing to compromise, particularly on issues that are minor to you but major to others.	____	____
10.	On controversial issues, it is important to delay or avoid your involvement if possible.	____	____

Scoring Key:

According to the author of this instrument, a complete organizational politician will answer "true" to all 10 questions. Organizational politicians with fundamental ethical standards will answer "false" to questions 5 and 6, which deal with deliberate lies and uncharitable behaviour. Individuals who regard manipulation, incomplete disclosure, and self-serving behaviour as unacceptable will answer "false" to all or almost all of the questions.

Source: J. F. Byrnes, "The Political Behavior Inventory." Reprinted by permission of Dr. Joseph F. Byrnes, Bentley College, Waltham, Massachusetts.

BREAKOUT **GROUP** EXERCISES

Form small groups to discuss the following topics, as assigned by your instructor:

1. Describe an incident in which you tried to use political behaviour in order to get something you wanted. What influence tactics did you use?

2. In thinking about the incident described above, were your influence tactics effective? Why?

3. Describe an incident in which you saw someone engaging in politics. What was your reaction to observing the political behaviour? Under what circumstances do you think political behaviour is appropriate?

Understanding Bases of Power

Step 1:   Your instructor will divide the class into groups of about 5 or 6 (making sure there are at least 5 groups). Each group will be assigned 1 of the following bases of power: (1) coercive, (2) reward, (3) legitimate, (4) expert, (5) referent, (6) information. Refer to your text for discussion of these terms.

Step 2:   Each group is to develop a role play that highlights the use of the power assigned. The role play should be developed using the following scenario:

> You are the leader of a group that is trying to develop a website for a new client. One of your group members, who was assigned the task of researching and analyzing the websites of your client's competition, has twice failed to bring the analysis to scheduled meetings, even though the member knew the assignment was due. Consequently, your group is falling behind in getting the website developed. As leader of the group, you have decided to speak with this team member and to use your specific brand of power to influence the individual's behaviour.

Step 3:   Each group should select 1 person to play the group leader, and another to play the member who has not done the assignment. You have 10 minutes to prepare an influence plan.

Step 4:   Each group will conduct its role play. In the event of multiple groups' being assigned the same power base, 1 of the groups may be asked to volunteer. While you are watching the other groups' role plays, try to put yourself in the place of the person being influenced, to see whether that type of influence would cause you to change your behaviour.

Immediately after each role play, while the next one is being set up, you should pretend that you were the person being influenced, and then record your reaction using the questionnaire below. To do this, take out a sheet of paper and tear it into 5 (or 6) pieces. At the top of each piece of paper, write the type of influence that was used. Then write the letters A, B, C, and D in a column, and indicate which number on the scale (see below) reflects the influence attempt.

Reaction to Influence Questionnaire

For each role play, think of yourself being on the receiving end of the influence attempt described and record your own reaction.

Type of power used _____

A. As a result of the influence attempt, I will . . .

| **definitely not comply** | 1 | 2 | 3 | 4 | 5 | **definitely comply** |

B. Any change that does come about will be . . .

| **temporary** | 1 | 2 | 3 | 4 | 5 | **long-lasting** |

C. My own personal reaction is . . .

| **resistant** | 1 | 2 | 3 | 4 | 5 | **accepting** |

D. As a result of this influence attempt, my relationship with my group leader will probably be . . .

| **worse** | 1 | 2 | 3 | 4 | 5 | **better** |

Step 5:   For each influence type, 1 member of each group will take the pieces of paper from group members and calculate the average group score for each of the 4 questions. For efficiency, this should be done while the role plays are being conducted.

continued

Step 6: Your instructor will collect the summaries from each group, and then lead a discussion based on these results.

Step 7: Discussion.

1. Which kind of influence is most likely to result immediately in the desired behaviour?
2. Which will have the longest-lasting effects?
3. What effect will using a particular base of power have on the ongoing relationship?
4. Which form of power will others find most acceptable? Least acceptable? Why?
5. Are there some situations in which a particular type of influence strategy might be more effective than others?

Source: This exercise was inspired by one found in Judith R. Gordon, *Organizational Behavior,* 2nd ed. (Englewood Cliffs, NJ: Prentice Hall, 1992), pp. 499–502.

ETHICAL **DILEMMA** EXERCISE

Swapping Personal Favours?

Jack Grubman was a powerful man on Wall Street. As a star analyst of telecom companies for the Salomon Smith Barney unit of Citigroup, his recommendations carried a lot of weight with investors.

For years, Grubman had been negative about the stock of AT&T. But in November 1999, he upgraded his opinion on the stock. According to email evidence, it appears that Grubman's decision to upgrade AT&T was not based on the stock's fundamentals. There were other factors involved.

At the time, his boss at Citigroup, Sanford Weill, was in the midst of a power struggle with co-CEO John Reed to become the single head of the company. Meanwhile, Salomon was looking for additional business to increase its revenues. Getting investment banking business fees from AT&T would be a big plus toward improving revenues. Salomon's efforts at getting that AT&T business would definitely be improved if Grubman would upgrade his opinion on the stock. Furthermore, Weill sought Grubman's upgrade to win favour with AT&T CEO Michael Armstrong, who sat on Citigroup's board. Weill wanted Armstrong's backing in his efforts to oust Reed.

Grubman had his own concerns. Although he was earning tens of millions a year in his job, he was a man of modest background. He was the son of a city employee in Philadelphia. He wanted the best for his twin daughters, which included entry to an exclusive New York City nursery school—a school that a year earlier had reportedly turned down Madonna's daughter. Weill made a call on Grubman's behalf to the school and pledged a $1 million donation from Citigroup.

At approximately the same time, Weill also asked Grubman to "take a fresh look" at his neutral rating on AT&T. Shortly after being asked to review his rating, Grubman turned positive, raised his rating, and AT&T awarded Salomon an investment-banking job worth nearly $45 million.

Did Sanford Weill do anything unethical? How about Jack Grubman? What do you think?

Source: Based on D. Kadlec, "Did Sandy Play Dirty?" *Time Online Edition,* November 25, 2002.

CASE INCIDENT

The Power of Bill Fowler at Blackmer/Dover Resources

Blackmer/Dover Resources' plant makes heavy-duty pumps designed to move commodities such as refined oil and chocolate. The plant has 160 employees.

Historically, management assigned employees to operate the same machine for months or even years at a time. In this way, each employee became intimately familiar with a narrow task. And employees used their expertise to earn more money. Until 1997, about half the workforce at the plant earned a premium, on top of their hourly wages, based on the number of pumps or pump parts they produced. The old system gave them a strong incentive to conceal output-enhancing tricks they had learned, even from co-workers.

Today, the plant's employees receive a straight hourly wage. To make the plant more flexible, management encourages workers to learn a variety of jobs and accept moves to different parts of the factory floor. Many of the plant's older employees, however, have not welcomed the change. One of those is Bill Fowler.

Fowler is 56 years old and has worked at the Blackmer plant for 24 years. Fowler does not like changing jobs and he does not like telling anyone anything about what he does. "I don't want to move around," he says, "because I love my routine—it helps me get through the day."

Fowler's job is cutting metal shafts for industrial pumps. It's a precision task: A minor error could render a pump useless. Fowler is outstanding at what he does. He is known for the accuracy of his cuts. His bosses also say he can be hours faster than anyone else in readying his giant cutting machines to shift from making one type of pump shaft to another. Management would love to incorporate Fowler's know-how into the manufacturing process, but he refuses to share his secrets even with fellow workers. "If I gave away my tricks, management could use [them] to speed things up and keep me at a flat-out pace all day long," says Fowler.

Employees like Fowler worry when they read about companies soliciting employees' expert advice in the name of making their plants more competitive, and then turn around and move jobs to lower-wage locations abroad. Blackmer's top management, however, says they have no plans to relocate jobs or otherwise hurt workers. They merely want to pool employees' knowledge to make the plant stronger. "We've realized that to get competitive, we need to start asking these guys what they know," says Blackmer's president.

Questions

1. Explain Bill Fowler's behaviour in power terms.

2. What, if anything, does this case say about trust and power?

3. What does this case say regarding implementing knowledge-management systems?

4. What, if anything, can management do to change Fowler's behaviour?

Source: This case is based on T. Aeppel, "On Factory Floors, Top Workers Hide Secrets to Success," *Wall Street Journal*, July 1, 2002, p. A1.

 VIDEO CASE INCIDENT

Jean Brault and the Sponsorship Scandal

The curtain was pulled back on a Canadian political scandal as Jean Brault testified at the Gomery inquiry. The sponsorship-kickback scheme toppled a government weeks after the Gomery Commission issued a report that outlined a story of greed, politics, and misconduct involving overspending, kickbacks, and fraudulent billing by communications agencies in Quebec.

At the heart of the scandal is advertising executive Jean Brault, who has come a long way since he started his advertising agency, Groupaction, out of his basement in the 1980s. Groupaction became a multi-million dollar company, helped along the way by generous federal government contracts. Brault is facing fraud charges, and it is from his firm that the federal government is trying to recover $35 million. The floodgates of government sponsorship contracts opened after the 1995 Quebec referendum, paving the way for a story of misuse of taxpayers' money and leading to speculation of widespread political corruption.

Much of the deal making took place over lavish lunches and extravagant dinners. One episode included a dinner with Brault and his advertising executives the night before they were going to make a pitch for a big federal contract. The person they were going to pitch to, Chuck Guité, was also there. Although Brault said at the inquiry the contract was not mentioned over dinner, a short time after that meal together Brault's company was awarded the contract.

In 2001 Brault met with Joe Morselli, vice-president of fundraising for the Liberal Party, who requested a Liberal organizer be placed on Brault's company payroll. Brault refused, and instead offered to pay $5000/month in cash using a bizarre payment system reminiscent of the underworld.

Brault benefited for several years from the nearly $60 million in contracts from the sponsorship program and kept funnelling money back to the Liberal Party. But stress was getting to Brault, and in 2001 he had a falling out with Alain Renaud, a Liberal activist and lobbyist. Brault had been paying Renaud's fees and expenses of almost $1 million, and in return Renaud secured most of Brault's sponsorship and advertising contracts. After the dispute, they parted ways.

Tony Mignacca, a close associate of Alfonso Galiano, the former cabinet minister who had been in charge of the sponsorship program, began to pressure Brault to take Renaud back. Mignacca gave Brault the impression that Groupaction's account with Via Rail would be in jeopardy if he did not re-hire Renaud.

In 2002, Brault knew a federal advertising contract for the Department of Justice was coming up. Because Brault's firm was not ready to bid, he wanted a delay in the closing of the tender. He met with Morselli, proposing $100 000 if the competition was delayed. He paid $50 000 in cash, and the competition was delayed. He planned to pay the rest in April 2002, but by that time Auditor General Sheila Fraser had begun her investigation into Brault's firm. Facing a criminal trial, Jean Brault, the high-flying advertising man, has been brought back to earth.

Questions

1. Identify the power bases of the individuals involved in the sponsorship scandal: Jean Brault, Chuck Guité, Joe Morselli, Alain Renaud, Tony Mignacca, and Sheila Fraser.

2. What influence tactics did the prominent characters in the sponsorship saga use to try to pressure people to act in certain ways?

3. What factors contributed to the political behaviour evident in the sponsorship scandal?

Sources: "Brault Dissected," *The National*, April 7, 2005; "Guité Trial Begins as Brault Sent to Jail," Daily Courier (Kelowna), May 6, 2006, p. A8; G. Chiasson, "Advertising Scandal Fells Canadian Government," *Advertising Age*, December 5, 2005, p. 81; and J. Intini, "Ottawa's Crusader," *Maclean's*, December 27, 2004, p. 32.

From **Concepts** to **Skills**

Politicking

Forget, for a moment, the ethics of politicking and any negative impressions you may have of people who engage in organizational politics.[85] If you wanted to be more politically adept in your organization, what could you do? The following eight suggestions are likely to improve your political effectiveness.

1. *Frame arguments in terms of organizational goals.* Effective politicking requires camouflaging your self-interest. No matter that your objective is self-serving; all the arguments you marshal in support of it must be framed in terms of the benefits that the organization will gain. People whose actions appear to blatantly further their own interests at the expense of the organization's are almost universally denounced, are likely to lose influence, and often suffer the ultimate penalty of being expelled from the organization.

2. *Develop the right image.* If you know your organization's culture, you understand what the organization wants and values from its employees—in terms of dress; associates to cultivate, and those to avoid; whether to appear risk-taking or risk-aversive; the preferred leadership style; the importance placed on getting along well with others; and so forth. Then you are equipped to project the appropriate image. Because the assessment of your performance is not a fully objective process, both style and substance must be addressed.

3. *Gain control of organizational resources.* The control of organizational resources that are scarce and important is a source of power. Knowledge and expertise are particularly effective resources to control. They make you more valuable to the organization and therefore more likely to gain security, advancement, and a receptive audience for your ideas.

4. *Make yourself appear indispensable.* Because we are dealing with appearances rather than objective facts, you can enhance your power by appearing to be indispensable. That is, you don't have to really be indispensable as long as key people in the organization believe that you are. If the organization's prime decision makers believe there is no ready substitute for what you are giving the organization, they are likely to go to great lengths to ensure that your desires are satisfied.

5. *Be visible.* Because performance evaluation has a substantial subjective component, it is important that your manager and those in power in the organization be made aware of your contribution. If you are fortunate enough to have a job that brings your accomplishments to the attention of others, it may not be necessary to take direct measures to increase your visibility. But your job may require you to handle activities that are low in visi-

bility, or your specific contribution may be indistinguishable because you are part of a team endeavour. In such cases—without appearing to toot your own horn or create the image of a braggart—you will want to call attention to yourself by highlighting your successes in routine reports, having satisfied customers relay their appreciation to senior executives in your organization, being seen at social functions, being active in your professional associations, developing powerful allies who speak positively about your accomplishments, and similar tactics. Of course, the skilled politician actively and successfully lobbies to get those projects that will increase his or her visibility.

6. *Develop powerful allies.* It helps to have powerful people in your camp. Cultivate contacts with potentially influential people above you, at your own level, and in the lower ranks. They can provide you with important information that may not be available through normal channels. There will be times, too, when decisions will be made in favour of those with the greatest support. Having powerful allies can provide you with a coalition of support if and when you need it.

7. *Avoid "tainted" members.* In almost every organization, there are fringe members whose status is questionable. Their performance and/or loyalty is suspect. Keep your distance from such individuals. Given the reality that effectiveness has a large subjective component, your own effectiveness might be called into question if you are perceived as too closely associated with tainted members.

8. *Support your manager.* Your immediate future is in the hands of your current manager. Since he or she evaluates your performance, you will typically want to do whatever is necessary to have your manager on your side. You should make every effort to help your manager succeed, make her look good, support her if she is under siege, and spend the time to find out what criteria she will be using to assess your effectiveness. Do not undermine your manager, and do not speak negatively of her to others.

Assessing Skills

After you've read this chapter, take the following Self-Assessments on your enclosed CD-ROM:

35. How Power-Oriented Am I?

36. What's My Preferred Type of Power?

37. How Good Am I at Playing Politics?

38. How Well Do I Manage Impressions?

Practising Skills

You used to be the star marketing manager for Hilton Electronics Corporation. But for the past year, you have been outpaced again and again by Sean, a new manager in the design department who has been accomplishing everything expected of him and more. Meanwhile, your best efforts to do your job well have been sabotaged and undercut by Maria—your and Sean's manager. For example, before last year's international consumer electronics show, Maria moved $30 000 from your budget to Sean's. Despite your best efforts, your marketing team could not complete all the marketing materials normally developed to showcase all of your organization's new products at this important industry show. Also, Maria has chipped away at your staff and budget ever since. Although you have been able to meet most of your goals with fewer staff and less budget, Maria has continued to slice away resources from your group. Just last week, she eliminated two positions in your team of eight marketing specialists to make room for a new designer and some extra equipment for Sean. Maria is clearly taking away your resources while giving Sean whatever he wants and more. You think it's time to do something or soon you will not have any team or resources left. What do you need to do to make sure your division has the resources to survive and grow?

Reinforcing Skills

1. Keep a one-week journal of your behaviour describing incidents when you tried to influence others around you. Assess each incident by asking: Were you successful at these attempts to influence them? Why or why not? What could you have done differently?

2. Outline a specific action plan, based on concepts in this module, that would improve your career progression in the organization in which you currently work or an organization in which you think you would like to be employed.

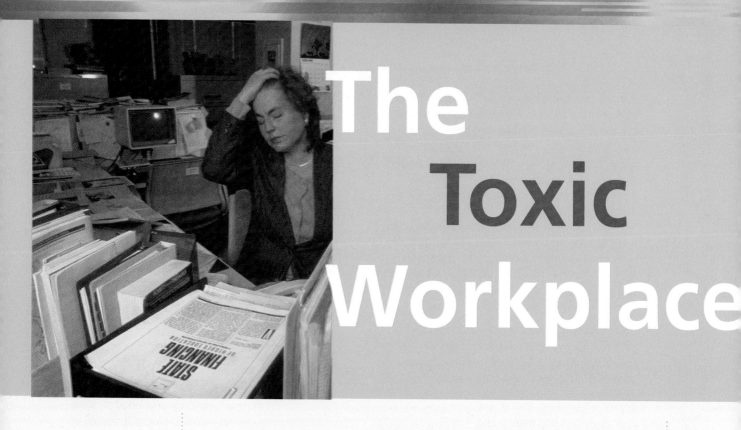

The Toxic Workplace

It's not unusual to find the following employee behaviours in today's workplace:

> *Answering the phone with a "yeah," neglecting to say thank you or please, using voice mail to screen calls, leaving a half cup of coffee behind to avoid having to brew the next pot, standing uninvited but impatiently over the desk of someone engaged in a telephone conversation, dropping trash on the floor and leaving it for the maintenance crew to clean up, and talking loudly on the phone about personal matters.*[1]

Some employers or managers fit the following descriptions:

> *In the months since [the new owner of the pharmacy] has been in charge [he] has made it clear that he is at liberty to fire employees at will . . . change their positions, decrease their bonus percentages, and refuse time-off and vacation choices. Furthermore, he has established an authoritarian work structure characterized by distrust, cut-backs on many items deemed essential to work comfort, disrespect, rigidity and poor-to-no-communication.*[2]

> *He walked all over people. He made fun of them; he intimidated them. He criticized work for no reason, and he changed his plans daily.*[3]

What's Happening in Our Workplaces?

Workplaces today are receiving highly critical reviews, being called everything from "uncivil" to "toxic."

Lynne Anderson and Christine Pearson, two management professors from St. Joseph's University and the University of North Carolina, respectively, note that "Historians may view the dawn of the twenty-first century as a time of thoughtless acts and rudeness: We tailgate, even in the slow lane; we dial wrong numbers and then slam the receiver on the innocent respondent; we break appointments with nonchalance."[4] The workplace has often been seen as one of the places where civility still ruled, with co-workers treating each other with a mixture of formality and friendliness, distance and politeness. However, with downsizing, re-engineering, budget cuts, pressures for increased productivity, autocratic work environments, and the use of part-time employees, there has been an increase in "uncivil and aggressive workplace behaviours."[5]

What does civility in the workplace mean? A simple definition of workplace civility is behaviour "involving politeness and regard for others in the workplace, within workplace norms for respect."[6] Workplace incivility then "involves acting with disregard for others in the workplace, in violation of workplace norms for respect."[7] Of course, different workplaces will have different norms for what determines mutual respect. For instance, in most restaurants, if the staff were rude to you when you were there for dinner, you would be annoyed, and perhaps even complain to the manager. However, at the Elbow Room Cafe in downtown Vancouver, if customers complain they are in a hurry, manager Patrick Savoie might well say, "If you're in a hurry, you should have gone to McDonald's."[8] Such a comeback is acceptable to the diners at the Elbow Room Cafe, because rudeness is its trademark.

Most work environments are not expected to be characterized by such rudeness. However, this has been changing in recent years. Robert Warren, a University of Manitoba marketing professor, notes that "simple courtesy has gone by the board."[9]

There is documented evidence of the rise of violence and threats of violence at work.[10] However, several studies have found that there is persistent negative behaviour in the workplace that is not of a violent nature.[11] For instance, a survey of 603 Toronto nurses found that 33 percent had experienced verbal abuse during the five previous days of work.[12]

Another study found that 78 percent of employees interviewed think that workplace incivility has increased in the past 10 years.[13] The researchers found that men are mostly to blame for this change: "Although men and women are targets of disrespect and rudeness in equal numbers . . . men instigate the rudeness 70 percent of the time."[14]

Rude behaviour is not confined to men, however. Professor André Roberge at Laval University suggests that some of the rudeness is generational. He finds that "young clerks often lack both knowledge and civility. Employers are having to train young people in simple manners because that is not being done at home."[15] Professor Warren backs this up: "One of the biggest complaints I hear from businesses when I go to talk about graduates is the lack of interpersonal skills."[16]

Workplace Violence

Recently, researchers have suggested that incivility may be the beginning of more negative behaviours in the workplace, including aggression and violence.[17]

Pierre Lebrun chose a deadly way to exhibit the anger he had stored up from his workplace.[18] He took a hunting rifle to Ottawa-Carleton–based OC Transpo and killed four public transit co-workers on April 6, 1999, before turning the gun on himself. Lebrun felt that he had been the target of harassment by his co-workers for years because of his stuttering. If this sounds like an unusual response for an irate employee, consider the circumstances at OC Transpo. "Quite apart from what's alleged or otherwise with Mr. Lebrun's situation, we know [OC Transpo's] had a very unhappy work environment for a long time," Al Loney, former chair of Ottawa-Carleton's transit commission, noted. A consultant's report produced the year before the shooting found a workplace with "rock-bottom morale and poor management." It was not uncommon for fights to break out in the unit where the four men were killed.

Workplace violence, according to the International Labour Organization (ILO), includes

any incident in which a person is abused, threatened or assaulted in circumstances relating to [his or her] work. These behaviours would originate from customers or co-workers at any level of the organization. This definition would include all forms of harassment, bullying, intimidation, physical threats, assaults, robbery and other intrusive behaviour.[19]

No Canadian statistics on anger at work are available.[20] However, studies show that anger pervades the US workplace. While 25 percent of Americans reported being "generally at least somewhat angry at work," 49 percent say that they felt "at least 'a little angry' at work."[21] A 2000 Gallup poll conducted in the United States found that 25 percent of the working adults surveyed felt like screaming or shouting because of job stress, 14 percent had considered hitting a co-worker, and 10 percent worry about colleagues becoming violent. This worry is not unfounded. Twenty employees are murdered each week in the United States.[22]

Canadian workplaces are not murder-free, however. In 2001, 60 murders occurred at work, 10 percent of all murders for the year.[23] Most of these workplace incidents were carried out by male spouses and partners of female employees. Surprisingly, Canada scores higher than the United States on workplace violence. In a recent ILO study involving 130 000 workers in 32 countries, Argentina was ranked the most violent. Romania was second, France third, and Canada fourth. The United States placed ninth.[24]

Sixty-four percent of union representatives who were surveyed recently reported an increase in workplace aggression, based on their review of incident reports, grievance files, and other solid evidence.[25] The ILO, in a separate 1998 study, found that, per capita, the rate of assault at work for Canadian women is four times that of American women.[26] To understand the seriousness of this situation, consider that one quarter of Nova Scotia teachers surveyed reported that they faced physical violence at work during the 2001–2002 school year.[28]

What Causes Incivility (and Worse) in the Workplace?

If employers and employees are acting with less civility toward each other, what is causing this to happen?

Managers and employees often have different views of the employee's role in the organization. Jeffrey Pfeffer, a professor of organizational behaviour at the Graduate School of Business at Stanford University, notes that many companies don't really value their employees: "Most managers, if they're being honest with themselves, will admit it: When they look at their people, they see costs, they see salaries, they see benefits, they see overhead. Very few companies look at their people and see assets."[29]

Most employees, however, like to think that they are assets to their organizations. The realization that they are simply costs and not valued members of an organization can cause frustration for employees.

In addition, "employers' excessive demands and top-down style of management are contributing to the rise of 'work rage,'" claims Gerry Smith of Toronto-based WarrenShepell Consultants.[30] He is the author of the recently released *Work Rage*.[31] He cites demands coming from a variety of sources: "overtime, downsizing, rapid technological changes, company restructuring and difficulty balancing the demands of job and home."[32] Smith worries about the consequences of these demands: "If you push people too hard, set unrealistic expectations and cut back their benefits, they're going to strike back."[33]

Smith's work supports the findings of a study that reported the most common cause of anger is the actions of supervisors or managers.[34] Other common causes of anger identified by the researchers include lack of productivity by co-workers and others; tight deadlines; heavy workload; interaction with the public; and bad treatment.

The Psychological Contract

Some researchers have looked at this frustration in terms of a breakdown of the psychological contract formed between employees and employers. Employers and employees begin to develop psychological contracts as they are first introduced to each other in the hiring process.[35] These continue over time as the employer and the employee come to understand each other's expectations about the amounts and quality of work to be performed and the types of rewards to be given. For instance, when an employee is continually asked to work late and/or be available at all hours through pagers and email, the employee may assume that doing so will result in greater rewards or faster promotion down the line. The

FactBox[27]

- In 2000, only 49% of working Canadians said they were committed to their employers. In 1991, the level of commitment was 62%.

- More Americans report commitment to their employers than Canadians: 55% of Americans vs. 49% of Canadians.

- Of those who experience rudeness, 12% quit their jobs in response, 22% decrease their work effort, and 52% lose work time worrying about it.

- Employees over the age of 55 express the highest degree of commitment to their employers.

employer may have had no such intention, and may even be thinking that the employee should be grateful simply to have a job. Later, when the employee does not get expected (though never promised) rewards, he or she is disappointed.

Sandra Robinson, an organizational behaviour professor at the Sauder School of Business at the University of British Columbia, and her colleagues have found that when a psychological contract is violated (perceptually or actually), the relationship between the employee and the employer is damaged. This can result in the loss of trust.[36] The breakdown in trust can cause employees to be less ready to accept decisions or obey rules.[37] The erosion of trust can also lead employees to take revenge on the employers. So they don't carry out their end of a task. Or they refuse to pass on messages. They engage in any number of subtle and not-so-subtle behaviours that affect the way work gets done—or prevents work from getting done.

The Toxic Organization

Pfeffer suggests that companies have become "toxic places to work."[38] He notes that companies, particularly in Silicon Valley, ask their employees to sign contracts on the first day of work indicating the employee's understanding that the company has the right to fire at will and for any reason. Some employers also ask their employees to choose between having a life and having a career. Pfeffer relates a joke people used to tell about Microsoft: "We offer flexible time—you can work any 18 hours you want."[39] This kind of attitude can be toxic to employees, though this does not imply that Microsoft is a toxic employer.

What does it mean to be a toxic organization? The late professor Peter Frost of the Sauder School of Business at the University of British Columbia notes that there will always be pain in organizations, but that sometimes it becomes so intense or prolonged that conditions within the organization begin to break down. In other words, the situation becomes toxic. This is not dissimilar to what the liver or kidneys do when toxins become too intense in a human body.[40]

What makes organizations toxic? Like Pfeffer, professors Frost and Robinson identify a number of factors. Downsizing and organizational change are two main factors, particularly in recent years. Sometimes

Do You Have a Toxic Manager?

Below are some of the toxic behaviours of managers and the workplace cultures that allow these behaviours to thrive.

Managerial Toxic Behaviour

- *Actor behaviour.* These managers act out anger rather than discuss problems. They slam doors, sulk, and make it clear they are angry, but refuse to talk about it.
- *Fragmentor behaviour.* These managers see no connection between what they do and the outcome, and take no responsibility for their behaviour.
- *Me-first behaviour.* These managers make decisions based on their own convenience.
- *Mixed-messenger behaviour.* These managers present themselves one way but their behaviour doesn't match what they say.
- *Wooden-stick behaviour.* These managers are extremely rigid and controlling.
- *Escape-artist behaviour.* These managers don't deal with reality, often lying, or at the extreme, escaping through drugs or alcohol.

Workplace Culture That Fosters This Behaviour

- *Macho culture.* People don't discuss problems. The emphasis is to "take it like a man."
- *Specialist culture.* Employees who are technically gifted or great in their fields don't have to consider how their behaviour or work affects anyone.
- *Elitist culture.* Promotions and rewards are not based on your work but on who your buddies are.
- *Office-politics culture.* Promotions and rewards are based on flattery and positioning.
- *Change-resistant culture.* Upper management struggles to maintain the status quo regardless of the outcome.
- *Workaholic culture.* Employees are forced to spend more time at the office than necessary.

Source: L. McClure, *Risky Business* (Binghamton, NY: Haworth Press, 1996).

organizations experience unexpected events—such as the sudden death of a key manager, an unwise move by senior management, strong competition from a start-up company—that lead to toxicity. Other organizations are toxic throughout their systems due to policies and practices that create distress. Such factors as unreasonable stretch goals or performance targets, or unrelenting internal competition, can create toxicity. There are also toxic managers who lead through insensitivity, vindictiveness, and failure to take responsibility, or they are control freaks or are unethical. The inset *Do You Have a Toxic Manager?* on page 253 lists some types of toxic managers and the workplace culture that fosters their behaviour.

What Are the Effects of Incivility and Toxicity in the Workplace?

In general, researchers have found that the effects of workplace anger are sometimes subtle: a hostile work environment and the tendency to do only enough work to get by.[41]

Those who feel chronic anger in the workplace are more likely to report "feelings of betrayal by the organization, decreased feelings of loyalty, a decreased sense that respondent values and the organization's values are similar, a decreased sense that the employer treated the respondent with dignity and respect, and a decreased sense that employers had fulfilled promises made to respondents."[42] So do these feelings make a difference? Apparently so. Researchers have found that those who felt angry with their employers were less likely to put forth their best efforts, more likely to be competitive toward other employees, and less likely to suggest "a quicker and better way to do their job."[43] All of these actions tend to decrease the productivity possible in the workplace.

It's not just those who work for an organization who are affected by incivility and toxicity. Poor service, from indifference to rudeness to outright hostility, characterizes many transactions in Canadian businesses. "Across the country, better business bureaus, provincial government consumer-help agencies and media ombudsmen report a lengthening litany of complaints about contractors, car dealers, repair shops, moving companies, airlines and department stores."[44] This suggests that customers and clients may well be feeling the impact of internal workplace dynamics.

The Toxin Handler

Employees of toxic organizations suffer pain from their experiences in toxic environments. In some organizations, mechanisms, often informal, are set up to deal with the results of toxicity.

Frost and Robinson identified a special role that some employees play in trying to relieve the toxicity within an organization: the toxin handler. This person tries to mitigate the pain by softening the blow of downsizing, or change, or the behaviour of the toxic leader. Essentially the toxin handler helps others around him or her deal with the strains of the organization, by counselling, advising, shielding employees from the wrath of angry managers, reinterpreting the managers' messages to make them less harsh, etc.

So who takes on this role? Certainly no organization to date has a line on its organizational chart for "the toxin handler." Often the role emerges as part of an individual's position in an organization, for instance, a manager in the human resource department. In many cases, however, handlers are pulled into the role "bit by bit—by their colleagues, who turn to them because they are trustworthy, calm, kind and nonjudgmental."[45]

Frost and Robinson, in profiling these individuals, suggest that toxin handlers are predisposed to say yes, have a high tolerance for pain, a surplus of empathy, and when they notice people in pain they have a need to make the situation right. But these are not individuals who thrive simply on dealing with the emotional needs of others. Quoting one of the managers in their study, Frost and Robinson cite the full range of activities of most toxin handlers: "These people are usually relentless in their drive to accomplish organizational targets and rarely lose focus

How Toxin Handlers Alleviate Organizational Pain

- They listen empathically.
- They suggest solutions.
- They work behind the scenes to prevent pain.
- They carry the confidences of others.
- They reframe difficult messages.

Source: P. Frost and S. Robinson, "The Toxic Handler: Organizational Hero—and Casualty," *Harvard Business Review,* July–August 1999, p. 101 (Reprint 99406).

FACE**OFF**

Manners are an over-romanticized concept. The big issue isn't that employees need to be concerned about their manners. Rather, employers should be paying better wages.

The Golden Rule, "Do unto others as you would have others do unto you," should still have a role in today's workplace. Being nice pays off.

on business issues. Managing emotional pain is one of their means."[46]

The inset *How Toxin Handlers Alleviate Organizational Pain* on page 254 identifies the many tasks that toxin handlers take on in an organization. Frost and Robinson suggest that these tasks will probably need to be handled forever, and they recommend that organizations take steps to actively support people performing this role.

Research Exercises

1. Look for data on violence and anger in the workplace in other countries. How do these data compare with the Canadian and American data presented here? What might you conclude about how violence and anger in the workplace are expressed in different cultures?

2. Identify three Canadian organizations that are trying to foster better and/or less toxic environments for their employees. What kind of effect is this having on the organizations' bottom lines?

Your Perspective

1. Is it reasonable to suggest, as some researchers have, that young people today have not learned to be civil to others or do not place a high priority on doing so? Do you see this as one of the causes of incivility in the workplace?

2. What should be done about managers who create toxicity in the workplace while being rewarded because they achieve bottom-line results? Should bottom-line results justify their behaviour?

Want to Know More?

If you'd like to read more on this topic, see Peter Frost, *Toxic Emotions at Work* (Cambridge, MA: Harvard Business School Press, 2003); P. Frost and S. Robinson, "The Toxic Handler: Organizational Hero—and Casualty," *Harvard Business Review,* July–August 1999, pp. 96–106 (Reprint 99406); and A. M. Webber, "Danger: Toxic Company," *Fast Company,* November 1998, pp. 152–157. You can find the latter article at www.fastcompany.com/online/19/toxic.html. It contains an interview with Professor Jeffrey Pfeffer, who discusses examples of toxic organizations.

CHAPTER **8**

Leadership

A major US city is hit by a deadly hurricane, and then suffers serious flooding. Does anyone have the leadership skills needed to rescue people and provide order?

1 What is the difference between a manager and a leader?

2 Are there specific traits, behaviours, and situations that affect how one leads?

3 How does a leader lead with vision?

4 Can a person be an informal leader?

5 What is self-leadership?

6 What are some of the contemporary issues in leadership?

Millions of people around the world were glued to their television sets in September 2005, watching the devastation of Hurricane Katrina unfold.[1] While the storm damaged parts of Mississippi, Alabama, and Louisiana, it was the damage to New Orleans that got the most press coverage. The entire city had to be evacuated because of severe flooding, causing thousands of people, mostly poor and black, to be stranded at the city's Superdome and Convention Center.

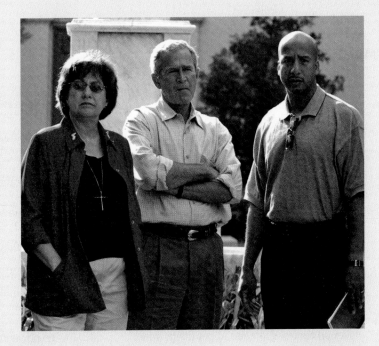

For many of those watching people waving from rooftops begging to be rescued, and people from the Convention Center and Superdome begging for food and water, the questions that arose were, Who was in charge? Why wasn't help coming faster? There was plenty of blame to go around, and the obvious leaders, Louisiana governor Kathleen Blanco, President George W. Bush, and New Orleans Mayor Ray Nagin, shown here, were all singled out for criticism. Subsequent investigations of what went wrong suggested that these leaders did not do enough to minimize the damage of the storm, starting right from the top with President Bush.

In this chapter, we examine the various studies on leadership to determine what makes an effective leader. We first consider the traits, behaviours, and situations that affect one's ability to lead, and then we consider visionary leadership. We then look at how leadership is being spread throughout the organization, and how you might lead yourself, through self-management. Finally, we consider contemporary issues in leadership.

ARE MANAGERS AND LEADERS THE SAME?

Leadership and *management* are two terms that are often confused. What is the difference between them?

John Kotter of the Harvard Business School argues that "managers promote stability while leaders press for change and only organizations that embrace both sides of the contradiction can survive in turbulent times."[2]

Professor Rabindra Kanungo at McGill University sees a growing consensus emerging "among management scholars that the concept of 'leadership' must be distinguished from the concept of 'supervision/management.'"[3] Exhibit 8-1 on page 258 illustrates Kanungo's distinctions between management and leadership. Leaders provide vision and strategy; managers implement that vision and strategy, coordinate and staff the organization, and handle day-to-day problems.

1 What is the difference between a manager and a leader?

Harvard Business School
www.hbs.edu

OB IS FOR EVERYONE

* Have you ever wondered if there was one right *way* to lead?
* Is a leader always necessary?
* Can anyone be a leader?
* How do you manage yourself?

EXHIBIT 8-1 Distinguishing Leadership from Management	
Management	**Leadership**
1. Engages in day-to-day caretaker activities: Maintains and allocates resources	Formulates long-term objectives for reforming the system: Plans strategy and tactics
2. Exhibits supervisory behaviour: Acts to make others maintain standard job behaviour	Exhibits leading behaviour: Acts to bring about change in others congruent with long-term objectives
3. Administers subsystems within organizations	Innovates for the entire organization
4. Asks how and when to engage in standard practice	Asks what and why to change standard practice
5. Acts within established culture of the organization	Creates vision and meaning for the organization
6. Uses transactional influence: Induces compliance in manifest behaviour using rewards, sanctions, and formal authority	Uses transformational influence: Induces change in values, attitudes, and behaviour using personal examples and expertise
7. Relies on control strategies to get things done by subordinates	Uses empowering strategies to make followers internalize values
8. Status quo supporter and stabilizer	Status quo challenger and change creator

Source: R. N. Kanungo, "Leadership in Organizations: Looking Ahead to the 21st Century," *Canadian Psychology* 39, no. 1–2 (1998), p. 77.

In our discussion of leadership, we will focus on two major tasks of those who lead in organizations: managing those around them to get the day-to-day tasks done (leadership as supervision) and inspiring others to do the extraordinary (leadership as vision).

LEADERSHIP AS SUPERVISION

As Hurricane Katrina rushed closer to the New Orleans coastline, people in authority in both Louisiana and Washington were trying to figure out how best to handle the situation. Some wondered whether hundreds of thousands of people should be evacuated from New Orleans before the storm hit or whether everyone could simply ride out the storm. Michael Brown, then head of the Federal Emergency Management Agency (FEMA), sent a small emergency response team to Louisiana to review evacuation plans the weekend before the levees broke. Frustrated that Mayor Ray Nagin did not seem to be acting quickly enough to get New Orleans evacuated, Brown called President George W. Bush to advise him of the situation. He also asked the president to phone the mayor directly to tell him to evacuate the people of New Orleans. The president's response, "Mike, you want me to call the Mayor?" illustrates the different roles of managers and leaders. The president was not expecting to micromanage an evacuation plan and did not really consider it his role. As the "big picture person," his job might have been to make sure that strategies were developed for emergency situations, not to develop the strategies or implement them. Nevertheless, did President Bush do all that was needed to make sure his followers could carry out their tasks?

2 Are there specific traits, behaviours, and situations that affect how one leads?

In this section we discuss theories of leadership that were developed before 1980. These early theories focused on the supervisory nature of leadership—that is, how leaders managed the day-to-day functioning of employees. The three general types of theories that emerged were (1) trait theories, which propose leaders have a particular set of traits that makes them different from nonleaders; (2) behavioural theories, which propose that particular behaviours make for better leaders; and (3) contingency theories, which propose the situation has an effect on leaders. When you think about these theories, remember that although they have been considered "theories of leadership," they rely on an older understanding of what "leadership" means, and they do not convey Kanungo's distinction between leadership and supervision.

Trait Theory: Are Leaders Different from Others?

Have you ever wondered whether there is some fundamental personality difference that makes some people "born leaders"? **Trait theories of leadership** emerged in the hope that if it were possible to identify the traits of leaders, it would be easier to select people to fill leadership roles.

The media have long been believers in trait theories. They identify people such as Nelson Mandela, Richard Branson of the Virgin Group, and Steve Jobs of Apple as leaders, and then describe them in terms such as *charismatic, enthusiastic, decisive,* and *courageous.* The media are not alone. Exhibit 8-2 on page 260 shows the findings of a recent survey of 200 CEOs, and what they cited as the most important leadership traits.

The search for personality, social, physical, or intellectual traits that would describe leaders and differentiate them from nonleaders goes back to research done by psychologists in the 1930s. However, until recently, research efforts at isolating leadership traits have reached few conclusions.[4] A breakthrough, of sorts, came when researchers began organizing traits around the Big Five personality framework (see Chapter 2, page 44).[5] They found that most of the dozens of traits that emerged in various leadership reviews fall under one of the Big Five personality traits (extraversion, agreeableness, conscientiousness, emotional stability, and openness to experience). This approach resulted in consistent and strong support for traits as predictors of leadership.

Comprehensive reviews of the leadership literature, when organized around the Big Five, have found that extraversion is the most important trait of effective leaders.[6] But results show that extraversion is more strongly related to leader emergence than to leader effectiveness. This is not totally surprising since sociable and dominant people are more likely to assert themselves in group situations. Conscientiousness and openness to experience also showed strong and consistent relationships to leadership, but not as strong as extraversion. The traits of agreeableness and emotional stability do not appear to offer much help in predicting leadership.

Recent studies indicate that emotional intelligence (EI) is an additional factor to consider in the emergence of a leader.[7] The work on EI suggests that leaders need more than the basic traits of intelligence and job-relevant knowledge.[8] It is the possession of the five components of EI—self-awareness, self-management, self-motivation, empathy, and social skills—that allows an individual to become a star performer. Without EI, a person can have outstanding training, a highly analytical mind, a long-term vision, and an endless supply of terrific ideas, but still not make a great leader.

Based on the latest findings, we offer two conclusions. First, traits can predict leadership. Second, traits do a better job at predicting the emergence of leaders and the appearance of leadership than in actually distinguishing between *effective* and *ineffective* leaders.[9] The fact that an individual exhibits the traits and others consider that person to be a leader does not necessarily mean that the leader is successful at getting his or her group to achieve its goals.

trait theories of leadership
Theories that propose traits—personality, social, physical, or intellectual—differentiate leaders from nonleaders.

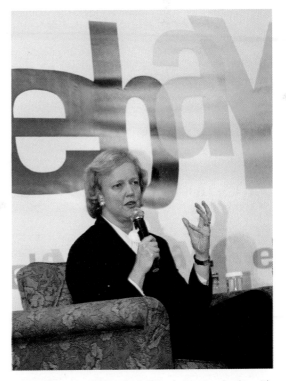

Meg Whitman, president and CEO of eBay, is a leader with high emotional intelligence. Since eBay founder Pierre Omidyar chose Whitman to transform his start-up into a global enterprise, she has emerged as a star performer in a job that demands a high degree of social interaction with employees and customers throughout the world. Whitman is described as self-confident, trustworthy, culturally sensitive, a high achiever, and expert at building teams and leading change. Shown here, Whitman interacts with customers during an eBay Live convention.

EXHIBIT 8-2   What CEOs Identify as Key Leadership Traits

Quality	CEOs Rating It Most Important (%)
Communication skills	52
Ability to motivate people	47
Honesty	34
Ability to listen	25
Team-building expertise	24
Analytical skills	19
Aggressiveness in business	10

Source: Survey conducted by American Express for the National Quality Institute. Reported in R. Nutt, "Survey Finds Leadership Key," *Vancouver Sun*, June 1, 2000, p. D6.

What Types of Traits Are Preferred in Leaders?

Remember the GLOBE study we discussed in Chapter 3? As part of that study, researchers surveyed managers in 62 countries to find out what attributes they liked and disliked in leaders. The study uncovered 22 leader attributes that were universally liked, 8 that were universally disliked, and 35 over which there was a lot of disagreement.[10] Exhibit 8-3 identifies some of these different attributes.

The results of this study suggest that

- Universally liked attributes should be used by leaders working in any culture

- Universally disliked attributes should be avoided by leaders

- Attributes over which there is a lot of disagreement should be used cautiously, based on specific cultures

EXHIBIT 8-3   Leadership Attributes: A Cross-Cultural View

Leader Attributes Universally Liked	Leader Attributes Universally Disliked	Leader Attributes Over Which There Was Most Disagreement
Trustworthy	Noncooperative	Subdued
Dynamic	Irritable	Intragroup conflict avoider
Motive arouser	Egocentric	Cunning
Decisive	Ruthless	Sensitive
Intelligent	Dictatorial	Provocateur
Dependable	Loner/self-centred	Self-effacing
Plans ahead		Willful
Excellence oriented		
Team builder		
Encouraging		

Source: D. N. Den Hartog, R. J. House, P. J. Hanges, S. A. Ruiz-Quintanilla, and P. W. Dorfman, "Culture Specific and Cross-culturally Generalizable Implicit Leadership Theories: Are Attributes of Charismatic/Transformational Leadership Universally Endorsed?" *Leadership Quarterly* 10, no. 2 (Summer 1999), pp. 219–256.

This chapter's *Point/Counterpoint* on page 285 raises further issues on the extent to which leadership is affected by national culture issues. *Case Incident—Moving from Colleague to Supervisor* on page 288 helps you think about the difficulties one has when moving from being a co-worker to taking on leadership responsibilities.

Behavioural Theories: Do Leaders Behave in Particular Ways?

Limited success in the study of traits led researchers to look at the behaviours that specific leaders exhibit. They wondered if there was something unique in the way that effective leaders behave. They also wondered if it was possible to *train* people to be leaders.

The three best-known **behavioural theories of leadership** are the Ohio State University studies that were conducted starting in the late 1940s, the University of Michigan studies conducted at about the same time, and Blake and Mouton's Leadership Grid, which reflects the behavioural definitions of both the Ohio and Michigan studies. All three approaches consider two main dimensions by which managers can be characterized: attention to production and attention to people.

behavioural theories of leadership Theories that propose that specific behaviours differentiate leaders from nonleaders.

The Ohio State Studies

In the Ohio State studies, these two dimensions are known as *initiating structure* and *consideration*.[11] **Initiating structure** refers to the extent to which a leader is likely to define and structure his or her role and the roles of employees in order to attain goals; it includes behaviour that tries to organize work, work relationships, and goals. For instance, leaders using this style may develop specific output goals or deadlines for employees.

Consideration is defined as the extent to which a leader is likely to have job relationships characterized by mutual trust, respect for employees' ideas, and regard for their feelings. A leader who is high in consideration shows concern for followers' comfort, well-being, status, and satisfaction. For instance, leaders using this style may create more flexible hours, or flextime, to make it easier for employees to manage family issues during work hours.

initiating structure The extent to which a leader is likely to define and structure his or her role and the roles of employees in order to attain goals.

consideration The extent to which a leader is likely to have job relationships characterized by mutual trust, respect for employees' ideas, and regard for their feelings.

The Michigan Studies

Researchers at the University of Michigan, whose work is referred to as "the Michigan studies," also developed two dimensions of leadership behaviour that they labelled *employee-oriented* and *production-oriented*.[12] **Employee-oriented leaders** emphasize interpersonal relations. They take a personal interest in the needs of their subordinates and accept individual differences among members. **Production-oriented leaders**, in contrast, tend to emphasize the technical or task aspects of the job. They are mainly concerned with making sure the group accomplishes its tasks, and the group members are simply a means to that end.

employee-oriented leader A leader who emphasizes interpersonal relations.

production-oriented leader A leader who emphasizes the technical or task aspects of the job.

The Leadership Grid

Blake and Mouton developed a graphic portrayal of a two-dimensional view of leadership style.[13] They proposed a **Leadership Grid** based on the styles of "concern for people" and "concern for production," which essentially represent the Ohio State dimensions of consideration and initiating structure, or the Michigan dimensions of employee orientation and production orientation.

The grid, shown in Exhibit 8-4 on page 262, has 9 possible positions along each axis, creating 81 different positions in which the leader's style may fall, but emphasis has been placed on 5: impoverished management (1,1); authority-obedience management (9,1); middle-of-the-road management (5,5); country club management (1,9); and team management (9,9). The grid shows the dominating factors in a leader's thinking with respect to how to get results from people, without focusing on what the specific results are.

Leadership Grid A two-dimensional grid outlining 81 different leadership styles.

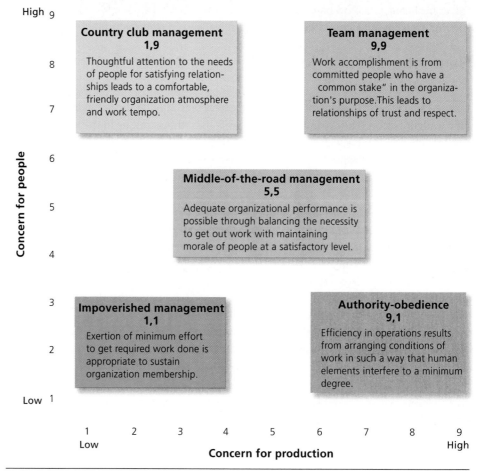

EXHIBIT 8-4 **The Leadership Grid**

Source: Reprinted by permission of *Harvard Business Review.* Based on an exhibit from "Breakthrough in Organization Development" by R. R. Blake, J. S. Mouton, L. B. Barnes, and L. E. Greiner (November–December 1964). Copyright © 1964 by the President and Fellows of Harvard College; all rights reserved.

 RESEARCH FINDINGS   Behavioural Theories of Leadership

A lengthy review of the results of behavioural studies supports the idea that people-oriented behaviour by leaders is related to employee satisfaction and motivation, and leader effectiveness; meanwhile, production-oriented behaviour by leaders is slightly more strongly related to performance by the leader, the group, and the organization.[14] The research also provides some insights into when leaders should be production oriented and when they should be people oriented:[15]

- When subordinates experience a lot of pressure because of deadlines or unclear tasks, leaders who are people oriented will increase employee satisfaction and performance.

- When the task is interesting or satisfying, there is less need for leaders to be people oriented.

- When it's clear how to perform the task and what the goals are, leaders who are people oriented will increase employee satisfaction, while those who are task oriented will increase dissatisfaction.

- When people don't know what to do or individuals don't have the knowledge or skills to do the job, it's more important for leaders to be production oriented than people oriented.

This chapter's *CBC Video Case Incident* gives you an opportunity to further explore the behaviours of leaders and their implications.

Contingency Theories: Does the Situation Matter?

> ✳ *Have you ever wondered if there was one right way to lead?*

As research on leadership developed, it became clear that predicting leadership success was more complex than simply isolating a few traits or preferable behaviours. Starting in the 1960s, leadership theories began to examine the situational factors that affect a leader's ability to act. This research pointed out that not all leaders can lead in every situation.[16] This was clearly illustrated by the failure of President George W. Bush, Louisiana governor Kathleen Blanco, and New Orleans Mayor Ray Nagin to demonstrate leadership during the Hurricane Katrina crisis. Their leadership skills might have been better displayed in other types of situations.

Situational, or contingency, theories of leadership try to isolate critical situational factors that affect leadership effectiveness. The theories consider the degree of structure in the task being performed, the quality of leader-member relations, the leader's position power, group norms, information availability, employee acceptance of leader's decisions, employee maturity, and the clarity of the employee's role.[17]

We discuss four situational theories below: the Fiedler contingency model, Hersey and Blanchard's situational leadership theory, path-goal theory, and substitutes for leadership. All of these theories focus on the relationship of the leader to followers, and there is broad support for the idea that this relationship is important.[18]

situational, or contingency, theories Theories that propose that leadership effectiveness depends on the situation.

Fiedler Contingency Model

The first comprehensive contingency model for leadership was developed by Fred Fiedler.[19] The **Fiedler contingency model** proposes that effective group performance depends on the proper match between the leader's style and the degree to which the situation gives control to the leader.

Fiedler created the *least preferred co-worker (LPC) questionnaire* to determine whether individuals were mainly interested in good personal relations with co-workers, and thus *relationship-oriented*, or mainly interested in productivity, and thus *task-oriented*. Fiedler assumed that an individual's leadership style is fixed. Therefore, if a situation requires a task-oriented leader and the person in that leadership position is relationship oriented, either the situation has to be modified or the leader must be removed and replaced for optimum effectiveness to be achieved.

Fiedler identified three contingency dimensions that together define the situation a leader faces:

- *Leader-member relations.* The degree of confidence, trust, and respect members have in their leader.

- *Task structure.* The degree to which the job assignments are procedurized (that is, structured or unstructured).

- *Position power.* The degree of influence a leader has over power variables such as hiring, firing, discipline, promotions, and salary increases.

Fiedler contingency model A theory that proposes that effective group performance depends on the proper match between the leader's style and the degree to which the situation gives control to the leader.

Fiedler stated that the better the leader-member relations, the more highly structured the job, and the stronger the position power, the more control the leader has. He suggested that task-oriented leaders perform best in situations of high and low control, while relationship-oriented leaders perform best in moderate control situations.[20] In a high-control situation, a leader can "get away" with task orientation, because the relationships are good and followers are easily influenced.[21] In a low-control situation (which is marked by poor relations, ill-defined task, and low influence), task orientation may be the only thing that makes it possible to get something done. In a moderate-control situation, the leader's relationship orientation may smooth the way to getting things done.

Hersey and Blanchard's Situational Leadership Theory

situational leadership theory (SLT) A theory that proposes that effective leaders adapt their leadership style according to how willing and able a follower is to perform tasks.

Paul Hersey and Ken Blanchard have developed a leadership model that has gained a strong following among management development specialists.[22] This model—called **situational leadership theory (SLT)**—has been included in leadership training programs at more than 400 of the *Fortune* 500 companies; and more than one million managers a year from a wide variety of organizations are taught its basic elements.[23]

SLT views the leader-follower relationship as similar to that of a parent and child. Just as a parent needs to give up control as a child becomes more mature and responsible, so too should leaders. Hersey and Blanchard identify four specific leader behaviours—from highly directive to highly laissez-faire. The most effective behaviour depends on a follower's ability and motivation. This is illustrated in Exhibit 8-5. SLT says that if a follower is *unable and unwilling* to do a task, the leader needs to give clear and specific directions (in other words, be highly directive). If a follower is *unable and willing,* the leader needs to display high task orientation to compensate for the follower's lack of ability, and high relationship orientation to get the follower to "buy into" the leader's desires (in other words, "sell" the task). If the follower is *able and unwilling,* the leader needs to adopt a supportive and participative style. Finally, if the employee is both *able and willing,* the leader does not need to do much (in other words, a laissez-faire approach will work).

EXHIBIT 8-5   Hersey and Blanchard's Situational Leadership Theory

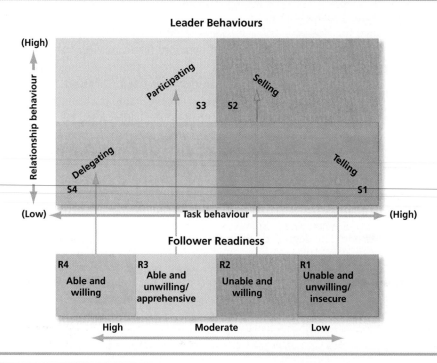

Both the Fiedler contingency model and Hersey and Blanchard's SLT have some intuitive appeal. Blanchard's work, for instance, is widely applied in the workplace. However, both theories have received far less empirical support, and Fiedler's theory has been found more difficult to apply in the work situation than the next model we consider, path-goal theory.[24]

Path-Goal Theory

Currently, one of the most respected approaches to leadership is **path-goal theory**. Developed by University of Toronto professor Martin Evans in the late 1960s, it was later expanded on by Robert House (formerly at the University of Toronto, but now at the Wharton School of Business at the University of Pennsylvania). Path-goal theory is a contingency model of leadership that extracts key elements from the Ohio State leadership research on initiating structure and consideration and from the expectancy theory of motivation.[25]

The essence of the theory is that it is the leader's job to assist followers in attaining their goals and to provide the necessary direction and/or support to ensure that their individual goals are compatible with the overall goals of the group or organization. The term *path-goal* derives from the belief that effective leaders both clarify the path to help their followers achieve their work goals and make the journey along the path easier by reducing roadblocks and pitfalls.

According to this theory, leaders should follow three guidelines to be effective:[26]

- *Determine the outcomes subordinates want.* These might include good pay, job security, interesting work, and the autonomy to do one's job.

- *Reward individuals with their desired outcomes* when they perform well.

- *Let individuals know what they need to do to receive rewards* (that is, the path to the goal), remove any barriers that would prevent high performance, and express confidence that individuals have the ability to perform well.

Path-goal theory identifies four leadership behaviours that might be used in different situations to motivate individuals:

- The *directive leader* lets followers know what is expected of them, schedules work to be done, and gives specific guidance as to how to accomplish tasks. This closely parallels the Ohio State dimension of initiating structure. This behaviour is best used when individuals have difficulty doing tasks or the tasks are ambiguous. It would not be very helpful when used with individuals who are already highly motivated, have the skills and abilities to do the task, and understand the requirements of the task.

- The *supportive leader* is friendly and shows concern for the needs of followers. This is essentially synonymous with the Ohio State dimension of consideration. This behaviour is often recommended when individuals are under stress or otherwise show that they need to be supported.

- The *participative leader* consults with followers and uses their suggestions before making a decision. This behaviour is most appropriate when individuals need to buy in to decisions.

- The *achievement-oriented leader* sets challenging goals and expects followers to perform at their highest level. This behaviour works well with individuals who like challenges and are highly motivated. It would be less effective with less capable individuals or those who are highly stressed from overwork.

As Exhibit 8-6 on page 266 illustrates, path-goal theory proposes two types of contingency variables that affect the leadership behaviour–outcome relationship:

path-goal theory A theory that says it is the leader's job to assist followers in attaining their goals and to provide the necessary direction and/or support to ensure that their individual goals are compatible with the overall goals.

Path-Goal Theory
http://faculty.css.edu/dswenson/web/LEAD/path-goal.html

EXHIBIT 8-6 Path-Goal Theory

CONTINGENCY FACTORS

Environmental
- Task structure
- Formal authority system
- Work group

Leader's Behaviour
- Directive
- Supportive
- Participative
- Achievement-oriented

Outcomes
- Performance
- Satisfaction

Subordinate
- Locus of control
- Experience
- Perceived ability

environmental variables that are outside the control of the employee and variables that are part of the personal characteristics of the employee. House assumes that leaders are flexible and can display any or all of these behaviours, depending on the situation. Some situations may in fact need more than one style from the leader. The theory proposes that employee performance and satisfaction are likely to be positively influenced when the leader compensates for things lacking in either the employee or the work setting. However, the leader who spends time explaining tasks when those tasks are already clear or when the employee has the ability and experience to handle them without interference is likely to be ineffective because the employee will see such directive behaviour as redundant or even insulting. Research generally supports path-goal theory.[27]

One question that arises from contingency theories is whether leaders can actually adjust their behaviour to various situations. As we know, individuals differ in their behavioural flexibility. Some people show considerable ability to adjust their behaviour to external, situational factors; they are adaptable. Others, however, exhibit high levels of consistency regardless of the situation. High self-monitors are usually able to adjust their leadership styles to suit changing situations better than low self-monitors.[28] Clearly, if an individual's leadership style range is very narrow and he or she cannot or will not adjust (that is, the person is a low self-monitor), that individual will be successful only in very specific situations suitable to his or her style. To find out more about your style of leadership, see the *Learning About Yourself Exercise* on page 286.

Substitutes for Leadership

* Is a leader always necessary?

The previous three theories argue that leaders are needed, but that leaders should consider the situation in determining the style of leadership to adopt. However, numerous studies collectively demonstrate that, in many situations, leaders' actions are irrelevant. Certain individual, job, and organizational variables can act as *substitutes* for leadership or *neutralize* the leader's ability to influence his or her followers.[29]

If employees have appropriate experience, training, or "professional" orientation or if employees are indifferent to organizational rewards, the effect of leadership can be

EXHIBIT 8-7   Substitutes and Neutralizers for Leadership

Characteristics of Individual	Effect on Leadership
Experience/training	Substitutes for task-oriented leadership
Professionalism	Substitutes for relationship-oriented and task-oriented leadership
Indifference to rewards	Neutralizes relationship-oriented and task-oriented leadership

Characteristics of Job	
Highly structured task	Substitutes for task-oriented leadership
Provides its own feedback	Substitutes for task-oriented leadership
Intrinsically satisfying	Substitutes for relationship-oriented leadership

Characteristics of Organization	
Explicit formal goals	Substitutes for task-oriented leadership
Rigid rules and procedures	Substitutes for task-oriented leadership
Cohesive work groups	Substitutes for relationship-oriented and task-oriented leadership

Source: Based on S. Kerr and J. M. Jermier, "Substitutes for Leadership: Their Meaning and Measurement," *Organizational Behavior and Human Performance*, December 1978, p. 378.

replaced or neutralized. Experience and training, for instance, can replace the need for a leader's support or ability to create structure and reduce task ambiguity. Jobs that are inherently unambiguous and routine, provide their own feedback, or are intrinsically satisfying generally require less hands-on leadership. Organizational characteristics such as explicit formalized goals, rigid rules and procedures, and cohesive work groups can replace formal leadership (see Exhibit 8-7). Recent research has supported the importance of ability and intrinsic satisfaction in considering performance outcomes.[30]

Can You Be a Better Follower?

Thus far we have concentrated on how leaders must adapt their styles to the needs of their followers. This underscores the importance of the followers' role in the way leadership is exercised. Only recently have we begun to recognize that in addition to having leaders who can lead, successful organizations need followers who can follow.[31] In fact, it's probably fair to say that all organizations have far more followers than leaders, so ineffective followers may be more of a handicap to an organization than ineffective leaders. The Far Side cartoon shown in Exhibit 8-8 gives you some indication of what can happen when someone finally realizes that he or she is "a follower, too."

An understanding of how to be a follower is important, because almost all roles in an organization require one to be a follower in some settings. Obviously lower-level employees are followers to their supervisors. But the supervisor is a follower to his or her manager, who is a follower to the CEO. The CEO in a public corporation is a follower to the board of directors. Even the best leaders have to be followers sometimes.

EXHIBIT 8-8

THE FAR SIDE   By GARY LARSON

"Well, what d'ya know! . . . *I'm* a follower, too!"

Source: THE FAR SIDE copyright 1990 & 1991 Farworks, Inc./Dist. by Universal Press Syndicate. Reprinted with permission. All rights reserved.

What qualities do effective followers have? One writer focuses on four:[32]

- *They manage themselves well.* They are able to think for themselves. They can work independently and without close supervision.

- *They are committed to a purpose outside themselves.* Effective followers are committed to something—a cause, a product, a work team, an organization, an idea—in addition to the care of their own lives. Most people like working with colleagues who are emotionally, as well as physically, committed to their work.

- *They build their competence and focus their efforts for maximum impact.* Effective followers master skills that will be useful to their organizations, and they hold higher performance standards than their jobs or work groups require.

- *They are courageous, honest, and credible.* Effective followers establish themselves as independent, critical thinkers whose knowledge and judgment can be trusted. They hold high ethical standards, give credit where credit is due, and are not afraid to own up to their mistakes.

These points suggest that there is a relationship between leadership and followership, and that taking responsibility for one's own behaviour is beneficial for both one's self and the organization.

INSPIRATIONAL LEADERSHIP

As people around the world watched the aftermath of Hurricane Katrina from the safety of their homes, many wondered, Why isn't anyone sending in food or water? The implicit question people were asking was, Why wasn't someone just taking charge and doing something rather than waiting for others to act? Both New Orleans mayor Ray Nagin and Louisiana governor Kathleen Blanco were quick to criticize President Bush, and the president's staff just as quickly tried to explain that it was not the role of the federal government to be the first responder. People who lead with vision do not wonder why someone else is not acting—rather, they make sure action is taken. Without pointing any fingers of blame, it is easy to see that in the early days after the levees broke, none of the official leaders was prepared to rise to the occasion and lead with vision. What does it take for a person to lead with vision? What characteristics does such a person need?

3 How does a leader lead with vision?

The leadership theories that we have discussed were developed at a time when most organizations were structured in traditional hierarchies where there were classic lines of command. While this form still dominates in Canada's "Most Respected Corporations,"[33] there are organizations trying to be innovative, faster moving, and more responsive to employees who are highly educated and intelligent, and who want more say in the workplace. Thus, new styles of leadership are evolving to meet the demands of these organizations. The more recent approaches to leadership move away from the supervisory tasks of leaders and focus on vision-setting activities. Today, leadership theories also try to explain how certain leaders can achieve extraordinary levels of performance from their followers, and they stress symbolic and emotionally appealing leadership behaviours.[34] In what follows, we consider transactional leadership, transformational leadership, and charismatic leadership.

From Transactional to Transformational Leadership

transactional leaders Leaders who guide or motivate their followers in the direction of established goals by clarifying role and task requirements.

Most of the leadership theories presented thus far in this chapter have concerned **transactional leaders**. Such leaders guide or motivate their followers in the direction of established goals by clarifying role and task requirements. In some styles of transactional leadership, the leader uses rewarding and recognizing behaviours. This approach results in performance that meets expectations, though rarely does one see results that exceed expectations.[35] In other styles of transactional leadership, the leader emphasizes correction and possible punishment rather than rewards and recognition. This style "results in performance below expectations, and discourages innovation and initiative in the workplace."[36] Of course, leaders should not ignore poor performance, but effective leaders emphasize how to achieve expectations rather than dwell on mistakes.

Some leaders inspire followers to transcend their own self-interests for the good of the organization and have a profound and extraordinary effect on their followers. These are **transformational leaders**, such as Matthew Barrett, chairman of Barclays PLC, Britain's second-largest bank, and formerly CEO of Bank of Montreal; Frank Stronach, chairman of the board of Aurora, Ontario-based Magna International; and Mogens Smed, CEO of Calgary-based DIRTT (Doing It Right This Time) and former CEO of SMED International. Other Canadians who have frequently been cited as charismatic leaders include René Lévesque, the late Quebec premier; Lucien Bouchard, former Bloc Québécois leader; Michaëlle Jean, Governor General; Pierre Trudeau, the late prime minister; and Craig Kielburger, the Canadian teenager who founded Free The Children to promote children's rights and combat exploitation of child labour. What links these individuals is that they pay attention to the concerns and developmental needs of individual followers. Transformational leaders change followers' awareness of issues by helping them look at old problems in new ways, and they are able to excite, arouse, and inspire followers to exert extra effort to achieve group goals.[37]

Transformational leadership is sometimes identified separately from **charismatic leadership** in the literature, although McGill's Kanungo notes that the two formulations do not differ in that charismatic leaders are also transformational leaders. Relying on his judgment, we use the two concepts interchangeably. As Kanungo notes, the charismatic leader "critically examines the status quo with a view to developing and articulating future strategic goals or vision for the organization and then leading organizational members to achieve these goals through empowering strategies."[38] While not all transformational leaders are charismatic in personality, both transformational and charismatic leaders work to empower their followers to reach higher goals.

Transactional and transformational leadership should not be viewed as opposing approaches to getting things done.[39] Transformational leadership is built *on top of* transactional leadership—it produces levels of employee effort and performance that go beyond what would occur with a transactional approach alone. Exhibit 8-9 on page 270 outlines the difference between transactional and transformational (or charismatic) leaders. Would you be able to be a charismatic leader? We give you tips in this chapter's *From Concepts to Skills* on pages 290–291.

While the idea of charismatic leadership was developed based on North American observations, professors Dale Carl of the School of Business Management at Ryerson University and Mansour Javidan at the University of Calgary also suggest that charismatic

transformational leaders
Leaders who inspire followers to go beyond their own self-interests for the good of the organization and have a profound and extraordinary effect on their followers.

charismatic leadership
Leadership that critically examines the status quo with a view to developing and articulating future strategic goals or vision for the organization, and then leading organizational members to achieve these goals through empowering strategies.

Through his charismatic leadership, Steve Jobs achieved unwavering loyalty and commitment from the technical staff he oversaw at Apple Computer during the late 1970s and early 1980s. However, as the company grew, this style was less effective, and he was forced out of Apple in 1985. In 1996, with Apple doing poorly, Jobs was brought back to lead the company once again with his vision and charisma. With such innovations as the iPod and the iPod shuffle, Jobs' visionary leadership continues to make Apple successful.

EXHIBIT 8-9   Characteristics of Transactional and Transformational Leaders

Transactional Leader

Contingent rewards: Contracts exchange of rewards for effort, promises rewards for good performance, recognizes accomplishments.

Management by exception (active): Watches and searches for deviations from rules and standards, takes corrective action.

Management by exception (passive): Intervenes only if standards are not met.

Laissez-faire: Abdicates responsibilities, avoids making decisions.

Transformational Leader

Charisma: Provides vision and sense of mission, instills pride, gains respect and trust.

Inspiration: Communicates high expectations, uses symbols to focus efforts, expresses important purposes in simple ways.

Intellectual stimulation: Promotes intelligence, rationality, and careful problem solving.

Individualized consideration: Gives personal attention, treats each employee individually, coaches, advises.

Source: B. M. Bass, "From Transactional to Transformational Leadership: Learning to Share the Vision," *Organizational Dynamics,* Winter 1990, p. 22. Reprinted by permission of the publisher. American Management Association, New York. All rights reserved.

leadership is expressed as relatively similar in a variety of countries, including Canada, Hungary, India, Turkey, Austria, Singapore, Sweden, and Venezuela.[40] This finding indicates that there may be some universal aspects of this style of leadership.

Sharing a Vision

Perhaps one of the key components of charismatic leadership is the ability to articulate a vision. A review of various definitions finds that a vision differs from other forms of direction setting in several ways:

> *A vision has clear and compelling imagery that offers an innovative way to improve, which recognizes and draws on traditions, and connects to actions that people can take to realize change. Vision taps people's emotions and energy. Properly articulated, a vision creates the enthusiasm that people have for sporting events and other leisure-time activities, bringing the energy and commitment to the workplace.*[41]

The key properties of a vision seem to be inspirational possibilities that are value-centred and realizable, with superior imagery and articulation.[42] Visions should be able to create possibilities that are inspirational and unique, and offer a new order that can produce organizational distinction. A vision is likely to fail if it does not offer a view of the future that is clearly and demonstrably better for the organization and its members. Desirable visions fit the times and circumstances and reflect the uniqueness of the organization. People in the organization must also believe that the vision is attainable. It should be perceived as challenging yet doable. Visions that have clear articulation and powerful imagery are more easily grasped and accepted. *Case Incident—Anne Mulcahy at Xerox* on the CD-ROM that accompanies this textbook discusses how visionary leadership helped turn Xerox around. *Case Incident—Mogens Smed: Charismatic Leader of SMED International* on the CD-ROM that accompanies this text describes how Mogens Smed shares his vision with his employees.

 RESEARCH FINDINGS   Charismatic Leadership

A number of studies demonstrate the effectiveness of charismatic and transformational leadership.[43] We consider the impact of this leadership style on company performance and individual performance.

Company Performance   Do vision and charismatic leadership really make a difference? Several studies provide positive evidence that they do:

- One study contrasted 18 visionary companies with 18 comparable nonvisionary firms over a 65-year period.[44] The visionary companies performed 6 times better than the comparison group, based on standard financial criteria, and their stocks performed 15 times better than the general market.

- In a study of 250 executives and managers at a major financial services company, Jane Howell (at the Richard Ivey School of Business at the University of Western Ontario) and her colleagues found that "transformational leaders had 34 percent higher business unit performance results than other types of leaders."[45]

- An unpublished study by Robert House and some colleagues of 63 American and 49 Canadian companies (including Nortel Networks, Molson, Gulf Canada [now ConocoPhillips], and Manulife Financial) found that "between 15 and 25 percent of the variation in profitability among the companies was accounted for by the leadership qualities of their CEO."[46] That is, charismatic leaders led more profitable companies in the 1990s. This may explain the high compensation packages for CEOs that we discussed in Chapter 4.

Individual Performance   An increasing body of research shows that people working for charismatic leaders are motivated to exert extra work effort and, because they like their leaders, they express greater satisfaction.[47]

To learn more about how to be transformational/charismatic yourself, see the *Working With Others Exercise* on page 287.

The evidence supporting the superiority of transformational leadership over the transactional variety is overwhelmingly impressive. For instance, a number of studies of US, Canadian, and German military officers found, at every level, that transformational leaders were evaluated as more effective than their transactional counterparts.[48] Managers at FedEx who were rated by their followers as exhibiting more transformational leadership were evaluated by their immediate supervisors as higher performers and more promotable.[49] Nevertheless, transformational leadership should be used with some caution in non–North American contexts, because its effectiveness may be affected by cultural values concerning leadership.[50]

In summary, the overall evidence indicates that transformational leadership correlates more strongly than transactional leadership with lower turnover rates, higher productivity, and higher employee satisfaction.[51] One caveat to this research is a study by Professor Timothy DeGroot of McMaster University and his colleagues. They found that charismatic leadership had a greater impact on team performance than on individual performance, and they suggest that the positive findings of previous studies are the result of charismatic leaders' providing a better team environment for everyone, which then resulted in higher performance.[52]

The Downside of Charismatic Leadership

When organizations are in need of great change, charismatic leaders are often able to inspire their followers to meet the challenges of change. Be aware that a charismatic leader may become a liability to an organization once the crisis is over and the need for dramatic change subsides.[53] Why? Because then the charismatic leader's overwhelming self-confidence can be a liability. He or she is unable to listen to others, becomes uncomfortable when challenged by aggressive employees, and begins to hold an unjustifiable belief in his or her "rightness" on issues. Some would argue that Jean Chrétien's behaviour leading up to his decision to announce that he would eventually step down as prime minister, thus preventing a divisive leadership review in February 2003, would fit this description.

Many have argued that the recent accounting scandals and high-profile bankruptcies facing North American companies, including Enron and WorldCom, point to some of the dangers of charismatic leadership. WorldCom's Bernard Ebbers and Enron's Kenneth Lay "seemed almost a breed apart, blessed with unique visionary powers" when their companies were increasing stock prices at phenomenal rates in the 1990s.[54]

Harvard Business School professor Rakesh Khurana argues that an inordinate number of today's chief executives have been "chosen for their ability to articulate messianic 'visions' for their companies; inspire employees to do whatever it takes to realize these grand designs; and imbue investors with faith in their own talents."[55] These traits, however, might have led to the corporate scandals that unfolded in recent years. Charismatic leadership, by its very nature, silences criticism. Thus, employees follow the lead of their visionary CEOs unquestioningly. Professor David Leighton, of the Richard Ivey School of Business at the University of Western Ontario, notes that even the boards of directors and auditors were reluctant to challenge these CEOs. He also suggests that Canada's "more balanced culture," which is less likely to turn CEOs into heroes, may help protect the country from some of the scandals that the United States faced.[56]

Is Charismatic Leadership Always Necessary?

A recent study of 29 companies that went from good to great (their cumulative stock returns were all at least three times better than the general stock market over 15 years) found that a key difference in successful charismatic leaders may be the fact that they are not *ego-driven*.[57] Although the leaders of these firms were fiercely ambitious and driven, their ambition was directed toward their company rather than themselves. They generated extraordinary results, but with little fanfare or hoopla. They took responsibility for mistakes and poor results but gave credit for successes to other people. They also prided themselves on developing strong leaders inside the firm who could direct the company to greater heights after they were gone. These individuals have been called **level 5 leaders** because they have four basic leadership qualities—individual capability, team skills, managerial competence, and the ability to stimulate others to high performance—plus a fifth dimension: a paradoxical blend of personal humility and professional will. Level 5 leaders channel their ego needs away from themselves and into the goal of building a great company. So while level 5 leaders are highly effective, they tend to be people you have never heard of and who get little notoriety in the business press—people like Orin Smith at Starbucks, Kristine McDivitt of Patagonia, John Whitehead of Goldman Sachs, and Jack Brennan of Vanguard. This study is important because it confirms that leaders do not necessarily need to be charismatic to be effective, especially where charisma is enmeshed in an outsized ego.

The current mood seems to be for CEOs with less vision, and more ethical and corporate responsibility. It seems clear that future research on charismatic leadership will need to provide greater insight into how this style relates to ethical and business behaviour.

level 5 leaders Leaders who are fiercely ambitious and driven, whose ambition is directed toward their company rather than themselves.

DISPERSED LEADERSHIP: SPREADING LEADERSHIP THROUGHOUT THE ORGANIZATION

US Army Lieutenant General Russel Honoré was perhaps the first leader to inspire calm in New Orleans, as people struggled to get help and others struggled to help out.[58] Clear leadership, with clear statements of what people should do, had not come from the obvious leaders in the situation: President George W. Bush, Governor Kathleen Blanco, and Mayor Ray Nagin. While these latter were elected politicians, chosen by their constituents to lead them, Honoré had no direct connection to the people he was about to save. Instead, he was a no-nonsense military man. When he arrived on the scene in New Orleans, he did not wait to find out what the other leaders wanted him to do: He assessed the situation and made decisions about the best way to get things under control.

One of the major issues facing Honoré when he arrived in Louisiana was how to evacuate the Superdome, where more than 20 000 people had gone to escape the storm. Once there, they became stranded when the New Orleans levees broke. With no electricity, and little food and water, Mayor Nagin complained bitterly that no one was sending the buses needed to get the people relocated. Honoré's junior officers did not provide much hope that the job could be done quickly—they told him it would take days. Honoré was not prepared to wait that long, and 24 hours after he gave orders he managed to clear the Superdome and put people on buses to shelters in other states. How is it that people who are not officially in charge can also be effective leaders?

Transformational leadership theory focuses on heroic leaders, leaders in the top echelons of their organizations, and also on individuals rather than teams. The following sections aim to explain how leadership can be spread throughout an organization through mentoring and team leadership. Even if you are not a manager or someone thinking about leadership in a corporate situation, this discussion offers important insights into how

4 Can a person be an informal leader?

✳ *Can anyone be a leader?*

you can take on a leadership role in an organization. Moreover, in today's flatter organizations, you may well be expected to show leadership characteristics, even if you are not a formal leader. The work of Lieutenant General Russel Honoré illustrates this point. Although he was a leader in the army, he had no formal authority to take charge in New Orleans. That was the job of politicians. Still, he saw what needed to be done and did it.

As you consider the ways that roles can spread to people who are not managers, be aware that not all organizations engage in this practice, and even within organizations, not all managers are happy with sharing their power with those under them. Gifted leaders often recognize that they actually have more power if they share power. That is, sharing power enables them to build coalitions and teams that work together for the overall good of the organization. There are other managers, though, who fear the loss of any power.

Mentoring

Many leaders create mentoring relationships. A **mentor** is often a senior employee who sponsors and supports a less-experienced employee (a protégé). The mentoring role includes coaching, counselling, and sponsorship.[59] As a coach, mentors help develop their protégés' skills. As counsellors, mentors provide support and help bolster protégés' self-confidence. And as sponsors, mentors actively intervene on behalf of their protégés, lobby to get their protégés visible assignments, and politic to get their protégés rewards such as promotions and salary increases.

mentor A senior employee who sponsors and supports a less-experienced employee.

Successful mentors are good teachers. They can present ideas clearly, listen well, and empathize with the problems of their protégés. They also share experiences with the protégés, act as role models, share contacts, and provide guidance through the political maze of the organization. They provide advice on how to survive and get ahead in the organization and act as a sounding board for ideas that protégés may be hesitant to share with their direct supervisors. Mentors vouch for their protégés, answer for them in the highest circles within the organization, and make appropriate introductions.

Some organizations have formal mentoring programs, in which mentors are officially assigned to new or high-potential employees. For instance, Montreal-based Bell Canada introduced Mentor Match in late 2002 to bring together senior and junior employees. The mentors meet one-on-one for about an hour a month, to build a stronger understanding of leadership and organizational knowledge for the younger employees.[60] However, in contrast to Bell Canada's formal system, most organizations rely on informal mentoring—with senior managers personally selecting employees as protégés or junior employees asking senior employees to mentor them.

Bell Canada
www.bell.ca

The most effective mentoring relationships exist outside the immediate boss–subordinate interface.[61] The boss–subordinate context has an inherent conflict of interest and tension, mostly attributable to managers' direct evaluation of the performance of subordinates, that limits openness and meaningful communication.

Why would a leader want to be a mentor? There are personal benefits to the leader as well as benefits for the organization. The mentor–protégé relationship gives the mentor unfiltered access to the attitudes and feelings of lower-ranking employees. Protégés can be an excellent source of information on potential problems; they can provide early warning signals to upper managers because they short-circuit the formal channels. So the mentor–protégé relationship is a valuable communication channel that allows mentors to learn about problems before they become common knowledge to others in upper management. In addition, in terms of leader self-interest, mentoring can provide personal satisfaction to senior executives. It gives them the opportunity to share with others the knowledge and experience that they have developed over many years.

From the organization's standpoint, mentoring provides a support system for high-potential employees. Where mentors exist, protégés are often more motivated, better grounded politically, and less likely to quit. A recent comprehensive review of the research, for instance, found that mentoring provided substantial benefits to protégés.[62] Specifically, mentored employees had higher compensation, a larger number of promotions, and were more satisfied with their careers than their nonmentored counterparts.

Are all employees in an organization equally likely to participate in a mentoring relationship? Unfortunately the answer is no.[63] The evidence indicates that minorities and women are less likely to be chosen as protégés than are white males and thus they are less likely to accrue the benefits of mentorship. Mentors tend to select protégés who are similar to themselves in criteria such as background, education, gender, race, ethnicity, and religion. "People naturally move to mentor and can more easily communicate with those with whom they most closely identify."[64]

In a twist to the typical mentoring-down idea, Procter & Gamble introduced a Mentoring Up program to help senior managers become more aware of what female managers can contribute to the organization. In its program, mid-level female managers mentor senior-level male executives. The program has led to fewer departures of female managers and has exposed women to top decision makers.[65]

Coaching

A number of organizations have introduced coaching, which is different from mentoring. "Mentoring, at its best, involves a longer term relationship in which there is an emotional attachment between mentor and protégé."[66] By contrast, coaching is often more task oriented and short term. Coaching is used by senior and middle managers in particular, although other managers use coaching as part of their leadership style. A good coach

- Emphasizes self-development and self-discovery of the person being coached

- Offers the person being coached constructive feedback on how to improve

- Meets regularly with the person being coached

- Is a good listener

- Challenges the person being coached to perform

- Sets realistic standards for the person being coached to achieve.[67]

Providing Team Leadership

Increasingly leadership is taking place within a team context. As teams grow in popularity, the role of the leader in guiding team members takes on more importance.[68] Also, because of its more collaborative nature, the role of team leader differs from the traditional leadership role performed by front-line supervisors.

Many leaders are not equipped to handle the move to team leader. As one prominent consultant noted, "Even the most capable managers have trouble making the transition because all the command-and-control type things they were encouraged to do before are no longer appropriate. There's no reason to have any skill or sense of this."[69] This same consultant estimated that "probably 15 percent of managers are natural team leaders; another 15 percent could never lead a team because it runs counter to their personality. [They are unable to put aside their dominating style for the good of the team.] Then there's that huge group in the middle: team leadership doesn't come naturally to them, but they can learn it."[70]

Effective team leaders need to build commitment and confidence, remove obstacles, create opportunities, and be part of the team.[71] They have to learn skills such as the patience to share information, the willingness to trust others, the ability to give up authority, and an understanding of when to intervene. New team leaders may try to retain too much control at a time when team members need more autonomy, or they may abandon their teams at times when the teams need support and help.[72]

After Hurricane Katrina devastated many areas of the southern United States, the Vancouver Urban Search and Rescue Team sent a group of 46 men to help with evacuations. The team is a self-contained unit that can bring all of its own supplies to a disaster area, in addition to supplies to help out others. The team members were the first rescuers to get to St. Bernard Parish in New Orleans. They received great praise for their team leadership in helping Americans in a time of real need.

Roles of Team Leaders

A recent study of 20 organizations that reorganized themselves around teams found certain common responsibilities that all leaders had to assume. These included coaching, facilitating, handling disciplinary problems, reviewing team/individual performance, training, and communicating.[73] Many of these responsibilities apply to managers in general. A more meaningful way to describe the team leader's job is to focus on two priorities: managing the team's relations with outsiders and facilitating the team process.[74] We have divided these priorities into four specific roles that team leaders play:

- *Liaisons with outsiders.* Outsiders include upper management, other internal teams, customers, and suppliers. The leader represents the team to other constituencies, secures needed resources, clarifies others' expectations of the team, gathers information from the outside, and shares this information with team members.

- *Troubleshooters.* When the team has problems and asks for assistance, team leaders sit in on meetings and try to help resolve the problems. This rarely relates to technical or operational issues because the team members typically know more about the tasks being done than does the team leader. The leader contributes by asking penetrating questions, by helping the team discuss problems, and by getting needed resources from external constituencies. For instance, when a team in an aerospace firm found itself short-handed, its team leader took responsibility for getting more staff. He presented the team's case to upper management and got the approval through the company's human resource department.

- *Conflict managers.* When disagreements surface, team leaders help process the conflict. What is the source of the conflict? Who is involved? What are the issues? What resolution options are available? What are the advantages and disadvantages of each? By getting team members to address questions such as these, the leader minimizes the disruptive aspects of intrateam conflicts.

- *Coaches.* They clarify expectations and roles, teach, offer support, cheerlead, and do whatever else is necessary to help team members improve their work performance.

LEADING ONE'S SELF

When the death toll after Hurricane Katrina was around 900 in New Orleans and 1100 overall, rather than the tens of thousands officials had feared at the start of the catastrophe, most people breathed a sigh of relief. What kept the toll so low? Two factors were largely responsible. First, people took charge of themselves and their families, doing what they could to get themselves evacuated before the storm hit. People also did what they could to help others evacuate—making it their own responsibility to help their poor, sick, and elderly neighbours move to safety. That the death toll was so low illustrates the importance of individuals' taking leadership responsibility when the situation demands. So, how can individuals practise leadership on a daily basis even if they do not hold official positions of leadership?

5 What is self-leadership?

Thus far we have discussed the role of leadership as if it were mainly a one-way street: Leadership is something someone at the top does and, one hopes, those at the bottom—the followers—follow. However, there are two provocative issues for you to consider when thinking about leadership. The first is the issue of self-leadership, or taking responsibility for your own actions. The second is learning how to be a leader, even if only in small areas of your work or personal life.

Exhibit 8-10 on page 277 gives a lighthearted look at what it means to be a team leader.

Self-Leadership (or Self-Management)

✳ *How do you manage yourself?*

A growing trend in organizations is the focus on self-leadership, or self-management.[75] With self-leadership, individuals and teams set goals, plan and implement tasks, evaluate performance, solve their own problems, and motivate themselves. Several factors call for self-leadership: reduced levels of supervision, more offices in the home, more teamwork, and growth in service and professional employment where individuals are often required to make decisions on the spot. Following from our previous discussion of substitutes for leadership, self-management can also be a substitute or neutralizer for leadership from others.

Despite the lack of studies of self-leadership techniques in organizational settings, self-leadership strategies have been shown to be successful in nonorganizational settings.[76] Those who practise self-leadership look for opportunities to be more effective in the workplace and improve their career success. Their behaviour is self-reinforced—that is, they provide their own sense of reward and feedback after carrying out their accomplishments. Moreover, self-reinforced behaviour is often maintained at a higher rate than behaviour that is externally regulated.[77]

What does self-leadership look like? Though "individuals in organizations are regularly taught how to lead subordinates, groups, and even organizations, they rarely receive instruction on how to lead themselves."[78] Few empirical studies of this kind have been carried out in the workplace,[79] but a 1999 study of 305 managers at a large retailing organization in the Midwestern United States identified four behaviours that can be considered

EXHIBIT 8-10

Source: DILBERT reprinted by permission of United Features Syndicate, Inc.

self-leadership: *planning, access management, catch-up activities,* and *emotions management.*[80] The *Learning About Yourself Exercise* on page 286 describes these behaviours in greater detail. How do leaders create self-leaders? The following have been suggested:[81]

- *Model self-leadership.* Practise self-observation, setting challenging personal goals, self-direction, and self-reinforcement. Then display these behaviours and encourage others to rehearse and then produce them.

- *Encourage employees to create self-set goals.* Support employees in developing quantitative, specific goals; having such goals is the most important part of self-leadership.

- *Encourage the use of self-rewards to strengthen and increase desirable behaviours.* By contrast, limit self-punishment only to occasions when the employee has been dishonest or destructive.

- *Create positive thought patterns.* Encourage employees to use mental imagery and self-talk to further stimulate self-motivation.

- *Create a climate of self-leadership.* Redesign the work to increase the natural rewards of a job and focus on these naturally rewarding features of work to increase motivation.

- *Encourage self-criticism.* Encourage individuals to be critical of their own performance.

The underlying assumptions of self-leadership are that people are responsible, capable, and able to exercise initiative without the external constraints of bosses, rules, or regulations. Given the proper support, individuals can monitor and control their own behaviour. Self-leadership is different from empowerment in that empowerment creates the conditions to make decisions. Self-leadership is far more extensive than empowerment in what employees accomplish, because self-leaders also set their own goals.

Leading Without Authority

We have discussed how to be a follower and how to manage yourself, but what if your goal is to be a leader, even if you do not have the authority (or formal appointment) to be one? For instance, what if you wanted to convince the dean of your school to introduce new business courses that were more relevant, or you wanted to convince the president of the company where you work that she should start thinking about more environmentally friendly strategies in dealing with waste? How do you effectively lead in a student group, in which everyone is a peer?

Leadership at the grassroots level in organizations does happen. Harvard Business School professor Rosabeth Moss Kanter discusses examples of people who saw something in their workplace that needed changing and took the responsibility to do so upon themselves in her book *The Change Masters.*[82] Employees were more likely to take on extra responsibility when organizations permitted initiative at all levels of the organization rather than making it a tool of senior executives only.

Leading without authority simply means exhibiting leadership behaviour even though you do not have a formal position or title that might encourage others "to obey." Neither Martin Luther King Jr. nor Mahatma Gandhi operated from a position of authority, yet each was able to inspire many to follow him in the quest for social justice. The workplace can be an opportunity for leading without authority as well. As Ronald Heifetz of Harvard's Kennedy School of Government notes, "leadership means taking responsibility for hard problems beyond anyone's expectations."[83] It also means not waiting for the coach's call.[84]

What are the benefits of leading without authority? Heifetz has identified three:[85]

- *Latitude for creative deviance.* Because one does not have authority and the trappings that go with authority, it is easier to raise harder questions and look for less traditional solutions.

- *Issue focus.* Leading without authority means that one can focus on a single issue rather than be concerned with the great number of issues that those in authority face.

- *Front-line information.* Leading without authority means that one is closer to the detailed experiences of some of the stakeholders, such as co-workers. Thus more information is available to this kind of leader.

Not all organizations will support this type of leadership, and some have been known to actively suppress it. Still others will look aside, neither encouraging nor discouraging it. Nevertheless, you may want to reflect on the possibility of engaging in leadership behaviour simply because you see a need rather than because you are required to act.

CONTEMPORARY ISSUES IN LEADERSHIP

Louisiana governor Kathleen Blanco found herself under severe criticism when the state seemed to have greater difficulties with its emergency evacuation plans compared with two other states hit by Hurricane Katrina: Mississippi and Alabama (states led by men).[86] Michael Brown, then director of the Federal Emergency Management Agency (FEMA), even described Blanco's response to the disaster as "confused" compared with the governors of the two other states.

In the early days after the levees broke, Blanco expressed some frustration that aides to President George W. Bush did not seem to respond to her pleas for help in a timely manner. FEMA director Brown asked her: "What do you need? Help me help you." Blanco's communications director, Robert Mann, said Blanco could not believe that FEMA could not anticipate some of the state's needs. "It was like walking into an emergency room bleeding profusely and being expected to instruct the doctors how to treat you," he said. Could gender differences in leadership styles and communication have played any role in how the reactions to Hurricane Katrina played out?

6 What are some of the contemporary issues in leadership?

Is there a moral dimension to leadership? Do men and women rely on different leadership styles, and if so, is one style inherently superior to the other? What are the challenges of online leadership? In this section, we briefly address these contemporary issues in leadership.

Is There a Moral Dimension to Leadership?

The topic of leadership and ethics has received surprisingly little attention. Only very recently have ethicists and leadership researchers begun to consider the ethical implications in leadership.[87] Why now? One reason may be the growing general interest in ethics throughout the field of business. Another reason may be the discovery by probing biographers that some of our past leaders suffered from ethical shortcomings. Regardless, no contemporary discussion of leadership is complete without addressing its ethical dimension.

Ethics relates to leadership in a number of ways. Transformational leaders, for instance, have been described by one authority as encouraging moral virtue when they try to change the attitudes and behaviours of followers.[88] Charisma, too, has an ethical component. Unethical leaders are more likely to use their charisma to enhance power over followers, directed toward self-serving ends. We prefer to believe that ethical leaders use their charisma in a socially constructive way to serve others.[89] Consider, too, the issue of abuse of power by leaders—for example, when they give themselves large salaries and bonuses while also trying to cut costs by laying off long-time employees.

Leadership effectiveness needs to address the means that a leader uses in trying to achieve goals, as well as the content of those goals. For instance, at Enron, employees were driven by the top executives to keep Enron stock prices up, at whatever cost. "The driver was this unbelievable desire to keep portraying Enron as something very different and keep the track record going and going," said Forrest Hoglund, who ran Enron's oil and gas exploration until 1999.[90] To achieve these goals, executives inflated revenues and hid debts. CEO and chair Kenneth Lay thus led his subordinates to achieve stock price goals no matter how this was accomplished. Anyone who questioned what the company was doing was ignored or dismissed.

Ethical leadership must also address the content of a leader's goals. Are the changes that the leader seeks for the organization morally acceptable? Is a business leader effective if he or she builds an organization's success by selling products that damage the health of their users, such as tobacco executives have done? Is a military leader successful when winning a war that should not have been fought in the first place?

Professor James Clawson of the Darden Graduate School of Business, University of Virginia, suggests that there are four cornerstones to a "moral foundation of leadership":[91]

- *Truth telling*. Leaders who tell the truth as they see it allow for a mutual, fair exchange to occur.

- *Promise keeping*. Leaders need to be careful about the commitments they make, and then careful to keep those commitments.

- *Fairness*. Leaders who are equitable ensure that followers get their fair share for their contributions to the organization.

- *Respect for the individual*. Leaders who tell the truth, keep promises, and are fair show respect for followers. Respect means treating people with dignity.

Moral leadership comes from within the individual, and in general means treating people well, and with respect. This chapter's *Ethical Dilemma Exercise* on pages 287–288 raises some provocative issues about whether we should consider just the ends toward which a leader strives, or the means as well.

Gender: Do Men and Women Lead Differently?

An extensive review of the literature suggests two conclusions.[92] First, the similarities between male and female leaders tend to outweigh the differences. Second, what differences there are seem to be that women fall back on a more democratic leadership style while men feel more comfortable with a directive style.

George Cooke, CEO of Toronto-based Dominion of Canada General Insurance, believes in promoting women to senior positions. He is noteworthy for this: Dominion is well above the national average in the percentage of women who have made it to the executive ranks of Canada's top companies.

The similarities among men and women leaders should not be completely surprising. Almost all the studies looking at this issue have treated managerial positions as synonymous with leadership roles. Both male and female managers have characteristics that set them apart from the general population. Just as people who choose careers in law enforcement or civil engineering have a lot in common, so do individuals who choose managerial careers. People with traits associated with leadership—such as intelligence, confidence, and sociability—are more likely to be perceived as leaders and encouraged to pursue careers where they can exert leadership. This is true regardless of gender. Similarly, organizations tend to recruit and promote people who project leadership attributes into leadership positions. The result is that, regardless of gender, those who achieve formal leadership positions in organizations tend to be more alike than different.

Despite the previous conclusion, studies indicate some differences in the inherent leadership styles of women and men. A recent Conference Board of Canada study found that "women are particularly strong in managing interpersonal relationships and their approach is more consensual."[93] Other studies have shown that women tend to adopt a style of shared leadership. They encourage participation, share power and information, and try to enhance followers' self-worth. They prefer to lead through inclusion and rely on their charisma, expertise, contacts, and interpersonal skills to influence others. Men, on the other hand, are more likely to use a directive command-and-control style. They rely on the formal authority of their position for their influence base.

Given that men have historically held the great majority of leadership positions in organizations, it is tempting to assume that the differences noted between men and women would automatically work to favour men. They do not. In today's organizations, flexibility, teamwork, trust, and information sharing are replacing rigid structures, competitive individualism, control, and secrecy. The best leaders listen, motivate, and provide support to their people. Many women seem to do those things better than men. As a specific example, the expanded use of cross-functional teams in organizations means that effective leaders must become skilled negotiators. The leadership styles women typically use can make them better at negotiating, as they are less likely than men to focus on wins, losses, and competition. They tend to treat negotiations in the context

EXHIBIT 8-11 **Where Female Managers Do Better: A Scorecard**

None of the five studies set out to find gender differences. They stumbled on them while compiling and analyzing performance evaluations.

Skill (Each check mark denotes which group scored higher on the respective studies.)	MEN	WOMEN
Motivating others		✓ ✓ ✓ ✓ ✓
Fostering communication		✓ ✓ ✓ ✓ *
Producing high quality work		✓ ✓ ✓ ✓ ✓
Strategic planning	✓ ✓	✓ ✓ *
Listening to others		✓ ✓ ✓ ✓ ✓
Analyzing issues	✓ ✓	✓ ✓ *

* In one study, women's and men's scores in these categories were statistically even.

Data: Hagberg Consulting Group, Management Research Group, Lawrence A. Pfaff, Personnel Decisions International Inc., Advanced Teamware Inc.

Source: R. Sharpe, "As Leaders, Women Rule," *BusinessWeek,* November 20, 2000, p. 75. Reprinted by permission of Business Week.

of a continuing relationship—trying hard to make the other party a winner in his or her own and others' eyes.

Although it's interesting to see how men's and women's leadership styles differ, a more important question is whether they differ in effectiveness. Although some researchers have shown that men and women tend to be equally effective as leaders,[94] an increasing number of studies have shown that women executives, when rated by their peers, employees, and bosses, score higher than their male counterparts in a wide variety of measures, including getting extra effort from subordinates and overall effectiveness in leading. Subordinates also report more satisfaction with the leadership given by women.[95] See Exhibit 8-11 for a scorecard on where female managers do better, based on a summary of five studies. Why these differences? One possible explanation is that in today's organizations, flexibility, teamwork and partnering, trust, and information sharing are rapidly replacing rigid structures, competitive individualism, control, and secrecy. In these types of workplaces, effective managers must use more social and interpersonal behaviours. They must listen, motivate, and provide support to their people. They must inspire and influence rather than control. Women seem to do those things better than men.[96]

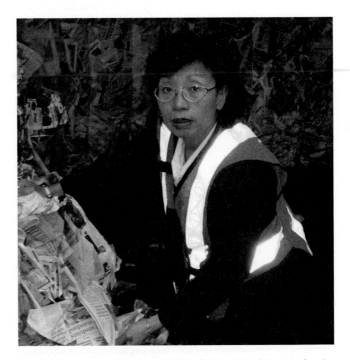

Emmie Wong Leung, founder and CEO of International Paper Industries (IPI) of North Vancouver, which collects, processes, and sells waste paper to offshore buyers, has been exporting to the United States, Hong Kong, Japan, China, the Philippines, India, and Indonesia for more than 20 years. She says: "I think an old-boys' network operates all over the world, but you can get them to accept you."

What Are the Challenges of Online Leadership?

Organizations are facing more telecommuting by employees, more contracting out, more mergers, and increasing globalization. Students often take courses online. It is becoming more common, then, that the person doing the leading is not necessarily in the same building, let alone the same organization or country, as the person being led.

How do you lead people who are physically separated from you and for whom interactions are basically reduced to written digital communications? This is a question that, to date, has received minimal attention from organizational behaviour researchers.[97] Leadership research has been directed almost exclusively to face-to-face and verbal situations. But we cannot ignore the reality that today's managers and employees are increasingly linked by networks rather than by geographical proximity. Obvious examples include co-workers who regularly use email to communicate with each other, managers who oversee virtual projects or teams, and students who take courses online.

If leadership is important for inspiring and motivating dispersed employees, we need to offer some guidance on how leadership might function in this context. Keep in mind, however, that there is limited research on this topic. So our intention here is not to provide you with definitive guidelines for leading online. Rather, it's to introduce you to an increasingly important issue and to get you to think about how leadership changes when relationships are defined by network interactions.

In face-to-face communications, harsh *words* can be softened by nonverbal action. A smile and comforting gestures, for instance, can lessen the blow behind strong words like *disappointed, unsatisfactory, inadequate,* or *below expectations.* That nonverbal component does not exist with online interactions. The *structure* of words in a digital communication has the power to motivate or demotivate the receiver.

Leaders need to be sure the *tone* of their email correctly reflects the emotions they want to send. Is the message formal or informal? Does it match the verbal style of the sender? Does it convey the appropriate level of importance or urgency? The fact that many people's writing styles are very different from their interpersonal styles is certainly a potential problem.

Jane Howell at the Richard Ivey School of Business, University of Western Ontario, and one of her former students, Kate Hall-Merenda, have considered the issues of leading from a distance.[98] They note that physical distance can create many potential problems, with employees feeling isolated, forgotten, and perhaps not cared about. It may result in lowered productivity. Their study of 109 business leaders and 371 followers in a large financial institution found that physical distance makes it more difficult for managers and employees to develop high-quality relationships.

Howell and Hall-Merenda suggest that some of the same characteristics of transformational leaders are appropriate for long-distance managing. In particular, they emphasize the need to articulate a compelling vision to employees and to communicate that vision in an inspiring way. Encouraging employees to think about ways to strive toward that vision is another important task of the leader. Their research also indicates that communication does not have to be done face to face as long as the vision is communicated clearly in some fashion.

This discussion leads us to the tentative conclusion that, for an increasing number of managers, good interpersonal skills may include the ability to communicate support and leadership through written words on a computer screen and to read emotions in others' messages. In this "new world" of communications, writing skills are likely to become an extension of interpersonal skills.

Summary and Implications

1 What is the difference between a manager and a leader? Managers promote stability, while leaders press for change. Leaders provide vision and strategy; managers implement that vision and strategy, coordinate and staff the organization, and handle day-to-day problems.

2 Are there specific traits, behaviours, and situations that affect how one leads? Early leadership theories were concerned with supervision and sought to find out if there were ways to identify leaders. Trait theories examined whether any traits were universal among leaders. While there are some common traits, leaders are more different than the same in terms of traits. Emotional intelligence is one of the few traits that has been found to be extremely important for leadership success. Other research has tried to discover whether some behaviours create better leaders than others. The findings were mixed, suggesting that leaders need to be both task oriented and people oriented. The mixed findings led researchers to contingency theories that consider the effect of the situations in which leadership is applied. This research tells us that leaders need to adjust their behaviours, depending on the situation and the needs of employees. Contingency theories were an important contribution to the study of leadership.

3 **How does a leader lead with vision?** The more recent approaches to leadership move away from the supervisory tasks of leaders and focus on vision-setting activities. These theories try to explain how certain leaders can achieve extraordinary performance levels from their followers, and they stress symbolic and emotionally appealing leadership behaviours. These leaders, known as *charismatic* or *transformational leaders,* inspire followers to go beyond their own self-interests for the good of the organization.

4 **Can a person be an informal leader?** There are several approaches to being a leader even if one does not hold a formal position of leadership. Mentoring is one way to be an informal leader. Mentors sponsor and support less-experienced employees, coaching and counselling them about their jobs. A person can also act as an informal leader on a team.

5 **What is self-leadership?** With self-leadership, individuals and teams set goals, plan and implement tasks, evaluate performance, solve their own problems, and motivate themselves. The supervisor plays a much-reduced role. Self-leadership can also include leadership at the grassroots level in an organization, where one does not have actual authority. Leading without authority simply means exhibiting leadership behaviour even though you do not have a formal position or title that might encourage others "to obey."

6 **What are some of the contemporary issues in leadership?** One of the major issues in leadership today is whether there is a moral dimension to leadership. Moral leadership comes from within the individual, and, in general, means treating people well and with respect. Another hot issue in leadership is the question of whether men and women use different leadership styles, and, if that is the case, whether one style is inherently superior to the other. The literature suggests two conclusions. First, the similarities between men and women tend to outweigh the differences. Second, what differences there are seem to relate to women's falling back on a more democratic leadership style and men's feeling more comfortable with a directive style. Yet another interesting issue in leadership is providing leadership online. Leadership demands are different when one does not have the opportunity for face-to-face interaction. For an increasing number of leaders, good interpersonal skills may include the ability to communicate support and leadership through written words on a computer screen and to read emotions in others' messages.

OB AT WORK

For Review

1. Trace the development of leadership research.

2. Describe the strengths and weaknesses of trait theories of leadership.

3. What is the Leadership Grid? Contrast its approach to leadership with the approaches of the Ohio State and Michigan studies.

4. What are the contingency variables in path-goal theory?

5. When might leaders be irrelevant?

6. What characteristics define an effective follower?

7. What are the differences between transactional and transformational leaders?

8. Describe the strengths and weaknesses of a charismatic leader.

9. What is moral leadership?

10. Why do you think effective female and male managers often exhibit similar traits and behaviours?

For Critical Thinking

1. Reconcile path-goal theory and substitutes for leadership.

2. What kind of activities could a full-time college or university student pursue that might lead to the perception that he or she is a charismatic leader? In pursuing those activities, what might the student do to enhance this perception?

3. Based on the low representation of women in upper management, to what extent do you think that organizations should actively promote women into the senior ranks of management?

4. Is there an ethical problem if leaders focus more on looking like leaders than actually being leaders? Discuss.

5. "Leaders make a real difference in an organization's performance." Build an argument in support of this statement. Then build an argument against this statement.

OB for You

- It is easy to imagine that theories of leadership are more important to those who are leaders or who plan in the near future to become leaders. However, leadership opportunities occur throughout an organization. You have no doubt seen student leaders who did not necessarily have any formal authority be extremely successful.

- Leaders are not born. They learn how to lead by paying attention to situations and what needs to be done.

- There is no one best way to lead. It is important to consider the situation and the needs of the people who will be led.

- Sometimes no leader is needed—the individuals in the group simply work well enough together that each takes turns at leadership without appointing a formal leader.

POINT

Leadership Is Culturally Bound

Leaders must adapt their styles to different national cultures. What works in China is not likely to work in Canada or France.[99] Can you imagine, for instance, executives at a large department store chain in Canada, such as The Bay, being effective by humiliating their employees? But that approach works at the Asia Department Store in central China.[100] Executives there blatantly brag about practising "heartless" management, requiring new employees to undergo two to four weeks of military-type training in order to increase their obedience, and conducting the store's in-house training sessions in a public place where employees can openly suffer embarrassment from their mistakes.

National culture affects leadership style by way of the follower. Leaders cannot choose their styles at will. They are constrained by the cultural conditions that their followers have come to expect. For instance, Korean leaders are expected to be paternalistic toward employees; Arab leaders who show kindness or generosity without being asked to do so are seen by other Arabs as weak; and Japanese leaders are expected to be humble and speak infrequently.[101]

Consistent with the contingency approach, leaders need to adjust their styles to the unique cultural aspects of a country. For example, a manipulative or autocratic style is compatible with high power distance, and we find high power distance scores in Russia and Spain, and Arab, Far Eastern, and most Latin countries. Power distance rankings should also be good indicators of employee willingness to accept participative leadership. Participation is likely to be most effective in low power distance cultures as exist in Norway, Finland, Denmark, and Sweden.

COUNTERPOINT

Leadership Transcends Culture

The GLOBE research program, which we introduced in Chapter 3, has gathered data on approximately 18 000 middle managers in 825 organizations, covering 62 countries. It is the most comprehensive cross-cultural study of leadership ever undertaken. So its findings should not be quickly dismissed. It is illuminating that one of the results coming from the GLOBE study is that there are some universal aspects to leadership. Specifically, a number of the elements making up transformational leadership appear to be associated with effective leadership regardless of what country the leader is in.[102] This conclusion is very important because it flies in the face of the contingency view that leadership style needs to adapt to cultural differences.

What elements of transformational leadership appear universal? Vision, foresight, providing encouragement, trustworthiness, dynamism, positiveness, and proactiveness. The results led two members of the GLOBE team to conclude that "effective business leaders in any country are expected by their subordinates to provide a powerful and proactive vision to guide the company into the future, strong motivational skills to stimulate all employees to fulfill the vision, and excellent planning skills to assist in implementing the vision."[103]

What might explain the universal appeal of these transformational leader attributes? It has been suggested that pressures toward common technologies and management practices, as a result of global competition and multinational influences, may make some aspects of leadership universally accepted. If this is true, we may be able to select and train leaders in a universal style and thus significantly raise the quality of leadership worldwide.

LEARNING ABOUT **YOURSELF** EXERCISE

Are You a Self-Manager?

To determine your self-management initiative, rate each of the following items, from 1 ("Never Do This") to 7 ("Always Do This").

	Never Do This						Always Do This
Planning							
1. I plan out my day before beginning to work.	1	2	3	4	5	6	7
2. I try to schedule my work in advance.	1	2	3	4	5	6	7
3. I plan my career carefully.	1	2	3	4	5	6	7
4. I come to work early to plan my day.	1	2	3	4	5	6	7
5. I use lists and agendas to structure my workday.	1	2	3	4	5	6	7
6. I set specific job goals on a regular basis.	1	2	3	4	5	6	7
7. I set daily goals for myself.	1	2	3	4	5	6	7
8. I try to manage my time.	1	2	3	4	5	6	7
Access Management							
1. I control the access subordinates have to me in order to get my work done.	1	2	3	4	5	6	7
2. I use a special place at work where I can work uninterrupted.	1	2	3	4	5	6	7
3. I hold my telephone calls when I need to get things done.	1	2	3	4	5	6	7
Catch-up Activities							
1. I come in early or stay late at work to prevent distractions from interfering with my work.	1	2	3	4	5	6	7
2. I take my work home with me to make sure it gets done.	1	2	3	4	5	6	7
3. I come in on my days off to catch up on my work.	1	2	3	4	5	6	7
Emotions Management							
1. I have learned to manage my aggressiveness with my subordinates.	1	2	3	4	5	6	7
2. My facial expression and conversational tone are important in dealing with subordinates.	1	2	3	4	5	6	7
3. It's important for me to maintain a "professional" manager-subordinate relationship.	1	2	3	4	5	6	7
4. I try to keep my emotions under control.	1	2	3	4	5	6	7

Scoring Key:

Higher scores mean a higher degree of self-management. For the overall scale, scores of 100 or higher represent high scores. For each area, the following represent high scores: planning, scores of 48 or higher; access management, scores of 18 or higher; catch-up activities, scores of 18 or higher; and emotions management, scores of 24 or higher.

Source: M. Castaneda, T. A. Kolenko, and R. J. Aldag, "Self-Management Perceptions and Practices: A Structural Equations Analysis," *Journal of Organizational Behavior* 20, 1999. Table 4, pp. 114–115. Copyright © John Wiley & Sons, Inc. Reproduced with permission.

BREAKOUT **GROUP** EXERCISES

Form small groups to discuss the following topics, as assigned by your instructor:

1. Identify an example of someone you think of as a good leader (currently or in the past). What traits did he or she have? How did these traits differ from someone you identify as a bad leader?

2. Identify a situation in which you were in a leadership position (in a group, in the workplace, within your family, etc.). To what extent were you able to use a contingency approach to leadership? What made that easier or more difficult for you?

3. When you have worked in student groups, how frequently have leaders emerged in the group? What difficulties occur when leaders are leading peers? Are there ways to overcome these difficulties?

WORKING WITH **OTHERS** EXERCISE

Being Charismatic

From Concepts to Skills on pages 290–291 suggests how to become charismatic. In this exercise, you will use that information to practise projecting charisma.

a. The class should break into pairs.

b. Student A's task is to "lead" Student B through a new-student orientation to your college or university. The orientation should last about 10 to 15 minutes. Assume Student B is new to your college or university and is unfamiliar with the campus. Student A should try to project himself or herself as charismatic.

c. Roles now reverse and Student B's task is to "lead" Student A in a 10- to 15-minute program on how to study more effectively for college or university exams. Take a few minutes to think about what has worked well for you, and assume that Student A is a new student interested in improving his or her study habits. This time, Student B should try to project himself or herself as charismatic.

d. When both role plays are complete, each pair should assess how well it did in projecting charisma and how it might improve.

Source: This exercise is based on J. M. Howell and P. J. Frost, "A Laboratory Study of Charismatic Leadership," *Organizational Behavior and Human Decision Processes,* April 1989, pp. 243–269.

ETHICAL **DILEMMA** EXERCISE

Do the Ends Justify the Means?

The power that comes from being a leader can be used for evil as well as for good. When you assume the benefits of leadership, you also assume ethical burdens. But many highly successful leaders have relied on questionable tactics to achieve their ends. These include manipulation, verbal attacks, physical intimidation, lying, fear, and control. Consider a few examples:

- Bill Clinton was viewed as a charismatic US president. Yet he lied when necessary and "managed" the truth.

- Former Prime Minister Jean Chrétien successfully led Canada through 10 years of economic change. Those close to him were committed and loyal followers. Yet concerns were raised recently that he might have been

continued

willing to quietly spend millions of dollars in sponsorship money to manage the Quebec situation.

- Jack Welch, former head of General Electric (GE), provided the leadership that made GE the most valuable company in America. He also ruthlessly preached firing the lowest-performing 10 percent of the company's employees every year.

- Former IBM chair Lou Gerstner oversaw the reemergence of IBM as a powerhouse in the computer industry. He was not, however, easy to work for. He believed in never relaxing or in letting others enjoy life.

Should leaders be judged solely on their end achievements? Or do the means they choose also reflect on their leadership qualities? Are employees, shareholders, and society too quick to excuse leaders who use questionable means if they are successful in achieving their goals? Is it impossible for leaders to be ethical *and* successful?

Source: Based on C. E. Johnson, *Meeting the Ethical Challenges in Leadership* (Thousand Oaks, CA: Sage, 2001), pp. 4–5.

CASE INCIDENT

Moving from Colleague to Supervisor

Cheryl Kahn, Rob Carstons, and Linda McGee have something in common. They all were promoted within their organizations into management positions. As well, each found the transition a challenge.

Kahn was promoted to director of catering for the Glazier Group of restaurants. With the promotion, she realized that things would never be the same again. No longer would she be able to participate in water-cooler gossip or shrug off an employee's chronic lateness. She says she found her new role daunting. "At first I was like a bulldozer knocking everyone over, and that was not well received. I was saying, 'It's my way or the highway.' And was forgetting that my friends were also in transition." She admits that this style alienated just about everyone with whom she worked.

Carstons, a technical manager at IBM, talks about the uncertainty he felt after being promoted to a manager from a junior programmer. "It was a little bit challenging to be suddenly giving directives to peers, when just the day before you were one of them. You try to be careful not to offend anyone. It's strange walking into a room and the whole conversation changes. People don't want to be as open with you when you become the boss."

McGee is now president of Medex Insurance Services. She started as a customer service representative with the

company, then leapfrogged over colleagues in a series of promotions. Her fast rise created problems. Colleagues "would say, 'Oh, here comes the big cheese now.' God only knows what they talked about behind my back."

Questions

1. A lot of new managers err in selecting the right leadership style when they move into management. Why do you think this happens?

2. If new managers don't know what leadership style to use, what does this say about leadership and leadership training?

3. Which leadership theories, if any, could help new leaders deal with this transition?

4. Do you think it's easier or harder to be promoted internally into a formal leadership position than to come into it as an outsider? Explain.

Source: Based on D. Koeppel, "A Tough Transition: Friend to Supervisor," *New York Times,* March 16, 2003, p. BU-12.

CBC ◉ VIDEO CASE INCIDENT

How Bad Is Your Boss?

No matter where you work, you cannot escape the boss. He or she can be demanding, can be out of touch, and can stress you out.

Shaun Belding, a consultant and author, developed a quiz about the seven deadly sins of being a boss. Answer yes or no to the following questions to find out how bad your boss really is:

	Yes	No
1. Has your boss ever embarrassed you in front of co-workers?	——	——
2. Does your boss have a tough time making decisions?	——	——
3. Is your boss a poor communicator?	——	——
4. Does your boss hog the limelight when things go well but look to blame others when things go wrong?	——	——
5. Does your boss argue about everything?	——	——
6. Is your boss unclear about what he or she expects of you?	——	——
7. Does your boss pile on the work?	——	——

If you answered yes to one or two questions, you have a stressful boss the odd time. If you answered yes to three to six questions, you have a bad boss and need to take action. If you confront the boss, make sure you can substantiate your claims. If you answered yes to all seven questions, you have the boss from hell and should leave the workplace.

Jack Welsh, named the toughest boss ever, built General Electric (GE) into a $400 billion powerhouse. He likens the boss's role to that of a gardener: "But some of the garden has weeds, and you have to cut those weeds out." He cut 100 000 of those weeds out of GE in massive layoffs in the 1980s, and every year he pruned by cutting out the bottom 10 percent of his workforce. His approach has been controversial, but Welsh makes no apologies. He adds that a boss is only as good as the number of employees he or she

has helped develop. A unit will sink if the boss does not build up great people.

Can you train a boss to be better? Robert Lemieux is the director of sales at the Delta Chelsea in Toronto. He has goals of reaching vice-president or president of the hotel, and knows he has to be a great boss to achieve that success. So, Lemieux is going to Boss Boot Camp. His drill sergeant, Lindsay Sukornyk, runs a coaching company on how to be a better manager. She meets with Lemieux's employees to hear about his leadership style.

Employees see Lemieux as extremely professional, self-contained, caring, and very intuitive in his leadership style. On the other hand, he sometimes appears standoffish and too busy to speak with employees. He also has a tendency to over-promise and under-deliver because of time constraints and competing demands. Lemieux should try to relinquish control, Sukornyk suggests.

Can Lemieux change his ways? He has owned up to his weaknesses and promises to do less talking and more listening. Lemieux feels the first team meeting with the new agenda was very powerful. It allowed employees to communicate how he could be a more effective leader—and they are committed to keeping him on task.

Questions

1. Would you identify Jack Welsh as a charismatic leader? Explain.

2. Is Robert Lemieux a manager or a leader? Explain.

3. If you were speaking in front of a room of top executives, what advice would you offer about why being a bad boss does not make good business sense?

Sources: "How Bad Is Your Boss?" *CBC Venture,* January 17, 2006, 14763; S. MacNaull, "Coping With an Employee Crunch," *Daily Courier* (Kelowna), January 21, 2006, p. B1; and G. Lowe, "Trust Is Tops," *Canadian Business,* April 10/23, 2006, pp. 85–86.

From **Concepts**
to **Skills**

Practising to Be Charismatic

In order to be charismatic in your leadership style, you need to engage in the following behaviours:[104]

1. *Project a powerful, confident, and dynamic presence.* This has both verbal and nonverbal components. Use a captivating and engaging tone of voice. Convey confidence. Talk directly to people, maintain direct eye contact, and hold your body posture in a way that says you are sure of yourself. Speak clearly, avoid stammering, and avoid sprinkling your sentences with noncontent phrases such as "ahhh" and "you know."

2. *Articulate an overarching goal.* You need to share a vision for the future, develop an unconventional way of achieving the vision, and have the ability to communicate the vision to others.

    The vision is a clear statement of where you want to go and how you are going to get there. You need to persuade others that the achievement of this vision is in their self-interest.

    You need to look for fresh and radically different approaches to problems. The road to achieving your vision should be seen as novel but also appropriate to the context.

    Charismatic individuals not only have a vision; they are also able to get others to buy into it. The real power of Martin Luther King Jr. was not that he had a dream but that he could articulate it in terms that made it accessible to millions.

3. *Communicate high performance expectations and confidence in others' ability to meet these expectations.* You need to demonstrate your confidence in people by stating ambitious goals for them individually and as a group. You then convey absolute belief that they will achieve their expectations.

4. *Be sensitive to the needs of followers.* Charismatic leaders get to know their followers individually. You need to understand their individual needs and develop intensely personal relationships with each. This is done by encouraging them to express their points of view, being approachable, genuinely listening to and caring about their concerns, and asking questions so that followers can learn what is really important to them.

Assessing Skills

After you've read this chapter, take the following Self-Assessments on your enclosed CD-ROM:

25. How Good Am I at Personal Planning?

29. What's My Leadership Style?

30. How Charismatic Am I?

32. Do Others See Me as Trustworthy?

Practising Skills

You recently graduated from college with your degree in business administration. You have spent the past two summers working at London Mutual Insurance (LMI), filling in as an intern on a number of different jobs while employees took their vacations. You have received and accepted an offer to join LMI full time as supervisor of the policy-renewal department.

LMI is a large insurance company. In the headquarters office alone, where you will be working, there are more than 1500 employees. The company believes strongly in the personal development of its employees. This translates into a philosophy, emanating from the top executive offices, of trust and respect for all LMI employees. The company is also regularly at the top of most lists of "best companies to work for," largely because of its progressive work/life programs and strong commitment to minimizing layoffs.

In your new job, you will direct the activities of 18 policy-renewal clerks. Their jobs require little training and are highly routine. A clerk's responsibility is to ensure that renewal notices are sent on current policies, to tabulate any changes in premiums, to advise the sales division if a policy is to be cancelled as a result of nonresponse to renewal notices, and to answer questions and solve problems related to renewals.

The people in your work group range in age from 19 to 62, with a median age of 25. For the most part, they are high school graduates with little previous working experience. They earn between $1850 and $2400 a month. You will be replacing a long-time LMI employee, Jan Allison. Jan is retiring after 37 years with LMI, the past 14 spent as a policy-renewal supervisor. Because you spent a few weeks in Jan's group last summer, you are familiar with Jan's style and are acquainted with most of the department members. But people don't know you very well and are suspicious of the fact that you are fresh out of university and have little experience in the department. And the reality is that you got this job because management wanted someone with a post-secondary degree to oversee the department. Your most vocal critic is Lillian Lantz. Lillian is well into her 50s, has been a policy-renewal clerk for over 12 years, and—as the person who has worked the longest in the department—carries a lot of weight with group members. It will be very hard to lead this department without Lillian's support.

Using your knowledge of leadership concepts, which leadership style would you choose and why?

Reinforcing Skills

1. Think of a group or team to which you currently belong or of which you have been a part. What type of leadership style did the leader of this group appear to exhibit? Give some specific examples of the types of leadership behaviours he or she used. Evaluate the leadership style. Was it appropriate for the group? Why or why not? What would you have done differently? Why?

2. Observe two sports teams (either college or professional—one that you consider successful and the other unsuccessful). What leadership styles appear to be used in these teams? Give some specific examples of the types of leadership behaviours you observe. How would you evaluate the leadership style? Was it appropriate for the team? Why or why not? To what degree do you think leadership style influenced the team's outcomes?

CHAPTER 9
Decision Making, Creativity, and Ethics

Nike's decision to manufacture shoes overseas has prompted critics to claim that it exploits workers in poor countries. Did Nike make a rational decision, and is the decision socially responsible?

1 Is there a right way to make decisions?

2 How do people actually make decisions?

3 What factors affect group decision making?

4 Should the leader make the decision or encourage the group to participate?

5 How can we get more creative decisions?

6 What is ethics and how can it be used for better decision making?

7 What is corporate social responsibility?

N ike's first "Corporate Responsibility Report," published in October 2001, confessed that making Nike's runners is "tedious, hard and doesn't offer a wonderful future."[1] Readers may have been startled to learn that employees in overseas factories making Nike products were being harassed by supervisors. Employees were also asked to work far more overtime than rules permitted. Finally, the company admitted to knowing far too little about day-to-day life in the factories, because it was not monitoring the situation closely enough.

These admissions might have seemed shocking to anyone who had not expected Nike to acknowledge what critics have been saying for years: Nike benefits from unfair labour practices in foreign-owned plants to which it subcontracts work. The company has since been trying to improve conditions at its overseas operations.

Nike's decision to publish a corporate responsibility report is just one example of the many decisions com-

panies face every day. Nike had also decided to move its manufacturing to low-wage countries, an action that has brought the company much criticism. So can organizations learn to make better decisions?

In this chapter, we describe how decisions in organizations are made. Decision making affects people at all levels of the organization, and is done by both individuals and groups. Thus, we consider the special characteristics of individual and group decision making. We also look at how creativity, ethics, and social responsibility are linked to decision making.

HOW SHOULD DECISIONS BE MADE?

After completing its first corporate responsibility report, Nike increased training for both managers and employees at its overseas operations.[2] Managers were told that treating employees properly would lead to "improved productivity, reduced labour turnover and less sick leave." Nike thus evaluated its problem and came up with ways to resolve it, in order to reduce criticism of its labour practices. How do individuals and companies make decisions?

A **decision** is the choice made from two or more alternatives. Decision making occurs as a reaction to a problem or an opportunity. A **problem** is a discrepancy between some current state of affairs and some desired state, requiring consideration of alternative

1 Is there a right way to make decisions?

Nike Canada
www.nike.com/canada/

decision The choice made from two or more alternatives.

problem A discrepancy between some current state of affairs and some desired state.

opportunity An occasion that gives rise to thoughts about new ways of proceeding.

courses of action.[3] An **opportunity** occurs when something unplanned happens, giving rise to thoughts about new ways of proceeding.

Whenever any of us make a decision, we have a process that we go through to help us arrive at that decision. Some of us take a very rational approach, with specific steps by which we analyze parts of the decision, others rely on intuition, and some just decide to put two or more alternatives into a hat and pull one out.

Knowing how to make decisions is an important part of everyday life. Below we consider various decision-making models that apply to both individual and group choices. (Later in the chapter, we discuss special aspects of group decision making.) We start with the *rational model*, which describes decision making in the ideal world, a situation that rarely exists. We then look at alternatives to the rational model and how decisions actually get made.

The Rational Decision-Making Process

rational Refers to choices that are consistent and value-maximizing within specified constraints.

The **rational** decision maker makes consistent, high-quality choices within specified constraints.[4] These choices are made following a six-step **rational decision-making model**.[5]

The Rational Model

rational decision-making model A six-step decision-making model that describes how individuals should behave in order to maximize some outcome.

The six steps in the rational decision-making model are listed in Exhibit 9-1.

First, the decision maker must *define the problem*. If you calculate your monthly expenses and find you are spending $50 more than your monthly earnings, you have defined a problem. Many poor decisions can be traced to the decision maker overlooking a problem or defining the wrong problem.

Once a decision maker has defined the problem, he or she needs to *identify the criteria* that will be important in solving the problem. In this step, the decision maker determines what is relevant in making the decision. This step brings the decision maker's interests, values, and personal preferences into the process. Identifying criteria is important because people can have different ideas about what is relevant. Also keep in mind that any factors not identified in this step are considered irrelevant to the decision maker.

To understand the types of criteria that might be used to make a decision, consider the many sponsorship requests the Toronto-based Canadian Imperial Bank of Commerce (CIBC) receives each year. In making a decision about whether or not to support a request, the bank considers the following criteria:[6]

- Strategic fit with CIBC's overall goals and objectives
- Ability to achieve youth customer–segment marketing objectives
- Tangible and intangible benefits of the proposal, such as goodwill, reputation, and cost/potential revenue
- Organizational impact
- Business risks (if any)

If the sponsorship request does not meet these criteria, it is not funded.

The criteria identified are rarely all equal in importance. So the third step requires the decision maker to *allocate weights to the criteria* in order to give them the correct priority in the decision.

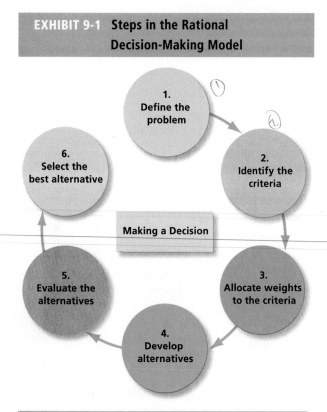

EXHIBIT 9-1   Steps in the Rational Decision-Making Model

1. Define the problem
2. Identify the criteria
3. Allocate weights to the criteria
4. Develop alternatives
5. Evaluate the alternatives
6. Select the best alternative

Making a Decision

The fourth step requires the decision maker to *develop alternatives* that could succeed in resolving the problem. No attempt is made in this step to appraise these alternatives, only to list them.

Once the alternatives are listed, the decision maker must *evaluate the alternatives*. The strengths and weaknesses of each alternative become evident as they are compared with the criteria and weights established in the second and third steps.

The final step in this model requires the decision maker to *select the best alternative.* This is done by evaluating each alternative against the weighted criteria and selecting the alternative with the highest total score.

Assumptions of the Model

The rational decision-making model we just described contains a number of assumptions.[7] Let's briefly outline those assumptions.

- *Problem clarity.* The problem is clear and unambiguous. The decision maker is assumed to have complete information regarding the decision situation.

- *Known options.* It is assumed the decision maker can identify all the relevant criteria and list all the workable alternatives. The decision maker is also aware of all possible implications of each alternative.

- *Clear preferences.* Rationality assumes that the criteria and alternatives can be ranked and weighted to reflect their importance.

- *Constant preferences.* It is assumed that the specific decision criteria are constant and that the weights assigned to them are stable over time.

- *No time or cost constraints.* The decision maker can obtain full information about criteria and alternatives because it is assumed that there are no time or cost constraints.

- *Maximum payoff.* The decision maker will choose the alternative that yields the highest perceived value.

HOW DO INDIVIDUALS ACTUALLY MAKE DECISIONS?

Chaichana Homsombat, a 21-year-old employee at Pan Asia Footwear Public Company in Thailand, the world's third-largest Nike subcontractor factory, explains his job: "Each of us has to work constantly. The faster we meet the assigned quota, the earlier we can go home."[8] Homsombat's quota is to pack 1296 pairs of runners into boxes each workday.

The deputy managing director of the plant, Boonrawd Indamanee, says the quotas improve productivity. A human rights inspector at the plant wonders whether employees are really getting a fair day's pay under the quota system. The management does not want trade unions in the plant, but the inspector fears that "Workers don't know their rights. They simply accept whatever is given to them." Thus when asked if the company gives benefits to employees, one responded: "The uniform. We get three of them when we join the company and two more each year." If employees are not aware of their rights, or do not have full information about them, or have few alternatives, are they really able to make an informed decision about how to behave?

The situation at the Nike plant in Thailand raises some questions: Do decision makers actually follow the rational model? Do they carefully assess problems, identify all relevant criteria, use their creativity to identify all workable alternatives, and painstakingly evaluate every alternative to find an optimizing choice?

2 How do people actually make decisions?

When decision makers are faced with a simple problem and few alternative courses of action, and when the cost of searching out and evaluating alternatives is low, the rational model provides a fairly accurate description of the decision process.[9] However, such situations are the exception. Most decisions in the real world do not follow the rational model. For instance, people are usually content to find an acceptable or reasonable solution to their problem rather than an optimizing one. As such, decision makers generally make limited use of their creativity. Choices tend to be confined to the problem symptom and to the current alternative. As one expert in decision making has concluded: "Most significant decisions are made by judgment, rather than by a defined prescriptive model."[10]

In the following sections, we identify areas where the reality of decision making conflicts with the rational model.[11] None of these ways of making decisions should be considered *irrational*; they are simply departures from the rational model that occur when information is unavailable or too costly to collect.

Problem Identification

Most of the decisions that get made reflect only the problems that decision makers see. Problems do not arrive with flashing neon lights to identify themselves. One person's *problem* may even be another person's *acceptable status quo*. So how do decision makers identify and select problems?

Problems that are visible tend to have a higher probability of being selected than ones that are important.[12] Why? We can offer at least two reasons. First, it's easier to recognize visible problems. They are more likely to catch a decision maker's attention. This explains why politicians are more likely to talk about the "crime problem" than the "illiteracy problem." Second, remember that we are concerned with decision making in organizations. Decision makers want to appear competent and "on top of problems." This motivates them to focus attention on problems that are visible to others.

Do not ignore the decision maker's self-interest. If a decision maker faces a conflict between selecting a problem that is important to the organization and one that is important to the decision maker, self-interest tends to win out.[13] This also ties in with the issue of visibility. It is usually in a decision maker's best interest to attack high-profile problems. It conveys to others that things are under control. Moreover, when the decision maker's performance is later reviewed, the evaluator is more likely to give a high rating to someone who has been aggressively attacking visible problems than to someone whose actions have been less obvious.

Bounded Rationality in Considering Alternatives

✳ *Do people really consider every alternative when making a decision?*

When you considered which college or university to attend, did you look at every possible alternative? Did you carefully identify all the criteria that were important to your decision? Did you evaluate each alternative against the criteria in order to find the school that is best for you? The answer to these questions is probably "no." But don't feel bad, because few people selected their educational institution this way.

It is difficult for individuals to identify and consider every possible alternative available to them. Realistically speaking, people are limited by their ability to interpret, process, and act on information. This is called **bounded rationality**.[14]

bounded rationality Limitations on a person's ability to interpret, process, and act on information.

Because of bounded rationality, individuals are not able to discover and consider every alternative for a decision. Instead, they identify a limited list of the most obvious choices. In most cases, these will include familiar criteria and previously tested solutions. Rather than carefully reviewing and evaluating each alternative in great detail, individuals will settle on an alternative that is "good enough"—one that meets an acceptable level of performance. The first alternative that meets the "good enough" criterion ends the search. So decision makers choose a final solution that **satisfices** rather than optimizes; that is, they seek a solution that is both satisfactory and sufficient. In practice this might mean that rather than interviewing 10 job candidates for a position, a manager interviews one at a time until one that is "good enough" is interviewed—that is, the first job candidate encountered who meets the minimum criteria for the job. The federal government has proposed this rule for its own hiring, as *OB in the Workplace* shows.

satisfice   To provide a solution that is both satisfactory and sufficient.

OB IN THE WORKPLACE

Ottawa May Stop Hiring "Best Qualified"

Is hiring the "best-qualified" person too much work?   Executives and middle managers working in the federal government think so.[15] They argue that "being qualified and competent for a particular job should be enough" even though the person may not be the best possible candidate.

Public servants asked for the rules on hiring to be loosened so that they could actually start hiring and filling positions rather than spending so much time finding the "best-qualified" person. They find those searches excruciating and exhausting. When managers follow the federal guidelines for hiring, it can take six months or more to fill a position.

Steve Hindle, president of the Professional Institute of the Public Service of Canada, explains why hiring someone who is qualified is probably good enough: "If people are honest, what they want is someone who is qualified, but the idea of finding the best? Do we have the time, tools and money needed to find the very best? You want someone competent and good and if they're the best, that's great."

However, not everyone agrees that changing the rules for hiring is a good idea. The public sector unions worry that favouritism may become more common. But they do agree that the current system has too much red tape. ⊼

Intuition

> ✳ *Is it okay to use intuition when making decisions?*

Irene Khoo has just committed her corporation to spending more than $40 million to build a new plant in New Westminster, BC, to manufacture electronic components for satellite communication equipment. As the vice-president of operations for her firm, Khoo reviewed a comprehensive analysis of five possible plant locations developed by a site-location consulting firm she had hired. This report ranked the New Westminster location third among the five alternatives. After carefully reading the report and its conclusions, Khoo decided against the consultant's recommendation. When asked to explain her decision, Khoo said, "I looked the report over very carefully. Despite its recommendation, I felt that the numbers didn't tell the whole story. Intuitively, I just sensed that New Westminster would prove to be the best bet over the long run."

Intuitive decision making, like that used by Irene Khoo, has recently come out of the closet and gained some respectability. Experts no longer automatically assume that using intuition to make decisions is irrational or ineffective.[16] There is growing recognition that rational analysis has been overemphasized and that, in certain instances, relying on intuition can improve decision making.

What do we mean by intuitive decision making? There are a number of ways to conceptualize intuition.[17] For instance, some consider it a form of extrasensory power or sixth

intuitive decision making   A
subconscious process created out of
a person's many experiences.

sense, and some believe it is a personality trait that a limited number of people are born with. For our purposes, we define **intuitive decision making** as a subconscious process created out of distilled experience. It does not necessarily operate independently of rational analysis; rather, the two complement each other. Those who use intuition effectively often rely on their experiences to help guide and assess their intuitions. That is why many managers are able to rely on intuition.

A study of 60 experienced professionals holding high-level positions in major US organizations found that many of them used intuition to help them make workplace decisions.[18] Twelve percent said they always used it, while 47 percent said they often used intuition. Only 10 percent said they rarely or seldom used intuition. More than 90 percent of managers said they were likely to use a mix of intuition and data analysis when making decisions.

When asked the types of decisions for which they most often used intuition, 40 percent reported that they used it to make people-related decisions such as hiring, performance appraisal, harassment complaints, and safety issues. The managers said they also used intuition for quick or unexpected decisions so they could avoid delays. They also were more likely to rely on intuition in novel situations that had a lot of uncertainty.

The results from this study suggest that intuitive decisions are best applied when time is short, when policies, rules, and guidelines do not give clear-cut advice, when there is a great deal of uncertainty, and when detailed numerical analysis needs a check and balance.

Intuition can be wrong, so it is important to develop one's intuition. Often, good intuition is really the result of recognizing the pattern in a situation and drawing upon previously learned information associated with that pattern to arrive quickly at a decision. The result is that the intuitive decision maker can decide rapidly with what appears to be very limited information. Decision making can be improved by analyzing one's decisions after the fact, to develop a better understanding of when good and bad decisions have been made.

So what does all of this tell us? Based on our discussion above, you should consider the following when making decisions:

- Make sure that you define the problem as best you can.

- Be clear on the factors that you will use to make your decision.

- Be sure to collect enough alternatives so that you can clearly differentiate among them.

Judgment Shortcuts

heuristics   Judgment shortcuts in
decision making.

In examining the ways that people make decisions, two eminent psychologists, Daniel Kahneman (the 2002 winner of the Nobel Prize in economic sciences) and Amos Tversky discovered that individuals often rely on **heuristics**, or judgment shortcuts, to simplify the decision process, rather than going through all of the steps of the rational decision-making model.[19] People tend to rely too heavily on experience, impulses, gut feelings, and convenient "rules of thumb" when they make decisions. In many instances, these shortcuts are helpful. However, in others, they may lead to poor decisions.

★ Why is it that we sometimes make bad decisions?

A growing body of research tells us that decision makers allow systematic biases and errors to creep into their judgments.[20] These come out of attempts to shortcut the decision process. In what follows, we discuss some of the most common judgment shortcuts to alert you to mistakes that are often made when making decisions.

EXHIBIT 9-2   Examples of Decision Biases

Scenario 1: Answer part A before reading part B.

A: Threatened by a superior enemy force, the general faces a dilemma. His intelligence officers say his soldiers will be caught in an ambush in which 600 of them will die unless he leads them to safety by one of two available routes. If he takes the first route, 200 soldiers will be saved. If he takes the second, there's a one-third chance that 600 soldiers will be saved and a two-thirds chance that none will be saved. Which route should he take?

B: The general again has to choose between two escape routes. But this time his aides tell him that if he takes the first, 400 soldiers will die. If he takes the second, there's a one-third chance that no soldiers will die, and a two-thirds chance that 600 soldiers will die. Which route should he take?

Scenario 2:

Linda is 31, single, outspoken, and very bright. She majored in philosophy in university. As a student, she was deeply concerned with discrimination and other social issues and participated in antinuclear demonstrations. Which statement is more likely?:

a. Linda is a bank teller.

b. Linda is a bank teller and active in the feminist movement.

Source: K. McKean, "Decisions, Decisions," *Discover,* June 1985, pp. 22–31.

Framing

Kahneman and Tversky discovered that even when people are trying to be coldly logical, they give radically different answers to the same question if it is posed in different ways.[21] For instance, consider choices A and B in Scenario 1 in Exhibit 9-2. Most people come to an opposite conclusion for A and B, even though the problems are identical. The only difference is that the first states the problem in terms of lives saved, while the second states it in terms of lives lost.

This judgment error is called **framing**, and it refers to how the selective use of perspective alters the way we might view a situation in formulating a decision.

framing   Error in judgment that arises from the selective use of perspective (that is, the way that a set of ideas, facts, or information is presented) that alters the way we view a situation in formulating a decision.

Statistical Regression to the Mean

Sometimes people make judgments while ignoring **statistical regression to the mean**, the statistical observation that a very good performance is often followed by a lesser performance, while a lesser performance is often followed by a very good performance; the result is average performance over time. This heuristic may be of particular interest to those trying to decide whether rewards or punishments work better with employees, colleagues, children, and even friends. Although many studies indicate that rewards are a more effective teaching tool than punishment, Kahneman was once faced with a student who begged to differ on this point. "I've often praised people warmly for beautifully executed manoeuvres, and the next time they almost always do worse. And I've screamed at people for badly executed manoeuvres, and by and large the next time they improve." Regression to the mean helps us understand that each person has an average performance level, so the highs and the lows balance out. Performance improvements happen over the long term. Thus, in this example, it would be helpful to realize that screaming is less likely to result in long-term improvements in behaviour and also tends to damage the relationship between people.

statistical regression to the mean   The statistical observation that an above-average performance is often followed by a lesser performance, while a below-average performance is more likely followed by a better performance; the result is average performance over time.

Availability Heuristic

The **availability heuristic** is the tendency for people to base their judgments on information that is readily available to them rather than complete data. Events that evoke emotions, that are particularly vivid, or that have occurred more recently tend to be more available in our memories. As a result, we tend to overestimate unlikely events such as

availability heuristic   The tendency for people to base their judgments on information that is readily available to them rather than complete data.

an airplane crash, compared with more likely events such as car crashes. The availability heuristic can also explain why managers, when doing annual performance appraisals, tend to give more weight to recent behaviours of an employee than to those behaviours of six or nine months ago.

Representative Heuristic

Many youngsters in Canada dream of playing hockey in the National Hockey League (NHL) when they grow up. In reality, they have a better chance of becoming medical doctors than they do of playing in the NHL, but these kids are suffering from a **representative heuristic**. They tend to assess the likelihood of an occurrence by trying to match it with a pre-existing category.[22] They heard about someone from their neighbourhood who went to the NHL 25 years ago, and imagine that anyone from their neighbourhood can do the same. In the workplace, individuals use this heuristic to make any number of decisions. For instance, if three graduates from the same university were hired and turned out to be poor performers, a manager might predict that a current job applicant from the same university would not be a good employee. The manager is assuming that the small sample of graduates previously employed represents all graduates from that university. Scenario 2 in Exhibit 9-2 on page 299 gives another example of representativeness. In that case, Linda is assumed to be a bank teller and a feminist, given her concerns about social issues, even though the probability of both situations' being true is much less than the probability that she is just a bank teller.

Ignoring the Base Rate

Yet another judgment error that people make is **ignoring the base rate**, which is ignoring the statistical likelihood that an event might happen. For instance, if you were planning to become an entrepreneur and were asked whether your business would succeed, you would almost undoubtedly respond with a resounding "yes." Individuals believe they will beat the odds, even when, in the case of founding a business, the failure rate is close to 90 percent. Ignoring the base rate is not due to inexperience of the decision maker. Professors Glen Whyte of the Joseph L. Rotman School of Management (University of Toronto) and Christina Sue-Chan of the I. H. Asper School of Business (University of Manitoba) found that even experienced human resource managers ignore the base rate when asked in an experiment to make hiring decisions.[23] They suggest the importance of reminding people of what the base rate is before asking them to make decisions.

People who ignore the base rate tend to do so because they take an *inside view* of a problem, simply assessing the facts of their situation as they know them and creating projections based on that. By contrast, people who take an *outside view* deliberately ignore the specific facts of their situation and instead consider the statistics for similar situations; this approach helps them better predict the likelihood of success of their situation.[24]

Escalation of Commitment

Some decision makers escalate commitment to a failing course of action.[25] **Escalation of commitment** is an increased commitment to a previous decision despite negative information. For example, a friend has been dating a man for about four years. Although she admits that things are not going too well in the relationship, she is determined to marry the man. When asked to explain this seemingly nonrational choice of action, she responds: "I have a lot invested in the relationship."

Individuals escalate commitment to a failing course of action when they view themselves as responsible for the failure. That is, they "throw good money after bad" to

---

representative heuristic   The tendency for people to assess the likelihood of an occurrence by trying to match it with a pre-existing category.

National Hockey League (NHL)
www.nhl.com

ignoring the base rate   Error in judgment that arises from ignoring the statistical likelihood that an event might happen.

I. H. Asper School of Business, University of Manitoba
http://umanitoba.ca/management/indexGo.html

escalation of commitment
An increased commitment to a previous decision despite negative information.

demonstrate that their initial decision was not wrong and to avoid having to admit they made a mistake.

Many organizations have suffered large losses because a manager was determined to prove his or her original decision was right by continuing to commit resources to what was a lost cause from the beginning.

Overconfidence Bias

It's been said that "no problem in judgment and decision making is more prevalent and more potentially catastrophic than overconfidence."[26]

When we are given factual questions and asked to judge the probability that our answers are correct, we tend to be far too optimistic. This is known as the **overconfidence bias**. For instance, studies have found that when people say they are 65 to 70 percent confident that they are right, they were actually correct only about 50 percent of the time.[27] And when they say they are 100 percent sure, they tended to be 70 to 85 percent correct.[28]

From an organizational standpoint, one of the more interesting findings related to overconfidence is that those individuals whose intellectual and interpersonal abilities are *weakest* are most likely to overestimate their performance and ability.[29] So as managers and employees become more knowledgeable about an issue, they are less likely to display overconfidence.[30] Overconfidence is most likely to occur when individuals are considering issues or problems that are outside their area of expertise.

overconfidence bias
Overestimating the accuracy of our predictions.

Anchoring Bias

The **anchoring bias** is a tendency to fixate on initial information as a starting point. Once set, we then fail to adequately adjust for subsequent information.[31] The anchoring bias occurs because our minds appear to give a disproportionate amount of emphasis to the first information they receive. So initial impressions, ideas, prices, and estimates carry undue weight relative to information received later.[32]

Professional people such as advertising writers, managers, politicians, real estate agents, and lawyers widely rely on anchoring—they create first impressions to persuade people to act in particular ways. For instance, in a mock jury trial, one set of jurors was asked by the plaintiff's attorney to make an award in the range of $15 million to $50 million. Another set of jurors was asked to make an award in the range of $50 million to $150 million. Consistent with the anchoring bias, the median awards were the first numbers heard by the jurors: $15 million in the first condition and $50 million in the second condition.[33]

When making decisions, you should consider whether you are falling into any of the judgment and bias traps described above. In particular, understanding the base rates and making sure that you collect information beyond that which is immediately available to you will provide you with more alternatives from which to frame a decision. It is also useful to consider whether you are sticking with a decision simply because you have invested time in that particular alternative, even though it may not be wise to continue. *OB in Action—Reducing Biases and Errors in Decision Making* provides you with some ideas for improving your decision making. To learn more about your decision-making style, see the *Learning About Yourself Exercise* on pages 324–325.

anchoring bias A tendency to fixate on initial information as a starting point.

OB IN ACTION

Reducing Biases and Errors in Decision Making

→ **Focus on goals**. Clear goals make decision making easier and help you eliminate options that are inconsistent with your interests.

→ **Look for information that disconfirms** your **beliefs**. When we deliberately consider various ways we could be wrong, we challenge our tendencies to think we are smarter than we actually are.

→ **Don't create meaning** out of random events. Ask yourself if patterns can be meaningfully explained or whether they are mere coincidence. Don't attempt to create meaning out of coincidence.

→ **Increase** your **options**. The more alternatives you can generate, and the more diverse those alternatives, the greater your chance of finding an outstanding one.

Source: S. P. Robbins, *Decide & Conquer: Making Winning Decisions and Taking Control of Your Life* (Upper Saddle River, NJ: Financial Times/Prentice Hall, 2004), pp. 164–168.

3 What factors affect group decision making?

GROUP DECISION MAKING

While a variety of decisions in both life and organizations are made at the individual level, the belief—characterized by juries—that two heads are better than one has long been accepted as a basic component of North America's and many other countries' legal systems. This belief has expanded to the point that, today, many decisions in organizations are made by groups, teams, or committees. In this section, we will review group decision making and compare it with individual decision making.

Groups vs. the Individual

Decision-making groups may be widely used in organizations, but does that mean group decisions are preferable to those made by an individual alone? The answer to this question depends on a number of factors we consider below.[34] See Exhibit 9-3 for a summary of our major points.

Strengths of Group Decision Making

Groups generate *more complete information and knowledge.* By combining the resources of several individuals, groups bring more input into the decision process. Groups can bring an *increased diversity of views* to the decision process, and, thus, the opportunity to consider more approaches and alternatives. In terms of decision outcomes, the evidence indicates that a group will almost always outperform even the best individual. So groups generate *higher quality decisions.*[35] Group decisions also tend to be more *accurate.* If *creativity* is important, groups tend to be more creative in their decisions than individuals.[36] Groups also lead to *increased acceptance of a solution.* Many decisions fail after the final choice is made because people do not accept them. Group members who participated in making a decision are likely to support the decision enthusiastically and encourage others to accept it.

Weaknesses of Group Decision Making

Despite the advantages noted, group decisions involve certain drawbacks. First, they are *time-consuming.* Groups typically take more time to reach a solution than an individual would. Thus, group decisions are not always efficient. Second, there are *conformity pressures* in groups. The desire of group members to be accepted and considered an asset to the group can result in quashing any overt disagreement. Third, group discussion can be *dominated by one or a few members.* If this dominant coalition is composed of low- and medium-ability members, the group's overall effectiveness will diminish. Finally, group decisions suffer from *ambiguous responsibility.* In an individual decision, it is clear who is accountable for the final outcome. In a group decision, the responsibility of any single member is watered down.

EXHIBIT 9-3 Group vs. Individual Decision Making		
Criteria of Effectiveness	**Groups**	**Individuals**
More complete information	✔	
Diversity of views	✔	
Decision quality	✔	
Accuracy	✔	
Creativity	✔	
Degree of acceptance	✔	
Speed		✔
Efficiency		✔

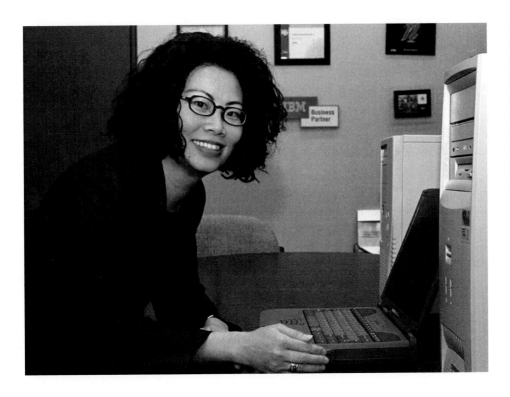

Molly Mak was chosen president of a national information technology solutions provider, Calgary-based Onward Computer Systems, by other partners in the firm after she showed that she had the vision and determination to lead the company to greater growth and profits. She says that consensus is not always possible, especially when it is important to get things accomplished under tight time constraints.

Groupthink and Groupshift

Two by-products of group decision making have received a considerable amount of attention by organizational behaviour (OB) researchers: groupthink and groupshift. As we will show, these two phenomena have the potential to affect the group's ability to appraise alternatives objectively and arrive at quality solutions.

Groupthink

Have you ever felt like speaking up in a meeting, classroom, or informal group, but decided against it? One reason might have been shyness. On the other hand, you might have been a victim of **groupthink**, a phenomenon in which group pressures for conformity prevent the group from critically appraising unusual, minority, or unpopular views. It describes a deterioration in an individual's mental efficiency, reality testing, and moral judgment as a result of group pressures.[37]

We have all seen the symptoms of the groupthink phenomenon:[38]

- *Illusion of invulnerability.* Group members become overconfident among themselves, allowing them to take extraordinary risks.

- *Assumption of morality.* Group members believe highly in the moral rightness of the group's objectives and do not feel the need to debate the ethics of their actions.

- *Rationalization.* Group members rationalize any resistance to the assumptions they have made. No matter how strongly the evidence may contradict their basic assumptions, members behave so as to reinforce those assumptions continually.

- *Stereotyping outgroups.* People outside the group who criticize decisions and actions are viewed as "enemies" who don't know what they are talking about.

- *Minimized doubts.* Group members who have doubts or hold differing points of view seek to avoid deviating from what appears to be group consensus by keeping silent about misgivings and even minimizing to themselves the importance of their doubts.

groupthink A phenomenon in which group pressures for conformity prevent the group from critically appraising unusual, minority, or unpopular views.

- *Illusion of unanimity.* If someone does not speak, it's assumed that he or she is in full agreement. In other words, abstention becomes viewed as a yes vote.

- *Mindguards.* One or more members of the team become self-appointed guardians to make sure that negative or inconsistent information does not reach team members.

- *Peer pressure.* Group members apply direct pressure on those who momentarily express doubts about any of the group's shared views or who question the alternative favoured by the majority.

As the Bre-X scandal was unfolding in early 1997, many people who possibly should have known better refused to accept the initial evidence that there might not be any gold at the Busang, Indonesia, mine. Because investors and the companies involved had convinced themselves that they were sitting on the gold find of the twentieth century, they were reluctant to challenge their beliefs when the first evidence of tampered core samples was produced. More recently, forecasters seemed to be suffering from groupthink as they pronounced the economy in recession, as this *OB in the Street* shows.

OB IN THE STREET

Recession: Are We There Yet?

How many economic forecasters does it take to change the economy?   In early 2002, economic forecasters were absolutely astonished by all the good news they heard on the economic front in Canada and the United States. They were surprised that the economies of both countries had grown in the fourth quarter and by the job growth in Canada during January and February. They were even surprised that Canada's manufacturers and exporters had had a great January. They were surprised because they had been predicting either a recession at worst, or a recession with jobless recovery at best.

Forecasters started painting a gloomy picture after September 11, 2001, anticipating that the US national crisis would have a long-lasting impact on the world economy. Even as evidence failed to support this gloomy picture, forecasters struggled to find evidence that they were right.

Groupthink may well explain the forecasters' lingering negative predictions. The forecasters were from the financial industry, which was harder hit than most industries, except for the technology sector. Wall Street economists also lived next door to the World Trade Center, so this had a greater impact. Rather than search more widely for evidence, they looked more locally, at the economy right around Wall Street.

Stock prices and corporate profits fell significantly during much of 2001, and this is what they focused on. Meanwhile, housing prices and consumer spending continued to rise. The analysts figured this was a temporary upturn before the large downturn they were predicting. They also failed to notice that personal income continued to rise throughout the year.

In short, forecasters were calling for a recession. They convinced each other it was coming. "[Those] who didn't buy the line and suggested that maybe this was only a very sharp slowdown, invited ridicule."[39]

The forecasters were suffering from some of the symptoms of groupthink. They rationalized resistance, suggesting it was everyone else who did not understand the economic numbers. They applied peer pressure to each other, ridiculing those who suggested that a recession might not occur. This might have led some analysts to minimize their doubts and keep silent. All of these behaviours led forecasters to appear unanimous in their views on the coming recession.

With groupthink, individuals who hold a position that differs from that of the dominant majority are under pressure to suppress, withhold, or modify their true feelings and beliefs. As members of a group, we find it more pleasant to be in agreement—to be a positive part of the group—than to be a disruptive force, even if disruption is necessary to improve the effectiveness of the group's decisions.

Does groupthink attack all groups? No. It seems to occur most often where there is a clear group identity, where members hold a positive image of their group, which they want to protect, and where the group perceives a collective threat to this positive image.[40] So groupthink is less a way to suppress dissenters than a means for a group to protect its positive image.

What can managers do to minimize groupthink?[41]

- *Encourage group leaders to play an impartial role.* Leaders should actively seek input from all members and avoid expressing their own opinions, especially in the early stages of deliberation.

- *Appoint one group member to play the role of devil's advocate.* This member's role is to overtly challenge the majority position and offer divergent perspectives.

- *Stimulate active discussion of diverse alternatives* to encourage dissenting views and more objective evaluations.

While considerable anecdotal evidence indicates the negative implications of groupthink in organizational settings, not much actual empirical work has been conducted in organizations in this area.[42] In fact, researchers of groupthink have been criticized for suggesting that its effect is uniformly negative[43] and for overestimating the link between the decision-making process and its outcome.[44] A study of groupthink using 30 teams from five large corporations suggests that elements of groupthink may affect decision making differently. For instance, the illusion of invulnerability, belief in inherent group morality, and the illusion of unanimity were positively associated with team performance.[45] The most recent research suggests that we should be aware of groupthink conditions that lead to poor decisions, while realizing that not all groupthink symptoms harm decision making.

Groupshift

Evidence suggests that there are differences between the decisions groups make and the decisions that might be made by individual members within the group.[46] In some cases, group decisions are more conservative than individual decisions. More often, group decisions are riskier than individual decisions.[47] In either case, participants have engaged in **groupshift**, a phenomenon in which the initial positions of individual group members become exaggerated because of the interactions of the group.

What appears to happen in groups is that the discussion leads to a significant shift in the positions of members toward a more extreme position toward the direction in which they were already leaning before the discussion. So conservative types become more cautious and more aggressive types assume more risk. The group discussion tends to exaggerate the initial position of the group.

Groupshift can be viewed as a special case of groupthink. The group's decision reflects the dominant decision-making norm that develops during the group's discussion. Whether the shift in the group's decision is toward greater caution or more risk depends on the dominant pre-discussion norm.

The greater shift toward risk has generated several explanations for the phenomenon.[48] It has been argued, for instance, that the discussion creates familiarity among the

groupshift A phenomenon in which the initial positions of individual group members become exaggerated because of the interactions of the group.

members. As they become more comfortable with each other, they also become bolder and more daring. Another argument is that our society values risk, that we admire individuals who are willing to take risks, and that group discussion motivates members to show that they are at least as willing as their peers to take risks. The most plausible explanation of the shift toward risk, however, seems to be that the group diffuses responsibility. Group decisions free any single member from accountability for the group's final choice. Greater risk can be taken because even if the decision fails, no one member can be held wholly responsible.

How should you use the findings on groupshift? You should recognize that group decisions exaggerate the initial position of the individual members, that the shift has been shown more often to be toward greater risk, and that whether a group will shift toward greater risk or caution is a function of the members' pre-discussion inclinations.

Group Decision-Making Techniques

Groups can use a variety of techniques to stimulate decision making. We outline four of them below.

Interacting Groups

interacting groups Typical groups, where members interact with each other face to face.

The most common form of group decision making takes place in **interacting groups**. In these groups, members meet face to face and rely on both verbal and nonverbal interaction to communicate with each other. All kinds of groups use this technique frequently, from groups organized to develop a class project, to a work team, to a senior management team. But as our discussion of groupthink demonstrates, interacting groups often censor themselves and pressure individual members toward conformity of opinion. *Brainstorming*, the *nominal group technique*, and *electronic meetings* have been proposed as ways to reduce many of the problems inherent in the traditional interacting group.

Brainstorming

brainstorming An idea-generation process that specifically encourages any and all alternatives while withholding any criticism of those alternatives.

Brainstorming is meant to overcome pressures for conformity within the interacting group that prevent the development of creative alternatives.[49] It achieves this by using an idea-generation process that specifically encourages any and all alternatives while withholding any criticism of those alternatives.

You have no doubt engaged in brainstorming when you have tried to come up with ideas for how to present a project for class. In a typical brainstorming session, a half-dozen to a dozen people sit around a table. The group leader, or even another team member, states the problem in a clear manner so that all participants understand it. Members then "freewheel" as many alternatives as they can in a given period of time. No criticism is allowed, and all the alternatives are recorded for later discussion and analysis. With one idea stimulating others and judgments of even the most bizarre suggestions withheld until later, group members are encouraged to "think the unusual."

Jerilyn Wright & Associates
www.jwadesign.com

A more recent variant of brainstorming is electronic brainstorming, which is done by people interacting on computers to generate ideas. For example, Calgary-based Jerilyn Wright & Associates uses electronic brainstorming to help clients design their workspaces through software that has been adapted for office-space design.[50]

Executive Decision Centre,
Queen's University
http://business.queensu.ca/qedc/

The Executive Decision Centre at Queen's University was "one of the first electronic [decision-making] facilities in North America and the first to be made accessible to the public."[51] Professor Brent Gallupe, the founding director and another facilitator at the centre have conducted more than 600 decision-making sessions with a variety of North American organizations, including GlaxoSmithKline, Bombardier, DuPont, Imperial Oil, the Department of National Defence and Canadian Forces, the Canadian Security Intelligence Service, and the United Way. The strength of the Queen's system is that participants simultaneously interact via computer terminals, all responses are anonymous, and the speed allows for generating numerous ideas in a short time. Whitby, Ontario-based McGraw-Hill Ryerson has become a regular user since finding that one of its divisions experienced a surge in sales after visiting the Queen's centre. "They came up with a better, more soundly developed strategy, with more commitment on the part of the people. People feel very committed to the outcomes of the process because they don't feel like they've been strong-armed into the outcomes. They've had a voice in it," says John Dill, former president and CEO of McGraw-Hill Ryerson.

However, brainstorming is not always the right strategy to use. For example, president and CEO Terry Graham of Scarborough, Ontario-based Image Processing Systems (now part of Photon Dynamics), which won Canada's 1997 Export Award, saw brainstorming backfire when doing business in China. He says that meetings with Chinese business people "are definitely not for brainstorming. We learned this lesson the hard way. Our team thought we could show our creativity by placing fresh alternatives in front of an important manager. It was two years before the company would talk to us again."[52] Brainstorming, we should also note, is merely a process for generating ideas. The following two techniques go further by offering methods of actually arriving at a preferred solution.[53]

Nominal Group Technique

The **nominal group technique** restricts discussion or interpersonal communication during the decision-making process; thus the term *nominal* (which means "in name only"). Group members are all physically present, as in a traditional committee meeting, but members operate independently. Specifically, a problem is presented and then the following steps take place:

- Members meet as a group, but before any discussion takes place each member independently writes down his or her ideas about the problem.

- After this silent period, each member presents one idea to the group. Group members take turns presenting a single idea until all ideas have been presented and recorded. No discussion takes place until all ideas have been recorded.

- The group then discusses the ideas for clarity and evaluates them.

- Each group member silently and independently ranks the ideas. The idea with the highest overall ranking determines the final decision.

The steps of the nominal group technique are illustrated in Exhibit 9-4. The chief advantage of this technique is that it permits the group to meet formally but does not restrict independent thinking as the interacting group does.

A number of studies suggest that brainstorming by nominal groups is more effective than brainstorming by interacting groups. However, recent research suggests that nominal groups generate more ideas and more original ideas, but not necessarily more quality ideas.[54]

nominal group technique A group decision-making method in which individual members meet face to face to pool their judgments in a systematic but independent fashion.

EXHIBIT 9-4 Nominal Group Technique

Team members receive description of problem.	**Individual Activity**	**Group Activity**	**Individual Activity**
	Individuals silently write down possible solutions.	Individuals take turns describing solutions to each other. Group then discusses and evaluates ideas.	Individuals silently rank (or vote on) each solution presented.

EXHIBIT 9-5 Evaluating Group Effectiveness

Effectiveness Criteria	Type of Group			
	Interacting	Brainstorming	Nominal	Electronic
Number of ideas	Low	Moderate	High	High
Quality of ideas	Low	Moderate	High	High
Social pressure	High	Low	Moderate	Low
Money costs	Low	Low	Low	High
Speed	Moderate	Moderate	Moderate	High
Task orientation	Low	High	High	High
Potential for interpersonal conflict	High	Low	Moderate	Low
Feelings of accomplishment	High to low	High	High	High
Commitment to solution	High	Not applicable	Moderate	Moderate
Development of group cohesiveness	High	High	Moderate	Low

Source: Based on J. K. Murnighan, "Group Decision Making: What Strategies Should You Use?" *Academy of Management Review,* February 1981, p. 61.

Electronic Meetings

electronic meeting A meeting in which members interact on computers, allowing for anonymity of comments and aggregation of votes.

The most recent approach to group decision making blends the nominal group technique with sophisticated computer technology.[55] It's called the computer-assisted group, or **electronic meeting**. Once the technology is in place, the concept is simple. As many as 50 people sit around a horseshoe-shaped table, which is empty except for a series of computer terminals. Issues are presented to the participants, and they type their responses onto their computer monitors. Individual comments, as well as total votes, are displayed on a projection screen in the room.

The major advantages of the electronic meeting are anonymity, honesty, and speed. Participants can anonymously type any messages they want, and they flash on the screen for all to see at the push of buttons on participants' keyboards. This type of meeting also allows people to be brutally honest without penalty. In addition, it is fast because chit-chat is eliminated, discussions do not digress, and many participants can "talk" at once without stepping on one another's toes. The future of group meetings undoubtedly will include extensive use of this technology.

Each of these four group-decision techniques has its own strengths and weaknesses. The choice of one technique over another will depend on what criteria you want to emphasize and the cost-benefit trade-off. For instance, as Exhibit 9-5 indicates, the interacting group is effective for building group cohesiveness, brainstorming keeps social pressures to a minimum, the nominal group technique is an inexpensive means for generating a large number of ideas, and electronic meetings process ideas quickly.

THE INFLUENCE OF THE LEADER ON GROUP DECISION MAKING

4 Should the leader make the decision or encourage the group to participate?

You are the head of your own business or the manager of your division at work, and you are trying to decide whether you should make a decision by yourself or involve the members of your team. Is there anything that can inform you about whether it is better for the leader to make a decision alone or get everyone involved in the decision-making process?

The **leader-participation model** presents the various actions a leader might take with respect to the decision-making processes of the group he or she leads.[56] The model provides a sequential set of rules that should be followed to determine the form and amount of participation desired by the manager or group leader in decision making, as dictated by the situation. It is a complex decision tree incorporating eight contingency variables that identify which of five leadership styles to use when making decisions.

The five leadership styles the model proposes leaders can use in a given situation are Autocratic I (AI), Autocratic II (AII), Consultative I (CI), Consultative II (CII), and Group II (GII). Thus the group leader or manager has the following alternatives from which to choose when deciding how involved to be with decisions that affect a work group:

AI: You solve the problem or make a decision yourself using whatever facts you have at hand.

AII: You obtain the necessary information from employees and then decide on the solution to the problem yourself. You may or may not tell them about the nature of the situation you face. You seek only relevant facts from them, not their advice or counsel.

CI: You share the problem with relevant employees one-on-one, getting their ideas and suggestions. However, the final decision is yours alone.

CII: You share the problem with your employees as a group, collectively obtaining their ideas and suggestions. Then you make the decision, which may or may not reflect your employees' influence.

GII: You share the problem with your employees as a group. Your goal is to help the group concur on a decision. Your ideas are not given any greater weight than those of others.

The original leader-participation model has been revised to include 12 contingency variables, 8 problem types, and 5 leadership styles, and is too complex to describe in detail in a basic OB textbook. There is a computer program that cuts through the complexity of the new model. The major decision factors include the quality of the decision required, the degree of commitment needed from participants, and the time available to make the decision.

Research testing of the original leader-participation model was very encouraging.[57] We have every reason to believe that the revised model provides an excellent guide to help managers choose the most appropriate leadership style in different situations.

CREATIVITY IN ORGANIZATIONAL DECISION MAKING

"Canada is not a very creative culture," according to a National Research Council report written by Professor David Bentley of the English Department at the University of Western Ontario.[58] The report suggests that concrete steps need to be taken to promote a culture of innovation, and improve the creativity of individuals. The report gives a number of suggestions for improving creativity, including using metaphors, empathetic thinking, and imagining to help see things in new ways.

Bentley's call for improving creativity is consistent with a survey showing that 58 percent of large public companies and entrepreneurs recognize a link between creative thinking within the organization and having a competitive edge.[59] "It [creative thinking] will not necessarily spell the difference between success and failure. But it is one of those tangential issues that can add a few cents per share profit," noted the head of an Ontario agriproducts company, who was not identified by the survey. Moreover, research

leader-participation model A leadership theory that provides a set of rules to determine the form and amount of participative decision making in different situations.

5 How can we get more creative decisions?

shows that the organizational benefits of individual creativity include "higher-quality products, more effective decision making, better group performance, and more innovative solutions to organizational problems."[60] A variety of definitions exist for the concept of creativity, with some viewing it as a characteristic of a person while others view it as a process.[61] Most contemporary researchers and theorists use a definition that addresses either the product or the outcome of the product development process.[62] In our next discussion, we consider **creativity** as the process of creating products, ideas, or procedures that are novel or original and are potentially relevant or useful to an organization.[63]

creativity The process of creating novel products, ideas, or procedures that are potentially relevant or useful to an organization.

Factors That Affect Individual Creativity

> ✴ *Why are some people more creative than others?*

People differ in their inherent creativity. Albert Einstein, Marie Curie, Thomas Edison, Pablo Picasso, and Wolfgang Amadeus Mozart were individuals of exceptional creativity. In more recent times, Canadian artist Emily Carr, legendary Canadian concert pianist Glenn Gould, basketball star Michael Jordan, and Canadian author Margaret Atwood have been noted for the creative contributions they have made to their fields. Not surprisingly, exceptional creativity is scarce. For example, a study of lifetime creativity of 461 men and women found that less than 1 percent were exceptionally creative.[64] But 10 percent were highly creative and about 60 percent were somewhat creative. These results suggest that most of us have creative potential, if we can learn to unleash it.

Edward De Bono
www.edwdebono.com

A large body of literature has examined the personal attributes associated with creative achievement.[65] In general, "these studies have demonstrated that a stable set of core personal characteristics, including broad interests, attraction to complexity, intuition, aesthetic sensitivity, toleration of ambiguity, and self-confidence, relate positively and consistently to measures of creative performance across a variety of domains."[66] While personality and cognitive skills are linked to creativity,[67] the task itself plays an important role. Individuals are more creative when they are motivated by intrinsic interest, challenge, task satisfaction, and self-set goals.[68] Those who are extrinsically motivated are more likely to look for the most efficient solution to a problem in order to receive the desired rewards. Those who are intrinsically motivated may take more time exploring issues and situations, which gives them the opportunity to see things in a different light.[69] The setting also makes a difference, and those settings that provide opportunities, absence of constraints,[70] and rewards[71] encourage creativity.

There is some evidence that the brain is set up to think linearly, rather than laterally, and yet lateral thinking is needed for creative thinking. Edward De Bono, a leading authority on creative and conceptual thinking for over 25 years, has written a number of books on this topic, including *Six Thinking Hats* and *The Mechanism of Mind*.[72] He has identified various tools for helping one use more lateral thinking. De Bono's "six thinking hats" concept is a simple yet powerful tool that is intended to change the way people think. He suggests that innovative and creative problem-solving can develop from working through

Creativity and the bottom line can go hand in hand. In fact, at Vancouver-based Big House Communications, creativity rules. Big House develops communications, including websites, for other companies. It is known for giving clients several alternatives: traditional, wacky, and fun. The company must be doing something right. It is 10 years old, which makes it *really* old for this type of business.

decisions using each of the frameworks represented by the individual hats. The hats are metaphors for different kinds of thinking.[73]

- The *white hat* represents impartial thinking, focusing strictly on the facts.

- The *red hat* represents expression of feelings, passions, intuitions, emotions.

- The *black hat* stands for a critical, deliberate, evaluating outlook.

- The *yellow hat* represents an optimistic, upbeat, positive outlook.

- The *green hat* represents creativity, inspiration, imagination, and the free flow of new concepts.

- The *blue hat* represents control, an overall "managerial" perspective of the process.

Each hat has its own place in the decision-making process. De Bono suggests that we use all six in order to fully develop our capacity to think more creatively. Groups could do the same by assigning each person to the role of one of the hats. For more suggestions on solving problems creatively, see *From Concepts to Skills* on pages 328–329.

Organizational Factors That Affect Creativity

In two decades of research analyzing the link between the work environment and creativity, six organizational factors have been found to affect creativity:[74]

- *Challenge.* When people are matched up with the right assignments, their expertise and skills can be brought to the task of creative thinking. Individuals should be stretched, but not overwhelmed.

- *Freedom.* To be creative, once a person is given a project, he or she needs the freedom to determine the process. In other words, let the person decide how to tackle the problem. This heightens intrinsic motivation.

- *Resources.* Time and money are the two main resources that affect creativity. Thus, managers need to allot these resources carefully.

Videogame maker Electronic Arts (EA) created an on-site labyrinth to help employees unleash their creative potential. EA encourages video and computer game developers to wander the maze when their creativity levels are running low. While walking the maze, they can think about their challenges in divergent ways for designing innovative products.

- *Work-group features.* In Chapter 5, our discussion of group composition and diversity concluded that diverse groups were likely to come up with more creative solutions. In addition to ensuring a diverse group of people, team members need to share excitement about the goal, must be willing to support each other through difficult periods, and must recognize one another's unique knowledge and perspectives.

- *Supervisory encouragement.* To sustain passion, most people need to feel that what they are doing matters to others. Managers can reward, collaborate, and communicate to nurture the creativity of individuals and teams.

- *Organizational support.* Creativity-supporting organizations reward creativity, and also make sure that there is information sharing and collaboration. They make sure that negative political problems do not get out of control.

Five organizational factors have been found that can block your creativity at work:

- *Expected evaluation.* Focusing on how your work is going to be evaluated.

- *Surveillance.* Being watched while you are working.

- *External motivators.* Focusing on external, tangible rewards.

- *Competition.* Facing win-lose situations with peers.

- *Constrained choice.* Being given limits on how you can do your work.[75]

WHAT ABOUT ETHICS IN DECISION MAKING?

At the Pan Asia Footwear Public Company in Thailand, managers set quotas in order to keep productivity high.[76] The difficulty, as one inspector points out, is "Shoes with complex details sometimes can't be finished in eight hours. This means that staff might work 10 hours for an eight-hour wage." The company does not pay overtime when this happens, because the employee has not met the quota on time. Employees are not paid by the hour. They simply receive a flat fee for a day's work. How can we determine whether this is an ethical practice by the company?

6 What is ethics and how can it be used for better decision making?

ethics The study of moral values or principles that guide our behaviour and inform us whether actions are right or wrong.

No contemporary discussion of decision making would be complete without the inclusion of ethics, because ethical considerations should be an important criterion in organizational decision making. **Ethics** is the study of moral values or principles that guide our behaviour and inform us whether actions are right or wrong. Ethical principles help us "do the right thing." In this final section, we present three ways to frame decisions ethically and examine the factors that shape an individual's ethical decision-making behaviour. We also examine organizational responses to the demand for ethical behaviour, as well as consideration of ethical decisions when doing business in other cultures. To learn more about your ethical decision-making approach, see the *Ethical Dilemma Exercise* on page 326. To consider the extent to which ethical decision making blurs the lines between work and personal life, see *Case Incident—Bankers' Excess Gets Them Fired* on the CD-ROM that accompanies this textbook.

Four Ethical Decision Criteria

utilitarianism A decision focused on outcomes or consequences that emphasizes the greatest good for the greatest number.

An individual can use four different criteria in making ethical choices.[77] The first is the *utilitarian* criterion, in which decisions are made solely on the basis of their outcomes or consequences. The goal of **utilitarianism** is to provide the greatest good for the greatest number. This view tends to dominate business decision making. It is consistent with goals such as efficiency, productivity, and high profits. By maximizing profits, for instance, a business executive can argue that he or she is securing the greatest good for the greatest number—as he or she hands out dismissal notices to 15 percent of the employees.

BMO Nesbitt Burns ignored unethical behaviour by an employee because the company stood to gain from the behaviour, as *Focus on Ethics* shows.

BMO Nesbitt Burns
www.bmonesbittburns.com

FOCUS ON **ETHICS**

Making Profits at the Expense of Clients

Can profits really drive unethical decisions?   In spring 2001, BMO Nesbitt Burns in Winnipeg agreed to pay the highest fine in Manitoba securities history ($100 000 plus $60 000 toward investigation costs) after being investigated by the Manitoba Securities Commission, the Investment Dealers Association (IDA), and the Canadian Banking Ombudsman for ignoring unethical behaviour by one of its investment brokers over several years.[78]

These investigations stemmed from continuing complaints about broker Randolph McDuff's behaviour, for which the company took little action. McDuff was first investigated by BMO Nesbitt Burns in March 1999 for trading in clients' accounts without their permission. McDuff admitted he had made unauthorized trades in client accounts; a compliance officer noted that "McDuff did not seem to understand that a client must be contacted prior to a trade being executed." The head of compliance at Nesbitt Burns' head office in Toronto recommended that McDuff be fired.

However, McDuff was not fired. Instead he was fined $2000 and warned that "any further occurrences may result in termination of employment." This was not the first incident of unethical behaviour by McDuff. An internal document dated January 28, 1999, noted, "We have experienced a large increase in the amount of settlements [anticipated and settled]" regarding McDuff.

Nevertheless, Tom Waitt, senior vice-president of BMO Nesbitt Burns' Prairie division and McDuff's supervisor in Manitoba, urged the head office to avoid taking drastic action, and to supervise McDuff closely instead. A memo McDuff wrote to his supervisor in September 1999 may explain why the Winnipeg office was so interested in ignoring his behaviour: "I know there is this great big cloud over my head and that head office wants me out of here. Does head office forget about my contributions to this firm over the years? In addition to providing for more than 15% of the office revenue consistently over the past five years, I have been an advocate of Nesbitt Burns . . . Rookies and marketers are still amazed at my work ethic. Some have said that it inspires them to work harder."

Decision makers, particularly in for-profit organizations, tend to feel safe and comfortable when they use utilitarianism. Many questionable actions can be justified when framed as being in the "best interests" of the organization and stockholders. But many critics of business decision makers argue that this perspective should change because it can result in ignoring the rights of some individuals, particularly those with minority representation in the organizations.[79]

A second ethical criterion is *rights*. This criterion calls on individuals to make decisions consistent with fundamental liberties and privileges as set forth in documents such as the Canadian Charter of Rights and Freedoms. An emphasis on rights in decision making means respecting and protecting the basic rights of individuals, such as the rights to privacy, free speech, and due process. For instance, this criterion would be used to protect whistle-blowers when they report unethical or illegal practices by their organizations to the media or to government agencies on the grounds of their right to free speech.

Canadian Charter of Rights and Freedoms
www.canadianheritage.gc.ca/progs/
pdp-hrp/canada/freedom_e.cfm

Stewart Leibl, president of Perth's, a Winnipeg dry-cleaning chain, is a founding sponsor of the Koats for Kids program. The company's outlets are a drop-off point for no-longer-needed children's coats, which Perth's cleans free of charge before distributing them to children who have no winter coats. Leibl is going beyond utilitarian criteria when he says, "We all have a responsibility to contribute to the society that we live in." He is also looking at social justice.

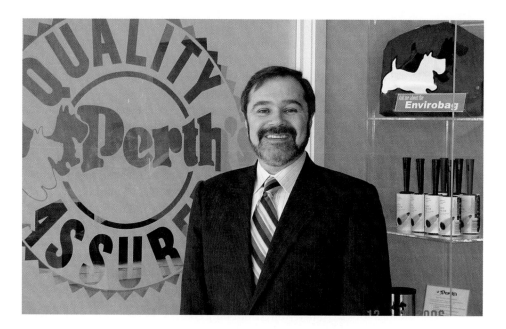

A third ethical criterion is *justice*. This criterion requires individuals to impose and enforce rules fairly and impartially so there is an equitable distribution of benefits and costs. Union members typically favour this criterion. It justifies paying people the same wage for a given job, regardless of performance differences, and it uses seniority as the primary determination in making layoff decisions. A focus on justice protects the interests of the underrepresented and less powerful, but it can encourage a sense of entitlement that reduces risk-taking, innovation, and productivity.

A fourth ethical criterion is *care*. The ethics of care can be stated as follows: "The morally correct action is the one that expresses care in protecting the special relationships that individuals have with each other."[80] Care as an ethical criterion came out of feminist literature[81] to address the idea that the male-dominated view of ethics was too impersonal and ignored the relationships among individuals.[82] The care criterion suggests that individuals should be aware of the needs, desires, and well-being of those to whom they are closely connected. Recent research does not suggest that men and women differ in their use of justice vs. care in making decisions.[83] However, this criterion does remind us of the difficulty of being impartial in all decisions.

Factors That Influence Ethical Decision-Making Behaviour

✳ *Why do some people make more ethical decisions than others?*

What accounts for unethical behaviour in organizations? Is it immoral individuals or work environments that promote unethical activity? The answer is *both!* The evidence indicates that ethical or unethical actions are largely a function of both the individual's characteristics and the environment in which he or she works.[84] The model in Exhibit 9-6 on page 315 illustrates factors affecting ethical decision making and emphasizes three factors: stage of moral development, locus of control, and the organizational environment.

Stages of Moral Development

stages of moral development
The developmental stages that explain a person's capacity to judge what is morally right.

Stages of moral development assess a person's capacity to judge what is morally right.[85] Research suggests that there are three levels of moral development, and each level has two stages.[86] The higher one's moral development, the less dependent he or she is on outside influences and thus the more he or she will be predisposed to behave ethically. The first level is the preconventional level, the second is the conventional

EXHIBIT 9-6 Factors Affecting Ethical Decision-Making Behaviour

level, and the highest level is the principled level. These levels and their stages are described in Exhibit 9-7.

The research indicates that people proceed through the stages one step at a time, though they do not necessarily reach the highest stage.[87] Most adults are at a mid-level of moral development—they are strongly influenced by peers and will follow an organization's rules and procedures. Those individuals who have progressed to the higher stages place increased value on the rights of others, regardless of the majority's opinion, and are likely to challenge organizational practices they personally believe are wrong. Those at the higher stages are most likely to make ethical decisions using the criteria of rights, justice, and care, which we discuss earlier.

Locus of Control

Research indicates that people with an external *locus of control* (that is, they believe their lives are controlled by outside forces, such as luck or chance) are less likely to take

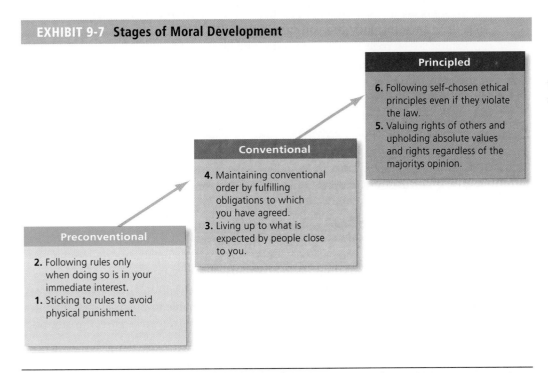

EXHIBIT 9-7 Stages of Moral Development

Principled

6. Following self-chosen ethical principles even if they violate the law.
5. Valuing rights of others and upholding absolute values and rights regardless of the majority's opinion.

Conventional

4. Maintaining conventional order by fulfilling obligations to which you have agreed.
3. Living up to what is expected by people close to you.

Preconventional

2. Following rules only when doing so is in your immediate interest.
1. Sticking to rules to avoid physical punishment.

Source: Based on L. Kohlberg, "Moral Stages and Moralization: The Cognitive-Developmental Approach," in *Moral Development and Behaviour: Theory, Research, and Social Issues,* ed. T. Lickona (New York: Holt, Rinehart and Winston, 1976), pp. 34–35.

responsibility for the consequences of their behaviour and are more likely to rely on external influences to determine their behaviour. Those with an internal locus of control (they believe they are responsible for their destinies), on the other hand, are more likely to rely on their own internal standards of right and wrong to guide their behaviour.

Organizational Environment

The *organizational environment* refers to an employee's perception of organizational expectations. Does the organizational culture encourage and support ethical behaviour by rewarding it or discourage unethical behaviour by punishing it? Characteristics of an organizational environment that are likely to foster high ethical decision making include written codes of ethics; high moral behaviour by senior management; realistic performance expectations; performance appraisals that evaluate means as well as ends; visible recognition and promotions for individuals who display high moral behaviour; and visible punishment for those who act unethically. An organization that has policies to protect **whistle-blowers**—individuals who report unethical practices to the press or government agencies—also makes it possible for people to speak out if they observe questionable activities. WestJet, for example, as discussed in this chapter's *CBC Video Case Incident*, introduced a whistle-blowing policy after being taken to court by Air Canada and Jetsgo for questionable practices. Unfortunately, many people who speak out against irregularities end up being punished for doing so, which is why strong company policies are necessary.

In summary, people who lack a strong moral sense are much less likely to make unethical decisions if they are constrained by an organizational environment that frowns on such behaviours. Conversely, righteous individuals can be corrupted by an organizational environment that permits or encourages unethical practices. In the next section, we consider how to formulate an ethical decision.

whistle-blowers   Individuals who report unethical practices by their employers to outsiders.

Corporate Espionage in the Canadian Airline Industry

Making Ethical Decisions

While there are no clear-cut ways to differentiate ethical from unethical decision making, there are some questions you should consider.

Exhibit 9-8 on page 317 illustrates a decision tree to guide ethical decisions. This tree is built on three of the ethical decision criteria—utilitarianism, rights, and justice—presented earlier. The first question you need to answer addresses self-interest vs. organizational goals.

The second question concerns the rights of other parties. If the decision violates the rights of someone else (his or her right to privacy, for instance), then the decision is unethical.

The final question that needs to be addressed relates to whether the decision conforms to standards of equity and justice. The department head who raises the performance evaluation of a favoured employee and lowers the evaluation of a disfavoured employee—and then uses these evaluations to justify giving the former a big raise and nothing to the latter—has treated the disfavoured employee unfairly.

Unfortunately, the answers to the questions in Exhibit 9-8 are often argued in ways to make unethical decisions seem ethical. Powerful people, for example, can become very adept at explaining self-serving behaviours in terms of the organization's best interests. Similarly, they can persuasively argue that unfair actions are really fair and just. Our point is that immoral people can justify almost any behaviour. Those who are powerful, articulate, and persuasive are the most likely to be able to get away with unethical actions successfully. When faced with an ethical dilemma, try to answer the questions in Exhibit 9-8 truthfully.

Organizational Response to Demands for Ethical Behaviour

During the 1990s, an explosion in the demand for more ethics occurred in Canada and the United States. A second explosion occurred in 2002, after the Enron, WorldCom, and

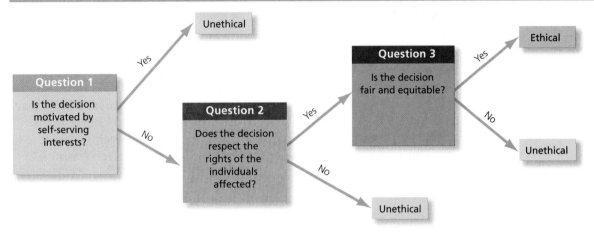

EXHIBIT 9-8   Is a Decision Ethical?

Source: Based on G. F. Cavanagh, D. J. Moberg, and M. Valasquez, "The Ethics of Organizational Politics," *Academy of Management Journal,* June 1981, pp. 363–374.

other accounting scandals. In Canada, more than 120 ethics specialists now offer services as in-house moral arbitrators, mediators, watchdogs, and listening posts. Some work at Canada's largest corporations, including the CIBC, Canada Post, Magna International, Royal Bank of Canada, and McDonald's Canada. These corporate ethics officers hear about issues such as colleagues making phone calls on company time, managers yelling at their employees, product researchers being asked to fake data to meet a deadline, or a company wanting to terminate a contract because the costs are higher than antici-pated. Ethics professor Wayne Norman of the Université de Montréal believes that ethics officers are a positive trend, noting, "all sorts of studies show the companies that take ethics seriously tend to be more successful."[88]

Many corporations are also developing codes of ethics. For example, about 60 per-cent of Canada's 650 largest corporations have some sort of ethics code.[89] Having a cor-porate ethics policy is not enough; employees must be instructed in how to follow the policy. Yet only about 39 percent of Canadian firms provided training in ethical decision making in 2000, although this was up from 21 percent in 1997. While no comparable Canadian data are available, a survey of employees in US businesses with ethics codes found that 75 percent of those surveyed had observed ethical or legal violations in the previous 12 months, including deceptive sales practices, unsafe working conditions, sexual harassment, conflicts of interest, and environmental violations.[90] Companies with codes of ethics may not do enough monitoring. For instance, David Nitkin, president of Toronto-based EthicScan Canada, an ethics consultancy, notes that "only about 15% of [larger Canadian corporations with codes of ethics] have designated an ethics officer or ombuds-man" or provide an ethics hotline, and that less than 10 percent offer whistle-blower protection.[91] *OB in Action—Developing a Meaningful Code of Ethics* shows how to implement codes of ethics in organizations.

Only 14 percent of companies evaluate their ethics-related performance, suggesting that most are not focused on improving

Canada Post
www.canadapost.ca

McDonald's Canada
www.mcdonalds.ca

OB IN ACTION

Developing a Meaningful Code of Ethics

→ Clearly **state basic principles** and expectations.

→ Realistically **focus on potential ethical dilem-mas** that employees face.

→ **Distribute** the **code** to all employees.

→ **Train individuals** so that they understand the code.

→ **Enforce penalties** for violating the code.

Source: Based on W. E. Stead, D. L. Worrell, and J. G. Stead, "An Integrative Model for Understanding and Managing Ethical Behavior in Business Organizations," *Journal of Business Ethics* 9, no. 3 (March 1990), pp. 233–242.

ethics in the workplace.[92] However, a small group of companies is even starting a new trend in monitoring ethical practices, hiring an ethical auditor, much as they would hire a financial auditor. The ethical auditor is hired to "double-check an organization's perception of its own morals."[93] Vancouver City Savings Credit Union (Vancity), Bell Canada, Tetra Pak, British Telecom, the University of Toronto, and The Body Shop have all brought in ethical auditors.

Another way to encourage ethical behaviour is to create mechanisms that encourage employees to speak up when they see wrongdoing. Toronto-based BBDO Canada encourages "candour moments." Employees are empowered "to call each other on behaviour that goes against company values, even junior employees who want to be candid with managers," says the ad agency's president and CEO, Gerry Frascione.[94]

What About National Culture?

We have already shown that there are differences between Canada and the United States in the legal treatment of ethics violations and the creation of an ethical corporate culture. However, it is important to note that what is considered unethical in one country may not be viewed similarly in another country. The reason is that there are no global ethical standards. Contrasts between Asia and the West provide an illustration.[95] In Japan, people doing business together often exchange gifts, even expensive ones. This is part of Japanese tradition. When North American and European companies started doing business in Japan, most North American executives were not aware of the Japanese tradition of exchanging gifts and wondered whether this was a form of bribery. Most have come to accept this tradition now and have even set different limits on gift giving in Japan from other countries.[96]

In another instance illustrating the differences between Asia and North America, a manager of a large US company that operates in China caught an employee stealing. Following company policy, she fired the employee and turned him over to the local authorities for his act. Later she discovered, much to her horror, that the former employee had been executed for the theft.[97] These examples indicate that standards for ethical behaviour and the consequences of particular acts are not universally similar. The fact that standards for ethical behaviour and the consequences of particular acts are not universal presents a variety of problems for those doing business in other countries.

BBDO Canada
www.bbdo.ca

United Parcel Service (UPS) Canada
www.ups.com/canada/
engindex.html

United Parcel Service (UPS) Canada, based in Fredericton, New Brunswick, wants to make sure that its employees approach ethical dilemmas with the confidence to make the right decisions. Therefore, the company conducts an ethics training program for all of its employees, from senior managers to service providers.

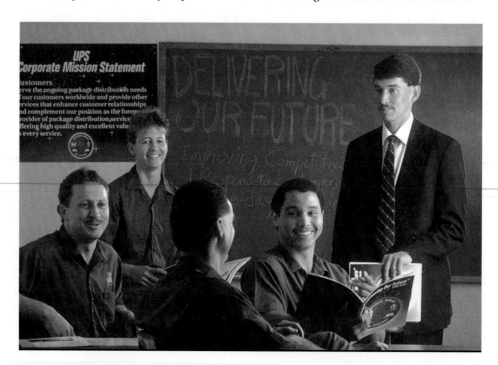

Companies operating branches in foreign countries are faced with tough decisions about how to conduct business under ethical standards that differ from those in Canada. For instance, Canadian companies must decide whether they want to operate in countries such as China, Burma, and Nigeria, which abuse human rights. Although the Canadian government permits investing in these countries, it also encourages companies to act ethically.

While ethical standards may seem ambiguous in the West, criteria defining right and wrong are actually much clearer in the West than in Asia. John McWilliams, senior vice-president, general counsel, and secretary for Calgary-based Nexen, notes that requests for bribes are not necessarily direct: "Usually, they don't say, 'Give me X thousands of dollars and you've got the deal.' It's a lot more subtle than that."[98] Michael Davies, vice-president and general counsel for Mississauga-based General Electric Canada, offers an example: "A payment [is] made to an administrative official to do the job that he's supposed to do. In other words, you pay a fellow over the counter $10 when you're in the airport in Saudi Arabia to get on the flight you're supposed to get on, because, otherwise, he's going to keep you there for two days."

Bribing foreign public officials is widespread. The US government reported that between 1994 and 2001, bribery was uncovered in more than 400 competitions for international contracts.[99] The need for global organizations to establish ethical principles for decision makers in all countries may be critical if high standards are to be upheld and if consistent practices are to be achieved.

Nexen
www.nexeninc.com

General Electric Canada
www.ge.com/ca

CORPORATE SOCIAL RESPONSIBILITY

In 1999 Nike gave a $7.7 million (US) grant to the International Youth Foundation (IYF) to establish an organization called the Global Alliance for Workers and Communities.[100] Global Alliance, founded to improve working conditions in overseas factories, has been critical of Nike, publishing a report in 2001 on abuses in Indonesian factories making Nike products. "Verbal abuse was the most marked, with 30 percent of the workers having personally experienced and 56 percent having observed the problem. An average of 7 percent of workers reported receiving unwelcome sexual comments and 3 percent reported being physically abused," the report said.

Nike admitted that it was unaware of these problems when the 2001 report was published. The company has since increased training for both managers and employees at its overseas facilities to avoid some of the abuses in the factories, and a 2003 report noted significant progress.[101] Maria Eitel, the company's vice-president for corporate responsibility, says: "The factory managers are telling us that as they increase their work around social responsibility, they are seeing improvements." To what extent should companies be held socially responsible?

Corporate social responsibility is defined as an organization's responsibility to consider the impact of its decisions on society. Thus, organizations may try to better society, through such things as charitable contributions or providing better wages to employees working in offshore factories. Organizations may engage in these practices because they feel pressured by society to do so, or they may seek ways to improve society because they feel it is the right thing to do.

7 What is corporate social responsibility?

corporate social responsibility
An organization's responsibility to consider the impact of its decisions on society.

Eighty percent of Canadians feel that Ottawa should establish standards for corporate social responsibility and require corporations to report on how they are meeting guidelines, according to a recent survey.[102] Many Canadian companies are feeling the pressure to demonstrate social responsibility as well. The Environics Group recently found that 49 percent of the 25 000 consumers interviewed worldwide made product decisions on the basis of companies' social responsibility.[103] This exceeded the 40 percent who made decisions based on brand quality and reputation. Moreover, 23 percent said they had punished a company in the previous year for not meeting what they thought were its social obligations.

Not everyone agrees with the position of organizations assuming social responsibility. For example, economist Milton Friedman remarked in *Capitalism and Freedom* that "few trends could so thoroughly undermine the very foundations of our free society as the acceptance by corporate officials of a social responsibility other than to make as much money for their stockholders as possible."[104]

Joel Bakan, professor of law at the University of British Columbia, author of *The Corporation*,[105] and co-director of the documentary of the same name, is more critical of organizations than Friedman, though he finds that current laws support corporate behaviour that some might find troubling. Bakan suggests that today's corporations have many of the same characteristics as a psychopathic personality (self-interested, lacking empathy, manipulative, and reckless in their disregard of others). Bakan notes that even though companies have a tendency to act psychopathically, this is not why they are fixated on profits. Rather, the only legal responsibility corporations have is to maximize organizational profits for stockholders. He suggests more laws and more restraints need to be put in place if corporations are to behave with more social responsibility, as current laws direct corporations to be responsible to their shareholders and make little mention of responsibility toward other stakeholders.

Interestingly enough, a recent study shows that MBA students change their views about social responsibility during the course of their program.[106] Students from 13 international business schools, including the Richard Ivey School of Business at the University of Western Ontario and the Schulich School of Business at York University, were asked at the beginning and the end of their MBA programs about their attitudes toward corporate social responsibility. At the start of their program, 40 percent reported that one of the primary responsibilities of a company is to produce useful, high quality goods and services. By the time the students graduated, only 30 percent of them thought this was a valuable corporate goal. Instead, 75 percent of the students suggested that a company's primary responsibility was to maximize shareholder value.

Some Canadian companies do practise social responsibility, however. Both Vancouver-based Vancity and Bolton, Ontario-based Husky Injection Molding Systems have "taken comprehensive steps to include customer, employee, community and environmental concerns in both long-term planning and day-to-day decision making."[107] Vancity's electronic banking arm, Citizens Bank, has an "Ethical Policy," which states, for instance, that the bank is against excessive environmental harm and will not do business with companies that either violate the fundamental rights of children or are involved in weapons.[108] This chapter's *Case Incident—Syncrude Wants to Be a Good Neighbour* on page 327 describes a socially responsible approach to running a business located near an Aboriginal community. For more on the debate about social responsibility vs. concentrating on the bottom line, see this chapter's *Point/Counterpoint* on page 323.

Vancity
www.vancity.com

Husky Injection Molding Systems
www.husky.ca

SUMMARY AND IMPLICATIONS

SNAPSHOT SUMMARY

1 How Should Decisions Be Made?
The Rational Decision-Making Process

➤

1 Is there a right way to make decisions? The rational decision-making model describes the six steps individuals take to make decisions: (1) Define the problem, (2) identify the criteria, (3) allocate weights to the criteria, (4) develop alternatives, (5) evaluate the alternatives, and (6) select the best alternative. This is an ideal model, and not every decision thoroughly follows these steps.

2 How do people actually make decisions? Most decisions in the real world do not follow the rational model. For instance, people are usually content to find an acceptable or reasonable solution to their problem rather than an optimizing one. Thus decision makers may rely on bounded rationality, satisficing, intuition, and judgment shortcuts in making decisions.

3 What factors affect group decision making? Groups generate more complete information and knowledge, they offer increased diversity of views, they generate higher quality decisions, and they lead to increased acceptance of a solution. However, group decisions are time-consuming. They also lead to conformity pressures, and the group discussion can be dominated by one or a few members. Finally, group decisions suffer from ambiguous responsibility, and the responsibility of any single member is watered down.

4 Should the leader make the decision or encourage the group to participate? The revised leader-participation model uses a decision tree to determine whether a leader should make a decision alone or incorporate some level of group participation. The major factors considered in the model include the quality of the decision required, the degree of commitment needed from participants, and the time available to make the decision.

5 How can we get more creative decisions? While there is some evidence that individuals vary in their ability to be creative, we also know that individuals are more creative when they are motivated by intrinsic interest, challenge, task satisfaction, and self-set goals. Five organizational factors have been found that can block creativity at work: (1) *expected evaluation*—focusing on how work is going to be evaluated; (2) *surveillance*—being watched while working; (3) *external motivators*—emphasizing external, tangible rewards; (4) *competition*—facing win-lose situations with peers; and (5) *constrained choice*—being given limits on how to do the work.

6 What is ethics and how can it be used for better decision making? Ethics is the study of moral values or principles that guide our behaviour and inform us whether actions are right or wrong. Ethical principles help us "do the right thing." An individual can use four different criteria in making ethical choices. The first is the *utilitarian* criterion, in which decisions are made solely on the basis of their outcomes or consequences. The second is *rights*; this ethical criterion focuses on respecting and protecting the basic rights of individuals. The third is *justice*; this ethical criterion requires individuals to impose and enforce rules fairly and impartially so there is an equitable distribution of benefits and costs. The fourth is *care*; this ethical criterion suggests that we should be aware of the needs, desires, and well-being of those to whom we are closely connected. There are advantages and disadvantages to each of these criteria.

7 What is corporate social responsibility? Corporate social responsibility is defined as an organization's responsibility to consider the impact of its decisions on society. Thus, organizations may try to better society, through such things as charitable contributions or providing better wages to employees working in offshore factories. Organizations may engage in these practices because they feel pressured by society to do so, or they may seek ways to improve society because they feel it is the right thing to do.

For Review

1. What is the rational decision-making model? Under what conditions is it applicable?

2. Describe organizational factors that might constrain decision makers.

3. What role does intuition play in effective decision making?

4. What is groupthink? What is its effect on decision-making quality?

5. What is groupshift? What is its effect on decision-making quality?

6. Identify five organizational factors that block creativity at work.

7. Describe the four criteria that individuals can use in making ethical decisions.

8. Are unethical decisions more a function of the individual decision maker or the decision maker's work environment? Explain.

9. What is corporate social responsibility, and why do companies engage in it?

For Critical Thinking

1. "For the most part, individual decision making in organizations is an irrational process." Do you agree or disagree? Discuss.

2. What factors do you think differentiate good decision makers from poor ones? Relate your answer to the six-step rational decision-making model.

3. Have you ever increased your commitment to a failed course of action? If so, analyze the follow-up decision to increase your commitment and explain why you behaved as you did.

4. If group decisions consistently achieve better-quality outcomes than those achieved by individuals, how did the phrase "a camel is a horse designed by a committee" become so popular and ingrained in our culture?

OB for You

- In some decision situations, you might consider following the rational decision-making model. This will ensure that you examine a wider variety of options before committing to a particular decision.

- Analyze decision situations and be aware of your biases. We all bring biases to the decisions we make. Combine rational analysis with intuition. As you gain experience, you should feel increasingly confident in using your intuition with your rational analysis.

- Use creativity-stimulation techniques. You can improve your overall decision-making effectiveness by searching for innovative solutions to problems. This can be as basic as telling yourself to think creatively and to look specifically for unique alternatives.

- When making decisions, you should consider their ethical implications. A quick way to do this is to ask yourself: Would I be embarrassed if this action were printed on the front page of the local newspaper?

POINT

COUNTERPOINT

Organizations Should Just Stick to the Bottom Line

The major goals of organizations are and should be efficiency, productivity, and high profits. By maximizing profits, businesses ensure that they will survive and thus make it possible to provide employment. Doing so is in the best interests of the organization, employees, and stockholders. Moreover, it is up to individuals to show that they are concerned about the environment through their investment and purchasing activities, not for corporations to lead the way.

Let's examine some of the reasons why it is not economically feasible to place all of the burden of protecting the environment on the shoulders of big business.

Studies show that environmental regulations are too costly. The Conference Board of Canada has suggested that environmental regulations cost Canadian companies $580 million to $600 million a year.[109] The Fraser Institute in Vancouver reported that all regulations, including those designed to protect the environment, cost Canadian industry $103 billion a year.[110] Environmental regulations can also be harmful to jobs. In British Columbia, the Forest Practices Code is said to have added $1 billion a year to harvesting costs and resulted in a number of job cuts.

While businesses are concerned with the high cost that results from environmental regulations, the general public is not completely supportive of protecting the environment either, particularly if it will inconvenience them.[111]

Companies would be better off sticking to the bottom line, and governments should stay away from imposing costly environmental regulations on business. Stringent environmental standards cause trade distortions, and governments rarely consider the cost of complying with regulations. Companies should be allowed to take their lead from shareholders and customers. If these constituencies want businesses to pay for environmental protection, they will indicate this by investing in firms that do so. Until they do, the cost of environmental legislation is simply too high.

Environmental Responsibility Is Part of the Bottom Line

Going green makes good economic sense. The studies reported in the *Point* argument tend to overstate the cost of environmental regulations.[112] They do not consider the benefits to society of those regulations.

A closer look at a few companies that have devoted efforts to being more environmentally friendly will illustrate the benefits of this approach. When the Quaker Oats Company of Canada started working toward a "greener" work environment, its plant in Peterborough, Ontario, saved more than $1 million in three years through various environmental initiatives.[113] As another example, Toronto-based Inco spent $600 million to change the way it produces nickel at its Sudbury, Ontario, operations in order to be less devastating to the local environment. Its smelting process is one of the most energy efficient and environmentally friendly in the world. Inco continues to work to restore the appearance of Sudbury. Trees have grown back, the wildlife has returned, and the air is clean. Sudbury has even been listed as one of the 10 most desirable places to live in Canada. While Inco invested a lot of money to change its production process, Doug Hamilton, controller at Inco's Ontario division in Sudbury, has said, "Our Sulphur Dioxide Abatement Program was an awesome undertaking. Not only did this investment allow us to capture 90 percent of the sulphur in the ore we mine, but the new processes save the company $90 million a year in production costs. That strikes me as a pretty smart investment."[114] London, Ontario-based 3M Canada started a Pollution Prevention Pays (3P) program more than 20 years ago.[115] The program emphasizes stopping pollution at the source to avoid the expense and effort of cleaning it up or treating it after the fact. The recycling program at 3M Canada's tape plant in Perth, Ontario, reduced its waste by 96 percent and saved the company about $650 000 annually. The capital cost for the program was only $30 000.

The examples of Quaker Oats, Inco, and 3M show that companies that are environmentally friendly have an advantage over their competitors. If organizations control their pollution costs better than their competitors, they will use their resources more efficiently and therefore increase profitability.

LEARNING ABOUT **YOURSELF** EXERCISE

Decision-Making Style Questionnaire

Circle the response that comes closest to the way you usually feel or act. There are no right or wrong responses to any of these items.

1. I am more careful about
    a. people's feelings   **b.** their rights

2. I usually get along better with
    a. imaginative people   **b.** realistic people

3. It is a higher compliment to be called
    a. a person of real feeling   **b.** a consistently reasonable person

4. In doing something with other people, it appeals more to me
    a. to do it in the accepted way   **b.** to invent a way of my own

5. I get more annoyed at
    a. fancy theories   **b.** people who do not like theories

6. It is higher praise to call someone
    a. a person of vision   **b.** a person of common sense

7. I more often let
    a. my heart rule my head   **b.** my head rule my heart

8. I think it is a worse fault
    a. to show too much warmth   **b.** to be unsympathetic

9. If I were a teacher, I would rather teach
    a. courses involving theory   **b.** factual courses

Which word in the following pairs appeals to you more? Circle *a* or *b*.

10. **a.** Compassion   **b.** Foresight

11. **a.** Justice   **b.** Mercy

12. **a.** Production   **b.** Design

13. **a.** Gentle   **b.** Firm

14. **a.** Uncritical   **b.** Critical

15. **a.** Literal   **b.** Figurative

16. **a.** Imaginative   **b.** Matter-of-fact

Scoring Key:

Mark each of your responses on the following scales. Then use the point value column to arrive at your score. For example, if you answered *a* to the first question, you would check *1a* in the Feeling column. This response receives zero points when you add up the point value column. Instructions for classifying your scores are indicated following the scales.

Sensation	Point Value	Intuition	Point Value	Thinking	Point Value	Feeling	Point Value
2b _____	1	2a _____	2	1b _____	1	1a _____	0
4a _____	1	4b _____	1	3b _____	2	3a _____	1
5a _____	1	5b _____	1	7b _____	1	7a _____	1
6b _____	1	6a _____	0	8a _____	0	8b _____	1
9b _____	2	9a _____	2	10b _____	2	10a _____	1
12a _____	1	12b _____	0	11a _____	2	11b _____	1
15a _____	1	15b _____	1	13b _____	1	13a _____	1
16b _____	2	16a _____	0	14b _____	0	14a _____	1

Maximum Point Value	(10)		(7)		(9)		(7)

Circle *Intuition* if your Intuition score is equal to or greater than your Sensation score. Circle *Sensation* if your Sensation score is greater than your Intuition score. Circle *Feeling* if your Feeling score is greater than your Thinking score. Circle *Thinking* if your Thinking score is greater than your Feeling score.

A high score on *Intuition* indicates you see the world in holistic terms. You tend to be creative. A high score on *Sensation* indicates that you are realistic and see the world in terms of facts. A high score on *Feeling* means you make decisions based on gut feeling. A high score on *Thinking* indicates a highly logical and analytical approach to decision making.

Source: Based on a personality scale developed by D. Hellriegel, J. Slocum, and R. W. Woodman, *Organizational Behavior,* 3rd ed. (St. Paul, MN: West Publishing, 1983), pp. 127–141, and reproduced in J. M. Ivancevich and M. T. Matteson, *Organizational Behavior and Management,* 2nd ed. (Homewood, IL: BPI/Irwin, 1990), pp. 538–539.

BREAKOUT **GROUP** EXERCISES

Form small groups to discuss the following topics, as assigned by your instructor:

1. Apply the rational decision-making model to deciding where your group might eat dinner this evening. How closely were you able to follow the rational model in making this decision?

2. The company that makes your favourite snack product has been accused of being weak in its social responsibility efforts. What impact will this have on your purchase of any more products from that company?

3. You have seen a classmate cheat on an exam or an assignment. Do you do something about this or ignore it?

WORKING WITH **OTHERS** EXERCISE

The Lifeboat Exercise

1. Your ship has crashed. Luckily your group has found a lifeboat. However there are 10 people who are currently surrounding your lifeboat and asking to join you. Unfortunately, your lifeboat has room for only 3 additional people beyond those in your group. (If you have 6 people in your group, your boat can fit 9, etc.)

continued

2. Here is what you know about the 10 people surrounding your lifeboat:

An elderly couple

A newlywed couple

A 7-year-old child

A minister

A doctor

A naval officer

A man in his 30s

A wounded woman

3. As a group, decide what to do with the 10 people. How would you arrive at your decision? What ethical criteria would you use to make your decision?

Source: Unknown.

ETHICAL **DILEMMA** EXERCISE

Five Ethical Decisions: What Would You Do?

Assume you are a middle manager in a company with about 1000 employees. How would you respond to each of the following situations?

1. You are negotiating a contract with a potentially very large customer whose representative has hinted that you could almost certainly be assured of getting his business if you gave him and his wife an all-expenses-paid cruise to the Caribbean. You know the representative's employer would not approve of such a "payoff," but you have the discretion to authorize such an expenditure. What would you do?

2. You have the opportunity to steal $100 000 from your company with absolute certainty that you would not be detected or caught. Would you do it?

3. Your company policy on reimbursement for meals while travelling on company business is that you will be repaid for your out-of-pocket costs, which are not to exceed $50 a day. You do not need receipts for these expenses—the company will take your word. When travelling, you tend to eat at fast-food places and rarely spend more than $15 a day. Most of your colleagues submit reimbursement requests in the range of $45 to $50 a day regardless of what their actual expenses are. How much would you request for your meal reimbursements?

4. You want to get feedback from people who are using one of your competitor's products. You believe you will get much more honest responses from these people if you disguise the identity of your company. Your boss suggests you contact possible participants by using the fictitious name of the Consumer Marketing Research Corporation. What would you do?

5. You have discovered that one of your closest friends at work has stolen a large sum of money from the company. Would you do nothing? Go directly to an executive to report the incident before talking about it with the offender? Confront the individual before taking action? Make contact with the individual with the goal of persuading that person to return the money?

6. You are in the process of hiring a new assistant, and your number-one client in terms of dollar value in sales has suggested that his sister-in-law would be ideal for the job. You have interviewed her, but believe that another candidate you interviewed is better qualified. You are concerned that if you don't hire the client's sister-in-law, however, you may lose some or all of your client's business.

Source: Several of these scenarios are based on D. R. Altany, "Torn Between Halo and Horns," *IndustryWeek*, March 15, 1993, pp. 15–20.

CASE INCIDENT

Syncrude Wants to Be a Good Neighbour

Fort McMurray, Alberta-based Syncrude is "the largest non-governmental employer of Aboriginal people in Canada." The company, the largest producer of light sweet crude oil from oil sand, is strongly committed to working with the Aboriginal community. According to Syncrude's website, "Commitment to the Aboriginal people of our region is not only motivated by our responsibility as a good corporate citizen, but by our desire to be a good neighbour."

In order to make sure that members of the Aboriginal community are employable, Syncrude provides them with skill training before they are even considered for hiring. This makes it possible for Aboriginal people to compete for jobs in the oil sands industry on an equal footing with nonAboriginal people. Nora Flett, Syncrude's Aboriginal development program coordinator, explains that companies cannot just hire Aboriginal people directly without training, "because you don't just take someone from a small community, put them in a big corporation environment and expect that people will survive there, because that's quite a bit of a culture shock."

In addition to being sensitive to the employment needs of the Aboriginal community, Syncrude is committed to being a good neighbour in the community. The company gives preference to local suppliers to help the local population benefit economically from Syncrude's presence. Syncrude supports literacy programs for schools. As well, employment counsellors offer advice about the company, helping Aboriginal families learn about the company and what is expected of its employees.

Questions

1. What benefits do you think Syncrude might derive from being a good neighbour in Fort McMurray?

2. Should the company engage in practices that help the Aboriginal community, even if it means that the return to shareholders is not as large?

3. How does social responsibility explain what Syncrude does?

Sources: A. Kellogg, "Punch the Query 'Canada's Best Major Corporate Citizen' into Google on Your Computer and It's Likely the Image of Eric Newell Will Pop Up," *Calgary Herald,* November 30, 2003, p. C2; C. Petten, "Syncrude, Cameco Strike Gold With PAR," *Windspeaker,* March 2002, pp. B7–B8; http://www.syncrude.com/community/aboriginal.html; and http://www.syncrude.com/business/business_04.html#4b.

CBC **VIDEO CASE** INCIDENT

Corporate Espionage in the Canadian Airline Industry

Sneaky moves, claims of corporate espionage, and shredded documents. This is not a fictitious spy thriller, but a true story of rivalry in the Canadian airline business. The companies involved are Air Canada, its arch enemy WestJet Airlines, and rival Jetsgo. All were locked in a ruthless battle for passengers.

The story began when one of the founders of WestJet, Mark Hill, gained access to Air Canada's protected website through a password from a former Air Canada employee. In the website, Hill found information on Air Canada's routes and the number of passengers on planes.

This kind of corporate snooping happens a lot more than people think, especially in high-tech firms, very competitive industries, and industries that are at the cutting edge of development. "Information is power," Hill says. "One of the reasons we were so successful is that we knew more about this business than the other discount airlines that were trying to get going around this time," he adds.

Air Canada might never have known that Hill had accessed its protected website, except a whistle-blower from WestJet tipped Air Canada off. By the time he was revealed, Hill had accessed the website 243 000 times in less than a year.

In another twist in this tale, Air Canada sent private investigators to Hill's home in Victoria, BC, to do a little digging of their own. The investigators dumped all the shredded paper in Hill's garbage into their pickup truck, which caught a neighbour's attention. The neighbour informed the police and Hill. A few weeks later, the private investigators were back for more garbage, but this time Hill was ready for them, with a camera. His pictures showed up on the front page of one of Canada's national newspapers, proof of Air Canada's "dumpster digging."

After Air Canada pieced together the retrieved shredded documents, it launched a $220-million lawsuit against WestJet, accusing it of a malicious attempt to take away business and schedule competing flights. WestJet responded with a countersuit, accusing Air Canada of trespassing and stealing private property. Michel Leblanc, president of the discount airline Jetsgo, claimed some of his company's private documents were also found in Hill's garbage. Jetsgo filed a lawsuit against WestJet for $50 million.

WestJet President Clive Beddoe eventually apologized to his employees and shareholders about the situation. Beddoe said, "I have to take responsibility for this event as I should have known what Mark Hill was doing. Neither I nor the board condone this sort of activity. . . . Furthermore, we have introduced a new corporate whistle-blowing policy . . . we have no intention of letting a situation like this happen again." Hill subsequently resigned from the company.

By the end of May 2006, WestJet and Air Canada had settled their dispute, with WestJet paying $5.5 million for Air Canada's investigation and legal fees, and $10 million to children's charities. Jetsgo filed for bankruptcy in March 2005.

Questions

1. Using the four ethical decision-making criteria (utilitarianism, rights, justice, and care), assess the ethics of WestJet Airlines' and Air Canada's actions.

2. What were the factors influencing ethical or unethical decision-making behaviour of the main characters in this airline saga?

3. What could WestJet do to prevent this type of ruthless, corporate espionage behaviour in the future?

Sources: "Corporate Espionage—Under the Radar," *CBC Venture,* October 31, 2004, VA2085A, 925; M. McClearn, E. Pooley, and J. Gray, "Spy vs. Spy," *Canadian Business,* January 31–February 13, 2005), pp. 32–45; and "Air Canada, WestJet Settle Spying Lawsuit," *CBC News,* May 30, 2006, http://www.cbc.ca/story/business/national/2006/05/29/westjet-aircansettle.html (accessed June 9, 2006).

From **Concepts** to **Skills**

Solving Problems Creatively

You can be more effective at solving problems creatively if you use the following 10 suggestions:[116]

1. *Think of yourself as creative.* Research shows that if you think you can't be creative, you won't be. Believing in your ability to be creative is the first step to becoming more creative.

2. *Pay attention to your intuition.* Every individual has a subconscious mind that works well. Sometimes answers will come to you when you least expect them. Listen to that "inner voice." In fact, most creative people will keep notepads near their beds and write down ideas when the thoughts come to them.

3. *Move away from your comfort zone.* Every individual has a comfort zone in which certainty exists. But creativity and the known often do not mix. To be creative, you need to move away from the status quo and focus your mind on something new.

4. *Determine what you want to do.* This includes such things as taking time to understand a problem before beginning to try to resolve it, getting all the facts in mind, and trying to identify the most important facts.

5. *Think outside the box.* Use analogies whenever possible (e.g., could you approach your problem like a fish out of water and look at what the fish does to cope? Or can you use the things you have to do to find your way when it's foggy to help you solve your problem?). Use different problem-solving strategies, such as verbal, visual, mathematical, or theatrical. Look at your problem from a different perspective or ask yourself what someone else, like your grandmother, might do if faced with the same situation.

6. *Look for ways to do things better.* This may involve trying consciously to be original, not worrying about looking foolish, keeping an open mind, being alert to odd or puzzling facts, thinking of unconventional

ways to use objects and the environment, discarding usual or habitual ways of doing things, and striving for objectivity by being as critical of your own ideas as you would be of someone else's.

7. *Find several right answers.* Being creative means continuing to look for other solutions even when you think you have solved the problem. A better, more creative solution just might be found.

8. *Believe in finding a workable solution.* Like believing in yourself, you also need to believe in your ideas. If you don't think you can find a solution, you probably won't.

9. *Brainstorm with others.* Creativity is not an isolated activity. Bouncing ideas off of others creates a synergistic effect.

10. *Turn creative ideas into action.* Coming up with creative ideas is only part of the process. Once the ideas are generated, they must be implemented. Keeping great ideas in your mind, or on papers that no one will read, does little to expand your creative abilities.

Assessing Skills

After you've read this chapter, take the following Self-Assessments on your enclosed CD-ROM:

    5. How Creative Am I?

    20. What's My Decision-Making Style?

    22. How Do My Ethics Rate?

Practising Skills

Every time the phone rings, your stomach clenches and your palms start to sweat. And it's no wonder! As sales manager for Brinkers, a machine tool parts manufacturer, you are besieged by calls from customers who are upset about late deliveries. Your boss, Carter Hererra, acts as both production manager and scheduler. Every time your sales representatives negotiate a sale, it's up to Carter to determine whether production can actually meet the delivery date the customer specifies. Carter invariably says, "No problem." The good thing about this is that you make a lot of initial sales. The bad news is that production hardly ever meets the shipment dates that Carter authorizes. He doesn't seem to be all that concerned about the aftermath of late deliveries. He says, "Our customers know they're getting outstanding quality at a great price. Just let them try to match that anywhere. It can't be done. So even if they have to wait a couple of extra days or weeks, they're still getting the best deal they can." Somehow the customers do not see it that way, and they let you know about their unhappiness. Then it's up to you to try to smooth over the relationship. You know this problem has to be taken care of, but what possible solutions are there? After all, how are you going to keep from making your manager angry or making the customers angry? Use your knowledge of creative problem solving to come up with solutions.

Reinforcing Skills

1. Take 20 minutes to list as many medical or health-care-related jobs as you can that begin with the letter *r* (for instance, radiologist, registered nurse). If you run out of listings before time is up, it's OK to quit early. But try to be as creative as you can.

2. List on a piece of paper some common terms that apply to both *water* and *finance*. How many were you able to come up with?

CHAPTER 10
Organizational Culture and Change

How does a for-profit Crown corporation with a $7-million deficit get back in the black? Changing its culture is part of the answer.

1 What is the purpose of organizational culture?

2 How do you create and maintain organizational culture?

3 What kind of organizational culture might suit you?

4 Can organizational culture have a downside?

5 How do organizations manage change?

6 Why do people and organizations resist change?

When David Dingwall was appointed president and CEO of the Ottawa-based Royal Canadian Mint in March 2003, the mint was a for-profit Crown corporation that had a $7-million deficit.[1] He described the culture that led to this deficit: "There was no discipline. There was no focus. There was no accountability and there was no transparency." He also noted that there was no urgency in wanting to help customers.

Dingwall noted that business processes "were essentially broken or non-existent. We had a very unprofitable jewellery line business; I'm talking about high-end jewellery that you or I would not buy for our spouses because we'd have to mortgage our house. In our foreign circulation coin we were floundering." Dingwall observed that the organization's culture needed to be changed if it was to become a profitable business.

Although Dingwall resigned amidst controversy in September 2005, he was later cleared of wrongdoing. Most reports reviewing his performance agreed that he had significantly turned around the fortunes of the Mint. Auditor General Sheila Fraser, in her 2005 performance review of the Mint, gave "good marks to management for introducing a 'lean enterprise' initiative to control costs." After completing a government-requested investigation in spring 2006 of the circumstances surrounding Dingwall's severance pay, George Adams, a retired

Ontario Superior Court judge, reported that as head of the Mint, Dingwall "had performed his job well." What did Dingwall do to change the culture of the Mint?

In this chapter, we show that every organization has a culture. We examine how that culture reveals itself and the impact it has on the attitudes and behaviours of members of that organization. An understanding of what makes up an organization's culture and how culture is created, sustained, and learned enhances our ability to explain and predict the behaviour of people at work. We also look at different approaches organizations take to managing change.

WHAT IS ORGANIZATIONAL CULTURE?

When Henry Mintzberg, professor at McGill University and one of the world's leading management experts, was asked to compare organizational structure and corporate culture, he said, "Culture is the soul of the organization—the beliefs and values, and how they are manifested. I think of the structure as the skeleton, and as the flesh and blood. And culture is the soul that holds the thing together and gives it life force."[2]

Mintzberg's metaphor provides a clear image of how to think about culture. Culture provides stability to an organization and gives employees a clear understanding of "the

1. What is the purpose of organizational culture?

Royal Canadian www.mint.ca

Henry Ming.com
www.henr

positive
hes to change?

way things are done around here." Culture sets the tone for how organizations operate and how individuals within the organization interact. Think of the different impressions you have when a receptionist tells you that "Ms. Dettweiler" will be available in a moment, while at another organization you are told that "Emma" will be with you as soon as she gets off the phone. It's clear that in one organization the rules are more formal than in the other.

As we discuss organizational culture, you may want to remember that organizations differ considerably in the cultures they adopt. Consider the different cultures of Calgary-based WestJet Airlines and Montreal-based Air Canada. WestJet is viewed as having a "young, spunky, can-do environment, where customers will have more fun."[3] Air Canada, by contrast, is considered less helpful and friendly. One analyst even suggested that Air Canada staff "tend to make their customers feel stressed" by their confrontational behaviour.[4] Our discussion of culture should help you understand how these differences across organizations occur.

Culture provides stability to an organization and gives employees a clear understanding of "the way things are done around here." It sets the tone for how organizations operate and how individuals within the organization interact. Thus, it has an impact on the employees who work for the firm.

As you start to think about different organizations where you might work, you will want to consider their cultures. An organization that expects employees to work 15 hours a day may not be one in which you would like to work. An understanding of culture might help you discover the firm's expectations before you accept a job, or it might help you understand why you like (or don't like) the college or university you attend.

Below, we propose a specific definition and review several issues that revolve around this definition. *From Concepts to Skills* on pages 363–364 tells you how to read an organization's culture. You may want to complete the *Learning About Yourself Exercise* on page 359, which assesses whether you would be more comfortable in a formal, rule-oriented culture or a more informal, flexible culture.

Definition of Organizational Culture

Organizational culture is the pattern of shared values, beliefs, and assumptions considered appropriate for thinking and acting within an organization. The key features of culture are as follows:

organizational culture
The pattern of shared values, beliefs, and assumptions considered appropriate for thinking and acting within an organization.

- Culture is shared by the members of the organization.
- Culture helps members of the organization solve and understand the things that the organization encounters, both internally and externally.
- Because the assumptions, beliefs, and expectations that make up culture have worked over time, members of the organization believe they are valid. Therefore, they are taught to people who join the organization.
- These assumptions, beliefs, and expectations strongly influence how people perceive, think, feel, and behave within the organization.[5]

Not every group develops a culture, although any group that has existed for a while and has shared learnings will likely have a culture. Groups that experience high turnover (so that learnings are not passed down to new members very effectively) and groups that have not experienced any challenging events may not develop cultures.

Levels of Culture

Because organizational culture has multiple levels,[6] the metaphor of an iceberg has often been used to describe it.[7] However, a simmering volcano may better represent the layers of culture: beliefs, values, assumptions bubble below the surface, producing

WestJet Airlines
www.westjet.com

Air Canada
www.aircanada.com

EXHIBIT 10-1 Layers of Culture

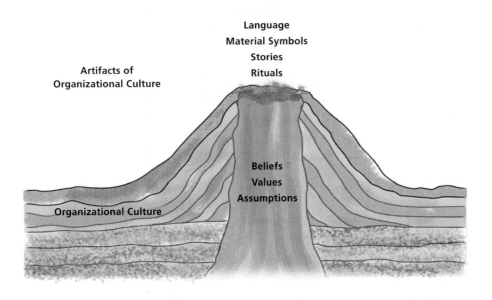

observable aspects of culture at the surface. Exhibit 10-1 reminds us that culture is very visible at the level of **artifacts**. These are what you see, hear, and feel when you encounter an organization's culture. You may notice, for instance, that employees in two offices have very different dress policies, or one office displays great works of art while another posts company mottos on the wall.

Exhibit 10-1 also shows us that beliefs, values, and assumptions, unlike artifacts, are not always readily observable. Instead, we rely on the visible artifacts (material symbols, special language used, rituals carried out, and stories told to others) to help us uncover the organization's beliefs, values, and assumptions. **Beliefs** are the understandings of how objects and ideas relate to each other. **Values** are the stable, long-lasting beliefs about what is important. For instance, Winnipeg-based Palliser Furniture, a

artifacts Aspects of an organization's culture that you see, hear, and feel.

beliefs The understandings of how objects and ideas relate to each other.

values The stable, long-lasting beliefs about what is important.

Montreal-based PEAK Financial Group sends employees to "The Academy," an intensive three-day orientation for all new hires. Afterward, all employees join together in a welcome ceremony, where new employees are asked to give a two-minute speech telling who they are and why they chose to work at PEAK. PEAK's programs make sure that employees feel part of the culture from day one and feel comfortable interacting with one another. Here we see Robert Frances (right), president and CEO, welcoming a new employee during a staff meeting.

manufacturer of wooden and upholstered furniture, promotes the following corporate values: "demonstrating integrity in all relationships, promoting the dignity and value of each other, and striving for excellence."[8] **Assumptions** are the taken-for-granted notions of how something should be. When basic assumptions are held by the entire group, members will have difficulty conceiving of another way of doing things. For instance, in Canada, some students hold a basic assumption that universities should not consider costs when setting tuition but that they should keep tuition low for greater access by students. Beliefs, values, and assumptions, if we can uncover them, help us understand why organizations do the things that we observe.

assumptions The taken-for-granted notions of how something should be.

Characteristics of Culture

Research suggests that seven primary characteristics capture the essence of an organization's culture:[9]

- *Innovation and risk-taking.* The degree to which employees are encouraged to be innovative and take risks.
- *Attention to detail.* The degree to which employees are expected to work with precision, analysis, and attention to detail.
- *Outcome orientation.* The degree to which management focuses on results, or outcomes, rather than on the techniques and processes used to achieve these outcomes.
- *People orientation.* The degree to which management decisions take into consideration the effect of outcomes on people within the organization.
- *Team orientation.* The degree to which work activities are organized around teams rather than individuals.
- *Aggressiveness.* The degree to which people are aggressive and competitive rather than easygoing and supportive.
- *Stability.* The degree to which organizational activities emphasize maintaining the status quo in contrast to growth.

Each of these characteristics exists on a continuum from low to high. For instance, the Royal Canadian Mint, discussed in this chapter's vignette, is high on innovation and risk-taking, and high on people orientation and team orientation. But the Mint is low on stability, as its goal is to be able to move quickly when opportunities arise.

When individuals consider their organizations according to these seven characteristics, they get a composite picture of the organizations' culture. This picture becomes the basis for feelings of shared understanding that members have about the organization, how things are done in it, and the way members are supposed to behave. Exhibit 10-2 on page 335 demonstrates how these characteristics can be mixed to create highly diverse organizations.

Culture's Functions

What does organizational culture do?

Culture performs a number of functions within an organization:

- It has a boundary-defining role because it creates distinction between one organization and others.
- It conveys a sense of identity to organization members.
- It helps create commitment to something larger than an individual's self-interest.
- It enhances stability; it is the social glue that helps hold the organization together by providing appropriate standards for what employees should say and do.

EXHIBIT 10-2 Contrasting Organizational Cultures

Organization A	Organization B
• Managers must fully document all decisions. • Creative decisions, change, and risks are not encouraged. • Extensive rules and regulations exist for all employees. • Productivity is valued over employee morale. • Employees are encouraged to stay within their own departments. • Individual effort is encouraged.	• Management encourages and rewards risk-taking and change. • Employees are encouraged to run with " ideas, and failures are treated as "learning experiences." • Employees have few rules and regulations to follow. • Productivity is balanced with treating its people right. • Team members are encouraged to interact with people at all levels and functions. • Many rewards are team-based.

- It serves as a control mechanism that guides and shapes the attitudes and behaviour of employees, and helps them make sense of the organization.

This last function is of particular interest to us.[10] As the following quotation makes clear, culture defines the rules of the game:

> *Culture by definition is elusive, intangible, implicit, and taken for granted. But every organization develops a core set of assumptions, understandings, and implicit rules that govern day-to-day behaviour in the workplace. Until newcomers learn the rules, they are not accepted as full-fledged members of the organization. Transgressions of the rules on the part of high-level executives or front-line employees result in universal disapproval and powerful penalties. Conformity to the rules becomes the primary basis for reward and upward mobility.[11]*

The role of culture in influencing employee behaviour appears to be increasingly important in today's workplace.[12] As organizations widen spans of control, flatten structures, introduce teams, reduce formalization, and empower employees, the *shared meaning* provided by a strong culture ensures that everyone is pointed in the same direction. Geoffrey Relph, IBM Canada's marketing director of professional services, compared the culture of his previous company (GE Appliances in Louisville, Kentucky) with that of IBM: "The priorities in GE are: 'Make the financial commitments. Make the financial commitments. Make the financial commitments.' At IBM, the company's attention is divided among customer satisfaction, employee morale, and positive financial results."[13] These two cultures give employees and managers different messages about where they should direct their attention. Recent research suggests, moreover, that employees are more likely to behave appropriately when there are clear norms about behaviour, rather than general guidelines, such as "be honest."[14]

IBM Canada
www.ibm.com/ca/en/

Culture can also influence people's ethical behaviour. When lower-level employees see their managers padding expense reports, this sends a signal that the firm tolerates such dishonest behaviour. Firms that emphasize individual sales records may encourage unhealthy competition among sales staff, including "misplacing" phone messages and not being helpful to someone else's client. Toronto-based GMP Securities, on the other hand, emphasizes the importance of a teamwork culture, so that individuals are not competing against one another and engaging in questionable activities. Founding partner Brad Griffiths notes that "the corporate culture is to make an environment where everybody feels they're involved. We want to be successful, but not at the expense of the individual."[15] For further discussion of the effect of culture on ethical behaviour, see this chapter's *Ethical Dilemma Exercise* on pages 360–361.

GMP Securities
www.gmpsecurities.com

Do Organizations Have Uniform Cultures?

Organizational culture represents a common perception held by the organization's members. This was made explicit when we defined culture as a system of *shared* meaning. We should expect, therefore, that individuals with different backgrounds or at different levels in the organization will tend to describe the organization's culture in similar terms.[16]

However, the fact that organizational culture has common properties does not mean that there cannot be subcultures within it. Most large organizations have a dominant culture and numerous sets of subcultures.[17]

dominant culture A system of shared meaning that expresses the core values shared by a majority of the organization's members.

A **dominant culture** expresses the core values that are shared by a majority of the organization's members. When we talk about an *organization's culture,* we are referring to its dominant culture. It is this macro view of culture that gives an organization its distinct personality.[18] **Subcultures** tend to develop in large organizations to reflect common problems, situations, or experiences that members face. These subcultures are likely to be defined by department designations and geographical separation.

subcultures Minicultures within an organization, typically defined by department designations and geographical separation.

An organization's purchasing department, for example, can have a subculture that is unique to the members of that department. It will include the **core values**—the primary, or dominant, values in the organization—plus additional values unique to members of the purchasing department. Similarly, an office or unit of the organization that is physically separated from the organization's main operations may take on a different personality. Again, the core values are basically retained but modified to reflect the distinct situation of the separated unit.

core values The primary, or dominant, values that are accepted throughout the organization.

If organizations had no dominant culture and were composed only of numerous subcultures, the value of organizational culture as an independent variable would be significantly lessened. This is because there would be no uniform interpretation of what represented appropriate and inappropriate behaviour. It is the "shared meaning" aspect of culture that makes it such a potent device for guiding and shaping behaviour. That is what allows us to say that Microsoft's culture values aggressiveness and risk-taking,[19] and then to use that information to better understand the behaviour of Microsoft executives and employees. But we cannot ignore the reality that as well as a dominant culture, many organizations have subcultures that can influence the behaviour of members. Some strong subcultures can even make it difficult for managers to introduce organizational change. This sometimes happens in unionized environments, and can occur in nonunionized environments as well. To learn more about how to identify the culture of an organization, see *From Concepts to Skills* on pages 363–364.

CREATING AND SUSTAINING AN ORGANIZATION'S CULTURE

To address the problems of the culture he faced when he started at the Royal Canadian Mint, president and CEO David Dingwall needed to make a number of changes.[20] He introduced a lean enterprise model and a new management team, including a new chief financial officer as well as a new vice-president of sales and marketing. He made $15 million in cuts, including getting rid of the jewellery business, reducing inventory by 50 percent and lowering travel and advertising expenses. He also reduced the time it took to get a product to market from more than 460 days to just 150, with the aim of becoming even faster in the future. To show that he was intent on creating a new culture, Dingwall involved employees in the changes. He encouraged them to help figure out how to create better work processes. Employees helped map out the steps for change and then implemented them. Dingwall complimented the employees on the job they did. "We had inventory savings. We had time savings. We were able to redirect some of our labour to other projects."

Dingwall recognized the importance of acknowledging good performance from employees. He wanted employees to meet customer demands quickly and efficiently. He suggested that the old culture at the Mint was partially responsible for not encouraging new ideas and initiatives by employees. "One of the big things I found at the Mint was a real reluctance to celebrate," he said.

Dingwall gave each of his vice-presidents a budget for celebrating achievements. "I am sure there was some celebration in the past, but now if you don't have celebrations in your operations I want to know why. That is the difference." In what other ways might Dingwall have created a high-performance culture at the Mint?

An organization's culture does not pop out of thin air. Once established, it rarely fades away. Exhibit 10-3 summarizes how an organization's culture is established and sustained. The original culture derives from the founder's philosophy. This in turn strongly influences the criteria used in hiring. The actions of the current top management set the general climate of what is acceptable behaviour and what is not. How employees are to be socialized will depend both on the degree of success an organization achieves in matching new employees' values to its own in the selection process and on top management's preference for socialization methods. We describe each part of this process below.

2 How do you create and maintain organizational culture?

How a Culture Begins

✳ *Is culture the same as rules?*

An organization's current customs, traditions, and general way of doing things largely owe to what it has done before and how successful those previous endeavours have been. This leads us to the ultimate source of an organization's culture: its founders.[21]

The founders traditionally have a major impact on that organization's early culture. They have a vision of what the organization should be. They are not constrained by previous customs or ideologies. Because new organizations are typically small, it is possible for the founders to impose their vision on all organizational members.

A culture can be created in three ways.[22] First, founders hire and keep only employees who think and feel the way they do. Second, they indoctrinate and socialize these employees to their way of thinking and feeling. Finally, the founders' behaviour acts as a role model, encouraging employees to identify with the founders and internalize those beliefs, values, and assumptions. When the organization succeeds, the founders' vision is seen as a primary determinant of that success. At that point, the founders' entire personality becomes embedded in the culture of the organization.

For example, Microsoft's culture is largely a reflection of its co-founder, chair, and chief software architect (and former CEO), Bill Gates. Gates is personally aggressive, competitive, and highly disciplined. Those are the same characteristics often used to describe the software giant he founded. Other contemporary examples of founders who

Bill Gates, Microsoft
www.microsoft.com/billgates/default.asp

EXHIBIT 10-3   How Organizational Cultures Form

IKEA founder Ingvar Kamprad grew up in a poor farming area in Sweden where people worked hard and lived frugally. He combined the lessons he learned growing up with his vision of helping people live a better life at home by offering them affordable, functional, and well-designed furniture. He named his company IKEA by combining his initials plus the first letters of Elmtaryd and Agunnaryd, the farm and village where he grew up. The success of IKEA in expanding to more than 220 stores in 35 countries stems from Kamprad's vision.

Ted Rogers, Rogers Communications
www.rogers.com/english/aboutrogers/historyofrogers/index.html

have had an immeasurable impact on their organizations' cultures are Ted Rogers of Toronto-based Rogers Communications, Frank Stronach of Aurora, Ontario-based Magna International, Anita Roddick of The Body Shop, and Richard Branson of the Virgin Group.

Keeping a Culture Alive

Once a culture is in place, human resource practices within the organization act to maintain it by giving employees a set of similar experiences.[23] For example, the selection process, performance evaluation criteria, training and career development activities, and promotion procedures ensure that new employees fit in with the culture, rewarding those who support it and penalizing (even expelling) those who challenge it. Three forces play a particularly important part in sustaining a culture: *selection* practices, the actions of *top management,* and *socialization* methods. Let's take a closer look at each.

Selection

The explicit goal of the selection process is to identify and hire individuals who have the knowledge, skills, and abilities to perform the jobs within the organization successfully. Typically, more than one candidate will meet any given job's requirements. The final decision as to who is hired is significantly influenced by the decision maker's judgment of how well each candidate will fit into the organization. This attempt to ensure a proper match, either deliberately or inadvertently, results in the hiring of people who have values consistent with those of the organization, or at least a good portion of those values.[24]

At the same time, the selection process provides information about the organization to applicants. If they perceive a conflict between their values and those of the organization, they can remove themselves from the applicant pool. Selection, therefore, becomes a two-way street, allowing the employer or applicant to look elsewhere if there appears to be a mismatch. In this way, the selection process sustains an organization's culture by selecting out those individuals who might attack or undermine its core values. *OB in the Workplace* on page 339 shows how one company's use of multiple interviews ensures that applicants are right for the job.

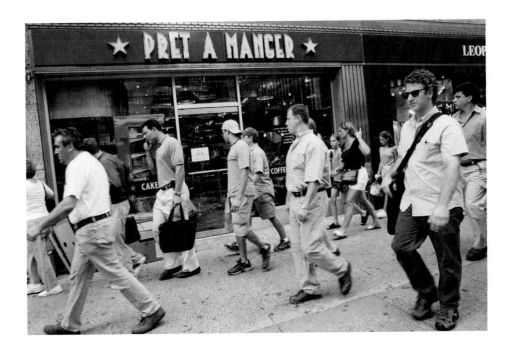

At Pret A Manger, a British sandwich shop chain, job applicants spend a trial day working at a shop, after which the shop's team of employees decide whether the applicants would make good additions to the staff.

OB IN THE WORKPLACE

Surviving Procter & Gamble's Intensive Screening Process

How does a company make sure an applicant is right for the job? Applicants for entry-level positions in brand management at household products maker Procter & Gamble (P&G) move through an exhaustive application and screening process. Their interviewers are part of an elite group who have been selected and trained extensively via lectures, videotapes, films, practice interviews, and role plays to identify applicants who will successfully fit in at P&G. Applicants are interviewed in depth for such qualities as their ability to "turn out high volumes of excellent work," "identify and understand problems," and "reach thoroughly substantiated and well-reasoned conclusions that lead to action." P&G values rationality and seeks applicants who demonstrate that quality. University and college applicants have two interviews and write a general-knowledge test on campus before being flown back to head office for three more one-on-one interviews and a group interview at lunch. Each encounter seeks corroborating evidence of the traits that the firm believes correlate highly with "what counts" for success at P&G.[25]

Top Management

The actions of top management also have a major impact on the organization's culture.[26] Through what they say and how they behave, senior executives establish norms that filter down through the organization. These norms establish whether risk-taking is desirable; how much freedom managers should give their employees; what is appropriate dress; what actions will pay off in terms of pay raises, promotions, and other rewards; and the like.

As we noted earlier, managers at the Royal Canadian Mint didn't seem to value celebrating employees' positive actions before David Dingwall took over. The manager of Sheraton Suites Calgary Eau Claire discovered how important changing the culture of the organization was to improve its performance, as *OB in the Workplace* on page 340 shows.

OB IN THE WORKPLACE

Employees Have Feelings Too

Sheraton Suites Calgary
Eau Claire
www.sheratonsuites.com

Can a culture change help with turnover problems?   Sheraton Suites Calgary Eau Claire had turnover problems almost from the time it opened.[27] Though the hotel ranked third out of 210 Sheratons across Canada in a 1999 customer satisfaction survey, its key employees kept leaving.

General manager Randy Zupanski wanted to improve employee morale and he hired a consulting group to uncover problems in the workplace through a series of seminars. The consultants uncovered interesting concerns. The hotel management had focused on team process, encouraging and rewarding team behaviour. However, the team culture was having a negative effect on many employees. They did not feel that they were being recognized and rewarded for what they were doing as individuals.

Zupanski and his managers introduced changes to the hotel's culture. They made the recognition program more personal, rewarding such things as attendance, performance, and extra work. Some employees received an extra day off with pay for their hard work.

The result, said the hotel's human resource manager, was an incredible change in atmosphere. Individual employees felt less stressed and more rewarded, which led to overall performance improvements by everyone. Customer satisfaction improved so much that the Eau Claire Sheraton received the Highest Overall Guest Satisfaction award among 230 Sheratons in North America in 2001, 2002, 2003, and 2004; it was also named #1 Sheraton Worldwide Hotel of the Year in 2005. Zupanski noted that working together to change the hotel's culture brought "us together and brought trust and understanding into the team atmosphere."

The example of Sheraton Suites Calgary Eau Claire shows that being aware of how culture affects individual performance can help managers identify specific practices that lead to poor morale. However, we would not want to leave you with the impression that changing culture is easy. In fact, it is a difficult process. For a specific example of the difficulties of culture change, see *Case Incident—EnCana's New Culture Presents Challenges* on the CD-ROM that accompanies this textbook. We discuss the process of changing culture later in this chapter.

Socialization

No matter how effectively the organization recruits and selects new employees, they are not fully trained in the organization's culture when they start their jobs. Because they are unfamiliar with the organization's culture, new employees may disturb the beliefs and customs that are in place. The organization will, therefore, want to help new employees adapt to its culture. This adaptation process is called **socialization**.[28]

socialization   The process that adapts new employees to an organization's culture.

New employees at the Japanese electronics company Sanyo are socialized through a particularly long training program. At their intensive five-month course, trainees eat and sleep together in company-subsidized dorms and are required to vacation together at company-owned resorts. They learn the Sanyo way of doing everything—from how to speak to managers to proper grooming and dress.[29] The company considers this program essential for transforming young employees, fresh out of school, into dedicated *kaisha senshi,* or corporate warriors.

Sanyo Canada
www.sanyocanada.com

As we discuss socialization, keep in mind that the new employee's entry into the organization is the most critical stage. This is when the organization seeks to mould the outsider into an employee "in good standing." Those employees who fail to learn the essential role behaviours risk being labelled "nonconformists" or "rebels," which often leads to their being fired. The organization continues to socialize every employee, though maybe not as explicitly, throughout his or her career in the organization. This further contributes to sustaining the culture. (Sometimes, however, employees are not fully socialized. For instance, you will note in Exhibit 10-4 that the cartoon employees had learned they were supposed to wear checkerboard caps to work, but clearly didn't know why.)

EXHIBIT 10-4

"I don't know how it started, either. All I know is that it's part of our corporate culture."

Source: Drawing by Mick Stevens in *The New Yorker*, October 3, 1994. Copyright © 1994 by *The New Yorker Magazine*, Inc. Reprinted by permission.

MATCHING PEOPLE WITH ORGANIZATIONAL CULTURES

There is now a substantive body of evidence to demonstrate that organizations try to select new members who fit well with the organizations' cultures.[30] Most job candidates similarly try to find organizations where their values and personality will fit in.

Research by Goffee and Jones provides some interesting insights into different organizational cultures and guidance for prospective employees.[31] They have identified four distinct cultural types. Let's take a look at their cultural framework and how you can use it to select an employer where you will best fit.

Goffee and Jones argue that two dimensions underlie organizational culture. The first is *sociability*. This is a measure of friendliness. High sociability means people do kind things for one another without expecting something in return and they relate to each other in a friendly, caring way. In terms of the characteristics of organizational culture presented at the beginning of this chapter, sociability is consistent with a high people orientation, high team orientation, and focuses on processes rather than outcomes.

The second dimension is *solidarity*. It considers the strength of the group's task orientation. High solidarity means people can overlook personal biases and rally behind common interests and common goals. Again, referring back to our earlier discussion of the characteristics of culture, solidarity is consistent with high attention to detail and high aggressiveness. Exhibit 10-5 on page 342 illustrates a matrix with these two dimensions rated as either high or low. They create four distinct cultural types:

3 What kind of organizational culture might suit you?

✳ *What kind of organizational culture would work best for you?*

- *Networked culture (high on sociability, low on solidarity).* Organizations with this type of culture view members as family and friends. People know and like each other. People willingly give assistance to others and openly share information. The major downside to this culture is that the focus on friendships can lead to a tolerance for poor performance and creation of political cliques.

EXHIBIT 10–5 Four-Culture Typology

Source: Adapted from R. Goffee and G. Jones, *The Character of a Corporation: How Your Company's Culture Can Make or Break Your Business* (New York: HarperBusiness, 1998), p. 21.

Unilever and Heineken are examples of companies with networked cultures. Heineken, for example, has more than 60 000 employees but retains the feeling of friendship and family more typical in small firms. The company's highly social culture produces a strong sense of belonging and often a passionate identification with its product. Family businesses can often have this type of culture, although not all family businesses would have a networked culture.

- *Mercenary culture (low on sociability, high on solidarity).* Organizations with this type of culture are fiercely goal-focused. People are intense and determined to meet goals. They have a zest for getting things done quickly and a powerful sense of purpose. A mercenary culture is not just about winning; it is about destroying the enemy. This focus on goals and objectivity leads to a minimal degree of politicking. The major downside to this culture is that it can lead to an almost inhumane treatment of people who are perceived as low performers.

Enron, Mars, Campbell Company of Canada, and Komatsu Canada (the Japanese heavy-equipment manufacturer) have classic mercenary cultures. At Virginia-based candy manufacturer Mars, for instance, meetings are concerned almost totally with work issues. There is little tolerance for socializing or small talk.

- *Fragmented culture (low on sociability, low on solidarity).* Organizations with this type of culture are made up of individualists. Commitment is first and foremost to individual members and their job tasks. There is little or no identification with the organization. In a fragmented culture, employees are judged solely on their productivity and the quality of their work. The major downside to this culture is that it can lead to excessive critiquing of others and an absence of collegiality and cooperation. Some large accounting and law firms have this type of culture.

Most top-tier universities and some large accounting and law firms take on the properties of fragmented cultures. Professors at major universities, for instance, are judged on their research and scholarship. Senior professors with big reputations do not need to be friendly to their peers or attend social functions to retain their status. Similarly, law partners who bring in new clients and win cases need to expend little energy getting to know co-workers or being visible in the office.

- *Communal culture (high on sociability, high on solidarity).* Organizations with this type of culture value both friendship and performance. People have a feeling of belonging, but there is still a ruthless focus on goal achievement. Leaders of these cultures tend to be inspirational and charismatic, with a clear vision of the organizations' future. The major downside to this culture is that it often consumes employees' lives. Its charismatic leaders frequently expect to create disciples rather than followers, resulting in a work climate that is almost "cult-like." Apple under Steve Jobs, particularly in its early years, is an example of a communal culture, as are Hewlett-Packard Canada, Johnson & Johnson Canada, and consulting firm Bain & Company. HP historically has been large and very goal-focused. Yet it is also a company known for its strong family feel. The "HP Way" is a set of values the company has developed that govern how people should behave and interact with each other. The HP Way's value of trust and community encourages loyalty to the company. The company returns that loyalty to employees as long as they perform well. Many start-ups exhibit a communal culture. During the height of the dot-com era, 20-something employees thought nothing of working around the clock, even sleeping and eating at their workplaces.

How important is the culture-person fit? In a study of accounting firms, new employees whose personalities meshed with the company were 20 percent less likely to leave their jobs in the first three years than those who did not fit as well.[32] *OB in Action—Finding Your Culture* provides a checklist to help you find the culture in which you might be most comfortable.

OB IN ACTION

Finding Your Culture

How do you know which culture is a good fit for you?

✔ *You are cut out for a **networked culture** if you possess good social skills and empathy; you like to forge close, work-related friendships; you thrive in a relaxed and convivial atmosphere; and you are not obsessed with efficiency and task performance.*

✔ *You are well matched to a **mercenary culture** if you are goal-oriented, thrive on competition, like clearly structured work tasks, enjoy risk-taking, and are able to deal openly with conflict.*

✔ *You are likely to fit in well in a **fragmented culture** if you are independent, have a low need to be part of a group atmosphere, are analytical rather than intuitive, and have a strong sense of self that is not easily undermined by criticism.*

✔ *You might fit in with a **communal culture** if you have a strong need to identify with something bigger than yourself, enjoy working in teams, and are willing to put the organization above family and personal life.*

THE LIABILITIES OF ORGANIZATIONAL CULTURE

When David Dingwall took over as president and CEO of the Royal Canadian Mint, he faced a large deficit and inefficient business processes.[33] Dingwall recognized the need to streamline the Mint's activities, but also knew that he might face great resistance by employees. The culture of the organization before he arrived was generally accepted by the employees.

Dingwall knew that part of what he had to do to change the culture was to get the employees onside with the changes. "I gave a commitment to all of our employees that nobody, but nobody, would lose their job as a result of the lean enterprise. And some of them didn't believe that, but when they saw that we were walking the walk, that we weren't laying people off as a result of lean enterprise (practices), then it became more believable. We started to see the exhilaration from employees in terms of improving our processes," he says.

At the end of 2004, just 20 months after Dingwall started, the Mint was set to have an unprecedented good year. The Winnipeg plant doubled its staff during 2004, allowing it to operate day and night. Revenue was $330 million, considerably higher than the Mint's $250-million revenue in 2003. Net income for 2004 was $13 million, wiping out the deficit Dingwall faced when he started. How does culture affect an employee's willingness to contribute to the organization?

We have treated organizational culture in a nonjudgmental manner thus far. We have not said that it is good or bad, only that it exists. Many of its functions, as outlined, are valuable for both the organization and the employee. Culture enhances organizational commitment and increases the consistency of employee behaviour. These are clearly benefits to an organization. From an employee's standpoint, culture is valuable because it reduces ambiguity. It tells employees how things are done and what is important. However, we should not ignore the potentially dysfunctional aspects of culture, especially of a strong culture, on an organization's effectiveness. *Focus on Ethics* on page 344 discusses how Enron's pressure-cooker culture led to the company's ultimate collapse.

4 Can organizational culture have a downside?

FOCUS ON **ETHICS**

Pressure-Cooker Culture Leads to Enron's Demise

Would employees knowingly do wrong for their employer? "At Enron, losers fell by the wayside but victors stayed in the game," wrote two *Washington Post* reporters.[34] The "winner-take-all" culture demanded that employees do whatever they could to make Enron's stock price continually rise. Executives thus took risks with investments and accounting procedures, inflating revenues and hiding debts. Those who could not (or would not) play this game were forced out. As the company's annual report stated, "We insist on results."

"The driver was this unbelievable desire to keep portraying Enron as something very, very different and keep the track record going and going," said Forrest Hoglund, a former senior manager.

Enron's culture set up an in-crowd and an out-crowd, and employees knew whether they were "in" or "out." Everyone wanted to be liked in the organization, according to Sally Ison, another employee. "You do everything you can do to keep that."

Employees were even willing to blatantly acknowledge they were doing wrong among themselves, according to Margaret Ceconi, a former Enron Energy Services (EES) manager, who was only briefly employed by Enron. After she was laid off, she wrote a memo to Kenneth Lay, former chair of Enron, and phoned federal regulators twice. In her memo to Lay she said, "EES has knowingly misrepresented EES' earnings," and, she added, "This is common knowledge among all the EES employees, and is actually joked about . . . [Enron] must investigate all these goings-on." 🕴

Enron's culture led its employees to engage in various unethical accounting practices. Consistent with what happened at Enron, recent research suggests that cultures that strongly emphasize competition can lead to negative organizational consequences.[35]

We now consider culture's impact on change, diversity, and mergers and acquisitions.

Culture as a Barrier to Change

Culture is a liability when the shared values do not agree with those that will further the organization's effectiveness. Employees are less likely to have shared values when the organization's environment is dynamic. When the environment is undergoing rapid change, the organization's entrenched culture may no longer be appropriate. Consistency of behaviour is an asset to an organization when it faces a stable environment. However, it may burden the organization and make it difficult to respond to changes in the environment. For many organizations with strong cultures, practices that led to previous successes can lead to failure when those practices no longer match up well with environmental needs.[36] When employees at the Royal Canadian Mint failed to act rapidly to create a commemorative coin for Canadian golfer Mike Weir, then president and CEO David Dingwall felt this underscored the Mint's reluctance to respond to a competitive environment. Consistent with this, research shows that overly friendly cultures may prevent managers from making important strategic decisions for fear of harming relationships.[37] This chapter's *Point/Counterpoint* on page 358 further explores the question of whether a culture can change.

Culture as a Barrier to Diversity

Hiring new employees who, because of race, gender, disability, or other differences, are not like the majority of the organization's members creates a paradox.[38] Management wants the new employees to accept the organization's core cultural values. Otherwise, these employees are unlikely to fit in or be accepted. But at the same time, management wants to openly acknowledge and demonstrate support for the differences that these employees bring to the workplace.

Strong cultures put considerable pressure on employees to conform. They limit the range of values and styles that are acceptable. It is no coincidence that employees at Disney theme parks appear to be almost universally attractive, clean, and wholesome looking, with bright smiles. That's the image the Walt Disney Company seeks. It selects employees who will maintain that image. Once the theme-park employees are on the job, a strong culture—supported by formal rules and regulations—ensures that they will act in a relatively uniform and predictable way.

The Walt Disney Company
http://disney.go.com

A strong culture that ignores prejudice can even undermine formal corporate diversity policies. A widely publicized example is the Texaco case in the United States, in which senior managers made disparaging remarks about minorities and, as a result of legal action on behalf of 1400 employees, paid a settlement of $246 million.[39] Organizations seek out and hire diverse individuals because of the new strengths they bring to the workplace. Yet these diverse behaviours and strengths are likely to diminish in strong cultures as people try to fit in. Strong cultures, therefore, can be liabilities when they effectively eliminate the unique strengths that people of different backgrounds bring to the organization. Moreover, strong cultures can also be liabilities when they support institutional bias or become insensitive to people who are different.

1996 Texaco Discrimination Case
www.courttv.com/archive/legaldocs/business/texaco/

Culture as a Barrier to Mergers and Acquisitions

Historically, the key factors that management looked at in making merger or acquisition decisions were related to financial advantages or product synergy. In recent years, cultural compatibility has become the primary concern.[40] While a favourable financial statement or product line may be the initial attraction of an acquisition candidate, whether the acquisition actually works seems to have more to do with how well the two organizations' cultures match up.

A number of mergers fail within the first several years, and the primary cause is often conflicting organizational cultures.[41] Even if mergers do not fail, the impact on employees can be devastating. For instance, employees from Andersen Canada merged with Toronto-based Deloitte & Touche LLP Canada in June 2002, after they were basically forced out of work with little notice as the Enron scandal unfolded. Colin Taylor, CEO and managing partner of Deloitte in Canada, noted that "given the circumstances, you have a lot of employees worried, anxious, traumatized even. They are in shock that a professional service firm of this size would have this happen to them so quickly."[42] Andersen's employees were not in a very good bargaining position when accepted into Deloitte. Unlike mergers where the two merging organizations fight over the name of the new company, and who gets what titles, Andersen's employees were concerned about having any jobs at all. This may affect how comfortable Andersen employees feel with the Deloitte culture as time passes.

Deloitte
www.deloitte.com

Strategies for Merging Cultures

Organizations can use several strategies when considering how to merge the cultures of two organizations:[43]

- *Assimilation.* The entire new organization is determined to take on the culture of one of the merging organizations. This strategy works best when one of the organizations has a relatively weak culture. However, if a culture is simply imposed on an organization, it rarely works.

- *Separation.* The organizations remain separate, and keep their individual cultures. This strategy works best when the organizations have little overlap in the industries in which they operate.

- *Integration.* A new culture is formed by merging parts of each of the organizations. This strategy works best when aspects of each organization's culture need to be improved.

While an integration strategy may take a lot of work, it can pay off, as *OB in the Workplace* shows.

OB IN THE WORKPLACE

Agrium Creates Its Own Culture Through Blending

Can an organization successfully merge many companies together?   Calgary-based Agrium, a fertilizer producer with production plants in Canada, the United States, and Argentina, grew aggressively during the 1990s through a series of mergers and acquisitions, which included companies such as Western Farm Services and Nu-West Industries.[44] Agrium grew out of the fertilizer division of Vancouver-based Cominco (now Teck Cominco), and then absorbed fertilizer divisions and spin-off companies from the mining and oil-and-gas industries, including Esso, Sherritt, and Unocal.

Since Agrium is the result of multiple mergers of companies, employees created a rule that if anyone mentions a former employer, he or she must contribute money to a fund. The fund is used for a "team-building event," in which employees go out together for lunch or dinner.

CEO Michael Wilson's explanation of the company's approach to merging cultures suggests that Agrium has used an integration strategy. "We take the best of the mining culture, which is very proactive, decisive, willing to act, willing to take appropriate risks . . . We blend it with the oil-and-gas culture [which is] very thorough in its analysis, in dotting of the i's and crossing of the t's, in making sure everyone's marching at the same pace." Wilson adds the culture of Dow Chemicals to the mix, where he worked for 18 years and learned "how to build collaboration across very strong business units, how to get results when you don't have full accountability."

Agrium has performed well in recent years, and Wilson sees this as a measure of a successful organizational culture. However, he believes that success is more than just earnings: "I have a saying, 'You have to be happy, healthy, and wise,' in that order." Wilson goes on to say, "There's nothing nicer than when you're at a convention with all your competition. And you look over your team, it's the bottom of the cycle, business is tough, and they're smiling. And you look over to the competition and they're all depressed because business is tough. And that's one measure right there: Is your team happy?"

APPROACHES TO MANAGING CHANGE

⑤ How do organizations manage change?

Our discussion of organizational culture as well as the issues that arise when organizations merge leads to a fundamental question for all organizations: How can change be managed? In what follows, we consider several approaches to managing change: Lewin's classic three-step model of the change process, Kotter's eight-step plan for implementing change, action research, and appreciative inquiry. We should also note that recent research emphasizes the need in change processes to manage the "hard stuff" as well as the "soft," or people, issues in order to be successful.[45] This chapter's *CBC Video Case Incident* examines how a company introduced and managed change.

Corporate Cuture Meets G.A.P. Adventures

change agents People who act as catalysts and assume the responsibility for managing change.

Who is responsible for managing change in an organization? The answer is **change agents**.[46] Change agents can be managers or nonmanagers, employees of the organization, or outside consultants.

EXHIBIT 10-6 Lewin's Three-Step Change Model

Unfreezing → Moving → Refreezing

Lewin's Three-Step Model

Assuming that an organization has uncovered a need for change, how does it engage in the change process? Kurt Lewin argued that successful change in organizations should follow three steps, which are illustrated in Exhibit 10-6: **unfreezing** the status quo, **moving** to a new state, and **refreezing** the new change to make it permanent.[47] The value of this model can be seen in the following example, where the management of a large company decided to reorganize its marketing function in Western Canada.

The oil company had three regional offices in the West, located in Winnipeg, Calgary, and Vancouver. The decision was made to consolidate the marketing divisions of the three regional offices into a single regional office to be located in Calgary. The reorganization meant transferring more than 150 employees, eliminating some duplicate managerial positions, and instituting a new hierarchy of command. As you might guess, such a huge move was difficult to keep secret. The rumours preceded the announcement by several months. The decision itself was made unilaterally. It came from the executive offices in Toronto. Those people affected had no say whatsoever in the choice. For anyone in Vancouver or Winnipeg who might have disliked the decision and its consequences—the problems involved in transferring to another city, pulling youngsters out of school, making new friends, having new co-workers, undergoing the reassignment of responsibilities—the only recourse was to quit. The status quo was about to change.

The status quo can be considered an equilibrium state. To move from this equilibrium—to overcome the pressures of both individual resistance and group conformity—unfreezing is necessary. Exhibit 10-7 shows that unfreezing can occur in one of three ways. The **driving forces**, which direct behaviour away from the status quo, can be increased. The **restraining forces**, which hinder movement from the existing equilibrium, can be decreased. A third alternative is to *combine the first two approaches.*

The oil company's management expected employee resistance to the consolidation and outlined its alternatives. Management could use positive incentives to encourage employees to accept the change. For instance, the company could offer pay increases to those who accept the transfer. It could also offer to pay all moving expenses. Management might offer low-cost mortgage funds to allow employees to buy new homes in Calgary. Of course, management might also consider unfreezing acceptance of the status quo by removing restraining forces. Employees could be counselled individually. Each employee's concerns and apprehensions could be heard and specifically clarified. Assuming that most of the fears are unjustified, the counsellor could assure the employees that there was nothing to fear and then demonstrate, through tangible evidence, that restraining forces are unwarranted. If resistance is extremely high, management may have to resort to both reducing resistance and increasing the attractiveness of the alternative so the unfreezing can succeed.

Once the consolidation change has been implemented, if it is to be successful, the new situation must be refrozen so that it can be sustained over time. Unless this last step is taken, there is a very high chance that the change will be short-lived and that

unfreezing Change efforts to overcome the pressures of both individual resistance and group conformity.

moving Efforts to get employees involved in the change process.

refreezing Stabilizing a change intervention by balancing driving and restraining forces.

driving forces Forces that direct behaviour away from the status quo.

restraining forces Forces that hinder movement away from the status quo.

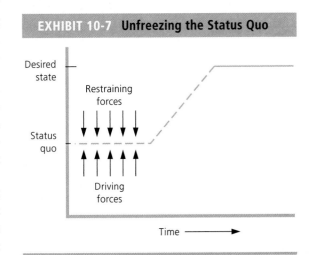

EXHIBIT 10-7 Unfreezing the Status Quo

employees will try to revert to the previous state of equilibrium. The objective of refreezing, then, is to stabilize the new situation by balancing the driving and restraining forces.

How could the oil company's management refreeze its consolidation change? It could systematically replace temporary forces with permanent ones. For instance, management might impose a new bonus system tied to the specific changes desired. The formal rules and regulations governing behaviour of those affected by the change could also be revised to reinforce the new situation. Over time, of course, the work group's own norms will evolve to sustain the new equilibrium. But until that point is reached, management will have to rely on more formal mechanisms. The *Working With Others Exercise* on page 360 gives you the opportunity to identify driving and restraining forces for another company experiencing problems with change and to make some recommendations for change.

A key feature of Lewin's three-step model is its conception of change as an episodic activity, with a beginning, a middle, and an end. However, the structure of today's workplaces requires change to take place as an ongoing, if not chaotic, process. Certainly the adjustment that companies have made to the realities of e-commerce indicates a more chaotic change, rather than a controlled and planned change.

Kotter's Eight-Step Plan for Implementing Change

John Kotter, professor of leadership at Harvard Business School, built on Lewin's three-step model to create a more detailed approach for implementing change.[48]

Kotter began by listing common failures that occur when managers try to initiate change. These include the inability to create a sense of urgency about the need for change; failure to create a coalition for managing the change process; the absence of a vision for change and to effectively communicate that vision; not removing obstacles that could impede the achievement of the vision; failure to provide short-term and achievable goals; the tendency to declare victory too soon; and not anchoring the changes in the organization's culture.

Kotter then established eight sequential steps to overcome these problems. These steps are listed in Exhibit 10-8.

Notice how Exhibit 10-8 builds on Lewin's model. Kotter's first four steps essentially represent the "unfreezing" stage. Steps 5 through 7 represent "moving." The final step works on "refreezing." Kotter's contribution lies in providing managers and change agents with a more detailed guide for implementing change successfully.

EXHIBIT 10-8 Kotter's Eight-Step Plan for Implementing Change

1. Establish a sense of urgency by creating a compelling reason for why change is needed.

2. Form a coalition with enough power to lead the change.

3. Create a new vision to direct the change and strategies for achieving the vision.

4. Communicate the vision throughout the organization.

5. Empower others to act on the vision by removing barriers to change and encouraging risk-taking and creative problem solving.

6. Plan for, create, and reward short-term "wins" that move the organization toward the new vision.

7. Consolidate improvements, reassess changes, and make necessary adjustments in the new programs.

8. Reinforce the changes by demonstrating the relationship between new behaviours and organizational success.

Source: Based on J. P. Kotter, *Leading Change* (Boston: Harvard Business School Press, 1996).

Action Research

Action research refers to a change process based on the systematic collection of data and then selection of a change action based on what the analyzed data indicate.[49] The importance of this approach is that it provides a scientific method for managing planned change.

The process of action research, carried out by a change agent, consists of five steps:

1. *Diagnosis.* The change agent gathers information about problems, concerns, and needed changes from members of the organization by asking questions, reviewing records, and listening to the concerns of employees.

2. *Analysis.* The change agent organizes the information gathered into primary concerns, problem areas, and possible actions.

3. *Feedback.* The change agent shares with employees what has been found during diagnosis and analysis. The employees, with the help of the change agent, develop action plans for bringing about any needed change.

4. *Action.* The employees and the change agent carry out the specific actions to correct the problems that have been identified.

5. *Evaluation.* The change agent evaluates the action plan's effectiveness, using the data gathered initially as a benchmark.

Action research provides at least two specific benefits for an organization. First, it is problem-focused. The change agent objectively looks for problems and the type of problem determines the type of change action. While this may seem intuitively obvious, a lot of change activities are not done this way. Rather, they are solution-centred. The change agent has a favourite solution—for example, implementing flextime, teams, or a process re-engineering program—and then seeks out problems that his or her solution fits. Second, because action research so heavily involves employees in the process, resistance to change is reduced. In fact, once employees have actively participated in the feedback stage, the change process typically takes on a momentum of its own. The employees and groups that have been involved become an internal source of sustained pressure to bring about the change.

Appreciative Inquiry

✳ Are there positive approaches to change?

Most organizational change approaches start from a negative perspective: The organization has problems that need solutions. **Appreciative inquiry** accentuates the positive.[50] Rather than looking for problems to fix, this approach seeks to identify the unique qualities and special strengths of an organization, which can then be built on to improve performance. That is, it focuses on an organization's successes rather than on its problems.

Advocates of appreciative inquiry argue that problem-solving approaches always ask people to look backward at yesterday's failures, to focus on shortcomings, and they rarely result in new visions. Instead of creating a climate for positive change, action research and organizational development (OD) techniques such as survey feedback and process consultation end up placing blame and generating defensiveness. Proponents of appreciative inquiry claim it makes more sense to refine and enhance what the organization is already doing well. This allows the organization to change by playing to its strengths and competitive advantages.

action research A change process based on the systematic collection of data and then selection of a change action based on what the analyzed data indicate.

appreciative inquiry An approach to change that seeks to identify the unique qualities and special strengths of an organization, which can then be built on to improve performance.

The appreciative inquiry process essentially consists of four steps, or "Four D's," often played out in a large-group meeting over a two- or three-day time period, and overseen by a trained change agent:

- *Discovery.* The idea is to find out what people think are the strengths of the organization. For instance, employees are asked to recount times they felt the organization worked best or when they specifically felt most satisfied with their jobs.

- *Dreaming.* The information from the discovery phase is used to speculate on possible futures for the organization. For instance, people are asked to envision the organization in five years and to describe what is different.

- *Design.* Based on the dream articulation, participants focus on finding a common vision of how the organization will look and agree on its unique qualities.

- *Destiny.* In this final step, participants discuss how the organization is going to fulfill its dream. This typically includes the writing of action plans and the development of implementation strategies.

Appreciative inquiry has proven an effective change strategy in organizations such as Toronto-based Orchestras Canada, Ajax, Ontario-based Nokia Canada, Burnaby, BC-based TELUS, Calgary-based EnCana, and Toronto-based CBC.

The use of appreciative inquiry in organizations is relatively recent, and it has not yet been determined when it is most appropriately used for organizational change.[51] However, it does give us the opportunity of viewing change from a much more positive perspective.

RESISTANCE TO CHANGE

6 Why do people and organizations resist change?

One of the most well-documented findings from studies of individual and organizational behaviour is that organizations and their members resist change. In a sense, this is positive. It provides a degree of stability and predictability to behaviour. If there were no resistance, organizational behaviour would take on characteristics of chaotic randomness. Resistance to change can also be a source of functional conflict. For example, resistance to a reorganization plan or a change in a product line can stimulate a healthy debate over the merits of the idea and result in a better decision. However, there is a definite downside to resistance to change: It hinders adaptation and progress.

Resistance to change does not necessarily surface in standard ways. Resistance can be overt, implicit, immediate, or deferred. It is easiest for management to deal with resistance when it is overt and immediate. For instance, a change is proposed, and employees respond immediately by voicing complaints, engaging in work slowdowns, threatening to go on strike, or the like. The greater challenge is managing resistance that is implicit or deferred. Implicit resistance efforts are more subtle—loss of loyalty to the organization, loss of motivation to work, increased errors or mistakes, increased absenteeism due to "sickness"—and hence more difficult to recognize. Similarly, deferred actions cloud the link between the source of resistance and the reaction to it. A change may produce what appears to be only a minimal reaction at the time it is initiated, but then resistance surfaces weeks, months, or even years later. Or a single change that in and of itself might have little impact becomes the straw that breaks the camel's back. Reactions to change can build up and then explode in some response that seems totally out of proportion to the change action it follows. The resistance, of course, has merely been deferred and stockpiled. What surfaces is a response to the accumulation of previous changes.

Let's look at the sources of resistance. For analytical purposes, we have categorized them as individual and organizational sources. In the real world, the sources often overlap.

Individual Resistance

✶ How do you respond to change?

Individual sources of resistance to change reside in basic human characteristics such as perceptions, personalities, and needs. This chapter's *Case Incident—GreyStar Art & Greetings Makes Technological Changes* on page 361 looks at an individual who resists change in the workplace. Exhibit 10-9 summarizes five reasons why individuals may resist change:

- *Habit.* To cope with life's complexities, we rely on habits or programmed responses. But when confronted with change, this tendency to respond in our accustomed ways becomes a source of resistance.

- *Security.* People with a high need for security are likely to resist change because it threatens their feelings of safety.

- *Economic factors.* Changes in job tasks or established work routines can arouse economic fears if people are concerned that they will not be able to perform the new tasks or routines to their previous standards, especially when pay is closely tied to productivity.

- *Fear of the unknown.* Change substitutes ambiguity and uncertainty for the known. This is also referred to as the "status quo bias," in which individuals assume that their current state is better than whatever the changed state might be.[52]

- *Selective information processing.* Individuals are guilty of selectively processing information in order to keep their perceptions intact. They hear what they want to hear, and they ignore information that challenges the world they have created.

Cynicism

In addition to simple resistance to change, employees often feel cynical about the change process, particularly if they have been through several rounds of change, and nothing appears (to them) to have changed. Three researchers from Ohio State University identified sources of cynicism in the change process of a large unionized manufacturing plant.[53] The major elements contributing to the cynicism were as follows:

- Feeling uninformed about what was happening

- Lack of communication and respect from one's manager

EXHIBIT 10-9   Sources of Individual Resistance to Change

- Lack of communication and respect from one's union representative

- Lack of opportunity for meaningful participation in decision making

The researchers also found that employees with negative personalities were more likely to be cynical about change. While organizations might not be able to change an individual's personality, they certainly have the ability to provide greater communication and respect, as well as opportunities to take part in decision making. The researchers found that cynicism about change led to such outcomes as lower commitment, less satisfaction, and reduced motivation to work hard. Exhibit 10-10 illustrates why some employees, particularly Dilbert, may have reason to feel cynical about organizational change.

Organizational Resistance

> * *What makes organizations resist change?*

Organizations, by their very nature, are conservative.[54] They actively resist change. You do not have to look far to see evidence of this phenomenon. Government agencies want to continue doing what they have been doing for years, whether the need for their service changes or remains the same. Organized religions are deeply entrenched in their history. Attempts to change church doctrine require great persistence and patience. Educational institutions, which exist to open minds and challenge established ways of thinking, are themselves extremely resistant to change. Most school systems are using essentially the same teaching technologies today that they were 50 years ago. Similarly, most business firms appear highly resistant to change. Half of the 309 human resource executives of Canadian firms who took part in a 1998 survey rated their companies' ability to manage change as "fair."[55] One-third of them said that their ability to manage change was their weakest skill, and only 25 percent of the companies made a strong effort to train leaders in the change process. When organizations refuse to change with the times, they can fail, as was the case with Eaton's, which never really adjusted to the arrival of Wal-Mart. When Eaton's was founded in 1869 by Irish immigrant Timothy Eaton, it was regarded as a "new wave" department store. Eaton's continued to set that pace for many years, but by the early 1980s, the store was considered dowdy rather than fashionable.[56]

Six major sources of organizational resistance to change (shown in Exhibit 10-11 on page 353) have been identified:[57]

- *Structural inertia.* Organizations have built-in mechanisms—such as their selection processes and formal regulations—to produce stability. When an organiza-

EXHIBIT 10-10

DILBERT BY SCOTT ADAMS

Source: Dilbert, by Scott Adams. August 3, 1996. DILBERT reprinted by permission of United Feature Syndicate, Inc.

tion is confronted with change, this structural inertia acts as a counterbalance to sustain stability.

- *Limited focus of change.* Organizations are made up of a number of interdependent subsystems. One cannot be changed without affecting the others. So limited changes in subsystems tend to be nullified by the larger system.

- *Group inertia.* Even if individuals want to change their behaviour, group norms may act as a constraint.

- *Threat to expertise.* Changes in organizational patterns may threaten the expertise of specialized groups.

- *Threat to established power relationships.* Any redistribution of decision-making authority can threaten long-established power relationships within the organization.

- *Threat to established resource allocations.* Groups in the organization that control sizable resources often see change as a threat. They tend to be content with the way things are.

Overcoming Resistance to Change

Michael Adams, president of Environics Research Group in Toronto, has noted that Canadians have become more resistant to change in recent years.[58] Between 1983 and the mid-1990s, Canadians reported that they "felt confident in their ability to cope with change." This trend has reversed in recent years. Half of Canadians aged 15 to 33 now "feel left behind and over-whelmed by the pace of life and the prevalence of technology." Those who feel left behind tend to be those who are not college- or university-educated, highly skilled, or adaptive.

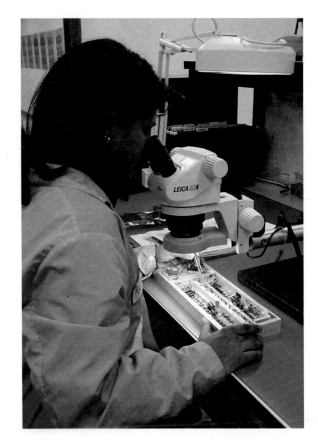

Though most people and organizations resist change, at Advantech AMT, located in Montreal, Quebec, change is the norm. François Binette, chief finance officer, says that "Managing change forms an intrinsic part of our corporate DNA and it is this environment that has allowed us to consistently develop unique and innovative products."

It probably cannot be emphasized enough that in order to break down resistance to change, it is essential to communicate a sense of urgency in the need for change. Doing so provides a framework for people to understand why the change is occurring.

EXHIBIT 10-11   Sources of Organizational Resistance to Change

- Threat to established resource allocations
- Structural inertia
- Threat to established power relationships
- Organizational Resistance
- Limited focus of change
- Threat to expertise
- Group inertia

Also, it is important to communicate and celebrate early successes to keep the momentum going, as change is a lengthy process. Kotter and Schlesinger have identified six tactics organizations use to deal with resistance to change:[59]

- *Education and communication.* Resistance can be reduced through communicating with employees to help them see the logic of a change. Communication can be achieved through one-on-one discussions, memos, group presentations, or reports.

- *Participation and involvement.* It is difficult for individuals to resist a change decision in which they have participated. Before making a change, those opposed can be brought into the decision process. Assuming that the participants have the expertise to make a meaningful contribution, their involvement can reduce resistance, obtain commitment, and increase the quality of the change decision.

- *Facilitation and support.* Organizations undergoing change can offer a range of supportive efforts to reduce resistance such as employee counselling and therapy, new-skills training, or a short paid leave of absence.

- *Negotiation and agreement.* Another way for organizations to deal with potential resistance to change is to exchange something of value for less resistance. For instance, if the resistance is centred in a few powerful individuals, a specific reward package can be negotiated that will meet their individual needs.

- *Manipulation and co-optation.* Manipulation refers to covert influence attempts. Twisting and distorting facts to make them appear more attractive, withholding undesirable information, and creating false rumours to get employees to accept a change are all examples of manipulation. Co-optation, on the other hand, is a form of both manipulation and participation. It seeks to "buy off" the leaders of a resistance group by giving them a key role in the change decision.

- *Explicit and implicit coercion.* Coercion is the application of direct threats or force upon the resisters. If the corporate management is determined to close a manufacturing plant should employees not acquiesce to a pay cut, then coercion would be the label attached to its change tactic. Other examples of coercion are threats of transfer, loss of promotions, negative performance evaluations, and poor letters of recommendation.

Exhibit 10-12 on page 355 describes when each of these approaches is best used, and the advantages and drawbacks of each.

The Politics of Change

No discussion of resistance to change would be complete without a brief mention of the politics of change. Because change invariably threatens the status quo, it inherently implies political activity.[60]

Politics suggests that the demand for change is more likely to come from employees who are new to the organization (and have less invested in the status quo) or managers who are slightly removed from the main power structure. Those managers who have spent their entire careers with a single organization and eventually achieve a senior position in the hierarchy are often major impediments to change. Change itself is a very real threat to their status and position. Yet they may be expected to implement changes to demonstrate that they are not merely caretakers.

By trying to bring about change, senior managers can symbolically convey to various constituencies—stockholders, suppliers, employees, customers—that they are on top of problems and adapting to a dynamic environment. Of course, as you might guess,

EXHIBIT 10-12 **Strategies for Overcoming Resistance to Change**

Approach	Commonly Used in Situations	Advantages	Drawbacks
Education + communication	Where there is a lack of information or inaccurate information and analysis.	Once persuaded, people will often help with the implementation of the change.	Can be very time-consuming if lots of people are involved.
Participation + involvement	Where the initiators do not have all the information they need to design the change, and where others have considerable power to resist.	People who participate will be committed to implementing change, and any relevant information they have will be integrated into the change plan.	Can be very time-consuming if participants design an inappropriate change.
Facilitation + support	Where people are resisting because of adjustment problems.	No other approach works as well with adjustment problems.	Can be time-consuming, expensive, and still fail.
Negotiation + agreement	Where someone or some group will clearly lose out in a change, and where that group has considerable power to resist.	Sometimes it is a relatively easy way to avoid major resistance.	Can be too expensive in many cases if it alerts others to negotiate for compliance.
Manipulation + co-optation	Where other tactics will not work, or are too expensive.	It can be a relatively quick and inexpensive solution to resistance problems.	Can lead to future problems if people feel manipulated.
Explicit + implicit coercion	Where speed is essential, and the change initiators possess considerable power.	It is speedy and can overcome any kind of resistance.	Can be risky if it leaves people angry with the initiators.

Source: Methods for dealing with resistance to change, J. P. Kotter and L. A. Schlesinger, "Choosing Strategies for Change," *Harvard Business Review,* March–April 1979, p. 111, Exhibit 1. Reprinted with permission.

when forced to introduce change, these long-time power holders tend to introduce changes that do not fundamentally challenge the status quo. Radical change is too threatening. This, incidentally, explains why boards of directors that recognize the need for the rapid introduction of fundamental, radical change in their organizations often turn to outside candidates for new leadership.[61]

You may remember that we discussed politics in Chapter 7 and gave some suggestions on how to more effectively encourage people to go along with your ideas. That chapter also indicated how individuals acquire power, which provides further insight into the ability of some individuals to resist change.

SUMMARY AND IMPLICATIONS

1 **What is the purpose of organizational culture?** Organizational culture is the pattern of shared values, beliefs, and assumptions considered the appropriate way to think and act within an organization. Culture provides stability to an organization and gives employees a clear understanding of "the way things are done around here."

2 **How do you create and maintain organizational culture?** The original culture of an organization is derived from the founder's philosophy. That philosophy then influences what types of employees are hired. The culture of the organization is then reinforced by top management, who signal what is acceptable behaviour and what is not.

SNAPSHOT SUMMARY

1 What Is Organizational Culture?

Definition of Organizational Culture

Levels of Culture

③ **What kind of organizational culture might suit you?** There is no one right organizational culture because individuals vary in the type of cultures with which they are comfortable. Organizational cultures can be analyzed in terms of their members' friendliness (*sociability*) and the degree to which their members are task oriented (*solidarity*). These dimensions combine to create four distinct cultural types: *networked, mercenary, fragmented,* and *communal*.

④ **Can organizational culture have a downside?** Many of culture's functions are valuable for both the organization and the employee. Culture enhances organizational commitment and increases the consistency of employee behaviour. Culture also reduces ambiguity for employees by telling them what is important and how things are done. However, a strong culture can have a negative effect, such as Enron's pressure-cooker culture, which led to the company's ultimate collapse. Culture can act as a barrier to change, it can make it difficult to create an inclusive environment, and it can hinder the success of mergers and acquisitions.

⑤ **How do organizations manage change?** Kurt Lewin argued that successful change in organizations should follow three steps: *unfreezing* the status quo, *moving* to a new state, and *refreezing* the new change to make it permanent. John Kotter built on Lewin's three-step model to create a more detailed eight-step plan for implementing change. Another approach to managing change is action research. *Action research* refers to a change process based on the systematic collection of data and the selection of a change action based on what the analyzed data indicate. Some organizations use appreciative inquiry to manage change. *Appreciative inquiry* seeks to identify the unique qualities and special strengths of an organization, which can then be built on to improve performance.

⑥ **Why do people and organizations resist change?** Individuals resist change because of basic human characteristics such as perceptions, personalities, and needs. Organizations resist change because they are conservative, and because change is difficult. The status quo is often preferred by those who feel they have the most to lose if change goes ahead.

For Review

1. How can an outsider assess an organization's culture?

2. What defines an organization's subcultures?

3. Can an employee survive in an organization if he or she rejects its core values? Explain.

4. What benefits can socialization provide for the organization? For the new employee?

5. Describe four cultural types and the characteristics of employees who fit best with each.

6. How can culture be a liability to an organization?

7. How does Lewin's three-step model of change deal with resistance to change?

8. How does Kotter's eight-step plan for implementing change deal with resistance to change?

9. What are the factors that lead individuals to resist change?

10. What are the factors that lead organizations to resist change?

For Critical Thinking

1. How are an individual's personality and an organization's culture similar? How are they different?

2. Is socialization brainwashing? Explain.

3. Can you identify a set of characteristics that describes your college's or university's culture? Compare them with several of your peers' lists. How closely do they agree?

4. "Resistance to change is an irrational response." Do you agree or disagree? Explain.

OB for You

- Carefully consider the culture of any organization at which you are thinking of being employed. You will feel more comfortable in cultures that share your values and expectations.

- When you work in groups on student projects, the groups create mini-cultures of their own. Be aware of the values and norms that are being supported early on in the group's life, as these will greatly influence the group's culture.

- Be aware that change is a fact of life. If you need to change something in yourself, be aware of the importance of creating new systems to replace the old. Saying you want to be healthier, without specifying that you intend to go to the gym three times a week, or eat five servings of fruits and vegetables a day, means that change likely will not occur. It's important to specify goals and behaviours as part of that change.

POINT

 COUNTERPOINT

Organizational Culture Doesn't Change

An organization's culture develops over many years and is rooted in deeply held values to which employees are strongly committed. In addition, there are a number of forces continually operating to maintain a given culture. These would include written statements about the organization's mission and philosophy, the design of physical spaces and buildings, the dominant leadership style, hiring criteria, past promotion practices, entrenched rituals, popular stories about key people and events, the organization's historical performance evaluation criteria, and the organization's formal structure.

Selection and promotion policies are particularly important devices that work against cultural change. Employees chose the organization because they perceived their values as a "good fit" with those of the organization. They become comfortable with that fit and will strongly resist efforts to disturb the equilibrium.

Those in control in organizations will also select senior managers who will continue the current culture. Even attempts to change a culture by going outside the organization to hire a new chief executive are unlikely to be effective. The evidence indicates that the culture is more likely to change the executive than the other way around. Why? It's too entrenched, and change becomes a potential threat to member self-interest. In fact, a more pragmatic view of the relationship between an organization's culture and its chief executive would be to note that the practice of filling senior-level management positions from the ranks of current managerial employees ensures that those who run the organization have been fully indoctrinated in the organization's culture. Promoting from within provides stability and lessens uncertainty. When a company's board of directors selects as a new chief executive officer an individual who has spent 30 years in the company, it virtually guarantees that the culture will continue unchanged.

Our argument, however, should not be viewed as saying that culture can never be changed. In the unusual case when an organization confronts a survival-threatening crisis—a crisis universally acknowledged as a true life-or-death situation—members of the organization will be responsive to efforts at cultural change. However, anything less than a crisis is unlikely to be effective in bringing about cultural change.

How to Change an Organization's Culture

Changing an organization's culture is extremely difficult, but cultures can be changed. The evidence suggests that cultural change is most likely to occur when most or all of the following conditions exist:

- *A dramatic crisis.* This is the shock that undermines the status quo and calls into question the relevance of the current culture. Examples of these crises might be a surprising financial setback, the loss of a major customer, or a dramatic technological breakthrough by a competitor. The *Columbia* space-shuttle disaster was a dramatic crisis for NASA. A $7-million deficit was a dramatic crisis for the Royal Canadian Mint.

- *Turnover in leadership.* New top leadership, which can provide an alternative set of key values, may be perceived as more capable of responding to the crisis. This would definitely be the organization's chief executive, but also might need to include all senior management positions. The recent rush to hire outside CEOs after the Enron and WorldCom scandals illustrates attempts to create more ethical climates through the introduction of new leadership. At NASA, some of the top leadership was moved to other positions after the *Columbia* disaster. A new CEO at the Royal Canadian Mint, who was determined to turn around a deficit situation, brought about many changes to that organization.

- *Young and small organization.* The younger the organization is, the less entrenched its culture will be. Similarly, it's easier for management to communicate its new values when the organization is small. This point helps explain the difficulty that multibillion-dollar corporations have in changing their cultures.

- *Weak culture.* The more widely held a culture is and the higher the agreement among members on its values, the more difficult it will be to change. A strong culture has been one of the problems facing NASA. Conversely, weak cultures are more open to change than strong ones.

Efforts directed at changing organizational culture do not usually yield immediate or dramatic results. For, in the final analysis, cultural change is a lengthy process—measured in years, not months. But we can ask the question "Can culture be changed?" and the answer is "Yes!"

What Kind of Organizational Culture Fits You Best?

For each of the following statements, circle the level of agreement or disagreement that you personally feel:

SA = **Strongly agree**
A = **Agree**
U = **Uncertain**
D = **Disagree**
SD = **Strongly disagree**

1. I like being part of a team and having my performance assessed in terms of my contribution to the team.   SA A U D SD

2. No person's needs should be compromised in order for a department to achieve its goals.   SA A U D SD

3. I like the thrill and excitement of taking risks.   SA A U D SD

4. If a person's job performance is inadequate, it's irrelevant how much effort he or she made.   SA A U D SD

5. I like things to be stable and predictable.   SA A U D SD

6. I prefer managers who provide detailed and rational explanations for their decisions.   SA A U D SD

7. I like to work where there isn't a great deal of pressure and where people are essentially easygoing.   SA A U D SD

Scoring Key:

For items 1, 2, 3, 4, and 7, score as follows: Strongly Agree = +2, Agree = +1, Uncertain = 0, Disagree = −1, Strongly Disagree = −2.

For items 5 and 6, reverse the score (Strongly Agree = −2, and so on).

Add up your total. Your score will fall somewhere between +14 and −14.

What does your score mean? The lower your score, the more comfortable you will be in a formal, mechanistic, rule-oriented, and structured culture. This is often associated with large corporations and government agencies. Positive scores indicate a preference for informal, humanistic, flexible, and innovative cultures, which are more likely to be found in research units, advertising firms, high-tech companies, and small businesses.

Form small groups to discuss the following topics, as assigned by your instructor:

1. Identify artifacts of culture in your current or previous workplace. From these artifacts, would you conclude that the organization has a strong or weak culture?

2. Have you or someone you know worked somewhere where the culture was strong? What was your reaction to that strong culture? Did you like that environment, or would you prefer to work where there is a weaker culture? Why?

3. Reflect on either the culture of one of your classes or the culture of the organization where you work, and identify characteristics of that culture that could be changed. How might these changes be made?

WORKING WITH OTHERS EXERCISE

The Beacon Aircraft Company

Objectives

1. To illustrate how forces for change and stability must be managed in organizational change programs.

2. To illustrate the effects of alternative change techniques on the relative strength of forces for change and forces for stability.

The Situation

The marketing division of the Beacon Aircraft Company has undergone two reorganizations in the past two years. Initially, its structure changed from a functional one, in which employees were organized within departments, to a matrix form, in which employees from several different functions reported both to their own manager and to a project manager. But the matrix structure did not satisfy some functional managers. They complained that the structure confused the authority and responsibility relationships.

In reaction to these complaints, the marketing manager revised Beacon's structure back to the functional form. This new structure had a marketing group and several project groups. The project groups were managed by project managers with a few general staff members, but no functional specialists, such as people from marketing, were assigned to these groups.

After the change, some problems began to surface. Project managers complained that they could not obtain adequate assistance from functional staff members. It not only took more time to obtain necessary assistance, but it also created problems in establishing stable relationships with functional staff members. Since these problems affected their services to customers, project managers demanded a change in the organizational structure—

probably again toward a matrix structure. Faced with these complaints and demands from project managers, the vice-president is pondering another reorganization. He has requested an outside consultant to help him in the reorganization plan.

The Procedure

1. Divide yourselves into groups of 5 to 7 and take the role of consultants.

2. Each group identifies the driving and restraining forces found in the firm. List these forces.

The Driving Forces	The Restraining Forces
_____	_____
_____	_____
_____	_____
_____	_____
_____	_____

3. Each group develops a set of strategies for increasing the driving forces and another set for reducing the restraining forces.

4. Each group prepares a list of changes it wants to introduce.

5. The class reassembles and hears each group's recommendations.

Source: Adapted from K. H. Chung and L. C. Megginson, *Organizational Behavior,* Copyright © 1981 by K. H. Chung and L. C. Megginson. Reprinted by permission of HarperCollins Publishers, Inc.

ETHICAL DILEMMA EXERCISE

Cultural Characteristics and Unethical Behaviour

An organization's culture socializes people. It subtly conveys to members that certain actions are acceptable, even though they may be illegal. For instance, when executives

at General Electric (GE), Westinghouse, and other manufacturers of heavy electrical equipment illegally conspired to set prices in the early 1960s, the defendants invariably testified that they came new to their jobs, found price-fixing as an established way of life, and simply entered into it as they did into other aspects of their jobs. One GE manager noted that every one of his bosses had directed him to meet with the competition: "It had become so common and gone on for so many years that I think we lost sight of the fact that it was illegal."

The strength of an organization's culture has an influence on the ethical behaviour of its managers. A strong culture will exert more influence on managers than a weak one. If the culture is strong and supports high ethical standards, it should have a very powerful positive influence on a manager's ethical behaviour. However, in a weak culture, managers are more likely to rely on subculture norms to guide their behaviour. Work groups and departmental standards will more strongly influence ethical behaviour in organizations that have weak overall cultures.

It is also generally acknowledged that the characteristics of a culture affect ethical behaviour. Assuming this is true, what would a culture look like that would shape high ethical standards? What could top management do to strengthen that culture? Do you think it's possible for a manager with high ethical standards to uphold those standards in an organizational culture that tolerates, or even encourages, unethical practices?

Source: P. C. Yeager, "Analyzing Corporate Offenses: Progress and Prospects," in *Business Ethics: Research Issues and Empirical Studies,* ed. W. C. Frederick and L. E. Preston (Greenwich, CT: JAI Press, 1990), p. 174.

CASE INCIDENT

GreyStar Art & Greetings Makes Technological Changes

Tammy Reinhold didn't believe the rumours. Now that the rumours were confirmed, she was in denial. "I can't believe it," she said. "I've worked as a greeting-card artist here for over 15 years. I love what I do. Now they tell me that I'm going to have to do all my work on a computer."

Tammy was not alone in her fear. The company's other two artists, Mike Tomaski and Maggie Lyall, were just as concerned. Each had graduated from art school near the top of his or her class. They came to work for GreyStar Art & Greetings right out of school—Mike in 1985, Tammy in 1991, and Maggie in 1997. They chose the company, which had been around for more than 50 years, because of its reputation as a good place to work. The company also had never had a layoff.

GreyStar Art & Greetings is a small maker of greeting cards and specialty wrapping paper. It has modest resources and modest ambitions. Management has always pursued progress slowly. Artists do much of their work by hand. Today, however, the company installed three high-powered Mac computers equipped with the latest graphics and photo-manipulation software, including Photoshop, Quark, and Illustrator.

Courtland Grey, the company's owner, called Tammy, Mike, and Maggie into his office this morning. He told them about the changes that were going to be made. Grey acknowledged that the three were going to have a lot to learn to be able to do all their work on computers. But he stressed that the changes would dramatically speed up the art-production and photo-layout processes and eventually result in significant cost savings. He offered to send the three to a one-week course specifically designed to train artists in the new technology and software. He also said he expected all of the company's art and photo operations to be completely digitalized within three months.

Tammy is not stupid. She has been following the trends in graphic art. More and more work is being done on computers. She just thought, as did Mike and Maggie, that she might escape having to learn these programs. After all, GreyStar Art & Greetings is not Hallmark. But Tammy was wrong. Technology is coming to GreyStar Art & Greetings and there isn't much she can do about it. Other than complain or look for another job!

Questions

1. Explain Tammy's resistance.

2. Evaluate the way Courtland Grey handled this change.

3. What, if anything, would you have done differently if you had been Grey?

CBC 🐦 VIDEO CASE INCIDENT

Corporate Culture Meets G.A.P Adventures

Bruce Poon Tip, owner of G.A.P Adventures, is one of Canada's most successful entrepreneurs. G.A.P Adventures is a travel company that offers eco-friendly tours with a difference—adventure and adrenaline.

Poon Tip has managed to take G.A.P Adventures from a business with 2 employees to one with more than 70 employees and over $12 million in annual sales—in 10 years.

Since the company's beginnings, Poon Tip has run G.A.P Adventures as more of a family business than a corporation. He considers himself better at building than maintaining businesses and wants to move on to new challenges in expanding and diversifying G.A.P Adventures' operations. Poon Tip believes it's time to take G.A.P Adventures to a new corporate level.

It's the 1990s. G.A.P Adventures' staff is at the annual spring retreat in Ontario's cottage country. To the surprise of all, Poon Tip announces a new division and the development of a travel TV show, and introduces a new "hired gun." Poon Tip has hired Dave Bowen, an aggressive marketing director with a corporate background, from one of G.A.P Adventures' biggest competitors. He wants Bowen to shake up the company, which he is concerned is not putting enough emphasis on the customer.

Bowen's challenge is to bring corporate discipline to the company without losing employee enthusiasm. Bowen uses his New York savvy and southern charm to transform G.A.P Adventures' corporate culture. The inefficient, handwritten reservation system is organized and converted to a high-tech reservation system, and reservation policies are formalized. The company's annual brochure will include more large, glossy pictures, more exciting titles, and only brief tour descriptions. Bowen insists that it's important to gain the interest of the customer first with the positive aspects of the tour, and then give the details (such as long bus rides) later.

How has G.A.P Adventures fared since the change to a corporate culture? Although some G.A.P employees have left the company, others have adjusted to a work environment that is more serious, more controlled, and less relaxed

and open. G.A.P Adventures' 1999 sales were $12.9 million, up from just $500,000 five years earlier. The events of September 11 made 2001 a financially challenging year for many travel companies, yet it was a profitable year for G.A.P Adventures.

This year's annual spring retreat is a bit different—the staff is staying in the executive suites of the upscale Blue Mountain resort in Ontario. Poon Tip announces another surprise: The company will be split into two divisions: the G.A.P division and the Real Tours division. The G.A.P division will market the company's own brand: G.A.P tours. The new Real Tours division will market other contracted-out tours. G.A.P Adventures has also partnered with Signature Vacations to market G.A.P tours. The reservation system is also changing, with a new IT company supporting it. Where will G.A.P Adventures' journey in the world of corporate culture take it next?

Questions

1. What benefits can come from bringing an "outsider," such as Dave Bowen, into a growing company like G.A.P Adventures? In your opinion, was Bowen a good fit for G.A.P, or should someone more suited to the company's existing organizational culture have been brought in?

2. Did G.A.P Adventures have a strong or weak culture before Bowen was hired? Justify your answer.

3. The impact of Bowen's changes around the workplace quickly caused two key employees to quit G.A.P Adventures. Why do you think these employees were so resistant to the new changes to G.A.P's culture?

Sources: Based on "Corporate Culture Meets G.A.P Adventures," *CBC Venture,* June 23, 2002, 833; G.A.P Adventures: World Wide Adventure Travel and Eco Tour website, http://www.gap.ca (accessed January 13, 2006); http://www.profitguide.com/magazine/article.jsp?content=261 (accessed January 13, 2006).

How to "Read" an Organization's Culture

The ability to read and assess an organization's culture can be a valuable skill.[62] If you are looking for a job, you will want to choose an employer whose culture is compatible with your values and in which you will feel comfortable. If you can accurately assess a prospective employer's culture before you make your decision, you may be able to save yourself a lot of grief and reduce the likelihood of making a poor choice. Similarly, you will undoubtedly have business transactions with numerous organizations during your professional career. You will be trying to sell a product or service, negotiate a contract, arrange a joint venture, or you may merely be seeking out which individual in an organization controls certain decisions. The ability to assess another organization's culture can be a definite plus in successfully completing these pursuits.

For the sake of simplicity, we will approach the problem of reading an organization's culture from that of a job applicant. We will assume you are interviewing for a job. Here is a list of things you can do to help learn about a potential employer's culture:

- Observe the physical surroundings. Pay attention to signs, pictures, style of dress, length of hair, degree of openness between offices, and office furnishings and arrangements.

- With whom are you meeting? Just the person who would be your immediate manager? Or potential colleagues, managers from other departments, or senior executives? Afterwards, based on what they revealed, to what degree do people other than the immediate manager have input into hiring decisions?

- How would you characterize the style of the people you met? Formal? Casual? Serious? Jovial?

- Does the organization have formal rules and regulations printed in a human resource policy manual? If so, how detailed are these policies?

- Ask questions of the people you meet. The most valid and reliable information tends to come from asking the same questions of many people (to see how closely their responses align) and by talking with boundary spanners. *Boundary spanners* are employees whose

work links them to the external environment. This includes jobs such as human resource interviewer, salesperson, purchasing agent, labour negotiator, public relations specialist, and company lawyer.

Questions that will give you insights into organizational processes and practices might include the following:

- What is the background of the founders?

- What is the background of current senior managers? What are their functional specializations? Were they promoted from within or hired from outside?

- How does the organization integrate new employees? Is there an orientation program? Training? If so, could you describe these features?

- How does your manager define his or her job success? (Amount of profit? Serving customers? Meeting deadlines? Acquiring budget increases?)

- How would you define fairness in terms of reward allocations?

- Can you identify some people here who are on the "fast track"? What do you think has put them on the fast track?

- Can you identify someone who seems to be considered a deviant in the organization? How has the organization responded to this person?

- Can you describe a decision that someone made here that was well received?

- Can you describe a decision that did not work out well? What were the consequences for the decision maker?

- Could you describe a crisis or critical event that has occurred recently in the organization? How did top management respond? What was learned from this experience?

Assessing Skills

After you've read this chapter, take the following Self-Assessments on your enclosed CD-ROM:

4. How Well Do I Handle Ambiguity?

49. How Well Do I Respond to Turbulent Change?

50. How Stressful Is My Life?

51. Am I Burned Out?

Practising Skills

You are the nursing supervisor at a community hospital employing both emergency-room and floor nurses. Each of these teams of nurses tends to work almost exclusively with others doing the same job. In your professional reading, you have come across the concept of cross-training nursing teams and giving them more varied responsibilities, which in turn has been shown to both improve patient care and lower costs. You call the two team leaders, Sue and Scott, into your office to explain that you want the nursing teams to move to this approach. To your surprise, they are both opposed to the idea. Sue says she and the other emergency-room nurses feel they are needed in the ER, where they fill the most vital role in the hospital. They work special hours when needed, do whatever tasks are required, and often work in difficult and stressful circumstances. They think the floor nurses have relatively easy jobs for the pay they receive. Scott, the leader of the floor nurse team, tells you that his group believes the ER nurses lack the special training and extra experience that the floor nurses bring to the hospital. The floor nurses claim they have the heaviest responsibilities and do the most exacting work. Because they have ongoing contact with patients and families, they believe they should not be called away from vital floor duties to help the ER nurses complete their tasks. Now that you are faced with this resistance, how can you most effectively introduce the cross-training model?

Reinforcing Skills

1. Choose two courses that you are taking this term, ideally in different faculties, and describe the culture of the classroom in each. What are the similarities and differences? What values about learning might you infer from your observations of culture?

2. Compare the atmosphere or feeling you get from various organizations. Because of the number and wide variety that you will find, it will probably be easiest for you to do this exercise using restaurants, retail stores, or banks. Based on the atmosphere that you observe, what type of organizational culture do you think these organizations might have? If you can, interview three employees at each organization for their descriptions of their organization's culture.

3. Think about changes (major and minor) that you have dealt with over the past year. Perhaps these changes involved other people and perhaps they were personal. Did you resist the change? Did others resist the change? How did you overcome your resistance or the resistance of others to the change?

4. Interview a manager at three different organizations about a change he or she has introduced. What was the manager's experience in bringing in the change? How did the manager manage resistance to the change?

ENDNOTES

Chapter 1

1. Opening vignette based on Social Capital Partners, "Launching a Social Enterprise: Early Learnings from Inner City Renovation," ICR Learnings Report.

2. C. R. Farquhar and J. A. Longair, *Creating High-Performance Organizations With People*, Report # R164–96 (Ottawa: The Conference Board of Canada, 1996).

3. Statistics in remainder of paragraph from Industry Canada, "Key Small Business Statistics," July 2005, http://strategis.gc.ca/sbstatistics.

4. Social Capital Partners, "Launching a Social Enterprise: Early Learnings from Inner City Renovation," ICR Learnings Report.

5. See, for example, M. J. Driver, "Cognitive Psychology: An Interactionist View"; R. H. Hall, "Organizational Behavior: A Sociological Perspective"; and C. Hardy, "The Contribution of Political Science to Organizational Behavior," all in J. W. Lorsch, ed., *Handbook of Organizational Behavior* (Englewood Cliffs, NJ: Prentice Hall, 1987), pp. 62–108.

6. R. Weinberg and W. Nord, "Coping With 'It's All Common Sense,'" *Exchange* 7, no. 2 (1982), pp. 29–33; R. P. Vecchio, "Some Popular (but Misguided) Criticisms of the Organizational Sciences," *Organizational Behavior Teaching Review* 10, no. 1 (1986–1987), pp. 28–34; and M. L. Lynn, "Organizational Behavior and Common Sense: Philosophical Implications for Teaching and Thinking" (paper presented at the 14th Annual Organizational Behavior Teaching Conference, Waltham, MA, May 1987).

7. This insight courtesy of an anonymous reviewer.

8. C. Thompson, "State of the Union," *Report on Business*, April 1998, pp. 73–82.

9. B. Livesey, "Making Nice," *Report on Business*, March 1998, pp. 96–104.

10. "50 Best Employers in Canada," *Report on Business*, December 23, 2005, p. 49.

11. R. T. Mowday, L. W. Porter, and R. M. Steers, *Employee Organization Linkages: The Psychology of Commitment, Absenteeism, and Turnover* (New York: Academic Press, 1982).

12. C. R. Farquhar and J. A. Longair, *Creating High-Performance Organizations With People*, Report # R164–96 (Ottawa: The Conference Board of Canada, 1996).

13. C.R. Farquhar and J.A. Longair, *Creating High-Performance Organizations With People*, Report # R164–96 (Ottawa: The Conference Board of Canada, 1996).

14. "People Power," *Canadian Business Review*, Spring 1996, p. 42.

15. Social Capital Partners, "Launching a Social Enterprise: Early Learnings from Inner City Renovation," ICR Learnings Report.

16. W. Marsden, "Ad Exec Brault Gets 2½ Years in Jail," *Gazette* (Montreal), May 6, 2006.

17. T. A. Wright, R. Cropanzano, P. J. Denney, and G. L. Moline, "When a Happy Worker Is a Productive Worker: A Preliminary Examination of Three Models," *Canadian Journal of Behavioural Science* 34, no. 3 (July 2002), pp. 146–150.

18. R. O'Flanagan, "Sears Employees Consider Joining Steelworkers," *Sudbury Star*, July 8, 2005, p. A3.

19. Angus Reid Group, *Workplace 2000: Working Toward the Millennium*, Fall 1997.

20. B. Dumaine, "The New Non-Manager Managers," *Fortune*, February 22, 1993, pp. 80–84.

21. "Wanted: Teammates, Crew Members, and Cast Members: But No Employees," *Wall Street Journal*, April 30, 1996, p. A1.

22. S. Ross, "U.S. Managers Fail to Fit the Bill in New Workplace: Study," *Reuters News Agency*, November 19, 1999.

23. *OB in the Workplace* based on P. Verburg, "Prepare for Takeoff," *Canadian Business*, December 25, 2000, pp. 94–96+.

24. The Conference Board of Canada, *Employability Skills Profile*, 1998.

25. T. Belford, "Strategy for the New Economy," *Financial Post* (*National Post*), March 14, 2005, p. FP9.

26. D. Nebenzahl, "People Skills Matter Most," *Gazette* (Montreal), September 20, 2004, p. B.1.

27. See, for instance, R. R. Thomas Jr., "From Affirmative Action to Affirming Diversity," *Harvard Business Review*, March–April 1990, pp. 107–117; B. Mandrell and S. Kohler-Gray, "Management Development That Values Diversity," *Personnel*, March 1990, pp. 41–47; J. Dreyfuss, "Get Ready for the New Work Force," *Fortune*, April 23, 1990, pp. 165–181; and I. Wielawski, "Diversity Makes Both Dollars and Sense," *Los Angeles Times*, May 16, 1994, p. I1–3.

28. *Focus on Diversity* based on M. O'Brien, "Heritage Room for Native Cadets," *Leader-Post* (Regina), December 5, 2000, p. A3.

29. See, for instance, E. E. Kossek and S. A. Lobel, eds., *Managing Diversity* (Cambridge, MA: Blackwell, 1996); J. A. Segal, "Diversify for Dollars," *HR Magazine*, April 1997, pp. 134–140; and "Strength Through Diversity for Bottom-Line Success," *Working Women*, March 1999, pp. 67–77.

30. E. Beauchesne, "Stats Can Misjudges Canada's Productivity," *CanWest News*, April 27, 2006, p. 1; and K. Beckman, P. M. Darby, D. Lemaire, and Y. St-Maurice, *Death by a Thousand Paper Cuts: The Effect of Barriers to Competition on Canadian Productivity* (Ottawa: The Conference Board of Canada, April 2006).

31. P. Drucker, *Management: Tasks, Responsibilities, Practices* (New York: Harper and Row, 1974).

32. D. W. Organ, *Organizational Citizenship Behavior: The Good Soldier Syndrome* (Lexington, MA: Lexington Books, 1988), p. 4.

33. M. G. Ehrhart and S. E. Naumann, "Organizational Citizenship Behavior in Work Groups: A Group Norms Approach," *Journal of Applied Psychology* 89, no. 6 (December 1, 2004), pp. 960–974.

34. "Corporate Culture," *Canadian HR Reporter* 17, no. 21 (December 6, 2004), pp. 7–11.

35. See, for example, P. M. Podsakoff and S. B. MacKenzie, "Organizational Citizenship Behavior and Sales Unit Effectiveness," *Journal of Marketing Research*, August 1994, pp. 351–363; P. M. Podsakoff, M. Ahearne, and S. B. MacKenzie, "Organizational Citizenship Behavior and the Quantity and Quality of Work Group

Performance," *Journal of Applied Psychology*, April 1997, pp. 262–270; L. A. Bettencourt, K. Gwinner, and M. L. Meuter, "A Comparison of Attitude, Personality, and Knowledge Predictors of Service-Oriented Organizational Citizenship Behaviors," *Journal of Applied Psychology* 86, 2001, pp. 29–41; and E. W. Morrison, "Organizational Citizenship Behavior as a Critical Link Between HRM Practices and Service Quality," *Human Resource Management* 35, 1996, pp. 493–512.

36. J. Pfeffer, and J. F. Veiga, "Putting People First for Organizational Success," *Academy of Management Executive* 13, no. 2 (May 1999), pp. 37–48. See also L. Bassi and D. McMurrer, "How's Your Return on People?" *Harvard Business Review* 82, no. 3 (March 2004), p. 18.

37. M. A. Huselid, "The Impact of Human Resource Management Practices on Turnover, Productivity, and Corporate Financial Performance," *Academy of Management Journal* 38, 1995, p. 647.

38. L. Blimes, K. Wetzker, and P. Xhonneux, "Value in Human Resources," *Financial Times*, February 1997, p. 10.

39. M. Kaeter, "The Age of the Specialized Generalist," *Training*, December 1993, pp. 48–53; and N. Templin, "Auto Plants, Hiring Again, Are Demanding Higher-Skilled Labor," *Wall Street Journal*, March 11, 1994, p. A1.

40. R. E. Quinn, *Beyond Rational Management: Mastering the Paradoxes and Competing Demands of High Performance* (San Francisco: Jossey-Bass, 1991); R. E. Quinn, S. R. Faerman, M. P. Thompson, and M. R. McGrath, *Becoming a Master Manager: A Competency Framework* (New York: John Wiley and Sons, 1990); K. Cameron and R. E. Quinn, *Diagnosing and Changing Organizational Culture: Based on the Competing Values Framework* (Reading, MA: Addison Wesley Longman, 1999).

41. R. E. Quinn, S. R. Faerman, M. P. Thompson, and M. R. McGrath, *Becoming a Master Manager: A Competency Framework* (New York: John Wiley and Sons, 1990).

42. D. Maley, "Canada's Top Women CEOs," *Maclean's*, October 20, 1997, pp. 52+.

43. Written by Nancy Langton and Joy Begley © 1999. (The events described are based on an actual situation, although the participants, as well as the centre, have been disguised.)

Chapter 2

1. Opening vignette based on P. Stock, "Mutual Back-Scratchers: Longstanding Liberal Policies Are Linked to the Feds' Civil Service Morale Crisis," *Report Newsmagazine*, June 25, 2001, pp. 17–18; A. Thompson, "Who Protects the Protectors?" *Toronto Star*, May 26, 2001, pp. K1, K4; "Canada's Human Rights Watchdog Considers Changes in Wake of Scathing Report," *Canadian Press Newswire*, May 18, 2001; and "Women Working at Canadian Human Rights Watchdog Face Discrimination: Report," *Canadian Press Newswire*, May 12, 2001.

2. A. Thompson, "Who Protects the Protectors?" *Toronto Star*, May 26, 2001, pp. K1, K4.

3. T. Cole, "Who Loves Ya?" *Report on Business Magazine*, April 1999, pp. 44–60.

4. P. Stock, "Mutual Back-Scratchers: Longstanding Liberal Policies Are Linked to the Feds' Civil Service Morale Crisis," *Report Newsmagazine*, June 25, 2001, pp. 17–18.

5. A. Thompson, "Who Protects the Protectors?" *Toronto Star*, May 26, 2001, pp. K1, K4.

6. R. Weitzer and S. A. Tuch, "Racially Biased Policing: Determinants of Citizen Perceptions," *Social Forces* 83, no. 3 (March 2005),

pp. 1009–1030; J. Hagan, C. Shedd, and M. R. Payne, "Race, Ethnicity, and Youth Perceptions of Criminal Injustice," *American Sociological Review* 70, no. 3 (June 2005), pp. 381–407.

7. P. Glick, S. Larsen, C. Johnson, and H. Branstiter, "Evaluations of Sexy Women in Low- and High-Status Jobs," *Psychology of Women Quarterly*, December 2005, pp. 389–395.

8. H. H. Kelley, "Attribution in Social Interaction," in *Attribution: Perceiving the Causes of Behavior*, ed. E. Jones et al. (Morristown, NJ: General Learning Press, 1972).

9. See L. Ross, "The Intuitive Psychologist and His Shortcomings," in *Advances in Experimental Social Psychology*, vol. 10, ed. L. Berkowitz (Orlando, FL: Academic Press, 1977), pp. 174–220; and A. G. Miller and T. Lawson, "The Effect of an Informational Option on the Fundamental Attribution Error," *Personality and Social Psychology Bulletin*, June 1989, pp. 194–204.

10. M. L. A. Hayward, V. P. Rindova, and T. G. Pollock, "Believing One's Own Press: The Causes and Consequences of CEO Celebrity," *Strategic Management Journal* 25, no. 7 (July 2004), pp. 637–653.

11. N. Epley and D. Dunning, "Feeling 'Holier Than Thou': Are Self-Serving Assessments Produced by Errors in Self- or Social Predictions?" *Journal of Personality and Social Psychology*, March 2001.

12. M. Goerke, J. Moller, and S. Schulz-Hardt, "'It's Not My Fault—but Only I Can Change It': Counterfactual and Prefactual Thoughts of Managers," *Journal of Applied Psychology* 89, no. 2 (April 2004), pp. 279–292.

13. B. McKenna, "Modern Suicides Hold Little Glory," *Globe and Mail*, June 2, 1998, p. A14.

14. S. Nam, "Cultural and Managerial Attributions for Group Performance" (PhD diss., University of Oregon), cited in R. M. Steers, S. J. Bischoff, and L. H. Higgins, "Cross-Cultural Management Research," *Journal of Management Inquiry*, December 1992, pp. 325–326.

15. *Focus on Diversity* based on A. Kerr, "Illness Can Be a Workplace Handicap," *Globe and Mail*, July 15, 2002.

16. S. E. Asch, "Forming Impressions of Personality," *Journal of Abnormal and Social Psychology*, July 1946, pp. 258–290.

17. J. S. Bruner and R. Tagiuri, "The Perception of People," in *Handbook of Social Psychology*, ed. E. Lindzey (Reading, MA: Addison-Wesley, 1954), p. 641.

18. A. Parducci, "Category Judgment: A Range-Frequency Model," *Psychological Review* 72, no. 6 (November 1965), pp. 407–418; D. M. O'Reilly, R. A. Leitch, and D. H. Wedell, "The Effects of Immediate Context on Auditors' Judgments of Loan Quality," *Auditing* 23, no. 1 (2004), pp. 89–105; and J. DeCoster and H. M. Claypool, "A Meta-Analysis of Priming Effects on Impression Formation Supporting a General Model of Information Biases," *Personality & Social Psychology Review* 8, no. 1 (2004), pp. 2–27.

19. See, for example, C. M. Judd and B. Park, "Definition and Assessment of Accuracy in Social Stereotypes," *Psychological Review*, January 1993, pp. 109–128.

20. K. D. Elsbach, and R. M. Kramer, "Assessing Creativity in Hollywood Pitch Meetings: Evidence for a Dual-Process Model of Creativity Judgments," *Academy of Management Journal* 46, no. 3 (2003), pp. 283–301.

21. M. Gladwell, *Blink: The Power of Thinking Without Thinking* (New York: Little, Brown, 2005).

22. See, for example, S. T. Fiske, D. N. Beroff, E. Borgida, K. Deaux, and M. E. Heilman, "Use of Sex Stereotyping Research in Price Waterhouse vs. Hopkins," *American Psychologist*, 1991, pp. 1049–1060; G. N. Powell, "The Good Manager: Business

Students' Stereotypes of Japanese Managers Versus Stereotypes of American Managers," *Group & Organizational Management,* 1992, pp. 44–56; and K. J. Gibson, W. J. Zerbe, and R. E. Franken, "Job Search Strategies for Older Job Hunters: Addressing Employers' Perceptions," *Canadian Journal of Counselling,* 1992, pp. 166–176.

23. J. T. Jost and A. C. Kay, "Complementary Justice: Effects of 'Poor but Happy' and 'Poor but Honest' Stereotype Exemplars on System Justification and Implicit Activation of the Justice Motive," *Journal of Personality and Social Psychology* 85, no. 5 (2003), pp. 823–837.

24. J. C. Ziegert and P. J. Hanges, "Employment Discrimination: The Role of Implicit Attitudes, Motivation, and a Climate for Racial Bias," *Journal of Applied Psychology* 90, no. 3 (May 2005), pp. 553–562; and D. Pager and L. Quillian, "Walking the Talk? What Employers Say Versus What They Do," *American Sociological Review* 70, no. 3 (June 2005), pp. 355–380.

25. K. May, "Action Vowed on Unrest: Agency Head Refuses to Quit," *Calgary Herald,* May 19, 2001, p. A13.

26. See, for example, E. C. Webster, *Decision Making in the Employment Interview* (Montreal: McGill University, Industrial Relations Centre, 1964).

27. See, for example, R. D. Bretz Jr., G. T. Milkovich, and W. Read, "The Current State of Performance Appraisal Research and Practice: Concerns, Directions, and Implications," *Journal of Management,* June 1992, pp. 323–324; and P. M. Swiercz, M. L. Icenogle, N. B. Bryan, and R. W. Renn, "Do Perceptions of Performance Appraisal Fairness Predict Employee Attitudes and Performance?" in *Proceedings of the Academy of Management,* ed. D. P. Moore (Atlanta: Academy of Management, 1993), pp. 304–308.

28. J. Schaubroeck and S. S. K. Lam, "How Similarity to Peers and Supervisor Influences Organizational Advancement in Different Cultures," *Academy of Management Journal* 45, no. 6 (2002), pp. 1120–1136.

29. A. M. Owens, "People Who Exercise Are More Highly Regarded: Study," *National Post,* February 10, 2001, p. A2.

30. See, for example, D. Eden, *Pygmalion in Management* (Lexington, MA: Lexington, 1990); D. Eden, "Leadership and Expectations: Pygmalion Effects and Other Self-Fulfilling Prophecies," *Leadership Quarterly,* Winter 1992, pp. 271–305; D. B. McNatt, "Ancient Pygmalion Joins Contemporary Management: A Meta-Analysis of the Result," *Journal of Applied Psychology,* April 2000, pp. 314–322; O. B. Davidson and D. Eden, "Remedial Self-Fulfilling Prophecy: Two Field Experiments to Prevent Golem Effects Among Disadvantaged Women," *Journal of Applied Psychology,* June 2000, pp. 386–398; and D. B. McNatt, "Ancient Pygmalion Joins Contemporary Management: A Meta-Analysis of the Result," *Journal of Applied Psychology* 85, no. 2 (April 2000), pp. 314–322.

31. D. Eden and A. B. Shani, "Pygmalion Goes to Boot Camp: Expectancy, Leadership, and Trainee Performance," *Journal of Applied Psychology,* April 1982, pp. 194–199.

32. G. W. Allport, *Personality: A Psychological Interpretation* (New York: Holt, Rinehart and Winston, 1937), p. 48.

33. See also R. Hogan, "Personality Psychology for Organizational Researchers," chapter 1 in *Personality and Organizations,* ed. B. Schneider, D. B. Smith, A. P. Brief, and J. P. Walsh (Mahwah, NJ: Laurence Erlebaum Associates, 2004).

34. R. C. Carson, "Personality," in *Annual Review of Psychology,* vol. 40, ed. M. R. Rosenzweig and L. W. Porter (Palo Alto, CA: Annual Reviews, 1989), pp. 228–229.

35. See A. H. Buss, "Personality as Traits," *American Psychologist,* November 1989, pp. 1378–1388; and D. G. Winter, O. P. John,

A. J. Stewart, E. C. Klohnen, and L. E. Duncan, "Traits and Motives: Toward an Integration of Two Traditions in Personality Research," *Psychological Review,* April 1998, pp. 230–250.

36. R. R. McCrae and A. Terracciano, "Universal Features of Personality Traits from the Observer's Perspective: Data from 50 Cultures," *Journal of Personality and Social Psychology* 88, no. 3 (2005), pp. 547–561.

37. See R. R. McCrae and P. T. Costa Jr., "Reinterpreting the Myers-Briggs Type Indicator from the Perspective of the Five Factor Model of Personality," *Journal of Personality,* March 1989, pp. 17–40; and C. Fitzgerald and L. K. Kirby, eds., *Developing Leaders: Research and Applications in Psychological Type and Leadership Development* (Palo Alto, CA: Davies-Black Publishing, 1997).

38. See, for example, J. M. Digman, "Personality Structure: Emergence of the Five-Factor Model," in *Annual Review of Psychology,* vol. 41, ed. M. R. Rosenzweig and L. W. Porter (Palo Alto, CA: Annual Reviews, 1990), pp. 417–440; R. R. McCrae and O. P. John, "An Introduction to the Five-Factor Model and Its Applications," *Journal of Personality,* June 1992, pp. 175–215; L. R. Goldberg, "The Structure of Phenotypic Personality Traits," *American Psychologist,* January 1993, pp. 26–34; P. H. Raymark, M. J. Schmit, and R. M. Guion, "Identifying Potentially Useful Personality Constructs for Employee Selection," *Personnel Psychology,* Autumn 1997, pp. 723–736; and O. Behling, "Employee Selection: Will Intelligence and Conscientiousness Do the Job?" *Academy of Management Executive,* 12, 1998, pp. 77–86.

39. D. J. Ozer and V. Benet-Martinez, "Personality and the Prediction of Consequential Outcomes," *Annual Review of Psychology* 57, no. 1 (2006), pp. 401–421.

40. See, for instance, M. R. Barrick and M. K. Mount, "The Big Five Personality Dimensions and Job Performance: A Meta-Analysis," *Personnel Psychology* 44, 1991, pp. 1–26; R. P. Tett, D. N. Jackson, and M. Rothstein, "Personality Measures as Predictors of Job Performance: A Meta-Analytic Review," *Personnel Psychology,* Winter 1991, pp. 703–742; T. A. Judge, J. J. Martocchio, and C. J. Thoresen, "Five-Factor Model of Personality and Employee Absence," *Journal of Applied Psychology,* October 1997, pp. 745–755; O. Behling, "Employee Selection: Will Intelligence and Conscientiousness Do the Job?" *Academy of Management Executive,* February 1998, pp. 77–86; and F. S. Switzer III and P. L. Roth, "A Meta-Analytic Review of Predictors of Job Performance for Salespeople," *Journal of Applied Psychology,* August 1998, pp. 586–597.

41. See, for instance, S. L. Kichuk and W. H. Wiesner, "Work Teams: Selecting Members for Optimal Performance," *Canadian Psychology* 39, no. 1–2 (1999), pp. 23–32; M. R. Barrick and M. K. Mount, "The Big Five Personality Dimensions and Job Performance: A Meta-Analysis," *Personnel Psychology* 44, 1991, pp. 1–26; D. Ones, C. Viswesvaran, and F. Schmidt, "Meta-Analysis of Integrity Test Validities: Findings and Implications for Personnel Selection and Theories of Job Performance [Monograph]," *Journal of Applied Psychology* 47, no. 1 (1993), pp. 147–156; and R. T. Hogan, J. Hogan, and B. W. Roberts, "Personality Measurement and Employment Decisions: Questions and Answers, *American Psychologist* 51, no. 5 (1996), pp. 469–477.

42. T. A. Judge and R. Ilies, "Relationship of Personality to Performance Motivation: A Meta-Analytic Review," *Journal of Applied Psychology* 87, no. 4 (2002), pp. 797–807.

43. D. W. Organ, "Personality and Organizational Citizenship Behavior," *Journal of Management,* Summer 1994, pp. 465–478; D. W. Organ and K. Ryan, "A Meta-Analytic Review of Attitudinal and Dispositional Predictors of Organizational Citizenship Behavior," *Personnel Psychology,* Winter 1995, pp. 775–802; and M. A. Konovsky and D. W. Organ, "Dispositional and Contextual

Determinants of Organizational Citizenship Behavior," *Journal of Organizational Behavior,* May 1996, pp. 253–266.

44. J. B. Rotter, "Generalized Expectancies for Internal Versus External Control of Reinforcement," *Psychological Monographs* 80, no. 609 (1966).

45. P. E. Spector, C. L. Cooper, J. I. Sanchez, et al., "Locus of Control and Well-Being at Work: How Generalizable Are Western Findings?" *Academy of Management Journal* 45, no. 2 (2002), pp. 453–456, presents the results of studies done of five continents.

46. P. E. Spector, "Behavior in Organizations as a Function of Employee's Locus of Control," *Psychological Bulletin,* May 1982, p. 493; D. R. Norris and R. E. Niebuhr, "Attributional Influences on the Job Performance-Job Satisfaction Relationship," *Academy of Management Journal,* June 1984, pp. 424–431; and P. C. Nystrom, "Managers' Salaries and Their Beliefs About Reinforcement Control," *Journal of Social Psychology,* August 1983, pp. 291–292.

47. J. B. Rotter, "Generalized Expectancies for Internal Versus External Control of Reinforcement," *Psychological Monographs* 80, no. 609 (1966).

48. R. G. Vleeming, "Machiavellianism: A Preliminary Review," *Psychological Reports,* February 1979, pp. 295–310.

49. R. Christie and F. L. Geis, *Studies in Machiavellianism* (New York: Academic Press, 1970), p. 312; and N. V. Ramanaiah, A. Byravan, and F. R. J. Detwiler, "Revised Neo Personality Inventory Profiles of Machiavellian and Non-Machiavellian People," *Psychological Reports,* October 1994, pp. 937–938.

50. R. Christie and F. L. Geis, *Studies in Machiavellianism* (New York: Academic Press, 1970).

51. Based on J. Brockner, *Self-Esteem at Work* (Lexington, MA: Lexington Books, 1988), chapters 1–4; and N. Branden, *Self-Esteem at Work* (San Francisco: Jossey-Bass, 1998).

52. J. V. Wood, S. A. Heimpel, I. R. Newby-Clark, and M. Ross, "Snatching Defeat from the Jaws of Victory: Self-Esteem Differences in the Experience and Anticipation of Success," *Journal of Personality and Social Psychology* 89, no. 5 (2005), pp. 764–780.

53. D. P. Schmitt and J. Allik, "Simultaneous Administration of the Rosenberg Self-Esteem Scale in 53 Nations: Exploring the Universal and Culture-Specific Features of Global Self-Esteem," *Journal of Personality and Social Psychology* 89, no. 4 (2005), pp. 623–642.

54. D. De Cremer, B. van Knippenberg, D. van Knippenberg, D. Mullenders, and F. Stinglhamber, "Rewarding Leadership and Fair Procedures as Determinants of Self-Esteem," *Journal of Applied Psychology* 90, no. 1 (2005), pp. 3–12.

55. See M. Snyder, *Public Appearances/Private Realities: The Psychology of Self-Monitoring* (New York: W. H. Freeman, 1987).

56. See M. Snyder, *Public Appearances/Private Realities: The Psychology of Self-Monitoring* (New York: W. H. Freeman, 1987).

57. M. Kilduff and D. V. Day, "Do Chameleons Get Ahead? The Effects of Self-Monitoring on Managerial Careers," *Academy of Management Journal,* August 1994, pp. 1047–1060.

58. D. V. Day, D. J. Schleicher, A. L. Unckless, and N. J. Hiller, "Self-Monitoring Personality at Work: A Meta-Analytic Investigation of Construct Validity," *Journal of Applied Psychology,* April 2002, pp. 390–401.

59. R. N. Taylor and M. D. Dunnette, "Influence of Dogmatism, Risk-Taking Propensity, and Intelligence on Decision-Making Strategies for a Sample of Industrial Managers," *Journal of Applied Psychology,* August 1974, pp. 420–423.

60. I. L. Janis and L. Mann, *Decision Making: A Psychological Analysis of Conflict, Choice, and Commitment* (New York: Free Press, 1977).

61. N. Kogan and M. A. Wallach, "Group Risk Taking as a Function of Members' Anxiety and Defensiveness," *Journal of Personality,* March 1967, pp. 50–63.

62. M. Friedman and R. H. Rosenman, *Type A Behavior and Your Heart* (New York: Alfred A. Knopf, 1974), p. 84 (emphasis in original).

63. M. Friedman and R. H. Rosenman, *Type A Behavior and Your Heart* (New York: Alfred A. Knopf, 1974), pp. 84–85.

64. K. A. Matthews, "Assessment of Type A Behavior, Anger, and Hostility in Epidemiological Studies of Cardiovascular Disease," in *Measuring Psychological Variables in Epidemiologic Studies of Cardiovascular Disease,* NIH Publication No. 85-2270, ed. A. M. Ostfield and E. D. Eaker (Washington, DC: US Department of Health and Human Services, 1985).

65. M. Friedman and R. H. Rosenman, *Type A Behavior and Your Heart* (New York: Alfred A. Knopf, 1974), p. 86.

66. J. Schaubroeck, D. C. Ganster, and B. E. Kemmerer, "Job Complexity, 'Type A' Behavior, and Cardiovascular Disorder," *Academy of Management Journal* 37, April 1994, pp. 426–439.

67. J. M. Crant, "Proactive Behavior in Organizations," *Journal of Management* 26, no. 3 (2000), p. 436.

68. S. E. Seibert, M. L. Kraimer, and J. M. Crant, "What Do Proactive People Do? A Longitudinal Model Linking Proactive Personality and Career Success," *Personnel Psychology,* Winter 2001, p. 850; and J. A. Thompson, "Proactive Personality and Job Performance: A Social Capital Perspective," *Journal of Applied Psychology* 90, no. 5 (2005), pp. 1011–1017.

69. T. S. Bateman and J. M. Crant, "The Proactive Component of Organizational Behavior: A Measure and Correlates," *Journal of Organizational Behavior,* March 1993, pp. 103–118; A. L. Frohman, "Igniting Organizational Change from Below: The Power of Personal Initiative," *Organizational Dynamics,* Winter 1997, pp. 39–53; and J. M. Crant and T. S. Bateman, "Charismatic Leadership Viewed from Above: The Impact of Proactive Personality," *Journal of Organizational Behavior,* February 2000, pp. 63–75.

70. J. M. Crant, "Proactive Behavior in Organizations," *Journal of Management* 26, no. 3 (2000), p. 436.

71. See, for instance, R. C. Becherer and J. G. Maurer, "The Proactive Personality Disposition and Entrepreneurial Behavior Among Small Company Presidents," *Journal of Small Business Management,* January 1999, pp. 28–36.

72. S. E. Seibert, J. M. Crant, and M. L. Kraimer, "Proactive Personality and Career Success," *Journal of Applied Psychology,* June 1999, pp. 416–427; and S. E. Seibert, M. L. Kraimer, and J. M. Crant, "What Do Proactive People Do? A Longitudinal Model Linking Proactive Personality and Career Success," *Personnel Psychology,* Winter 2001, p. 850.

73. F. Kluckhohn and F. L. Strodtbeck, *Variations in Value Orientations* (Evanston, IL: Row Peterson, 1961).

74. J. Pickard, "Misuse of Tests Leads to Unfair Recruitment," *People Management* 2, no. 25 (1996), p. 7.

75. J. Pickard, "Misuse of Tests Leads to Unfair Recruitment," *People Management* 2, no. 25 (1996), p. 7.

76. See N. H. Frijda, "Moods, Emotion Episodes and Emotions," in *Handbook of Emotions,* ed. M. Lewis and J. M. Haviland (New York: Guildford Press, 1993), pp. 381–403.

77. H. M. Weiss and R. Cropanzano, "Affective Events Theory," in *Research in Organizational Behavior,* vol. 18, ed. B. M. Staw and L. L. Cummings (Greenwich, CT: JAI Press, 1996), pp. 17–19.

78. N. H. Frijda, "Moods, Emotion Episodes and Emotions," in *Handbook of Emotions,* ed. M. Lewis and J. M. Haviland (New York: Guildford Press, 1993), p. 381. This point is further explored in

L. J. Barclay, D. P. Skarlicki, and S. D. Pugh, "Exploring the Role of Emotions in Injustice Perceptions and Retaliation, *Journal of Applied Psychology* 90, no. 4 (2005), pp. 629–643, who find that the experience of injustice can result in varied emotions.

79. H. M. Weiss and R. Cropanzano, "Affective Events Theory," in *Research in Organizational Behavior*, vol. 18, ed. B. M. Staw and L. L. Cummings (Greenwich, CT: JAI Press, 1996), pp. 20–22.

80. Cited in R. D. Woodworth, *Experimental Psychology* (New York: Holt, 1938).

81. S. P. Brown, R. A. Westbrook, et al. "Good Cope, Bad Cope: Adaptive and Maladaptive Coping Strategies Following a Critical Negative Work Event," *Journal of Applied Psychology* 90, no. 4 (2005), pp. 792–798.

82. A. Hochschild, *The Managed Heart: The Commercialization of Human Feeling* (Berkeley, CA: University of California Press, 1983); J. Van Maanen and G. Kunda, "Real Feelings: Emotional Expression and Organizational Culture," in *Research in Organizational Behavior*, vol. 11, ed. L. L. Cummings and B. M. Staw (Greenwich, CT: JAI Press, 1989), pp. 43–103; and B. A. Turner, "Sociological Aspects of Organizational Symbolism," *Organization Studies* 7, 1986, pp. 101–115.

83. A. Hochschild, *The Managed Heart: The Commercialization of Human Feeling* (Berkeley, CA: University of California Press, 1983); R. I. Sutton and A. Rafaeli, "Untangling the Relationship Between Displayed Emotions and Organizational Sales: The Case of Convenience Stores," *Academy of Management Journal* 31, 1988, pp. 461–487; A. Rafaeli, "When Cashiers Meet Customers: An Analysis of the Role of Supermarket Cashiers," *Academy of Management Journal* 32, 1989, pp. 245–273; A. Rafaeli and R. I. Sutton, "The Expression of Emotion in Organizational Life," in *Research in Organizational Behavior*, vol. 11, ed. L. L. Cummings and B. M. Staw (Greenwich, CT: JAI Press, 1989), pp. 1–42; A. Rafaeli and R. I. Sutton, "Busy Stores and Demanding Customers: How Do They Affect the Display of Positive Emotion?" *Academy of Management Journal* 33, 1990, pp. 623–637; A. Rafaeli and R. I. Sutton, "Emotional Contrast Strategies as Means of Social Influence: Lessons from Criminal Interrogators and Bill Collectors," *Academy of Management Journal* 34, 1991, pp. 749–775; R. I. Sutton, "Maintaining Norms About Expressed Emotions: The Case of Bill Collectors," *Administrative Science Quarterly* 36, 1991, pp. 245–268; and J. A. Morris and D. C. Feldman, "The Dimensions, Antecedents, and Consequences of Emotional Labor," *Academy of Management Review*, October 1996, pp. 986–1010.

84. A. Hochschild, *The Managed Heart: The Commercialization of Human Feeling* (Berkeley, CA: University of California Press, 1983); R. I. Sutton and A. Rafaeli, "Untangling the Relationship Between Displayed Emotions and Organizational Sales: The Case of Convenience Stores," *Academy of Management Journal* 31, 1988, pp. 461–487; A. Rafaeli, "When Cashiers Meet Customers: An Analysis of the Role of Supermarket Cashiers," *Academy of Management Journal* 32, 1989, pp. 245–273; A. Rafaeli and R. I. Sutton, "The Expression of Emotion in Organizational Life," in *Research in Organizational Behavior*, vol. 11, ed. L. L. Cummings and B. M. Staw (Greenwich, CT: JAI Press, 1989), pp. 1–42; A. Rafaeli and R. I. Sutton, "Busy Stores and Demanding Customers: How Do They Affect the Display of Positive Emotion?" *Academy of Management Journal* 33, 1990, pp. 623–637; A. Rafaeli and R. I. Sutton, "Emotional Contrast Strategies as Means of Social Influence: Lessons from Criminal Interrogators and Bill Collectors," *Academy of Management Journal* 34, 1991, pp. 749–775; and R. I. Sutton, "Maintaining Norms About Expressed Emotions: The Case of Bill Collectors," *Administrative Science Quarterly* 36, 1991, pp. 245–268.

85. A. A. Grandey, "When 'The Show Must Go On': Surface Acting and Deep Acting as Determinants of Emotional Exhaustion and Peer-Rated Service Delivery," *Academy of Management Journal* 46, no. 1 (2003), pp. 86–96.

86. H. Willmott, "Strength Is Ignorance; Slavery Is Freedom: Managing Culture in Modern Organizations," *Journal of Management Studies* 30, 1993, pp. 515–552; and S. Fineman, "Emotion and Organizing," in *Handbook of Organizational Studies*, ed. S. Clegg (London: Sage, 1996), pp. 543–564.

87. A. Hochschild, *The Managed Heart: The Commercialization of Human Feeling* (Berkeley, CA: University of California Press, 1983).

88. J. Van Maanen and G. Kunda, "Real Feelings: Emotional Expression and Organizational Culture," in *Research in Organizational Behavior*, vol. 11, ed. L. L. Cummings and B. M. Staw (Greenwich, CT: JAI Press, 1989), pp. 43–103.

89. V. Waldron and K. Krone, "The Experience and Expression of Emotion in the Workplace: A Study of a Corrections Organization," *Management Communication Quarterly* 4, 1991, pp. 287–309.

90. C. Bains, "Safeway Clerks' Forced Smiles Seen as Flirtation," *Vancouver Sun*, September 3, 1998, pp. A1, A2.

91. N. M. Ashkanasy, and C. S. Daus, "Emotion in the Workplace: The New Challenge for Managers," *Academy of Management Executive* 16, no. 1 (2002), pp. 76–86.

92. This section is based on Daniel Goleman, *Emotional Intelligence* (New York: Bantam, 1995); J. D. Mayer and G. Geher, "Emotional Intelligence and the Identification of Emotion," *Intelligence*, March–April 1996, pp. 89–113; J. Stuller, "EQ: Edging Toward Respectability," *Training*, June 1997, pp. 43–48; R. K. Cooper, "Applying Emotional Intelligence in the Workplace," *Training & Development*, December 1997, pp. 31–38; "HR Pulse: Emotional Intelligence," *HR Magazine*, January 1998, p. 19; M. Davies, L. Stankov, and R. D. Roberts, "Emotional Intelligence: In Search of an Elusive Construct," *Journal of Personality and Social Psychology*, October 1998, pp. 989–1015; and D. Goleman, *Working With Emotional Intelligence* (New York: Bantam, 1999).

93. T. Sy, S. Cote, and R. Saavedra, "The Contagious Leader: Impact of the Leader's Mood on the Mood of Group Members, Group Affective Tone, and Group Processes," *Journal of Applied Psychology* 90, no. 2 (March 2005), pp. 295–305.

94. K. S. Law, C. S. Wong, and L. J. Song, "The Construct and Criterion Validity of Emotional Intelligence and Its Potential Utility for Management Studies," *Journal of Applied Psychology* 89, no. 3 (June 2004), pp. 483–496; T. A. Judge, A. E. Colbert, and R. Ilies, "Intelligence and Leadership: A Quantitative Review and Test of Theoretical Propositions," *Journal of Applied Psychology* 89, no. 3 (June 2004), pp. 542–552; J. D. Mayer and G. Geher, "Emotional Intelligence and the Identification of Emotion," *Intelligence*, March–April 1996, pp. 89–113; and M. Davies, L. Stankov, and R. D. Roberts, "Emotional Intelligence: In Search of an Elusive Construct," *Journal of Personality and Social Psychology*, October 1998, pp. 989–1015.

95. R. Bar-On, "Emotional and Social Intelligence: Insights from the Emotional Quotient Inventory," in *Handbook of Emotional Intelligence*, ed. R. Bar-On and J. Parker (San Francisco, CA: Jossey-Bass, 2000).

96. J. Rowlands, "Soft Skills Give Hard Edge," *Globe and Mail*, June 9, 2004, p. C8.

97. D. Goleman, *Working With Emotional Intelligence* (New York: Bantam, 1999).

98. R. McQueen, "New CEO Brings Fresh Style to BMO: Tony Comper Slowly Stepping Out of the Shadows," *Financial Post* (*National Post*), November 10, 1999, p. C3.

99. S. L. Robinson and R. J. Bennett, "A Typology of Deviant Workplace Behaviors: A Multidimensional Scaling Study," *Academy of Management Journal*, April 1995, p. 556.

100. S. L. Robinson and R. J. Bennett, "A Typology of Deviant Workplace Behaviors: A Multidimensional Scaling Study," *Academy of Management Journal*, April 1995, pp. 555–572.

101. Based on A. G. Bedeian, "Workplace Envy," *Organizational Dynamics*, Spring 1995, p. 50.

102. A. G. Bedeian, "Workplace Envy," *Organizational Dynamics*, Spring 1995, p. 54.

103. H. M. Weiss and R. Cropanzano, "Affective Events Theory," in *Research in Organizational Behavior*, vol. 18, ed. B. M. Staw and L. L. Cummings (Greenwich, CT: JAI Press, 1996), p. 55.

104. Some of the points in this argument are from R. J. House, S. A. Shane, and D. M. Herold, "Rumors of the Death of Dispositional Research Are Vastly Exaggerated," *Academy of Management Review*, January 1996, pp. 203–224.

105. Based on A. Davis-Blake and J. Pfeffer, "Just a Mirage: The Search for Dispositional Effects in Organizational Research," *Academy of Management Review*, July 1989, pp. 385–400.

106. Based on V. P. Richmond, J. C. McCroskey, and S. K. Payne, *Nonverbal Behavior in Interpersonal Relations*, 2nd ed. (Englewood Cliffs, NJ: Prentice Hall, 1991), pp. 117–138; and L. A. King, "Ambivalence Over Emotional Expression and Reading Emotions in Situations and Faces," *Journal of Personality and Social Psychology*, March 1998, pp. 753–762.

Chapter 3

1. Taken from the website of Procter & Gamble: http://www.pg.com.

2. S. H. Schwartz, "Universals in the Content and Structure of Values: Theoretical Advances and Empirical Tests in 20 Countries," in *Advances in Experimental Social Psychology*, ed. M. P. Zanna (New York: Academic Press, 1992), p. 4.

3. M. Rokeach and S. J. Ball-Rokeach, "Stability and Change in American Value Priorities, 1968–1981," *American Psychologist*, May 1989, pp. 775–784.

4. M. Rokeach, *The Nature of Human Values* (New York: Free Press, 1973), p. 6.

5. J. M. Munson and B. Z. Posner, "The Factorial Validity of a Modified Rokeach Value Survey for Four Diverse Samples," *Educational and Psychological Measurement*, Winter 1980, pp. 1073–1079; and W. C. Frederick and J. Weber, "The Values of Corporate Managers and Their Critics: An Empirical Description and Normative Implications," in *Business Ethics: Research Issues and Empirical Studies*, ed. W. C. Frederick and L. E. Preston (Greenwich, CT: JAI Press, 1990), pp. 123–144.

6. W. C. Frederick and J. Weber, "The Values of Corporate Managers and Their Critics: An Empirical Description and Normative Implications," in *Business Ethics: Research Issues and Empirical Studies*, ed. W. C. Frederick and L. E. Preston (Greenwich, CT: JAI Press, 1990), pp. 123–144.

7. W. C. Frederick and J. Weber, "The Values of Corporate Managers and Their Critics: An Empirical Description and Normative Implications," in *Business Ethics: Research Issues and Empirical Studies*, ed. W. C. Frederick and L. E. Preston (Greenwich, CT: JAI Press, 1990), p. 132.

8. K. Hodgson, *A Rock and a Hard Place: How to Make Ethical Business Decisions When the Choices Are Tough* (New York: AMACOM, 1992), pp. 66–67.

9. G. Hofstede, *Culture's Consequences: International Differences in Work Related Values* (Beverly Hills, CA: Sage, 1980); G. Hofstede, *Cultures and Organizations: Software of the Mind* (London: McGraw-Hill, 1991); and G. Hofstede, "Cultural Constraints in Management Theories," *Academy of Management Executive*, February 1993, pp. 81–94.

10. G. Hofstede and M. H. Bond, "The Confucius Connection: From Cultural Roots to Economic Growth," *Organizational Dynamics*, Spring 1988, pp. 12–13.

11. R. J. House, P. J. Hanges, M. Javidan, P. W. Dorfman, and V. Gupta, *Culture, Leadership, and Organizations: The GLOBE Study of 62 Societies* (Thousand Oaks, CA: Sage Publications, 2004).

12. G. Hofstede and M. H. Bond, "The Confucius Connection: From Cultural Roots to Economic Growth," *Organizational Dynamics*, Spring 1988, pp. 12–13; and G. Hofstede, "Cultural Constraints in Management Theories," *Academy of Management Executive*, February 1993, pp. 81–94.

13. B. Meglino, E. C. Ravlin, and C. L. Adkins, "A Work Values Approach to Corporate Culture: A Field Test of the Value Congruence Process and Its Relationship to Individual Outcomes," *Journal of Applied Psychology* 74, 1989, pp. 424–432.

14. B. Z. Posner, J. M. Kouzes, and W. H. Schmidt, "Shared Values Make a Difference: An Empirical Test of Corporate Culture," *Human Resource Management* 24, 1985, pp. 293–310; and A. L. Balazas, "Value Congruency: The Case of the 'Socially Responsible' Firm," *Journal of Business Research* 20, 1990, pp. 171–181.

15. C. A. O'Reilly, J. Chatman, and D. Caldwell, "People and Organizational Culture: A Q-Sort Approach to Assessing Person-Organizational Fit," *Academy of Management Journal* 34, 1991, pp. 487–516.

16. C. Enz and C. K. Schwenk, "Performance and Sharing of Organizational Values" (paper presented at the annual meeting of the Academy of Management, Washington, DC, 1989).

17. E. Anderssen and M. Valpy, "Face the Nation: Canada Remade," *Globe and Mail*, June 7, 2003, pp. A10–A11.

18. G. Schellenberg, *Immigrants in Canada's Census Metropolitan Areas*, Catalogue no. 89-613-MIE—No. 003 (Ottawa: Statistics Canada, August 2004).

19. Statistics Canada, "2001 Census: *Census of Population: Language, Mobility and Migration*," *The Daily*, December 10, 2002.

20. Statistics Canada, "2001 Census: *Census of Population: Language, Mobility and Migration*," *The Daily*, December 10, 2002.

21. Statistics Canada, "Ethnic Diversity Survey, 2002," *The Daily*, September 29, 2003.

22. The Pew Research Center for the People & the Press, *Views of a Changing World 2003* (Washington, DC: The Pew Research Center for the People & the Press, June 2003).

23. M. Adams, *Fire and Ice: The United States, Canada and the Myth of Converging Values* (Toronto: Penguin Canada, 2003).

24. M. Adams, *Fire and Ice: The United States, Canada and the Myth of Converging Values* (Toronto: Penguin Canada, 2003).

25. R. N. Kanungo and J. K. Bhatnagar, "Achievement Orientation and Occupational Values: A Comparative Study of Young French and English Canadians," *Canadian Journal of Behavioural Science* 12, 1978, pp. 384–392; M. W. McCarrey, S. Edwards, and R. Jones, "The Influence of Ethnolinguistic Group Membership, Sex and Position Level on Motivational Orientation of Canadian Anglophone and Francophone Employees," *Canadian Journal of Behavioural Science* 9, 1977, pp. 274–282; M. W. McCarrey, S. Edwards, and R. Jones, "Personal Values of Canadian Anglophone and Francophone Employees and Ethnolinguistic

Group Membership, Sex and Position Level," *Journal of Psychology* 104, 1978, pp. 175–184; S. Richer and P. Laporte, "Culture, Cognition and English-French Competition," in *Readings in Social Psychology: Focus on Canada*, ed. D. Koulack and D. Perlman (Toronto: Wiley and Sons, 1973); and L. Shapiro and D. Perlman, "Value Differences Between English and French Canadian High School Students," *Canadian Ethnic Studies* 8, 1976, pp. 50–55.

26. R. N. Kanungo and J. K. Bhatnagar, "Achievement Orientation and Occupational Values: A Comparative Study of Young French and English Canadians," *Canadian Journal of Behavioural Science* 12, 1978, pp. 384–392.

27. V. Mann-Feder and V. Savicki, "Burnout in Anglophone and Francophone Child and Youth Workers in Canada: A Cross-Cultural Comparison," *Child & Youth Care Forum* 32, no. 6 (December 2003), p. 345.

28. R. N. Kanungo and J. K. Bhatnagar, "Achievement Orientation and Occupational Values: A Comparative Study of Young French and English Canadians," *Canadian Journal of Behavioural Science* 12, 1978, pp. 384–392.

29. V. Mann-Feder and V. Savicki, "Burnout in Anglophone and Francophone Child and Youth Workers in Canada: A Cross-Cultural Comparison," *Child & Youth Care Forum* 32, no. 6 (December 2003), pp. 337–354.

30. H. C. Jain, J. Normand, and R. N. Kanungo, "Job Motivation of Canadian Anglophone and Francophone Hospital Employees," *Canadian Journal of Behavioural Science*, April 1979, pp. 160–163; R. N. Kanungo, G. J. Gorn, and H. J. Dauderis, "Motivational Orientation of Canadian Anglophone and Francophone Managers," *Canadian Journal of Behavioural Science*, April 1976, pp. 107–121.

31. M. Major, M. McCarrey, P. Mercier, and Y. Gasse, "Meanings of Work and Personal Values of Canadian Anglophone and Francophone Middle Managers," *Canadian Journal of Administrative Sciences*, September 1994, pp. 251–263.

32. G. Bouchard, F. Rocher, and G. Rocher, *Les Francophones Québécois* (Montreal, PQ: Bowne de Montréal, 1991).

33. A. Derfel, "Boy, Are We Stressed Out! Quebec Has Highest Rate of Work Absenteeism," *Gazette* (Montreal), May 29, 2003, http://www.canada.com/montreal/montrealgazette/story.asp?id=5D0D7 AF8-DFCB-44D5-ABE4-DA4DACA11DEA (accessed May 29, 2003).

34. P. La Novara, "Culture Participation: Does Language Make a Difference?" *Focus on Culture* 13, no. 3, Catalogue no. 87-004-XIE (Ottawa: Statistics Canada, 2002).

35. Statistics Canada, *2001 Census*. Cited in Industry Canada, "Aboriginal Business Canada," http://strategis.ic.gc.ca/epic/internet/inabc-eac.nsf/en/ab00313e.html#a_ftn1 (accessed April 24, 2006).

36. C. Howes, "The New Native Tycoons: Armed With a New Sense of Entrepreneurialism, Aboriginals Across Canada Have Begun Cashing in on Energy, Forestry, Mining and Other Sectors, and Are Creating Businesses at a Rate Faster Than the National Average," *Financial Post* (*National Post*), January 27, 2001, p. D5.

37. L. Redpath and M. O. Nielsen, "A Comparison of Native Culture, Non-Native Culture and New Management Ideology," *Canadian Journal of Administrative Sciences* 14, no. 3 (1997), p. 327.

38. G. C. Anders and K. K. Anders, "Incompatible Goals in Unconventional Organizations: The Politics of Alaska Native Corporations," *Organization Studies* 7, 1986, pp. 213–233; G. Dacks, "Worker-Controlled Native Enterprises: A Vehicle for Community Development in Northern Canada?" *Canadian Journal of Native Studies* 3, 1983, pp. 289–310; L. P. Dana, "Self-

Employment in the Canadian Sub-Arctic: An Exploratory Study," *Canadian Journal of Administrative Sciences* 13, 1996, pp. 65–77.

39. L. Redpath and M. O. Nielsen, "A Comparison of Native Culture, Non-Native Culture and New Management Ideology," *Canadian Journal of Administrative Sciences* 14, no. 3 (1997), p. 327.

40. R. B. Anderson, "The Business Economy of the First Nations in Saskatchewan: A Contingency Perspective," *Canadian Journal of Native Studies* 2, 1995, pp. 309–345.

41. E. Struzik, "'Win-Win Scenario' Possible for Resource Industry, Aboriginals," *Edmonton Journal*, April 6, 2003, p. A12.

42. Discussion based on L. Redpath and M. O. Nielsen, "A Comparison of Native Culture, Non-Native Culture and New Management Ideology," *Canadian Journal of Administrative Sciences* 14, no. 3 (1997), pp. 327–339.

43. Discussion based on L. Redpath and M. O. Nielsen, "A Comparison of Native Culture, Non-Native Culture and New Management Ideology," *Canadian Journal of Administrative Sciences* 14, no. 3 (1997), pp. 327–339.

44. D. Grigg and J. Newman, "Five Ways to Foster Bonds, Win Trust in Business," *Ottawa Citizen*, April 23, 2003, p. F12.

45. T. Chui, K. Tran, and J. Flanders, "Chinese Canadians: Enriching the Cultural Mosaic," *Canadian Social Trends*, no. 76, Spring 2005.

46. Statistics Canada, "Canada's Visible Minority Population in 2017," *The Daily*, March 22, 2005.

47. I. Y. M. Yeung and R. L. Tung, "Achieving Business Success in Confucian Societies: The Importance of Guanxi (Connections)," *Organizational Dynamics: Special Report*, 1998, pp. 72–83.

48. I. Y. M. Yeung and R. L. Tung, "Achieving Business Success in Confucian Societies: The Importance of Guanxi (Connections)," *Organizational Dynamics: Special Report*, 1998, p. 73.

49. Material in this section based on the work of M. Adams, *Sex in the Snow* (Toronto: Penguin Books, 1997); and M. Adams, *Fire and Ice: The United States, Canada and the Myth of Converging Values* (Toronto: Penguin Canada, 2003).

50. D. Tapscott, *Growing Up Digital: The Rise of the Net Generation* (New York: McGraw-Hill, 1998).

51. W. Howe and N. Strauss, *Millennials Rising: The Next Great Generation* (New York: Vintage, 2001).

52. "Get Used to It: The Net Generation Knows More Than Its Parents," *Financial Post* (*National Post*), February 8, 2000, p. C10.

53. W. Howe and N. Strauss, *Millennials Rising: The Next Great Generation* (New York: Vintage, 2001).

54. Statistics Canada, "Census of Population," *The Daily*, February 11, 2003.

55. See http://www.pg.com/en_CA.

56. A. Kerr, "Female Architects Seen Running for Exits," *Globe and Mail*, May 6, 2002, p. B11.

57. Vignette based on E. Louie, "She Has a Knife And She Knows How to Use It," *New York Times*, June 5, 2002, p. F1.

58. G. Shaw, "Canada Lags World on Job Quality," *Vancouver Sun*, September 18, 2004, p. F5.

59. V. H. Vroom, *Work and Motivation* (New York: Wiley, 1964); and M. T. Iaffaldano and P. M. Muchinsky, "Job Satisfaction and Job Performance: A Meta-Analysis," *Psychological Bulletin*, March 1985, pp. 251–273.

60. C. N. Greene, "The Satisfaction-Performance Controversy," *Business Horizons*, February 1972, pp. 31–41; E. E. Lawler III, *Motivation in Organizations* (Monterey, CA: Brooks/Cole, 1973); and M. M. Petty, G. W. McGee, and J. W. Cavender, "A Meta-Analysis of the Relationship Between Individual Job Satisfaction and

Individual Performance," *Academy of Management Review,* October 1984, pp. 712–721.

61. L. Rhoades and R. Eisenberger, "Perceived Organizational Support: A Review of the Literature," *Journal of Applied Psychology* 87, no. 4 (2002), pp. 698–714.

62. C. Ostroff, "The Relationship Between Satisfaction, Attitudes, and Performance: An Organizational Level Analysis," *Journal of Applied Psychology,* December 1992, pp. 963–974.

63. D. W. Organ, *Organizational Citizenship Behavior: The Good Soldier Syndrome* (Lexington, MA: Lexington Books, 1988), p. 4.

64. D. W. Organ, *Organizational Citizenship Behavior: The Good Soldier Syndrome* (Lexington, MA: Lexington Books, 1988); C. A. Smith, D. W. Organ, and J. P. Near, "Organizational Citizenship Behavior: Its Nature and Antecedents," *Journal of Applied Psychology,* 1983, pp. 653–663.

65. J. Farh, C. Zhong, and D. W. Organ, "Organizational Citizenship Behavior in the People's Republic of China," *Academy of Management Proceedings,* 2000, pp. OB: D1–D6; J. Farh, C. Zhong, and D. W. Organ, "Organizational Citizenship Behavior in the People's Republic of China," *Organization Science* 15, no. 2 (2004), pp. 241–253.

66. J. M. George and A. P. Brief, "Feeling Good–Doing Good: A Conceptual Analysis of the Mood at Work—Organizational Spontaneity Relationship," *Psychological Bulletin* 112, 2002, pp. 310–329; and S. Wagner and M. Rush, "Altruistic Organizational Citizenship Behavior: Context, Disposition and Age," *Journal of Social Psychology* 140, 2002, pp. 379–391.

67. S. D. Salamon and Y. Deutsch, "OCB as a Handicap: An Evolutionary Psychological Perspective," *Journal of Organizational Behavior* 27, no. 2 (2006), pp. 185–199.

68. P. E. Spector, *Job Satisfaction: Application, Assessment, Causes, and Consequences* (Thousand Oaks, CA: Sage, 1997), pp. 57–58.

69. P. M. Podsakoff, S. B. MacKenzie, J. B. Paine, and D. G. Bachrach, "Organizational Citizenship Behaviors: A Critical Review of the Theoretical and Empirical Literature and Suggestions for Future Research," *Journal of Management* 26, no. 3 (2000), pp. 513–563.

70. See T. S. Bateman and D. W. Organ, "Job Satisfaction and the Good Soldier: The Relationship Between Affect and Employee 'Citizenship,'" *Academy of Management Journal,* December 1983, pp. 587–595; C. A. Smith, D. W. Organ, and J. P. Near, "Organizational Citizenship Behavior: Its Nature and Antecedents," *Journal of Applied Psychology,* October 1983, pp. 653–663; and A. P. Brief, *Attitudes in and Around Organizations* (Thousand Oaks, CA: Sage, 1998), pp. 44–45.

71. D. W. Organ and R. H. Moorman, "Fairness and Organizational Citizenship Behavior: What Are the Connections?" *Social Justice Research* 6, no. 1 (March 1993), pp. 5–18.

72. D. W. Organ and K. Ryan, "A Meta-Analytic Review of Attitudinal and Dispositional Predictors of Organizational Citizenship Behavior," *Personnel Psychology,* Winter 1995, p. 791.

73. J. Farh, P. M. Podsakoff, and D. W. Organ, "Accounting for Organizational Citizenship Behavior: Leader Fairness and Task Scope Versus Satisfaction," *Journal of Management,* December 1990, pp. 705–722; R. H. Moorman, "Relationship Between Organizational Justice and Organizational Citizenship Behaviors: Do Fairness Perceptions Influence Employee Citizenship?" *Journal of Applied Psychology,* December 1991, pp. 845–855; and M. A. Konovsky and D. W. Organ, "Dispositional and Contextual Determinants of Organizational Citizenship Behavior," *Journal of Organizational Behavior,* May 1996, pp. 253–266.

74. D. W. Organ, "Personality and Organizational Citizenship Behavior," *Journal of Management,* Summer 1994, p. 466.

75. J. L. Farh, C. B. Zhong, and D. W Organ, "Organizational Citizenship Behavior in the People's Republic of China," *Organization Science* 15, no. 2 (March–April 2004), pp. 241–253.

76. See, for instance, E. Naumann and D. W. Jackson Jr., "One More Time: How Do You Satisfy Customers?" *Business Horizons,* May–June 1999, pp. 71–76; D. J. Koys, "The Effects of Employee Satisfaction, Organizational Citizenship Behavior, and Turnover on Organizational Effectiveness: A Unit-Level, Longitudinal Study," *Personnel Psychology,* Spring 2001, pp. 101–114; and J. Griffith, "Do Satisfied Employees Satisfy Customers? Support-Services Staff Morale and Satisfaction Among Public School Administrators, Students, and Parents," *Journal of Applied Social Psychology,* August 2001, pp. 1627–1658.

77. M. J. Bitner, B. H. Booms, and L. A. Mohr, "Critical Service Encounters: The Employee's Viewpoint," *Journal of Marketing,* October 1994, pp. 95–106.

78. E. A. Locke, "The Nature and Causes of Job Satisfaction," in *Handbook of Industrial and Organizational Psychology,* ed. M. D. Dunnette (Chicago: Rand McNally, 1976), p. 1331; S. L. McShane, "Job Satisfaction and Absenteeism: A Meta-Analytic Re-Examination," *Canadian Journal of Administrative Science,* June 1984, pp. 61–77; R. D. Hackett and R. M. Guion, "A Reevaluation of the Absenteeism–Job Satisfaction Relationship," *Organizational Behavior and Human Decision Processes,* June 1985, pp. 340–381; K. D. Scott and G. S. Taylor, "An Examination of Conflicting Findings on the Relationship Between Job Satisfaction and Absenteeism: A Meta-Analysis," *Academy of Management Journal,* September 1985, pp. 599–612; R. D. Hackett, "Work Attitudes and Employee Absenteeism: A Synthesis of the Literature" (paper presented at the 1988 National Academy of Management Conference, Anaheim, CA, August 1988); and R. P. Steel and J. R. Rentsch, "Influence of Cumulation Strategies on the Long-Range Prediction of Absenteeism," *Academy of Management Journal,* December 1995, pp. 1616–1634.

79. J. L. Cotton and J. M. Tuttle, "Employee Turnover: A Meta-Analysis and Review With Implications for Research," *Academy of Management Review* 11, 1986, pp. 55–70; R. W. Griffeth and P. W. Hom, "The Employee Turnover Process," *Research in Personnel and Human Resources Management* 13, 1995, pp. 245–293; P. W. Hom, F. Caranikas-Walker, G. E. Prussia, and R. W. Griffeth, "A Meta-Analytical Structural Equations Analysis of a Model of Employee Turnover," *Journal of Applied Psychology* 77, 1992, pp. 890–909; P. W. Hom and R. W. Griffeth, *Employee Turnover* (Cincinnati, OH: South-Western College, 1995); W. H. Mobley, R. W. Griffeth, H. H. Hand, and B. Meglino, "Review and Conceptual Analysis of the Employee Turnover Process," *Psychological Bulletin* 86, 1979, pp. 493–522; J. L. Price, *The Study of Turnover* (Ames, IA: Iowa State University Press, 1977); R. P. Steel and N. K. Ovalle, "A Review and Meta-analysis of Research on the Relationship Between Behavioral Intentions and Employee Turnover," *Journal of Applied Psychology* 69, 1984, pp. 673–686; and R. P. Tett and J. P. Meyer, "Job Satisfaction, Organizational Commitment, Turnover Intention, and Turnover: Path Analyses Based on Meta-Analytical Findings," *Personnel Psychology* 46, 1993, pp. 259–293.

80. T. A. Judge, "Does Affective Disposition Moderate the Relationship Between Job Satisfaction and Voluntary Turnover?" *Journal of Applied Psychology,* June 1993, pp. 395–401.

81. S. M. Puffer, "Prosocial Behavior, Noncompliant Behavior, and Work Performance Among Commission Salespeople," *Journal of Applied Psychology,* November 1987, pp. 615–621; J. Hogan and R. Hogan, "How to Measure Employee Reliability," *Journal of Applied Psychology,* May 1989, pp. 273–279; and C. D. Fisher and E. A. Locke, "The New Look in Job Satisfaction Research and Theory," in *Job Satisfaction,* ed. C. J. Cranny, P. C. Smith, and E. F. Stone (New York: Lexington Books, 1992), pp. 165–194.

82. S. M. Puffer, "Prosocial Behavior, Noncompliant Behavior, and Work Performance Among Commission Salespeople," *Journal of Applied Psychology*, November 1987, pp. 615–621; J. Hogan and R. Hogan, "How to Measure Employee Reliability," *Journal of Applied Psychology*, May 1989, pp. 273–279; and C. D. Fisher and E. A. Locke, "The New Look in Job Satisfaction Research and Theory," in *Job Satisfaction*, ed. C. J. Cranny, P. C. Smith, and E. F. Stone (New York: Lexington Books, 1992), pp. 165–194.

83. R. B. Freeman, "Job Satisfaction as an Economic Variable," *American Economic Review*, January 1978, pp. 135–141.

84. G. J. Blau and K. R. Boal, "Conceptualizing How Job Involvement and Organizational Commitment Affect Turnover and Absenteeism," *Academy of Management Review*, April 1987, p. 290.

85. N. J. Allen and J. P. Meyer, "The Measurement and Antecedents of Affective, Continuance, and Normative Commitment to the Organization," *Journal of Occupational Psychology* 63, 1990, pp. 1–18; and J. P. Meyer, N. J. Allen, and C. A. Smith, "Commitment to Organizations and Occupations: Extension and Test of a Three-Component Conceptualization," *Journal of Applied Psychology* 78, 1993, pp. 538–551.

86. K. Bentein, R. Vandenberg, C. Vandenberghe, and F. Stinglhamber, "The Role of Change in the Relationship Between Commitment and Turnover: A Latent Growth Modeling Approach," *Journal of Applied Psychology* 90, no. 3 (2005), pp. 468–482.

87. J. P. Meyer, S. V. Paumonen, I. R. Gellatly, R. D. Goffin, and D. N. Jackson, "Organizational Commitment and Job Performance: It's the Nature of the Commitment That Counts," *Journal of Applied Psychology* 74, 1989, pp. 152–156; L. M. Shore and S. J. Wayne, "Commitment and Employee Behavior: Comparison of Affective and Continuance Commitment With Perceived Organizational Support," *Journal of Applied Psychology* 78, 1993, pp. 774–780.

88. D. M. Rousseau, "Organizational Behavior in the New Organizational Era," in *Annual Review of Psychology* 48, ed. J. T. Spence, J. M. Darley, and D. J. Foss (Palo Alto, CA: Annual Reviews, 1997), p. 523.

89. "Do as I Do," *Canadian Business*, March 12, 1999, p. 35.

90. J. R. Katzenback and J. A. Santamaria, "Firing up the Front Line," *Harvard Business Review*, May–June 1999, p. 109.

91. C. Hult, "Organizational Commitment and Person-Environment Fit in Six Western Countries," *Organization Studies* 26, no. 2 (2005), pp. 249–270.

92. E. A. Locke, "The Nature and Causes of Job Satisfaction," in *Handbook of Industrial and Organizational Psychology*, ed. M. D. Dunnette (Chicago: Rand McNally, 1976), pp. 1319–1328.

93. See, for instance, T. A. Judge and S. Watanabe, "Another Look at the Job Satisfaction–Life Satisfaction Relationship," *Journal of Applied Psychology*, December 1993, pp. 939–948; R. D. Arvey, B. P. McCall, T. J. Bouchard Jr., and P. Taubman, "Genetic Influences on Job Satisfaction and Work Values," *Personality and Individual Differences*, July 1994, pp. 21–33; and D. Lykken and A. Tellegen, "Happiness Is a Stochastic Phenomenon," *Psychological Science*, May 1996, pp. 186–189.

OB on the Edge: Stress at Work

1. Information in this paragraph based on S. McKay, "The Work-Family Conundrum," *Financial Post Magazine*, December 1997, pp. 78–81; and J. Mawhinney, "Style With Heart and Soul," *Toronto Star*, September 1, 2005, p. E04.

2. Paragraph based on "'You'd Drink Too,' Charged School Bus Driver Says," *National Post*, March 4, 2002, p. A7.

3. Statistics Canada, "Life Stress, by Sex, Household Population Aged 18 and Over, Canada, Provinces, Territories, Health Regions and Peer Groups, 2000/01," www.statcan.ca/english/freepub/82-221-XIE/00503/tables/html/2336.htm (accessed August 4, 2005).

4. A. Marchand, P. Durand, and A. Demers, "Work and Mental Health: The Experience of the Quebec Workforce Between 1987 and 1998," *Work* 25, no. 2, 2005, pp. 135–142.

5. I. Phaneuf, "Drug Company Study Finds Rise in Work-Related Stress," *Vancouver Sun*, May 5, 2001, p. D15.

6. V. Galt, "Statscan Studies Workplace Stress," *Globe and Mail*, June 26, 2003, p. B3.

7. R. B. Mason, "Taking Health Care to Factory Floor Proves Smart Move for Growing Ontario Company," *Canadian Medical Association Journal*, November 15, 1997, pp. 1423–1424.

8. L. Duxbury and C. Higgins, *2001 National Work-Life Conflict Study*, as reported in J. Campbell, "'Organizational Anorexia' Puts Stress on Employees," *Ottawa Citizen*, July 4, 2002.

9. K. Harding, "Balance Tops List of Job Desires," *Globe and Mail*, May 7, 2003, pp. C1, C6.

10. V. Galt, "Productivity Buckling Under the Strain of Stress, CEOs Say," *Globe and Mail*, June 9, 2005, p. B1.

11. "Canadian Workers Among Most Stressed," *Worklife Report* 14, no. 2 (2002), pp. 8–9.

12. N. Ayed, "Absenteeism Up Since 1993," *Canadian Press Newswire*, March 25, 1998.

13. N. Ayed, "Absenteeism Up Since 1993," *Canadian Press Newswire*, March 25, 1998.

14. H. Selye, *The Stress of Life* (New York: McGraw-Hill, 1976); and H. Selye, *Stress Without Distress* (Philadelphia, PA: J. B. Lippincott, 1974).

15. R. DeFrank and J. M. Ivancevich, "Stress on the Job: An Executive Update," *Academy of Management Executive*, August 1998, pp. 55–66.

16. E. Church, "Work Winning Out Over Family in the Struggle for Balance," *Globe and Mail*, February 13, 2002, pp. B1, B2.

17. W. Stueck, "Firms Not 'Family Friendly': Study," *Globe and Mail*, July 4, 2002, p. B4.

18. These key changes and the unattributed quotations in this section are taken from R. DeFrank and J. M. Ivancevich, "Stress on the Job: An Executive Update," *Academy of Management Executive*, August 1998, pp. 55–66.

19. P. Demont and A. M. Tobin, "One in Three Canadians Say They're Workaholics," *Vancouver Sun*, November 10, 1999, pp. A1, A2.

20. D. Stonehouse, "Caught in the E-Mailstrom: You Know Things Are Getting out of Hand When a Guy With an Online Newsletter Pulls the Plug," *Vancouver Sun*, June 8, 2002, pp. H3, H4.

21. S. McKay, "The Work-Family Conundrum," *Financial Post Magazine*, December 1997, pp. 78–81; and A. Davis, "Respect Your Elders: Pressure on the Healthcare System Means Elderly Patients Aren't Staying in Hospitals as Long as They Used To," *Benefits Canada* 26, no. 8 (2002), p. 13.

22. L. T. Thomas and D. C. Ganster, "Impact of Family-Supportive Work Variables on Work-Family Conflict and Strain: A Control Perspective," *Journal of Applied Psychology* 80, 1995, pp. 6–15.

23. H. Selye, *The Stress of Life* (New York: McGraw-Hill, 1976).

24. R. S. Schuler, "Definition and Conceptualization of Stress in Organizations," *Organizational Behavior and Human Performance*, April 1980, p. 191; and R. L. Kahn and P. Byosiere, "Stress in

Organizations," *Organizational Behavior and Human Performance,* April 1980, pp. 604–610.

25. KPMG Canada, compensation letter, July 1998.

26. B. D. Steffy and J. W. Jones, "Workplace Stress and Indicators of Coronary-Disease Risk," *Academy of Management Journal* 31, 1988, p. 687.

27. C. L. Cooper and J. Marshall, "Occupational Sources of Stress: A Review of the Literature Relating to Coronary Heart Disease and Mental Ill Health," *Journal of Occupational Psychology* 49, no. 1 (1976), pp. 11–28.

28. J. R. Hackman and G. R. Oldham, "Development of the Job Diagnostic Survey," *Journal of Applied Psychology,* April 1975, pp. 159–170.

29. J. L. Xie and G. Johns, "Job Scope and Stress: Can Job Scope Be Too High?" *Academy of Management Journal,* October 1995, pp. 1288–1309.

30. S. J. Motowidlo, J. S. Packard, and M. R. Manning, "Occupational Stress: Its Causes and Consequences for Job Performance," *Journal of Applied Psychology,* November 1987, pp. 619–620.

31. See, for instance, R. C. Cummings, "Job Stress and the Buffering Effect of Supervisory Support," *Group & Organization Studies,* March 1990, pp. 92–104; M. R. Manning, C. N. Jackson, and M. R. Fusilier, "Occupational Stress, Social Support, and the Cost of Health Care," *Academy of Management Journal,* June 1996, pp. 738–750; and P. D. Bliese and T. W. Britt, "Social Support, Group Consensus and Stressor-Strain Relationships: Social Context Matters," *Journal of Organizational Behavior,* June 2001, pp. 425–436.

32. See L. R. Murphy, "A Review of Organizational Stress Management Research," *Journal of Organizational Behavior Management,* Fall–Winter 1986, pp. 215–227.

33. R. Williams, *The Trusting Heart: Great News About Type A Behavior* (New York: Times Books, 1989).

34. T. H. Macan, "Time Management: Test of a Process Model," *Journal of Applied Psychology,* June 1994, pp. 381–391.

35. See, for example, G. Lawrence-Ell, *The Invisible Clock: A Practical Revolution in Finding Time for Everyone and Everything* (Seaside Park, NJ: Kingsland Hall, 2002).

36. J. Kiely and G. Hodgson, "Stress in the Prison Service: The Benefits of Exercise Programs," *Human Relations,* June 1990, pp. 551–572.

37. E. J. Forbes and R. J. Pekala, "Psychophysiological Effects of Several Stress Management Techniques," *Psychological Reports,* February 1993, pp. 19–27; and G. Smith, "Meditation, the New Balm for Corporate Stress," *BusinessWeek,* May 10, 1993, pp. 86–87.

38. *FactBox* based on P. Demont and A. M. Tobin, "One in Three Canadians Say They're Workaholics," *Vancouver Sun,* November 10, 1999, pp. A1, A2; E. Beauchesne, "Lost Work Cost Placed at $10b: Growing Stress Levels Are Cited as a Leading Factor in the Rise in Absenteeism in Canada," *Vancouver Sun,* September 2, 1999, p. A3; L. Ramsay, "Caught Between the Potty and the PC," *National Post,* November 9, 1998, p. D9; V. Galt, "Just Don't Call Them 'Workaholics'" *Globe and Mail,* April 8, 2002, pp. B1, B2; S. McGovern, "No Rest for the Weary," *The Gazette* (Montreal), August 19, 2003, p. B1; and D. McMurdy, "People Get Stress Relief Express-Style," *Financial Post* (*National Post*), January 15, 2005, p. IN1.

39. D. Etzion, "Moderating Effects of Social Support on the Stress-Burnout Relationship," *Journal of Applied Psychology,* November 1984, pp. 615–622; and S. Jackson, R. Schwab, and R. Schuler, "Toward an Understanding of the Burnout Phenomenon," *Journal of Applied Psychology* 71, no. 4 (November 1986), pp. 630–640.

40. H. Staseson, "Can Perk Help Massage Bottom Line? On-Site Therapeutic Sessions Are Used by an Increasingly Diverse Group of Employers Hoping to Improve Staff Performance," *Globe and Mail,* July 3, 2002, p. C1.

41. B. Bouw, "Employers Embrace Wellness at Work: Fitness Programs Gaining Popularity as Companies Look to Boost Productivity With Healthier Staff," *Globe and Mail,* April 10, 2002, p. C1.

42. "Wellness Programs Offer Healthy Return, Study Finds," *Report Bulletin,* #224, October 2001, p. 1.

43. H. Staseson, "Can Perk Help Massage Bottom Line? On-Site Therapeutic Sessions Are Used by an Increasingly Diverse Group of Employers Hoping to Improve Staff Performance," *Globe and Mail,* July 3, 2002, p. C1.

44. B. Bouw, "Employers Embrace Wellness at Work: Fitness Programs Gaining Popularity as Companies Look to Boost Productivity With Healthier Staff," *Globe and Mail,* April 10, 2002, p. C1.

45. P. M. Wright, "Operationalization of Goal Difficulty as a Moderator of the Goal Difficulty-Performance Relationship," *Journal of Applied Psychology,* June 1990, pp. 227–234; E. A. Locke and G. P. Latham, "Building a Practically Useful Theory of Goal Setting and Task Motivation: A 35-Year Odyssey," *American Psychologist* 57, no. 9 (2002), pp. 705–717; K. L. Langeland, C. M. Johnson, and T. C. Mawhinney, "Improving Staff Performance in a Community Mental Health Setting: Job Analysis, Training, Goal Setting, Feedback, and Years of Data," *Journal of Organizational Behavior Management,* 1998, pp. 21–43.

46. See W. A. Anthony and C. W. Anthony, *The Art of Napping at Work* (Burdett, NY: Larson Publications, 2000); J. E. Brody, "New Respect for the Nap, a Pause That Refreshes," *New York Times,* January 4, 2000, p. D7; and "Nappers of the World, Lie Down and Be Counted!" *Training,* May 2000, p. 24.

47. See, for instance, R. A. Wolfe, D. O. Ulrich, and D. F. Parker, "Employee Health Management Programs: Review, Critique, and Research Agenda," *Journal of Management,* Winter 1987, pp. 603–615; D. L. Gebhardt and C. E. Crump, "Employee Fitness and Wellness Programs in the Workplace," *American Psychologist,* February 1990, pp. 262–272; and C. E. Beadle, "And Let's Save 'Wellness.' It Works," *New York Times,* July 24, 1994, p. F9.

Chapter 4

1. Opening vignette based on M. Beamish, "Lions Know Practice Makes Perfect," *Nanaimo Daily News,* August 23, 2005, p. B3; M. Sekeres, "Two Sides to Buono," *Kamloops Daily News,* September 8, 2005, p. A13; L. Little, "Lions Must Shore Up Offensive Line," *Vancouver Sun,* November 23, 2005, p. E1.

2. G. P. Latham and C. C. Pinder, "Work Motivation Theory and Research at the Dawn of the Twenty-First Century," *Annual Review of Psychology* 56, no. 1 (2005), pp. 485–516; and C. C. Pinder, *Work Motivation in Organizational Behavior* (Upper Saddle River, NJ: Prentice Hall, 1998), p. 11. See also E. A. Locke and G. P. Latham, "What Should We Do About Motivation Theory? Six Recommendations for the Twenty-First Century," *Academy of Management Review* 29, no. 3 (July 1, 2004), pp. 388–403.

3. D. McGregor, *The Human Side of Enterprise* (New York: McGraw-Hill, 1960). For an updated analysis of Theory X and Theory Y constructs, see R. J. Summers and S. F. Cronshaw, "A Study of McGregor's Theory X, Theory Y and the Influence of Theory X, Theory Y Assumptions on Causal Attributions for Instances of

Worker Poor Performance," in *Organizational Behavior*, ed. S. L. McShane, ASAC 1988 Conference Proceedings, 9, part 5, Halifax, 1988, pp. 115–123.

4. K. W. Thomas, *Intrinsic Motivation at Work* (San Francisco: Berrett-Koehler, 2000); and K. W. Thomas, "Intrinsic Motivation and How It Works," *Training*, October 2000, pp. 130–135.

5. S. E. DeVoe and S. S. Iyengar, "Managers' Theories of Subordinates: A Cross-cultural Examination of Manager Perceptions of Motivation and Appraisal of Performance," *Organizational Behavior and Human Decision Processes* 93, no. 1 (January 2004), pp. 47–61.

6. C. P. Alderfer, "An Empirical Test of a New Theory of Human Needs," *Organizational Behavior and Human Performance*, May 1969, pp. 142–175.

7. D. C. McClelland, *The Achieving Society* (New York: Van Nostrand Reinhold, 1961); J. W. Atkinson and J. O. Raynor, *Motivation and Achievement* (Washington, DC: Winston, 1974); D. C. McClelland, *Power: The Inner Experience* (New York: Irvington, 1975); M. J. Stahl, *Managerial and Technical Motivation: Assessing Needs for Achievement, Power, and Affiliation* (New York: Praeger, 1986); and D. G. Winter, "The Motivational Dimensions of Leadership: Power, Achievement, and Affiliation," in *Multiple Intelligences and Leadership*, ed. R. E. Riggio, S. E. Murphy, and F. J. Pirozzolo (Mahwah, NJ: Lawrence Erlbaum, 2002), pp. 119–138.

8. A. H. Maslow, *Motivation and Personality* (New York: Harper and Row, 1954).

9. G. P. Latham and C. C. Pinder, "Work Motivation Theory and Research at the Dawn of the Twenty-First Century," *Annual Review of Psychology* 56, no. 1 (2005), pp. 485–516.

10. R. Hogan and R. Warremfeltz, "Educating the Modern Manager," *Academy of Management Journal*, 2003, pp. 74–84.

11. K. Korman, J. H. Greenhaus, and I. J. Badin, "Personnel Attitudes and Motivation," in *Annual Review of Psychology*, ed. M. R. Rosenzweig and L. W. Porter (Palo Alto, CA: Annual Reviews, 1977), p. 178; and M. A. Wahba and L. G. Bridwell, "Maslow Reconsidered: A Review of Research on the Need Hierarchy Theory," *Organizational Behavior and Human Performance*, April 1976, pp. 212–240.

12. C. P. Alderfer, "An Empirical Test of a New Theory of Human Needs," *Organizational Behavior and Human Performance*, May 1969, pp. 142–175.

13. C. P. Schneider and C. P. Alderfer, "Three Studies of Measures of Need Satisfaction in Organizations," *Administrative Science Quarterly*, December 1973, pp. 489–505; and I. Borg and M. Braun, "Work Values in East and West Germany: Different Weights, but Identical Structures," *Journal of Organizational Behavior* 17, special issue (1996), pp. 541–555.

14. J. P. Wanous and A. Zwany, "A Cross-Sectional Test of Need Hierarchy Theory," *Organizational Behavior and Human Performance*, May 1977, pp. 78–97.

15. D. C. McClelland, *The Achieving Society* (New York: Van Nostrand Reinhold, 1961); J. W. Atkinson and J. O. Raynor, *Motivation and Achievement* (Washington, DC: Winston, 1974); D. C. McClelland, *Power: The Inner Experience* (New York: Irvington, 1975); and M. J. Stahl, *Managerial and Technical Motivation: Assessing Needs for Achievement, Power, and Affiliation* (New York: Praeger, 1986).

16. D. C. McClelland, *The Achieving Society* (New York: Van Nostrand Reinhold, 1961).

17. D. C. McClelland, *Power: The Inner Experience* (New York: Irvington, 1975); D. C. McClelland and D. H. Burnham, "Power Is the Great Motivator," *Harvard Business Review*, March–April 1976, pp. 100–110; and R. E. Boyatzis, "The Need for Close Relationships and the Manager's Job," in *Organizational Psychology:*

Readings on Human Behavior in Organizations, 4th ed., ed. D. A. Kolb, I. M. Rubin, and J. M. McIntyre (Upper Saddle River, NJ: Prentice Hall, 1984), pp. 81–86.

18. D. G. Winter, "The Motivational Dimensions of Leadership: Power, Achievement, and Affiliation," in *Multiple Intelligences and Leadership*, ed. R. E. Riggio, S. E. Murphy, and F. J. Pirozzolo (Mahwah, NJ: Lawrence Erlbaum, 2002), pp. 119–138.

19. F. Herzberg, B. Mausner, and B. Snyderman, *The Motivation to Work* (New York: Wiley, 1959).

20. R. J. House and L. A. Wigdor, "Herzberg's Dual-Factor Theory of Job Satisfaction and Motivations: A Review of the Evidence and Criticism," *Personnel Psychology*, Winter 1967, pp. 369–389; D. P. Schwab and L. L. Cummings, "Theories of Performance and Satisfaction: A Review," *Industrial Relations*, October 1970, pp. 403–430; R. J. Caston and R. Braito, "A Specification Issue in Job Satisfaction Research," *Sociological Perspectives*, April 1985, pp. 175–197; and J. Phillipchuk and J. Whittaker, "An Inquiry into the Continuing Relevance of Herzberg's Motivation Theory," *Engineering Management Journal* 8, 1996, pp. 15–20.

21. Based on L. Ullrich, "Anything but Glamorous at 4 a.m.: No Security, Insane Hours, No Pension and Zero Benefits," *Province* (Vancouver), August 3, 2005, p. A40.

22. V. H. Vroom, *Work and Motivation* (New York: John Wiley, 1964).

23. J. Choudhury, "The Motivational Impact of Sales Quotas on Effort," *Journal of Marketing Research*, February 1993, pp. 28–41; and C. C. Pinder, *Work Motivation* (Glenview, IL: Scott Foresman, 1984), chapter 7.

24. A. Grimes, "Lessons from the Locker Room: Vancouver's Top Coaches Share Their Keys to Success With Business Leaders," Vancouver Board of Trade, April 6, 2006, http://www.boardoftrade.com/vbot_speech.asp?pageID=174&speechID=914&off-set=&speechfind (accessed May 1, 2006).

25. "Workplace 2000: Working Toward the Millennium," *Angus Reid Group*, Fall 1997, p. 14.

26. See http://www.radical.ca.

27. See, for example, H. G. Heneman III and D. P. Schwab, "Evaluation of Research on Expectancy Theory Prediction of Employee Performance," *Psychological Bulletin*, July 1972, pp. 1–9; T. R. Mitchell, "Expectancy Models of Job Satisfaction, Occupational Preference and Effort: A Theoretical, Methodological and Empirical Appraisal," *Psychological Bulletin*, November 1974, pp. 1053–1077; and L. Reinharth and M. A. Wahba, "Expectancy Theory as a Predictor of Work Motivation, Effort Expenditure, and Job Performance," *Academy of Management Journal*, September 1975, pp. 502–537.

28. See, for example, L. W. Porter and E. E. Lawler III, *Managerial Attitudes and Performance* (Homewood, IL: Richard D. Irwin, 1968); D. F. Parker and L. Dyer, "Expectancy Theory as a Within-Person Behavioral Choice Model: An Empirical Test of Some Conceptual and Methodological Refinements," *Organizational Behavior and Human Performance*, October 1976, pp. 97–117; H. J. Arnold, "A Test of the Multiplicative Hypothesis of Expectancy-Valence Theories of Work Motivation," *Academy of Management Journal*, April 1981, pp. 128–141; J. P. Wanous, T. L. Keon, and J. C. Latack, "Expectancy Theory and Occupational/Organizational Choices: A Review and Test," *Organizational Behaviour and Human Performance*, August 1983, pp. 66–86; and W. Van Eerde and H. Thierry, "Vroom's Expectancy Models and Work-Related Criteria: A Meta-Analysis," *Journal of Applied Psychology* 81, October 1996, pp. 575–586.

29. P. C. Earley, *Face, Harmony, and Social Structure: An Analysis of Organizational Behavior Across Cultures* (New York: Oxford

University Press, 1997); R. M. Steers and C. Sanchez-Runde, "Culture, Motivation, and Work Behavior," in *Handbook of Cross-cultural Management*, ed. M. Gannon and K. Newman (London: Blackwell, 2001), pp. 190–215; and H. C. Triandis, "Motivation and Achievement in Collectivist and Individualistic Cultures," in *Advances in Motivation and Achievement*, vol. 9, ed. M. Maehr and P. Pintrich (Greenwich, CT: JAI Press, 1995), pp. 1–30.

30. E. A. Locke, "Toward a Theory of Task Motivation and Incentives," *Organizational Behavior and Human Performance*, May 1968, pp. 157–189; and G. H. Seijts, G. P. Latham, K. Tasa, and B. Latham, "Goal Setting and Goal Orientation: An Integration of Two Different yet Related Literatures," *Academy of Management Journal* 47, no. 2 (2004), pp. 227–239.

31. E. A. Locke, K. N. Shaw, L. M. Saari, and G. P. Latham, "Goal Setting and Task Performance: 1969–1980," *Psychological Bulletin*, July 1981, p. 126.

32. P. C. Earley, P. Wojnaroski, and W. Prest, "Task Planning and Energy Expended: Exploration of How Goals Influence Performance," *Journal of Applied Psychology*, February 1987, pp. 107–114.

33. E. A. Locke and G. P. Latham, *A Theory of Goal Setting and Task Performance* (Englewood Cliffs, NJ: Prentice Hall, 1980).

34. Based on http://www.profitguide.com/profit100/2005/article.asp?ID=1328&page=3 (accessed September 10, 2005).

35. R. Ilies and T. A. Judge, "Goal Regulation Across Time: The Effects of Feedback and Affect," *Journal of Applied Psychology* 90, no. 3 (May 2005), pp. 453–467.

36. A. Bandura, *Self-Efficacy: The Exercise of Control* (New York: Freeman, 1997).

37. E. A. Locke, E. Frederick, C. Lee, and P. Bobko, "Effect of Self-Efficacy, Goals, and Task Strategies on Task Performance," *Journal of Applied Psychology*, May 1984, pp. 241–251; M. E. Gist and T. R. Mitchell, "Self-Efficacy: A Theoretical Analysis of Its Determinants and Malleability," *Academy of Management Review*, April 1992, pp. 183–211; and A. D. Stajkovic and F. Luthans, "Self-Efficacy and Work-Related Performance: A Meta-Analysis," *Psychological Bulletin*, September 1998, pp. 240–261.

38. A. Bandura and D. Cervone, "Differential Engagement in Self-Reactive Influences in Cognitively-Based Motivation," *Organizational Behavior and Human Decision Processes*, August 1986, pp. 92–113.

39. J. R. Hollenbeck, C. R. Williams, and H. J. Klein, "An Empirical Examination of the Antecedents of Commitment to Difficult Goals," *Journal of Applied Psychology*, February 1989, pp. 18–23. See also J. C. Wofford, V. L. Goodwin, and S. Premack, "Meta-Analysis of the Antecedents of Personal Goal Level and of the Antecedents and Consequences of Goal Commitment," *Journal of Management*, September 1992, pp. 595–615; and M. E. Tubbs, "Commitment as a Moderator of the Goal-Performance Relation: A Case for Clearer Construct Definition," *Journal of Applied Psychology*, February 1993, pp. 86–97.

40. See R. E. Wood, A. J. Mento, and E. A. Locke, "Task Complexity as a Moderator of Goal Effects: A Meta Analysis," *Journal of Applied Psychology*, August 1987, pp. 416–425; R. Kanfer and P. L. Ackerman, "Motivation and Cognitive Abilities: An Integrative/Aptitude-Treatment Interaction Approach to Skill Acquisition," *Journal of Applied Psychology* 74, monograph (1989), pp. 657–690; T. R. Mitchell and W. S. Silver, "Individual and Group Goals When Workers Are Interdependent: Effects on Task Strategies and Performance," *Journal of Applied Psychology*, April 1990, pp. 185–193; and A. M. O'Leary-Kelly, J. J. Martocchio, and D. D. Frink, "A Review of the Influence of Group Goals on

Group Performance," *Academy of Management Journal*, October 1994, pp. 1285–1301.

41. Based on J. Morris, "QB Controversy Hits Lions," *Nelson Daily News*, August 8, 2005, p. 7; and M. Beamish, "Casey Printers Grumpy Over Contract Talk," *Nanaimo Daily News*, June 20, 2005, p. B3.

42. J. S. Adams, "Inequity in Social Exchanges," in *Advances in Experimental Social Psychology*, ed. L. Berkowitz (New York: Academic Press, 1965), pp. 267–300.

43. See, for example, E. Walster, G. W. Walster, and W. G. Scott, *Equity: Theory and Research* (Boston: Allyn and Bacon, 1978); and J. Greenberg, "Cognitive Reevaluation of Outcomes in Response to Underpayment Inequity," *Academy of Management Journal*, March 1989, pp. 174–184.

44. P. S. Goodman and A. Friedman, "An Examination of Adams' Theory of Inequity," *Administrative Science Quarterly*, September 1971, pp. 271–288; R. P. Vecchio, "An Individual-Differences Interpretation of the Conflicting Predictions Generated by Equity Theory and Expectancy Theory," *Journal of Applied Psychology*, August 1981, pp. 470–481; J. Greenberg, "Approaching Equity and Avoiding Inequity in Groups and Organizations," in *Equity and Justice in Social Behavior*, ed. J. Greenberg and R. L. Cohen (New York: Academic Press, 1982), pp. 389–435; E. W. Miles, J. D. Hatfield, and R. C. Huseman, "The Equity Sensitive Construct: Potential Implications for Worker Performance," *Journal of Management*, December 1989, pp. 581–588; R. T. Mowday, "Equity Theory Predictions of Behavior in Organizations," in *Motivation and Work Behavior*, 5th ed., ed. R. Steers and L. W. Porter (New York: McGraw-Hill, 1991), pp. 111–131; and R. T. Mowday and K. A. Colwell, "Employee Reactions to Unfair Outcomes in the Workplace: The Contributions of Adams' Equity Theory to Understanding Work Motivation," in *Motivation and Work Behavior*, 7th ed., ed. L. W. Porter, G. A. Bigley, and R. M. Steers (Burr Ridge, IL: Irwin/McGraw-Hill, 2003), pp. 65–82.

45. See, for example, K. S. Sauley and A. G. Bedeian, "Equity Sensitivity: Construction of a Measure and Examination of Its Psychometric Properties," *Journal of Management* 26, no. 5 (2000), pp. 885–910; and M. N. Bing and S. M. Burroughs, "The Predictive and Interactive Effects of Equity Sensitivity in Teamwork-Oriented Organizations," *Journal of Organizational Behavior*, May 2001, pp. 271–290.

46. J. Greenberg and S. Ornstein, "High Status Job Title as Compensation for Underpayment: A Test of Equity Theory," *Journal of Applied Psychology*, May 1983, pp. 285–297; and J. Greenberg, "Equity and Workplace Status: A Field Experiment," *Journal of Applied Psychology*, November 1988, pp. 606–613.

47. P. S. Goodman, "Social Comparison Process in Organizations," in *New Directions in Organizational Behavior*, ed. B. M. Staw and G. R. Salancik (Chicago: St. Clair, 1977), pp. 97–132; and J. Greenberg, "A Taxonomy of Organizational Justice Theories," *Academy of Management Review*, January 1987, pp. 9–22.

48. See, for instance, J. Greenberg, *The Quest for Justice on the Job* (Thousand Oaks, CA: Sage, 1996); R. Cropanzano and J. Greenberg, "Progress in Organizational Justice: Tunneling Through the Maze," in *International Review of Industrial and Organizational Psychology*, vol. 12, ed. C. L. Cooper and I. T. Robertson (New York: Wiley, 1997); and J. A. Colquitt, D. E. Conlon, M. J. Wesson, C. O. L. H. Porter, and K. Y. Ng, "Justice at the Millennium: A Meta-Analytic Review of the 25 Years of Organizational Justice Research," *Journal of Applied Psychology*, June 2001, pp. 425–445.

49. R. J. Bies and J. S. Moag, "Interactional Justice: Communication Criteria for Fairness," in *Research on Negotiation in Organizations*, vol. 1, ed. B. H. Sheppard (Greenwich, CT: JAI Press, 1986), pp. 43–55.

50. See, for example, R. C. Dailey and D. J. Kirk, "Distributive and Procedural Justice as Antecedents of Job Dissatisfaction and Intent to Turnover," *Human Relations*, March 1992, pp. 305–316; D. B. McFarlin and P. D. Sweeney, "Distributive and Procedural Justice as Predictors of Satisfaction With Personal and Organizational Outcomes," *Academy of Management Journal*, August 1992, pp. 626–637; M. A. Korsgaard, D. M. Schweiger, and H. J. Sapienza, "Building Commitment, Attachment, and Trust in Strategic Decision-Making Teams: The Role of Procedural Justice," *Academy of Management Journal*, February 1995, pp. 60–84; M. A. Konovsky, "Understanding Procedural Justice and Its Impact on Business Organizations," *Journal of Management* 26, no. 3 (2000), pp. 489–511; R. Cropanzano and D. E. Rupp, "An Overview of Organizational Justice: Implications for Work Motivation," in *Motivation and Work Behavior*, 7th ed., ed. L. W. Porter, G. A. Bigley, and R. M. Steers (Burr Ridge, IL: Irwin/McGraw-Hill, 2003), pp. 82–95; and L. J. Barclay, D. P. Skarlicki, and S. D. Pugh, "Exploring the Role of Emotions in Injustice Perceptions and Retaliation," *Journal of Applied Psychology* 90, no. 4 (2005), pp. 629–643.

51. W. Chan Kim and R. Mauborgne, "Fair Process: Managing in the Knowledge Economy," *Harvard Business Review*, July–August 1997, pp. 65–76.

52. A. S. Blinder, "Introduction," in *Paying for Productivity: A Look at the Evidence*, ed. A. S. Blinder (Washington, DC: Brookings Institution, 1990), p. 30.

53. D. P. Skarlicki and R. Folger, "Retaliation in the Workplace: The Roles of Distributive, Procedural and Interactional Justice," *Journal of Applied Psychology* 82, 1997, pp. 434–443.

54. J. Morris, "Quarterback Casey Printers Signs Deal With NFL's Kansas City Chiefs," *Canadian Press*, January 12, 2006, http://www.canada.com/topics/sports/football/cfl/argos/story.html?id=2e9159c5-fe96-4250-a6c6-922b7526703d&page=1 (accessed May 1, 2006).

55. R. de Charms, *Personal Causation: The Internal Affective Determinants of Behavior* (New York: Academic Press, 1968).

56. E. L. Deci, R. Koestner, and R. M. Ryan, "A Meta-Analytic Review of Experiments Examining the Effects of Extrinsic Rewards on Intrinsic Motivation," *Psychological Bulletin* 125, no. 6 (November 1999), pp. 627–668.

57. A. Kohn, *Punished by Rewards* (Boston: Houghton Mifflin, 1993).

58. J. B. Miner, *Theories of Organizational Behavior* (Hinsdale, IL: Dryden Press, 1980), p. 157; and A. Kohn, *Punished by Rewards* (Boston: Houghton Mifflin, 1993).

59. A. Kohn, *Punished by Rewards* (Boston: Houghton Mifflin, 1993).

60. B. Nelson, "Dump the Cash, Load on the Praise," *Personnel Journal* 75, July 1996, pp. 65–66.

61. J. Pfeffer, *The Human Equation: Building Profits by Putting People First* (Boston: Harvard Business School Press, 1998).

62. K. W. Thomas, E. Jansen, and W. G. Tymon Jr., "Navigating in the Realm of Theory: An Empowering View of Construct Development," in *Research in Organizational Change and Development*, vol. 10, ed. W. A. Pasmore and R. W. Woodman (Greenwich, CT: JAI Press, 1997), pp. 1–30.

63. Our definition of a formal recognition system is based on S. E. Markham, K. D. Scott, and G. H. McKee, "Recognizing Good Attendance: A Longitudinal, Quasi-Experimental Field Study," *Personnel Psychology*, Autumn 2002, p. 641.

64. Hewitt Associates, "Employers Willing to Pay for High Performance," news release, September 8, 2004, http://was4.hewitt.com/hewitt/resource/newsroom/pressrel/2004/09-08-04eng.htm (accessed October 9, 2004).

65. J. Buckstein, "In Praise of Praise in the Workplace," *Globe and Mail*, June 15, 2005, p. C1.

66. J. Buckstein, "In Praise of Praise in the Workplace," *Globe and Mail*, June 15, 2005, p. C1.

67. Based on S. Baille-Ruder, "Sweet Devotion: How Chocolatier R.C. Purdy Developed the Perfect Recipe for a Superstar Workforce," *Profit*, December 2004, pp. 44–51; L. Pratt, "Management Tip from the Top," *National Post*, July 26, 2004, p. FP9; B. Constantineau, "Staff Discounts Can Make a Good Employer Great," *Vancouver Sun*, July 16, 2005, p. A1; and http://www.purdys.com/employer.htm.

68. "Praise Beats Raise as Best Motivator, Survey Shows," *Vancouver Sun*, September 10, 1994.

69. S. L. Rynes, B. Gerhart, and L. Parks, "Personnel Psychology: Performance Evaluation and Pay for Performance," *Annual Review of Psychology* 56, no. 1 (2005), p. 572.

70. Based on S. E. Gross and J. P. Bacher, "The New Variable Pay Programs: How Some Succeed, Why Some Don't," *Compensation & Benefits Review*, January–February 1993, p. 51; and J. R. Schuster and P. K. Zingheim, "The New Variable Pay: Key Design Issues," *Compensation & Benefits Review*, March–April 1993, p. 28.

71. Hewitt Associates, "Employers Willing to Pay for High Performance," news release, September 8, 2004, http://was4.hewitt.com/hewitt/resource/newsroom/pressrel/2004/09-08-04eng.htm (accessed October 9, 2004); Hewitt Associates, "Hewitt Study Shows Pay-for-Performance Plans Replacing Holiday Bonuses," news release, December 6, 2005, http://was4.hewitt.com/hewitt/resource/newsroom/pressrel/2005/12-06-05eng.pdf (accessed April 29, 2006); and P. Brieger, "Variable Pay Packages Gain Favour: Signing Bonuses, Profit Sharing Taking Place of Salary Hikes," *Financial Post* (*National Post*), September 13, 2002, p. FP5.

72. J. Smilko and K. Van Neck, "Rewarding Excellence Through Variable Pay," *Benefits Quarterly* 20, no. 3 (Third Quarter 2004), pp. 21–25.

73. "More Than 20 Percent of Japanese Firms Use Pay Systems Based on Performance," *Manpower Argus*, May 1998, p. 7; and "Bonus Pay in Canada," *Manpower Argus*, September 1996, p. 5.

74. E. Beauchesne, "Pay Bonuses Improve Productivity, Study Shows," *Vancouver Sun*, September 13, 2002, p. D5; and The Conference Board of Canada, "Variable Pay Offers a Bonus for Unionized Workplaces," news release, September 12, 2002, http://www.conferenceboard.ca/press/2002/variable_pay.asp (accessed April 29, 2006).

75. "Hope for Higher Pay: The Squeeze on Incomes Is Gradually Easing Up," *Maclean's*, November 25, 1996, pp. 100–101.

76. "Bonus Pay in Canada," *Manpower Argus*, September 1996, p. 5.

77. "Risk and Reward: More Canadian Companies Are Experimenting With Variable Pay," *Maclean's*, January 8, 1996, pp. 26–27.

78. "Higher Salaries and Bonuses Key to Retaining Employees, Survey Finds," *Edmonton Journal*, April 15, 2006, p. F2.

79. See, for instance, S. C. Hanlon, D. G. Meyer, and R. R. Taylor, "Consequences of Gainsharing," *Group & Organization Management*, March 1994, pp. 87–111; J. G. Belcher Jr., "Gainsharing and Variable Pay: The State of the Art," *Compensation & Benefits Review*, May–June 1994, pp. 50–60; and T. M. Welbourne and L. R. Gomez Mejia, "Gainsharing: A Critical Review and a Future Research Agenda," *Journal of Management* 21, no. 3 (1995), pp. 559–609.

80. D. Beck, "Implementing a Gainsharing Plan: What Companies Need to Know," *Compensation & Benefits Review*, January–February 1992, p. 23.

81. T. M. Welbourne and L. R. Gomez-Mejia, "Gainsharing: A Critical Review and a Future Research Agenda," *Journal of Management* 21, no. 3 (1995), pp. 559–609.

82. M. Byfield, "Ikea's Boss Gives Away the Store for a Day," *Report Newsmagazine*, October 25, 1999, p. 47.

83. K. Cox, "Power Struggle Cost FPI Millions," *Globe and Mail*, February 21, 2002, p. B3.

84. See K. M. Young, ed., *The Expanding Role of ESOPs in Public Companies* (New York: Quorum, 1990); J. L. Pierce and C. A. Furo, "Employee Ownership: Implications for Management," *Organizational Dynamics*, Winter 1990, pp. 32–43; J. Blasi and D. L. Druse, *The New Owners: The Mass Emergence of Employee Ownership in Public Companies and What It Means to American Business* (Champaign, IL: Harper Business, 1991); F. T. Adams and G. B. Hansen, *Putting Democracy to Work: A Practical Guide for Starting and Managing Worker-Owned Businesses* (San Francisco: Berrett-Koehler, 1993); and A. A. Buchko, "The Effects of Employee Ownership on Employee Attitudes: An Integrated Causal Model and Path Analysis," *Journal of Management Studies*, July 1993, pp. 633–656.

85. A. Toulin, "Lowly Staff Join Bosses in Receiving Stock Options," *National Post*, March 1, 2001, pp. C1, C12.

86. A. A. Buchko, "The Effects of Employee Ownership on Employee Attitudes: An Integrated Causal Model and Path Analysis," *Journal of Management Studies*, July 1993, pp. 633–656.

87. C. M. Rosen and M. Quarrey, "How Well Is Employee Ownership Working?" *Harvard Business Review*, September–October 1987, pp. 126–132.

88. W. N. Davidson and D. L. Worrell, "ESOP's Fables: The Influence of Employee Stock Ownership Plans on Corporate Stock Prices and Subsequent Operating Performance," *Human Resource Planning*, 1994, pp. 69–85.

89. J. L. Pierce and C. A. Furo, "Employee Ownership: Implications for Management," *Organizational Dynamics*, Winter 1990, pp. 32–43; and S. Kaufman, "ESOPs' Appeal on the Increase," *Nation's Business*, June 1997, p. 43.

90. G. D. Jenkins Jr., N. Gupta, A. Mitra, and J. D. Shaw, "Are Financial Incentives Related to Performance? A Meta-Analytic Review of Empirical Research," *Journal of Applied Psychology*, October 1998, pp. 777–787.

91. T. Coupé, V. Smeets, and F. Warzynski, "Incentives, Sorting and Productivity along the Career: Evidence from a Sample of Top Economists," *Journal of Law, Economics, & Organization* 22, no. 1 (April 2006), pp. 137–167.

92. A. Kauhanen and H. Piekkola, "What Makes Performance-Related Pay Schemes Work? Finnish Evidence," *Journal of Management and Governance* 10, no. 2 (2006), pp. 149–177.

93. J. S. Ang, A.-S. Chen, and J. W. Lin, "Ascertaining the Effects of Employee Bonus Plans," *Applied Economics* 37, no. 12 (July 10, 2005), pp. 1439–1448; C. G. Hanson and W. D. Bell, *Profit Sharing and Profitability: How Profit Sharing Promotes Business Success* (London: Kogan Page Ltd., 1987); E. M. Doherty, W. R. Nord, and J. L. McAdams, "Gainsharing and Organizational Development: A Productive Synergy," *Journal of Applied Behavioral Science*, August 1989, pp. 209–230; and T. C. McGrath, "How Three Screw Machine Companies Are Tapping Human Productivity Through Gainsharing," *Employment Relations Today* 20, no. 4 (1994), pp. 437–447.

94. P. A. Siegel and D. C. Hambrick, "Pay Disparities Within Top Management Groups: Evidence of Harmful Effects on Performance of High-Technology Firms," *Organization Science* 16, no. 3 (May–June 2005), pp. 259–276; S. Kerr, "Practical, Cost-Neutral

95. A. D. Stajkovic and F. Luthans, "Differential Effects of Incentive Motivators on Work Performance," *Academy of Management Journal*, June 2001, pp. 580–590; and A. M. Dickinson, "Are We Motivated by Money? Some Results from the Laboratory," *Performance Improvement* 44, no. 3 (March 2005), pp. 18–24.

96. S. L. Rynes, B. Gerhart, and L. Parks, "Personnel Psychology: Performance Evaluation and Pay for Performance," *Annual Review of Psychology* 56, no. 1 (2005), p. 572.

97. E. Beauchesne, "Pay Bonuses Improve Productivity, Study Shows," *Vancouver Sun*, September 13, 2002, p. D5.

98. E. Beauchesne, "Pay Bonuses Improve Productivity, Study Shows," *Vancouver Sun*, September 13, 2002, p. D5.

99. V. Sanderson, "Sweetening Their Slice: More Hardware and Lumberyard Dealers Are Investing in Profit-Sharing Programs as a Way to Promote Employee Loyalty," *Hardware Merchandising*, May–June 2003, p. 66.

100. J. Pfeffer and N. Langton, "The Effects of Wage Dispersion on Satisfaction, Productivity, and Working Collaboratively: Evidence from College and University Faculty," *Administrative Science Quarterly* 38, no. 3 (1983), pp. 382–407.

101. "Risk and Reward: More Canadian Companies Are Experimenting With Variable Pay," *Maclean's*, January 8, 1996, pp. 26–27.

102. "Risk and Reward: More Canadian Companies Are Experimenting With Variable Pay," *Maclean's*, January 8, 1996, pp. 26–27.

103. P. K. Zingheim and J. R. Schuster, "Introduction: How Are the New Pay Tools Being Deployed?" *Compensation & Benefits Review*, July–August 1995, pp. 10–11.

104. *OB in the Street* based on "In Pursuit of Level Playing Fields," *Globe and Mail*, March 9, 2002, p. S1.

105. T. Denison, "Formula for Success," August 13, 2004, http://www.collegecolours.com/columns/004.html.

106. J. R. Hackman and G. R. Oldham, "Motivation Through the Design of Work: Test of a Theory," *Organizational Behavior and Human Performance*, August 1976, pp. 250–279.

107. J. R. Hackman and G. R. Oldham, *Work Redesign* (Reading, MA: Addison Wesley, 1980).

108. J. R. Hackman, "Work Design," in *Improving Life at Work*, ed. J. R. Hackman and J. L. Suttle (Santa Monica, CA: Goodyear, 1977), pp. 132–133.

109. J. R. Hackman, "Work Design," in *Improving Life at Work*, ed. J. R. Hackman and J. L. Suttle (Santa Monica, CA: Goodyear, 1977), p. 129.

110. H. Munro, "Transit Drivers Taking Fewer Sick Days," *Vancouver Sun*, June 2, 1999, p. B3.

111. V. Sanderson, "Sweetening Their Slice: More Hardware and Lumberyard Dealers Are Investing in Profit-Sharing Programs as a Way to Promote Employee Loyalty," *Hardware Merchandising*, May–June 2003, p. 66.

112. S. Kerr, "On the Folly of Rewarding A, While Hoping for B," *Academy of Management Executive* 9, no. 1 (1995), pp. 7–14.

113. "More on the Folly," *Academy of Management Executive* 9, no. 1 (1995), pp. 15–16.

114. J. A. Ross, "Japan: Does Money Motivate?" *Harvard Business Review*, September–October 1997. See also R. B. Money and J. L. Graham, "Salesperson Performance, Pay, and Job Satisfaction: Tests of a

Model Using Data Collected in the U.S. and Japan" (working paper, University of South Carolina, 1997).

115. N. J. Adler, *International Dimensions of Organizational Behavior*, 3rd ed. (Cincinnati, OH: South Western, 1997), p. 158.

116. A. Kohn, *Punished by Rewards* (Boston: Houghton Mifflin, 1993).

117. W. G. Ouchi, *Theory Z* (New York: Avon Books, 1982); "Bosses' Pay," *Economist*, February 1, 1992, pp. 19–22; and W. Edwards Deming, *Out of the Crisis* (Cambridge: MIT Center for Advanced Engineering Study, 1986).

118. J. Pfeffer, *The Human Equation: Building Profits by Putting People First* (Boston: Harvard Business School Press, 1998).

119. G. Hofstede, "Motivation, Leadership, and Organization: Do American Theories Apply Abroad?" *Organizational Dynamics*, Summer 1980, p. 55.

120. J. K. Giacobbe-Miller, D. J. Miller, and V. I. Victorov, "A Comparison of Russian and U.S. Pay Allocation Decisions, Distributive Justice Judgments, and Productivity Under Different Payment Conditions," *Personnel Psychology*, Spring 1998, pp. 137–163.

121. S. L. Mueller and L. D. Clarke, "Political-Economic Context and Sensitivity to Equity: Differences Between the United States and the Transition Economies of Central and Eastern Europe," *Academy of Management Journal*, June 1998, pp. 319–329.

122. A. Kohn, *Punished by Rewards* (Boston: Houghton Mifflin, 1993), p. 181.

123. A. Kohn, *Punished by Rewards* (Boston: Houghton Mifflin, 1993), p. 181.

124. A. Kohn, *Punished by Rewards* (Boston: Houghton Mifflin, 1993), p. 186. See also P. R. Scholtes, "An Elaboration of Deming's Teachings on Performance Appraisal," in *Performance Appraisal: Perspectives on a Quality Management Approach*, ed. G. N. McLean, S. R. Damme, and R. A. Swanson (Alexandria, VA: American Society for Training and Development, 1990); and H. H. Meyer, E. Kay, and J. R. P. French Jr., "Split Roles in Performance Appraisal," *Harvard Business Review*, 1965, excerpts reprinted in "HBR Retrospect," *Harvard Business Review*, January–February 1989, p. 26; W.-U. Meyer, M. Bachmann, U. Biermann, M. Hempelmann, F.-O. Ploeger, and H. Spiller, "The Informational Value of Evaluative Behavior: Influences of Praise and Blame on Perceptions of Ability," *Journal of Educational Psychology* 71, 1979, pp. 259–268; A. Halachmi and M. Holzer, "Merit Pay, Performance Targeting, and Productivity," *Review of Public Personnel Administration* 7, 1987, pp. 80–91.

125. A. S. Blinder, "Introduction," in *Paying for Productivity: A Look at the Evidence*, ed. A. S. Blinder (Washington, DC: Brookings Institution, 1990).

126. A. Kohn, *Punished by Rewards* (Boston: Houghton Mifflin, 1993), p. 187.

127. D. Tjosvold, *Working Together to Get Things Done: Managing for Organizational Productivity* (Lexington, MA: Lexington Books, 1986); P. R. Scholtes, *The Team Handbook: How to Use Teams to Improve Quality* (Madison, WI: Joiner Associates, 1988); and A. Kohn, *No Contest: The Case Against Competition*, rev. ed. (Boston: Houghton Mifflin, 1992).

128. E. L. Deci, "Applications of Research on the Effects of Rewards," in *The Hidden Costs of Rewards: New Perspectives on the Psychology of Human Motivation*, ed. M. R. Lepper and D. Green (Hillsdale, NJ: Erlbaum, 1978).

129. S. E. Perry, *San Francisco Scavengers: Dirty Work and the Pride of Ownership* (Berkeley: University of California Press, 1978).

130. A. Kohn, *Punished by Rewards* (Boston: Houghton Mifflin, 1993), p. 192.

131. T. H. Naylor, "Redefining Corporate Motivation, Swedish Style," *Christian Century*, May 30–June 6, 1990, pp. 566–570; R. A. Karasek, T. Thorell, J. E. Schwartz, P. L. Schnall, C. F. Pieper, and J. L. Michela, "Job Characteristics in Relation to the Prevalence of Myocardial Infarction in the US Health Examination Survey (HES) and the Health and Nutrition Examination Survey (HANES)," *American Journal of Public Health* 78, 1988, pp. 910–916; D. P. Levin, "Toyota Plant in Kentucky Is Font of Ideas for the U.S.," *New York Times*, May 5, 1992, pp. A1, D8.

132. M. Bosquet, "The Prison Factory," reprinted from *Le Nouvel Observateur* in *Working Papers for a New Society*, Spring 1973, pp. 20–27; J. Holusha, "Grace Pastiak's 'Web of Inclusion,'" *New York Times*, May 5, 1991, pp. F1, F6; J. Simmons and W. Mares, *Working Together: Employee Participation in Action* (New York: New York University Press, 1985); D. I. Levine and L. D'Andrea Tyson, "Participation, Productivity, and the Firm's Environment," in *Paying for Productivity: A Look at the Evidence*, ed. A. S. Blinder (Washington, DC: Brookings Institution, 1990); and W. F. Whyte, "Worker Participation: International and Historical Perspectives," *Journal of Applied Behavioral Science* 19, 1983, pp. 395–407.

133. K. O. Doyle, "Introduction: Money and the Behavioral Sciences," *American Behavioral Scientist*, July 1992, pp. 641–657.

134. S. Caudron, "Motivation? Money's Only No. 2," *IndustryWeek*, November 15, 1993, p. 33.

135. E. A. Locke, D. Feren, V. McCaleb, K. Shaw, and A. Denny, "The Relative Effectiveness of Four Methods of Motivating Employee Performance," in *Changes in Working Life*, ed. K. D. Duncan, M. M. Gruneberg, and D. Wallis (London: Wiley, 1980), pp. 363–383.

136. B. Filipczak, "Can't Buy Me Love," *Training*, January 1996, pp. 29–34.

137. See A. Mitra, N. Gupta, and G. D. Jenkins Jr., "The Case of the Invisible Merit Raise: How People See Their Pay Raises," *Compensation & Benefits Review*, May–June 1995, pp. 71–76.

Chapter 5

1. Opening vignette based on R. Ross, "Students Give Themselves the Gears," *Toronto Star*, February 25, 2002, http://www.torontostar.com/NASApp/cs/ContentServer?pagename=thestar/Layout/Article_Type1&c=Article&cid=1014591698117&call_page=TS_Business&call_pageid=968350072197&call_pagepath=Business/News&col=969048863851 (accessed February 25, 2002); and *Canada FIRST* website: http://www.canadafirst.org.

2. J. R. Katzenback and D. K. Smith, *The Wisdom of Teams: Creating the High-Performance Organization* (New York: Harper Business, 1999), p. 45.

3. J. R. Katzenback and D. K. Smith, *The Wisdom of Teams: Creating the High-Performance Organization* (New York: Harper Business, 1999), p. 214.

4. P. Booth, *Challenge and Change: Embracing the Team Concept*, Report 123-194 (Ottawa: The Conference Board of Canada, 1994).

5. Cited in C. Joinson, "Teams at Work," *HR Magazine*, May 1999, p. 30; and P. Strozniak, "Teams at Work," *IndustryWeek*, September 18, 2000, p. 47.

6. See, for example, D. Tjosvold, *Team Organization: An Enduring Competitive Advantage* (Chichester, UK: Wiley, 1991); S. A. Mohrman, S. G. Cohen, and A. M. Mohrman Jr., *Designing Team-Based Organizations* (San Francisco: Jossey-Bass, 1995); P. MacMillan, *The Performance Factor: Unlocking the Secrets of Teamwork* (Nashville, TN: Broadman and Holman, 2001); and E. Salas, C. A. Bowers, and E. Edens, eds., *Improving Teamwork in*

Organizations: Applications of Resource Management Training (Mahwah, NJ: Lawrence Erlbaum, 2002).

7. B. W. Tuckman, "Developmental Sequences in Small Groups," *Psychological Bulletin,* June 1965, pp. 384–399; B. W. Tuckman and M. C. Jensen, "Stages of Small-Group Development Revisited," *Group and Organizational Studies,* December 1977, pp. 419–427; and M. F. Maples, "Group Development: Extending Tuckman's Theory," *Journal for Specialists in Group Work,* Fall 1988, pp. 17–23.

8. R. C. Ginnett, "The Airline Cockpit Crew," in *Groups That Work (and Those That Don't),* ed. J. R. Hackman (San Francisco: Jossey-Bass, 1990).

9. C. J. G. Gersick, "Time and Transition in Work Teams: Toward a New Model of Group Development," *Academy of Management Journal,* March 1988, pp. 9–41; C. J. G. Gersick, "Marking Time: Predictable Transitions in Task Groups," *Academy of Management Journal,* June 1989, pp. 274–309; E. Romanelli and M. L. Tushman, "Organizational Transformation as Punctuated Equilibrium: An Empirical Test," *Academy of Management Journal,* October 1994, pp. 1141–1166; B. M. Lichtenstein, "Evolution or Transformation: A Critique and Alternative to Punctuated Equilibrium," in *Academy of Management Best Paper Proceedings,* ed. D. P. Moore (National Academy of Management Conference, Vancouver, 1995), pp. 291–295; and A. Seers and S. Woodruff, "Temporal Pacing in Task Forces: Group Development or Deadline Pressure?" *Journal of Management* 23, no. 2 (1997), pp. 169–187.

10. C. J. G. Gersick, "Time and Transition in Work Teams: Toward a New Model of Group Development," *Academy of Management Journal,* March 1988, pp. 9–41; M. J. Waller, J. M. Conte, C. B. Gibson, and M. A. Carpenter, "The Effect of Individual Perceptions of Deadlines on Team Performance," *Academy of Management Review,* October 2001, pp. 586–600; G. A. Okhuysen and M. J. Waller, "Focusing on Midpoint Transitions: An Analysis of Boundary Conditions," *Academy of Management Journal* 45, 2002, pp. 1056–1065; and M. J. Waller, M. E. Zellmer-Bruhn, and R. C. Giambatista, "Watching the Clock: Group Pacing Behavior Under Dynamic Deadlines," *Academy of Management Journal* 45, 2002, pp. 1046–1055.

11. A. Chang, P. Bordia, and J. Duck, "Punctuated Equilibrium and Linear Progression: Toward a New Understanding of Group Development," *Academy of Management Journal* 46, no. 1 (2003), pp. 106–117.

12. K. L. Bettenhausen, "Five Years of Groups Research: What We Have Learned and What Needs to Be Addressed," *Journal of Management* 17, 1991, pp. 345–381; and R. A. Guzzo and G. P. Shea, "Group Performance and Intergroup Relations in Organizations," in *Handbook of Industrial and Organizational Psychology,* 2nd ed., vol. 3, ed. M. D. Dunnette and L. M. Hough (Palo Alto, CA: Consulting Psychologists Press, 1992), pp. 269–313.

13. A. Chang, P. Bordia, and J. Duck, "Punctuated Equilibrium and Linear Progression: Toward a New Understanding of Group Development," *Academy of Management Journal* 46, no. 1 (2003), pp. 106–117; and S. G. S. Lim and J. K. Murnighan, "Phases, Deadlines, and the Bargaining Process," *Organizational Behavior and Human Decision Processes* 58, 1994, pp. 153–171.

14. See, for instance, D. L. Gladstein, "Groups in Context: A Model of Task Group Effectiveness," *Administrative Science Quarterly,* December 1984, pp. 499–517; J. R. Hackman, "The Design of Work Teams," in *Handbook of Organizational Behavior,* ed. J. W. Lorsch (Englewood Cliffs, NJ: Prentice Hall, 1987), pp. 315–342; M. A. Campion, G. J. Medsker, and C. A. Higgs, "Relations Between Work Group Characteristics and Effectiveness: Implications for Designing Effective Work Groups," *Personnel*

Psychology, 1993; and R. A. Guzzo and M. W. Dickson, "Teams in Organizations: Recent Research on Performance and Effectiveness," in *Annual Review of Psychology,* vol. 47, ed. J. T. Spence, J. M. Darley, and D. J. Foss, 1996, pp. 307–338.

15. D. E. Hyatt and T. M. Ruddy, "An Examination of the Relationship Between Work Group Characteristics and Performance: Once More into the Breach," *Personnel Psychology,* Autumn 1997, p. 555.

16. This model is based on D. R. Ilgen, J. R. Hollenbeck, M. Johnson, and D. Jundt, "Teams in Organizations: From Input-Process-Output Models to IMOI Models," *Annual Review of Psychology* 56, no. 1 (2005), pp. 517–543; M. A. Campion, E. M. Papper, and G. J. Medsker, "Relations Between Work Team Characteristics and Effectiveness: A Replication and Extension," *Personnel Psychology,* Summer 1996, pp. 429–452; D. E. Hyatt and T. M. Ruddy, "An Examination of the Relationship Between Work Group Characteristics and Performance: Once More into the Breach," *Personnel Psychology,* Autumn 1997, pp. 553–585; S. G. Cohen and D. E. Bailey, "What Makes Teams Work: Group Effectiveness Research from the Shop Floor to the Executive Suite," *Journal of Management* 23, no. 3 (1997), pp. 239–290; G. A. Neuman and J. Wright, "Team Effectiveness: Beyond Skills and Cognitive Ability," *Journal of Applied Psychology,* June 1999, pp. 376–389; and L. Thompson, *Making the Team* (Upper Saddle River, NJ: Prentice Hall, 2000), pp. 18–33.

17. *OB in the Street* based on M. Petrie, "Canada's Skeleton Crew Made Peace to Improve," *CanWest News Service,* February 21, 2005; and B. Graveland, "Pain Credits Team for Win," *Edmonton Journal,* February 22, 2005, p. D3.

18. M. Petrie, "Canada's Skeleton Crew Made Peace to Improve," *CanWest News Service,* February 21, 2005.

19. B. Graveland, "Pain Credits Team for Win," *Edmonton Journal,* February 22, 2005, p. D3.

20. See M. Mattson, T. V. Mumford, and G. S. Sintay, "Taking Teams to Task: A Normative Model for Designing or Recalibrating Work Teams" (paper presented at the National Academy of Management Conference, Chicago, August 1999); and G. L. Stewart and M. R. Barrick, "Team Structure and Performance: Assessing the Mediating Role of Intrateam Process and the Moderating Role of Task Type," *Academy of Management Journal,* April 2000, pp. 135–148.

21. G. Keenan, "Steely John: Dofasco Lifer John Mayberry Is Not Your Typical Steel CEO. He's Making Money," *Report on Business Magazine,* September 2002, pp. 12–15.

22. E. M. Stark, "Interdependence and Preference for Group Work: Main and Congruence Effects on the Satisfaction and Performance of Group Members," *Journal of Management* 26, no. 2 (2000), pp. 259–279; and J. W. Bishop, K. D. Scott, and S. M. Burroughs, "Support, Commitment, and Employee Outcomes in a Team Environment," *Journal of Management* 26, no. 6 (2000), pp. 1113–1132.

23. J. R. Hackman, *Leading Teams* (Boston: Harvard Business School Press, 2002).

24. D. Eden, "Pygmalion Without Interpersonal Contrast Effects: Whole Groups Gain from Raising Manager Expectations," *Journal of Applied Psychology,* August 1990, pp. 394–398.

25. J. M. George and K. Bettenhausen, "Understanding Prosocial Behavior, Sales, Performance, and Turnover: A Group-Level Analysis in a Service Context," *Journal of Applied Psychology,* December 1990, pp. 698–709; and J. M. George, "State or Trait: Effects of Positive Mood on Prosocial Behaviors at Work," *Journal of Applied Social Psychology,* April 1991, pp. 299–307.

26. W. Immen, "The More Women in Groups, the Better," *Globe and Mail,* April 27, 2005, p. C3.

27. J. L. Berdahl and C. Anderson, "Men, Women, and Leadership Centralization in Groups Over Time," *Group Dynamics: Theory, Research, and Practice* 9, no. 1 (2005), pp. 45–57.

28. R. Wageman, J. R. Hackman, and E. V. Lehman, "Development of the Team Diagnostic Survey" (working paper, Tuck School, Dartmouth College, Hanover, NH, 2004).

29. J. R. Hackman and R. Wageman, "A Theory of Team Coaching," *Academy of Management Review* 30, no. 2 (April 2005), pp. 269–287.

30. R. I. Beekun, "Assessing the Effectiveness of Sociotechnical Interventions: Antidote or Fad?" *Human Relations*, October 1989, pp. 877–897.

31. S. G. Cohen, G. E. Ledford, and G. M. Spreitzer, "A Predictive Model of Self-Managing Work Team Effectiveness," *Human Relations*, May 1996, pp. 643–676.

32. D. R. Ilgen, J. R. Hollenbeck, M. Johnson, and D. Jundt, "Teams in Organizations: From Input-Process-Output Models to IMOI Models," *Annual Review of Psychology* 56, no. 1 (2005), pp. 517–543.

33. K. T. Dirks, "Trust in Leadership and Team Performance: Evidence from NCAA Basketball," *Journal of Applied Psychology*, December 2000, pp. 1004–1012; and M. Williams, "In Whom We Trust: Group Membership as an Affective Context for Trust Development," *Academy of Management Review*, July 2001, pp. 377–396.

34. See S. T. Johnson, "Work Teams: What's Ahead in Work Design and Rewards Management," *Compensation & Benefits Review*, March–April 1993, pp. 35–41; and A. M. Saunier and E. J. Hawk, "Realizing the Potential of Teams Through Team-Based Rewards," *Compensation & Benefits Review*, July–August 1994, pp. 24–33.

35. D. L. Ferrin and K. T. Dirks, "The Use of Rewards to Increase and Decrease Trust: Mediating Processes and Differential Effects," *Organization Science* 14, no. 1 (January–February 2003), pp. 18–31.

36. J. Pfeffer and N. Langton, "The Effect of Wage Dispersion on Satisfaction, Productivity, and Working Collaboratively: Evidence from College and University Faculty," *Administrative Science Quarterly* 38, 1993, pp. 382–407.

37. M. Bloom, "The Performance Effects of Pay Dispersion on Individuals and Organizations," *Academy of Management Journal* 42, 1999, pp. 25–40.

38. For a more detailed breakdown on team skills, see M. J. Stevens and M. A. Campion, "The Knowledge, Skill, and Ability Requirements for Teamwork: Implications for Human Resource Management," *Journal of Management*, Summer 1994, pp. 503–530.

39. M. R. Barrick, G. L. Stewart, M. J. Neubert, and M. K. Mount, "Relating Member Ability and Personality to Work-Team Processes and Team Effectiveness," *Journal of Applied Psychology*, June 1998, pp. 377–391.

40. M. R. Barrick, G. L. Stewart, M. J. Neubert, and M. K. Mount, "Relating Member Ability and Personality to Work-Team Processes and Team Effectiveness," *Journal of Applied Psychology*, June 1998, pp. 377–391.

41. M. R. Barrick, G. L. Stewart, M. J. Neubert, and M. K. Mount, "Relating Member Ability and Personality to Work-Team Processes and Team Effectiveness," *Journal of Applied Psychology*, June 1998, pp. 377–391.

42. E. Sundstrom, K. P. Meuse, and D. Futrell, "Work Teams: Applications and Effectiveness," *American Psychologist*, February 1990, pp. 120–133.

43. See M. F. Peterson, P. B. Smith, A. Akande, S. Ayestaran, S. Bochner, V. Callan, N. Guk Cho, J. Correia Jesuino, M. D'Amorim, P.-H. François, K. Hofmann, P. L. Koopman, K. Leung, T. K. Lim, S. Mortazavi, J. Munene, M. Radford, A. Ropo, G. Savage, B. Setiadi, T. N. Sinha, R. Sorenson, and C. Viedge, "Role Conflict, Ambiguity, and Overload: A 21-Nation Study," *Academy of Management Journal*, April 1995, pp. 429–452.

44. See, for instance, M. Sashkin and K. J. Kiser, *Putting Total Quality Management to Work* (San Francisco: Berrett-Koehler, 1993); and J. R. Hackman and R. Wageman, "Total Quality Management: Empirical, Conceptual and Practical Issues," *Administrative Science Quarterly*, June 1995, pp. 309–342.

45. D. van Knippenberg, C. K. W. De Dreu, and A. C. Homan, "Work Group Diversity and Group Performance: An Integrative Model and Research Agenda," *Journal of Applied Psychology* 89, no. 6 (December 2004), pp. 1008–1022.

46. R. J. Ely and D. A. Thomas, "Cultural Diversity at Work: The Effects of Diversity Perspectives on Work Group Processes and Outcomes," *Administrative Science Quarterly* 46, 2001, pp. 229–273; K. A. Jehn, G. B. Northcraft, and M. A. Neale, "Why Some Differences Make a Difference: A Field Study of Diversity, Conflict, and Performance in Workgroups," *Administrative Science Quarterly* 44, 1999, pp. 741–763; and W. E. Watson, K. Kumar, and L. K. Michaelsen, "Cultural Diversity's Impact on Interaction Process and Performance: Comparing Homogeneous and Diverse Task Groups," *Academy of Management Journal* 36, 1993, pp. 590–602.

47. For a review, see K. Y. Williams and C. A. O'Reilly, "Demography and Diversity in Organizations: A Review of 40 Years of Research," in *Research in Organizational Behavior*, vol. 20, ed. B. M. Staw and L. L. Cummings (Greenwich, CT: JAI Press, 1998), pp. 77–140.

48. See, for instance, J. M. Sacco and N. Schmitt, "A Dynamic Multilevel Model of Demographic Diversity and Misfit Effects," *Journal of Applied Psychology* 90, no. 2 (March 2005), pp. 203–231.

49. E. Peterson, "Negotiation Teamwork: The Impact of Information Distribution and Accountability on Performance Depends on the Relationship Among Team Members," *Organizational Behavior and Human Decision Processes* 72, 1997, pp. 364–384.

50. J. Labianca, "The Ties That Blind," *Harvard Business Review* 82, no. 10 (October 2004), p. 19.

51. D. A. Harrison, K. H. Price, J. H. Gavin, and A. T. Florey, "Time, Teams, and Task Performance: Changing Effects of Surface- and Deep-Level Diversity on Group Functioning," *Academy of Management Journal* 45, no. 5 (2002), pp. 1029–1045; and J. S. Bunderson and K. M. Sutcliffe, "Comparing Alternative Conceptualizations of Functional Diversity in Management Teams: Process and Performance Effects," *Academy of Management Journal* 45, no. 5 (2002), pp. 875–893.

52. M. A. Neale, G. B. Northcraft, and K. A. Jehn, "Exploring Pandora's Box: The Impact of Diversity and Conflict on Work Group Performance," *Performance Improvement Quarterly* 12, no. 1 (1999), pp. 113–126.

53. See, for instance, M. Sashkin and K. J. Kiser, *Putting Total Quality Management to Work* (San Francisco: Berrett-Koehler, 1993); and J. R. Hackman and R. Wageman, "Total Quality Management: Empirical, Conceptual and Practical Issues," *Administrative Science Quarterly*, June 1995, pp. 309–342.

54. J. S. Bunderson and K. M. Sutcliffe, "Comparing Alternative Conceptualizations of Functional Diversity in Management Teams: Process and Performance Effects," *Academy of Management Journal* 45, no. 5 (2002), pp. 875–893, discusses some of the recent work in this area.

55. G. S. Van der Vegt, and J. S. Bunderson, "Learning and Performance in Multidisciplinary Teams: The Importance of Collective Team Identification," *Academy of Management Journal* 48, no. 3 (2005), pp. 532–547.

56. R. J. Ely and D. A. Thomas, "Cultural Diversity at Work: The Effects of Diversity Perspectives on Work Group Processes and Outcomes," *Administrative Science Quarterly* 46, 2001, pp. 229–273.

57. J. T. Polzer, L. P. Milton, and W. B. Swann Jr., "Capitalizing on Diversity: Interpersonal Congruence in Small Work Groups," *Administrative Science Quarterly* 47, no. 2 (2002), pp. 296–324.

58. *Focus on Diversity* based on B. L. Kelsey, "Increasing Minority Group Participation and Influence Using a Group Support System," *Canadian Journal of Administrative Sciences* 17, no. 1 (2000), pp. 63–75.

59. See D. R. Comer, "A Model of Social Loafing in Real Work Groups," *Human Relations*, June 1995, pp. 647–667.

60. E. Sundstrom, K. P. Meuse, and D. Futrell, "Work Teams: Applications and Effectiveness," *American Psychologist*, February 1990, pp. 120–133.

61. D. E. Hyatt and T. M. Ruddy, "An Examination of the Relationship Between Work Group Characteristics and Performance: Once More into the Breach," *Personnel Psychology*, Autumn 1997, p. 555; and J. D. Shaw, M. K. Duffy, and E. M. Stark, "Interdependence and Preference for Group Work: Main and Congruence Effects on the Satisfaction and Performance of Group Members," *Journal of Management* 26, no. 2 (2000), pp. 259–279.

62. R. Wageman, "Critical Success Factors for Creating Superb Self-Managing Teams," *Organizational Dynamics*, Summer 1997, p. 55.

63. M. A. Campion, E. M. Papper, and G. J. Medsker, "Relations Between Work Team Characteristics and Effectiveness: A Replication and Extension," *Personnel Psychology*, Summer 1996, p. 430.

64. M. A. Campion, E. M. Papper, and G. J. Medsker, "Relations Between Work Team Characteristics and Effectiveness: A Replication and Extension," *Personnel Psychology*, Summer 1996, p. 430.

65. K. Hess, *Creating the High-Performance Team* (New York: Wiley, 1987); J. R. Katzenbach and D. K. Smith, *The Wisdom of Teams* (Boston: Harvard Business School Press, 1993), pp. 43–64; and K. D. Scott and A. Townsend, "Teams: Why Some Succeed and Others Fail," *HR Magazine*, August 1994, pp. 62–67.

66. E. Weldon and L. R. Weingart, "Group Goals and Group Performance," *British Journal of Social Psychology*, Spring 1993, pp. 307–334.

67. R. A. Guzzo, P. R. Yost, R. J. Campbell, and G. P. Shea, "Potency in Groups: Articulating a Construct," *British Journal of Social Psychology*, March 1993, pp. 87–106; S. J. Zaccaro, V. Blair, C. Peterson, and M. Zazanis, "Collective Efficacy," in *Self-Efficacy, Adaptation and Adjustment: Theory, Research and Application*, ed. J. E. Maddux (New York: Plenum, 1995), pp. 308–330; and D. L. Feltz and C. D. Lirgg, "Perceived Team and Player Efficacy in Hockey," *Journal of Applied Psychology*, August 1998, pp. 557–564.

68. For some of the controversy surrounding the definition of cohesion, see J. Keyton and J. Springston, "Redefining Cohesiveness in Groups," *Small Group Research*, May 1990, pp. 234–254.

69. C. R. Evans and K. L. Dion, "Group Cohesion and Performance: A Meta-Analysis," *Small Group Research*, May 1991, pp. 175–186; B. Mullen and C. Cooper, "The Relation Between Group Cohesiveness and Performance: An Integration," *Psychological Bulletin*, March 1994, pp. 210–227; S. M. Gully, D. J. Devine, and D. J. Whitney, "A Meta-Analysis of Cohesion and Performance: Effects of Level of Analysis and Task Interdependence," *Small Group Research*, 1995, pp. 497–520; and P. M. Podsakoff, S. B. MacKenzie, and M. Ahearne, "Moderating Effects of Goal Acceptance on the Relationship Between Group Cohesiveness and Productivity," *Journal of Applied Psychology*, December 1997, pp. 974–983.

70. A. Chang and P. Bordia, "A Multidimensional Approach to the Group Cohesion–Group Performance Relationship," *Small Group Research*, August 2001, pp. 379–405.

71. Paragraph based on R. Kreitner and A. Kinicki, *Organizational Behavior*, 6th ed. (New York: Irwin, 2004), pp. 459–461.

72. K. M. Eisenhardt, J. L. Kahwajy, and L. J. Bourgeois III, "How Management Teams Can Have a Good Fight," *Harvard Business Review*, July–August 1997, p. 78.

73. K. Jehn, "A Multimethod Examination of the Benefits and Detriments of Intragroup Conflict," *Administrative Science Quarterly*, June 1995, pp. 256–282.

74. K. M. Eisenhardt, J. L. Kahwajy, and L. J. Bourgeois III, "How Management Teams Can Have a Good Fight," *Harvard Business Review*, July–August 1997, p. 78.

75. K. Hess, *Creating the High-Performance Team* (New York: Wiley, 1987).

76. See, for example, C. M. Fiol and E. J. O'Connor, "Identification in Face-to-Face, Hybrid, and Pure Virtual Teams: Untangling the Contradictions," *Organization Science* 16, no. 1 (January–February 2005), pp. 19–32; L. L. Martins, L. L. Gilson, and M. T. Maynard, "Virtual Teams: What Do We Know and Where Do We Go from Here?" *Journal of Management* 30, no. 6 (December 2004), pp. 805–835; D. Duarte and N. T. Snyder, *Mastering Virtual Teams: Strategies, Tools, and Techniques* (San Francisco: Jossey-Bass, 1999); M. L. Maznevski and K. M. Chudoba, "Bridging Space Over Time: Global Virtual Team Dynamics and Effectiveness," *Organization Science*, September–October 2000, pp. 473–492; and J. Katzenbach and D. Smith, "Virtual Teaming," *Forbes*, May 21, 2001, pp. 48–51.

77. K. Kiser, "Working on World Time," *Training*, March 1999, p. 30.

78. B. B. Baltes, M. W. Dickson, M. P. Sherman, C. C. Bauer, and J. S. LaGanke, "Computer-Mediated Communication and Group Decision Making: A Meta-Analysis," *Organizational Behaviour and Human Decision Processes* 87, no. 1 (2002), pp. 156–179.

79. J. M. Wilson, S. G. Straus, and B. McEvily, "All in Due Time: The Development of Trust in Computer-Mediated and Face-to-Face Teams," *Organizational Behavior and Human Decision Processes* 99, no. 1 (2006), pp. 16–33; and S. L. Jarvenpaa, K. Knoll, and D. E. Leidner, "Is Anybody Out There? Antecedents of Trust in Global Virtual Teams," *Journal of Management Information Systems*, Spring 1998, pp. 29–64.

80. This section based on A. Majchrzak, A. Malhotra, J. Stamps, and J. Lipnack, "Can Absence Make a Team Grow Stronger?" *Harvard Business Review* 82, no. 5 (May 2004), pp. 131–136.

81. B. L. Kirkman, B. Rosen, C. B. Gibson, P. E. Tesluk, and S. O. McPherson, "Five Challenges to Virtual Team Success: Lessons from Sabre, Inc.," *Academy of Management Executive* 16, no. 3 (2002), pp. 67–79.

82. P. J. Hinds and M. Mortensen. "Understanding Conflict in Geographically Distributed Teams: The Moderating Effects of Shared Identity, Shared Context, and Spontaneous Communication," *Organization Science* 16, no. 3 (2005), pp. 290–307.

83. D. Brown, "Innovative HR Ineffective in Manufacturing Firms," *Canadian HR Reporter*, April 7, 2003, pp. 1–2.

84. A. B. Drexler and R. Forrester, "Teamwork—Not Necessarily the Answer," *HR Magazine*, January 1998, pp. 55–58.

85. R. Forrester and A. B. Drexler, "A Model for Team-Based Organization Performance," *Academy of Management Executive*, August 1999, p. 47. See also S. A. Mohrman, with S. G. Cohen and A. M. Mohrman Jr., *Designing Team-Based Organizations* (San Francisco: Jossey-Bass, 1995); and J. H. Shonk, *Team-Based Organizations* (Homewood, IL: Business One Irwin, 1992).

86. Based on N. Katz, "Sports Teams as a Model for Workplace Teams: Lessons and Liabilities," *Academy of Management Executive*, August 2001, pp. 56–67.

87. Based on N. Katz, "Sports Teams as a Model for Workplace Teams: Lessons and Liabilities," *Academy of Management Executive*, August 2001, pp. 56–67.

88. Based on S. P. Robbins and P. L. Hunsaker, *Training in Interpersonal Skills*, 2nd ed. (Upper Saddle River, NJ: Prentice Hall, 1996), pp. 168–184.

Chapter 6

1. Opening vignette based on B. Livesey, "Heart of Steel," *Report on Business Magazine*, August 1997, pp. 20–27; D. McMurdy, "Dofasco Steel on Cutting Edge: Mayberry Banks on High-Tech to Boost Production," *Financial Post*, December 10, 2001, pp. FP1, FP7; J. Terrett, "Dofasco Engages Workforce to Profit in Tough Steel Market: Losses in Early 1990s Lead to Major Transformation," *Plant*, May 6, 2002, p. 15; and G. Keenan, "Dofasco Head Leaves Winning Strategy for Steel Maker," *Globe and Mail*, May 3, 2003, p. B3.

2. See, for example, K. W. Thomas and W. H. Schmidt, "A Survey of Managerial Interests With Respect to Conflict," *Academy of Management Journal*, June 1976, p. 317.

3. L. Ramsay, "Communication Key to Workplace Happiness," *Financial Post*, December 6/8, 1997, p. 58.

4. See http://www.isrsurveys.com/default.asp (accessed March 14, 2002).

5. D. K. Berlo, *The Process of Communication* (New York: Holt, Rinehart and Winston, 1960), p. 54.

6. *Focus on Ethics* based on "Big Mac Said Close to Settling Fries Suit," *Toronto Star*, March 8, 2002, http://www.torontostar.com/NASApp/cs/ContentServer?pagename=thestar/Layout/Article_Type1&c=Article&cid=1015542115092&call_page=TS_Business&call_pageid=968350072197&call_pagepath=Business/News&col=969048863851 (accessed March 9, 2002).

7. J. C. McCroskey, J. A. Daly, and G. Sorenson, "Personality Correlates of Communication Apprehension," *Human Communication Research*, Spring 1976, pp. 376–380.

8. See R. L. Daft and R. H. Lengel, "Information Richness: A New Approach to Managerial Behavior and Organization Design," in *Research in Organizational Behavior*, vol. 6, ed. B. M. Staw and L. L. Cummings (Greenwich, CT: JAI Press, 1984), pp. 191–233; R. E. Rice and D. E. Shook, "Relationships of Job Categories and Organizational Levels to Use of Communication Channels, Including Electronic Mail: A Meta-Analysis and Extension," *Journal of Management Studies*, March 1990, pp. 195–229; R. E. Rice, "Task Analyzability, Use of New Media, and Effectiveness," *Organization Science*, November 1992, pp. 475–500; S. G. Straus and J. E. McGrath, "Does the Medium Matter? The Interaction of Task Type and Technology on Group Performance and Member Reaction," *Journal of Applied Psychology*, February 1994, pp. 87–97; J. Webster and L. K. Trevino, "Rational and Social Theories as Complementary Explanations of Communication Media Choices: Two Policy-Capturing Studies," *Academy of Management Journal*, December 1995, pp. 1544–1572; and L. K. Trevino, J. Webster, and E. W. Stein, "Making Connections: Complementary Influences on Communication Media Choices, Attitudes, and Use," *Organization Science*, March–April 2000, pp. 163–182.

9. R. L. Daft, R. H. Lengel, and L. K. Trevino, "Message Equivocality, Media Selection, and Manager Performance: Implications for Information Systems," *MIS Quarterly*, September 1987, pp. 355–368.

10. "Virtual Pink Slips Start Coming Online," *Vancouver Sun*, July 3, 1999, p. D15.

11. Thanks are due to an anonymous reviewer for providing this elaboration.

12. J. Terrett, "Dofasco Engages Workforce to Profit in Tough Steel Market: Losses in Early 1990s Lead to Major Transformation," *Plant*, May 6, 2002, p. 15.

13. M. Swartz, "How Enron Blew It," *Texas Monthly*, November 2001.

14. Based on K. Cox, "Risley's Wagging Tongue Doomed FPI Deal," *Globe and Mail*, February 19, 2002, p. B14; and C. Jackson, "Liberal Leader Has Doubts About Bill," *Telegram*, June 7, 2005, p. A1.

15. S. I. Hayakawa, *Language in Thought and Action* (New York: Harcourt Brace Jovanovich, 1949), p. 292.

16. H. Weeks, "Taking the Stress Out of Stressful Conversations," *Harvard Business Review*, July–August 2001, pp. 112–119.

17. See, for instance, R. Hotch, "Communication Revolution," *Nation's Business*, May 1993, pp. 20–28; G. Brockhouse, "I Have Seen the Future," *Canadian Business*, August 1993, pp. 43–45; R. Hotch, "In Touch Through Technology," *Nation's Business*, January 1994, pp. 33–35; and P. LaBarre, "The Other Network," *IndustryWeek*, September 19, 1994, pp. 33–36.

18. T. Hamilton, "E-Mail Overload Swamps Workplace," *Toronto Star*, June 26, 2002, http://www.torontostar.com/NASApp/cs/ContentServer?pagename=thestar/Layout/ArticleType1&c=Article&cid=1022100352728&call_page=TS_Business&call_pageid=968350072197&call_pagepath=Business/News&col=969048863851 (accessed June 26, 2002).

19. K. Macklem, "You've Got Too Much Mail," *Maclean's*, January 30, 2006, pp. 20–21.

20. K. Macklem, "You've Got Too Much Mail," *Maclean's*, January 30, 2006, pp. 20–21.

21. K. Macklem, "You've Got Too Much Mail," *Maclean's*, January 30, 2006, pp. 20–21.

22. T. R. Kurtzberg, C. E. Naquin, and L. Y. Belkin, "Electronic Performance Appraisals: The Effects of E-Mail Communication on Peer Ratings in Actual and Simulated Environments," *Organizational Behavior and Human Decision Processes* 98, no. 2 (2005), pp. 216–226.

23. J. Kruger, N. Epley, J. Parker, and Z.-W. Ng, "Egocentrism Over E-Mail: Can We Communicate as Well as We Think?" *Journal of Personality and Social Psychology* 89, no. 6 (2005), pp. 925–936.

24. Derived from P. Kuitenbrouwer, "Office E-Mail Runs Amok," *Financial Post (National Post)*, October 18, 2001, p. FP11.

25. E. Church, "Employers Read E-Mail as Fair Game," *Globe and Mail*, April 14, 1998, p. B16.

26. J. Kay, "Someone Will Watch Over Me: Think Your Office E-Mails Are Private? Think Again," *National Post Business*, January 2001, pp. 59–64.

27. E. Church, "Employers Read E-Mail as Fair Game," *Globe and Mail*, April 14, 1998, p. B16.

28. A. Harmon, "Appeal of Instant Messaging Extends into the Workplace," *New York Times*, March 11, 2003, p. A1.

29. Report released by the Canadian Wireless Telecommunications Association, as reported in P. Wilson, "Record Growth of Text Messaging Continues in Canada," *Vancouver Sun*, March 23, 2005, p. D2.

30. Cited in C. Y. Chen, "The IM Invasion," *Fortune*, May 26, 2003, pp. 135–138.

31. A. Stuart, "IM Is Here. RU Ready 2 Try It?" *Inc.*, July 2003, pp. 7–8.

32. G. Buckler, "Instant Messaging Replacing Pagers in the Enterprise," *Computing Canada* 30, no. 4 (March 26, 2004), p. 18.

33. R. O. Crockett, "'The Office Gossips' New Water Cooler," *BusinessWeek*, June 24, 2003, p. 14.

34. R. L. Birdwhistell, *Introduction to Kinesics* (Louisville, KY: University of Louisville Press, 1952).

35. J. Fast, *Body Language* (Philadelphia: M. Evans, 1970), p. 7.

36. E. T. Hall, *The Hidden Dimension*, 2nd ed. (Garden City, NY: Anchor Books/Doubleday, 1966).

37. This section largely based on C. C. Pinder and K. P. Harlos, "Employee Silence: Quiescence and Acquiescence as Responses to Perceived Injustice," in *Research in Personnel and Human Resource Management*, ed. G. R. Ferris (Greenwich, CT: JAI, 2002), pp. 331–369; and P. Mornell, "The Sounds of Silence," *Inc.*, February 2001, pp. 117–118.

38. See D. Tannen, *You Just Don't Understand: Women and Men in Conversation* (New York: Ballantine Books, 1991); and D. Tannen, *Talking from 9 to 5* (New York: William Morrow, 1995).

39. D. Goldsmith and P. Fulfs, "You Just Don't Have the Evidence: An Analysis of Claims and Evidence in Deborah Tannen's *You Just Don't Understand*," in *Communications Yearbook*, vol. 22, ed. M. Roloff (Thousand Oaks, CA: Sage, 1999).

40. N. Langton, "Differences in Communication Styles: Asking for a Raise," in *Organizational Behavior: Experiences and Cases*, 4th ed., ed. D. Marcic (St. Paul, MN: West Publishing, 1995).

41. See M. Munter, "Cross-Cultural Communication for Managers," *Business Horizons*, May–June 1993, pp. 75–76.

42. N. Adler, *International Dimensions of Organizational Behavior*, 4th ed. (Cincinnati, OH: South Western, 2002), p. 94.

43. See, for instance, C. F. Fink, "Some Conceptual Difficulties in Theory of Social Conflict," *Journal of Conflict Resolution*, December 1968, pp. 412–460. For an updated review of the conflict literature, see J. A. Wall Jr. and R. R. Callister, "Conflict and Its Management," *Journal of Management* 21, no. 3 (1995), pp. 515–558.

44. L. L. Putnam and M. S. Poole, "Conflict and Negotiation," in *Handbook of Organizational Communication: An Inter-disciplinary Perspective*, ed. F. M. Jablin, L. L. Putnam, K. H. Roberts, and L. W. Porter (Newbury Park, CA: Sage, 1987), pp. 549–599.

45. K. W. Thomas, "Conflict and Negotiation Processes in Organizations," in *Handbook of Industrial and Organizational Psychology*, vol. 3, 2nd ed., ed. M. D. Dunnette and L. M. Hough (Palo Alto, CA: Consulting Psychologists Press, 1992), pp. 651–717.

46. K. Jehn, "A Multimethod Examination of the Benefits and Detriments of Intragroup Conflict," *Administrative Science Quarterly*, June 1995, pp. 256–282; K. A. Jehn, "A Qualitative Analysis of Conflict Types and Dimensions in Organizational Groups," *Administrative Science Quarterly*, September 1997, pp. 530–557; K. A. Jehn and E. A. Mannix, "The Dynamic Nature of Conflict: A Longitudinal Study of Intragroup Conflict and Group Performance," *Academy of Management Journal*, April 2001, pp. 238–251; C. K. W. De Dreu and A. E. M. Van Vianen, "Managing Relationship Conflict and the Effectiveness of Organizational Teams," *Journal of Organizational Behavior*, May 2001, pp. 309–328; and K. A. Jehn and C. Bendersky, "Intragroup Conflict in Organizations: A Contingency Perspective on the Conflict-Outcome Relationship," in *Research in Organizational Behavior*, vol. 25, ed. R. M. Kramer and B. M. Staw (Oxford, UK: Elsevier, 2003), pp. 199–210.

47. A. C. Amason, "Distinguishing the Effects of Functional and Dysfunctional Conflict on Strategic Decision Making: Resolving a Paradox for Top Management Teams," *Academy of Management Journal* 39, no. 1 (1996), pp. 123–148.

48. D. Tjosvold, "Cooperative and Competitive Goal Approach to Conflict: Accomplishments and Challenges," *Applied Psychology: An International Review* 47, no. 3 (1998), pp. 285–342.

49. K. W. Thomas, "Conflict and Negotiation Processes in Organizations," in *Handbook of Industrial and Organizational Psychology*, vol. 3, 2nd ed., ed. M. D. Dunnette and L. M. Hough (Palo Alto, CA: Consulting Psychologists Press, 1992), pp. 651–717.

50. C. K. W. De Dreu, A. Evers, B. Beersma, E. S. Kluwer, and A. Nauta, "A Theory-Based Measure of Conflict Management Strategies in the Workplace," *Journal of Organizational Behavior* 22, no. 6 (September 2001), pp. 645–668. See also D. G. Pruitt and J. Rubin, *Social Conflict: Escalation, Stalemate and Settlement* (New York: Random House, 1986).

51. C. K. W. De Dreu, A. Evers, B. Beersma, E. S. Kluwer, and A. Nauta, "A Theory-Based Measure of Conflict Management Strategies in the Workplace," *Journal of Organizational Behavior* 22, no. 6 (September 2001), pp. 645–668.

52. R. A. Baron, "Personality and Organizational Conflict: Effects of the Type A Behavior Pattern and Self-Monitoring," *Organizational Behavior and Human Decision Processes*, October 1989, pp. 281–296; A. Drory and I. Ritov, "Effects of Work Experience and Opponent's Power on Conflict Management Styles," *International Journal of Conflict Management* 8, 1997, pp. 148–161; R. J. Sternberg and L. J. Soriano, "Styles of Conflict Resolution," *Journal of Personality and Social Psychology*, July 1984, pp. 115–126; and R. J. Volkema and T. J. Bergmann, "Conflict Styles as Indicators of Behavioral Patterns in Interpersonal Conflicts," *Journal of Social Psychology*, February 1995, pp. 5–15.

53. *OB in the Street* based on "A Lesson in Design: Get It in Writing," *Vancouver Sun*, May 13, 2000, p. A22.

54. These ideas are based on S. P. Robbins, *Managing Organizational Conflict: A Nontraditional Approach* (Upper Saddle River, NJ: Prentice Hall, 1974), pp. 59–89.

55. Based on K. W. Thomas, "Toward Multidemensional Values in Teaching: The Example of Conflict Behaviours," *Academy of Management Review*, July 1977, p. 487; and C. K. W. De DDreu, A. Evers, B. Beersma, E. S. Kluwer, and A. Nauta, "A Theory-Based Measure of Conflict Management Strategies in the Workplace," *Journal of Organizational Behaviour* 22, no. 6 (September 2001). pp. 645–688.

56. R. D. Ramsey, "Interpersonal Conflicts," *SuperVision* 66, no. 4 (April 2005), pp. 14–17.

57. R. D. Ramsey, "Interpersonal Conflicts," *SuperVision* 66, no. 4 (April 2005), pp. 14–17.

58. M. A. Von Glinow, D. L. Shapiro, and J. M. Brett, "Can We Talk, and Should We? Managing Emotional Conflict in Multicultural Teams," *Academy of Management Review* 29, no. 4 (October 2004), pp. 578–592.

59. J. A. Wall Jr., *Negotiation: Theory and Practice* (Glenview, IL: Scott Foresman, 1985).

60. K. Harding, "A New Language, a New Deal," *Globe and Mail*, October 30, 2002, pp. C1, C10.

61. This model is based on R. J. Lewicki, "Bargaining and Negotiation," *Exchange: The Organizational Behavior Teaching Journal* 6, no. 2 (1981), pp. 39–40; and B. S. Moskal, "The Art of the Deal," *IndustryWeek*, January 18, 1993, p. 23.

62. R. Fisher and W. Ury, *Getting to Yes: Negotiating Agreement Without Giving In*, 2nd ed. (New York: Penguin Books, 1991).

63. P. H. Kim and A. R. Fragale, "Choosing the Path to Bargaining Power: An Empirical Comparison of BATNAs and Contributions in Negotiation," *Journal of Applied Psychology* 90, no. 2 (March 2005), pp. 373–381.

64. P. LeBrun, "Talks End Badly Thursday in Toronto," *Canadian Press,* February 10, 2005; A. Woods, "Season Down to Final Hours," *National Post,* February 11, 2005, pp. B8, B11.

65. M. H. Bazerman and M. A. Neale, *Negotiating Rationally* (New York: Free Press, 1992), pp. 67–68.

66. R. Fisher and W. Ury, *Getting to Yes: Negotiating Agreement Without Giving In,* 2nd ed. (New York: Penguin Books, 1991).

67. S. A. Hellweg and S. L. Phillips, "Communication and Productivity in Organizations: A State-of-the-Art Review," in *Proceedings of the 40th Annual Academy of Management Conference,* Detroit, 1980, pp. 188–192.

68. The points presented here were influenced by E. Van de Vliert, "Escalative Intervention in Small-Group Conflicts," *Journal of Applied Behavioral Science,* Winter 1985, pp. 19–36.

69. T. Davis and M. J. Landa, "A Contrary Look at Employee Performance Appraisal," *Canadian Manager,* Fall 1999, pp. 18–19+.

70. J. S. Lublin, "It's Shape-Up Time for Performance Reviews," *Wall Street Journal,* October 3, 1994, p. B1.

71. Much of this section is based on H. H. Meyer, "A Solution to the Performance Appraisal Feedback Enigma," *Academy of Management Executive,* February 1991, pp. 68–76.

72. B. Gates, *The Road Ahead* (New York: Viking, 1995), p. 86.

73. R. J. Burke, "Why Performance Appraisal Systems Fail," *Personnel Administration,* June 1972, pp. 32–40.

74. B. R. Nathan, A. M. Mohrman Jr., and J. Milliman, "Interpersonal Relations as a Context for the Effects of Appraisal Interviews on Performance and Satisfaction: A Longitudinal Study," *Academy of Management Journal,* June 1991, pp. 352–369.

75. R. Kreitner and A. Kinicki, *Organizational Behavior,* 6th ed. (New York: McGraw-Hill/Irwin, 2004), p. 335.

Chapter 7

1. Opening vignette based on T. Wharnsby, "How New IOC President Rogge Turned Scandalous Silver into Gold," *Globe and Mail,* February 17, 2002, http://www.globeandmail.com; "A Duo Deprived," *New York Times,* February 13, 2002, http://ea.nytimes.com/cgibin/email?REFURI=http://www.nytimes.com/2002/02/13/opinion/_13WED4.html (accessed February 17, 2002); and B. Smith, "Overhaul Proposed in Judging of Skaters," *Globe and Mail,* February 19, 2002, pp. A1, A10.

2. Based on B. M. Bass, *Bass & Stogdill's Handbook of Leadership,* 3rd ed. (New York: Free Press, 1990).

3. S. Prashad, "Fill Your Power Gap," *Globe and Mail,* July 23, 2003, p. C3.

4. T. B. Lawrence, M. K. Mauws, B. Dyck, and R. F. Kleysen, "The Politics of Organizational Learning: Integrating Power into the 4I Framework," *Academy of Management Review* 30, no. 1 (January 2005), pp. 180–191.

5. J. R. P. French Jr. and B. Raven, "The Bases of Social Power," in *Studies in Social Power,* ed. D. Cartwright (Ann Arbor: University of Michigan, Institute for Social Research, 1959), pp. 150–167. For an update on French and Raven's work, see D. E. Frost and A. J. Stahelski, "The Systematic Measurement of French and Raven's Bases of Social Power in Workgroups," *Journal of Applied Social Psychology,* April 1988, pp. 375–389; T. R. Hinkin and C. A. Schriesheim, "Development and Application of New Scales to Measure the French and Raven (1959) Bases of Social Power," *Journal of Applied Psychology,* August 1989, pp. 561–567; and G. E. Littlepage, J. L. Van Hein, K. M. Cohen, and L. L. Janiec, "Evaluation and Comparison of Three Instruments Designed to Measure Organizational Power and Influence Tactics," *Journal of Applied Social Psychology,* January 16–31, 1993, pp. 107–125.

6. B. H. Raven, "Social Influence and Power," in *Current Studies in Social Psychology,* ed. I. D. Steiner and M. Fishbein (New York: Holt, Rinehart and Winston, 1965), pp. 371–382.

7. D. Kipnis, *The Powerholders* (Chicago: University of Chicago Press, 1976), pp. 77–78.

8. E. A. Ward, "Social Power Bases of Managers: Emergence of a New Factor," *Journal of Social Psychology,* February 2001, pp. 144–147.

9. D. Hickson, C. Hinings, C. Lee, R. Schneck, and J. Pennings, "A Strategic Contingencies Theory of Intra-Organizational Power," *Administrative Science Quarterly* 16, 1971, pp. 216–229.

10. J. W. Dean Jr. and J. R. Evans, *Total Quality: Management, Organization, and Strategy* (Minneapolis-St. Paul, MN: West, 1994).

11. M. Folb, "Cause Celeb: From Deborah Cox to Maestro, Homegrown Talent Is Hocking Retail Fashion," *Marketing Magazine,* April 5, 1999, p. 13.

12. G. Yukl, H. Kim, and C. M. Falbe, "Antecedents of Influence Outcomes," *Journal of Applied Psychology* 81, no. 3 (June 1, 1996), pp. 309–317.

13. P. P. Carson, K. D. Carson, and C. W. Roe, "Social Power Bases: A Meta-Analytic Examination of Interrelationships and Outcomes," *Journal of Applied Social Psychology* 23, no. 14 (1993), pp. 1150–1169.

14. Cited in J. R. Carlson, D. S. Carlson, and L. L. Wadsworth, "The Relationship Between Individual Power Moves and Group Agreement Type: An Examination and Model," *S.A.M. Advanced Management Journal* 65, no. 4 (2000), pp. 44–51.

15. C. M. Falbe and G. Yukl, "Consequences for Managers of Using Single Tactics and Combinations of Tactics," *Academy of Management Journal* 35, 1992, pp. 638–652.

16. B. Smith, "Russian Refuses Extradition," *Globe and Mail,* http://www.globeandmail.com (accessed August 7, 2002).

17. R. E. Emerson, "Power-Dependence Relations," *American Sociological Review* 27, 1962, pp. 31–41.

18. Thanks are due to an anonymous reviewer for supplying this insight.

19. H. Mintzberg, *Power in and Around Organizations* (Englewood Cliffs, NJ: Prentice Hall, 1983), p. 24.

20. Based on R. A. Oppel Jr., "The Man Who Paid the Price for Sizing Up Enron," *New York Times,* March 27, 2002, http://www.nytimes.com/2002/03/27/business/27ENRO.html?ex=1018242314&ei=1&en=84c572c79afa6b2c (accessed March 27, 2002).

21. See, for example, D. Kipnis, S. M. Schmidt, C. Swaffin-Smith, and I. Wilkinson, "Patterns of Managerial Influence: Shotgun Managers, Tacticians, and Bystanders," *Organizational Dynamics,* Winter 1984, pp. 58–67; T. Case, L. Dosier, G. Murkison, and B. Keys, "How Managers Influence Superiors: A Study of Upward Influence Tactics," *Leadership and Organization Development Journal* 9, no. 4 (1988), pp. 25–31; D. Kipnis and S. M. Schmidt, "Upward-Influence Styles: Relationship With Performance Evaluations, Salary, and Stress," *Administrative Science Quarterly,* December 1988, pp. 528–542; G. Yukl and C. M. Falbe, "Influence Tactics and Objectives in Upward, Downward, and Lateral Influence Attempts," *Journal of Applied Psychology,* April 1990, pp. 132–140; G. Yukl, H. Kim, and C. M. Falbe, "Antecedents of

Influence Outcomes," *Journal of Applied Psychology*, June 1996, pp. 309–317; K. E. Lauterbach and B. J. Weiner, "Dynamics of Upward Influence: How Male and Female Managers Get Their Way," *Leadership Quarterly*, Spring 1996, pp. 87–107; K. R. Xin and A. S. Tsui, "Different Strokes for Different Folks? Influence Tactics by Asian-American and Caucasian-American Managers," *Leadership Quarterly*, Spring 1996, pp. 109–132; S. J. Wayne, R. C. Liden, I. K. Graf, and G. R. Ferris, "The Role of Upward Influence Tactics in Human Resource Decisions," *Personnel Psychology*, Winter 1997, pp. 979–1006; and C. A. Higgins and T. A. Judge, "The Effect of Applicant Influence Tactics on Recruiter Perceptions of Fit and Hiring Recommendations: A Field Study," *Journal of Applied Psychology* 89, no. 4 (August 2004), pp. 622–632.

22. This section adapted from G. Yukl, C. M. Falbe, and J. Y. Youn, "Patterns of Influence Behavior for Managers," *Group & Organization Studies* 18, no. 1 (March 1993), p. 7.

23. This section adapted from G. Yukl, C. M. Falbe, and J. Y. Youn, "Patterns of Influence Behavior for Managers," *Group & Organization Studies* 18, no. 1 (March 1993), p. 7.

24. Search of *Business Source Premier* and *Canadian Newsstand* articles conducted by Nancy Langton, September 2005.

25. This is the definition given by R. Forrester, "Empowerment: Rejuvenating a Potent Idea," *The Academy of Management Executive*, August 2000, pp. 67–80.

26. R. E. Quinn and G. M. Spreitzer, "The Road to Empowerment: Seven Questions Every Leader Should Consider," *Organizational Dynamics*, Autumn 1997, p. 38.

27. S. Wetlaufer, "Organizing for Empowerment: An Interview With AES's Roger Sant and Dennis Bakke," *Harvard Business Review*, January–February 1999, pp. 110–123.

28. C. Argyris, "Empowerment: The Emperor's New Clothes," *Harvard Business Review*, May–June 1998.

29. K. Kitagawa, *Empowering Employee–Learners With Essential Skills at Durabelt Inc.* (Ottawa: The Conference Board of Canada, March 2005).

30. J. Schaubroeck, J. R. Jones, and J. L. Xie, "Individual Differences in Utilizing Control to Cope With Job Demands: Effects on Susceptibility to Infectious Disease," *Journal of Applied Psychology*, April 2001, pp. 265–278.

31. Thanks are due to an anonymous reviewer for this insight.

32. "Delta Promotes Empowerment," *Globe and Mail*, May 31, 1999, Advertising Supplement, p. C5.

33. G. M. Spreitzer, "Psychological Empowerment in the Workplace: Dimensions, Measurement, and Validation," *Academy of Management Journal* 38, 1995, pp. 1442–1465; G. M. Spreitzer, M. A. Kizilos, and S. W. Nason, "A Dimensional Analysis of the Relationship Between Psychological Empowerment and Effectiveness, Satisfaction, and Strain," *Journal of Management* 23, 1997, pp. 679–704; and K. W. Thomas and W. G. Tymon, "Does Empowerment Always Work: Understanding the Role of Intrinsic Motivation and Personal Interpretation," *Journal of Management Systems* 6, 1994, pp. 39–54.

34. D. E. Hyatt and T. M. Ruddy, "An Examination of the Relationship Between Work Group Characteristics and Performance: Once More Into the Breach," *Personnel Psychology* 50, 1997, pp. 553–585; B. L. Kirkman and B. Rosen, "Beyond Self-Management: Antecedents and Consequences of Team Empowerment," *Academy of Management Journal* 42, 1999, pp. 58–74; P. E. Tesluck, D. J. Brass, and J. E. Mathieu, "An Examination of Empowerment Processes at Individual and Group Levels" (paper presented at the 11th annual conference of the Society of Industrial and Organizational Psychology, San Diego, 1996).

35. D. Kivell, "Support Employees' Efforts to Sustain Gains," *Plant*, February 20, 2006, p. 32.

36. C. Robert, T. M. Probst, J. J. Martocchio, and F. Drasgow, and J. J. Lawler, "Empowerment and Continuous Improvement in the United States, Mexico, Poland, and India: Predicting Fit on the Basis of the Dimensions of Power Distance and Individualism," *Journal of Applied Psychology* 85, no. 5 (2000), pp. 643–658.

37. W. A. Randolph and M. Sashkin, "Can Organizational Empowerment Work in Multinational Settings?" *Academy of Management Executive*, February 2002, pp. 102–115.

38. T. Lee and C. M. Brotheridge, "When the Prey Becomes the Predator: Bullying as Predictor of Reciprocal Bullying, Coping, and Well-Being" (working paper, University of Regina, 2005).

39. "More and More Workplaces Have Bullies," *Leader-Post* (Regina), December 14, 2004, p. A1.

40. M. Bridge, "Female Firefighters Claim Harassment," *Vancouver Sun*, March 22, 2006, p. A1.

41. "Employers Underestimate Extent of Sexual Harassment, Report Says," *Vancouver Sun*, March 8, 2001, p. D6.

42. N. Alcoba, "Students Face Sexual Harassment," *Vancouver Sun*, November 30, 2005, p. A8.

43. "Employers Underestimate Extent of Sexual Harassment, Report Says," *Vancouver Sun*, March 8, 2001, p. D6.

44. S. Lim and L. M. Cortina, "Interpersonal Mistreatment in the Workplace: The Interface and Impact of General Incivility and Sexual Harassment," *Journal of Applied Psychology* 90, no. 3 (2005), pp. 483–496.

45. *Janzen v. Platy Enterprises Ltd.* [1989] 10 C.H.R.R. D/6205 SCC.

46. The following section is based on J. N. Cleveland and M. E. Kerst, "Sexual Harassment and Perceptions of Power: An Under-Articulated Relationship," *Journal of Vocational Behavior*, February 1993, pp. 49–67.

47. J. Goddu, "Sexual Harassment Complaints Rise Dramatically," *Canadian Press Newswire*, March 6, 1998.

48. K. Von Hoffmann, "Forbidden Fruit: Student-Faculty Relationships," *Yale Herald*, October 17, 2003, p. 1.

49. See, for instance, "Car Dealership Settles Same Sex Harassment Lawsuit," *Associated Press*, June 28, 1999.

50. S. A. Culbert and J. J. McDonough, *The Invisible War: Pursuing Self-Interest at Work* (New York: John Wiley, 1980), p. 6.

51. H. Mintzberg, *Power in and Around Organizations* (Englewood Cliffs, NJ: Prentice Hall, 1983), p. 26.

52. T. Cole, "Who Loves Ya?" *Report on Business Magazine*, April 1999, p. 54.

53. D. Farrell and J. C. Petersen, "Patterns of Political Behavior in Organizations," *Academy of Management Review*, July 1982, p. 405. For a thoughtful analysis of the academic controversies underlying any definition of organizational politics, see A. Drory and T. Romm, "The Definition of Organizational Politics: A Review," *Human Relations*, November 1990, pp. 1133–1154.

54. P. Dawson and D. Buchanan, "The Way It Really Happened: Competing Narratives in the Political Process of Technological Change," *Human Relations* 58, no. 7 (2005), pp. 845–865; A. Spicer, "The Political Process of Inscribing a New Technology," *Human Relations* 58, no. 7 (2005), pp. 867–890; and J. Swan and H. Scarbrough, "The Politics of Networked Innovation," *Human Relations* 58, no. 7 (2005), pp. 913–943.

55. J. Pfeffer, *Power in Organizations* (Marshfield, MA: Pittman, 1981).

56. *OB in the Workplace* based on R. McQueen, "Hard Truths: To Capture a Corner Office, You Have to Play Politics and Know When to Lie," *National Post Business*, September 2000, pp. 51–52.

57. G. R. Ferris, G. S. Russ, and P. M. Fandt, "Politics in Organizations," in *Impression Management in Organizations*, ed. R. A. Giacalone and P. Rosenfeld (Newbury Park, CA: Sage, 1989), pp. 143–170; and K. M. Kacmar, D. P. Bozeman, D. S. Carlson, and W. P. Anthony, "An Examination of the Perceptions of Organizational Politics Model: Replication and Extension," *Human Relations*, March 1999, pp. 383–416.

58. K. M. Kacmar and R. A. Baron, "Organizational Politics: The State of the Field, Links to Related Processes, and an Agenda for Future Research," in *Research in Personnel and Human Resources Management*, vol. 17, ed. G. R. Ferris (Greenwich, CT: JAI Press, 1999); and M. Valle and L. A. Witt, "The Moderating Effect of Teamwork Perceptions on the Organizational Politics–Job Satisfaction Relationship," *Journal of Social Psychology*, June 2001, pp. 379–388.

59. G. R. Ferris, D. D. Frink, M. C. Galang, J. Zhou, K. M. Kacmar, and J. L. Howard, "Perceptions of Organizational Politics: Prediction, Stress-Related Implications, and Outcomes," *Human Relations*, February 1996, pp. 233–266; K. M. Kacmar, D. P. Bozeman, D. S. Carlson, and W. P. Anthony, "An Examination of the Perceptions of Organizational Politics Model; Replication and Extension," *Human Relations*, March 1999, p. 388; and J. M. L. Poon, "Situational Antecedents and Outcomes of Organizational Politics Perceptions," *Journal of Managerial Psychology* 18, no. 2 (2003), pp. 138–155.

60. C. Kiewitz, W. A. Hochwarter, G. R. Ferris, and S. L. Castro, "The Role of Psychological Climate in Neutralizing the Effects of Organizational Politics on Work Outcomes," *Journal of Applied Social Psychology*, June 2002, pp. 1189–1207; and J. M. L. Poon, "Situational Antecedents and Outcomes of Organizational Politics Perceptions," *Journal of Managerial Psychology* 18, no. 2 (2003), pp. 138–155.

61. K. M. Kacmar and R. A. Baron, "Organizational Politics: The State of the Field, Links to Related Processes, and an Agenda for Future Research," in *Research in Personnel and Human Resources Management*, vol. 17, ed. G. R. Ferris (Greenwich, CT: JAI Press, 1999); and M. Valle and L. A. Witt, "The Moderating Effect of Teamwork Perceptions on the Organizational Politics–Job Satisfaction Relationship," *Journal of Social Psychology*, June 2001, pp. 379–388.

62. R. W. Allen, D. L. Madison, L. W. Porter, P. A. Renwick, and B. T. Mayes, "Organizational Politics: Tactics and Characteristics of Its Actors," *California Management Review*, Fall 1979, pp. 77–83.

63. W. L. Gardner and M. J. Martinko, "Impression Management in Organizations," *Journal of Management*, June 1988, pp. 321–338; D. C. Gilmore and G. R. Ferris, "The Effects of Applicant Impression Management Tactics on Interviewer Judgments," *Journal of Management*, December 1989, pp. 557–564; M. R. Leary and R. M. Kowalski, "Impression Management: A Literature Review and Two-Component Model," *Psychological Bulletin*, January 1990, pp. 34–47; S. J. Wayne and K. M. Kacmar, "The Effects of Impression Management on the Performance Appraisal Process," *Organizational Behavior and Human Decision Processes*, February 1991, pp. 70–88; E. W. Morrison and R. J. Bies, "Impression Management in the Feedback-Seeking Process: A Literature Review and Research Agenda," *Academy of Management Review*, July 1991, pp. 522–541; S. J. Wayne and R. C. Liden, "Effects of Impression Management on Performance Ratings: A Longitudinal Study," *Academy of Management Journal*, February 1995, pp. 232–260; and C. K. Stevens and A. L. Kristof, "Making the Right Impression: A Field Study of Applicant Impression Management During Job Interviews," *Journal of Applied Psychology*, October 1995, pp. 587–606.

64. M. R. Leary and R. M. Kowalski, "Impression Management: A Literature Review and Two-Component Model," *Psychological Bulletin*, January 1990, p. 40.

65. W. L. Gardner and M. J. Martinko, "Impression Management in Organizations," *Journal of Management*, June 1988, p. 333.

66. R. A. Baron, "Impression Management by Applicants During Employment Interviews: The 'Too Much of a Good Thing' Effect," in *The Employment Interview: Theory, Research, and Practice*, ed. R. W. Eder and G. R. Ferris (Newbury Park, CA: Sage, 1989), pp. 204–215.

67. M. Snyder and J. Copeland, "Self-Monitoring Processes in Organizational Settings," in *Impression Management in the Organization*, ed. R. A. Giacalone and P. Rosenfeld (Hillsdale, NJ: Lawrence Erlbaum Associates, 1989), p. 11; E. D. Long and G. H. Dobbins, "Self-Monitoring, Impression Management, and Interview Ratings: A Field and Laboratory Study," in *Proceedings of the 52nd Annual Academy of Management Conference*, ed. J. L. Wall and L. R. Jauch (Las Vegas, August 1992), pp. 274–278; and A. Montagliani and R. A. Giacalone, "Impression Management and Cross-Cultural Adaption," *Journal of Social Psychology*, October 1998, pp. 598–608.

68. Z. I. Barsness, K. A. Diekmann, and M. D. L. Seidel, "Motivation and Opportunity: The Role of Remote Work, Demographic Dissimilarity, and Social Network Centrality in Impression Management," *Academy of Management Journal* 48, 2005, pp. 401–419.

69. R. A. Baron, "Impression Management by Applicants During Employment Interviews: The 'Too Much of a Good Thing' Effect," in *The Employment Interview: Theory, Research, and Practice*, ed. R. W. Eder and G. R. Ferris (Newbury Park, CA: Sage, 1989), pp. 204–215; D. C. Gilmore and G. R. Ferris, "The Effects of Applicant Impression Management Tactics on Interviewer Judgments," *Journal of Management*, December 1989, pp. 557–564; and C. K. Stevens and A. L. Kristof, "Making the Right Impression: A Field Study of Applicant Impression Management During Job Interviews," *Journal of Applied Psychology*, October 1995, pp. 587–606.

70. C. K. Stevens and A. L. Kristof, "Making the Right Impression: A Field Study of Applicant Impression Management During Job Interviews," *Journal of Applied Psychology*, October 1995, pp. 587–606.

71. S. J. Wayne and K. M. Kacmar, "The Effects of Impression Management on the Performance Appraisal Process," *Organizational Behavior and Human Decision Processes* 48, 1991, pp. 70–78; S. J. Wayne and G. R. Ferris, "Influence Tactics, Affect, and Exchange Quality in Supervisor-Subordinate Interactions," *Journal of Applied Psychology* 75, 1990, pp. 487–499; and G. R. Ferris, T. A. Judge, K. M. Rowland, and D. E. Fitzgibbons, "Subordinate Influence and the Performance Evaluation Process: Test of a Model," *Organizational Behavior and Human Decision Processes* 58, 1994, pp. 101–135.

72. S. J. Wayne and R. C. Liden, "Effects of Impression Management on Performance Ratings: A Longitudinal Study," *Academy of Management Journal* 38, 1995, pp. 232–260.

73. G. H. Dobbins and J. M. Russell, "The Biasing Effects of Subordinate Likeableness on Leaders' Responses to Poor Performers: A Laboratory and a Field Study," *Personnel Psychology* 39, 1986, pp. 759–777; and T. R. Mitchell and R. Wood, "Manager Behavior in a Social Context: The Impact of Impression Management on Attributions and Disciplinary Actions," *Organizational Behavior and Human Decision Processes*, December 1981, pp. 356–378.

74. D. V. Day, D. J. Schneider, and A. L. Unckless, "Self-Monitoring and Work-Related Outcomes: A Meta-Analysis" (paper presented at the 11th Annual Conference of the Society of Industrial and Organizational Psychology, San Diego, CA, 1996); and M. A. Warech, J. W. Smither, R. R. Reilly, R. E. Millsap, and S. P. Reilly, "Self-

Monitoring and 360-Degree Ratings," *Leadership Quarterly* 9, 1998, pp. 449–473.

75. M. A. Warech, J. W. Smither, R. R. Reilly, R. E. Millsap, and S. P. Reilly, "Self-Monitoring and 360-Degree Ratings," *Leadership Quarterly* 9, 1998, pp. 449–473.

76. D. V. Day, D. J. Schneider, and A. L. Unckless, "Self-Monitoring and Work-Related Outcomes: A Meta-Analysis" (paper presented at the 11th Annual Conference of the Society of Industrial and Organizational Psychology, San Diego, CA, 1996).

77. J. M. Maslyn and D. B. Fedor, "Perceptions of Politics: Does Measuring Different Foci Matter?" *Journal of Applied Psychology* 84, 1998, pp. 645–653; and L. G. Nye and L. A. Witt, "Dimensionality and Construct Validity of the Perceptions of Organizational Politics Scale," *Educational and Psychological Measurement* 53, 1993, pp. 821–829.

78. G. R. Ferris, D. D. Frink, D. I. Bhawuk, J. Zhou, and D. C. Gilmore, "Reactions of Diverse Groups to Politics in the Workplace," *Journal of Management* 22, 1996, pp. 23–44; K. M. Kacmar, D. P. Bozeman, D. S. Carlson, and W. P. Anthony, "An Examination of the Perceptions of Organizational Politics Model: Replication and Extension," *Human Relations* 52, 1999, pp. 383–416.

79. T. P. Anderson, "Creating Measures of Dysfunctional Office and Organizational Politics: The DOOP and Short-Form DOOP Scales," *Psychology: A Journal of Human Behavior* 31, 1994, pp. 24–34.

80. G. R. Ferris, D. D. Frink, D. I. Bhawuk, J. Zhou, and D. C. Gilmore, "Reactions of Diverse Groups to Politics in the Workplace," *Journal of Management* 22, 1996, pp. 23–44; K. M. Kacmar, D. P. Bozeman, D. S. Carlson, and W. P. Anthony, "An Examination of the Perceptions of Organizational Politics Model: Replication and Extension," *Human Relations* 52, 1999, pp. 383–416.

81. K. M. Kacmar, D. P. Bozeman, D. S. Carlson, and W. P. Anthony, "An Examination of the Perceptions of Organizational Politics Model: Replication and Extension," *Human Relations* 52, 1999, pp. 383–416; J. M. Maslyn and D. B. Fedor, "Perceptions of Politics: Does Measuring Different Foci Matter?" *Journal of Applied Psychology* 84, 1998, pp. 645–653.

82. M. Warshaw, "The Good Guy's (and Gal's) Guide to Office Politics," *Fast Company*, April 1998, p. 156.

83. G. Yukl, C. M. Falbe, and J. Y. Youn, "Patterns of Influence Behavior for Managers," *Group & Organization Studies* 18, no. 1 (March 1993), p. 7.

84. This is largely based on D. M. Rousseau, "The Idiosyncratic Deal: Flexibility versus Fairness?" *Organizational Dynamics*, Spring 2001, pp. 260–273.

85. *From Concepts to Skills* based on S. P. Robbins and P. L. Hunsaker, *Training in Interpersonal Skills: Tips for Managing People at Work*, 2nd ed. (Upper Saddle River, NJ: Prentice Hall, 1996), pp. 131–134.

OB on the Edge:
The Toxic Workplace

1. L. M. Anderson and C. M. Pearson, "Tit for Tat? The Spiraling Effect of Incivility in the Workplace," *Academy of Management Review* 24, no. 3 (1999), p. 453.

2. The source of this quotation is N. Giarrusso, "An Issue of Job Satisfaction," unpublished undergraduate term paper, Concordia University, Montreal, 1990. It is cited in B. E. Ashforth, "Petty Tyranny in Organizations: A Preliminary Examination of Antecedents and Consequences," *Canadian Journal of Administrative Sciences* 14, no. 2 (1997), pp. 126–140.

3. P. Frost and S. Robinson, "The Toxic Handler: Organizational Hero—and Casualty," *Harvard Business Review*, July–August 1999, p. 101 (Reprint 99406).

4. L. M. Anderson and C. M. Pearson, "Tit for Tat? The Spiraling Effect of Incivility in the Workplace," *Academy of Management Review* 24, no. 3 (1999), pp. 452–471.

5. L. M. Anderson and C. M. Pearson, "Tit for Tat? The Spiraling Effect of Incivility in the Workplace," *Academy of Management Review* 24, no. 3 (1999), pp. 452–471. For further discussion of this, see R. A. Baron and J. H. Neuman, "Workplace Violence and Workplace Aggression: Evidence on Their Relative Frequency and Potential Causes," *Aggressive Behavior* 22, 1996, pp. 161–173; C. C. Chen and W. Eastman, "Towards a Civic Culture for Multicultural Organizations," *Journal of Applied Behavioral Science* 33, 1997, pp. 454–470; J. H. Neuman and R. A. Baron, "Aggression in the Workplace," in *Antisocial Behavior in Organizations*, ed. R. A. Giacalone and J. Greenberg (Thousand Oaks, CA: Sage, 1997), pp. 37–67.

6. L. M. Anderson and C. M. Pearson, "Tit for Tat? The Spiraling Effect of Incivility in the Workplace," *Academy of Management Review* 24, no. 3 (1999), pp. 452–471.

7. L. M. Anderson and C. M. Pearson, "Tit for Tat? The Spiraling Effect of Incivility in the Workplace," *Academy of Management Review* 24, no. 3 (1999), pp. 452–471.

8. R. Corelli, "Dishing Out Rudeness: Complaints Abound as Customers Are Ignored, Berated," *Maclean's*, January 11, 1999, p. 44.

9. R. Corelli, "Dishing Out Rudeness: Complaints Abound as Customers Are Ignored, Berated," *Maclean's*, January 11, 1999, p. 44.

10. See, for example, "The National Labour Survey," The Canadian Initiative on Workplace Violence, March 2000, www.workplaceviolence.ca/research/survey1.pdf (accessed September 26, 2005).

11. R. A. Baron and J. H. Neuman, "Workplace Violence and Workplace Aggression: Evidence on Their Relative Frequency and Potential Causes," *Aggressive Behavior* 22, 1996, pp. 161–173; K. Bjorkqvist, K. Osterman, and M. Hjelt-Back, "Aggression Among University Employees," *Aggressive Behavior* 20, 1986, pp. 173–184; and H. J. Ehrlich and B. E. K. Larcom, *Ethnoviolence in the Workplace* (Baltimore, MD: Center for the Applied Study of Ethnoviolence, 1994).

12. J. Graydon, W. Kasta, and P. Khan, "Verbal and Physical Abuse of Nurses," *Canadian Journal of Nursing Administration*, November–December 1994, pp. 70–89.

13. C. M. Pearson and C. L. Porath, "Workplace Incivility: The Target's Eye View" (paper presented at the Annual Meeting of The Academy of Management, Chicago, August 10, 1999).

14. "Men More Likely to Be Rude in Workplace, Survey Shows," *Vancouver Sun*, August 16, 1999, p. B10.

15. R. Corelli, "Dishing Out Rudeness: Complaints Abound as Customers Are Ignored, Berated," *Maclean's*, January 11, 1999, p. 44.

16. R. Corelli, "Dishing Out Rudeness: Complaints Abound as Customers Are Ignored, Berated," *Maclean's*, January 11, 1999, p. 44.

17. R. A. Baron and J. H. Neuman, "Workplace Violence and Workplace Aggression: Evidence on Their Relative Frequency and Potential Causes," *Aggressive Behavior* 22, 1996, pp. 161–173; C. MacKinnon, *Only Words* (New York: Basic Books, 1994); J. Marks, "The American Uncivil Wars," *U.S. News & World Report*, April 22, 1996, pp. 66–72; and L. P. Spratlen, "Workplace Mistreatment: Its Relationship to Interpersonal Violence," *Journal of Psychosocial Nursing* 32, no. 12 (1994), pp. 5–6.

18. Information in this paragraph based on B. Branswell, "Death in Ottawa: The Capital Is Shocked by a Massacre That Leaves Five Dead," *Maclean's*, April 19, 1999, p. 18; "Four Employees Killed by Former Co-worker," *Occupational Health & Safety*, June 1999, pp. 14, 16; and "Preventing Workplace Violence," *Human Resources Advisor Newsletter, Western Edition*, May–June 1999, pp. 1–2.

19. W. M. Glenn, "An Employee's Survival Guide: An ILO Survey of Workplaces in 32 Countries Ranked Argentina the Most Violent, Followed by Romania, France and Then, Surprisingly, Canada," *Occupational Health & Safety*, April–May 2002, p. 28 passim.

20. D. Flavelle, "Managers Cited for Increase in 'Work Rage,'" *Vancouver Sun*, April 11, 2000, pp. D1, D11.

21. E. Girardet, "Office Rage Is on the Boil," *National Post*, August 11, 1999, p. B1.

22. S. James, "Long Hours Linked to Rising Toll from Stress," *Financial Post* (*National Post*), August 6, 2003, p. FP12.

23. S. Boyes, "Workplace Violence: Coping in a Dangerous World," *Canadian Consulting Engineer*, January–February 2002, pp. 51–52.

24. W. M. Glenn, "An Employee's Survival Guide: An ILO Survey of Workplaces in 32 Countries Ranked Argentina the Most Violent, Followed by Romania, France and Then, Surprisingly, Canada," *Occupational Health & Safety*, April–May 2002, p. 28 passim.

25. W. M. Glenn, "An Employee's Survival Guide: An ILO Survey of Workplaces in 32 Countries Ranked Argentina the Most Violent, Followed by Romania, France and Then, Surprisingly, Canada," *Occupational Health & Safety*, April–May 2002, p. 28 passim.

26. "Work Rage," *BCBusiness Magazine*, January 2001, p. 23.

27. Information for *FactBox* based on "Breeding Loyalty Pays for Employers," *Vancouver Sun*, April 22, 2000, p. D14; and "Men More Likely to Be Rude in Workplace, Survey Shows," *Vancouver Sun*, August 16, 1999, p. B10.

28. "A Quarter of Nova Scotia Teachers Who Responded to a Recent Survey Said They Faced Physical Violence at Work During the 2001–02 School Year," *Canadian Press Newswire*, February 14, 2003.

29. A. M. Webber, "Danger: Toxic Company," *Fast Company*, November 1998, pp. 152–157.

30. D. Flavelle, "Managers Cited for Increase in 'Work Rage,'" *Vancouver Sun*, April 11, 2000, pp. D1, D11.

31. G. Smith, *Work Rage* (Toronto: HarperCollins Canada, 2000).

32. "Work Rage," *BCBusiness Magazine*, January 2001, p. 23.

33. D. Flavelle, "Managers Cited for Increase in 'Work Rage,'" *Vancouver Sun*, April 11, 2000, pp. D1, D11.

34. D. E. Gibson and S. G. Barsade, "The Experience of Anger at Work: Lessons from the Chronically Angry" (paper presented at the Annual Meeting of the Academy of Management, Chicago, August 11, 1999).

35. H. Levinson, *Emotional Health in the World of Work* (Boston: South End Press, 1964); E. Schein, *Organizational Psychology* (Englewood Cliffs, NJ: Prentice Hall, 1980).

36. E. W. Morrison and S. L. Robinson, "When Employees Feel Betrayed: A Model of How Psychological Contract Violation Develops," *Academy of Management Journal* 22, 1997, pp. 226–256; S. L. Robinson, "Trust and Breach of the Psychological Contract," *Administrative Science Quarterly* 41, 1996, pp. 574–599; and S. L. Robinson, M. S. Kraatz, and D. M. Rousseau, "Changing Obligations and the Psychological Contract: A Longitudinal Study," *Academy of Management Journal* 37, 1994, pp. 137–152.

37. T. R. Tyler and P. Dogoey, "Trust in Organizational Authorities: The Influence of Motive Attributions on Willingness to Accept Decisions," in *Trust in Organizations*, ed. R. M. Kramer and T. R. Tyler (Thousand Oaks, CA: Sage, 1996), pp. 246–260.

38. A. M. Webber, "Danger: Toxic Company," *Fast Company*, November 1998, pp. 152–157.

39. A. M. Webber, "Danger: Toxic Company," *Fast Company*, November 1998, pp. 152–157.

40. P. Frost, *Toxic Emotions at Work* (Cambridge, MA: Harvard Business School Press, 2003).

41. "Men More Likely to Be Rude in Workplace, Survey Shows," *Vancouver Sun*, August 16, 1999, p. B10.

42. D. E. Gibson and S. G. Barsade, "The Experience of Anger at Work: Lessons from the Chronically Angry" (paper presented at the Annual Meeting of the Academy of Management, Chicago, August 11, 1999).

43. D. E. Gibson and S. G. Barsade, "The Experience of Anger at Work: Lessons from the Chronically Angry" (paper presented at the Annual Meeting of the Academy of Management, Chicago, August 11, 1999).

44. R. Corelli, "Dishing Out Rudeness: Complaints Abound as Customers Are Ignored, Berated," *Maclean's*, January 11, 1999, p. 44.

45. P. Frost and S. Robinson, "The Toxic Handler: Organizational Hero—and Casualty," *Harvard Business Review*, July–August 1999, p. 101 (Reprint 99406).

46. P. Frost and S. Robinson, "The Toxic Handler: Organizational Hero—and Casualty," *Harvard Business Review*, July–August 1999, p. 101 (Reprint 99406).

Chapter 8

1. R. Cohen, "New York Gets It Done; Bush and Cheney Don't," *New York Times*, February 15, 2006, http://www.nytimes.com (accessed April 29, 2006); and S. Shane and D. D. Kirkpatrick, "Unaware as Levees Fell, Officials Expressed Relief," *New York Times*, March 2, 2006, p. A16.

2. J. P. Kotter, "What Leaders Really Do," *Harvard Business Review*, May–June 1990, pp. 103–111.

3. R. N. Kanungo, "Leadership in Organizations: Looking Ahead to the 21st Century," *Canadian Psychology* 39, no. 1–2 (1998), p. 77. For more evidence of this consensus, see N. Adler, *International Dimensions of Organizational Behavior*, 3rd ed. (Cincinnati, OH: South Western College Publishing, 1997); R. J. House, "Leadership in the Twenty-First Century," in *The Changing Nature of Work*, ed. A. Howard (San Francisco: Jossey-Bass, 1995), pp. 411–450;

R. N. Kanungo and M. Mendonca, *Ethical Dimensions of Leadership* (Thousand Oaks, CA: Sage Publications, 1996); and A. Zaleznik, "The Leadership Gap," *Academy of Management Executive* 4, no. 1 (1990), pp. 7–22.

4. J. G. Geier, "A Trait Approach to the Study of Leadership in Small Groups," *Journal of Communication*, December 1967, pp. 316–323.

5. See T. A. Judge, J. E. Bono, R. Ilies, and M. Werner, "Personality and Leadership: A Review" (paper presented at the 15th Annual Conference of the Society for Industrial and Organizational Psychology, New Orleans, 2000); T. A. Judge, J. E. Bono, R. Ilies, and M. W. Gerhardt, "Personality and Leadership: A Qualitative and Quantitative Review," *Journal of Applied Psychology*, August 2002, pp. 765–780; and D. A. Hofmann and L. M. Jones, "Leadership, Collective Personality, and Performance," *Journal of Applied Psychology* 90, no. 3 (2005), pp. 509–522.

6. T. A. Judge, J. E. Bono, R. Ilies, and M. Werner, "Personality and Leadership: A Review" (paper presented at the 15th Annual Conference of the Society for Industrial and Organizational Psychology, New Orleans, 2000).

7. D. Goleman, *Working With Emotional Intelligence* (New York: Bantam, 1998); D. Goleman, "What Makes a Leader?" *Harvard Business Review*, November–December 1998, pp. 93–102; and D. Goleman, R. Boyatzis, and A. McKee, *Primal Leadership: Realizing the Power of Emotional Intelligence* (Cambridge, MA: Harvard Business School Press, 2002).

8. N. M. Ashkanasy and C. S. Daus, "Emotion in the Workplace: The New Challenge for Managers," *Academy of Management Executive* 16, no. 1 (2002), pp. 76–86.

9. T. A. Judge, J. E. Bono, R. Ilies, and M. Werner, "Personality and Leadership: A Review" (paper presented at the 15th Annual Conference of the Society for Industrial and Organizational Psychology, New Orleans, 2000); R. G. Lord, C. L. DeVader, and G. M. Alliger, "A Meta-Analysis of the Relation Between Personality Traits and Leadership Perceptions: An Application of Validity Generalization Procedures," *Journal of Applied Psychology*, August 1986, pp. 402–410; and J. A. Smith and R. J. Foti, "A Pattern Approach to the Study of Leader Emergence," *Leadership Quarterly*, Summer 1998, pp. 147–160.

10. D. N. Den Hartog, R. J. House, P. J. Hanges, S. A. Ruiz-Quintanilla, and P. W. Dorfman, "Culture Specific and Cross-Culturally Generalizable Implicit Leadership Theories: Are Attributes of Charismatic/Transformational Leadership Universally Endorsed?" *Leadership Quarterly* 10, no. 2 (Summer 1999), pp. 219–256.

11. R. M. Stogdill and A. E. Coons, eds., *Leader Behavior: Its Description and Measurement*, Research Monograph no. 88 (Columbus: Ohio State University, Bureau of Business Research, 1951). This research is updated in S. Kerr, C. A. Schriesheim, C. J. Murphy, and R. M. Stogdill, "Toward a Contingency Theory of Leadership Based upon the Consideration and Initiating Structure Literature," *Organizational Behavior and Human Performance*, August 1974, pp. 62–82; and C. A. Schriesheim, C. C. Cogliser, and L. L. Neider, "Is It 'Trustworthy'? A Multiple-Levels-of-Analysis Reexamination of an Ohio State Leadership Study, With Implications for Future Research," *Leadership Quarterly*, Summer 1995, pp. 111–145.

12. R. Kahn and D. Katz, "Leadership Practices in Relation to Productivity and Morale," in *Group Dynamics: Research and Theory*, 2nd ed., ed. D. Cartwright and A. Zander (Elmsford, NY: Row, Paterson, 1960).

13. R. R. Blake and A. A. McCanse, *Leadership Dilemmas—Grid Solutions* (Houston: Gulf Publishing Company, 1991); R. R. Blake and J. S. Mouton, "Management by Grid Principles or Situationalism: Which?" *Group and Organization Studies* 7 (1982), pp. 207–210.

14. T. A. Judge, R. F. Piccolo, and R. Ilies, "The Forgotten Ones? The Validity of Consideration and Initiating Structure in Leadership Research," *Journal of Applied Psychology* 89, no. 1 (February 2004), pp. 36–51; and R. T. Keller, "Transformational Leadership, Initiating Structure, and Substitutes for Leadership: A Longitudinal Study of Research and Development Project Team Performance," *Journal of Applied Psychology* 91, no. 1 (2006), pp. 202–210.

15. Based on G. Johns and A. M. Saks, *Organizational Behaviour*, 5th ed. (Toronto: Pearson Education Canada, 2001), p. 276.

16. A. J. Mayo and N. Nohria, "Zeitgeist Leadership," *Harvard Business Review* 83, no. 10 (2005), pp. 45–60.

17. See, for instance, P. M. Podsakoff, S. B. MacKenzie, M. Ahearne, and W. H. Bommer, "Searching for a Needle in a Haystack: Trying to Identify the Illusive Moderators of Leadership Behavior," *Journal of Management* 1, no. 3 (1995), pp. 422–470.

18. H. Wang, K. S. Law, R. D. Hackett, D. Wang, and Z. X. Chen, "Leader-Member Exchange as a Mediator of the Relationship Between Transformational Leadership and Followers' Performance and Organizational Citizenship Behavior," *Academy of Management Journal* 48, no. 3 (June 2005), pp. 420–432.

19. F. E. Fiedler, *A Theory of Leadership Effectiveness* (New York: McGraw-Hill, 1967).

20. Cited in R. J. House and R. N. Aditya, "The Social Scientific Study of Leadership: Quo Vadis?" *Journal of Management* 23, no. 3 (1997), p. 422.

21. G. Johns and A. M. Saks, *Organizational Behaviour*, 5th ed. (Toronto: Pearson Education Canada, 2001), pp. 278–279.

22. P. Hersey and K. H. Blanchard, "So You Want to Know Your Leadership Style?" *Training and Development Journal*, February 1974, pp. 1–15; and P. Hersey, K. H. Blanchard, and D. E. Johnson, *Management of Organizational Behavior: Leading Human Resources*, 8th ed. (Upper Saddle River, NJ: Prentice Hall, 2001).

23. Cited in C. F. Fernandez and R. P. Vecchio, "Situational Leadership Theory Revisited: A Test of an Across-Jobs Perspective," *Leadership Quarterly* 8, no. 1 (1997), p. 67.

24. **For controversy surrounding the Fiedler LPC scale, see** A. Bryman, "Leadership in Organizations," in *Handbook of Organization Studies*, ed. S. R. Clegg, C. Hardy, and W. R. Nord (London: Sage Publications, 1996), pp. 279–280; A. Bryman, *Leadership and Organizations* (London: Routledge & Kegan Paul, 1986); and T. Peters and N. Austin, *A Passion for Excellence* (New York: Random House, 1985). **For supportive evidence on the Fiedler model, see** L. H. Peters, D. D. Hartke, and J. T. Pohlmann, "Fiedler's Contingency Theory of Leadership: An Application of the Meta-Analysis Procedures of Schmidt and Hunter," *Psychological Bulletin*, March 1985, pp. 274–285; C. A. Schriesheim, B. J. Tepper, and L. A. Tetrault, "Least Preferred Co-Worker Score, Situational Control, and Leadership Effectiveness: A Meta-Analysis of Contingency Model Performance Predictions," *Journal of Applied Psychology*, August 1994, pp. 561–573; and R. Ayman, M. M. Chemers, and F. Fiedler, "The Contingency Model of Leadership Effectiveness: Its Levels of Analysis," *Leadership Quarterly*, Summer 1995, pp. 147–167. **For evidence that LPC scores are not stable, see**, for instance, R. W. Rice, "Psychometric Properties of the Esteem for the Least Preferred Coworker (LPC) Scale," *Academy of Management Review*, January 1978, pp. 106–118; C. A. Schriesheim, B. D. Bannister, and W. H. Money, "Psychometric Properties of the LPC Scale: An Extension of Rice's Review," *Academy of Management Review*, April 1979, pp. 287–290; and J. K. Kennedy, J. M. Houston, M. A. Korgaard, and D. D. Gallo, "Construct Space of the Least Preferred Co-Worker (LPC) Scale," *Educational & Psychological Measurement*, Fall 1987, pp. 807–814. For difficulty in applying Fiedler's model, see E. H. Schein, *Organizational Psychology*, 3rd ed. (Englewood Cliffs, NJ: Prentice Hall, 1980), pp. 116–117; and B. Kabanoff, "A

Critique of Leader Match and Its Implications for Leadership Research," *Personnel Psychology*, Winter 1981, pp. 749–764. **For evidence that Hersey and Blanchard's model has received little attention from researchers, see** R. K. Hambleton and R. Gumpert, "The Validity of Hersey and Blanchard's Theory of Leader Effectiveness," *Group & Organizational Studies*, June 1982, pp. 225–242; C. L. Graeff, "The Situational Leadership Theory: A Critical View," *Academy of Management Review*, April 1983, pp. 285–291; R. P. Vecchio, "Situational Leadership Theory: An Examination of a Prescriptive Theory," *Journal of Applied Psychology*, August 1987, pp. 444–451; J. R. Goodson, G. W. McGee, and J. F. Cashman, "Situational Leadership Theory: A Test of Leadership Prescriptions," *Group & Organization Studies*, December 1989, pp. 446–461; W. Blank, J. R. Weitzel, and S. G. Green, "A Test of the Situational Leadership Theory," *Personnel Psychology*, Autumn 1990, pp. 579–597; and W. R. Norris and R. P. Vecchio, "Situational Leadership Theory: A Replication," *Group & Organization Management*, September 1992, pp. 331–342. **For evidence of partial support for the theory, see** R. P. Vecchio, "Situational Leadership Theory: An Examination of a Prescriptive Theory," *Journal of Applied Psychology*, August 1987, pp. 444–451; and W. R. Norris and R. P. Vecchio, "Situational Leadership Theory: A Replication," *Group & Organization Management*, September 1992, pp. 331–342. **For evidence of no support for Hersey and Blanchard, see** W. Blank, J. R. Weitzel, and S. G. Green, "A Test of the Situational Leadership Theory," *Personnel Psychology*, Autumn 1990, pp. 579–597.

25. M. G. Evans, "The Effects of Supervisory Behavior on the Path-Goal Relationship," *Organizational Behavior and Human Performance* 5, 1970, pp. 277–298; M. G. Evans, "Leadership and Motivation: A Core Concept," *Academy of Management Journal* 13, 1970, pp. 91–102; R. J. House, "A Path-Goal Theory of Leader Effectiveness," *Administrative Science Quarterly*, September 1971, pp. 321–338; R. J. House and T. R. Mitchell, "Path-Goal Theory of Leadership," *Journal of Contemporary Business*, Autumn 1974, p. 86; M. G. Evans, "Leadership," in *Organizational Behavior*, ed. S. Kerr (Columbus, OH: Grid Publishing, 1979); R. J. House, "Retrospective Comment," in *The Great Writings in Management and Organizational Behavior*, 2nd ed., ed. L. E. Boone and D. D. Bowen (New York: Random House, 1987), pp. 354–364; and M. G. Evans, "Fuhrungstheorien, Weg-ziel-theorie," in *Handworterbuch Der Fuhrung*, 2nd ed., ed. A. Kieser, G. Reber, and R. Wunderer, trans. G. Reber (Stuttgart, Germany: Schaffer Poeschal Verlag, 1995), pp. 1075–1091.

26. G. R. Jones, J. M. George, C. W. L. Hill, and N. Langton, *Contemporary Management* (Toronto: McGraw-Hill Ryerson, 2002), p. 392.

27. See J. C. Wofford and L. Z. Liska, "Path-Goal Theories of Leadership: A Meta-Analysis," *Journal of Management*, Winter 1993, pp. 857–876; M. G. Evans, "R.J. House's 'A Path-Goal Theory of Leader Effectiveness,'" *Leadership Quarterly*, Fall 1996, pp. 305–309; C. A. Schriesheim and L. L. Neider, "Path-Goal Leadership Theory: The Long and Winding Road," *Leadership Quarterly*, Fall 1996, pp. 317–321; A. Somech, "The Effects of Leadership Style and Team Process on Performance and Innovation in Functionally Heterogeneous Teams," *Journal of Management* 32, no. 1 (2006), pp. 132–157; and S. Yun, S. Faraj, and H. P. Sims, "Contingent Leadership and Effectiveness of Trauma Resuscitation Teams," *Journal of Applied Psychology* 90, no. 6 (2005), pp. 1288–1296.

28. L. R. Anderson, "Toward a Two-Track Model of Leadership Training: Suggestions from Self-Monitoring Theory," *Small Group Research*, May 1990, pp. 147–167; G. H. Dobbins, W. S. Long, E. J. Dedrick, and T. C. Clemons, "The Role of Self-Monitoring and Gender on Leader Emergence: A Laboratory and Field Study," *Journal of Management*, September 1990, pp. 609–618; and

S. J. Zaccaro, R. J. Foti, and D. A. Kenny, "Self-Monitoring and Trait-Based Variance in Leadership: An Investigation of Leader Flexibility Across Multiple Group Situations," *Journal of Applied Psychology*, April 1991, pp. 308–315.

29. S. Kerr and J. M. Jermier, "Substitutes for Leadership: Their Meaning and Measurement," *Organizational Behavior and Human Performance*, December 1978, pp. 375–403; J. P. Howell and P. W. Dorfman, "Substitutes for Leadership: Test of a Construct," *Academy of Management Journal*, December 1981, pp. 714–728; J. P. Howell, P. W. Dorfman, and S. Kerr, "Leadership and Substitutes for Leadership," *Journal of Applied Behavioral Science* 22, no. 1 (1986), pp. 29–46; J. P. Howell, D. E. Bowen, P. W. Dorfman, S. Kerr, and P. M. Podsakoff, "Substitutes for Leadership: Effective Alternatives to Ineffective Leadership," *Organizational Dynamics*, Summer 1990, pp. 21–38; P. M. Podsakoff, B. P. Niehoff, S. B. MacKenzie, and M. L. Williams, "Do Substitutes for Leadership Really Substitute for Leadership? An Empirical Examination of Kerr and Jermier's Situational Leadership Model," *Organizational Behavior and Human Decision Processes*, February 1993, pp. 1–44; P. M. Podsakoff and S. B. MacKenzie, "An Examination of Substitutes for Leadership Within a Levels-of-Analysis Framework," *Leadership Quarterly*, Fall 1995, pp. 289–328; P. M. Podsakoff, S. B. MacKenzie, and W. H. Bommer, "Transformational Leader Behaviors and Substitutes for Leadership as Determinants of Employee Satisfaction, Commitment, Trust, and Organizational Citizenship Behaviors," *Journal of Management* 22, no. 2 (1996), pp. 259–298; P. M. Podsakoff, S. B. MacKenzie, and W. H. Bommer, "Meta-Analysis of the Relationships Between Kerr and Jermier's Substitutes for Leadership and Employee Attitudes, Role Perceptions, and Performance," *Journal of Applied Psychology*, August 1996, pp. 380–399; and J. M. Jermier and S. Kerr, "'Substitutes for Leadership: Their Meaning and Measurement'—Contextual Recollections and Current Observations," *Leadership Quarterly* 8, no. 2 (1997), pp. 95–101.

30. R. T. Keller, "Transformational Leadership, Initiating Structure, and Substitutes for Leadership: A Longitudinal Study of Research and Development Project Team Performance," *Journal of Applied Psychology* 91, no. 1 (2006), pp. 202–210.

31. R. E. Kelley, "In Praise of Followers," *Harvard Business Review*, November–December 1988, pp. 142–148; E. P. Hollander, "Leadership, Followership, Self, and Others," *Leadership Quarterly*, Spring 1992, pp. 43–54; and I. Challeff, *The Courageous Follower: Standing Up to and for Our Leaders* (San Francisco: Berrett-Koehler, 1995).

32. R. E. Kelley, "In Praise of Followers," *Harvard Business Review*, November–December 1988, pp. 142–148.

33. V. Smith, "Leading Us On," *Report on Business Magazine*, April 1999, pp. 91–96.

34. A. Bryman, "Leadership in Organizations," in *Handbook of Organization Studies*, ed. S. R. Clegg, C. Hardy, and W. R. Nord (London: Sage Publications, 1996), pp. 276–292.

35. J. M. Howell and B. J. Avolio, "The Leverage of Leadership," in *Leadership: Achieving Exceptional Performance*, A Special Supplement Prepared by the Richard Ivey School of Business, *Globe and Mail*, May 15, 1998, pp. C1, C2.

36. J. M. Howell and B. J. Avolio, "The Leverage of Leadership," in *Leadership: Achieving Exceptional Performance*, A Special Supplement Prepared by the Richard Ivey School of Business, *Globe and Mail*, May 15, 1998, pp. C1, C2.

37. J. M. Howell and B. Shamir, "The Role of Followers in the Charismatic Leadership Process: Relationships and Their Consequences," *Academy of Management Review* 30, no. 1 (2005), pp. 96–112.

38. R. N. Kanungo, "Leadership in Organizations: Looking Ahead to the 21st Century," *Canadian Psychology* 39, no. 1–2 (1998), p. 78.

39. B. M. Bass, "Leadership: Good, Better, Best," *Organizational Dynamics,* Winter 1985, pp. 26–40; and J. Seltzer and B. M. Bass, "Transformational Leadership: Beyond Initiation and Consideration," *Journal of Management,* December 1990, pp. 693–703.

40. D. E. Carl and M. Javidan, "Universality of Charismatic Leadership: A Multi-Nation Study," *Academy of Management Proceedings,* 2001, pp. IM: B1–B6.

41. P. C. Nutt and R. W. Backoff, "Crafting Vision," *Journal of Management Inquiry,* December 1997, p. 309.

42. P. C. Nutt and R. W. Backoff, "Crafting Vision," *Journal of Management Inquiry,* December 1997, pp. 312–314.

43. For an overview of this research, see T. A. Judge and R. F. Piccolo, "Transformational and Transactional Leadership: A Meta-Analytic Test of Their Relative Validity," *Journal of Applied Psychology* 89, no. 5 (October 2004), pp. 755–768.

44. J. C. Collins and J. I. Porras, *Built to Last: Successful Habits of Visionary Companies* (New York: HarperBusiness, 1994).

45. J. M. Howell and B. J. Avolio, "The Leverage of Leadership," in *Leadership: Achieving Exceptional Performance,* A Special Supplement Prepared by the Richard Ivey School of Business, *Globe and Mail,* May 15, 1998, p. C2.

46. "Building a Better Boss," *Maclean's,* September 30, 1996, p. 41.

47. H. Wang, K. S. Law, R. D. Hackett, D. Wang, and Z. X. Chen, "Leader-Member Exchange as a Mediator of the Relationship Between Transformational Leadership and Followers' Performance and Organizational Citizenship Behavior," *Academy of Management Journal* 48, no. 3 (June 2005), pp. 420–432; T. Dvir, D. Eden, B. J. Avolio, and B. Shamir, "Impact of Transformational Leadership on Follower Development and Performance: A Field Experiment," *Academy of Management Journal* 45, no. 4 (2002), pp. 735–744; R. J. House, J. Woycke, and E. M. Fodor, "Charismatic and Noncharismatic Leaders: Differences in Behavior and Effectiveness," in *Charismatic Leadership in Organizations,* ed. J. A. Conger and R. N. Kanungo (Thousand Oaks, CA: Sage, 1998), pp. 103–104; and S. A. Kirkpatrick and E. A. Locke, "Direct and Indirect Effects of Three Core Charismatic Leadership Components on Performance and Attitudes," *Journal of Applied Psychology,* February 1996, pp. 36–51.

48. Cited in B. M. Bass and B. J. Avolio, "Developing Transformational Leadership: 1992 and Beyond," *Journal of European Industrial Training,* January 1990, p. 23.

49. J. J. Hater and B. M. Bass, "Supervisors' Evaluation and Subordinates' Perceptions of Transformational and Transactional Leadership," *Journal of Applied Psychology,* November 1988, pp. 695–702.

50. G. M. Spreitzer, K. H. Perttula, and K. Xin, "Traditionality Matters: An Examination of the Effectiveness of Transformational Leadership in the United States and Taiwan," *Journal of Organizational Behavior* 26, no. 3 (2005), pp. 205–227.

51. B. M. Bass and B. J. Avolio, "Developing Transformational Leadership: 1992 and Beyond," *Journal of European Industrial Training,* January 1990, p. 23; and J. M. Howell and B. J. Avolio, "The Leverage of Leadership," in *Leadership: Achieving Exceptional Performance,* A Special Supplement Prepared by the Richard Ivey School of Business, *Globe and Mail,* May 15, 1998, pp. C1, C2.

52. T. DeGroot, D. S. Kiker, and T. C. Cross, "A Meta-Analysis to Review Organizational Outcomes Related to Charismatic Leadership," *Canadian Journal of Administrative Sciences* 17, no. 4 (2000), pp. 356–371.

53. J. A. Conger, *The Charismatic Leader: Behind the Mystique of Exceptional Leadership* (San Francisco: Jossey-Bass, 1989); R. Hogan, R. Raskin, and D. Fazzini, "The Dark Side of Charisma," in *Measures of Leadership,* ed. K. E. Clark and M. B. Clark (West Orange, NJ: Leadership Library of America, 1990); D. Sankowsky, "The Charismatic Leader as Narcissist: Understanding the Abuse of Power," *Organizational Dynamics,* Spring 1995, pp. 57–71; and J. O'Connor, M. D. Mumford, T. C. Clifton, T. L. Gessner, and M. S. Connelly, "Charismatic Leaders and Destructiveness: An Historiometric Study," *Leadership Quarterly,* Winter 1995, pp. 529–555.

54. A. Elsner, "The Era of CEO as Superhero Ends Amid Corporate Scandals," *Globe and Mail,* July 10, 2002, p. C1.

55. R. Khurana, "Toward More Rational CEO Succession," *Chief Executive,* April 2003, p. 16.

56. G. Pitts, "Scandals Part of Natural Cycles of Excess," *Globe and Mail,* June 28, 2002, pp. B1, B5.

57. J. Collins, "Level 5 Leadership: The Triumph of Humility and Fierce Resolve," *Harvard Business Review,* January 2001, pp. 67–76; R. A. Minde and J. Groebel, eds., *Cooperation and Prosocial Behaviour* (Cambridge, UK: Cambridge University Press, 1991), p. 194; D. J. McAllister, "Affect- and Cognition-Based Trust as Foundations for Interpersonal Cooperation in Organizations," *Academy of Management Journal,* February 1995, p. 25; and D. M. Rousseau, S. B. Sitkin, R. S. Burt, and C. Camerer, "Not So Different After All: A Cross-Discipline View of Trust," *Academy of Management Review,* July 1998, pp. 393–404.

58. Based on D. Montgomery, "To Task-Force Leader, Results, Not Excuses, Matter," *Star-Telegram,* September 12, 2005, http://www.dfw.com/mld/dfw/ (accessed September 22, 2005).

59. See, for example, L. J. Zachary, *The Mentor's Guide: Facilitating Effective Learning Relationships* (San Francisco: Jossey-Bass, 2000); M. Murray, *Beyond the Myths and Magic of Mentoring: How to Facilitate an Effective Mentoring Process,* rev. ed. (New York: Wiley, 2001); and F. Warner, "Inside Intel's Mentoring Movement," *Fast Company,* April 2002, pp. 116–120.

60. *Mentoring: Finding a Perfect Match for People Development Briefing* (Ottawa: The Conference Board of Canada, June 2003).

61. J. A. Wilson and N. S. Elman, "Organizational Benefits of Mentoring," *Academy of Management Executive,* November 1990, p. 90; and J. Reingold, "Want to Grow as a Leader? Get a Mentor!" *Fast Company,* January 2001, pp. 58–60.

62. T. D. Allen, L. T. Eby, M. L. Poteet, E. Lentz, and L. Lima, "Career Benefits Associated With Mentoring for Protégés: A Meta-Analysis," *Journal of Applied Psychology,* February 2004, pp. 127–136.

63. See, for example, D. A. Thomas, "The Impact of Race on Managers' Experiences of Developmental Relationships: An Intra-Organizational Study," *Journal of Organizational Behavior,* November 1990, pp. 479–492; K. E. Kram and D. T. Hall, "Mentoring in a Context of Diversity and Turbulence," in *Managing Diversity,* ed. E. E. Kossek and S. A. Lobel (Cambridge, MA: Blackwell, 1996), pp. 108–136; M. N. Ruderman and M. W. Hughes-James, "Leadership Development Across Race and Gender," in *The Center for Creative Leadership Handbook of Leadership Development,* ed. C. D. McCauley, R. S. Moxley, and E. Van Velsor (San Francisco: Jossey-Bass, 1998), pp. 291–335; and B. R. Ragins and J. L. Cotton, "Mentor Functions and Outcomes: A Comparison of Men and Women in Formal and Informal Mentoring Relationships," *Journal of Applied Psychology,* August 1999, pp. 529–550.

64. J. A. Wilson and N. S. Elman, "Organizational Benefits of Mentoring," *Academy of Management Executive,* November 1990, p. 90.

65. D. Zielinski, "Mentoring Up," *Training* 37, no. 10 (October 2000), pp. 136–141.

66. J. M. Hunt and J. R. Weintraub, "Learning Developmental Coaching," *Journal of Management Education* 28, no. 1 (February 2004), pp. 39–61.

67. J. Mills, "Subordinate Perceptions of Managerial Coaching Practices," *Proceedings,* Academy of Management, Chicago, 1986, pp. 113–116.

68. See, for instance, J. H. Zenger, E. Musselwhite, K. Hurson, and C. Perrin, *Leading Teams: Mastering the New Role* (Homewood, IL: Business One Irwin, 1994); and M. Frohman, "Nothing Kills Teams Like Ill-Prepared Leaders," *IndustryWeek*, October 2, 1995, pp. 72–76.

69. See, for instance, M. Frohman, "Nothing Kills Teams Like Ill-Prepared Leaders," *IndustryWeek,* October 2, 1995, p. 93.

70. See, for instance, M. Frohman, "Nothing Kills Teams Like Ill-Prepared Leaders," *IndustryWeek,* October 2, 1995, p. 100.

71. J. R. Katzenbach and D. K. Smith, *The Wisdom of Teams: Creating the High-Performance Organization* (Boston, MA: Harvard Business School, 1993).

72. N. Steckler and N. Fondas, "Building Team Leader Effectiveness: A Diagnostic Tool," *Organizational Dynamics,* Winter 1995, p. 20.

73. R. S. Wellins, W. C. Byham, and G. R. Dixon, *Inside Teams* (San Francisco: Jossey-Bass, 1994), p. 318.

74. N. Steckler and N. Fondas, "Building Team Leader Effectiveness: A Diagnostic Tool," *Organizational Dynamics,* Winter 1995, p. 21.

75. C. C. Manz and H. P. Sims Jr., *The New SuperLeadership: Leading Others to Lead Themselves* (San Francisco: Berrett-Koehler Publishers, 2001).

76. A. Bandura, "Self-Reinforcement: Theoretical and Methodological Considerations," *Behaviorism* 4, 1976, pp. 135–155; P. W. Corrigan, C. J. Wallace, and M. L. Schade, "Learning Medication Self-Management Skills in Schizophrenia: Relationships With Cognitive Deficits and Psychiatric Symptoms," *Behavior Therapy,* Winter 1994, pp. 5–15; A. S. Bellack, "A Comparison of Self-Reinforcement and Self-Monitoring in a Weight Reduction Program," *Behavior Therapy* 7, 1976, pp. 68–75; T. A. Eckman, W. C. Wirshing, and S. R. Marder, "Technique for Training Schizophrenic Patients in Illness Self-Management: A Controlled Trial," *American Journal of Psychiatry* 149, 1992, pp. 1549–1555; J. J. Felixbrod and K. D. O'Leary, "Effect of Reinforcement on Children's Academic Behavior as a Function of Self-Determined and Externally Imposed Contingencies," *Journal of Applied Behavior Analysis* 6, 1973, pp. 141–150; A. J. Litrownik, L. R. Franzini, and D. Skenderian, "The Effects of Locus of Reinforcement Control on a Concept Identification Task," *Psychological Reports* 39, 1976, pp. 159–165; P. D. McGorry, "Psychoeducation in First-Episode Psychosis: A Therapeutic Process," *Psychiatry,* November 1995, pp. 313–328; G. S. Parcel, P. R. Swank, and M. J. Mariotto, "Self-Management of Cystic Fibrosis: A Structural Model for Educational and Behavioral Variables," *Social Science and Medicine* 38, 1994, pp. 1307–1315; G. E. Speidel, "Motivating Effect of Contingent Self-Reward," *Journal of Experimental Psychology* 102, 1974, pp. 528–530.

77. D. B. Jeffrey, "A Comparison of the Effects of External Control and Self-Control on the Modification and Maintenance of Weight," *Journal of Abnormal Psychology* 83, 1974, pp. 404–410.

78. M. Castaneda, T. A. Kolenko, and R. J. Aldag, "Self-Management Perceptions and Practices: A Structural Equations Analysis," *Journal of Organizational Behavior* 20, 1999, p. 102.

79. M. Castaneda, T. A. Kolenko, and R. J. Aldag, "Self-Management Perceptions and Practices: A Structural Equations Analysis," *Journal of Organizational Behavior* 20, 1999, p. 102.

80. M. Castaneda, T. A. Kolenko, and R. J. Aldag, "Self-Management Perceptions and Practices: A Structural Equations Analysis," *Journal of Organizational Behavior* 20, 1999, p. 102.

81. C. C. Manz and H. P. Sims Jr., *The New SuperLeadership: Leading Others to Lead Themselves* (San Francisco: Berrett-Koehler, 2001).

82. R. M. Kanter, *The Change Masters: Innovation and Entrepreneurship in the American Corporation* (New York: Simon and Schuster, 1983).

83. R. A. Heifetz, *Leadership Without Easy Answers* (Cambridge, MA: Harvard University Press, 1996), p. 205.

84. R. A. Heifetz, *Leadership Without Easy Answers* (Cambridge, MA: Harvard University Press, 1996), p. 205.

85. R. A. Heifetz, *Leadership Without Easy Answers* (Cambridge, MA: Harvard University Press, 1996), p. 188.

86. Based on D. D. Kirkpatrick and S. Shane, "Ex-FEMA Chief Tells of Frustration and Chaos," *New York Times,* September 15, 2005, http://www.nytimes.com/ (accessed September 15, 2005).

87. This section is based on R. B. Morgan, "Self- and Co-Worker Perceptions of Ethics and Their Relationships to Leadership and Salary," *Academy of Management Journal,* February 1993, pp. 200–214; J. B. Ciulla, "Leadership Ethics: Mapping the Territory," *Business Ethics Quarterly,* January 1995, pp. 5–28; E. P. Hollander, "Ethical Challenges in the Leader-Follower Relationship," *Business Ethics Quarterly,* January 1995, pp. 55–65; J. C. Rost, "Leadership: A Discussion About Ethics," *Business Ethics Quarterly,* January 1995, pp. 129–142; R. N. Kanungo and M. Mendonca, *Ethical Dimensions of Leadership* (Thousand Oaks, CA: Sage Publications, 1996); and M. Schminke, M. L. Ambrose, and D. O. Neubaum, "The Effect of Leader Moral Development on Ethical Climate and Employee Attitudes," *Organizational Behavior and Human Decision Processes* 97, no. 2 (July 2005), pp. 135–151.

88. J. M. Burns, *Leadership* (New York: Harper and Row, 1978).

89. J. M. Howell and B. J. Avolio, "The Ethics of Charismatic Leadership: Submission or Liberation?" *Academy of Management Executive,* May 1992, pp. 43–55.

90. J. Stephens and P. Behr, "Enron's Culture Fed Its Demise: Groupthink Promoted Foolhardy Risks," *Washington Post,* January 27, 2002, p. A01.

91. J. G. Clawson, *Level Three Leadership* (Upper Saddle River, NJ: Prentice Hall, 1999), pp. 46–49.

92. The material in this section is based on S. Helgesen, *The Female Advantage: Women's Ways of Leadership* (New York: Doubleday, 1990); A. H. Eagly and B. T. Johnson, "Gender and Leadership Style: A Meta-Analysis," *Psychological Bulletin,* September 1990, pp. 233–256; A. H. Eagly and S. J. Karau, "Gender and the Emergence of Leaders: A Meta-Analysis," *Journal of Personality and Social Psychology,* May 1991, pp. 685–710; J. B. Rosener, "Ways Women Lead," *Harvard Business Review,* November–December 1990, pp. 119–125; A. H. Eagly, M. G. Makhijani, and B. G. Klonsky, "Gender and the Evaluation of Leaders: A Meta-Analysis," *Psychological Bulletin,* January 1992, pp. 3–22; A. H. Eagly, S. J. Karau, and B. T. Johnson, "Gender and Leadership Style Among School Principals: A Meta-Analysis," *Educational Administration Quarterly,* February 1992, pp. 76–102; L. R. Offermann and C. Beil, "Achievement Styles of Women Leaders and Their Peers," *Psychology of Women Quarterly,* March 1992, pp. 37–56; R. L. Kent and S. E. Moss, "Effects of Size and Gender Role on Leader Emergence," *Academy of Management Journal,* October 1994, pp. 1335–1346; C. Lee, "The Feminization of Management," *Training,* November 1994, pp. 25–31; H. Collingwood, "Women as Managers: Not Just Different: Better," *Working Woman,* November 1995, p. 14; J. B. Rosener, *America's Competitive Secret: Women Managers* (New York: Oxford University

Press, 1995); and J. Cliff, N. Langton, and H. Aldrich, "Walking the Talk? Gendered Rhetoric vs. Action in Small Firms," *Organizational Studies* 26, no. 1 (2005), pp. 63–91.

93. B. Orser, *Creating High Performance Organizations: Leveraging Women's Leadership* (Ottawa: The Conference Board of Canada, 2000).

94. J. M. Norvilitis and H. M. Reid, "Evidence for an Association Between Gender-Role Identity and a Measure of Executive Function," *Psychological Reports*, February 2002, pp. 35–45; W. H. Decker and D. M. Rotondo, "Relationships Among Gender, Type of Humor, and Perceived Leader Effectiveness," *Journal of Managerial Issues*, Winter 2001, pp. 450–465; H. Aguinis and S. K. R. Adams, "Social-Role Versus Structural Models of Gender and Influence Use in Organizations: A Strong Inference Approach," *Group & Organization Management*, December 1998, pp. 414–446; and A. H. Eagly, S. J. Karau, and M. G. Makhijani, "Gender and the Effectiveness of Leaders: A Meta-Analysis," *Psychological Bulletin* 117, 1995, pp. 125–145.

95. A. H. Eagly, M. C. Johannesen-Schmidt, and M. L. van Engen, "Transformational, Transactional, and Laissez-Faire Leadership Styles: A Meta-Analysis Comparing Women and Men," *Psychological Bulletin* 129, no. 4 (July 2003), pp. 569–591; K. M. Bartol, D. C. Martin, and J. A. Kromkowski, "Leadership and the Glass Ceiling: Gender and Ethnic Influences on Leader Behaviors at Middle and Executive Managerial Levels," *Journal of Leadership & Organizational Studies*, Winter 2003, pp. 8–19; and R. Sharpe, "As Leaders, Women Rule," *BusinessWeek*, November 20, 2000, pp. 74–84.

96. K. M. Bartol, D. C. Martin, and J. A. Kromkowski, "Leadership and the Glass Ceiling: Gender and Ethnic Influences on Leader Behaviors at Middle and Executive Managerial Levels," *Journal of Leadership & Organizational Studies*, Winter 2003, pp. 8–19.

97. B. J. Avolio, S. Kahai, and G. E. Dodge, "E-Leadership: Implications for Theory, Research, and Practice," *Leadership Quarterly*, Winter 2000, pp. 615–668; and B. J. Avolio and S. S. Kahai, "Adding the 'E' to E-Leadership: How It May Impact Your Leadership," *Organizational Dynamics* 31, no. 4 (2003), 325–338.

98. J. Howell and K. Hall-Merenda, "Leading from a Distance," in *Leadership: Achieving Exceptional Performance*, A Special Supplement Prepared by the Richard Ivey School of Business, *Globe and Mail*, May 15, 1998, pp. C1, C2.

99. M. Javidan, P. W. Dorfman, M. S. Du Luque, and R. J. House, "In the Eye of the Beholder: Cross-Cultural Lessons in Leadership from Project GLOBE," *Academy of Management Perspectives* 20, no. 1 (2006), pp. 67–90.

100. "Military-Style Management in China," *Asia Inc.*, March 1995, p. 70.

101. R. J. House, "Leadership in the Twenty-First Century," in *The Changing Nature of Work*, ed. A. Howard (San Francisco: Jossey-Bass, 1995), pp. 442–444; and M. F. Peterson and J. G. Hunt, "International Perspectives on International Leadership," *Leadership Quarterly*, Fall 1997, pp. 203–231.

102. D. N. Den Hartog, R. J. House, P. J. Hanges, S. A. Ruiz-Quintanilla, and P. W. Dorfman, "Culture Specific and Cross-Culturally Generalizable Implicit Leadership Theories: Are Attributes of Charismatic/Transformational Leadership Universally Endorsed?" *Leadership Quarterly* 10, no. 2 (Summer 1999), pp. 219–256; and D. E. Carl and M. Javidan, "Universality of Charismatic Leadership: A Multi-Nation Study" (paper presented at the National Academy of Management Conference, Washington, DC, August 2001).

103. D. E. Carl and M. Javidan, "Universality of Charismatic Leadership: A Multi-Nation Study" (paper presented at the National Academy of Management Conference, Washington, DC, August 2001), p. 29.

104. Based on J. M. Howell and P. J. Frost, "A Laboratory Study of Charismatic Leadership," *Organizational Behavior and Human Decision Processes*, April 1989, pp. 243–269.

Chapter 9

1. Opening vignette based on M. Skapinker, "Why Nike Has Broken into a Sweat," *Financial Times*, March 6, 2002, http://news.ft.com/ft/gx.cgi/ftc?pagename=View&c=Article&cid=FT363BTGHYC&live=true (accessed March 12, 2002); and D. Simpson, "Ethics and Corporate Social Responsibility," advertising supplement, *Report on Business* Magazine, February 2002.

2. M. Skapinker, "Why Nike Has Broken into a Sweat," *Financial Times*, March 6, 2002, http://news.ft.com/ft/gx.cgi/ftc?pagename=View&c=Article&cid=FT363BTGHYC&live=true (accessed March 12, 2002).

3. W. Pounds, "The Process of Problem Finding," *Industrial Management Review*, Fall 1969, pp. 1–19.

4. See H. A. Simon, "Rationality in Psychology and Economics," *Journal of Business*, October 1986, pp. 209–224; and A. Langley, "In Search of Rationality: The Purposes Behind the Use of Formal Analysis in Organizations," *Administrative Science Quarterly*, December 1989, pp. 598–631.

5. For a review of the rational model, see E. F. Harrison, *The Managerial Decision Making Process*, 5th ed. (Boston: Houghton Mifflin, 1999), pp. 75–102.

6. T. Barry, "Smart Cookies: Why CIBC Said Yes to the Girl Guides," *Marketing Magazine*, May 31, 1999, pp. 11, 14.

7. J. G. March, *A Primer on Decision Making* (New York: Free Press, 1994), pp. 2–7.

8. Vignette based on "Quotas at Thailand Footwear Factory Promote Fast Work but Draw Fire," *Knight Ridder Tribune Business News*, March 18, 2002, p. 1.

9. D. L. Rados, "Selection and Evaluation of Alternatives in Repetitive Decision Making," *Administrative Science Quarterly*, June 1972, pp. 196–206.

10. M. Bazerman, *Judgment in Managerial Decision Making*, 3rd ed. (New York: Wiley, 1994), p. 5.

11. See, for instance, L. R. Beach, *The Psychology of Decision Making* (Thousand Oaks, CA: Sage, 1997).

12. See, for example, M. D. Cohen, J. G. March, and J. P. Olsen, "A Garbage Can Model of Organizational Choice," *Administrative Science Quarterly*, March 1972, pp. 1–25.

13. See J. G. Thompson, *Organizations in Action* (New York: McGraw-Hill, 1967), p. 123.

14. See H. A. Simon, *Administrative Behavior*, 4th ed. (New York: Free Press, 1997); and M. Augier, "Simon Says: Bounded Rationality Matters," *Journal of Management Inquiry*, September 2001, pp. 268–275. Individuals may also be constrained by time, which makes them focus their deliberations on fewer aspects of alternatives. For further discussion of this point, see J. W. Payne, J. R. Bettman, and E. J. Johnson, "Behavioral Decision Research: A Constructive Processing Perspective," *Annual Review of Psychology* 43, no. 1 (1992), pp. 87–131.

15. *OB in the Workplace* based on K. May, "Ottawa May Stop Hiring Best Qualified," *National Post*, March 4, 2002, p. A4.

16. W. H. Agor, "The Logic of Intuition: How Top Executives Make Important Decisions," *Organizational Dynamics*, Winter 1986, p. 5; W. H. Agor, ed., *Intuition in Organizations* (Newbury Park,

CA: Sage Publications, 1989); O. Behling and N. L. Eckel, "Making Sense Out of Intuition," *Academy of Management Executive*, February 1991, pp. 46–47; G. Klein, *Sources of Power: How People Make Decisions* (Cambridge: MIT Press, 1998); P. E. Ross, "Flash of Genius," *Forbes*, November 16, 1998, pp. 98–104; L. A. Burke and M. K. Miller, "Taking the Mystery Out of Intuitive Decision Making," *Academy of Management Executive*, November 1999, pp. 91–99; and N. Khatri and H. A. Ng, "The Role of Intuition in Strategic Decision Making," *Human Relations*, January 2000, pp. 57–86.

17. O. Behling and N. L. Eckel, "Making Sense Out of Intuition," *Academy of Management Executive*, February 1991, pp. 46–54.

18. L. A. Burke and M. K. Miller, "Taking the Mystery Out of Intuitive Decision Making," *Academy of Management Executive*, November 1999, pp. 91–99.

19. A. Tversky and K. Kahneman, "Judgment Under Uncertainty: Heuristics and Biases," *Science*, September 1974, pp. 1124–1131.

20. S. P. Robbins, *Decide & Conquer: Making Winning Decisions and Taking Control of Your Life* (Upper Saddle River, NJ: Financial Times/Prentice Hall, 2004), p. 13.

21. A. Tversky and K. Kahneman, "Judgment Under Uncertainty: Heuristics and Biases," *Science*, September 1974, pp. 1124–1131; and J. S. Hammond, R. L. Keeney, and H. Raiffa, "The Hidden Traps in Decision Making," *Harvard Business Review*, September–October 1998, pp. 47–58.

22. See A. Tversky and D. Kahneman, "Availability: A Heuristic for Judging Frequency and Probability," in *Judgment Under Uncertainty: Heuristics and Biases*, ed. D. Kahneman, P. Slovic, and A. Tversky (Cambridge, UK: Cambridge University Press, 1982), pp. 163–178.

23. G. Whyte and C. Sue-Chan, "The Neglect of Base Rate Data by Human Resources Managers in Employee Selection," *Revue Canadienne des Sciences de l'Administration* 19, no. 1 (2002), pp. 1–11.

24. D. Kahneman and D. Lovallo, "Timid Choices and Bold Forecasts—A Cognitive Perspective on Risk-Taking," *Management Science* 39, no. 1 (1993), pp. 17–31.

25. See B. M. Staw, "The Escalation of Commitment to a Course of Action," *Academy of Management Review*, October 1981, pp. 577–587; and H. Moon, "Looking Forward and Looking Back: Integrating Completion and Sunk-Cost Effects Within an Escalation-of-Commitment Progress Decision," *Journal of Applied Psychology*, February 2001, pp. 104–113.

26. S. Plous, *The Psychology of Judgment and Decision Making* (New York: McGraw Hill, 1993), p. 217.

27. S. Lichtenstein and B. Fischhoff, "Do Those Who Know More Also Know More About How Much They Know?" *Organizational Behavior and Human Performance*, December 1977, pp. 159–183.

28. B. Fischhoff, P. Slovic, and S. Lichtenstein, "Knowing With Certainty: The Appropriateness of Extreme Confidence," *Journal of Experimental Psychology: Human Perception and Performance*, November 1977, pp. 552–564.

29. J. Kruger and D. Dunning, "Unskilled and Unaware of It: How Difficulties in Recognizing One's Own Incompetence Lead to Inflated Self-Assessments," *Journal of Personality and Social Psychology*, November 1999, pp. 1121–1134.

30. B. Fischhoff, P. Slovic, and S. Lichtenstein, "Knowing With Certainty: The Appropriateness of Extreme Confidence," *Journal of Experimental Psychology: Human Perception and Performance*, November 1977, pp. 552–564.

31. See, for instance, A. Tversky and D. Kahneman, "Judgment Under Uncertainty: Heuristics and Biases," *Science*, September 1974, pp. 1124–1131.

32. J. S. Hammond, R. L. Keeney, and H. Raiffa, *Smart Choices* (Boston: HBS Press, 1999), p. 191.

33. R. Hastie, D. A. Schkade, and J. W. Payne, "Juror Judgments in Civil Cases: Effects of Plaintiff's Requests and Plaintiff's Identity on Punitive Damage Awards," *Law and Human Behavior*, August 1999, pp. 445–470.

34. See N. R. F. Maier, "Assets and Liabilities in Group Problem Solving: The Need for an Integrative Function," *Psychological Review*, April 1967, pp. 239–249; G. W. Hill, "Group Versus Individual Performance: Are N+1 Heads Better Than One?" *Psychological Bulletin*, May 1982, pp. 517–539; and A. E. Schwartz and J. Levin, "Better Group Decision Making," *Supervisory Management*, June 1990, p. 4.

35. See, for example, R. A. Cooke and J. A. Kernaghan, "Estimating the Difference Between Group Versus Individual Performance on Problem-Solving Tasks," *Group & Organization Studies*, September 1987, pp. 319–342; and L. K. Michaelsen, W. E. Watson, and R. H. Black, "A Realistic Test of Individual Versus Group Consensus Decision Making," *Journal of Applied Psychology*, October 1989, pp. 834–839.

36. See, for example, W. C. Swap and Associates, *Group Decision Making* (Newbury Park, CA: Sage, 1984).

37. I. L. Janis, *Groupthink* (Boston: Houghton Mifflin, 1982); W. Park, "A Review of Research on Groupthink," *Journal of Behavioral Decision Making*, July 1990, pp. 229–245; C. P. Neck and G. Moorhead, "Groupthink Remodeled: The Importance of Leadership, Time Pressure, and Methodical Decision Making Procedures," *Human Relations*, May 1995, pp. 537–558; and J. N. Choi and M. U. Kim, "The Organizational Application of Groupthink and Its Limits in Organizations," *Journal of Applied Psychology*, April 1999, pp. 297–306.

38. Based on I. L. Janis, *Groupthink: Psychological Studies of Policy Decisions and Fiascoes*, 2nd ed. (Boston: Houghton Mifflin, 1982), p. 244.

39. B. Little, "Forecasters Were Lost in a Fog of Pessimism," *Globe and Mail*, March 21, 2002, http://www.theglobeandmail.com (accessed March 21, 2002).

40. M. E. Turner and A. R. Pratkanis, "Mitigating Groupthink by Stimulating Constructive Conflict," in *Using Conflict in Organizations*, ed. C. De Dreu and E. Van de Vliert (London: Sage, 1997), pp. 53–71.

41. See N. R. F. Maier, *Principles of Human Relations* (New York: John Wiley, 1952); I. L. Janis, *Groupthink: Psychological Studies of Policy Decisions and Fiascoes*, 2nd ed. (Boston: Houghton Mifflin, 1982); and C. R. Leana, "A Partial Test of Janis' Groupthink Model: Effects of Group Cohesiveness and Leader Behavior on Defective Decision Making," *Journal of Management*, Spring 1985, pp. 5–17.

42. J. N. Choi and M. U. Kim, "The Organizational Application of Groupthink and Its Limitations in Organizations," *Journal of Applied Psychology* 84, 1999, pp. 297–306.

43. J. Longley and D. G. Pruitt, "Groupthink: A Critique of Janis' Theory," in *Review of Personality and Social Psychology*, ed. L. Wheeler (Newbury Park, CA: Sage, 1980), pp. 507–513; and J. A. Sniezek, "Groups Under Uncertainty: An Examination of Confidence in Group Decision Making," *Organizational Behavior and Human Decision Processes* 52, 1992, pp. 124–155.

44. C. McCauley, "The Nature of Social Influence in Groupthink: Compliance and Internalization," *Journal of Personality and Social Psychology* 57, 1989, pp. 250–260; P. E. Tetlock, R. S. Peterson, C. McGuire, S. Chang, and P. Feld, "Assessing Political Group Dynamics: A Test of the Groupthink Model," *Journal of Personality and Social Psychology* 63, 1992, pp. 781–796; S. Graham, "A Review of Attribution Theory in Achievement Contexts," *Educational Psychology Review* 3, 1991, pp. 5–39; and G. Moorhead and

J. R. Montanari, "An Empirical Investigation of the Groupthink Phenomenon," *Human Relations* 39, 1986, pp. 399–410.

45. J. N. Choi and M. U. Kim, "The Organizational Application of Groupthink and Its Limitations in Organizations," *Journal of Applied Psychology* 84, 1999, pp. 297–306.

46. See D. J. Isenberg, "Group Polarization: A Critical Review and Meta-Analysis," *Journal of Personality and Social Psychology,* December 1986, pp. 1141–1151; J. L. Hale and F. J. Boster, "Comparing Effect Coded Models of Choice Shifts," *Communication Research Reports,* April 1988, pp. 180–186; and P. W. Paese, M. Bieser, and M. E. Tubbs, "Framing Effects and Choice Shifts in Group Decision Making," *Organizational Behavior and Human Decision Processes,* October 1993, pp. 149–165.

47. See, for example, N. Kogan, and M. A. Wallach, "Risk Taking as a Function of the Situation, the Person, and the Group," in *New Directions in Psychology,* vol. 3 (New York: Holt, Rinehart and Winston, 1967); and M. A. Wallach, N. Kogan, and D. J. Bem, "Group Influence on Individual Risk Taking," *Journal of Abnormal and Social Psychology* 65, 1962, pp. 75–86.

48. R. D. Clark III, "Group-Induced Shift Toward Risk: A Critical Appraisal," *Psychological Bulletin,* October 1971, pp. 251–270.

49. A. F. Osborn, *Applied Imagination: Principles and Procedures of Creative Thinking* (New York: Scribner's, 1941). See also P. B. Paulus, M. T. Dzindolet, G. Poletes, and L. M. Camacho, "Perception of Performance in Group Brainstorming: The Illusion of Group Productivity," *Personality and Social Psychology Bulletin,* February 1993, pp. 78–89.

50. I. Edwards, "Office Intrigue: By Design, Consultants Have Workers Conspire to Create Business Environments Tailored to Getting the Job Done," *Financial Post Daily,* December 16, 1997, p. 25.

51. Information in this paragraph from G. Crone, "Electrifying Brainstorms," *Financial Post* (*National Post*), July 3, 1999, p. D11.

52. T. Graham, "The Keys to the Middle Kingdom: Experts Will Tell You It Takes Years of Patient Effort to Crack the Chinese Market, but That's Not Always the Case," *PROFIT,* December 1997/January 1998, p. 29.

53. See A. L. Delbecq, A. H. Van deVen, and D. H. Gustafson, *Group Techniques for Program Planning: A Guide to Nominal and Delphi Processes* (Glenview, IL: Scott, Foresman, 1975); and W. M. Fox, "Anonymity and Other Keys to Successful Problem-Solving Meetings," *National Productivity Review,* Spring 1989, pp. 145–156.

54. E. F. Rietzschel, B. A. Nijstad, and W. Stroebe, "Productivity Is Not Enough: A Comparison of Interactive and Nominal Brainstorming Groups on Idea Generation and Selection," *Journal of Experimental Social Psychology* 42, no. 2 (2006), pp. 244–251.

55. See, for instance, A. R. Dennis and J. S. Valacich, "Computer Brainstorms: More Heads Are Better Than One," *Journal of Applied Psychology,* August 1993, pp. 531–537; R. B. Gallupe and W. H. Cooper, "Brainstorming Electronically," *Sloan Management Review,* Fall 1993, pp. 27–36; and A. B. Hollingshead and J. E. McGrath, "Computer-Assisted Groups: A Critical Review of the Empirical Research," in *Team Effectiveness and Decision Making in Organizations,* ed. R. A. Guzzo and E. Salas (San Francisco: Jossey-Bass, 1995), pp. 46–78.

56. V. H. Vroom and P. W. Yetton, *Leadership and Decision Making* (Pittsburgh: University of Pittsburgh Press, 1973).

57. See, for example, R. H. G. Field, "A Test of the Vroom-Yetton Normative Model of Leadership," *Journal of Applied Psychology,* October 1982, pp. 523–532; C. R. Leana, "Power Relinquishment Versus Power Sharing: Theoretical Clarification and Empirical Comparison of Delegation and Participation," *Journal of Applied Psychology,* May 1987, pp. 228–233; J. T. Ettling and A. G. Jago, "Participation Under Conditions of Conflict: More on the Validity of the Vroom-Yetton Model," *Journal of Management Studies,* January 1988, pp. 73–83; and R. H. G. Field and R. J. House, "A Test of the Vroom-Yetton Model Using Manager and Subordinate Reports," *Journal of Applied Psychology,* June 1990, pp. 362–366.

58. W. Kondro, "Canada in Creativity Crisis: Study," *National Post,* May 25, 2001, pp. A2, A6.

59. "Theatrics in the Boardroom: Acting Classes Are Not Widely Accepted as Management Tools," *Financial Post,* March 4/6, 1995, pp. 24–25.

60. T. Kelley, *The Art of Innovation: Lessons in Creativity from IDEO, America's Leading Design Firm* (New York: Doubleday, 2001).

61. T. M. Amabile, "A Model of Creativity and Innovation in Organizations," in *Research in Organizational Behavior,* vol. 10, ed. B. M. Staw and L. L. Cummings (Greenwich, CT: JAI Press, 1988), pp. 123–167; and T. M. Amabile, "Motivating Creativity in Organizations," *California Management Review,* Fall 1997, p. 40.

62. T. M. Amabile, *The Social Psychology of Creativity* (New York: Springer-Verlag, 1983); T. M. Amabile, "A Model of Creativity and Innovation in Organizations," in *Research in Organizational Behavior,* vol. 10, ed. B. M. Staw and L. L. Cummings (Greenwich, CT: JAI Press, 1988), pp. 123–167; C. E. Shalley, "Effects of Productivity Goals, Creativity Goals, and Personal Discretion on Individual Creativity," *Journal of Applied Psychology* 76, 1991, pp. 179–185; R. W. Woodman, J. E. Sawyer, and R. W. Griffin, "Toward a Theory of Organizational Creativity," *Academy of Management Review* 18, 1993, pp. 293–321; and G. Zaltman, R. Duncan, and J. Holbek, *Innovation and Organizations* (London: Wiley, 1973).

63. G. R. Oldham and A. Cummings, "Employee Creativity: Personal and Contextual Factors at Work," *Academy of Management Journal* 39, 1996, pp. 607–634.

64. Cited in C. G. Morris, *Psychology: An Introduction,* 9th ed. (Upper Saddle River, NJ: Prentice Hall, 1996), p. 344.

65. F. B. Barron and D. M. Harrington, "Creativity, Intelligence, and Personality," *Annual Review of Psychology* 32, 1981, pp. 439–476; G. A. Davis, "Testing for Creative Potential," *Contemporary Educational Psychology* 14, 1989, pp. 257–274; C. Martindale, "Personality, Situation, and Creativity," in *Handbook of Creativity,* ed. J. A. Glover, R. R. Ronning, and C. R. Reynolds (New York: Plenum, 1989), pp. 211–232.

66. G. R. Oldham and A. Cummings, "Employee Creativity: Personal and Contextual Factors at Work," *Academy of Management Journal* 39, 1996, pp. 607–634; see also F. B. Barron and D. M. Harrington, "Creativity, Intelligence, and Personality," *Annual Review of Psychology* 32, 1981, pp. 439–476; H. G. Gough, "A Creative Personality Scale for the Adjective Check List," *Journal of Personality and Social Psychology* 37, 1979, pp. 1398–1405; C. Martindale, "Personality, Situation, and Creativity," in *Handbook of Creativity,* ed. J. A. Glover, R. R. Ronning, and C. R. Reynolds (New York: Plenum, 1989), pp. 211–232; and R. J. Sternberg, *Handbook of Creativity* (Cambridge: Cambridge University Press, 1999).

67. F. Barron and D. M. Harrington, "Creativity, Intelligence, and Personality," *Annual Review of Psychology* 32, 1981, pp. 439–476; M. Basadur and C. T. Finkbeiner, "Measuring Preference for Ideation in Creating Problem Solving Training," *Journal of Applied Behavioral Science* 21, 1985, pp. 37–49; M. Basadur, G. B. Graen, and S. G. Green, "Training in Creative Problem Solving: Effects on Ideation and Problem Finding and Solving in an Industrial Research Organization," *Organizational Behavior and Human Performance* 30, 1982, pp. 41–70; H. Gardner, *Frames of Mind.* (New York: Basic Books, 1993); M. A. Glynn, "Innovative Genius: A Framework for Relating Individual and Organizational Intelligences to Innovation," *Academy of Management Review* 21, 1996, pp. 1081–1111; R. Helson, B. Roberts, and G. Agronick, "Enduringness and Change in Creative Personality and the

Prediction of Occupational Creativity," *Journal of Personality and Social Psychology* 69, 1995, pp. 1173–1183; B. Singh, "Role of Personality Versus Biographical Factors in Creativity," *Psychological Studies* 31, 1986, pp. 90–92; and R. J. Sternberg, "A Three-Facet Model of Creativity," in *The Nature of Creativity: Contemporary Psychological Views*, ed. R. J. Sternberg (Cambridge: Cambridge University Press, 1988), pp. 125–147.

68. T. M. Amabile, "A Model of Creativity and Innovation in Organizations," in *Research in Organizational Behavior*, vol. 10, ed. B. M. Staw and L. L. Cummings (Greenwich, CT: JAI Press, 1988), pp. 123–167; T. M. Amabile, K. G. Hill, B. A. Hennessey, and E. M. Tighe, "The Work Preference Inventory: Assessing Intrinsic and Extrinsic Motivational Orientations," *Journal of Personality and Social Psychology* 66, 1994, pp. 950–967; M. A. Glynn and J. Webster, "Refining the Nomological Net of the Adult Playfulness Scale: Personality, Motivational, and Attitudinal Correlates for Highly Intelligent Adults," *Psychological Reports* 72, 1993, pp. 1023–1026; R. Kanfer, "Motivation Theory and Industrial/Organizational Psychology," in *Handbook of Industrial and Organizational Psychology*, vol. 1, ed. M. D. Dunnette (Palo Alto, CA: Consulting Psychologists Press, 1990), pp. 75–170; and R. Kanfer and P. L. Ackerman, "Motivation and Cognitive Abilities: An Integrative Aptitude-Treatment Interaction Approach to Skill Acquisition," *Journal of Applied Psychology Monograph* 74, 1989, pp. 657–690.

69. T. M. Amabile, "How to Kill Creativity," *Harvard Business Review*, September–October 1998, pp. 76–87.

70. T. M. Amabile, "A Model of Creativity and Innovation in Organizations," in *Research in Organizational Behavior*, vol. 10, ed. B. M. Staw and L. L. Cummings (Greenwich, CT: JAI Press, 1988), pp. 123–167; T. M. Amabile and S. S. Gryskiewicz, *Creativity in the R&D Laboratory*, Technical Report no. 10 (Greensboro, NC: Center for Creative Leadership, 1987); and G. R. Oldham and A. Cummings, "Employee Creativity: Personal and Contextual Factors at Work," *Academy of Management Journal* 39, 1996, pp. 607–634.

71. M. D. Mumford and S. B. Gustafson, "Creativity Syndrome: Integration, Application, and Innovation," *Psychological Bulletin* 103, 1988, pp. 27–43.

72. E. De Bono, *Six Thinking Hats* (Boston: Little, Brown, 1985); and E. De Bono, *The Mechanism of Mind* (New York: Simon and Schuster, 1969).

73. Adapted from E. De Bono, *Six Thinking Hats* (Boston: Little, Brown, 1985).

74. M. Amabile, "How to Kill Creativity," *Harvard Business Review*, September–October 1998, pp. 76–87; H.-S. Choi and L. Thompson, "Old Wine in a New Bottle: Impact of Membership Change on Group Creativity," *Organizational Behavior and Human Decision Processes* 98, no. 2 (2005), pp. 121–132; R. Florida and J. Goodnight, "Managing for Creativity," *Harvard Business Review* 83, no. 7 (2005), pp. 124+; L. L. Gilson, J. E. Mathieu, C. E. Shalley, and T. R. Ruddy, "Creativity and Standardization: Complementary or Conflicting Drivers of Team Effectiveness?" *Academy of Management Journal* 48, no. 3 (2005), pp. 521–531; and K. G. Smith, C. J. Collins, and K. D. Clark, "Existing Knowledge, Knowledge Creation Capability, and the Rate of New Product Introduction in High-Technology Firms," *Academy of Management Journal* 48, no. 2 (2005), pp. 346–357.

75. Cited in T. Stevens, "Creativity Killers," *IndustryWeek*, January 23, 1995, p. 63.

76. Vignette based on "Quotas at Thailand Footwear Factory Promote Fast Work but Draw Fire," *Knight Ridder Tribune Business News*, Mar 18, 2002, p. 1.

77. G. F. Cavanagh, D. J. Moberg, and M. Valasquez, "The Ethics of Organizational Politics," *Academy of Management Journal*, June 1981, pp. 363–374.

78. *Focus on Ethics* based on T. Tedesco, "Broker Shielded from Firing," *Financial Post* (*National Post*), April 10, 2001, pp. C1, C10; P. Brieger, "Manitoba Hits Brokerage for Poor Supervision: $160,000 Fine," *National Post*, May 10, 2001, p. C1; and D. DeCloet, "Punished Broker Acted as an Advisor to Watchdog," *Financial Post* (*National Post*), May 16, 2001, p. C4.

79. See, for example, T. Machan, ed., *Commerce and Morality* (Totowa, NJ: Rowman and Littlefield, 1988).

80. P. L. Schumann, "A Moral Principles Framework for Human Resource Management Ethics," *Human Resource Management Review* 11, Spring–Summer 2001, pp. 93–111.

81. See, for instance, R. S. Dillon, "Care and Respect," in *Explorations in Feminist Ethics: Theory and Practice*, ed. E. Browning Cole and S. Coultrap-McQuin (Bloomington, IN: Indiana University Press, 1992), pp. 69–81; C. Gilligan, *In a Different Voice: Psychological Theory and Women's Development* (Cambridge, MA: Harvard University Press, 1982); and M. C. Raugust, "Feminist Ethics and Workplace Values," in *Explorations in Feminist Ethics: Theory and Practice*, ed. E. Browning Cole and S. Coultrap-McQuin (Bloomington, IN: Indiana University Press, 1992), pp. 69–81.

82. P. L. Schumann, "A Moral Principles Framework for Human Resource Management Ethics," *Human Resource Management Review* 11, Spring–Summer 2001, pp. 93–111.

83. S. Jaffee and J. Hyde, "Gender Differences in Moral Orientation: A Meta-Analysis," *Psychological Bulletin*, September 2000, pp. 703–726.

84. L. K. Trevino, "Ethical Decision Making in Organizations: A Person-Situation Interactionist Model," *Academy of Management Review*, July 1986, pp. 601–617; and L. K. Trevino and S. A. Youngblood, "Bad Apples in Bad Barrels: A Causal Analysis of Ethical Decision Making Behavior," *Journal of Applied Psychology*, August 1990, pp. 378–385.

85. See L. Kohlberg, *Essays in Moral Development: The Philosophy of Moral Development*, vol. 1 (New York: Harper and Row, 1981); L. Kohlberg, *Essays in Moral Development: The Psychology of Moral Development*, vol. 2 (New York: Harper and Row, 1984); and R. S. Snell, "Complementing Kohlberg: Mapping the Ethical Reasoning Used by Managers for Their Own Dilemma Cases," *Human Relations*, January 1996, pp. 23–50.

86. L. Kohlberg, *Essays in Moral Development: The Philosophy of Moral Development*, vol. 1 (New York: Harper and Row, 1981); L. Kohlberg, *Essays in Moral Development: The Philosophy of Moral Development*, vol. 2 (New York: Harper and Row, 1984); and R. S. Snell, "Complementing Kohlberg: Mapping the Ethical Reasoning Used by Managers for Their Own Dilemma Cases," *Human Relations*, January 1996, pp. 23–49.

87. J. Weber, "Managers' Moral Reasoning: Assessing Their Responses to Three Moral Dilemmas," *Human Relations*, July 1990, pp. 687–702; and S. B. Knouse and R. A. Giacalone, "Ethical Decision-Making in Business: Behavioral Issues and Concerns," *Journal of Business Ethics*, May 1992, pp. 369–377.

88. D. Todd, "Business Responds to Ethics Explosion," *Vancouver Sun*, April 27, 1998, pp. A1, A7.

89. L. Bogomolny, "Good Housekeeping," *Canadian Business*, March 1, 2004, pp. 87–88.

90. "Ethics Programs Aren't Stemming Employee Misconduct," *Wall Street Journal*, May 11, 2000, p. A1.

91. L. Bogomolny, "Good Housekeeping," *Canadian Business*, March 1, 2004, pp. 87–88.

92. K. Doucet, "Canadian Organizations Not Meeting Ethics Expectations," *CMA Management* 74, no. 5 (2000), p. 10; and G. Crone, "UPS Rolls Out Ethics Program," *Financial Post* (*National Post*), May 26, 1999, p. C4.

93. D. Todd, "Ethics Audit: Credit Union Reveals All," *Vancouver Sun*, October 19, 1998, p. A5.

94. "Corporate Culture," *Canadian HR Reporter* 17, no. 21 (December 6, 2004), pp. 7–11.

95. W. Chow Hou, "To Bribe or Not to Bribe?" *Asia, Inc.*, October 1996, p. 104; and T. Jackson, "Cultural Values and Management Ethics: A 10-Nation Study," *Human Relations*, October 2001, pp. 1267–1302.

96. T. Donaldson, "Values in Tension: Ethics Away from Home," *Harvard Business Review*, September–October 1996, pp. 48–62.

97. P. Digh, "Shades of Gray in the Global Marketplace," *HR Magazine*, April 1997, pp. 91–98.

98. McWilliams and Davies quotations from A. Gillis, "How Can You Do Business in a Country Where Crooked Cops Will Kill You for a Song?" *Report on Business Magazine*, March 1998, p. 60.

99. M. McClearn, "African Adventure," *Canadian Business*, September 1, 2003, pp. 60–66.

100. Vignette based on M. Skapinker, "Why Nike Has Broken into a Sweat," *Financial Times*, March 6, 2002, http://news.ft.com/ft/gx.cgi/ftc?pagename=View&c=Article&cid=FT363BTGHYC&live=true (accessed March 12, 2002); and D. Simpson, "Ethics and Corporate Social Responsibility," advertising supplement, *Report on Business Magazine*, February 2002.

101. See http://www.theglobalalliance.org/workersurveys.htm (accessed May 15, 2006).

102. "Many Canadian Businesses and Citizens Want to See Tougher Federal Rules Governing Corporate Responsibility and It's Time for the Government to Take Action, Says a Social Justice Coalition," *Canadian Press Newswire*, January 24, 2002.

103. R. Littlemore, "Do the Right Thing: Would a Socially Responsible Company Do This?" *BCBusiness Magazine*, October 2001, pp. 30–33+.

104. M. Friedman, *Capitalism and Freedom* (Chicago: University of Chicago Press, 1962).

105. J. Bakan, *The Corporation* (Toronto: Big Picture Media Corporation, 2003).

106. D. Bradshaw, "How to Make an Idealist Think Again," *Financial Times*, April 5, 2002, http://news.ft.com/ft/gx.cgi/ftc?pagename=View&c=Article&cid=FT39XM6AOZC&live=true (accessed April 11, 2002).

107. R. Walker and S. Flanagan, "The Ethical Imperative: If You Don't Talk About a Wider Range of Values, You May Not Have a Bottom Line," *Financial Post 500*, 1997, pp. 28–36.

108. P. Foster, "Social Responsibility, Corporate Humbug," *Financial Post* (*National Post*), June 23, 1999, p. C7.

109. A. Howatson, *Lean Green: Benefits from a Streamlined Canadian Environmental Regulatory System* (Ottawa: The Conference Board of Canada, April 1996).

110. L. Jones and S. Graf, "Canada's Regulatory Burden: How Many Regulations? At What Cost?" *Fraser Forum*, August 2001, www.fraserinstitute.ca/shared/readmore.asp?sNar=pb&id=150 (accessed May 15, 2006).

111. R. Brunet, "To Survive and Thrive: Bled Dry by the NDP, BC Business Plots a New Course for the 21st Century," *British Columbia Report*, February 9, 1998, pp. 18–22.

112. G. Gallon, "Bunk Behind the Backlash: Highly Publicized Reports Exaggerate the Costs of Environmental Regulation," *Alternatives*, Fall 1997, pp. 14–15.

113. J. K. Grant, "Whatever Happened to Our Concern About the Environment?" *Canadian Speeches*, April 1997, pp. 37–42.

114. "The Business of Being Green," advertising supplement, *Canadian Business*, January 1996, pp. 41–56.

115. Minnesota Mining and Manufacturing Company (3M), "Pollution Prevention Pays: Moving Toward Environmental Sustainability," Brochure #78-6900-3343-2, St. Paul, MN, 1998; and J. K. Grant, "Whatever Happened to Our Concern About the Environment?" *Canadian Speeches*, April 1997, pp. 37–42.

116. Based on J. Calano and J. Salzman, "Ten Ways to Fire Up Your Creativity," *Working Woman*, July 1989, p. 94; J. V. Anderson, "Mind Mapping: A Tool for Creative Thinking," *Business Horizons*, January–February 1993, pp. 42–46; M. Loeb, "Ten Commandments for Managing Creative People," *Fortune*, January 16, 1995, pp. 135–136; and M. Henricks, "Good Thinking," *Entrepreneur*, May 1996, pp. 70–73.

Chapter 10

1. Opening vignette based on "Corporate Culture," *Canadian HR Reporter* 17, no. 21 (December 6, 2004), pp. 7–11; P. Kuitenbrouwer, "Making Money, and Enjoying It: Dingwall at the Mint," *Financial Post* (*National Post*), December 29, 2004, p. FP1; C. Clark, "Dingwall Severance in the Works," *Globe and Mail*, September 30, 2005, p. A5; and "Dingwall's Resignation Forced by Martin PMO According to Independent Report," *Canadian Press*, April 12, 2006.

2. "Organization Man: Henry Mintzberg Has Some Common Sense Observations About the Ways We Run Companies," *Financial Post*, November 22/24, 1997, pp. 14–16.

3. K. McArthur, "Air Canada Tells Employees to Crack a Smile More Often," *Globe and Mail*, March 14, 2002, pp. B1, B2.

4. K. McArthur, "Air Canada Tells Employees to Crack a Smile More Often," *Globe and Mail*, March 14, 2002, pp. B1, B2.

5. C. O'Reilly, "Corporations, Culture and Commitment: Motivation and Social Control in Organizations," *California Management Review* 31, no. 4 (1989), pp. 9–25.

6. E. Schein, "Coming to a New Awareness of Organizational Culture," *Sloan Management Review*, Winter 1984, pp. 3–16; E. Schein, *Organizational Culture and Leadership*, 2nd ed. (San Francisco, CA: Jossey-Bass, 1992); and E. Schein, "What Is Culture?" in *Reframing Organizational Culture*, ed. P. J. Frost, L. F. Moore, M. R. Louis, C. C. Lundberg, and J. Martin (Newbury Park, CA: Sage, 1991), pp. 243–253.

7. T. G. Stroup Jr., "Leadership and Organizational Culture: Actions Speak Louder Than Words," *Military Review* 76, no. 1 (January–February 1996), pp. 44–49; B. Moingeon and B. Ramanantsoa, "Understanding Corporate Identity: The French School of Thought," *European Journal of Marketing* 31, no. 5/6 (1997), pp. 383–395; A. P. D. Van Luxemburg, J. M. Ulijn, and N. Amare, "The Contribution of Electronic Communication Media to the Design Process: Communicative and Cultural Implications," *IEEE Transactions on Professional Communication* 45, no. 4 (December 2002), pp. 250–264; L. D. McLean, "Organizational Culture's Influence on Creativity and Innovation: A Review of the Literature and Implications for Human Resource Development," *Advances in Developing Human Resources* 7, no. 2 (May 2005), pp. 226–246; and V. J. Friedman and A. B. Antal, "Negotiating Reality: A Theory of Action Approach to Intercultural Competence," *Management Learning* 36, no. 1 (2005), pp. 69–86.

8. See http://www.palliser.com/companyinfo.html (accessed June 11, 2005).

9. Seven-item description based on C. A. O'Reilly III, J. Chatman, and D. F. Caldwell, "People and Organizational Culture: A Profile Comparison Approach to Assessing Person-Organization Fit," *Academy of Management Journal*, September 1991, pp. 487–516; and J. A. Chatman and K. A. Jehn, "Assessing the Relationship Between Industry Characteristics and Organizational Culture: How Different Can You Be?" *Academy of Management Journal*, June 1994, pp. 522–553. For a description of other popular measures, see A. Xenikou and A. Furnham, "A Correlational and Factor Analytic Study of Four Questionnaire Measures of Organizational Culture," *Human Relations*, March 1996, pp. 349–371. For a review of cultural dimensions, see N. M. Ashkanasy, C. P. M. Wilderom, and M. F. Peterson, eds., *Handbook of Organizational Culture and Climate* (Thousand Oaks, CA: Sage, 2000), pp. 131–145.

10. See C. A. O'Reilly and J. A. Chatman, "Culture as Social Control: Corporations, Cultures, and Commitment," in *Research in Organizational Behavior*, vol. 18, ed. B. M. Staw and L. L. Cummings (Greenwich, CT: JAI Press, 1996), pp. 157–200.

11. T. E. Deal and A. A. Kennedy, "Culture: A New Look Through Old Lenses," *Journal of Applied Behavioral Science*, November 1983, p. 501.

12. J. Case, "Corporate Culture," *Inc.*, November 1996, pp. 42–53.

13. T. Cole, "How to Stay Hired," *Report on Business Magazine*, March 1995, pp. 46–48.

14. S. L. Grover, "The Truth, the Whole Truth, and Nothing but the Truth: The Causes and Management of Workplace Lying," *Academy of Management Executive* 19, no. 2 (May 2005), pp. 148–157.

15. R. McQueen, "Bad Boys Make Good," *Financial Post*, April 4, 1998, p. 6.

16. The view that there will be consistency among perceptions of organizational culture has been called the "integration" perspective. For a review of this perspective and conflicting approaches, see D. Meyerson and J. Martin, "Cultural Change: An Integration of Three Different Views," *Journal of Management Studies*, November 1987, pp. 623–647; and P. J. Frost, L. F. Moore, M. R. Louis, C. C. Lundberg, and J. Martin, eds., *Reframing Organizational Culture* (Newbury Park, CA: Sage Publications, 1991).

17. See J. M. Jermier, J. W. Slocum Jr., L. W. Fry, and J. Gaines, "Organizational Subcultures in a Soft Bureaucracy: Resistance Behind the Myth and Facade of an Official Culture," *Organization Science*, May 1991, pp. 170–194; S. A. Sackmann, "Culture and Subcultures: An Analysis of Organizational Knowledge," *Administrative Science Quarterly*, March 1992, pp. 140–161; R. F. Zammuto, "Mapping Organizational Cultures and Subcultures: Looking Inside and Across Hospitals" (paper presented at the 1995 National Academy of Management Conference, Vancouver, August 1995); and G. Hofstede, "Identifying Organizational Subcultures: An Empirical Approach," *Journal of Management Studies*, January 1998, pp. 1–12.

18. T. A. Timmerman, "Do Organizations Have Personalities?" (paper presented at the 1996 National Academy of Management Conference, Cincinnati, OH, August 1996).

19. S. Hamm, "No Letup—and No Apologies," *BusinessWeek*, October 26, 1998, pp. 58–64.

20. Based on "Corporate Culture," *Canadian HR Reporter* 17, no. 21 (December 6, 2004), pp. 7–11; and P. Kuitenbrouwer, "Making Money, and Enjoying It: Dingwall at the Mint," *Financial Post* (*National Post*), December 29, 2004, p. FP1.

21. E. H. Schein, "The Role of the Founder in Creating Organizational Culture," *Organizational Dynamics*, Summer 1983, pp. 13–28.

22. E. H. Schein, "Leadership and Organizational Culture," in *The Leader of the Future*, ed. F. Hesselbein, M. Goldsmith, and R. Beckhard (San Francisco: Jossey-Bass, 1996), pp. 61–62.

23. See, for example, J. R. Harrison and G. R. Carroll, "Keeping the Faith: A Model of Cultural Transmission in Formal Organizations," *Administrative Science Quarterly*, December 1991, pp. 552–582.

24. See B. Schneider, "The People Make the Place," *Personnel Psychology*, Autumn 1987, pp. 437–453; J. A. Chatman, "Matching People and Organizations: Selection and Socialization in Public Accounting Firms," *Administrative Science Quarterly*, September 1991, pp. 459–484; D. E. Bowen, G. E. Ledford Jr., and B. R. Nathan, "Hiring for the Organization, Not the Job," *Academy of Management Executive*, November 1991, pp. 35–51; B. Schneider, H. W. Goldstein, and D. B. Smith, "The ASA Framework: An Update," *Personnel Psychology*, Winter 1995, pp. 747–773; and A. L. Kristof, "Person-Organization Fit: An Integrative Review of Its Conceptualizations, Measurement, and Implications," *Personnel Psychology*, Spring 1996, pp. 1–49.

25. R. Pascale, "The Paradox of 'Corporate Culture': Reconciling Ourselves to Socialization," *California Management Review*, Winter 1985, pp. 26–27.

26. D. C. Hambrick and P. A. Mason, "Upper Echelons: The Organization as a Reflection of Its Top Managers," *Academy of Management Review*, April 1984, pp. 193–206; B. P. Niehoff, C. A. Enz, and R. A. Grover, "The Impact of Top-Management Actions on Employee Attitudes and Perceptions," *Group and Organization Studies*, September 1990, pp. 337–352; and H. M. Trice and J. M. Beyer, "Cultural Leadership in Organizations," *Organization Science*, May 1991, pp. 149–169.

27. *OB in the Workplace* based on D. Sankey, "Listening to Employees Can Solve Most Workplace Woes," *Vancouver Sun*, December 2, 2000, p. D23; and http://www.sheratonsuites.com/awards.htm (accessed May 13, 2006).

28. See, for instance, J. P. Wanous, *Organizational Entry*, 2nd ed. (New York: Addison-Wesley, 1992); G. T. Chao, A. M. O'Leary-Kelly, S. Wolf, H. J. Klein, and P. D. Gardner, "Organizational Socialization: Its Content and Consequences," *Journal of Applied Psychology*, October 1994, pp. 730–743; B. E. Ashforth, A. M. Saks, and R. T. Lee, "Socialization and Newcomer Adjustment: The Role of Organizational Context," *Human Relations*, July 1998, pp. 897–926; D. A. Major, "Effective Newcomer Socialization into High-Performance Organizational Cultures," in *Handbook of Organizational Culture & Climate*, ed. N. M. Ashkanasy, C. P. M. Wilderom, and M. F. Peterson (Thousand Oaks, CA: Sage, 2000), pp. 355–368; and D. M. Cable and C. K. Parsons, "Socialization Tactics and Person-Organization Fit," *Personnel Psychology*, Spring 2001, pp. 1–23.

29. J. Impoco, "Basic Training, Sanyo Style," *U.S. News & World Report*, July 13, 1992, pp. 46–48.

30. B. Schneider, "The People Make the Place," *Personnel Psychology*, Autumn 1987, pp. 437–453; D. E. Bowen, G. E. Ledford Jr., and B. R. Nathan, "Hiring for the Organization, Not the Job," *Academy of Management Executive*, November 1991, pp. 35–51; B. Schneider, H. W. Goldstein, and D. B. Smith, "The ASA Framework: An Update," *Personnel Psychology*, Winter 1995, pp. 747–773; A. L. Kristof, "Person-Organization Fit: An Integrative Review of Its Conceptualizations, Measurement, and Implications," *Personnel Psychology*, Spring 1996, pp. 1–49; D. M. Cable and T. A. Judge, "Interviewers' Perceptions of Person–Organization Fit and Organizational Selection Decisions," *Journal of Applied Psychology*, August 1997, pp. 546–561; and J. Schaubroeck, D. C. Ganster, and J. R. Jones, "Organization and Occupation Influences in the Attraction-Selection-Attrition Process," *Journal of Applied Psychology*, December 1998, pp. 869–891.

31. This section is based on R. Goffee and G. Jones, *The Character of a Corporation: How Your Company's Culture Can Make or Break Your Business* (New York: HarperBusiness, 1998).

32. Jennifer Chatman's work, as reported in M. Siegel, "The Perils of Culture Conflict," *Fortune*, November 9, 1998, pp. 257–262.

33. Vignette based on "Corporate Culture," *Canadian HR Reporter* 17, no. 21 (December 6, 2004), pp. 7–11; and P. Kuitenbrouwer, "Making Money, and Enjoying It: Dingwall at the Mint," *Financial Post* (*National Post*), December 29, 2004, p. FP1.

34. J. Stephens and P. Behr, "Enron's Culture Fed Its Demise: Groupthink Promoted Foolhardy Risks," *Washington Post*, January 27, 2002, p. A01.

35. G. Probst and S. Raisch, "Organizational Crisis: The Logic of Failure," *Academy of Management Executive* 19, no. 1 (February 2005), pp. 90–105; D. L. Ferrin and K. T. Dirks, "The Use of Rewards to Increase and Decrease Trust: Mediating Processes and Differential Effects," *Organizational Science* 14, no. 1 (2003), pp. 18–31; J. R. Dunn and M. E. Schweitzer, "Too Good to Be Trusted? Relative Performance, Envy, and Trust," *Academy of Management Best Conference Paper Proceedings*, 2004, CM, pp. B1–B6.

36. See, for instance, D. Miller, "What Happens After Success: The Perils of Excellence," *Journal of Management Studies*, May 1994, pp. 11–38.

37. G. Probst and S. Raisch, "Organizational Crisis: The Logic of Failure," *Academy of Management Executive* 19, no. 1 (February 2005), pp. 90–105; R. Deshpande, J. U. Farley, and F. E. Webster, "Corporate Culture, Customer Orientation, and Innovativeness in Japanese Firms: A Quadrate Analysis," *Journal of Marketing* 57, no. 1 (1993), pp. 23–27; and C. Homburg and C. Pflesser, "A Multiple Layer Model of Market-Oriented Organizational Culture: Measurement Issues and Performance Outcomes," *Journal of Marketing Research* 37, no. 4 (2000), pp. 449–462.

38. See C. Lindsay, "Paradoxes of Organizational Diversity: Living Within the Paradoxes," in *Proceedings of the 50th Academy of Management Conference*, ed. L. R. Jauch and J. L. Wall (San Francisco, 1990), pp. 374–378; and T. Cox Jr., *Cultural Diversity in Organizations: Theory, Research & Practice* (San Francisco: Berrett-Koehler, 1993), pp. 162–170.

39. "Texaco: Lessons from a Crisis-in-Progress," *BusinessWeek*, December 2, 1996, p. 44; and M. A. Verespej, "Zero Tolerance," *IndustryWeek*, January 6, 1997, pp. 24–28.

40. A. F. Buono and J. L. Bowditch, *The Human Side of Mergers and Acquisitions: Managing Collisions Between People, Cultures, and Organizations* (San Francisco: Jossey-Bass, 1989); S. Cartwright and C. L. Cooper, "The Role of Culture Compatibility in Successful Organizational Marriages," *Academy of Management Executive*, May 1993, pp. 57–70; R. J. Grossman, "Irreconcilable Differences," *HR Magazine*, April 1999, pp. 42–48; J. Veiga, M. Lubatkin, R. Calori, and P. Very, "Measuring Organizational Culture Clashes: A Two-Nation Post-Hoc Analysis of a Cultural Compatibility Index," *Human Relations*, April 2000, pp. 539–557; and E. Krell, "Merging Corporate Cultures," *Training*, May 2001, pp. 68–78.

41. J. R. Carleton, "Cultural Due Diligence," *Training*, November 1997, p. 70; and D. Carey and D. Ogden, "A Match Made in Heaven? Find Out Before You Merge," *Wall Street Journal*, November 30, 1998, p. A22.

42. E. Church, "Andersen Name Fades into Canadian History," *Globe and Mail*, June 12, 2002.

43. K. W. Smith, "A Brand-New Culture for the Merged Firm," *Mergers and Acquisitions* 35, no. 6 (June 2000), pp. 45–50.

44. Based on "Corporate Culture," *Canadian HR Reporter* 17, no. 21 (December 6, 2004), pp. 7–11.

45. H. L. Sirkin, P. Keenan, and A. Jackson, "The Hard Side of Change Management," *Harvard Business Review* 83, no. 10 (October 1, 2005), pp. 108–118.

46. See, for instance, K. H. Hammonds, "Practical Radicals," *Fast Company*, September 2000, pp. 162–174; and P. C. Judge, "Change Agents," *Fast Company*, November 2000, pp. 216–226.

47. K. Lewin, *Field Theory in Social Science* (New York: Harper and Row, 1951).

48. J. P. Kotter, "Leading Changes: Why Transformation Efforts Fail," *Harvard Business Review*, March–April 1995, pp. 59–67; and J. P. Kotter, *Leading Change* (Boston: Harvard Business School Press, 1996).

49. See, for example, A. B. Shani and W. A. Pasmore, "Organization Inquiry: Towards a New Model of the Action Research Process," in *Contemporary Organization Development: Current Thinking and Applications*, ed. D. D. Warrick (Glenview, IL: Scott, Foresman, 1985), pp. 438–448; and C. Eden and C. Huxham, "Action Research for the Study of Organizations," in *Handbook of Organization Studies*, ed. S. R. Clegg, C. Hardy, and W. R. Nord (London: Sage, 1996).

50. See, for example, G. R. Bushe, "Advances in Appreciative Inquiry as an Organization Development Intervention," *Organizational Development Journal*, Summer 1999, pp. 61–68; D. L. Cooperrider and D. Whitney, *Collaborating for Change: Appreciative Inquiry* (San Francisco: Berrett-Koehler, 2000); R. Fry, F. Barrett, J. Seiling, and D. Whitney, eds., *Appreciative Inquiry & Organizational Transformation: Reports from the Field* (Westport, CT: Quorum, 2002); J. K. Barge and C. Oliver, "Working With Appreciation in Managerial Practice," *Academy of Management Review*, January 2003, pp. 124–142; and D. van der Haar and D. M. Hosking, "Evaluating Appreciative Inquiry: A Relational Constructionist Perspective," *Human Relations*, August 2004, pp. 1017–1036.

51. G. R. Bushe, "Advances in Appreciative Inquiry as an Organization Development Intervention," *Organization Development Journal* 17, no. 2 (Summer 1999), pp. 61–68.

52. W. Samuelson and R. Zeckhauser, "Status Quo Bias in Decision Making," *Journal of Risk Uncertainty* 1, 1988, pp. 7–59.

53. A. E. Reichers, J. P. Wanous, and J. T. Austin, "Understanding and Managing Cynicism About Organizational Change," *Academy of Management Executive* 11, 1997, pp. 48–59.

54. R. H. Hall, *Organizations: Structures, Processes, and Outcomes*, 4th ed. (Englewood Cliffs, NJ: Prentice Hall, 1987), p. 29.

55. J. Lee, "Canadian Businesses Not Good at Adjusting, Survey Says," *Vancouver Sun*, December 14, 1998, pp. C1, C2.

56. R. Starnes, "The Lucky Touch Wore Off: Timothy Eaton's Legacy Fell Victim to Its Conservative Image and Failure to Keep Pace With Trends," *Ottawa Citizen*, February 19, 2002, p. D1.

57. D. Katz and R. L. Kahn, *The Social Psychology of Organizations*, 2nd ed. (New York: John Wiley and Sons, 1978), pp. 714–715.

58. Paragraph based on M. Johne, "Wanted: a Few Good Egocentric, Self-Serving Risk-Takers," *Globe and Mail*, May 27, 2002, p. C1.

59. J. P. Kotter and L. A. Schlesinger, "Choosing Strategies for Change," *Harvard Business Review*, March–April 1979, pp. 106–114.

60. See J. Pfeffer, *Managing With Power: Politics and Influence in Organizations* (Boston: Harvard Business School Press, 1992),

pp. 7, 318–320; and D. Knights and D. McCabe, "When 'Life Is but a Dream': Obliterating Politics Through Business Process Reengineering?" *Human Relations*, June 1998, pp. 761–798.

61. See, for instance, W. Ocasio, "Political Dynamics and the Circulation of Power: CEO Succession in U.S. Industrial Corporations, 1960–1990," *Administrative Science Quarterly*, June 1994, pp. 285–312.

62. Ideas in *From Concepts to Skills* were influenced by A. L. Wilkins, "The Culture Audit: A Tool for Understanding Organizations," *Organizational Dynamics*, Autumn 1983, pp. 24–38; H. M. Trice and J. M. Beyer, *The Cultures of Work Organizations* (Englewood Cliffs, NJ: Prentice Hall, 1993), pp. 358–362; H. Lancaster, "To Avoid a Job Failure, Learn the Culture of a Company First," *Wall Street Journal*, July 14, 1998, p. B1; and M. Belliveau, "4 Ways to Read a Company," *Fast Company*, October 1998, p. 158.

GLOSSARY/SUBJECT INDEX

Key terms and the pages on which they are defined appear in **boldface**.

A

Aboriginal peoples
    Aboriginal culture,   16–17
    business partnerships with,   81
    values,   80–81
absenteeism,   54–55, 86
abuse of power,   232–234
accountability,   171
achievement-oriented leader,   265
acquisitions,   345
action,   349
action research A change process based on
    the systematic collection of data and then
    selection of a change action based on
    what the analyzed data indicate.   **349**
adjourning The final stage in group
    development for temporary groups,
    where attention is directed toward
    wrapping up activities rather than task
    performance.   **155**, 157
affective commitment The strength of an
    individual's emotional attachment to,
    identification with, and involvement in
    the organization.   **10**, 88
affective conflict Conflict that is emotional
    and aimed at a person rather than an
    issue.   **201**
aggressiveness,   334
agreeableness A personality factor that
    describes the degree to which someone
    is good-natured, cooperative, and
    trusting.   **44**
ambiguous responsibility,   302
analysis,   349
anchoring bias A tendency to fixate on
    initial information as a starting
    point.   **301**
anger,   103
Anglophone values,   79–80
appreciative inquiry An approach to
    change that seeks to identify the unique
    qualities and special strengths of an
    organization, which can then be built on
    to improve performance.   **349**–350
artifacts Aspects of an organization's
    culture that you see, hear, and feel.   **333**
Asian values,   81–82
assertiveness,   76
assimilation,   345
assumption of morality,   303
assumptions The taken-for-granted notions
    of how something should be.   **334**
attention to detail,   334
attitudes Positive or negative feelings about
    objects, people, or events.   **84**
    changing attitudes,   93
    job satisfaction,   85–88
    negative impact of,   84
    organizational commitment,   88–89
    versus values,   84

attribution theory The theory that when
    we observe what seems to be atypical
    behaviour by an individual, we attempt
    to determine whether it is internally or
    externally caused.   **34**
    consensus,   35
    consistency,   35
    described,   34–35, 35f
    development of, in U.S.   36
    distinctiveness,   35
    distortion of attributions,   36
    fundamental attribution error,   36
    rules for determining attribution,
        35
    self-serving bias,   36
authoritative command,   204
autonomy The degree to which the job
    provides substantial freedom,
    independence, and discretion to the
    individual in scheduling the work and
    determining the procedures to be used
    in carrying it out.   **132**
availability heuristic The tendency for
    people to base their judgments on
    information that is readily available to
    them rather than complete data.   **299**
avoidance,   202, 204

B

Baby Boomers,   82
balance,   24–25
bargaining. *See* negotiation
bargaining zone The zone between each
    party's resistance point, assuming there
    is overlap in this range.   **207**, 207f
bases of powFer
    coercive power,   222–223
    described,   222–223
    evaluation of,   225–226
    expert power,   224
    information power,   225
    legitimate power,   223
    measurement of,   222f
    and political behaviour,   235
    referent power,   224
    reward power,   223
BATNA The *b*est *a*lternative *to* a *n*egotiated
    *a*greement; the outcome an individual
    faces if negotiations fail.   **207**
behavioural symptoms of stress,   102
behavioural theories of leadership
    Theories that propose that specific
    behaviours differentiate leaders from
    nonleaders.   **261**
    Leadership Grid,   261–263, 262f
    Michigan studies,   261
    Ohio State studies,   261
    research findings,   262
beliefs The understandings of how objects
    and ideas relate to each other.   **333**
"best qualified" person,   297

biases
    anchoring bias,   301
    cultural bias,   51
    decision biases,   299f
    overconfidence bias,   301
    reducing, in decision making,   301
    self-serving bias,   36
Big Five personality factors,   44–46, 45f,
    163
body language,   196–197
bonuses,   127
bounded rationality Limitations on a
    person's ability to interpret, process, and
    act on information.   **296**–297
brainstorming An idea-generation process
    that specifically encourages any and all
    alternatives while withholding any
    criticism of those alternatives.   **306**–307
bribery,   94, 319
bullying,   232–233

C

Canadian-American value differences,   79f
Canadian workplace. *See* workplace
care,   314
case incidents
    "Emailing "Lazy" Employees,"   216
    "Frustrated at Age 32,"   147
    "Gourmet Foods Works on Employee
        Attitudes,"   95
    "GreyStar Art & Greetings Makes
        Technological Changes,"   361
    "How a UPS Manager Cut Turnover,"
        25
    "Moving from Colleague to
        Supervisor,"   288
    "The Power of Bill Fowler at
        Blackmer/Dover Resources,"
        246–247
    "The Rise and Fall of Dennis
        Kozlowski,"   68–69
    "Syncrude Wants to Be a Good
        Neighbour,"   327
    "A Virtual Team at T.A. Stearns,"
        180–181
CBC video case incidents
    "Air Canada Employee Morale Flies
        Low,"   147–148
    "Buggy Wars,"   216–217
    "Corporate Culture Meets G.A.P.
        Adventures,"   362
    "Corporate Espionage in the
        Canadian Airline Industry,"
        327–328
    "Diverging Ideologies,"   96
    "Earth Buddies,"   181–182
    "GM Woes,"   26
    "How Bad Is Your Boss?"   289
    "Jean Brault and the Sponsorship
        Scandal,"   247–248
    "NovaScotian Crystal,"   69–70

NAME AND ORGANIZATION INDEX

The page on which a weblink appears is printed in **boldface**.

A

Abbott Labs,   93
Adams, George,   331
Adams, J. Stacy,   120
Adams, Michael,   78, 82, 353
Advantech AMT,   352–353
AES,   123
Agrium,   346
Air Canada,   14, **332**
Alcan,   **81**
Alderfer, Clayton,   110, 112
Allport, Gordon,   41
Allstate,   93
American Management Association,   **14**
Andersen Canada,   345
Anderson, Lynne,   251
Angus Reid Group,   13, 115
Apple Computer,   152, 228, 259, 269, 343
Armstrong, Michael,   246
Arthur Andersen,   15
Asia Department Store,   285
AT&T,   152, 246
Athabasca University,   81
Atwood, Margaret,   310
Australian Airlines,   152
Avcorp Industries,   128

B

Bain & Company,   343
Bakan, Joel,   320
Bank of Montreal (BOM),   49, **54**, 127, 269
Barclays PLS,   269
Baril, Peter,   199
Barrett, Mathew,   49, 269
BBDO Canada,   **18, 318**
BC Lions,   106–**107**, 114, 118, 122
BCS Communications,   104, 105
Beddoe, Clive,   14
Bell Canada,   **273**, 318
Bell Labs,   54
Bell Mobility,   158
Ben & Jerry's,   89
Benimadhu, Prem,   126, 129
Bentley, David,   309
Berdahl, Jennifer,   162
Berezhnaya, Yelena,   221
Bettman, Gary,   208
Big House Communications,   310
Billingsley, Jason,   33
Binette, François,   353
Black Photo Corporation,   **9**
Blais, Daniel,   135
Blake, R.R.,   261
Blanchard, Ken,   263, 264–265
Blanco, Kathleen,   231, 257, 263, 272, 278

B (continued)

Bloomberg,   3
BMO Nesbitt Burns,   **313**
The Body Shop,   318, 338
Boehm, Paul,   159
Bombardier,   306
Bond, Michael,   75
Boston University,   189
Bouchard, Lucien,   269
Bradshaw, Patricia,   222
Branden, Nathaniel,   **48**
Branson, Richard,   49, 259, 338
Brault, Jean,   12
Bre-X,   **304**
Brennan, Jack,   272
British Airways,   49
British Telecom,   318
Brotheridge, Céleste,   233
Brown, Michael,   222–258, 278
Buono, Wally,   107–114
Busch, Pauline,   17
Bush, George W.,   41, 52, 222–258, 231, 257, 263, 272, 278

C

Calgary Stampeders,   113
California Sushi Academy,   85
Calvillo, Anthony,   119
Cameron, Kim,   27
Campbell Company of Canada,   342
Campbell Soup,   18
Canada Post,   **317**
Canadian Alliance,   187
Canadian Auto Workers (CAW),   185, **194**–195, 204
Canadian Banking Ombudsman,   313
Canadian Conservative Reform Alliance Party (CCRAP),   186
Canadian Football League (CFL),   106–107, 113
Canadian Human Rights Commission (CHRC),   30, **31**, 33, 34, 39
Canadian Imperial Bank of Canada (CIBC),   13, 294, 317
Canadian Institute for Health Information,   79
Canadian Interuniversity Sport (CIS),   131
Canadian Labour Congress,   **130**
Canadian Mental Health Association,   37
Canadian National Railway (CN),   **194**–195
Canadian Policy Research Network,   **85**
Canadian Security Intelligence Service,   306
Carbon Five,   229–230
Carbone, Arnold,   89
Carl, Dale,   269
Carr, Emily,   310

C (continued)

Carstons, Rob,   288
Carter, Vince,   225
Casino Windsor,   108
Catalyst Paper Corporation,   205
Cavanagh, Christina,   101, **193**, 194
Cavoukian, Ann,   195
CBC,   350
Ceconi, Margaret,   344
Centre de rénovation Pointe et Meunier,   135
Chinese University of Hong Kong,   75
Choi, Jin Nam,   16
Chrétien, Jean,   80, 271, 287
Chrysler,   225
Cinquanta, Ottavio,   222, 228, 234
Citigroup,   246
Citizens Bank,   320
City of Vancouver,   203
Clawson, James,   279
Clearwater Seafood,   191
Clinton, Bill,   287
CNN,   163
Coleman, Jon,   194
Cominco,   346
Communications, Energy and Paperworkers Union of Canada,   205
Community Ownership Solutions (COS),   3
Comper, Tony,   54
Cona, Donna,   198–199
The Conference Board of Canada,   **11**, 15, 126, 129, 153, 175, 233, 280, 323
ConocoPhillips,   271
Consortium for research on Emotional Intelligence,   259
Crisanti, Robyn,   104
Crooke, George,   279–280
Currie, Marie,   310

D

DaimlerChrysler AG,   152
Daly, Bill,   208
Darden Graduate School of Business,   279
Davidson, Lynda,   37
Davies, Michael,   319
De Bono, Edward,   **310**
DeGroot, Timothy,   271
Dell Canada,   19
Deloitte & Touche LLP,   **345**
Department of Justice,   127
Department of National Defence and Canadian Forces,   306
Deutsch, Yuval,   86
Dickenson, Dave,   118
Dill, John,   307
DiNatale, Lou,   240

LIST OF CANADIAN COMPANIES

PHOTO CREDITS

Author photographs: page xv, Gary Schwartz (top); courtesy of Stephen P. Robbins (bottom).

Chapter 1

Page 3: Reprinted by permission of Marty Donkervoort, President, Inner City Renovations, photo by Marty Donkervoort; page 4 (top):Malone & Co. Photography, Inc.; page 4 (left): Robert Wright Photography; page 4 (right): © 1999 Brian Coats/Brian Coats Photography; page 13: Reprinted by permission of RBC Financial Group.

Chapter 2

Page 31: Tom Hanson/CP Photo Archive; page 33: Ward Perrin/ *Vancouver Sun*; page 36: Amy Etra/PhotoEdit; page 42: Mark Richards; page 45: Reprinted with permission from *The Globe and Mail*; page 49: Courtesy of Richard Branson/Virgin Airlines; page 53: Joyce Ravid.

Chapter 3

Page 73: Courtesy Procter & Gamble; page 78: Patty Gower/*The Globe and Mail*; page 80: Courtesy of John Wells; page 83: Courtesy of Mainframe Entertainment Inc.; page 89: Copyright Kristine Larsen 2004, all rights reserved.

OB on the Edge: Stress at Work

Page 98: Keith Beatty/*The Toronto Star*.

Chapter 4

Page 107: Richard Lam/CP Photo Archive; page 114: Michael Stuparyk/*The Toronto Star*; page 120: Peter Blakely, SABA Press Photos Inc.; page 122: AP/Wide World Photos; page 125: Snap Promotions Inc.; page 127: Derwin Gowan/CP Photo Archive; page 132: © Mark Peterson/CORBIS.

Chapter 5

Page 151: Courtesy of Johanne Christensen; page 152: Courtesy of Xerox Canada Ltd.; page 160: Courtesy PEAK archives; page 163: Fred Prouser/Reuters/Landov; page 167: © Greg Girard/Contact Press Images; page 169: Nathan Denette/CP Photo Archive.

Chapter 6

Page 185: Gary Yokoyama/CP Photo Archive; page 186: Adrian Wyld/CP Photo Archive; page 189: Courtesy of Claude Norfolk/Photo by Larry Newland; page 193: Andrew Brusso; page 198: © Rolf Bruderer/CORBIS; page 199: Courtesy of Donna Cona Inc.; page 208: Adrian Wyld/CP Photo Archives; page 209: © Dave Bartruff/CORBIS.

Chapter 7

Page 221: Paul Chiasson/CP Photo Archive; page 223: Dilip Mehta/Contact Press Images Inc.; page 227: Alan Levenson; page 229: David G. McIntyre/Black Star; page 230: Carbon Five Inc.; page 231: Courtesy of Great Little Box Company Ltd.; page 237: Courtesy of Teranet.

OB on the Edge: The Toxic Workplace

Page 250: Peter Southwick/Picture Quest.

Chapter 8

Page 257: Daniel Acker/Bloomberg News/Landov; page 259: Laurent Fievet/Agence France Presse/Getty Images; page 269: Stuart Ramson/CP Photo Archive; page 275: Jason Reed/Reuters/Landov; page 280: Reprinted with permission from *The Globe and Mail*; page 281: Courtesy of Emmie Wong Leung.

Chapter 9

Page 293: © Steve Raymer/CORBIS; page 303: Photo by Patrick Price; page 310: Ian Lindsay/*The Vancouver Sun*; page 311: Michael Lewis; page 314: Courtesy of Stewart Leibl; page 318: Courtesy of United Parcel Service.

Chapter 10

Page 331: Andrew Vaughan/CP Photo Archive; page 333: PEAK Financial Group; page 338: AP/Wide World Photos; page 339: Frances M. Roberts/Richard B. Levin © Frances M. Roberts, all rights reserved; page 353: Advantech Microwave Technologies Inc.

"AS IS" LICENSE AGREEMENT AND LIMITED WARRANTY